POSTING OF WORKERS AND COLLECTIVE LABOUR LAW: THERE AND BACK AGAIN

Social Europe Series, Volume 33

POSTING OF WORKERS AND COLLECTIVE LABOUR LAW: THERE AND BACK AGAIN

Between Internal Market and Fundamental Rights

Marco Rocca

intersentia
Cambridge – Antwerp – Portland

Intersentia Ltd.
Sheraton House | Castle Park
Cambridge | CB3 0AX | United Kingdom
Tel.: +44 1223 370 170 | Email: mail@intersentia.co.uk

Distribution for the UK:
NBN International
Airport Business Centre, 10 Thornbury Road
Plymouth, PL6 7PP
United Kingdom
Tel: +44 1752 202 301 | Fax: +44 1752 202 331
Email: orders@nbninternational.com

Distribution for the USA and Canada:
International Specialized Book Services
920 NE 58th Ave Suite 300
Portland, OR 97213
USA
Tel.: +1 800 944 6190 (toll free)
Email: info@isbs.com

Distribution for Austria:
Neuer Wissenschaftlicher Verlag
Argentinierstraße 42/6
1040 Wien
Austria
Tel.: +43 1 535 61 03 24
Email: office@nwv.at

Distribution for other countries:
Intersentia Publishing nv
Groenstraat 31
2640 Mortsel
Belgium
Tel.: +32 3 680 15 50
Email: mail@intersentia.be

Posting of Workers and Collective Labour Law: There and Back Again. Between Internal Market and Fundamental Rights
Marco Rocca

ISBN 978-1-78068-307-2
D/2015/7849/39
NUR 825

British Library Cataloguing in Publication Data. A catalogue record for this book is available from the British Library.

FOREWORD

On the 27th of May 2014, Marco Rocca defended his Ph.D. thesis at the Law Faculty of the *Université Catholique de Louvain*. I had the privilege and the pleasure of being the supervisor of this thesis as well as the promotor of its author. The title of his thesis (Posting of workers and collective labour law: there and back again) refers to a phenomenon which has been regulated by a well-known EU Directive (96/71, PWD). This EU Directive essentially deals with the law applicable on an individual employment relation. It does not tackle the question whether or to which extent posted workers have access to the system of industrial relations of the Host State. However, in defining the law applicable to the individual employment relation, the Directive does take into account collective agreements which have been declared universally applicable for employers in the construction sector of the Host State.

By the end of 2007, the *Laval* judgement of the CJEU stirred the attention of labour lawyers around Europe for the impact of the PWD on existing systems of industrial relations in the Member States. Two subsequent judgment *Rüffert* and *Commission v Luxembourg* corroborated the impression that the freedom to provide services as fleshed out in the PWD restricted not just the ability of social partners but also of governmental actors to combat social competition between posted workers and workers of the Host State. Labour Law was being construed as a ceiling rather than as a floor. Though the case of the posted workers is not the first illustration of "negative integration" operated by economic freedoms to the detriment of fragments of the labour law *acquis* at member State level, it is unprecedented insofar as it affects a tension between fundamental economic freedoms and genuine fundamental rights. The subtitle of the Ph.D. thesis reads "between internal market and fundamental rights". Insofar as some of the fundamental rights are crucial for the empowerment of workers and the progressive development of labour law, the case of the posted workers raises serious question as to the commitment of the EU to uphold fundamental (workers) rights. It might even be said that the relation of values and objectives of the Union as fleshed out in Articles 2 and 3 of the TEU is in fact reversed, since some objectives cease to be instrumental to the values the EU seeks to promote.

Though the case law which has inspired the Ph.D. research project had already been commented by an impressive amount of leading labour law scholars at the very start of the project, the Ph.D. thesis stands out for its attempt to contextualise the case law through the concepts of industrial relations in comparison to the concepts of collective labour law. Furthermore, it situates the recent case law on posted workers in a broad historic perspective which predates the adoption of the PWD. During the drafting of the Ph.D. thesis, the tension between fundamental freedoms and fundamental rights within the EU became even more apparent due to the critical observations of supervising bodies of international instruments which enshrine these social rights within other international legal orders (Council of Europe, ILO). A tension between legal standards within the EU has thus amounted to a clash between legal orders and the (quasi) judicial bodies of these legal orders. The author also analyses the failed attempt of the EU (the so called "Monti II Proposal") to deal with the discomfort the cases generated. The period of the drafting process also coincides with the financial and economic crisis. The approach of the new economic governance to national systems of collective labour law is being confronted with the judicial interpretation of the PWD.

Marco Rocca is the very first Ph.D. student to have survived me as a supervisor. I already knew that the defence of a Ph.D. thesis can be an emotional event for anyone trying to defend such a *magnum opus* during several consecutive hours. Marco has helped me to understand that such an event is moving as well for a supervisor. The notion of a Ph.D. *student* is an unfortunate one. During 5 academic years Marco has been in fact one of my closest collaborators. His assistance in the preparation of many scientific projects (seminars, conferences and the functioning of our labour law department) was invaluable. Marco has been an ideal collaborator. He does not await an instruction, but he proposes to solve practical problems, before you have actually sensed and identified them. I only had to dissuade him not to ask to carry my bags, since in Belgium we don't consider assistants to be our "*portaborse*".

My decision to recruit him was one of my most fortunate professional decisions. I was happy enough to adopt that decision together with Pierre-Paul Van Gehuchten and Yves De Cordt who accepted my request to participate in a recruitment panel. Italy has generously offered its *meglio gioventù*. Marco has been able to integrate smoothly in a distinct academic environment enriching it with the grand tradition of Italian Academia. His double training as a lawyer at the University of Pisa and as a student enrolled in the prestigious *Scuola Superiore Sant'Anna* proved to be worthwhile. He has been able to function in two languages which were not his own by birth, teaching in French and publishing in English, (Italian) and French. His *magnum opus* provides proof of erudition profiting from the legal scholarship versed in all these European languages. His deeply rooted convictions which I was able to share to a large extent have helped him to be creative as a legal scholar, although never abandoning the technical skills of his art and reserving literate formula's to the original titles and subtitles of the various chapters. His confidence deprived of arrogance was reassuring to him and his supervisor. I am grateful to Pascale Vielle and Pierre-Paul Van Gehuchten for speaking out during the meetings of his *comité d'accompagnement* and to two outstanding European labour lawyers for joining the jury: Simon Deakin, "our" Doctor *honoris causa* and Giovanni Orlandini (whose scientific work so wonderfully combines the European law issues of posting of workers and collective labour law). Furthermore, Philippe Pochet's (General Director of ETUI and guest professor at UCL) membership of the Jury, was salutary due to the meta-legal approach of the Thesis.

I am extremely grateful to Alexia Autenne of our Research Department for giving Marco the opportunity to continue his post-doctoral years after finishing his Ph.D. thesis. I am confident that we will be able to learn and read more of him in the years to come, wherever Fate will guide him.

Filip Dorssemont

ACKNOWLEDGEMENTS

'Ci spetta il tepore dei bagni. Possano i giorni trascorrere senza meta. Non si prosegua l'azione secondo un piano'[1]
— Luther Blisset, *Q*

First of all, I would like to thank wholeheartedly my supervisor, Filip Dorssemont, for his support, his encouragement and, above all, for his warmth. Though he always respected my autonomy and intellectual freedom, I profited enormously from our frequent discussions about law, history, arts, food, beer and wine. Indeed, as I sit here finalising these acknowledgments, I still cannot quite believe my luck in finding such a supervisor.

I am grateful to Pierre-Paul Van Gehuchten and Pascale Vielle, who, together with my supervisor, have composed the enriching *comité d'accompagnement* of my thesis. I owe also a great deal to the members of the jury: Simon Deakin, Giovanni Orlandini and Philippe Pochet. Their comments and critiques have greatly improved the final version of my thesis.

Funding for this project was provided by the *Fonds Nationale de la Recherche Scientifique* (FNRS) and by the *Atelier de Droit Social* of the *Université Catholique de Louvain*. Their financial support made possible the completion of the thesis. Further thanks are due to all the colleagues of the *Centre de Recherche Interdisciplinaire Droit Entreprise et Société* (CRIDES) who welcomed me with open arms, dispelling the initial loneliness as soon as the first *diner du Centre*. Thanks, in particular, to the administrative staff, Catherine and Ariane, and to all the Ph.D. students and teaching assistants with whom I shared this epic quest: thanks to Auriane, my sister-in-research, to Aurélie, Elise, Alice, and to all the others.

I would also like to extend my thanks to the many wonderful researchers I met during the countless conferences and seminars which punctuated these years. If I should single any out, many thanks go to all the participants of the three editions of the Pontignano Seminar to which I had the occasion to participate.

As for every important achievement of my life, I owe a debt of gratitude to my friends, for their support … and for all the rest. True to the situation of our generation, this support came often from far away, our little fellowship having being scattered to the four corners of Europe (and beyond). This only makes me

[1] "We deserve the warmth of baths. May the days be aimless/Do not advance the action according to a plan."

all the more grateful for their continued presence in my life. Indeed, some of them went as far as to accept to proofread one or more chapters of my thesis, in a spectacular display of friendship if there ever was one. Thus, thanks to Alessandro, the brother in arms of many an online battle, to Cinzia, who often tries to interrupt those battles, to Rosa, my family-in-Brussels, and to the others who hopefully know that they are included here.

Special and heartfelt thanks go to my parents, Fabrizio Rocca and Elena Beisso, for their endless encouragement and for the pride they always showed for my work. Their own work as trade unionists and political activists has been and continues to be an inspiration to me. Thanks to my brother Luca, for counterbalancing all this inspiration with a healthy dose of chaos.

This research has been a truly transnational work. Indeed, it has been written as much in my office at the *Université* Catholique de Louvain as "up in the air". Hence, 400 flights (and counting) later, my final thanks go to Margherita. Thank you, for being the sanctuary island for the pirate ship of my soul.

CONTENTS

INTRODUCTION

This research deals with the complicated relationship between posting of workers in the EU and collective labour law. It does so from a legal perspective, though from time to time it does not refrain from looking at the economic and social context in order to better understand the legal construction of the said relationship. The first objective of this work is to provide a comprehensive picture of this relationship, from the first steps of the legal framework of posting, through the direct clash of 2007–2008,[1] to the present days.

Having clarified this background, the research has the ambition to examine the whole issue into its changing context. Such change stems both from legal innovations and from political and economical events. The analysis of those changes is meant to show two major tensions arising between the legal framework for posting of workers shaped by EU law and its context. The first tension will be identified in the mounting conflict between the said legal framework and (fundamental) collective social rights as protected by international documents.[2] In analysing the second tension I will look into the growing trend towards decentralisation of collective bargaining. The role of EU institutions[3] in fostering this trend will be highlighted, as those institutions appear to be putting their efforts in a self-conscious and coherent promotion (when not imposition) of decentralisation of collective bargaining.[4] Along this work I will show how such a *political* choice is at odds with the legal framework for posting of workers.

Hence, the main focus is on the *legal* aspects of the posting phenomenon and of its context. However, this will be complemented by the contribution of other social sciences. In particular, empirical and sociological data will be presented in order to provide a better understanding of the posting phenomenon. Political elements will be introduced when looking at the drafting process of relevant EU legislation, as well as in reflecting on the political impact of the tensions I just

1 I am referring here to the case law delivered by the Court of Justice between the end of 2007 and 2008. These decisions will be introduced in the next pages.

2 The European Convention of Human Rights, the European Social Charter and the relevant Conventions of the International Labour Organisation.

3 The EU Commission, the EU Council and the European Central Bank.

4 Either by the reforms imposed by the so-called Troika (EU Commission, ECB and International Monetary Fund) via Memoranda of Understanding, or by Country Specific Recommendations in the context of the European Semester. See in particular Chapter 8.

highlighted. Finally, the analysis of the present context[5] will profit from the contribution of economic research.

This Introduction provides the fundamental elements for understanding the research, by anticipating some key notion which will be presented in much greater detail along the rest of the work.[6]

POSTED WORKERS: WHAT'S IN A NAME?

As a first step in the domain of this research, it seems useful to spend a few words on the concept of "posting of workers" and of "posted worker". Indeed, these concepts cannot be considered as self-evident nor do they stem from some dark corner of the common sense.

However, this provisional definition will be limited to the actual legal text of Directive 96/71.[7] Furthermore, here I will only provide with a superficial glance, leaving the details to the next Chapters, both legal and empirical.[8]

Coming back to the definition of "posting of workers", one has to turn to Article 1 of the PWD. The first paragraph of this Article sets down three important elements which characterise the "posting of workers". First, the phenomenon takes place in the context of a "transnational provision of services".[9] This is in line with the legal basis of the directive.[10] Second (and third), Article 1(1) limits the application of the directive to "undertakings established in a Member State" which "post" workers to another Member State (henceforth, the "host state"). Hence, to be applied the PWD requires the existence of an employment relationship with the provider of services in the Member State of departure (henceforth the "home state").[11]

---

5 The reference here goes mainly to the Great Recession, to avoid the more generic and rather abused "crisis".

6 See in particular Chapter 4 and 5.

7 Directive 96/71/EC of the European Parliament and of the Council of 16 December 1996 concerning the posting of workers in the framework of the provision of services. Along this text I will refer to this Directive either as "Directive 96/71" or with its acronym "PWD" (*i.e.* Posting of Workers Directive).

8 Chapter 1 will deal with the empirical aspect of posting of workers, while Chapters 4 and 5 will deal with the PWD and with the case law of the Court of Justice of the European Union about posting of workers.

9 PWD, Article 1(1).

10 At the time of its adoption, Article 57(2) and Article 66 TEC (now respectively Article 53 and 62 TFEU). Article 57(2) authorised the Council to adopt harmonising directives, by qualified majority and in co-operation with the European Parliament, aimed at facilitating the activities of persons working as self-employed. Article 66 simply extended the content of (among other provisions) Article 57(2) to the area of the provision of services.

11 P. Davies, "Posted Workers: Single Market or Protection of National Labour Law Systems?", *Common Market Law Review* 34 (1997): 571–602, pp. 575–576; P. Rodière, *Droit Social de L'Union Européenne* (Paris: L.G.D.J., 1998), p. 418.

As regards the concept of "posting", one has to reach the third paragraph of Article 1 in order to find some clarification. Here the Directive identifies three categories of arrangements between the posting undertaking and the user undertaking. Without going much into details, this list can be summarised as follows. First, we have the situation in which the home undertaking provides services on its account and under its direction under a contract concluded with the party for whom the services are intended.[12] Thus Article 1(3)(a) envisages the situation of workers who are "sent" or "brought" to the host state in order to work directly under the direction of their home undertaking in the context of a provision of services. The second scenario can be described as "intra-group posting".[13] This means that one or more workers are sent to the host state in order to work in a different undertaking or establishment owned by the same group of the home undertaking. Still, the employment relationship continues with the home undertaking. Under the third and last category we find the case of "a temporary employment undertaking or placement agency"[14] established in the home state and supplying labour to an undertaking located in the host state. It is also important to note that the PWD leaves to the host state to determine who is a worker.[15] Finally, Article 2(2) defines as posted worker "a worker who, for a limited period, carries out his work in the territory of a Member State other than the State in which he normally works". This identifies two additional elements which define the posting phenomenon: on the one hand, the intrinsically temporary nature of the posting,[16] on the other, the requirement of a pre-existing working relationship habitually carried out in a (Member) State different from the host state.

As for the employment relationships *excluded* from the scope of the directive (and, hence, from our definition of "posting of workers"), the first explicit exclusion is provided by Article 1(2). This paragraph states that the PWD "shall not apply to merchant navy undertakings as regards seagoing personnel". On the implicit side, a number of exclusions stem quite evidently from the wording of the directive; as for example, the situations covered by the free movement of workers. A less evident exclusion is the situation in which one or more workers are sent to another Member State to render services directly to the home undertaking.[17]

---

12 M. Biagi, "The 'Posted Workers' EU Directive: from Social Dumping to Social Protectionism", in *Labour Law and Industrial Relations in the European Union*, ed. Roger Blanpain (The Hague: Kluwer Law International, 1998), 173–180, p. 175.

13 PWD, Article 1(3)(b).

14 Article 1(3)(c).

15 Article 2(2): "For the purposes of this Directive, the definition of a worker is that which applies in the law of the Member State to whose territory the worker is posted".

16 Though what "temporary" means in terms of actual duration is not further specified in the Directive.

17 Davies, "Posted Workers: Single Market or Protection of National Labour Law Systems?", p. 576.

THE CORE

The main reason to identify these "posted workers" as in the previous definition, can be traced back to a question of territorial application of labour law. This is obviously a somewhat simplified way to address the main drivers behind the PWD. Still, the literature is concordant[18] in identifying a specific case decided by the Court of Justice as (one of) the starting point(s) of the history of the PWD. In the *Rush Portuguesa* case,[19] the Court of Justice distinguished the posting of workers from the free movement of workers,[20] which would have implied the application of the full set of labour regulations of the host country. In such a situation, the rules stemming from private international law entailed at the time,[21] roughly speaking, the application of the rule of the habitual place where the work is carried out, *in casu* the home country.[22] This was considered as a threat of "social dumping" by the countries characterised by higher wages and labour standards. At the same time, the Court, in a *dictum*, left it open for the Member States to apply the full extent of their labour regulations. Thus, the *Rush Portuguesa* case managed to upset both parties (*i.e.* Member States interested in profiting from the competitive advantage granted by their lower wages and working conditions and Member States willing to deny this possibility), paving the way for a shared consensus about the need for a legislative intervention. At the same time, and quite

---

18 E. Kolehmainen, *The Posted Workers Directive: European Reinforcement of National Labour Protection* (Florence: European University Institute, 2002), p. 112; C. Barnard, *The Substantive Law of the EU: The Four Freedoms* (Oxford: Oxford University Press, 2007), p. 370; S. Evju and T. Novitz, "The Evolving Regulation: dynamics and Consequences", *FORMULA Working Paper* 33, no. 33 (2012): 1–89, p. 14.

19 Case C-113/89 of 27 March 1990. See *infra* for a summary and Chapter 5 for a more in-depth analysis.

20 See E. Sjödin, "Labour Market Regulation as Restrictions. A Developmental Study of ECJ Case Law at the Interface Between Free Movement and Posting of Workers", in *Cross-Border Services, Posting of Workers and Multilevel Governance*, ed. Stein Evju (Oslo: Institutt for privaterett, 2013), 19–84, pp. 30–31.

21 Convention 80/934/ECC on the law applicable to contractual obligations, known as the "Rome convention".

22 Article 6 of the Rome Convention: "[…] a contract of employment shall, in the absence of choice in accordance with Article 3, be governed: (a) by the law of the country in which the employee *habitually carries out his work* in performance of the contract, *even if he is temporarily employed in another country*; or (b) if the employee does not habitually carry out his work in any one country, by the law of the country in which the place of business through which he was engaged is situated; unless it appears from the circumstances as a whole that the contract is more closely connected with another country, in which case the contract shall be governed by the law of that country" (emphasis added). As the content of the Rome Convention has in the meantime been "transposed" in the Regulation 593/2008 of the European Parliament and of the Council of 17 June 2008 on the law applicable to contractual obligations (Rome I Regulation), the new text (Article 8) states that "To the extent that the law applicable to the individual employment contract has not been chosen by the parties, the contract shall be governed by the law of the country in which or, failing that, from which the employee habitually carries out his work in performance of the contract. The country where the work is habitually carried out shall not be deemed to have changed if he is temporarily employed in another country."

obviously, views differed greatly about the actual content of this intervention, so that it took several years of negotiations for the PWD to see the light.[23]

The compromise between these conflicting views (and interests), is particularly evident in the legal text of the PWD. Here I will concentrate on several other important points of the Directive in order to complete the sketched picture.

In a way, Article 3, concerning Terms and conditions of employment can be considered as the core of the PWD.[24] Article 3(1) lays down a list of (basic) employment conditions whose application to posted workers must be ensured by Member States. These "hard-core" conditions[25] are those labour standards whose observance could be of immediate interest for posted workers.[26] Article 3(7) and 3(10) provide for two "opening clauses" to the list of *minimum* conditions provided by Article 3(1). On the one hand, Article 3(7) lays down a "principle of favourability"[27] providing that the preceding paragraphs of Article 3 "shall not prevent application of terms and conditions of employment which are more favourable to workers". Though such a wording seems to provide a very broad exemption, it has been argued that the cited principle was only intended as referring to more favourable working conditions applied in the home state.[28] From the present point of view we know that the Court of Justice has indeed interpreted this passage as only covering conditions applicable in the home state.[29] On the other hand the first indent of Article 3(10) allows the host state to apply terms and conditions which are not covered by Article 3(1) in the case of public policy provisions, as long as this is done in compliance with the Treaty and on a basis of equality of treatment. At the time of the drafting of the PWD, Article 3(10) was saluted as an important widening of the regulatory competence of the host state.[30] A dozen years later this interpretation must be revised in the light of the

---

23 See Chapter 4 for the analysis of the drafting process of the Directive.

24 T. Van Peijpe, "Collective Labour Law After Viking, Laval, Rüffert, and Commission v. Luxembourg", *International Journal of Comparative Labour Law and Industrial Relations* 25, no. 2 (2009): 81–107, p. 87; S. Giubboni and G. Orlandini, *La Libera Circolazione Dei Lavoratori Nell'Unione Europea* (Bologna: Il Mulino, 2007), p. 106. Article 3 also took the lion's share in terms of case law, as it will be explained *infra*.

25 Working hours, holidays, minimum pay, the regulation of the conditions for the supply of workers by agencies, health and safety, the protective rules for pregnant workers, young mothers at work and of children and young persons, and equal treatment of men and women, and other provisions of non-discrimination.

26 Davies, "Posted Workers: Single Market or Protection of National Labour Law Systems?", p. 579.

27 S. Evju, "Posting Past and Present. The Posting of Workers Directive – Genesis and Current Contrasts", *FORMULA Working Paper* 8, no. 8 (2009): 1–65, p. 31.

28 Ibid. *Contra* see the Opinions of AG Mengozzi in Case C-341/05, *Laval un Partneri*, 18 December 2007, para. 197–199, and of AG Bot in Case C-346/06, *Rüffert*, para. 81–83. Also, C. Barnard, *EC Employment Law* (Oxford: Oxford University Press, 2000), p. 179 considers the Directive as only imposing the respect of *minimum* conditions and hence allowing the foreign services provider to retain its competitive advantage.

29 *Laval*, para. 79–81, *Rüffert*, para. 32–34; see *infra* and Chapter 5.

30 Davies, "Posted Workers: Single Market or Protection of National Labour Law Systems?", p. 582: "Article 3, taken as a whole, gives the host state considerable freedom to [...] apply to

case law of the Court of Justice. The CJEU made it clear that the scope of "public policy" cannot be freely and unilaterally decided by a given Member State: as it represents an exception to free movement principles, the imposition of standards on the ground of "public policy" is subject to the scrutiny of the Court of Justice and must be interpreted strictly.[31]

Another (and final) point worth stressing in this introduction is related to the type of sources of labour standards which are considered by the PWD. The Directive makes reference to "law, regulation or administrative provision".[32] As one turns to labour standards laid down by collective agreements, however, the picture gets more complicated. The same Article 3(1) includes "collective agreements or arbitration awards which have been declared universally applicable within the meaning of paragraph 8, insofar as they concern the activities referred to in the Annex".[33] Paragraph 8 first clarifies the meaning of "universally applicable", by referring to collective agreements whose observation is mandatory for "all undertakings in the geographical area and in the profession or industry concerned".[34] Second, for those host states lacking a system for declaring collective agreements "universally applicable", the same paragraph provides for two more options. The decision to avail themselves of either option however must be taken explicitly by the Member State.[35] The first indent allows Member States to base themselves on collective agreements which, although not "universally applicable", are "generally applicable to all similar undertakings in the geographical area and in the profession or industry concerned". This option has been interpreted as substituting the "test of obligation" with a test of "applicability in fact".[36] The second indent further broadens the categories of collective agreements which can be relied upon by the host state, including those agreements "which have been concluded by the most representative employers' and labour organisations at national level and which are applied throughout national territory". As the first option was characterised by a test of "applicability in fact", here the test is defined as one of "representative status" of the parties.[37] The provision is completed by

posted workers on ground of public policy terms and conditions of employment derived from their labour laws which go beyond the compulsory list laid down in Article 3(1)".

31 Case C-319/06, *Commission v. Luxembourg*, para. 26–33.

32 Article 3(1).

33 The Annex fundamentally comes down to the building sector in its broader sense, including the construction, repair, upkeep, alteration or demolition of buildings. The importance of the building sector for the posting phenomenon (or, better, vice versa) will be clarified by the data provided in Chapter 1.

34 Article 3(8).

35 "In the absence of a system for declaring collective agreements or arbitration awards to be of universal application within the meaning of the first sub paragraph, Member States may, *if they so decide*, base themselves on […]" (emphasis added). See Giubboni, and Orlandini, *La Libera Circolazione Dei Lavoratori Nell'Unione Europea*, p. 6.

36 Davies, "Posted Workers: Single Market or Protection of National Labour Law Systems?", p. 580.

37 Ibid.

a "safety net":[38] the application of labour standards set out by those collective agreements must not result in a situation violating the equality of treatment between undertakings in a similar position. Concluding this short introductory overview, it is important to remember that the question of the application of standards laid down by collective agreements is *prima facie* related only to the construction sector (as identified by the Annex of the PWD). This, however, is only true as regards the rules which the host state is obliged to apply to posted workers.[39] If one turns to the rules the host state is *permitted* to apply, the second indent of Article 3(10) allows Member States to extend the application of collective agreement to sectors of activity "other than those referred in the Annex". This enlargement is, once again, subject to the requirement of equality of treatment and of compliance with the Treaties.[40]

A FISTFUL OF CASES

The case law of the Court of Justice of the European Union (CJEU) represents a fundamental element for the study of the legal aspects of the posting phenomenon in the EU. As we will see, some important decisions have played a major role not only in shaping the legal framework of the phenomenon here at stake, but also in sparking the debate about posting workers. Indeed, as recalled *supra*, it was a decision of the Court of Justice which to some extent paved the way for the adoption of the PWD, though the influence of the case law upon the text itself is far from straightforward.

Thus, in order to provide for some background information, it is necessary to anticipate the description of some of those cases, since they will be often referred to in the next Chapters. Indeed, these cases played a major role in shaping the framework of posting of workers, clearly leaving their mark on its legal evolution. Their impact can hardly be overstated. Here I will summarise four important judgements delivered by the Court of Justice. In order to avoid to overburden the reader already in this Introduction, I will keep these brief paragraphs as descriptive as possible, leaving the legal analysis of the case law for the next Chapters.[41]

---

38 Evju, "Posting Past and Present. The Posting of Workers Directive – Genesis and Current Contrasts", p. 33.

39 Davies, "Posted Workers: Single Market or Protection of National Labour Law Systems?", p. 581.

40 Ibid., pp. 582–583.

41 A more detailed analysis of these cases, together with other decisions delivered by the CJEU on the topic, will be presented in Chapter 5.

RUSH PORTUGUESA

Rush Portuguesa was a Portuguese construction firm providing its services as a subcontractor on the TGV Atlantique construction site. In order to carry out the works, Rush brought its Portuguese employees to France.[42] It is important to note that, at the time when the facts took place, those workers were essentially third-country nationals, as the transitional arrangements for Portuguese accession were still in place.[43] Thus, these workers were not covered by the provisions of the Treaty about free movement of workers.

The French immigration authority found Rush Portuguesa in breach of the law, which required third-country nationals employed in France to obtain a work permit. Furthermore, these workers were paid below the French wage standards.[44] Rush was then fined by the *Office national d'immigration*. The preliminary question to the Court of Justice was raised in the subsequent administrative procedure, where Rush defended its position on the basis of the freedom to provide services.

The French judge asked three questions, which came down to the compatibility with the freedom to provide services of the French regulation about third-country nationals employed by service providers established in a Member State.

The Court held that the freedom to provide services entailed the right to do so "under the same conditions as are imposed by that State on its own nationals". From this perspective, the imposition of the requirement to obtain a work permit was considered a discriminatory restriction to the freedom to provide services.[45] The provisions about free movement of workers were not applicable to the case, because of the transitional arrangements following the accession of Portugal; the Court however stressed that these provisions did not apply to the case because the workers employed by Rush would return to their country of origin after the completion of their work. To this the Court added an important statement: this situation meant that posted workers did not, at any time, gain access to the labour market of the host Member State.[46]

---

42 Thus, reasoning in terms of the not-yet-existent Posting of Workers Directive, the case involves the first scenario of posting.

43 *Rush Portuguesa*, para. 4. See Barnard, *The Substantive Law of the EU: The Four Freedoms*, p. 369.

44 *Rush Portuguesa*, para. 3. See also R. Blanpain, *Freedom of Services in the European Union: Labour and Social Security Law: the Bolkestein Initiative* (The Hague: Kluwer Law International, 2006), p. 182 and R. Blanpain, *European Labour Law* (The Hague: Kluwer Law International, 2010), p. 373.

45 *Rush Portuguesa*, para. 11–12.

46 *Rush Portuguesa*, para. 15: "In fact, such workers return to their country of origin after the completion of their work without at any time gaining access to the labour market of the host Member State". Indeed, this is the only criterion used by the Court to distinguish the situation of posted workers from the one covered by the free movement of workers. One cannot fail to notice that this criterion draws an indeed thin line, with a number of foreseeable borderline situation. As Hellsten puts it, such a distinction seems artificial: "thinking [that] a worker moving on his own initiative for one day to the host state enters its labour market while a

Finally, to answer the concerns expressed by the French government, the Court made a statement which would have a major impact on the drafting process of the PWD. Indeed, the Court concluded that "Community law does not preclude Member States from extending their legislation, or collective labour agreements entered into by both sides of industry, to any person who is employed, even temporarily, within their territory, no matter in which country the employer is established; nor does Community law prohibit Member States from enforcing those rules by appropriate means".[47]

In brief

Foreign undertakings have the right to bring their own manpower when providing services in the territory of another Member State. The host state cannot impose conditions relating to the recruitment of manpower or the obtaining of work permits to these workers and/or to their employer. However, the host state is in principle entitled to extend its legislation and collective labour agreements to these workers. Posted workers do not gain at any time access to the host state labour market, save for those workers posted in the context of a provision of services specifically intended to make available labour in the host state.

LAVAL

In May 2004 the Latvian company Laval un Partneri posted workers to its (fully owned) subsidiary (L&P Baltic Bygg) in Sweden.[48] This subsidiary, following public tender, had to perform a number of contracts in the construction sector. Notably, it had to renovate a school building for the town of Vaxholm.[49] The subsidiary was not bound by a collective agreement with any Swedish trade union. Following the beginning of the renovation, the Swedish union of construction workers started contacts with both the representatives of the subsidiary and of the Latvian "mother company". However, Laval refused to sign a collective

---

worker posted for a ten years' project does not"; see J Hellsten, "On the Social Dimension in Posting of Workers", *Publication of Labour Administration*, no. 301 (2006): 1–134, p. 9.

47 *Rush Portuguesa*, para. 18.

48 The case falls into the second posting scenario, covered by Article 1(3)(b) of the Posting of Workers Directive.

49 A number of authors give full account of this case, see for example A.R. Ganesh, "Appointing Foxes to Guard Henhouses: the European Posted Workers' Directive", *Columbia Journal of European Law*, 2008, 123–142, pp. 126–127; Van Peijpe, "Collective Labour Law After Viking, Laval, Rüffert, and Commission v. Luxembourg", pp. 89 ff.; R. Eklund, "A Swedish Perspective on Laval", *Comparative Labor Law & Policy Journal* 29, no. 4 (2008): 551–572, pp. 551 ff.; Davies, "One Step Forward, Two Steps Back? The Viking and Laval Cases in the ECJ", *Industrial Law Journal* 37, no. 2 (June 2008): 126–148, pp. 127 ff.; J. Malmberg and T. Sigeman, "Industrial Action and EU Economic Freedoms: The Autonomous Collective Bargaining Model Curtailed by the European Court of Justice", *Common Market Law Review* 45 (2008): 1115, pp. 1120 and ff.

agreement, so that the negotiations basically failed. Thus, after giving prior notice, the Swedish construction union (soon joined by the electricians union), started a *blockade* against the construction site. This collective action meant, in very brief, that the workers affiliated to these unions refused to perform their contract for the part regarding the construction site of Laval. Such a situation rapidly made it impossible for Laval to perform the contract, so that it eventually went bankrupt.

The legal dispute started on 7 December 2004, when Laval brought an action before the Labour Court, asking for a prohibition of the collective action as well as for compensation from the unions. The Court denied Laval an "interlocutory decision" (roughly speaking, an interim injunction) to discontinue the action. However, even though the action was lawful under Swedish law,[50] in the following proceedings the Court found that issues touching upon EU law had to be solved, and hence asked the Court of Justice for a preliminary ruling. The Labour Court asked to the CJEU two different preliminary questions.[51] The first concerned the compatibility with EU law, and notably with the freedom to provide services and the PWD, of the collective action at stake. The second also concerned compatibility with these rules, but regarded a piece of Swedish legislation, the so-called *Lex Britannia*.[52] Without entering into details, this law, while forbidding collective action aimed at changing an existing collective agreement signed under Swedish law, allowed such actions in order to challenge "foreign" collective agreement.[53]

On 18 December 2007 the Court of Justice (hereinafter in this section, the Court) delivered its judgement. Here I will summarise the main arguments.

The PWD

The Court started with a rather lengthy analysis of the Posting of Workers Directive. In fact, the analysis seems indeed long if one considers that the Directive itself was not applicable to the claim, as it was addressed to the Swedish union, not to the Kingdom of Sweden.[54] Nevertheless, the Court took the occasion to "clarify" its interpretation of a number of key points of the PWD, touching some of the dispositions highlighted *supra*.

The Court referred to Article 3(8) of the Directive, in order to examine whether the Swedish system did fall into one of the categories which allowed the application to posted workers of employment conditions laid down in collective

---

50 Eklund, "A Swedish Perspective on Laval", p. 552.

51 Van Peijpe, "Collective Labour Law After Viking, Laval, Rüffert, and Commission v. Luxembourg", p. 90.

52 *Official Gazette* 1991:681, *Government Bill* 1990/91:162, om vissa fredspliktstegler.

53 Which was the case in *Laval*, at least after 14 September and 20 October 2004, when Laval signed two collective agreements with the Latvian building workers' union. See Eklund, "A Swedish Perspective on Laval", p. 552.

54 Davies, "One Step Forward, Two Steps Back? The Viking and Laval Cases in the ECJ", pp. 127–128.

agreements. The answer was negative.[55] Having no system to extend collective agreements, either universally or generally,[56] the Swedish system is based on a case by case negotiation of wages and working conditions. Thus, the posting employer was expected to enter into such negotiations with trade unions in order to establish the minimum conditions required by the Directive.[57] On this background, the Court found that the collective action, aimed at forcing the employer to sign a collective agreement, was not compatible with the PWD and the freedom to provide services. The Court reached this conclusion stressing in particular the uncertainty of both the duration and the eventual outcome of the process.[58] Moreover, the Court pointed out that a Member State willing to make use of one the "options" provided by Article 3(8) "*must* so decide",[59] in this sense implying the necessity of an explicit choice made by the Member State when transposing the PWD.[60]

The Court then moved to assess the actual content of collective agreements, to deal with the terms and working conditions applicable to posted workers. Here, the Court found that the collective agreement (whose signing by the posting employer was the aim of the collective action) established working conditions which were more favourable than the ones provided by Swedish law.[61] In the view of the Court this made those provisions incompatible with Article 3(1), which only covered *minimum* conditions. As for Article 3(7),[62] the Court held that it only covered the case of a posting employer signing a collective agreement *of its own accord*.[63] The Court also found that the collective agreement contained certain terms which fell outside the items provided by the list of Article 3(1).[64] Once again, this was considered in breach of the Directive, notwithstanding the fact that Article 3(10) explicitly allows the application of "terms and conditions of employment on matters other than those referred to in the first subparagraph of paragraph 1 in the case of public policy provisions". The Court considered that

---

55 *Laval*, para. 69–70 and 100.

56 See A. Adlercreutz and B. Nystrom, *Labour Law in Sweden* (Alphen aan den Rijn: Kluwer Law International, 2010), pp. 188–189; Malmberg and Sigeman, "Industrial Action and EU Economic Freedoms: The Autonomous Collective Bargaining Model Curtailed by the European Court of Justice"; J. Malmberg, "The Collective Agreement as an Instrument for Regulation of Wages and Employment Conditions", *Stability and Change in Nordic Labour Law* 43 (2002): 189–213.

57 Davies, "One Step Forward, Two Steps Back? The Viking and Laval Cases in the ECJ", p. 128.

58 *Laval*, para. 71.

59 Ibid., para. 66 (emphasis added).

60 Van Peijpe, "Collective Labour Law After Viking, Laval, Rüffert, and Commission v. Luxembourg", p. 91; Eklund, "A Swedish Perspective on Laval", p. 558.

61 *Laval*, para. 78.

62 Which, as we saw, allows the "application of terms and conditions of employment which are more favourable to workers".

63 *Laval*, para. 81.

64 Such as a number of pecuniary obligation, *e.g.*, insurance premiums; see Eklund, "A Swedish Perspective on Laval", p. 560.

trade unions could not avail themselves of this provision since they are not bodies governed by public law.[65]

The freedom to provide services

The Court went on to assess its *competence* to decide upon the issue, on the basis of the freedom to provide services.[66] The Court discarded[67] the objection that the EU had no competence to assess the right to strike, on the basis of the explicit exclusion provided by the Treaties.[68] Furthermore, the Court also discarded[69] the objection based on its lack of competence to decide upon fundamental rights. Indeed, the Court, while reassessing its legitimacy in solving a question involving a fundamental right, recognised the right to collective action as such. This was done on the basis of a number of international instruments.[70] However, having recognised this status for the right to take collective action, the Court affirmed that its exercise may nevertheless be subject to *certain restrictions*.[71] It is important also to stress the fact that the Court considered that Article 49 EC (now Article 56 TFEU), protecting the freedom to provide services, was applicable to trade unions, in view of their (alleged) quasi-regulatory nature.[72]

The Court takes the view that the recourse to collective action is liable to make it less attractive, or more difficult, for an undertaking to carry out its work

65 *Laval*, para. 84. The Court held that a Member State wishing to have recourse to Article 3(10) in order to extend the list of applied provisions must explicitly state it when transposing the directive.

66 Back then, Article 49 TCE, now Article 56 TFEU.

67 *Laval*, para. 86–88.

68 Article 137(5) TCE, now 153(5) TFEU.

69 *Laval*, para. 89–95.

70 Ibid., para. 90, which is worth quoting in full: "In that regard, it must be recalled that the right to take collective action is recognised both by various international instruments which the Member States have signed or cooperated in, such as the European Social Charter, signed at Turin on 18 October 1961 – to which, moreover, express reference is made in Article 136 EC- and Convention No 87 of the International Labour Organisation concerning Freedom of Association and Protection of the Right to Organise of 9 July 1948- and by instruments developed by those Member States at Community level or in the context of the European Union, such as the Community Charter of the Fundamental Social Rights of Workers adopted at the meeting of the European Council held in Strasbourg on 9 December 1989, which is also referred to in Article 136 EC, and the Charter of Fundamental Rights of the European Union proclaimed in Nice on 7 December 2000."

71 Ibid., para. 96.

72 Ibid., para. 98: "Furthermore, compliance with Article 49 EC is also required in the case of rules which are not public in nature but which are designed to regulate, collectively, the provision of services." This conception of trade unions was criticised as a misunderstanding of their role, since trade union action was essentially assimilated to an exercise of regulatory powers delegated by the State. See F. Dorssemont, "The Right to Take Collective Action Versus Fundamental Economic Freedoms in the Aftermath of Laval and Viking. Foes Are Forever", in *European Union Internal Market and Labour Law: Friends or Foes?*, ed. Marc De Vos, vol. 88 (Antwerp: Intersentia, 2009), 45–104, pp. 66–67; Davies, "One Step Forward, Two Steps Back? The Viking and Laval Cases in the ECJ", pp. 136–137.

in Sweden, thus constituting a *restriction* to the freedom to provide services.[73] This sets the stage for the assessment of the right to strike as a restriction to a fundamental freedom, which then requires a justification.[74] On the basis of its evaluation of the PWD which was summarised *supra*, the Court finds no such justification: this because of the uncertainty which characterised the Swedish system as to which obligations the service provider was obliged to comply with.[75] Thus, the collective action represents a restriction to the freedom to provide services which cannot be justified as it tries to "force" the employer to apply working conditions which go over and beyond the ones applicable under the PWD.

The Lex Britannia

The recalled provisions of the *Lex Britannia* constituted the object of the second preliminary question addressed to the Court. The answer to this question takes a much shorter part of the Court reasoning. These provisions were considered discriminatory.[76] Although the Court acknowledged that the *Lex Britannia* was aimed at fighting social dumping[77] , such a justification was not considered as sufficient. Indeed, the Court affirmed that this objective didn't fall in the categories which could in principle justify a discriminatory measure, stated in Article 46 TEC (now Article 52 TFEU).[78]

In brief

The exercise of the right to take collective action against a posting undertaking established in another Member State represents a restriction to the freedom to provide services. Such a collective action, if aimed at forcing the employer to sign a collective agreement setting wages and working conditions above the minima contained in the Posting of Workers Directive, or regulating topics going beyond the list of this Directive, cannot be justified in the light of the objectives of fighting against social dumping and/or of workers' protection. A rule excluding "foreign" collective agreements from the peace obligation stemming from the conclusion of a collective agreement in the host member state, is discriminatory and as such incompatible with the Treaty.

73 *Laval*, para. 99.
74 Ibid., para. 101. The Court however conceded that fighting against "possible social dumping" may in principle justify the restriction: *id.*, para. 103.
75 Ibid., para. 110.
76 Ibid., para. 112–120.
77 Ibid., para. 113.
78 Ibid., para. 119.

RÜFFERT

In the German state of Lower Saxony, a law required contractors awarded with public contracts to pay their workers a minimum level of pay.[79] This provision also extended to sub-contractors. This minimum level was identified by a regional collective agreement which had not been declared universally applicable. This collective agreement contained a higher minimum wage than the national one. In case of non compliance, the contractor would be fined for an amount up to the 10% of the contract. Such an eventuality materialised in the present case.

In autumn 2003 the state of Lower Saxony, following a public invitation to tender, awarded the German company Objekt und Bauregie a contract for a structural work in the building of Göttingen-Rosdorf prison. This company made use of a subcontractor located in Poland. In summer 2004 the subcontractor was accused of paying its workers well below the cited minimum level (around 46% of the minimum wage laid down in the regional collective agreement). At this point both the State of Lower Saxony and Objekt und Bauregie terminated the contract. After the first instance, the company was fined for a total around 85000 EUR. It was on the occasion of the appeal, where Mr. Dirk Rüffert acted as liquidator of Objekt und Bauregie, that the preliminary question was asked to the Court of Justice.

The German court basically asked whether the obligation to pay the minimum wage identified by the regional collective agreement was compatible with the freedom to provide services, in its application to posting of workers.[80] The Court took again the occasion to clarify the provisions of the PWD.

The Court found the method applied by Lower Saxony for fixing the minimum wage of posted workers to be in breach of the freedom to provide services. This particularly because the cited method did not respect the requirements of Articles 3(1) and 3(8) of the PWD.[81] Article 3(1) requires that the provisions to be applied to posted workers must have been laid out either by law (or administrative provisions) or, for the construction sector, by collective agreement declared universally applicable – within the meaning of Article 3(8). The Court found that the minimum wage applied by Lower Saxony was not laid down in legislation[82] nor by a universally applicable collective agreement.[83] Indeed, it must be noted that, while the national collective agreement for the construction sector had been

---

79 For a more complete account of the case see for example P. Davies, "Case C-346/06, Ruffert v. Land Niedersachsen [2008] IRLR 467 (ECJ)", *Industrial Law Journal* 37, no. 3 (September 2008): 293–295; Ganesh, "Appointing Foxes to Guard Henhouses: the European Posted Workers' Directive", pp. 127–128; Van Peijpe, "Collective Labour Law After Viking, Laval, Rüffert, and Commission V. Luxembourg", pp. 92–93.

80 Davies, "Case C-346/06, Ruffert v. Land Niedersachsen [2008] IRLR 467 (ECJ)", p. 295.

81 Van Peijpe, "Collective Labour Law After Viking, Laval, Rüffert, and Commission v. Luxembourg", p. 93.

82 *Rüffert*, para. 24.

83 Ibid., para. 25.

extended, the same was not true for the regional one.[84] On this basis the Court held that the different methods laid down in Article 3(8)[85] could only be used if a given Member State lacked a system to declare collective agreements universally applicable.[86] Furthermore, the Court pointed out that the regional collective agreement could not be considered as "generally applicable" since it covered only those enterprises carrying out public contracts.[87]

The Court also found that Article 3(7) could not be relied upon in order to justify the method chosen by Lower Saxony.[88] In fact, with a definitive clarification of this Article, the Court stated that this provision "cannot be interpreted as allowing the host Member State to make the provision of services in its territory conditional on the observance of terms and conditions of employment which go beyond the mandatory rules for minimum protection".[89] It is worth stressing that the Court so decides as the contrary interpretation would "amount to depriving the directive of its effectiveness".[90]

Finally the Court rejected the argument proposed by Lower Saxony that the measure was justified by the objective of ensuring the protection of workers.[91] In the view of the Court, the fact that the minimum wage would have been applied only to workers employed by undertakings carrying out public contract was a sufficient argument to counter the objection of Lower Saxony.[92]

In brief

A rule submitting the awarding of public contracts to the respect of wages and working conditions set in a given collective agreement entails a restriction of the freedom to provide services. Provided that such a collective agreement does not fall in any of the categories listed by Article 3(8) of the PWD and only covers public contracts, this restriction cannot be justified in view of the objective of workers' protection. The rule is thus incompatible with the Treaty. Also, the higher degree of protection cannot be covered by Article 3(7), as this Article only refers to wages and working conditions stemming from the application of legislation and collective agreements in force in the home state.

---

84 Indeed, in the German system, the *Land* of Lower Saxony was simply not competent for such an extension. See Ibid., p. 98–99.
85 Collective agreement "generally applicable" or signed by the most representative organisations.
86 *Rüffert*, para. 27.
87 Ibid., para. 29.
88 See also Davies, "Case C-346/06, Ruffert V Land Niedersachsen [2008] IRLR 467 (ECJ)", p. 295.
89 *Rüffert*, para. 33.
90 Ibid.
91 Ibid., para. 38.
92 Ibid., para. 40: "The case-file submitted to the Court contains no evidence to support the conclusion that the protection resulting from such a rate of pay [...] is necessary for a construction sector worker only when he is employed in the context of a public works contract but not when he is employed in the context of a private contract".

COMMISSION V. LUXEMBOURG (2008)

The Grand Duchy of Luxembourg had transposed the PWD in 2002.[93] This law diverged from the PWD on several aspects. Four of those were singled out by the infringement procedure started by the Commission.[94] First, the law of Luxembourg included a number of mandatory provisions which are not listed under Article 3(1) of the PWD. On this point, the Court explicitly defined Article 3(1) as setting out an exhaustive list of matters.[95] Furthermore, as Luxembourg relies upon Article 3(10) in order to justify the enlargement of the list[96] , the Court stated that the *scope* of the public policy exception cannot be *unilaterally* determined by a given Member State.[97] The Court also held that Article 3(10) could not be used to justify national requirements covering obligations already present in Community law. The law of the Grand Duchy did impose such obligations in the area of information to be given to the worker (covered by Directive 91/533/EEC[98]) as well as in the area of fixed-term work (covered by Directives 97/81/EC and 1999/EC.[99]

It is interesting to note that the Court, with respect of the automatic indexation of wages, considered such indexation as legitimate only as long as it concerned *the* minimum wage. On the contrary, the indexation of wages higher than the minimum could not be imposed to posting employers, since it fell outside the scope of Article 3(1).[100] The Court discarded the justification put forward by Luxembourg, namely that the measure was aimed at promoting good labour relations by maintaining the purchasing power of wages.[101]

---

93 Loi du 20 décembre 2002 portant: 1. Transposition de la directive 96/71/CE du Parlement européen et du Conseil du 16 décembre 1996 concernant le détachement de travailleurs effectué dans le cadre d'une prestation de services; 2. Réglementation du contrôle de l'application du droit du travail.

94 Here I will mainly deal with the first of those points, as the others are of a minor interest for the present research. For a more in-depth analysis see S. Krebber, "Case C-319/06, Commission v. Luxembourg, Judgment of the Court (First Chamber) of 19 June 2008,[2008] ECR I-4323", *Common Market Law Review* 46, no. 5 (2009): 1725; see also Ganesh, "Appointing Foxes to Guard Henhouses: the European Posted Workers' Directive"; Van Peijpe, "Collective Labour Law After Viking, Laval, Rüffert, and Commission v. Luxembourg".

95 *Commission v. Luxembourg*, para. 26.

96 Ibid., para. 28: "As is clear from Article 1(1) of the Law of 20 December 2002, which states that the provisions concerning matters referred to in points 1 to 14 thereof are mandatory provisions falling under national public policy, the Grand Duchy of Luxembourg intended to rely on the first indent of Article 3(10) of Directive 96/71."

97 Ibid., para. 30; also, as Article 3(10) provides for a derogation from the fundamental principle of freedom to provide services, it must be interpreted strictly, ibid.

98 Council Directive 91/533/EEC of 14 October 1991 on an employer's obligation to inform employees of the conditions applicable to the contract or employment relationship.

99 Council Directive 97/81/EC of 15 December 1997 concerning the Framework Agreement on part-time work concluded by UNICE, CEEP and the ETUC and Council Directive 1999/70/ EC of 28 June 1999 concerning the framework agreement on fixed-term work concluded by ETUC, UNICE and CEEP.

100 *Commission v. Luxembourg*, para. 47–48.

101 Ibid., para. 52–54.

The remaining issues identified by the infringement procedure did concern the monitoring scheme, the requirement of an "ad hoc" agent and the incomplete transposition of the PWD by the Grand Duchy of Luxembourg. As for the last point, Luxembourg acknowledged the violation, while submitting that the law had already been amended. Unsurprisingly, the Court considered that the change was not relevant in the case at hand, and thus confirmed the critique put forward by the Commission.[102] Both the monitoring scheme and the requirement of an "ad hoc" agent were considered as violating Article 49 (now Article 56).[103]

In brief

The exception of Article 3(10), covering public policy provisions, must be interpreted narrowly, as it is both an exception to the general rule of the freedom to provide services and to the exhaustive list of applicable conditions provided by the PWD. Member States are not free to unilaterally determine the provisions falling in the category of "public policy". In order to rely on this exception Member States must prove the existence of a genuine and sufficiently serious threat to a fundamental interest of society through appropriate evidence.

SETTING SAIL

The interest for the phenomenon of posting of workers has risen and fallen as the tide. In the last twenty years Europe witnessed two moments of high tide, the first at the beginning of the 90s and the second starting around 2007/2008. In both occasions the Court of Justice played a major role in starting the movement: we can roughly identify the starting point of the two high tides with the decisions, respectively, in *Rush Portuguesa* and in *Laval*. Both times, when the tide retreated, it left on the shore its legal debris: the first time the PWD emerged with the fall of the tide, while the second time a so-called Enforcement Directive[104] was added to the PWD, as well as, though only partially linked, a proposal for a Regulation about the relationship between (the right to take) collective action and fundamental freedoms.[105]

---

102 Ibid., para. 70 ff.

103 Ibid., para. 75 ff. and 83 ff. See Krebber, "Case C-319/06, Commission v. Luxembourg, Judgment of the Court (First Chamber) of 19 June 2008,[2008] ECR I-4323", pp. 1727–1728.

104 Directive 2014/67/EU of the European Parliament and of the Council on the enforcement of Directive 96/71/EC concerning the posting of workers in the framework of the provision of services and amending Regulation (EU) No 1024/2012 on administrative cooperation through the Internal Market Information System ("the IMI Regulation"), 15 May 2014.

105 Proposal for a Council Regulation on the exercise of the right to take collective action within the context of the freedom of establishment and the freedom to provide services, COM(2012) 130, 21 March 2012.

Another important correlation strikes the eye, observing the timing of these tides. In fact, both "starting points" can be situated roughly three years after the accession of new Member States to the EC/EU. Hence, the first tide was preceded by the accession of Spain and Portugal, while the second followed the 2004 accession of the "eastern" Member States, as well as of Cyprus and Malta. Although my intention is by no means to imply a *causation* relationship between the two facts, this correlation brings on the table an ever-present debate permeating the legal regulation of the posting phenomenon. I will refer to this argument as "social dumping", though this may not be completely pertinent.[106] With "social dumping, for the limited context of this research, I refer to the situation in which the posting of workers allows a service provider to gain a competitive advantage over its competitors by applying, to its workers, working conditions which are "lower" than the ones normally applied in the host state, and/or by avoiding the "normal" constraints implied by the industrial relations system of the host state.[107] A clear conflict of interest can be (and has been[108]) identified around this issue. Limiting our scope to the Member States as possible actors, on the one hand one has the position of the net *importers* of posted workers, which one can assume as characterised by better conditions of employment; those Member States, one can hypothesise, will have an interest in "protecting" their labour standards and, thus, to make it difficult to have recourse to social dumping through posting of workers. On the other hand, net *exporters* of posted workers will stand on the opposite position, having an interest to make it harder for the host state to apply the full set of its labour regulations. The two high tides both exemplify this situation, though one has to leave aside from this picture the UK, which for a political choice often represents an outlier as regards the EU intervention. Thus, one can see that during the discussion about the PWD it was for Portugal to play the role of the "exporter" of posted workers (a role which it had already played in the *Rush Portuguesa* case). Indeed, a scholar directly involved in the final drafting process under the Italian presidency, tells us that Portugal was in fact against the whole package of the PWD since it "was not a piece of legislation designed to promote freedom to provide services".[109] On the other side, it was particularly for France and Luxembourg to try to restrict as much as possible the

[106] For a review of definitions concerning this concept, see M. Bernaciak, "Social Dumping: political Catchphrase or Threat to Labour Standards?", *ETUI Working Paper* 6 (2012): 1–40.

[107] See Ibid., pp. 25–26. See also the Opinion of AG Mengozzi, para. 273. *Contra*, see the stance ultimately taken by the Court on the point in *Laval*, para. 75 (though the Court never refers to "social dumping", speaking instead of "unfair competition").

[108] Davies, "Posted Workers: Single Market or Protection of National Labour Law Systems?", p. 573; B. Bercusson, "The Trade Union Movement and the European Union: Judgment Day", *European Law Journal* 13, no. 3 (May 2007): 279–308, p. 305; Ganesh, "Appointing Foxes to Guard Henhouses: the European Posted Workers' Directive", p. 130.

[109] M. Biagi, "Fortune Smiles on the Italian EU Presidency: talking Half-Seriously About the Poste Workers and Parental Leave Directives", *The International Journal of Comparative Labour Law and Industrial Relations* 12, no. 2 (1996): 97–109, Biagi, "The 'Posted Workers' EU Directive': from Social Dumping to Social Protectionism", p. 175.

possibility for "social dumping". A similar situation can be identified by looking at the observations submitted by a number of Governments and Institutions during the *Laval* case.[110] A superficial glance at these interventions shows that the Lithuanian, Estonian, Latvian, Polish and Czech Governments argued that Sweden had incorrectly transposed the PWD.[111] On the contrary, the Austrian, Danish, Finnish French and Norwegian Governments supported the Kingdom of Sweden in its defence, joined, though with some specification, by the German and Spanish Governments.[112] It is evident that such an approach to the phenomenon of posting does stress the aspect of individual employment conditions over other possible (legal) tensions.

During the second high tide, posting of workers also found itself thrown in the middle of a vast debate sparkled by a *quartet* of cases decided by the Court of Justice. The debate is the one about the relationship between fundamental freedoms[113] and fundamental (especially, social) rights in the EU legal order. Indeed, three out of four cases composing the so-called *Laval quartet*[114] are cases dealing with the posting of workers.[115] Those cases stirred an enormous debate, which soon lost its contact with the posting of workers, to address the general issue of the cited relationship. It is important to note that the rights at stake, as we just saw in the preceding summaries of the cases, where often *collective* (fundamental) social rights, as the right to take collective action. Also, the issue of collective bargaining was of utmost importance in both *Laval* and *Rüffert*. This brings us closer to the perspective of the present research.

To put it shortly, the aim of this research is to analyse the relationship between posting of workers (or posted workers) and the collective dimension of labour law.[116] The perspective of the research is mainly a legal one, based on European and International labour law. However, empirical studies about posting of workers will be presented, to better define the actual reality of the phenomenon. Also, the theoretical framework of industrial relations studies will be taken into account. This in order to answer a number of questions.

---

110 The Kingdom of Belgium, the Czech Republic, the Kingdom of Denmark, the Federal Republic of Germany, the Republic of Estonia, the Kingdom of Spain, the French Republic, the Republic of Ireland, the Republic of Latvia, the Republic of Lithuania, the Republic of Austria, the Republic of Poland, the Republic of Finland and the Kingdom of Sweden, as well as EU Commission, the EFTA Surveillance Authority, the Republic of Iceland and the Kingdom of Norway.

111 Opinion of AG Mengozzi in *Laval*, para. 169.

112 Ibid., para. 167–168.

113 *I.e.* the free movement of goods (Article 28 TFEU) and of capitals (Article 63 TFEU), the freedom of establishment (Article 49 TFEU), the freedom to provide services (Article 56 TFEU). I will refer to these freedoms either as "fundamental freedoms" or as "market freedoms".

114 The expression is now commonly used to refer to those cases. See for example J. Malmberg, "Posting Post Laval International and National Responses", Center for Labor Studies (Uppsala, 2010).

115 *Laval*, *Rüffert* and *Commission v. Luxembourg*.

116 A definition, as well as a categorisation, of "collective labour law" will be presented in Chapter 3.

The starting point does not look bright. It is in fact a twofold start: on the one hand we have the PWD, which is mute as regards the collective aspects of posting of workers. True enough, the Directive does refer to the *content of* collective agreements, but it ignores the rest of collective labour law institutions. On the other hand, the Court of Justice didn't make things any easier when, as early as the *Rush Portuguesa* case, it stated that posted workers are never to be considered as gaining access to the labour market of the host state.[117] Ideally, our first task will be to analyse such a situation, in order to ascertain whether this clear-cut exclusion is tenable. This analysis will be carried out in the light of international and European standards regarding collective labour rights, as well as of the subsequent case law of the Court of Justice. Finally, the data provided by the empirical studies will be carefully considered, as they sometimes seem at odds with the legal understanding of the phenomenon which I just summarised.

Second, this research will try to assess the possible disruptive effect of posting of workers, in its present legal shape, as regards existing collective labour law practices and institutions. The focus here is evidently on the legal aspect;[118] the difficulties and hurdles which the posting phenomenon poses in sociological (and/or industrial relations) terms will be summarised,[119] but they only play a background role in the present research. This second task is intertwined with the debate about the relationship between fundamental rights and fundamental freedoms in the EU legal system, which I briefly recalled before. In this sense it is worth stressing that this debate, though it doesn't represent the main topic explored by this research, forms an integral and unavoidable part of my analysis.[120] The reason for this is indeed simple: following our definition of posting of workers provided above, one can see that the posting phenomenon takes place *necessarily* in the context of a transnational provision of services between two Member States of the EU. Thus, the (fundamental) freedom to provide services is always at stake.

In concluding this analysis, a perspective *de iure condito*, thus aimed at the interpretation of *existing* legislation, will be preferred to a more "creative" (or daring) approach. Though sticking to this preference won't always be possible, the present context makes the recourse of a *de jure condendo* perspective at risk of naiveté or lack of realism.

117 *Rush Portuguesa*, para. 15: "[...] In fact, such workers [posted workers] return to their country of origin after the completion of their work without at any time gaining access to the labour market of the host Member State".

118 I refrain from adding yet another definition here. The concept of "negative integration", as well as its meaning in our context, will be presented in Chapter 7.

119 See Chapter 1.

120 Though the issue will often surface along my research, Chapter 6 is where it will be mainly dealt with.

THE CONTEXT

Thus, to close this introduction, a few words about (some specific aspects of) the context. We already pointed out the coincidence of the "tides" of debate around posting with the moment of enlargement of the EU. Another, much unfortunate, coincidence is relevant. Regarding the second high tide, one can see as the whole debate, sparked by the decisions of the Court of Justice, started only a few month before the sudden bankruptcy of Lehman Brothers. Thus, the ensuing discussion was carried out right in the middle of the hard biting economic crisis. Evidently, the timing was not quite right for a debate about the extension of social rights. In general, the political debate at European level veered quickly towards the waters of fiscal profligacy, austerity and competitiveness. At the same time, in countries interested by Memoranda,[121] collective social rights (notably, collective bargaining) were in fact restricted.[122] Furthermore, the widespread high unemployment meant a lesser capacity for trade unions to mobilise their power resources, so that an important actor of any debate dealing with labour rights found its strength greatly undermined.

Shifting the attention to the legal context the situation does change. Indeed, in recent years some important collective social rights (as the right to take collective action and the right to collective bargaining) have been recognised as fundamental rights, or even *essential parts* of a human right, by the two "highest" judicial instances of the European area: the Court of Justice of the European Union (CJEU)[123] and the European Court of Human Rights (ECtHR).[124] Under this different light, it is even more striking that posting of workers in the EU legal order should be conceived, in legal terms, as a *vacuum* of collective social rights.

Now, as we saw before, the debate around posting of workers is intertwined with the issue of social dumping. This is especially due to a restricted number of cases which made their way to the media.[125] Thus, the whole idea of *vacuum* that I just summoned does push forward this perception of posted workers as "not playing by the rules". Obviously, the issue of social dumping is particularly perceived in Member States characterised by "higher" employment conditions,

---

121 The most striking example being Greece; see for example E. Achtsioglou, "Greece 2010–2012: labour in the Maelstrom of Deregulation", *Transfer: European Review of Labour and Research* 19, no. 1 (January 2013): 125–127, pp. 126–127.

122 See S. Clauwaert and I. Schomann, "The Crisis and National Labour Law Reforms – a Mapping Exercise", *Transfer: European Review of Labour and Research* 19, no. 1 (January 2013): 121–124, p. 122.

123 Case C-438/05, *Viking Line ABP v. The International Transport Workers' Federation and the Finnish Seaman's Union*; Case C-341/05, *Laval un Partneri*; Case C-271/08, *Commission v. Germany.*

124 *Demir and Baykara v. Turkey*, 12 November 2008, no. 34503/97; *Enerji Yapi-Yol Sen*, 21 April 2009, no. 68959/01.

125 See for example the Lindsey Oil Refinery dispute, as described by C. Barnard, "'British Jobs for British Workers': The Lindsey Oil Refinery Dispute and the Future of Local Labour Clauses in an Integrated EU Market", *Industrial Law Journal* 38, no. 3 (August 2009): 245–277.

and especially wages. Indeed, posting of workers is only a piece of the puzzle, and a small one at that, but somehow, for a number of coincidences that I tried to summarise in these pages, it has become an extremely visible piece. Such a visible piece pushing forward the idea of the EU legal system as the Trojan horse for the avoidance of established industrial relations practices, and hence for social dumping, is indeed dangerous. It has the potential to alienate the support for European integration of the workers in these "high wages" countries. The devil, for once leaving the details, is in the coincidences. In a period where Euroscepticism is increasing across the Member States,[126] and the European Union is put at strain by the division along the debtor/creditor line, this additional source of risk should not be overlooked. A legal solution to *allow* the different systems of industrial relations to integrate posted workers should thus play a role in winning back the support for the European integration.[127]

126 See for example, J.I. Torreblanca and M. Leonard, "The Continent-Wide Rise of Euroscepticism", *European Council of Foreign Relations Policy Memo*, 2013, 1–10.

127 As highlighted by the so-called "Monti Report": A New Strategy for the Single Market at the Service of Europe's Economy and Society, Report to the President of the European Commission José Manuel Barroso by Mario Monti, 9 May 2010, p. 68: "The revival of this divide [between advocates of greater market integration and those who feel that the call for economic freedoms and for breaking up regulatory barriers is code for dismantling social rights protected at national level] has the potential to alienate from the Single Market and the EU a segment of public opinion, workers' movements and trade unions, which has been over time a key supporter of economic integration."

CHAPTER 1

THE LONELINESS OF THE LONG DISTANCE RUNNER

Defining the Posting Phenomenon from "Black Letter Law" to Empirical Data

From a quantitative perspective, posting of workers is not the most important issue for labour lawyers or social actors in the European space. Indeed, the actual number of posted workers, although rather unclear, is lower than, for example, migrant workers in the EU. Notwithstanding this fact, from a qualitative point of view, the posting phenomenon is probably one of the most complex challenges of the whole social sphere in the European Union.

Reading the law as a consequence of the reality flowing underneath, the wording of Posting of Workers Directive (96/71/EC) does reveal the inherent complexity of the phenomenon of posting in the EU. Article 3 of the Directive represents the crux of this nature.[1]

---

[1] "Article 3 – Terms and conditions of employment
1. Member States shall ensure that, whatever the law applicable to the employment relationship, the undertakings referred to in Article 1 (1) guarantee workers posted to their territory the terms and conditions of employment covering the following matters which, in the Member State where the work is carried out, are laid down:
- by law, regulation or administrative provision, and/or
- by collective agreements or arbitration awards which have been declared universally applicable within the meaning of paragraph 8, insofar as they concern the activities referred to in the Annex:
(a) maximum work periods and minimum rest periods;
(b) minimum paid annual holidays;
(c) the minimum rates of pay, including overtime rates; this point does not apply to supplementary occupational retirement pension schemes;
(d) the conditions of hiring-out of workers, in particular the supply of workers by temporary employment undertakings;
(e) health, safety and hygiene at work;
(f) protective measures with regard to the terms and conditions of employment of pregnant women or women who have recently given birth, of children and of young people;
(g) equality of treatment between men and women and other provisions on non-discrimination.
[...]

Born as a compromise between the country of origin principle (stemming, at the risk of oversimplifying, from the application of private international law[2]) and the application of the host country regulations as a whole (a way paved by the Court of Justice in the *Rush Portuguesa* case[3]), the Directive places the posted workers into a limbo. As evidenced by the cited wording, working conditions of posted workers are regulated by the home country regulations, with the exception of conditions enumerated by Article 3.1 of the Directive (with the possible "deviations" provided by Articles 3.7 and 3.10). One can see this limbo depicted by the CJEU in Rush Portuguesa:

> 15. The situation is different, however, in a case such as that in the main proceedings where there is a temporary movement of workers who are sent to another Member State to carry out construction work or public works as part of a provision of services by their employer. In fact, such workers return to their country of origin after the completion of their work without at any time gaining access to the labour market of the host Member State.[4]

Thus posted workers are influencing two labour markets (the Home State with temporary emigration, the host State with temporary competition) while they're part of neither and regulated by both. The complexity is served.

From the point of view of industrial relations this situation of "transnational limbo" provides a tough challenge to European industrial relations systems, still mainly developed at national level. As an example, which I will develop further in the following sections, Dunlop, in his general theory of industrial relations, defines the scope of an industrial relations system as directly connected with wage determination,[5] proposing the idea of the "wage-setting unit" as identifying the limits of an industrial relations system.[6] It is evident that posted workers fit difficultly into the scope of an industrial relations system defined as such. Indeed

---

7. Paragraphs 1 to 6 shall not prevent application of terms and conditions of employment which are more favourable to workers.

[...]

10. This Directive shall not preclude the application by Member States, in compliance with the Treaty, to national undertakings and to the undertakings of other States, on a basis of equality of treatment, of:

– terms and conditions of employment on matters other than those referred to in the first subparagraph of paragraph 1 in the case of public policy provisions.

[...]"

2 A. Van Hoek and M Houwerzijl, "Comparative Study on the Legal Aspects of the Posting of Workers in the Framework of the Provision of Services in the European Union" (Brussels, 2011), pp. 9 ff.

3 Case C-113/89 of 27 March 1990.

4 *Rush Portuguesa*, para. 15.

5 J.T. Dunlop, *Industrial Relations Systems* (New York: Henry Holt; Company, 1958).

6 See also on this point J.T. Dunlop, "The Task of Contemporary Wage Theory", in *New Concepts in Wage Determination*, ed. W. Taylor and Frank C. Pierson (New York: McGraw Hill, 1957), 131–134.

their wage is set in their home state, but, afterwards, the framework established by the Directive implies the application of minimum wage regulations of the host state. Further complexity may arise from Article 3.7, *id est* from the application of "terms and conditions of employment which are more favourable to workers".

The Directive does not help to solve this knot, as it just looks at the outcomes of the industrial relations system of the host state to identify the applicable working conditions.[7]

Posted workers are thus confronted with the *outcomes* of the regulatory framework eventually provided by collective agreements. The Directive does not take into account that such regulations are the final product of a complex process, which takes place all around posted workers, in the form of collective bargaining and collective action.[8] In this sense the Directive is silent about every possible relationship of posted workers as actors with the industrial relations system of the host state.

The whole idea behind the regulations (legislative or judicial them may be) has its cornerstone on the aforementioned statement of *Rush Portuguesa*: the temporary presence of posted workers in the host state, implies (following the reasoning of the Court of Justice) their irrelevance for the labour market of the given country. This reasoning is proving itself too formalistic. There are situations in which, even if temporary, the presence of posted workers may amount to a degree of influence of the labour market (in which they supposedly never entered) such as to force the social actors to confront with those workers. This may be caused by qualitative or quantitative issues. Qualitative issues exert pressure on the industrial relations system because of working conditions below

---

7 "Article 3 Terms and conditions of employment
1. Member States shall ensure that, whatever the law applicable to the employment relationship, the undertakings referred to in Article 1 (1) guarantee workers posted to their territory the terms and conditions of employment covering the following matters which, in the Member State where the work is carried out, are laid down:
- by law, regulation or administrative provision, and/or
- by collective agreements or arbitration awards which have been declared universally applicable within the meaning of paragraph 8, insofar as they concern the activities referred to in the Annex
[...]
8. 'Collective agreements or arbitration awards which have been declared universally applicable' means collective agreements or arbitration awards which must be observed by all undertakings in the geographical area and in the profession or industry concerned. In the absence of a system for declaring collective agreements or arbitration awards to be of universal application within the meaning of the first subparagraph, Member States may, if they so decide, base themselves on:
- collective agreements or arbitration awards which are generally applicable to all similar undertakings in the geographical area and in the profession or industry concerned, and/or
- collective agreements which have been concluded by the most representative employers' and labour organizations at national level and which are applied throughout national territory."

8 Directive 96/71, recital 22: "Whereas this Directive is without prejudice to the law of the Member States concerning collective action to defend the interests of trades and professions."

(perceived) national standards. Quantitative issues can arise from a widespread and particularly visible use of posted workers. An example is the construction of a nuclear plant in Finland, where around 4000 posted workers were employed.[9] What is more, the concentration of posted workers in specific regions and sectors can amount to an effect (in distorting competition or undercutting minimum working conditions) that may be larger than the overall figures about the phenomenon across the EU.[10] Against the alleged "irrelevance" for national industrial relations system of posted workers one must keep in mind that neither migrant nor temporary workers are ignored by those systems. In fact, as we will see, the recent efforts of trade unions to organise those "new" groups of workers go in the very contrary direction.

However, after this comparison, the picture gets even more complicated, as the results of those organising efforts are, as for now, quite disappointing. Thus, in the posting phenomenon, we can find another layer of difficulties for an industrial relations system: to the first, legal, layer we should add the difficulties arising from the practical situation of posted workers as migrant and temporary workers. I will address these difficulties in the following sections.[11]

1.1 A THORNY PHENOMENON

Analysing those difficulties one can understand why a national system of industrial relations finds itself at a disadvantage when facing the posting phenomenon. The recourse to judges (and, as the highest instance, to the Court of Justice) represents an epiphenomenon of this difficulties.

Indeed, the recourse to the judge is something that brings the conflict outside the borders of the industrial relations system. It symbolically declares the inability of the social actors to reach an agreement via the means provided by industrial relations. This may be due to an irreconcilable conflict of interests or by an actual lack of means to exert pressure.

1.1.1 A DIAGONAL ISSUE?

Focusing on the latter issue, the phenomenon at stake fits nicely into the definition of *diagonal conflict*.[12] As opposed to vertical conflicts (where Community law

9 R. Pedersini and M. Pallini, *Posted Workers in the European Union* (Dublin: European Fondation for Improvement of Living; Working Conditions, 2010), p. 34.

10 J. Cremers, *In Search of Cheap Labour in Europe. Working and Living Conditions of Posted Workers*, CLR Studies (Brussels: European Institute for Construction Labour Research, 2011), p. 20.

11 Section 1.3 will focus on this parallel comparison of posted workers with both migrant and temporary ones.

12 C. Joerges, "Rethinking European Law's Supremacy", *EUI Working Paper* 12 (2005).

prevails over national law) and horizontal conflicts (which arise from differences among the Member States' systems), the term diagonal conflicts has been used to describe a structural characteristic of the European multi-level system: neither the European level nor a national level is in a position to address a specific problem in its entirety. This concept can be applied to our topic, even though we are not in the field of a "purely legal" conflict. Indeed the phenomenon of posting involves the EU level and the industrial relations systems of both the home and the host State: the Community holds powers that relate only to one segment of interdependent issues[13] while national systems hold partial powers that equally do not suffice to achieve a solution of problems autonomously,[14] as neither industrial relations system is *de facto* or *de jure* able to include posted workers.

For the Home State, this is largely due to the loose connection that posted workers have with it, often limited to the process of hiring by the service providers.[15] For the host State the reason is more multi-faced, involving both the legal construction of the phenomenon provided by the EU and by the CJEU, and the practical situation of posted workers.

1.1.2 STRETCHING THE SYSTEM OUTSIDE ITS BORDERS. UNTIL IT BREAKS

In accordance with the idea of the recourse to judges as a symptom of a difficulty lying underneath, I will now analyse several passages of the *Laval* decision[16] that are useful to identify these difficulties. In particular I will address the efforts of the Swedish trade union to include the service provider into the national system of industrial relations.[17]

So, in the beginning of this well known history, Laval un Partneri Baltic Bygg (henceforth, Laval), a Swedish subsidiary of a Latvian company, was awarded a public contract in order to build a school for the Swedish town of Vaxholm. In order to carry out this task, Laval had recourse to its own Latvian workforce, thus posting these workers to Sweden. In June 2004 the local branch (*Bygettan*) of the Swedish union of building workers (*Byggnads*) entered into talks with Laval

---

13 As the PWD can only refer to the outcomes of state-level instruments in setting the working conditions of posted workers, while being mutant on the surrounding processes. This is well exemplified by recital 22 of the directive, echoing the limitation provided by Article 153(5) TFEU.

14 C. Joerges and F. Rödl, "Informal Politics, Formalised Law and the Social Deficit of European Integration: Reflections After the Judgments of the ECJ in Viking and Laval", *European Law Journal* 15, no. 1 (January 2009): 1–19.

15 R. Pedersini, *Trade Union Strategies to Recruit New Groups of Workers* (Dublin: European Foundation for the Improvement of Living; Working Conditions, 2010), p. 13.

16 Case C-341/05, *Laval un Partneri*, 18 December 2007.

17 For a more in depth account of the facts see Van Peijpe, "Collective Labour Law After Viking, Laval, Rüffert, and Commission v. Luxembourg" and Eklund, "A Swedish Perspective on Laval".

in order to negotiate a collective agreement covering the construction work[18] in Vaxholm.[19] Thus we can see that, from the national industrial relations system point of view, it all started as a physiological collective bargaining procedure, with the trade union interested in the signing of a collective agreement establishing working conditions.[20] Still not surprisingly, this demand was accompanied by the threat of collective action.[21]

As Laval refused to sign the collective agreement, notice was given that a collective action would take place, in the form of a blockade of the building site.[22] Such a blockade started on 2 November 2004, followed by a secondary action performed by the Electricians' Union (which interested all the construction sites of Laval, including Vaxholm). After a period of blockade the two parties were still unable to reach an agreement thus a mediation meeting was arranged before the Swedish labour court.[23]

It was then in the context of the proceeding commenced by Laval before the Labour Court (*Arbetsdomstolen*) that the preliminary question was referred to the CJEU. This brought the dispute outside the borders of the system of industrial relations. Thus, looking at the Home State side, while keeping an eye on the host State, one can see summarised the complexity of the situation in paragraph 28:

---

18 It is interesting to note that at that time Laval was not bound by a collective agreement with any of the Swedish trade unions involved in the dispute. See Ibid., p. 551.

19 "It is clear from the file that, in June 2004, contacts were established between Byggettan, on the one hand, and Baltic and Laval, on the other, and negotiations were begun with a view to Laval's signing the collective agreement for the building sector. Laval asked for wages and other terms and conditions of employment to be defined in parallel with the negotiations, so that the level of pay and terms and conditions of employment would already be fixed by the time that agreement was signed. Byggettan agreed to this request, even though, generally, the negotiation of a collective agreement needs to have been completed before discussions on wages and other terms and conditions of employment are entered into in the framework of the mandatory social truce. Byggettan refused to allow the introduction of a system of monthly wages, but did agree to Laval's proposal on the principle of an hourly wage". *Laval*, para. 29.

20 "Bygettan ad demanded that Laval, first, sign the collective agreement for the building sector in respect of the Vaxholm site, and secondly, guarantee that the posted workers would receive an hourly wage of SEK 145 (approximately 16 EUR). That hourly wage was based on statistics on wages for the Stockholm (Sweden) region for the first quarter of 2004, relating to professionally qualified builders and carpenters". Ibid., para. 30.

21 Byggettan declared that it was prepared to take collective action forthwith in the event that Laval failed to agree to this. Ibid..

22 "Since those negotiations were not successful, Byggettan requested Byggnads to take measures to initiate the collective action against Laval announced at the meeting of 15 September 2004. Notice was given in October 2004". Ibid., para. 33.

23 "At the mediation meeting arranged on 1 December 2005 and at the conciliation hearing held before the Arbetsdomstolen on 20 December 2005, Laval was requested by Byggettan to sign the collective agreement for the building sector before the issue of wages was dealt with. If Laval had accepted that proposal, the collective action would have ceased immediately, and the social truce, which would have allowed negotiations on wages to begin, would have come into effect. Laval, however, refused to sign the agreement, since it was not possible for it to know in advance what conditions would be imposed on it in relation to wages". Ibid., para. 36.

> Laval, which had signed, on 14 September and 20 October 2004, in Latvia, collective agreements with the Latvian building sector's trade union, was not bound by any collective agreement entered into with Byggnads, Byggettan or Elektrikerna, none of whose members were employed by Laval. Around 65% of the Latvian workers concerned were members of the building workers' trade union in their State of origin.

From the file one cannot discover if there was any effort of the Swedish trade unions to "penetrate" the *monad* of posted workers nor to establish a contact with the Latvian unions involved in the collective agreements signed by Laval. The fact that Bygettan didn't have any member among the Latvian workers is not surprising; still, it makes the situation even more complicated from an industrial relations point of view.

The picture drawn by the cited passages shows that the Swedish trade unions did not try to *include* posted workers into their system of industrial relations. The aim of the dispute was limited to the application of working conditions, following the very idea of the Directive itself: posted workers may be the object of the results of a process of collective bargaining but they are not supposed to take part in this process.

The whole dispute seems to be more a struggle against the *negative integration*, than an effort to reach a *positive* one. Indeed the national industrial relations system (*in casu* represented by the Swedish trade unions) tried to defend its way of setting working conditions via collective bargaining and collective action at plant level against the idea embodied in the directive, which completely neglects this tradition of industrial relations.[24] As we know, the outcome of the procedure before the CJEU proved itself very negative for the Swedish system. This was mostly due to the interpretation delivered by the Court. Indeed, this interpretation comes from the very first "general" approach delivered by the Court in *Rush Portuguesa*. As, from the point of view of the CJEU, the Latvian workers are still in the Latvian labour market, and thus in the Latvian system of industrial relations, the *Laval* case sees the Swedish system of industrial relations trying to "stretch" itself outside its "natural" borders to cover these workers.

1.1.3 THE SOUND OF SILENCE

The legal reasoning delivered by the Court builds upon the Directive 96/71. In this sense we have to keep in mind the Directive itself is completely silent about every possible relationship of posted workers with a system of industrial relations. This is true for the system of the host State, but the relation with the home system is also neglected, while the peculiar situation of those workers would probably

---

24 Eklund, "A Swedish Perspective on Laval", p. 570.

require a specific attention. That being said the Directive does not consider posted workers even as *included* in the host State's system of industrial relations. While it is evident that EU legislation does not take into account those workers as *actors*, I will spend some more words to justify the extension of this reasoning to their possible role as "recipients" of industrial relations' practices.

The fact that the Directive makes reference to conditions which result from collective bargaining does not imply that posted workers are considered by the same Directive as included in the system of industrial relations of the host country. The Directive, instead, *allows* Member State to *make use* of working and employment conditions fixed by collective agreements, which respect certain conditions (see Articles 3.1 and 3.8). The difference may seem subtle but it is indeed important, both from a legal and sociological point of view. It is then apparent that the Directive does not extend the scope of those collective agreements to posted workers; on the contrary, it is the legal instrument transposing the directive that makes use of the contents of a collective agreement to regulate working conditions of posted workers. Thus those workers are objects of such a legal instrument, not of the process of collective bargaining and of the outcomes of this process. Anyhow, this is the only (although quite loose) reference to industrial relations present in the Directive. With respect with any other topic of industrial relations (basically, every topic of the subject) the Directive is utterly silent. A large share of the problems arising from the interpretation delivered by the CJEU comes from this silence.

1.2 THE BLACK BOX

Before moving on to analyse migrant and temporary workers, a little disclaimer is due. In speaking about the practical situation of posted workers one must keep in mind a first preliminary obstacle: the phenomenon is effectively shrouded by the clouds. Out of the metaphor, there is a substantial lack of information about the extent of the phenomenon. The European Commission addressed this lack of information at the time of the preparation of the "2007 Communication on Posting of workers in the framework of the provision of services: Maximising its benefits and potential while guaranteeing the protection of workers".[25] In its Communication, the Commission stressed that "there are no precise figures or estimates of posted workers in the EU".[26] The overall situation does not seem to have changed substantially in this respect. A Report of the European Foundation for the Improvement of Living and Working Conditions, dating 2010, reached the same conclusion, in admitting that "There is a substantial lack of data regarding the overall number and characteristics of posted workers throughout

[25] COM(2007) 304 final.
[26] Ibid., p. 3.

the EU".[27] Again, the Authors of the Report complained about the complete lack of information on the employment and working conditions of posted workers, even in countries where data collection is more developed.

Reliable data about the number of posted workers are available only for Czech Republic, Finland, Lithuania, Slovenia and -since 2008- Denmark.[28] This is an obstacle that hinders comparative analysis of the phenomenon. From a different perspective, several Member States have established a mandatory system of *ex ante* notification (Belgium, Greece, Lithuania, Luxembourg, Slovenia, Spain and, since 2009, Portugal) or registration (Finland and, since 2008, Denmark) of Community undertakings having recourse to posted workers on their territory in the context of a transnational provision of services. Other Member States, such as Belgium, Finland and Luxembourg, decided to impose to posting companies to have a representative in the host state and/or to keep all documentation related to the contracts of the posted workers in the host state's territory. Although potentially very useful for monitoring (and understanding) the phenomenon, these measures may be considered by the CJEU as impeding the free movement of services, and thus be declared incompatible with EU law.[29]

Once more, the wording of the 2010 Report clarifies the situation: "None of the national correspondents could provide information on either the basic quantitative aspects, in terms of total numbers and distribution by gender and sectors, or the qualitative elements of these workers' employment and working conditions. Information on the latter, which is of course crucial for effectively assessing the operation of the posting of workers within the EU, was completely absent from the national reports.".[30] What is more, even where reporting systems are in place, such administrative data are not publicly available.

As the lack of information about posted workers is complete when it comes to employment and working conditions, the issue of inspections and controls is quite pressing. The Report shows that, along with the usual lack of data, inspection services only rarely cover the posting of workers. As checks on the conditions applied to posted workers are, in effect, done only by the host-state inspection, the enforcement of regulations on posted workers depend almost exclusively on the quality and quantity of local administrative inspections in each host state. The Directive addressed the issue in Article 4.[31]

---

27 Pedersini and Pallini, *Posted Workers in the European Union*, p. 25.

28 Ibid.

29 See *infra*, p. 37.

30 Ibid., p. 9.

31 "Article 4 Cooperation on information
1. For the purposes of implementing this Directive, Member States shall, in accordance with national legislation and/or practice, designate one or more liaison offices or one or more competent national bodies.
2. Member States *shall make provision for cooperation between the public authorities which, in accordance with national legislation, are responsible for monitoring the terms and conditions of employment* referred to in Article 3. Such cooperation shall in particular consist in replying to

Unfortunately, *none* of the Member States had set up any kind of regulation of the checking and cooperation activity, at least at the time of the 2008 EU Commission Recommendation on "enhanced administrative cooperation in the context of the posting of workers in the framework of the provision of services".[32] The importance of this issue is stressed by recent studies about working conditions of Polish posted workers in Oslo.[33] The study showed as those workers face lower wages and working conditions than Polish migrant workers. Irregularities in working conditions were then present and widespread among posted workers, even though the study shows that the line between migrant[34] and posted is, in fact, a thin one, as only a minority (around 15%) of posted workers had effectively worked for their Polish employer in their home country.

1.2.1 RENEWED INTEREST AND FURTHER ANALYSIS

In the aftermath of the CJEU intervention, and especially after the widespread debate arising from the *Laval* case, the absence of reliable data about the posting phenomenon was directly addressed as an issue. Hence, on behalf of the European Commission and of the DG Employment, Social Affairs and Equal Opportunities, a study addressing both the economic and social effects of posting"[35] was prepared. This study, presented in 2011, helps shedding some light on the reality of the posting phenomenon, although many dark corners remain.

Study on the economic and social effects associated with the phenomenon of posting of workers in the EU

The most valuable contribution of this study, prepared by IDEA Consult and ECORYS Netherlands, to the analysis of posting of workers in the EU is represented by the provision of actual data and figures about the phenomenon. That being said the Authors of the study expressly underline the fact that, at EU level, data sources about cross-border posting are limited to the E101 social security forms.[36] This amount to a degree of uncertainty about the final results of the study, as

reasoned requests from those authorities for information on the transnational hiring-out of workers, including manifest abuses or possible cases of unlawful transnational activities."

32 2008/C 85/01.

33 See J. Hansen and S. Andersen, "East European Workers in the Building and Construction Industry. Recruitment Strategies and Effects on Wages, Employment Terms and Agreements" (Employment Relations Research Centre (FAOS), 2008).

34 The concept of "migrant" worker as opposed to "posted" identifies those workers covered by the provisions about free movement of workers.

35 IDEA Consult and ECORYS Netherlands, *Study on the Economic and Social Effects Associated with the Phenomenon of Posting of Workers in the EU Final Report, Labour* (European Commission, 2011).

36 In short, E101 is the name of a certificate which is used by all countries of the European Union. With this certificate, an employee who works outside its own country can prove that he or she

the actual precision of the measure of posting based on E101 certificates, as the Authors admit, may be questioned.[37] However the conclusion of the study is that, the E101 being the only administrative data source at EU level that can provide information about posting (both form receiving and sending perspective), this document still represent the best available instrument for those looking for a cross-country analysis of the phenomenon.[38] Keeping this foreword in mind, I will now look at the data provided by the study about the European level.

From these data sources, the study considers the number of posted workers to be around 1.06 million. The Authors stress that, although this number may suggest a small phenomenon, posted workers still represent almost a fifth (18.5%) of the whole stock of non-nationals EU citizens in the labour force.[39] Posting thus represents an important share of transnational labour mobility in the EU. What is more, the phenomenon does not affect evenly all the European countries, whether at the sending or receiving end, so that its importance may differ greatly from one country to another.

Figure 1.1 Number of E101 certificates by sending country (x 1,000), 2007

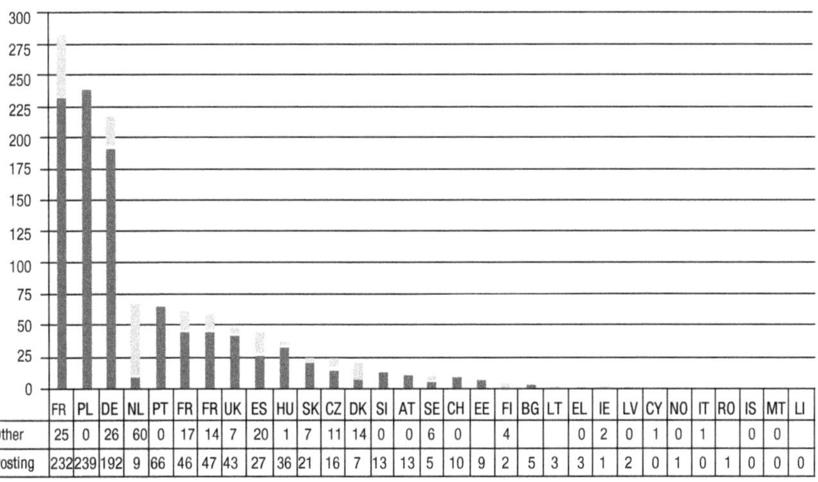

	FR	PL	DE	NL	PT	FR	FR	UK	ES	HU	SK	CZ	DK	SI	AT	SE	CH	EE	FI	BG	LT	EL	IE	LV	CY	NO	IT	RO	IS	MT	LI
Other	25	0	26	60	0	17	14	7	20	1	7	11	14	0	0	6	0		4			0	2	0	1	0	1		0	0	
Posting	232	239	192	9	66	46	47	43	27	36	21	16	7	13	13	5	10	9	2	5	3	3	1	2	0	1	0	1	0	0	0

Table 1.1 shows the distribution, in terms of total number of postings, between EU countries as regards the number of posted workers actually received during

is covered under it's home country social insurance legislation for e.g. old age pension, child benefit and unemployment. Each country has the certificate in its own language.

[37] In particular the study points out that A) the number of E101 certificates issued approximates the number of "postings" but this number may differ from the actual number of "posted workers", and B) some posting employer may not request the E101 certificate for his workers in case of very short-term posting.

[38] Ibid., p. 95.

[39] Ibid., p. 3.

year 2007. If we look at the number of E101 certificate issued for posting, we can see that the three main sending countries, namely Poland (22.7%), France (22.1%) and Germany (18.3%), account together for the majority (63.1%) of postings across the EU. Behind them, Belgium, Portugal and the United Kingdom show nearly 50.000 postings each, while the other countries reported much lower numbers. The study then stresses that although an important phenomenon in transnational labour mobility, posting is concentrated in a few countries. With a broader look, 66% of posted workers came from EU-15 while 33% from EU-12, thus accounting an average 0.37% of the active population of EU-15 sending countries and 0.74% of EU-12.[40]

Figure 1.2 Number of received postings by country (x 1,000), 2007

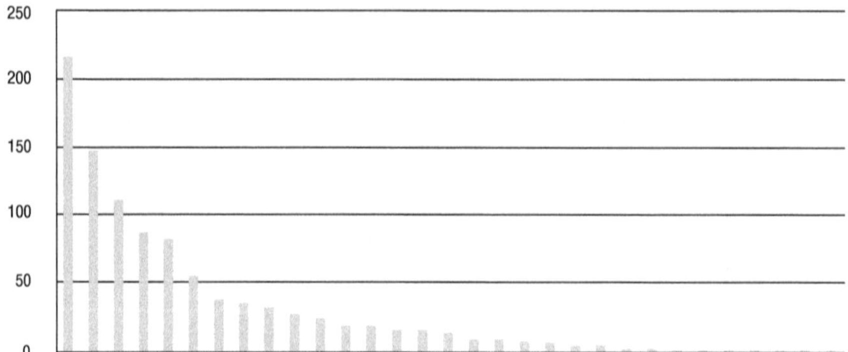

	DE	FR	BE	NL	ES	IT	AT	UK	NO	CH	LU	SE	FI	DK	CZ	PL	PT	RO	EL	HU	IE	LT	SK	SI	LV	BU	CY	IS	EE	MT	LI
2007	21	14	11	89	86	56	39	38	34	29	28	21	19	18	17	15	13	11	10	8	8	6	4	4	3	3	2	2	2	2	1

Source: IDEA Consult/Ecorys NL based on data collection of European Commission

Looking at the receiving side, Table 1.2 summarises the data for the year 2007 about the number of posted workers sent to the various countries. Again, from a quantitative point of view, those data show a phenomenon concentrated in a small number of European countries. Notably Germany (20.8%), France (14.2%), Belgium (10.8%), The Netherlands (8.5%) and Spain (5.3%) got the lion's share on the receiving hand. Hence, it is evident that EU-12 countries, and in particular Poland, present a net balance of postings with a strongly prevalent sending side. This is shown in Table 1.3.

In particular the study shows that Germany is the destination of choice for a large part (45.9%) of postings from EU-12, with France securing the second place with a much lower share (10.2%).

[40] Ibid., p. 75.

Figure 1.3 Net balance between sent and received postings (x 1,000), 2007

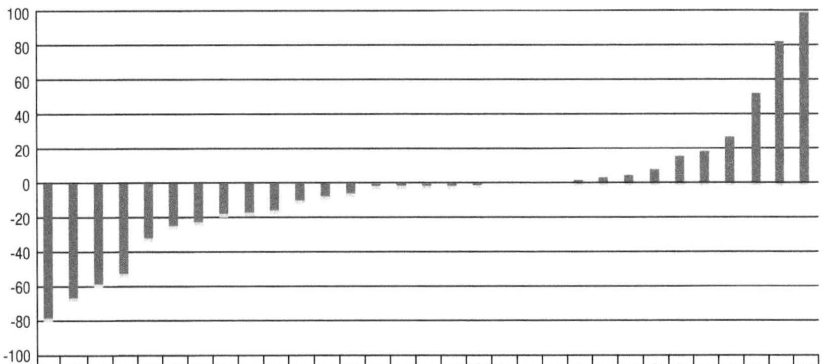

	NL	BE	ES	IT	NO	AT	DE	CH	FI	SE	DK	IE	EL	LT	CY	IC	RO	MT	CZ	LI	LV	BU	UK	EE	SI	SK	LU	HU	PT	FR	PO
■ Net posting	-79	-67	-60	-52	-33	-26	-25	-19	-16	-15	-11	-7	-6	-3	-2	-2	-2	-2	-1	-1	-1	2	5	7	9	17	19	28	53	83	224

Source: IDEA Consult/Ecorys NL based on data collection of European Commission

A major drawback of the study is however the lack of data about sectoral distribution. This is mainly due to the fact that many countries, including some of the most important ones in a sending perspective (notably Poland, France and Germany), did not provide data about the distinction by economic activity.[41] Still the study identifies the construction sector as the most affected by the posting phenomenon, with one worker out of four being posted in this context. Provided that this does not come as a surprise, the specific case of Belgium is interesting to stress the potential effect of sectoral concentration: indeed, data for year 2007 showed that the 11.3% of the whole workforce in the construction sector consisted of posted workers.

A second limit of the study, although a common one for inquiries about posting, is the absence of data on working conditions of posted workers. In this area the darkness is still complete, thus hindering a realistic assessment, from a quantitative point of view, about the application of Directive 96/71. What is more, this leaves open all the questions and doubts about the (ab)use of posting in order to undercut salaries and working conditions in the receiving country. It is interesting to note that the study, in analysing the main "drivers" for having recourse to posting (in the perspective of receiving companies in the host country[42]) identified "lower labour costs" as the *fil rouge* among the most important receiving countries.[43]

---

41 Ibid., p. 163.

42 The analysis is based on literature findings, the field research and the web-based survey which was distributed amongst representatives of employers federations. Ibid., p. 131.

43 Belgium, Denmark, France, Germany, The Netherlands, Spain. Ibid., p. 135.

Provided that the study does present a much larger scope, here I will just add a final comment. Both in the summary and in conclusions[44] the Authors affirm that the effects of posting on labour markets are negligible. However they add that significant effects can be observed "in sectors where posting is concentrated".[45] This is puzzling, as the study itself shows that posting *is* in fact a phenomenon characterised by a high degree of concentration. In fact, although the data about sectoral distribution are flawed by incompleteness, the study suggests that around a quarter of all the postings (in 2007) was sent in the construction sector.[46] Thus we can conclude that posting of workers is probably having an effect on this sector, especially in those regions more interested by the phenomenon. Under this light the study points out the possibility of a crowding-out effect for local workers.[47]

1.2.2 AN INTERIM WORD OF WARNING

At the end of the day, one has to conclude that the absence of reliable data makes it difficult to analyse the phenomenon from a quantitative point of view. Even though the quantitative aspect may not be the main issue of the posting phenomenon (as the impact on industrial relations may be strong even with just a few visible cases), the availability of reliable data on posted workers should be a precondition for a renewed interest about their specificities and their impact on the European systems of industrial relations.[48] It is evident that the simple access to the quantitative dimension of the phenomenon for the whole European area cannot be considered as sufficient. Sectoral distribution as well as working conditions and gender distribution are fundamental information whose unavailability clearly hinders the analysis of the phenomenon and of its impact.

Apart from this methodological problem, this situation has more direct effects on our topic. Indeed it is difficult to envisage the inclusion of posted workers into a system of industrial relations when their actual presence on the territory of the host state[49] remains unnoticed even to administrative authorities. In this sense the CJEU approach to registration, prior notification and monitoring procedures may prove itself an obstacle for the overcoming of this lack of data (and, therefore, of awareness). Indeed the Court has considered as infringing Article 56 TFEU a national measure requiring the foreign service provider "to send a prior

44 Ibid., p. 2 and p. 161.
45 Ibid., p. 161.
46 Ibid., p. 53.
47 Ibid., p. 173.
48 This has been stressed into another recent study, devoted to the juridical aspects of posting of workers. Van Hoek, and Houwerzijl, "Comparative Study on the Legal Aspects of the Posting of Workers in the Framework of the Provision of Services in the European Union", p. 31: "Indeed, effective policy making is impossible when no reliable data exist about the size and character of the phenomenon of posting in the framework of the PWD."
49 Ibid., p. 25.

declaration of posting, in so far as the employer must be notified of a registration number for the declaration before the planned posting may take place and the national authorities of that first State have a period of five working days from receipt of the declaration to issue that notification".[50] Such a measure, following the reasoning delivered by the Court, would amount to an administrative authorisation procedure. In the same case the Court suggests that an appropriate measure would be an obligation imposed on the service provider to inform local authorities of the presence of posted workers, of the duration of posing and of the provision of services justifying the deployment.[51] On a similar line of reasoning the Court held as incompatible with Article 49 TCE (now Article 56 TFEU) a measure that *could* amount to the obligation for the service provider to communicate on demand to the inspection service a series of information about posted workers prior to the commencement of the work.[52] Here the CJEU pointed out that the expression "prior to the commencement of work" could cover a "somewhat longer period preceding" the actual day on which the work commences (interpretation which had been put forward by the Grand Duchy of Luxembourg). Thus, back to *Santos*, we can see as, following the interpretation delivered by the Court of Justice, the monitoring of compliance with the social, welfare and wages legislation is an issue that the national authorities cannot deal with before the commencement of the provision of services, but only during the actual deployment of posted workers through inspection services.[53] Having this is mind it comes as no surprise that data about working conditions of posted workers are completely lacking.[54]

The situation does not improve if one looks at the monitoring of conditions applied to posted workers after the end of their deployment. Here the CJEU has referred several times to the aforementioned "Cooperation on Information" (Article 4 of the PWD) as the instrument to address all the necessities of monitoring of the host State authorities following the depart of posted workers from their territory.[55] As I already briefly recalled, the problem is that such a cooperation is still not very developed, to say the least, even after the 2008 EU Commission Recommendation on "Enhanced Administrative Cooperation in the Context of the Posting of Workers in the Framework of the Provision of Services".[56] That being said, it is puzzling to see how the Court in the *Commission*

50 Case C-515/08, *Santos Palhota*, 7 October 2010, para. 61.
51 Ibid., para. 51.
52 Case C-319/06, *Commission v. Luxembourg*, 19 June 2008, paras. 75–82.
53 *Santos Palhota*, para. 51.
54 Especially if we add to this that, even where system of prior information are in place, service providers deploying posted workers for short periods often "forget" to inform the local authorities. See Van Hoek, and Houwerzijl, "Comparative Study on the Legal Aspects of the Posting of Workers in the Framework of the Provision of Services in the European Union", p. 31.
55 See Joined Cases C-369/96 and C-376/96, *Arblade and Leloup*, 23 November 1999, par. 79, and Case C-319/06, *Commission v. Luxembourg*, 19 June 2008, par. 92.
56 2008/C 85/01.

v. Luxembourg decision of 2008 still made reference to such a system for cooperation and exchanges of information, with the same wording of the 9 years earlier *Arblade* decision (dating 1999).[57] Also the European Commission played a somewhat contradictory role on this subject, calling for the superfluousness of certain monitoring measures in the light of the possibility offered by the system for cooperation and information,[58] a system which by its own admission was still far from being implemented[59]

1.3 AT THE CROSSROAD OF DIFFICULTIES

Posted workers are a complex phenomenon for industrial relations. The transnational mobility, together with the limited duration of this mobility, makes it difficult to identify even the most basic component of industrial relations: an identifiable workplace, or, more precisely, an "industrial community".[60] The three different transnational measures that characterise the recourse to posted workers already show this difficulty.[61] Thus, in Article 1 of the Directive, under letter (a) we have a posting of workers under the account and direction of the service provider,

[57] Quite ironically the Court in *Arblade* affirmed that "[...] the organised system for cooperation and exchanges of information between Member States, as provided for in Article 4 of Directive 96/71 will *shortly* render superfluous the retention of the document in the host Member State after the employer has ceased to employ workers there" (emphasis added).

[58] See for example Case C-490/04, *Commission v. Germany.* Here the Commission did argue against the obligation for the foreign service providers to translate the relevant social documents into German: "the general obligation to translate the relevant documents has been made superfluous by the system of cooperation between the Member States provided for in Article 4 of Directive 96/71", para. 59.

[59] This confusing policy has been criticised by the European trade union movement. See ETUC and EFBWW, 2007, Joint response of ETUC and EFBWW to the Communication "Guidance on the posting of workers in the framework of the provision of services", COM(2006) 159.

[60] I borrow the concept from M.J. Piore, *Birds of Passage: Migrant Labor and Industrial Societies* (Cambridge: Cambridge University Press, 1980), p. 54. See in the same sense, F. Dorssemont, "Collectief arbeidsrechtelijke aspecten van internationale detachering", in *Handboek Europese Detachering En Vrij Verkeer van Diensten*, ed. Yves Jorens (Bruges: die Keure, 2009), 525–576.

[61] "Article 1 Scope
[...]
3. This Directive shall apply to the extent that the undertakings referred to in paragraph 1 take one of the following transnational measures:
(a) post workers to the territory of a Member State on their account and under their direction, under a contract concluded between the undertaking making the posting and the party for whom the services are intended, operating in that Member State, provided there is an employment relationship between the undertaking making the posting and the worker during the period of posting; or
(b) post workers to an establishment or to an undertaking owned by the group in the territory of a Member State, provided there is an employment relationship between the undertaking making the posting and the worker during the period of posting; or
(c) being a temporary employment undertaking or placement agency, hire out a worker to a user undertaking established or operating in the territory of a Member State, provided there is an employment relationship between the temporary employment undertaking or placement agency and the worker during the period of posting."

following a service contract between service provider and an undertaking in host State; we can thus envisage the existence of two different industrial communities.

Under letter (b) we have a posting of workers within a trans-national undertaking or group of undertakings, thus we face one single, although transnational, industrial community.

Under letter (c) we have a posting of workers carried out by a temporary employment undertaking or placement agency of agency workers, with posted workers working under the direction of the user undertaking in the host State; in this case we have a single industrial community in the host State.[62]

In studying the relationship of such a phenomenon with industrial relations these peculiarities hinder an easy answer to every classical question on the subject. Thus, I will try to anchor the unknown to the known via a process of analogy. I will build this analogy on the three vertices of a triangle: at the apex the posted workers, at the other vertices temporary workers and migrant workers. The reasons of this choice should be self-explanatory: posted workers do share some characteristics with both groups. On the one hand, they're migrant workers, "strangers in a strange land", with all the obstacles that this situation involves (starting from language barriers). On the other hand their presence on the working site is inherently temporary,[63] being otherwise deemed to find its regulation under the freedom of establishment/freedom of movement. Unfortunately for trade unions (and thus, for industrial relations) these two groups already represent two difficult challenges for the recruiting and involvement of workers. In order to develop this analogy, in the following sections I will give an overview of the strategies put in place by trade unions in the effort to include[64] these groups of workers.

1.3.1 "NEW" GROUPS OF WORKERS AND TRADE UNIONS

A report of the European Foundation for the Improvement of Living and Working Conditions[65] identifies, among other groups, temporary and migrant workers as "difficult groups" for trade unions. However, before passing to the analysis of difficulties and strategies, a preliminary remark is necessary: the distinction of

---

62 Ibid., pp. 532–533.

63 Coming back to the juridical for a little note, we have to point out that this limit in time is not precise. The directive itself does not identify a maximum period of permanence in the host State for posted workers: this lack of precision has been criticised by the trade union movement. See "ETUC response to ECJ judgements Viking and Laval", 4 March 2008, www.etuc.org/a/4704M; "ETUC Resolution on conditions for free movement: more protection of workers and fair competition", 28 April 2009, www.etuc.org/a/6212.

64 Both in terms of unionisation and of protection of their interests.

65 Pedersini, *Trade Union Strategies to Recruit New Groups of Workers*, p. 16. "Besides young people, the most challenging groups of workers for unionisation are migrants and people employed on temporary contracts, as well as workers in high skilled sectors."

these "difficult groups" is not easy nor clear-cut. Indeed, migrant workers tend to be employed with atypical employment contracts; the same is true about young workers (another group identified by the report as difficult ground for trade unions). In this sense, it is not always easy to disentangle the effects of each individual factor. That being said, there are factors which are connected with the status of migrant or temporary worker, as well as strategies clearly directed towards those groups. In giving account of these issues, I will start with temporary workers.

Temporary workers and trade unions

It is not the aim of this section to review the whole history of the relationship between non-standard workers and trade unionism. Briefly, it is true that trade unions have long defended the standard employment contract as the "correct" form of employment. In many cases they have openly opposed non-standard employment contracts, considering them as an instrument to undercut working conditions and salaries.[66] However, recent analysis of the strategies developed by trade unions to organise and represent non-standard workers clearly show as this trend has changed, in many cases performing a complete U-turn.[67] In particular, the intervention at EU level in the negotiations of the Fixed Term Work Directive[68] represents a tangible result of this process. In analysing these issues I will refer to "temporary" workers to include both employees working under a fixed term contract and temporary agency workers, as well as all the other forms of employment that amount to a theoretical shorter duration than the standard open-end contract of employment.

Looking at temporary workers one can see as in most European countries union density among them is lower than among workers employed with "standard" employment contracts,[69] with the notable exception of countries characterised by the so called "Ghent system".[70] Quantitative data are not available for every country in the EU; however, I will focus more on qualitative issues, giving account of the barriers to unionisation identified by the reports.

The first set of barriers is the one related to the absence of a definite industrial community. From the available data it is possible to notice a high rate of turnover in the workforce hired with temporary employment contracts. This amounts to

66 Ibid., p. 31.

67 Ibid.; K. Vandaele and J. Leschke, *Following the 'Organising Model' of British Unions? Organising Non-Standard Workers in Germany and the Netherlands* (European Trade Union Institute, 2010).

68 Council Directive 1999/70/EC of 28 June 1999 concerning the framework agreement on fixed-term work concluded by ETUC, UNICE and CEEP, OJ L 175 , 10/07/1999 P.0043–0048.

69 A. Scheele, *Non-Permanent Employment, Quality of Work and Industrial Relations* (Dublin: European Foundation for the Improvement of Living; Working Conditions, 2002).

70 Belgium, Denmark, Finland and Sweden, where differences in unionisation between standard and non-standard workers are less pronounced.

a different perception of the social pressure exerted by the peers, when present. Temporary workers tend to have less stable or less frequent contact with fellow workers and are thus less interested to comply with "social norms" of union membership. However, one must keep in mind that this factor may be less important when considering temporary workers employed in sectors where employer resistance to union presence in the workplace is higher or more effective due to type-of-contract segmentation.

Another aspect of the "industrial community problems" is the fragmentation of the workplace. In fact, temporary workers are predominantly employed in sectors which are characterised by a workforce scattered through a number of small workplaces. Apart from employers resistances, this situation, which is per se difficult for trade unions, keeps down involvement of temporary workers as the very union availability at the workplace may not be granted. Furthermore, organising temporary workers may prove costly for trade unions because of this scattered configuration of the workplace.

From another perspective, temporary workers may not be interested into trade unions activities because of their frequent transition to unemployment. Indeed, temporary employment contract are not always the stepping stone to a standard contract, and, as the present crisis has proved, they're most likely used as an instrument to reduce the work-force during economic downturns. Because of this temporary workers have less incentives to join a trade union, as in most cases they are not interested in organising unemployed or in providing services to them.

To summarise, we can identify barriers to the organising and involving temporary workers by trade unions:

- High rate of turnover
- Employers resistance in the sectors most interested by the phenomenon
- Fragmentation of the workplace
- Frequent transitions to unemployment

Trade unions and migrant workers

Turning our gaze to migrants[71] we can see a similar pattern in trade union's acceptance of the phenomenon. Indeed, migrants were considered, for quite a

[71] Here I will refer to "migrants" or "migrant workers" in a very broad sense, including all those workers that accede to another country, either EU citizens or third country nationals, in order to establish themselves. This is aimed at excluding employer-driven mobility and mobility related to the temporary provision of a service, as well as other forms of cross-border activities (as, for example, international transport workers).

long time, as a danger for workers and trade unionism.[72] This approach can be exemplified by this passage, coming from the UK and dating 1991:

> Immigrants would form a new cheap labour pool, undermining the trade unions' traditional bargaining power for their white workers.[73]

This stance was linked to the conception of migrants as the equivalent of what Marx referred to as the "reserve army of labour",[74] which would be used to undermine the power of trade unions. This idea brought many scholars to foresee that in time of economic decline migrant workers would return to their home country.[75] As everyone can see in present times, these predictions have proven fallacious.

However, as we saw for temporary workers, the approach of trade unions to the issue of migrant workers has markedly changed in more recent times. This was partly due to the evidence recalled in the previous paragraph (migrant workers are not returning to their home country in period of high unemployment), and partly to a shift in the approach of trade unions to the issue. On the politics side, trade unions figured out that a more strict legislation on the access of (using the EU language) "third country nationals" would just increase the number of "illegals", thus increasing the number of people prone to accept even lower working conditions (and, quite obviously, less likely to unionise, even when legislation allows them to). Two other motives can be put forward here. The first is the recognition of the shift from a national to a "trans-nationalised" labour market, which made evident that policies attempting to regain control on the phenomenon of migrations at national level are deemed to prove themselves futile.[76]

The second reason is related to this recognition. As the decline of trade unions has been a tendency in almost every European country since the 80s,[77] the inclusion and organisation of "new groups of workers" (and here again the history of migrant workers crosses that of temporary ones) appeared as the only possibility for workers' organisations to survive.

After this shift, however, trade unions found that migrant workers weren't an easy group to organise. Apart from the experience of migrants coming to the

---

72 G. Avci and C. McDonald, "Chipping Away at the Fortress: Unions, Immigration and the Transnational Labour Market", *International Migration* 38, no. 2 (June 2000): 191–213.

73 *Annual Conference Report*, TUC, London, 1991, p. 312.

74 See on the point S. Castles and G. Kosack, *Immigrant Workers and Class Structures in Western Europe* (Oxford: Oxford University Press, 1985).

75 A. Portes and J. Walton, *Labor, Class, and the International System* (New York: Academic Press, 1981).

76 Avci and McDonald, "Chipping Away at the Fortress: Unions, Immigration and the Transnational Labour Market", p. 203.

77 J. Visser, "Union Membership Statistics in 24 Countries", *Monthly Labor Review* 129, no. 1 (2006): 38–49.

UK from the former colonies, which commonly spoke English, and were familiar with British social institutions,[78] other groups all across the European countries do present a number of difficulties for the efforts of trade unions.

In analysing those obstacles I will not take into account the whole discourse about, racism, xenophobia and similar contextual/political situations. Instead I will just look to the difficulties reported by trade unions in their efforts to involve and organise migrant workers.

At the first place we find the problem of the language. It is not uncommon that migrant workers do not speak the language of their country of arrival.[79] For trade unions activities this means a much more difficult access to traditional channels of information, as well as a quite strong barrier even for the very individual approach by trade union members or officers.

Another important issue, which could be defined as "cultural", came from the distrust towards trade unions that characterises certain groups (in particular the ones who experienced the soviet regimes). However, this aspect must not be overly stressed, as an inquiry, dating 2007, among Polish and Lithuanian workers in the UK showed a quite high degree of "sympathy" for trade unions.[80]

That being said, the respondents identified more practical reasons which hindered their interest in joining a trade union: costs, lack of information and brevity of stay. While the importance of the first is difficult to assess, the second seems to be mostly linked to other factors (language, trade union presence). The third is more interesting, confirming the trend of union membership increasing with length of service[81] (and age).

Looking at occupations, many migrant workers are concentrated in "elementary occupations" and/or working for an agency.[82] From an industrial relations point of view, this may amount in a more effective employers' pressure against unionisation, as those occupations are characterised by a high rate of turnover and by the presence of a vast "reserve army of labour". Indeed a high share of migrant worker is occupied into sectors that are badly organised[83] (such as hotels and restaurants, agriculture, cleaning and personal service), at least in most European countries. In considering employers' pressure one must

78 See J. Wrench, "Trade Union Responses to Immigrants and Ethnic Inequality in Denmark and the UK: the Context of Consensus and Conflict", *European Journal of Industrial Relations* 10, no. 1 (March 2004): 7–30.

79 As an example, a quite recent inquiry among Polish and Lithuanian workers in the UK showed as nearly one third of the respondents described their English as "basic only" or "none", and one half described it as "adequate". See B. Anderson, N. Clark, and V. Parutis, "New EU Members?: Migrant Workers' Challenges and Opportunities to UK Trades Unions: a Polish and Lithuanian Case Study" (London: TUC, 2007), p. 6.

80 Ibid., p. 22. What is more, among those not interested in joining a trade union, less than 10% gave ideological reasons or bad experiences of unions as reason for not joining.

81 See H. Grainger, "Trade Union Membership 2005", *DTI Publications*, 2005.

82 B. Anderson et al., "Central and East European Migrants in Low-Wage Employment in the UK", *Joseph Rowntree Foundation* (London: Joseeph Rowntree Foundation, 2006), p. 6.

83 Ibid., p. 22.

keep in mind that the legal permanence of migrants in another country is often interwoven with the ability to prove an employment relationship.

A last "obstacle" hindering the involvement of migrant workers into the system of industrial relations, is the tendency to have recourse to their community when looking for help and information. This behaviour, that is partly an effect of the other difficulties, keeps them less connected to the "industrial community". This is partly connected to the recognised importance of personal networks as important factors in migration,[84] and partly to the issue of language: it is evident that migrants who got a good command of the language of their arrival country find it easier to contact trade unions (as well as other possible actors, like labour inspectors or lawyers).

In sum, barriers to organising and involving migrant workers can be summarised as follows:

- Language barriers
- Attitude towards trade unions
- Duration of stay, if limited
- Possible efficient employer's pressure against unionisation
- Recourse to different means of problem-solving (community).

1.3.2 IT'S HARD TO FIND A WAY, WHATEVER...

As we saw, the interest of trade unions towards these two groups follows, to a certain extent, a similar "pattern": from refusal to commitment. However, the barriers that I tried to summarise in the previous Sections brought trade unions to rethink their approach to those groups and to develop new strategies in order to involve workers coming from those groups, or, at least, to try to involve them.

It is evident that the approach to these "difficult" groups is inherently linked to the actual structure, tradition and organisation of trade unions, factors which do present enormous differences in the various European countries. However I will stress the similarities between the approaches put in place to overcome the recalled barriers. In doing so I will organise these measures around two poles, making use of the two "ideal-types" of "servicing approach" and "organising approach".[85]

In brief, the "servicing approach" has been defined as the traditional model followed by trade unions. This approach does rely on trade union activity external to the workplace to support members, thus focusing on full-time officers.

---

84 D. Massey et al., "Theories of International Migration: A Review and Appraisal", *Population and Development Review* 19, no. 3 (1993): 431–466, pp. 448–449.

85 See J.E. Dolvik and J. Waddington, "Organizing Marketized Services: Are Trade Unions Up to the Job?", *Economic and Industrial Democracy* 25, no. 1 (February 2004): 9–40.

Similarly, recruiting and retention activities are left to full-time officers.[86] In this sense, the servicing model is based on a rather passive form of membership, the members being "dependent" on full-time officers and union bureaucracy. Even though this model is facing increasing difficulties, due to decentralisation of collective bargaining and proliferation of employment at small sites, the "servicing approach" is still widespread all across Europe, especially in those countries characterised by the "Ghent system".

On the other hand, the "organising approach" is focused on the recruitment, involvement and empowerment of new members at workplace level. Indeed, even though a certain support from trade union may be necessary for achieving recognition, the organising approach assumes that workplace representatives perform many of the duties undertaken by full-time officers within the servicing approach, the provision of training and specialist advice remaining the only external support provided by the union. The model tends to adopt several approaches and tactics towards recruiting campaigns and encouragement of union activity among members, putting emphasis on grass-root mobilisation.[87]

Unions' strategies addressed to temporary workers

It is quite difficult do disentangle measures specifically addressed to this group from those generically intended to increase membership among "atypical workers". However, it is possible to identify several "trends" among trade unions[88] in this field. One trend is the one based on the setting up of specific unions for workers with "atypical" work contracts. This may be achieved in different ways, as the specific union can be more or less linked to the mother confederation/federation, and use innovative structure and instruments in order to meet the need of those workers. An interesting example in this sense is the Dutch experience of De Unie, which is, in short, an internet-based union (with reduced membership fees). Other (more "classical") experiences come from Greece, where unions for atypical workers have been set up mainly at sectoral level (as the Seasonal Fire-fighters Union) and from Italy, where a specific union was set up at national level (the NIdiL, New Identities of Work, set up by the Italian General Confederation of Labour, CGIL).

A different strategy, is the one based on the provision of specific services aimed at atypical workers. These services may include advice on legal issues, pensions, pay levels, access to credit and job vacancies, training and career development. Depending on the national context these services may include union's support

86 Ibid., pp. 21–22.

87 See in general Vandaele and Leschke, *Following the 'Organising Model' of British Unions? Organising Non-Standard Workers in Germany and the Netherlands.*

88 In this analysis I will rely mainly on the report issued by the European Foundation for the Improvement of Living and Working Conditions and by the ETUI: see Ibid. and Pedersini, *Trade Union Strategies to Recruit New Groups of Workers.*

in the process of transformation of atypical contracts into standard ones. This strategy, however, is often linked with the one previously identified as new specifically created trade unions may be better equipped to understand atypical workers need and provide the correct answer in terms of services.

On a different level, several unions engaged in country-wide strategies aimed at improving working conditions of atypical workers. This has been done either via lobbying and pressure on the political actors or through information and awareness-raising campaigns targeted at workers, members, employers or politicians.

Looking at these strategies, while sticking to the ideal-types definition provided before, it seems that the issue has been mainly addressed through the servicing model. This, compared to the increasing interest for the organising approach, can be interpreted as leading to a (although superficial) conclusion: when dealing with those "volatile" workers, the organising approach may not be able to overcome the barriers identified in the previous section, especially due to the difficulty to actually get into contact with "atypical" workers.[89]

Unions' strategies addressed to migrant workers

Turning to migrant workers, one must keep in mind, as stated above, that in many cases these workers are employed with atypical contracts, thus presenting both sets of difficulties. Here I will try to identify the strategies specifically aimed at migrant workers as such.

At first place we find informative campaigns directed towards migrant workers, which can be put in place through direct contact with migrants or via trade union's website or materials. To overcome the linguistic barrier, trade unions can have recourse to translators. These campaigns can be directed to the information about individual and collective rights, as well as about the role of trade unions. In Norway, the Norwegian United Federation of Trade Unions (*Fellesforbundet*) completed these "informative" efforts with the provision of Norwegian language classes for foreign workers. Closely linked to informative campaigns are the strategies involving direct contact with migrant workers. This can be done either by contact at the workplace or trough personal visits to migrants' homes. Here again union officers may have to overcome the linguistic barrier.

As for temporary/atypical workers, specific services may be provided in order to intercept the needs of migrant workers. These services are often not confined to the classical ones; on the contrary they can include help to obtain working permits, visa or to overcome other immigration-related issues. The creation of

---

89 Vandaele and Leschke, *Following the 'Organising Model' of British Unions? Organising Non-Standard Workers in Germany and the Netherlands*, pp. 30–32.

specific trade unions for migrant workers is less widespread than for atypical workers. However a recent experience in this sense must be cited:

> In September 2004, Germany's Trade Union for Building, Forestry, Agriculture and the Environment (IG BAU) announced the foundation of a European Migrant Workers Union. The new union addresses posted and seasonal workers in all industries, but in the initial phase will concentrate on migrant workers in construction and agriculture who work for a limited period of time in one or several EU Member States. The aim is to provide those workers with legal assistance and advice, support them in the event of sickness or accident, help them to receive correct payment for work done and promote the provision of better accommodation. The European Migrant Workers Union is thought to be the first such organisation to be formed within the European trade union movement.[90]

Another approach is closely linked to the "nature" of migrant workers. The so-called "network approach" is based on the collaboration with associations and NGOs engaged in migrant issues. This approach, however, need to be developed alongside with informational campaigns or direct contacts, being just an instrument to actually get into contact with migrant workers. This approach has sometimes been further developed in the national experiences dealing with more stable, more identified migrant communities (such as the black minorities in the UK[91]). The idea here is to explore the "community dimension", linking the action of trade unions with community actors and leaders in a logic of coalition building aimed at the improving of the overall living conditions of migrant communities and/or minorities.

At the end of this bird's eye review of strategies on these two fronts of trade union activities among the European countries, a final word of warning is needed. Both groups are still identified, in more recent reports[92] as challenging groups, and – at least in most countries – as under-unionised ones, with the notable exception of stable communities of migrant workers. This doesn't mean, obviously, that these strategies did fail, but still they were not sufficient to allow trade unions to finally pierce the veil of these group of workers.

---

90 H. Dribbusch, "European Migrant Workers Union Founded", Dublin European Foundation. However, the initiative did not meet widespread success, see I. Greer, Z. Ciupijus and N. Lillie, "The European Migrant Workers Union and the Barriers to Transnational Industrial Citizenship", *European Journal of Industrial Relations* 19, no. 1 (February 2013): 5–20, p. 2 and ff.

91 M.M. Lucio and R. Perrett, "The Diversity and Politics of Trade Unions' Responses to Minority Ethnic and Migrant Workers: The Context of the UK", *Economic and Industrial Democracy* 30, no. 3, (July 2009): 324–347.

92 Pedersini, *Trade Union Strategies to Recruit New Groups of Workers*, p. 16.

1.3.3 A LITTLE BIT HARDER

In order to complete the analogy, I will now stress differences and similarities between posted workers and the two groups identified in the previous Section. In doing so, however, I will have to cope with the substantial lack of empirical data on the posting phenomenon in the EU, an hurdle that I already stressed before. Because of this the figure of "posted workers" will be built mainly upon its legal definition, as well as through the disputes that made their way to the Court of Justice of the EU and/or to the media; along with these "indirect" representations, I will, obviously, use the data available.

I have already recalled the relevant parts of the PWD at the beginning of this chapter. Here I will just summarise the characteristics of posted workers stemming from the legal wording of the Directive. In brief, these characteristics are the one of trans-nationality and that of the temporary character of the employment in the host member state. However, as the former characteristic is pretty clear, the latter is, at least, vague. Indeed, in the Directive we cannot find a time limit for the worker to be considered as being temporary employed in the host country.

Without the help of quantitative data on employment duration of posted workers, the question of temporariness will remain unanswered. One can see as two (*Laval* and *Rüffert*) out of three among the ground-breaking cases came from the construction sector, which implies a long lasting duration of building sites. In the same sector we can find the construction procedure of the Olkiluoto 3 nuclear power plant in Finland. The working site, started in 2005 (with operation expected to start in 2010[93]), saw a widespread use of posted workers coming both from inside and outside the EU.[94] Such long lasting working operation may cast some doubts about the very idea of posting as an activity carried out "for a limited period",[95] but still, as we ignore the turnover rate among those workers, one cannot take this for granted, not even for posted workers employed in the construction sector.

Looking at the Olkiluoto site from another angle, a sociological inquiry on the conditions of foreign workers employed on the construction site[96] showed that these workers tend to live in a "separate community", without contacts with Finnish people. This research identified the lack of linguistic skill[97] (while no solution was offered to these workers to address the issue; *i.e.* no language classes were organised for them) and the distance from "usual" networks (families, trade unions and so on) as key factors in determining this isolation. What is more,

---

93 The project however suffered a number of delays, the start of operation being now expected for 2018.

94 Pedersini and Pallini, *Posted Workers in the European Union*, p. 34.

95 Posting of Workers Directive, Article 2.

96 A. Kontula, *Näkymätön Kylä* (Helsinki: Into, 2010). For a more concise account see N. Lillie and M. Sippola, "National Unions and Transnational Workers: the Case of Olkiluoto 3, Finland", *Work, Employment & Society* 25, no. 2 (June 2011): 292–308.

97 See also Ibid., p. 301.

the research stressed the dependency from the employer for every possible need, from housing (provided by the company), to services. In addition, the research emphasises, that complaints from the posted workers would lead nowhere as the ones complaining would just be sent back home.[98]

This situation of "isolation" is perfectly depicted in another case, which was covered by the media: the dispute at of East Lindsey,[99] a refinery in Lincolnshire, UK. In that occasion TOTAL awarded a French company (IREM) a contract to build the plant's de-sulphurisation unit. IREM was intended to supply its own skilled workforce, consisting of Portuguese and Italian workers, as it did. However, here I will not indulge on the legal aspects of the dispute, which touch the respect of minimum wages and other working conditions of those posted workers. Instead I will just focus on the recalled "isolation" aspect: those workers were living on a barge moored near their working site for the whole duration of the contract.

To finalise this picture I will look again at the EIRO report on posted workers.[100] I already analysed the report, dating 2010, to stress the unavailability of data. However, one can still make use of data available for specific areas and from specific countries. Thus, one can conclude that the majority of national reports which can provide, trough available data or reliable estimation, actual numbers (including both the case of workers being posted abroad and of foreigners arriving in the country), indicated the construction sector as the most interested by the posting phenomenon, with catering, manufacturing and civil engineering also cited as significant in several experiences.[101] Where data are available about distribution by gender, a widespread predominance of males is shown.

This isolation marks a clear difference between posted workers and temporary ones. While the latter normally accede an existing industrial community, the former, as we saw, tend form a separated community. Obviously another factor of divergence is the linguistic barrier, if present. Both factors are mainly due to the nature of the posting of workers, being a situation of mobility employer-driven.[102] In this sense, it is easier for the employer to provide housing and services keeping the posted-workforce together and close to the working site.

---

98 Kontula, *Näkymätön Kylä*, as reported by Greenpeace International, www.greenpeace.org/international/en/news/Blogs/nuclear-reaction/nuclear-news-two-euro-wages-at-olkiluoto/blog/12000.

99 For a full account of the dispute, see BBC News, 29 Jan – 3 Feb 2009; S. Milne, *The Guardian*, 5 February 2009.

100 Pedersini and Pallini, *Posted Workers in the European Union*.

101 Ibid., pp. 7–11.

102 See E. Çaro et al., "Work/Life Experience of Posted Migrant Construction Workers in a Pan-European Labour Market", August (2013): 1–17, pp. 1–2, available at www.academia.edu/4244828/Posted_Workers_Transnational_Lives_in_a_pan-European_Labour_Market.

The employer's intervention in the mobility of workers differentiates posted mobility from the one of migrant workers too.[103] Indeed, migrant workers tend to move along already established, although informal, channels. In doing so they can profit from an existing network after their arrival in the new country. What is more, difficult it may be to find another job, the (legal) presence of migrant workers in the "host" state is not tied to a specific employment contract. On the contrary, posted workers would be immediately sent back to their home country in case of lay-off (or non-renewal of the temporary contract). However, as regards the attitude towards trade unions, the situation of posted workers appears much more close to the one of migrant workers which intend to came back to their home country. Unfortunately for trade unions, this group is probably the most difficult to involve. Indeed, they lack of incentives both in overcoming the linguistic barrier (as the newly acquired language will probably be worthless after their return) and in actually joining a trade union, as the improvement of working conditions via the collective instruments becomes more interesting in the medium-long run.

Thus, from an industrial relations point of view, we can see that posted workers share some of the hurdles which characterise the two groups analysed, while lacking more positive aspects characterising the same groups. In respect of migrant workers, their experience of mobility "eludes" stable networks and communities, while, in respect of temporary workers, they tend to be isolated in the workplace too (even when they share it with national workers, which is not always the case). To summarise the identified characteristics, which make posted workers a though challenge for every system of industrial relations:

- High rate of turnover.[104]
- Language barriers.
- Permanence limited in time, and precarious.
- Isolation of both working and living community (and also from the home country).
- Efficient means of anti-unions pressure for employers.

It is very difficult to assess trade unions' strategies addressed exclusively at posted workers. In fact many of these strategies are in fact aimed at reaching foreign workers in general.[105] This is due to two main factors. The first is the scarce concern about the issue of posted workers, which made its way to social actors' discussions just after the CJEU intervention of 2007–2008, while migrant workers

103 This also represents the fundamental difference between posted workers and temporary *migrant* workers (the ones defined by Piore as "target earners"). See Piore, *Birds of Passage: Migrant Labor and Industrial Societies*, pp. 50 ff., especially p. 61.

104 Most of the (few) reports and inquiries on the subject do stress this factor; however the lack of data about duration of employment of posted workers makes it difficult to confirm this assumption.

105 Pedersini and Pallini, *Posted Workers in the European Union*, p. 30.

are high on the agenda since the very foundation of the European Community; the other reason is a more concrete one, as it is difficult even to know the actual presence of the individual foreign worker in the host state.

However, reading the EIRO reports, the specific issue of posted workers is reported as significant for trade unions in Denmark, Finland, Norway and the UK. The strategies put in place in these countries can be classified as information campaign, efforts of recruitment, transnational cooperation with foreign trade unions and monitoring of employment and working conditions in workplaces with posted workers. Information campaigns are mostly addressed at overcoming the linguistic barrier, by providing translated materials, websites and setting up dedicated telephone numbers. The Danish report[106] states that "initiatives to recruit posted workers in construction and, agriculture and nursery are numerous", but it concludes that "according to the unions, however, it is a difficult task in itself to find and approach posted workers", casting some doubts on the effectiveness of those campaigns. Another interesting strategy is to strengthen the cooperation with administrative bodies and/or social inspectorates,[107] here again focusing on the monitoring and enforcement of working conditions more than to the actual inclusion of posted workers into a system of industrial relation.

All in all, these obstacles to the actual involvement of posted workers would remain in place and equally effective even in the case of an aspiration in this sense on the side of posted workers.[108] Such a situation explains why, in the clash between national industrial relations system and the posting phenomenon, the attention is focused on the posting *employer*. Indeed, it is only through the inclusion of the employer that the posting phenomenon can be covered by the industrial relations system of the host state. Hence, one should keep this in mind while analysing the legal disputes arising, in particular, at the EU level.

---

106 Www.eurofound.europa.eu/eiro/studies/tn0908038s/dk0908039q.htm.

107 Cremers, *In Search of Cheap Labour in Europe. Working and Living Conditions of Posted Workers*, p. 36.

108 E. Çaro et al., "Work/Life Experience of Posted Migrant Construction Workers in a Pan-European Labour Market", p. 5: "Even when the workers show willingness to integrate, barriers such as long working hours, isolation in remote/rural areas, language barriers, and lack of information about institutional structure, make it unfeasible in the short time frames they intend to remain. Employer involvement in organising the migration process both reflects and reinforces this tendency", available at www.academia.edu/4244828/Posted_Workers_Transnational_Lives_in_a_pan-European_Labour_Market.

CHAPTER 2

INDUSTRIAL RELATIONS AND THE LAW – AN OVERVIEW

Industrial Relations Theories and Their Encounters with the Legal Phenomenon

The clash between national industrial relations systems and the temporary presence of foreign workers is not a completely new issue. As a provocative example one can see that the question was addressed at the Congress of the International Workingmen's Association (1867).[1] This clash has always represented a threat to the functioning of industrial relations, both in terms of pressure upon working conditions and of a shift into the established constituency of trade unions. Thus we can see that the "posting phenomenon" considered in its practical aspect,[2] is not something *per se* unknown to the history of industrial relations. It is then necessary to identify the element(s) differentiating this phenomenon from the previous history of industrial relations in Europe. The most staggering cases came out only at the end of 2007.[3] Hence, one could argue that this novelty is connected with the process of enlargement of the EU, seen as a factor of pressure upon working conditions and as a driver for increased competition between the different national systems. Indeed, the role played by such a background cannot be denied. However, if we look at our ground-breaking case, *Laval*, a major role is played by the legal construction. It is the law, both EU law and its interpretation delivered by the CJEU, that caused the discrepancy between the facts (showing a classical collective dispute involving foreign workers) and the outcome (the impossibility of the industrial relations system of functioning along its traditional way). As

---

1 "Until today these associations had remained purely local, while the power of capital, thanks to new industrial inventions, is increasing day by day; furthermore in many cases national associations have become powerless: a study of the struggle waged by the English working class reveals that, in order to oppose their workers, the employers either *bring in workers from abroad* or else transfer manufacture to countries where there is a cheap labour force." (emphasis added), K. Marx and F. Engels, *Marx and Engels Collected Works – Volume 20* (New York: International Publishers, 1986), p. 421.

2 *Id est*, workers being employed abroad for a definite period of time.

3 The facts, however, took place in 2004–2005.

it has been pointed out in the context of a recent research project on posting,[4] the "systematic and large scale way for employers to (more or less legally) access cheap labour and avoid national labour laws and collective agreements" probably represents the most relevant novelty of the posting phenomenon. Thus, I will devote this chapter to the relationship between the law and industrial relations. In order to do so, however, I will first address the concept of "industrial relations".

2.1 INDUSTRIAL RELATIONS

In making reference to the concept of "industrial relations" one has to define the actual boundaries of such a concept. It must however be noted that, as stressed by prominent specialists in this field, the study of industrial relations has always been characterised by a somewhat "pragmatic approach", which thus disregarded theorisation and conceptualisation. This is well illustrated by the dictum (cited by Edwards[5] and attributed to the "Oxford school" of industrial relations scholars): "an ounce of fact is worth a ton of theory". Dunlop complained about this lack of theory in the very introduction of his seminal work,[6] which was in fact aimed at achieving a general theory capable of integrating the expanding factual experience in the field. Finally Hyman denounced the same problem, pointing at the fact that "those who glory in their pragmatism and insist that they are immune from theory are simply unaware of their own preconceptions and presuppositions".[7]

Industrial relations emerged as a field of study around the beginning of the 20th century. At that moment its scope stretched as far as to essentially include the whole topic of the employer-employee relationship.[8] This broader approach has more recently been defined as the original paradigm of industrial relations.[9]

---

4 E. Çaro et al., "Work/Life Experience of Posted Migrant Construction Workers in a Pan-European Labour Market", p. 6, available at https://www.academia.edu/4244828/Posted_Workers_Transnational_Lives_in_a_pan-European_Labour_Market. See also N. Lillie and I. Greer, "Industrial Relations, Migration, and Neoliberal Politics: The Case of the European Construction Sector", *Policy & Society* 35 (2007): 551–581.

5 P. Edwards, "The Employment Relationship and the Field of Industrial Relations", in *Industrial Relations: theory and Practice*, ed. Paul Edwards (New York: John Wiley & Sons, 2003), 1–36, p. 30.

6 "Mountains of facts have been piled up on the plains of human ignorance [...] The result is a glut of raw material. Great piles of facts are lying around unutilized, or utilized only in an occasional and partial manner", Dunlop, *Industrial Relations Systems*, p. vi, citing Julian Huxley.

7 R. Hyman, *Industrial Relations: a Marxist Introduction* (Macmillan, 1975), p. 2. The author continues citing Keynes in a similar dictum: "practical men, who believe themselves to be quite exempt from any intellectual influences, are usually the slaves of some defunct economist".

8 B. Kaufman, "The Core Principle and Fundamental Theorem of Industrial Relations", *The International Journal of Comparative Labour Law and Industrial Relations* 23, no. 1 (2007): 5–33, p. 9: "all the behaviours, outcomes, practices and institutions that emanate from or impinge on the employment relationship".

9 B. Kaufman, "Paradigms in Industrial Relations: Original, Modern and Versions In-Between", *British Journal of Industrial Relations* 46, no. 2 (June 2008): 314–339, p. 323.

Opposed to such a paradigm, a modern one has been identified, characterised by a narrower focus.[10] Following this paradigm the core of modern industrial relations is then to be found in the study of trade unions, collective bargaining and labour-management relations.[11] In fact, the concept of "collective bargaining" had been identified as a key element of industrial relations since the founding work of the Webbs, *Industrial Democracy*.[12] Once these core elements of interest are identified, it is possible to affirm that the conceptual focus of modern industrial relations is the analysis of the processes of creation of *rules* governing work relations.[13] Or, with a different formulation, the focal point of the study of industrial relations is the activity to "generate rules governing behaviour in the workplace".[14]

However it must be noted that the focus on *processes* as a shared characteristic of modern industrial relations cannot be taken for granted. Some important authors in fact put the focus of industrial relations on the *network of rules* governing the employment relationship or the workplace. Such a vision is present in Dunlop,[15] and reaffirmed by Flanders.[16] One can see as the focus on the institutional aspect[17] of industrial relations tends to enlarge once again its field of interest. This tendency can be summarised with the wording of Clegg, who defines

---

10 Though it should be evident that the choice of words to identify these paradigms, and the very definition of what characterises one paradigm or the other, is by no means neutral.

11 Ibid., p. 317. The reference here goes only to the definition provided by the author, even though the opposition between original and modern paradigm of industrial relations is proposed in the context of a plea to come back to the former in order to overcome the growing difficulties of the latter.

12 R. Hyman, *The Political Economy of Industrial Relations: Theory and Practice in a Cold Climate* (Macmillan, 1989), p. 4. The term is reported as having been coined by the Webbs by P. Edwards, *The Employment Relationship and the Field of Industrial Relations* in Edwards, "The Employment Relationship and the Field of Industrial Relations", p. 4.

13 Hyman, *Industrial Relations: a Marxist Introduction*, p. 12. The author here provides its own definition as follow: "industrial relations is the study of *process of control over work relations*; and among these processes, those involving collective worker organisation and action are of particular concern". One can see how the modern approach to industrial relations is re-asserted by such a definition.

14 T. Colling and M. Terry, "Work, the Employment Relationship and the Field of Industrial Relations", in *Industrial Relations. Theory and Practice*, ed. T. Colling and M. Terry (New York: John Wiley & Sons, 2010), 1–24, p. 9. See also A. Bevort and A. Jobert, *Sociologie Du Travail: les Relations Professionelles* (Paris: Armand Colin, 2008), p. 3: "Les relations professionelles désignent, dans l'univers du travail, l'ensemble des relations qui s'établissent entre trois catégories d'acteurs: les pouviors publics, les salariés et leurs répresentants, les employeurs et leurs organisations. Elles ont pour objet l'élaboration de règles de contenu comme celles portant sur le salaire, le temps de travail, les garanties d'emploi, et de règles de procédure comme celles relatives à la negociation, aux accords, aux conflicts, aux modes de répresentation des salariés".

15 Dunlop, *Industrial Relations Systems*, p. 383. However, at page 5, the same Author refers to the "full range of *rule-making* governing the work place" (emphasis added).

16 A. Flanders, *Industrial Relations: What Is Wrong with the System? An Essay on Its Theory and Future* (London: Faber; Faber, 1965), p. 10: "The study of industrial relations [...] may therefore be described as a study of the institutions of job regulation."

17 See DWP Ruiter, "A Basic Classification of Legal Institutions", *Ratio Juris* 10, no. 4 (December 1997): 357–371, p. 358, who defines institutions as "systems of rules that provide frameworks for social action within larger ruler-governed settings".

industrial relations as "the study of the rules governing employment".[18] Apart from the previously mentioned difficulties created by such a broad definition, this approach has been criticised as being excessively *static*. The focus on rules and regulation would imply an underlying evaluative preference for stability and regularity in the workplace.[19]

The concept of "industrial relations" is hence used in the sense entailed by the "modern paradigm", keeping in mind the focus on procedures for the adoption of rules.

2.1.1 MODERN INDUSTRIAL RELATIONS

In analysing the modern paradigm of industrial relations Kaufman proposed a list of 10 items representing the shared foundations of the studies devoted to this approach.[20] Here I will refer to this list. However, this choice is simply dictated by the need to provide some structure to the assessment of the main elements characterising an industrial relations approach. In this sense, these elements will mainly provide the occasion to further explore several important aspects of such an approach. The list reads as follows:

- Conflict of interests in the employment relationship.
- The employer has a power advantage over the worker.
- Labour is not a commodity.
- Industrial democracy is needed in workforce governance.
- Pluralism in the employment relationship is the best/most practical model.
- Focus on unions, collective bargaining and labour-management relations.
- Unitarism and human resources are separate from industrial relations.
- Ideologically soft on union and hard on non-union employers.
- Theoretical roots in union studies and labour institutionalism.
- Origin in the 30s and institutionalisation in the early post-Second World War period.

---

18 H. Clegg, *The Changing System of Industrial Relations in Great Britain* (Oxford: Blackwell, 1979), p. 1.

19 Hyman, *Industrial Relations: a Marxist Introduction*, p. 11. That being said, it must be noted how, in a more recent contribution, the same Author seems to accept a definition more rules-oriented: "We may define industrial relations as the regulation of work and employment, provided that we understand regulation (control by rule, according to the dictionary) in its broadest sense as encompassing a complex web of social processes and a terrain of actual or potential resistance and struggle." R. Hyman, "European Integration and Industrial Relations: a Case of Variable Geometry?", *Antipode*, 2001, p. 8.

20 Kaufman, "Paradigms in Industrial Relations: Original, Modern and Versions In-Between", p. 320.

Thus, to further clarify the industrial relations approach it is useful to go through those items. Some are however less relevant for the present work, being focused on ideological and theoretical aspects, and will not be treated extensively.

Conflict of interests in the employment relationship

Although Kaufman puts the notion of the inevitable conflict as the first shared item of modern industrial relations approaches,[21] such a concept needs a more in-depth analysis. In fact, along the notion of "conflict of interests" one can see the demarcation lines of three different visions of industrial relations or "frames of reference".[22]

At the one end of the spectrum one can find the unitary view, which postulates the identity of interest between employer and employees.[23] From this point of view the eventual conflict arising between employer and employees is seen as a pathological occurrence.[24] However, modern industrial relations approaches tend to consider the unitarist view as an old fashioned[25] model of the employment relationship, aimed (although not explicitly) at promoting a top-down workforce governance centred on management dominance,[26] or at allowing "enlightened" employers to adopt an attitude of paternalistic benevolence.[27]

The second approach is the pluralist one. The pluralist perspective sees conflict as inevitable,[28] due to the variety of organisation struggling to shape the rules governing the work relationship.[29] In doing so this approach accepts the divergence of interests between employers and employees. However such divergences are implicitly or explicitly considered as not hindering the collaboration to continue,

---

21 As Edwards puts it, the employment relationship is characterised by "structured antagonism". See P. Edwards, *Conflict at Work: A Materialist Analysis of Workplace Relations* (Oxford: Blackwell Pub, 1986).

22 See the distinction made by Fox between unitary and pluralist approaches: A. Fox, *Industrial Sociology and Industrial Relations* (London: H.M.S.O., 1966).

23 Edwards, "The Employment Relationship and the Field of Industrial Relations", p. 10.

24 See C. Crouch, *Trade Unions: The Logic of Collective Action* (Waukegan: Fontana Press, 1982), p. 18, where the unitary view on conflict is described as "[any conflict that may occur is seen as] the result of misunderstanding or mischief; in other words, as pathological".

25 What is more, an unitarist view of workers-employers relationship has historically been associated with many of the 20th century worst regimes, as stressed in O. Kahn-Freund, *Labour and the Law*, 2nd revise (London: Stevens & Sons Ltd, 1977), p. 16.

26 "From a modern industrial relations perspective, unitarism is unworkable in practice and becomes a smokescreen for employer control and union avoidance", Kaufman, "Paradigms in Industrial Relations: Original, Modern and Versions In-Between", p. 322.

27 Or, for the unenlightened ones, "to hinder their workers in exercising their freedom of organisation, to refuse negotiations with genuine trade unions and to set up sham organisation controlled by management", Kahn-Freund, *Labour and the Law*, p. 16.

28 Edwards, "The Employment Relationship and the Field of Industrial Relations", p. 11.

29 Clegg, *The Changing System of Industrial Relations in Great Britain*, p. 1: "whenever there are separate sources of authority there is the risk of conflict".

through compromises that can benefit *both* parties.[30] The underlying assumption is the existence of a shared consensus between employees and employers upon procedural issues.[31] Thus, the pluralist approach calls for a compromise in front of the necessity of conflicts; to quote the famous dictum by Flanders: "the paradox, whose truth managements have found it so difficult to accept, is that they can only regain control by sharing it".[32] For a lawyer's perspective, the pluralist view permeates in the work of Otto Kahn-Freund. In describing the "legitimate expectations" protected by labour law, Kahn-Freund points out clearly that those are necessarily conflicting.[33] However, he adds, such a conflict can be adjusted through "give and take". There is, in this position, an underlying preference for a neutral vision of the conflicting interests: "management's interest in planning production and in being protected against its interruption is the exact equivalent to the worker's interest in planning his and his family life and in being protected against an interruption in his mode of existence".[34] In reading the passages where Kahn-Freund affirms his preference for the pluralist view,[35] one can clearly see the demarcation line drawn between the assumption of the unavoidable conflict of interests[36] and the common interest for a shared allegiance to a procedural framework where those conflicts should take place.[37]

At the other end of the spectrum stands the so called "radical" approach. Developed as a critique of the pluralist approach,[38] the radical one foster a vision of industrial relations as a domain characterised by a "persistent generation of conflict and disorder within the very institutions and procedures designed to bring order and stability to employer-employee relationship".[39] This unavoidable disorder[40] is caused by the necessary antagonism between workers' and employers'

---

30 A. Fox, "Industrial Relations: a Social Critique of Pluralist Ideology", in *Man and Organization: The Search for Explanation and Social Relevance*, ed. John Child (Allen & Unwin, 1973), 264, p. 196.

31 See A. Fox, *Beyond Contract: Work, Power and Trust Relations* (London: Faber, 1974), who speaks of a "basic procedural consensus".

32 A. Flanders, *Management and Unions* (London: Faber, 1970), p. 172.

33 Kahn-Freund, *Labour and the Law*, p. 49.

34 Ibid., p. 49. "All this is palpably obvious, except for a person blinded by class hatred either way" continues the author. This very passage will be harshly criticised by Hyman, as allowing the workers only to ask for "reasonable" improvements of their conditions. See Hyman, *Industrial Relations: a Marxist Introduction*, p. 82.

35 Kahn-Freund, *Labour and the Law*, p. 15.

36 "Any approach to the relations between management and labour is fruitless unless the divergence of their interests is plainly recognised and articulated", Ibid., p. 15.

37 Ibid., p. 16: "there is however, one interest that management and labour have in common: it is that the inevitable and necessary conflicts should be regulated from time to time by reasonably predictable procedures".

38 Sometimes this amounted in fact to an auto-critique, see Fox, "Industrial Relations: a Social Critique of Pluralist Ideology".

39 Hyman, *The Political Economy of Industrial Relations: Theory and Practice in a Cold Climate*, p. 86.

40 "The wage-labour relationship contains a constant potential for disorder", Hyman, *Industrial Relations: a Marxist Introduction*, p. 197.

interests,[41] an antagonism which is considered as including the very foundations of the economic system. Hence the critique to the pluralist approach, accused to consider the divisions of interests between workers and employers as relatively superficial when compared with common interests and shared values.[42] A second critique can be identified in relation with the notion of "win-win" compromises present in the pluralist approach. The radical view considers this idea as inextricably rooted to a specific economic cycle, where sustained growth allowed for a considerable margin in employers' concessions; on the contrary, a context of economic "crisis" would make extremely difficult the peaceful accommodation of opposing interests.[43]

In the end, provided that the unitary view has not many followers left in the field of industrial relations studies,[44] the conflicting nature of the interests expressed in the work relationship seems indeed to be an integral part of the industrial relations approach, although with the cited differences between the pluralist view and the radical one.

The employer has a power advantage over the worker

The second item on the list entails the asymmetrical nature of the work relationship. The industrial relations approach considers the individual employer as intrinsically having a power advantage over the individual worker. In fact, the individual worker has normally no bargaining power, having to accept the conditions which the employer offers.[45] Thus, the obligations arising from the work relationship are relatively precise for the employer (pay the specified wage and bonuses, respect the various legal regulations etc.) and there is little that he is required to do which is not formally prescribed, either by law or contract. On the contrary, the obligations of the worker are generally imprecise and elastic.[46] To summarise very briefly: "in order to provide for themselves and their families, most workers have no choice but to engage in paid work and, in practice, many workers will have relatively limited choices between potential employers. In contrast employers enjoy considerable resources and can often replace unwilling

41 Edwards, "The Employment Relationship and the Field of Industrial Relations", p. 11.

42 Hyman, *Industrial Relations: a Marxist Introduction*, p. 196.

43 Hyman, *The Political Economy of Industrial Relations: Theory and Practice in a Cold Climate*, p. 87. Here Hyman also denounces the "procedural bias" of the pluralist approach, which, in neglecting the relevance of the substantial demands, would became less and less useful to understand the real world of industrial relations.

44 On the contrary it must be noted that the unitary view inspires much of the human resources approach. See Edwards, "The Employment Relationship and the Field of Industrial Relations", p. 10.

45 Kahn-Freund, *Labour and the Law*, p. 6.

46 Hyman, *Industrial Relations: a Marxist Introduction*, p. 24: "rather than agreeing to expend a given amount of effort, the employee surrenders his capacity of work".

workers with other people or with technology".[47] It is upon this background that Khan-Freund stated that "on the labour side, power is collective power".[48] It is so that a collection of organised workers (whether this collection goes under the name of "trade union" or not) can represent a countervailing power for the employer, while the individual worker can be so only in the most peculiar situations (*e.g.* a highly skilled craftsman, a top rank scientist). In general it can be safely assumed that workers have to unite in order to consolidate and mobilise their collective power, if any.

It is evident that in dealing with the negotiation of rules, power relationships are inextricably intertwined with the study of industrial relations. However, Flanders did criticise the founding fathers of industrial relations exactly because of their scarce attention to the power struggle between workers and employers underlying the process of collective bargaining.[49] This has been justified as the natural consequence of industrial relations being a field of study and, as such, not meant to debate the fundamentals of concepts developed by other branches (politics, sociology, economics, psychology). One can also consider, once again, the pragmatic nature of industrial relations studies as a reason of this lack of theorisation.

Hyman considers the unceasing power struggle as the "central feature of industrial relations",[50] and defines the concept of power as "the ability of an individual or group to control his (their) physical and social environment; and, as part of this process, the ability to influence the decisions which are and are not taken by others".[51] Collateral to this unceasing struggle is the distinction drawn between two aspects of power: "power for" and "power over". The former is defined as a resource that can be used in order to achieve the interests of a community, while the latter represents the ability to exert power over others.[52] However, it is evident that in a domain characterised by necessarily conflicting interests, power will normally be a "power over". Speaking of "pure bargaining power", Dunlop

---

47 Colling and Terry, "Work, the Employment Relationship and the Field of Industrial Relations", p. 8.

48 Kahn-Freund, *Labour and the Law*, p. 6.

49 "There is hardly any consideration in the whole of the Webbs' writing of an employer's interest in collective bargaining [...] Today, with advantage of hindsight, it is easy to appreciate the inadequacy of any theory of either the nature or the growth of collective bargaining which sees it only as a method of trade unionism and overlooks in its development the role of employers and their associations", Flanders, *Management and Unions*, pp. 214–215, as cited in Hyman, *Industrial Relations: a Marxist Introduction*, p. 107.

50 Ibid., p. 26.

51 Ibid., p. 26. The author continues: "This ability is typically founded on a privileged access or control over material and ideological resources. Ownership and control over means of production clearly involves power [...]. The ability to call on certain generally accepted beliefs and values [...] is likewise a source of power."

52 Ibid., pp. 26–27.

spoke of "the ability to get favourable bargains apart from market conditions".[53] More importantly, Dunlop seems to consider the "power context" of an industrial relations system just as "the product of public policy", which prescribes the status and role of each actor inside the system.[54]

More recently, the underlying view of power in industrial relations studies has been summarised as follows:[55]

- Power is a capacity to pursue ones own interests, and it can be activated through individual or collective means;
- Power involves the capacity to oppose the actions of others (reactive power) and to pursue ones own objectives (proactive power);[56]
- As in other areas of social life, power is embedded in continuing relationships, and establishing "interests" is never easy;
- Power resources can shift over time;
- Those resources are not fixed things but are also developed through use;
- Power resides in organisational routines and assumptions as well as in overt actions.

Thus power can be embodied in both material and "ideological" resources. It is important to note, in a lawyer's perspective, that the concept of "power" here does not necessarily entails a juridical relationship ("authority"). Still, for example, property rights over means of production do constitute the basis for a power resource. On the other side we find the more subtle "ideological" resources, which represent the ability to call on values and ideologies shared by the industrial relations system or the broader society.[57] Hyman refers to those values with the example of the "belief that there will always be masters and men".

As this brief overview clearly shows, the question of the asymmetry in the work relationship is less problematical, although different approaches to the previous point (conflict of interests) may amount to a divergence in analysing the underlying question of power.

---

53 J.T. Dunlop, *Wage Determination Under Trade Unions* (London: Macmillan Co, 1944), p. 77. The expression is interesting also in connection with the item treated in the next paragraph. See *infra*, "Labour is not a commodity".

54 Dunlop, *Industrial Relations Systems*, pp. 98–99.

55 Edwards, "The Employment Relationship and the Field of Industrial Relations", p. 12.

56 This distinction is somewhat similar to the one between "power over" and "power for". In fact we can consider that an expression of the "reactive power" does always entails a struggle to achieve a certain "power over" the others, whose actions one wants to oppose.

57 Hyman, *Industrial Relations: a Marxist Introduction*, p. 26.

Labour is not a commodity

The wording "labour is not a commodity" echoes the ILO Declaration of Philadelphia,[58] which, in its first article, expresses the very same concept.[59] Modern industrial relations pursues its studies in the way traced by this declaration.[60]

Borrowing the term "fictional commodity" from Polanyi's masterpiece,[61] the industrial relations approach distinguishes labour from other commodities: "Buy a kilo of potatoes and they become physically your property, while the seller parts company with them for good. But the employer does not buy a worker: that is what distinguishes wage-labour from slavery".[62] This distinction is founded on several aspects that, in the view of industrial relations, characterise the "labour commodity".

The fundamental assumption is that unlike other commodities, "labour" is inextricably embodied in a human being. A corollary of this assumption is that, notwithstanding the formal wording of an employment contract, the employer does not buy a certain amount of "labour". What he buys is the "capacity to work" or "labour power" of the worker[63] as well as his/her promise to use this capacity for a certain amount of time and to comply with reasonable standards of diligence and efficiency.[64]

Those two characteristics amount to a number of consequences. Industrial relations specialists focus especially on one of these: the issue of indeterminacy. As I just recalled, the labour contract does not entail an exchange of goods or services; instead it involves the exchange of money for the capacity to provide labour power.[65] What is more, the employer generally has an interest to retain a wide margin of discretion in terms of flexible use of the workforce,[66] while

58 "Declaration concerning the aims and purposes of the International Labour Organisation", adopted at the 26th meeting of the International Labour organisation in Philadelphia, 10 May 1944. For an essay about the meaning of the "spirit" of this declaration see A. Supiot, *L'esprit de Philadelphie: La Justice Sociale Face Au Marché Total* (Paris: Seuil, 2010).

59 Article 1: "The Conference reaffirms the fundamental principles on which the organisation is based and, in particular, that:
(a) labour is not a commodity [...]."

60 Kaufman, "The Core Principle and Fundamental Theorem of Industrial Relations", p. 28.

61 K. Polanyi, *The Great Transformation: The Political and Economic Origins of Our Time* (Boston: Beacon Press, 1957).

62 R. Hyman, "The Europeanisation – or the Erosion – of Industrial Relations", *Industrial Relations Journal*, 2001, p. 3.

63 Hyman, *Industrial Relations: a Marxist Introduction*, p. 24.

64 Hyman, "The Europeanisation – or the Erosion – of Industrial Relations", pp. 3–4.

65 Colling and Terry, "Work, the Employment Relationship and the Field of Industrial Relations", p. 8. See also Edwards, "The Employment Relationship and the Field of Industrial Relations", p. 14: "In the labour contract, the worker sells an ability to work, which is translated into actual labour only during the course of the working day".

66 Hyman, *The Political Economy of Industrial Relations: Theory and Practice in a Cold Climate*, pp. 20–21.

over-detailed job description are normally considered counter-productive.[67] As Commons put it, from the point of view of the contract, "[the contract of employment]is not a contract, it is a continuing implied renewal of contracts at every minute and hour".[68] Upon this background it must be finally noted that the employer may have an interest not to enforce a strict compliance solely through the subjugation inherent in the employment relationship, as this may push the worker to react by lowering his commitment should the opportunity arise. This is especially true in the area of so called "emotional workers" (*e.g.* call centres, customer services), where the employer may be interested in having the customers encounter "contented" workers.[69]

The industrial relations approach to the nature of labour does inevitably reverberate upon the analysis of the concept of "labour market". In fact the very existence of a "market" *stricto sensu* is denied by this approach. Indeed the labour market is seen as a domain encompassing something more and different from the mere economic process of supply and demand: the wage-labour relation is considered as the result of a social and political struggle[70] as well as the outcome of an economic process. Furthermore, the behaviour of this peculiar market is different from other markets, again, due to the impossibility to separate the labour commodity from the human being. In this sense, to cite just two examples, in the labour market prices (i.e., wages) show a higher degree of rigidity and perform a role which is broader of the simple allocative function.[71] This vision finds its roots also in the historical analysis developed by Polanyi, which demonstrates that labour markets have never been allowed to function as "real" markets (i.e., markets driven only by the demand-supply forces): "The labor market was allowed to retain its main function only on condition that wages and conditions of work, standards and regulations should be such as would safeguard the human character of the alleged commodity, labor".[72] In fact we can safely say that humanitarian grounds have also played a role in rejecting an approach based on a complete freedom of contracts in the relationship worker-employer.[73]

As a final note, it is interesting to stress how the peculiar nature of the labour-commodity is not only a reality studied *by* industrial relations analysis, but also the product *of* industrial relations in practice. It is evident that union representation, collective bargaining and collective actions do limit the reach of market relations. In fact, industrial relations practices can be analysed as being

67 D. Marsden, *A Theory of Employment Systems: Micro-Foundations of Societal Diversity* (Oxford: Oxford University Press, 1999), p. 15.

68 J.R. Commons, *Legal Foundations of Capitalism* (New York: McMillan, 1924), p. 285.

69 Colling and Terry, "Work, the Employment Relationship and the Field of Industrial Relations", p. 8.

70 Hyman, "The Europeanisation – or the Erosion – of Industrial Relations", p. 7.

71 Kaufman, "Paradigms in Industrial Relations: Original, Modern and Versions In-Between", p. 321.

72 Polanyi, *The Great Transformation: The Political and Economic Origins of Our Time*, p. 177.

73 Hyman, "The Europeanisation – or the Erosion – of Industrial Relations", p. 7.

aimed at the de-commodification[74] of labour. In this sense the cited Article of the Declaration of Philadelphia can be read as an objective and not as a simple recognition. Thus, the nature of a shared value of the assumption "labour is not a commodity" or, at least, "labour is a (very) peculiar commodity", cannot be denied without denying a large part of industrial relations practices.

Focus on unions, collective bargaining and labour-management relations

In opening his famous work on trade unions and collective bargaining, Clegg stated that "trade unions are regarded as one of the most powerful forces shaping our society and determining our future".[75] Almost twenty years later, Hyman stressed that such an opening would be inconceivable in a text written in the 90s.[76] This trend has not stopped in present days. However, the focus on unions and labour-management relations can still be considered a shared item through industrial relations studies. That being said, it has been noted that modern industrial relations reacted to the shrinking in unionisation and collective bargaining coverage by broadening its field of interest to include alternative forms of collective representation and involvement as well as trans-national and supra-national forms of collective employee regulation.[77]

Here I will not re-state what I already explained before, in defining the modern industrial relations approach. As I already described, such an approach bears as a central point the focus on labour-management relations, as well as on unions and collective bargaining.

That being said, it is interesting to look at some more recent contributions, in order to assess how this shared item may have shifted in response to the cited transformations.

In particular, in a context of decreasing strikes and union activity, the field of industrial relations has been challenged by the approaches proposed by "human resource management" and "organisational behaviour".[78] This has been explained with the narrowly construed approach of modern industrial relations:

---

74 A concept used in ibid., p. 10, and borrowed from G. Esping-Andersen, *The Three Worlds of Welfare Capitalism* (Princeton University Press, 1990). In the context of this research I will often refer to the role of de-commodification which is played by collective bargaining. In this sense I do not consider that collective bargaining, by creating the conditions for the buying and selling of work, is an instrument for commodifying labour power. Quite the contrary, by making it so that the price (and regulation in general) of labour is *not* fixed by the mere rules of demand and offer, collective bargaining, in the meaning I accept for this work, performs a fundamental role in de-commodifying labour.

75 H. Clegg, *Trade Unionism Under Collective Bargaining: A Theory Based on Comparisons of Six Countries* (Oxford: Blackwell Publishers, 1976), p. 1.

76 R. Hyman, "Theory and Industrial Relations", *British Journal of Industrial Relations* 32, no. 2 (June 1994): 165–180, p. 178.

77 Kaufman, "Paradigms in Industrial Relations: Original, Modern and Versions In-Between", p. 321.

78 Colling and Terry, "Work, the Employment Relationship and the Field of Industrial Relations", p. 3.

a field of study strictly associated with a particular institution (*in casu*, trade unions) is condemned to share the fortunes of this institution.[79] As Keller puts it: "Discussions of the future of industrial relations always tend to turn into a debate on the future of trade unions".[80]

Thus, it is interesting to look at the response proposed by Kaufman. This response involves the distinction that I presented in the beginning of this section, between the original industrial relations approach and the modern one. In fact, it explicitly involves a move back to the original approach, a strategic repositioning of industrial relations into a much more broader field of study to avoid its reduction to insignificance.[81]

As I already briefly summarised, the field of study of the "original" approach to industrial relations is the entire employment relationship. As stated in the Survey of Research in the Field of Industrial Relations prepared by the Social Science Research Council (United States) in 1928: "the focal point of the field is the employer-employee relationship". Although the concept of "core" may seem not quite properly used when referring to such a broad domain, Kaufman defines the "core" subject of the original approach as: "all the behaviors, outcomes, practices and institutions that emanate from or impinge on the employment relationship".[82] Central to this definition is the concept of "labour problem", meaning all the shortcomings necessarily arising from labour markets and employment relationships:[83] to formulate solutions to those "labour problems" is considered to be the very purpose of (original) industrial relations. In developing his argument for this repositioning of industrial relations,[84] Kaufman also identifies the core principle of original industrial relations: the rejection of the

[79] Kaufman, "Paradigms in Industrial Relations: Original, Modern and Versions In-Between", p. 315.

[80] B. Keller, "The German Approach to Industrial Relations: A Literature Review", *European Journal of Industrial Relations* 2, no. 2 (July 1996): 199–210.

[81] Kaufman, "The Core Principle and Fundamental Theorem of Industrial Relations", pp. 6–7.

[82] Ibid., p. 9.

[83] Those "maladjustment, defects and shortcomings" are generated by the fact that the labour market does not function as a "perfect" market by the sole force of demand/supply encounter.

[84] It is not the aim of this brief outline to give a complete account of the proposition developed by Kaufman. See B. Kaufman, "The Social Welfare Objectives and Ethical Principles of Industrial Relations", in *The Ethics of Human Resources and Industrial Relations*, ed. J. Budd and J. Scoville (Champaign: Labour; Employment Relations Association, 2005), 23–59; Kaufman, "The Core Principle and Fundamental Theorem of Industrial Relations"; Kaufman, "Paradigms in Industrial Relations: Original, Modern and Versions In-Between"; Kaufman, "The Theoretical Foundation of Industrial Relations and Its Implications for Labor Economics and Human Resource Management", *Industrial and Labor Relations Review* 64, no. 1 (2010). The fundamental theorem of industrial relations is then identified as follows: "Free labour markets without the balance, fairness social protection and macroeconomic guidance offered by the institutions of industrial relations and the visible hand of state management will necessarily create or perpetuate conditions that undermine their own effectiveness and survival. The purpose of industrial relations is to make the market system and capitalism work better. To accomplish this goal, industrial relations seeks to humanize, stabilize, professionalize, democratize, and balance the market system through new, expanded and reformed institutions."

orthodox competitive demand/supply labour market model as the appropriate framework for analysing and understanding the key features and outcomes of the employment relationship; or, with just a shift in its formulation, the proposition that labour is not a commodity.[85] One can see as these principles are perfectly compatible (if not overlapping) with those underlying the studies which go under the label of "modern" industrial relations.

It is interesting, in the end of this paragraph, to look at two recent textbooks of industrial relations through the distinction between the original paradigm of industrial relations and the modern one. The first one is the collective work of the so called "Warwick school" (the Industrial Relations Research Unit at the University of Warwick) of industrial relations.[86] In the introductory chapter the authors and editors pay tribute to the proposal developed by Kaufman, in including every rule (whether legal or not) governing the employment relation.[87] This vision is developed through the book. However, as a side note, in looking at the chapters one can see a large part of the texts are devoted to "classical" industrial relations topics, as actors and procedures of rule-making. The second text is a French textbook from Bevort and Jobert.[88] Here the *relations professionnelles* are described with a much more classical approach, which looks to the processes of rule-making as the first and most important object of industrial relations.[89]

In sum, the focus on collective aspects can still be considered a very important part (if not the most important) of an industrial relations approach. For what it matters here, I will continue to apply the industrial relations framework as developed through the definitions arising from the "modern" approach; thus, from a lawyer perspective and at with a hint of oversimplification, the area interested is the one which goes under the name of "collective labour law".

2.1.2 AN INDUSTRIAL RELATIONS SYSTEM

The transnational situation is an inherent characteristic of the posting phenomenon as regulated by EU law. Strictly intertwined with this concept comes then the question of limits and boundaries of a system. Legal rules make it easy to identify the moment when the posted worker leaves his home country (and legal system) and accedes the host one. However the answer is less evident if

85 Kaufman, "The Core Principle and Fundamental Theorem of Industrial Relations", pp. 20–22.
86 Colling and Terry, "Work, the Employment Relationship and the Field of Industrial Relations".
87 Ibid., pp. 9–10. See also page 16: "Our argument so far has acknowledged the need for industrial relations analysis to move beyond the concerns that dominated the subject for half a century and to rediscover a more expansive and inclusive approach to employment relations."
88 Bevort and Jobert, *Sociologie du Travail: les relations professionnelles.*
89 Ibid., p. 3: "Analyser les relations professionnelles, c'est décrire les règles et les institutions qui les portent, s'interroger sur la genèse, expliquer les processus d'interaction et d'échange entre les acteurs dont elles sont les produit, analyser l'ensemble des pratiques qui se nouent autour d'elles, pour les appliquer, les transformer, les supprimer."

one turns his gaze to the dimension of industrial relations. Thus, does the worker leave its own system of industrial relations as he puts his feet in the Host country?

Formulated as such the question summons, with the wording "system of industrial relations" a concept which has been central in the evolution of the discipline of industrial relations. The reference here goes obviously to the seminal work of John Henry Dunlop.[90]

Even though Dunlop never founded what one may call "a school" of industrial relations, he has represented the fundamental theoretical reference until the half of the 70s. Hyman traced this success back to the necessity of American academics to justify their studies to their colleagues, after the decline of the post-war strike wave.[91] Developed as a sub-system of the social sphere (parallel and different from, although close to, the economic one), industrial relations are construed as a set of institutions, practices and procedures aimed to the production of a "web of rules" regulating the employment relations. Such a system is composed by three categories of actors (managers, workers, governmental agencies) which are inserted in a context characterised by three set of variables (technical context, market and budgetary constraints, power context and status of the actors). The whole system of industrial relations is then considered as standing on a floor of shared values (ideology) which defines the role of every actor.[92] In particular, Dunlop conceives the system as strongly distinct from its context (i.e. contextual variables are not influenced by the actors of industrial relations), while the context itself is the main explanation for the structure, the behaviour and the developments of the industrial relations system.[93]

For the present work it is interesting to look at two issues related to this concept: first, the nature of the "industrial relations system" as a tool for analysis; second the question of the scope of a given system. Consequently I will not even try to give a full account of Dunlop's work and theorisation. Still, on the background drawn in the preceding sections, one must keep in mind the author's position about industrial relations. In fact, the central feature of the industrial relations system is presented by Dunlop both as "rule making"[94] (thus, with a focus on the process) and as "web of rules".[95] One can see as his position is somewhat blurred in respect of the positions that I sketched before.

---

90 Dunlop, *Industrial Relations Systems*.

91 Hyman, *The Political Economy of Industrial Relations: Theory and Practice in a Cold Climate*, p. 121.

92 M. Lallement, *Sociologie des relations professionnelles* (Paris: La Découverte, 1996), pp. 39–40.

93 Bevort and Jobert, *Sociologie du Travail: les relations professionnelles*, p. 6: "Dunlop établit une distinction forte entre le système lui même [...] et son contexte formé des variables techniques, économiques et politiques. Selon lui, ce contexte et ses transformations déterminent principalement le fonctionnement du système de relations professionnelles."

94 Dunlop, *Industrial Relations Systems*, p. 5: "the full range of rule-making governing the work place is [...] central to an industrial relations system".

95 Ibid., p. viii: "the theoretical framework is concerned with analysing the workings of industrial relations system".

Theory, device, taxonomy

It has been argued that the concept of "industrial relations system" should be used only as an heuristic device for structuring data.[96] In fact, Dunlop himself presents the concept of "industrial relations system" indifferently (and sometimes in the very same sentence) as:[97]

- a general theory;[98]
- an explanatory device;[99]
- a taxonomy.[100]

Here this concept is introduced basically because of its second "use". The explanatory function of the concept of "industrial relations system" is indeed interesting in dealing with the complex issue of posted workers, and especially with their relationship with the two different "systems" involved in regulating their working conditions: the Home system and the Host one.

Scope

In this sense, an extremely interesting question analysed by Dunlop is the one related to the *scope* of the industrial relations system. That being said, it is fruitless to look for a precise definition of boundaries and frontiers in Dunlop's work. Evidently, as a tool aimed at understanding the most various frameworks for industrial relations, the definition of the scope of a given industrial relations system is stated in a markedly fuzzy way: "the concept of an industrial-relations system is deliberately variable in scope, it may be used to characterise an immediate work place, an enterprise, a sector, or a country as a whole";[101] however such grouping cannot be arbitrary, as the components of the system "must reflect a considerable degree of cohesiveness and formal or informal interdependence".[102] Cohesiveness and interdependence are then two elements of the existence of an industrial relations system. To these one can add "unity" or "consistency".[103] Looking at the

96 G. Bain and H. Clegg, "A Strategy for Industrial Relations Research in Great Britain", *British Journal of Industrial Relations* 12, no. 1 (1974): 91–113, p. 92.

97 S.J. Wood et al., "The 'Industrial Relations System' Concept As a Basis for Theory in Industrial Relations", *British Journal of Industrial Relations* 13, no. 3 (November 1975): 291–308, p. 292.

98 "The present volume presents a general theory of industrial relations", Dunlop, *Industrial Relations Systems*, p. vii.

99 "It [the present volume] seeks to provide tools of analysis to interpret and to gain understanding of the widest possible range of industrial relations facts and practices", ibid., p. vii.

100 "[the volume] develops a systematic body of ideas for arranging and interpreting the known facts of worker-management-government interactions; it also provides a set of concepts fitted together that require the collection of new facts, presented in new categories", ibid., p. 380.

101 Ibid., pp. 385–386.

102 Ibid., p. 386.

103 Ibid., p. 388.

phenomenon at stake in the present research, posted workers represent an evident challenge to the "cohesiveness" of a given industrial relations system, due to the elements highlighted in the previous Chapter.

However, with a different definition, Dunlop makes reference to the question of wage determination as a defining feature of a system. This means that one can trace the boundaries of an industrial relations system along the "wage setting unit".[104] This second approach, although more precise than the previously enumerated characteristics, is not exempt from difficulties, as more often than not the "wage" is defined at different levels of a national "system" (*e.g.*, countrywide minimum wage, sectoral wages and workplace bargaining on performance pay). In fact, this seems to be the case of the issue here at stake, with the additional issue of the multi-national nature of the sources regulating posted workers' working conditions. Still, one might argue on this basis that posted workers do fall into the industrial relations system which is responsible for the ultimate setting of their wages. Hence, in the case where (minimum) wages of the host state do apply, the definition proposed by Dunlop would consider posted workers as falling into the scope of the industrial relations system of this state.

2.2 INDUSTRIAL RELATIONS AND THE LAW

The point here is not only to analyse the disruptive effect that judicial intervention may have on an established industrial relations practice. Kahn-Freund (although taken from a completely different context) referred to judicial intervention in critical terms, and called for a legislative intervention that would "redress the balance which had been upset by court decision capable of exercising the most injurious influence on the relations between capital and labour".[105] What I will try to analyse here is the relationship between the system of industrial relations and the set of rules which can be identified as "the law". This includes the interpretation provided by judges. The necessary degree of abstraction required by such an analysis notwithstanding, I will recall the peculiarities of our topic when needed. This is made necessary by the specificity of the European system that often fits uncomfortably into theories focused on the nation state.

The influence of the legal system has been somewhat disregarded by specialists of industrial relations. In many works, the legal system is analysed just as a given part of the context.[106] A *fil rouge* links this vision to the approach of Kahn-Freund;

---

104 Ibid., p. 387.

105 Kahn-Freund, *Labour and the Law*, pp. 1–2. As a side note, it is interesting here to stress the fact that in the present case the "Parliament" summoned by Kahn-Freund could not intervene to redress the balance, as it is well known that the competences of the EU in the field of industrial relations are very limited, if not completely absent (as for collective action, for the most *striking* example).

106 Dunlop, *Industrial Relations Systems*, p. 127–128.

in its seminal work, the German-British lawyer carve a very humble role for the law in shaping industrial relations. This position is inextricably linked with the issue of power,[107] as it is evident from the wording of the Author: "Where labour is weak -and its strength or weakness depends largely on factor outside the control of the law- Acts of Parliament, however well intentioned and well designed, can do something, but cannot do much to modify the power relation between labour and management".[108] More recently, Hyman has expressed a similar position, affirming the limited efficacy of law when not "internalised" by industrial relations actors.[109] This, however, leaves unanswered the question of the possible power-shifting effect of legal regulations, which conversely Khan-Freund had explicitly (though not completely) denied.

Such a vision has been criticised as assuming too impermeable a relationship between industrial relations and the law. This critique, based on the national experiences characterised by corporatist/tripartite structure in industrial relations,[110] build especially on the possibility for social actors to influence and modify the legal framework.[111]

In general the question of the role of the state and the law has been confined to the regulation of working conditions, or to the role of the State as employer.[112] If we look at the influences that Edwards recognises as exerted by the State on industrial relations, we can summarise them as follows:

- Laws establishing minimum wages and working conditions;
- Role of employer of public sector workers;
- Relationships with unions either through laws or bilateral arrangements;
- Trilateral relationship involving both unions and employers' associations;
- Shape employers conduct through mandatory collective bargaining.

Still, the question of the eventual effect on power relationship emerges only indirectly in the reference to laws influencing trade unions.[113] On the contrary, the relationship of trade unions with the state has always been a debated topic, and in

---

107 See *supra*, p. 59.

108 Kahn-Freund, *Labour and the Law*, p. 8. On the same tone, the author continues: "The law has important functions in labour relations, but they are secondary if compared with the impact of the labour market (supply and demand) and, which is relevant here, with the spontaneous creation of a social power on the workers' side to balance that of management."

109 Hyman, "The Europeanisation – or the Erosion – of Industrial Relations", p. 9.

110 For this classification, see C Crouch, *Industrial Relations and European State Traditions* (Oxford: Oxford University Press, 1993).

111 See É. Léonard, "Le modèle belge et l'Union européenne", in *Dynamiques de La Concertation Sociale*, ed. Étienne Arcq et al. (CRISP, 2010), 389–404, pp. 390–391; see also the critique to the "static" nature of the theory developed by Dunlop, summarised by I. da Costa, "La théorie des relations industrielles aux Etats-Unis. De Dunlop au débat actuel", in *Les Systèmes de Relations Professionnelles*, ed. Jean-Daniel Reynaud et al. (Paris: Editions du Centre National de la Recherche Scientifique, 1990), pp. 25 ff.

112 Bevort and Jobert, *Sociologie du Travail: les relations professionnelles*, pp. 13–14.

113 Edwards, "The Employment Relationship and the Field of Industrial Relations", p. 10.

particular a subject for those analysis focused on the notions of corporatism or of political exchange.[114] This is however a very different topic from the influence of state intervention (through laws or judges) *on* the industrial relations system, and more specifically on the power relationships inside the system.

In his oft-quoted analysis of evolutionary patterns of workplace representation among the EC countries, Sorge deals, although not directly, with a similar question.[115] Indeed, Sorge argues that state intervention has, in certain evolutionary patterns,[116] strengthened systems of workplace representation or created such machineries almost from scratch. Evidently such evolutions entail a shift (or the creation) of power resources; in the sense explained by Edwards,[117] (a shift in) the capacity to pursue one's interests or to oppose decisions taken by others is necessarily involved in these legal interventions.

2.2.1 WHAT HUMP?

Thus, why is this aspect often disregarded? As Hyman puts it, legal intervention cannot *create* organisation: "It may be added that the law itself can scarcely generate organisation in a vacuum".[118] Thus, the idea that "on the labour side power is collective power", *id est* the already recalled focus on unions and labour-management relations[119] probably represents the main reason. Another important reason can be traced into the "path dependency" of a large part of industrial relations specialists. As shown by the academic literature cited along this Chapter, the lion's share of the scholarship comes from Anglo-Saxon experiences. These experiences have represented, in every taxonomy, the purest examples of the *laissez faire* approach on the state's side, and of the voluntarist one on the social actors' side.[120] However, if we look to a "continental" text book, the chapter devoted

114 Hyman, *The Political Economy of Industrial Relations: Theory and Practice in a Cold Climate*, p. 202.

115 See A. Sorge, "The Evolution of Industrial Democracy in the Countries of the European Community", *British Journal of Industrial Relations* 14, no. 3 (1976): 274–294.

116 Ibid., p. 290.

117 See *supra*, p. 61.

118 Hyman, *The Political Economy of Industrial Relations: Theory and Practice in a Cold Climate*, p. 220, "It seems to serve labour best" the author continues, "when it reinforces, stabilises and perhaps generalises the achievements of *prior* struggles within the politics of production. And where the material basis of workplace organisational strength is undermined, the law is unlikely to function indefinitely as an effective substitute."

119 See *supra*, p. 64.

120 See for example Sorge, "The Evolution of Industrial Democracy in the Countries of the European Community", p. 290: "Social sources of conflict were more or less pragmatically and voluntarily recognised, and voluntary institutions for articulation of conflict were created; this is true of Britain, Ireland and Denmark." See also Kahn-Freund, *Labour and the Law*, pp. 24–25.

to the state's role in the *relations professionnelles* does not analyse its possible role in shaping power relations; neither the judicial intervention is examined.[121]

Dunlop limits its analysis about the relation between trade unions and government agencies to the appraisal of the existence a wide diversity of arrangements through the various national experiences.[122] In fact the power context is considered as important to those rules which define (for example) the right to strike and lock-out or the procedures for settling disputes; on the contrary, the power-shifting effect of those rules is not analysed.[123] In looking at the development of an industrial relations system, Dunlop focuses his attention on the economic development, as well as on the sequence of national social changes and on the decisions of the industrialising elite.[124] While it is evident that many of these developments will take the form of changes in legal regulations and institutions, this aspect is never dealt with in the analysis. That being said, in another part of its work, Dunlop carves out a fundamental role for legislation in shaping the whole power context of an industrial relations system: "the status of any one of the actors in an industrial relations system is defined to mean the prescribed functions of that actor and the relations with other actors in the same system. These prescribed functions and relations may be largely imposed upon an industrial relations system from outside by the community, as in the case of *legislation*".[125] Such an approach seems to entail a vision of power as "descending" mainly from public policy. Notwithstanding the fact that this definition would completely obliterate power at lower levels, the definition of power as a contextual variable prevents the author from every analysis of its effects and developments in time.

The intervention of the CJEU in *Laval* may at least have the merit to call for a renewed analysis of this relationship. There, a judicial intervention, coming from the outside of the industrial relations system, does indeed impact on established practices. As I tried to summarise here, it would be hard to find a similar concern through the works of industrial relations specialists. Even more that legislative/regulatory intervention, the impact of judicial decisions is almost completely disregarded.[126]

---

121 Bevort and Jobert, *Sociologie du Travail: les relations professionnelles*, pp. 71–91.

122 Dunlop, *Industrial Relations Systems*, p. 113–115. The reference to "agencies of government" is not limited to their action as parties in tripartite bargaining, as Dunlop explicitly refers to "the power of governments to direct the affairs of labor organisations, to control their finances, to prevent their formation or to dissolve the organisations, or to enhance their standing and functions in the community". Such a focus seems much closer to the subject matter of this Section.

123 Ibid., p. 127.

124 Ibid., pp. 313–318.

125 Ibid., pp. 98–99, emphasis added.

126 This is true even for the labour movement: along their history it is hard to find an occasion where trade unions organised a collective action directed towards a judicial body. Difficulties created by a judicial decisions have generally be dealt with through pressure on the legislative power.

2.2.2 QUESTIONS OF POWER

On the lawyers' side the intervention of the CJEU in the "*Laval* quartet" has been thoroughly analysed.[127] Still, the question of the effects of this judicial intervention upon power resources is not something that one can find in the production of law specialists. However, although under different wording, similar issues have found their way into the legal analysis. With a little effort of generalisation one can make abstraction from the specific dispute.

Novitz, Hayes and Reed[128] did propose a categorisation of the effects that a judicial intervention (negative for trade unions as the *Laval* quartet has been) can have upon trade unions' action. In particular they proposed to classify those (negative) effects under three distinct categories: the "chilling effect", the "ripple effect" and the "disruptive effect".

The chilling effect[129] refers to the hampering of the ability of trade unions to take lawful industrial action. Turning back our gaze to industrial relations authors, we can see that industrial action (often described with its most common manifestation: the strike) is considered as the "sanction" of an industrial relations system,[130] fundamental to the process of collective bargaining: "serious negotiations involves the overt or implicit threat of collective action". Putting this on the background of power relations that I have summarised before,[131] the limitation of the ability to have recourse to collective action evidently entails a reduction of "the ability to influence the decisions which are and are not taken by others"[132] and of "the capacity to oppose the actions of others".[133]

The ripple effect[134] is identified in the undermining of collective bargaining. Indeed, making it harder to secure the application of agreed conditions clearly represents another shift of power resources. In fact, collective agreements are the practical epiphenomena of trade union's power, intended as "the ability of an individual or group to control his (their) physical and social environment"[135] as well as the proactive "capacity to pursue one's interests.[136]

---

127 See *infra*, Chapter 5, p. 184.

128 T. Novitz, L. Hayes and H. Reed, "Applying the Laval Quartet in a UK Context: chilling, Ripple and Distruptive Effects on Industrial Relations", in *Reconciling Fundamental Social Rights and Economic Freedoms After Viking, Laval and Rüffert*, ed. Andreas Bücker and Wiebke Warneck (Baden-Baden: Nomos Publishers, 2011), 195–244.

129 Ibid., pp. 227–230.

130 Hyman, *Industrial Relations: a Marxist Introduction*, p. 189.

131 See *supra*, p. 61.

132 Ibid., p. 26.

133 Edwards, "The Employment Relationship and the Field of Industrial Relations", p. 12.

134 Novitz, Hayes, and Reed, "Applying the Laval Quartet in a UK Context: chilling, Ripple and Distruptive Effects on Industrial Relations", pp. 230–235.

135 Hyman, *Industrial Relations: a Marxist Introduction*, p. 26.

136 Edwards, "The Employment Relationship and the Field of Industrial Relations", p. 12.

Finally, the disruptive effect[137] depicts the ultimate outcome of the two previous effects, involving the very role of trade unions in society. With their weapons (collective action) and tools (collective bargaining) seriously undermined trade unions are deemed to loose attractiveness for workers. This amounts to the disruption of established practices and pushes workers towards less institutionalised means for expressing their eventual unhappiness (*e.g.* wildcat strikes[138]).

Thus, an industrial relations system (whose scope can be as limited as a single industry or as large as to include an entire country) can be shaped by legislative action or, *in casu*, by judicial decision. This is achieved through the shift of power resources caused by the legal intervention. The infamous *Taff Vale* case[139] represents a stark example. There an act of parliament was needed to redress the shift and preserve the practices of the industrial relations system.[140] For a number of different reasons, such a solution is hard to envisage at the EU level, so that the power-shifting effects of judicial intervention are free to unleash their full potential.[141]

2.3 A FURTHER LOOK TO AN ANECDOTE

Finally, it is time to turn to the facts of *Laval* in order to put them into the framework sketched so far. One can see clearly the cited struggle for de-commodification of labour power carried out in the behaviour of the Swedish trade unions. Such a struggle is embodied into the demand for the application of collectively agreed working conditions, in order to take those conditions "out of competition". To better understand this issue, however, we need to undertake a little *detour* to analyse the main characteristics of the Swedish system.[142]

---

137 Novitz, Hayes and Reed, "Applying the Laval Quartet in a UK Context: chilling, Ripple and Distruptive Effects on Industrial Relations", pp. 235–239.

138 Ibid., p. 239.

139 *Taff Vale Ry. v. Amalg. Soc. of Ry. Servants* [1901] A.C. 426. To summarise very briefly, the decision stated that a trade union was liable with its funds to pay damages for torts committed by those acting on its behalf. See Kahn-Freund, *Labour and the Law*, pp. 231–232.

140 The Trade Disputes Act of 1906.

141 This argument will be developed in Chapter 7. See *infra*, p. 281.

142 This choice is dictated by the fundamental role that the *Laval* case plays for the present research.

2.3.1 AN AUTONOMOUS COLLECTIVE BARGAINING MODEL

The Swedish system of collective bargaining has been described as a an autonomous collective bargaining model.[143] This definition is based on two fundamental characteristics: the central role played by collective agreements in establishing working conditions and the absence of both legally established minimum wages and legal instruments to extend *erga omnes* the application of collective agreements.[144] It is evident that, to pursue the cited aim of de-commodification, such a system relies on a high degree of organisation which characterise workers and employers alike.[145]

Figure 2.1 Trade union density in Sweden

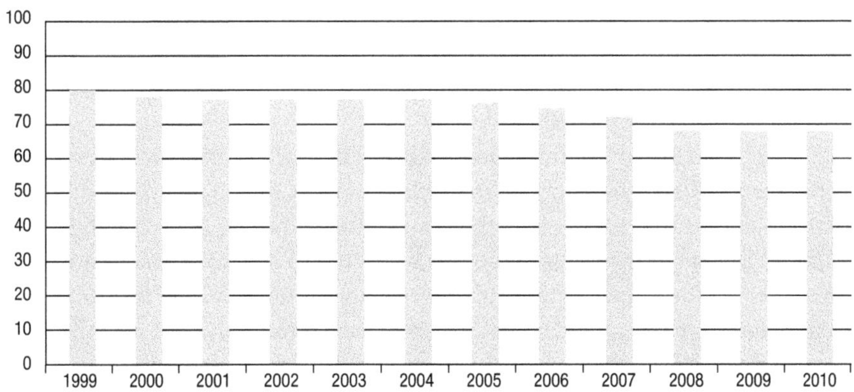

Source: OECD.Stat

A fundamental principle of the Swedish labour market implies the obligation to apply the provisions of collective agreements also to employees belonging to non-signatory unions and to wholly non-unionised employees that perform work covered by the agreement. The reason for this principle is considered to be the necessity to avoid the hiring of cheaper non-organised labour.[146] Thus, in Sweden each business sector is generally regulated by a collective agreement covering

143 Malmberg and Sigeman, "Industrial Action and EU Economic Freedoms: The Autonomous Collective Bargaining Model Curtailed by the European Court of Justice", p. 1117.

144 Adlercreutz and Nystrom, *Labour Law in Sweden*, pp. 188–189.

145 See Table 2.1 for trade union density. As of 2008 employers density was reported as above 80%. Source: J. Visser, ICTWSS database 3.0.

146 Malmberg, "The Collective Agreement as an Instrument for Regulation of Wages and Employment Conditions", pp. 203–210.

about three-fourths of all employees, and indirectly shaping all the individual employment contracts for non-unionised employees.[147]

On this background, trade unions deal with non-organised employers, including foreign service providers, by trying to conclude with them a "tie-in agreement" or "application agreement", which would replicate the contents of the sectoral collective agreement without forcing the employer to became part of the employers' association. Such an agreement can contain additional clauses but the remaining content is wholly dependent on what has been agreed between the parties to the national agreement (this is true also for its interpretation).[148] Unions may request the employer to sign a tie-in agreement even if he does not employ any of their members:[149] in this case it would be hard to conceive a strike as an effective way to force the employer into signing the agreement. Thus the Swedish system relies (and here one gradually approaches the facts of *Laval*) on a broad recognition of the possibility, for the unions, to have recourse to sympathy actions in order to put pressure on the recalcitrant employer. These sympathy actions may vary as regards their practical execution, but they normally involve the refusal of union members employed by other employers to carry out their activities in relation to the non-organised employer.[150]

Apart from briefly outlining the Swedish system, these characteristics can be considered as identifying (to a greater or lesser extent) the shared understanding of the Swedish social actors about their own system. Thus we can (roughly) speak of these elements as the "ideology" of the Swedish system of industrial relations.[151] This is yet another aspect of the clash between the national and the transnational, as the foreign service provider does not share such understandings with the Host country's actors.

Finally, one can see that the absence of legal instruments to enforce the application of collective agreements on non-organised employers makes the Swedish system reliant on the actual ability of trade unions to put pressure on these employers. The crux then is the power relation between trade unions and the employer.

---

147 R. Eklund, T. Sigeman and L. Carlson, *Swedish Labour and Employment Law: Cases and Materials* (Lustu Forlag, 2008), p. 17.

148 "A tie-in agreement is a standard collective agreement concluded between a trade union and employers who are not already bound by a collective agreement, and who are not members of any employer organisation. A tie-in agreement shall have the same content as the national collective agreement": Eklund, "A Swedish Perspective on Laval", p. 555.

149 Malmberg and Sigeman, "Industrial Action and EU Economic Freedoms: The Autonomous Collective Bargaining Model Curtailed by the European Court of Justice", p. 1117.

150 This is known as a blockade, listed as industrial action in the §41 of the Co-determination Act, SFS 1976:580. An English translation can be found in the Appendix of Eklund, Sigeman, and Carlson, *Swedish Labour and Employment Law: Cases and Materials*.

151 Dunlop, *Industrial Relations Systems*, p. 16.

2.3.2 HARDEST LAW

It is then on this stage that the *Laval* case takes place. One can see as the Swedish system reacted to the presence of the foreign (posted) workers through its traditional instruments and procedures. As I already summarised in the Introduction,[152] the employer was invited to sign the tie-in agreement: the Swedish trade unions were acting in order to de-commodificate the provision of labour, trying to level the playing field as regards working conditions. The same applies to the subsequent blockade and to the sympathy action carried out by the electricians' union. Which was then the outcome from the perspective of the Swedish industrial relations system? It is safe to affirm that the collective action was successful.[153] The employer did not change his mind and an agreement could not be reached, but the system re-affirmed its integrity. If one considers an industrial relations system as a legal order[154] it is apparent that in the present case such legal order, facing a violation of its own set of rules[155] reacted with a sanction[156] (the collective action) seeking the restoration of its "legality". As the violation did not end, the perpetrator had thus to be "removed" from the legal order. At the end of the industrial dispute the outcome was the impossibility *de facto* of employing workers in violation of the web of rules established by the actors, which is, plainly, the aim of an industrial relation system.[157]

It is then clear that, until the dispute was confined on the Swedish soil, the national system of industrial relation, though incapable of including posted workers, was able to defend its own traditional functioning and rule-setting role. That being said, it is well known that the dispute was not a successful one for the Swedish trade unions nor for the whole system of industrial relations. In fact, someone argued that the system itself was being curtailed by the combination of EU law and the interpretation provided by the CJEU.[158] Thus, it is between Brussels and Luxembourg and not in Sweden that we can find the reason why the previously described situation turned into a defeat for the Swedish trade unions. The bottom line here is that the "power shift" witnessed in the dispute at stake is largely due to the *legal* framework for posting of workers.

---

152 See p. 9.

153 Dorssemont, "The Right to Take Collective Action Versus Fundamental Economic Freedoms in the Aftermath of Laval and Viking. Foes Are Forever", p. 1.

154 See on this point G. Giugni, *Introduzione Allo Studio Dell'autonomia Collettiva* (Milano: Giuffrè, 1960).

155 Dunlop, *Industrial Relations Systems*, p. 13.

156 Hyman, *Industrial Relations: a Marxist Introduction*, pp. 189–190.

157 Hyman, "The Europeanisation – or the Erosion – of Industrial Relations", p. 10.

158 Malmberg and Sigeman, "Industrial Action and EU Economic Freedoms: The Autonomous Collective Bargaining Model Curtailed by the European Court of Justice".

CHAPTER 3
COLLECTIVE LABOUR LAW

Defining the Scope of "Collective Labour Law" as well as its Main Elements

In this Chapter I will present the main conceptual framework for my research, *i.e.* collective labour law. Coming on top of the previous chapters, this analytical tool will then take into account the data provided by the first chapter and the insights offered by industrial relations theories in order to explore how the legal framework of collective labour law welcomed the posting phenomenon, ultimately being put on strain by it.

It goes without saying that an in-depth analysis of collective labour law, whether of a given country or on a cross-country perspective, goes far beyond the scope and the aims of this chapter. My purpose here is to present the core aspects and (a) structure of collective labour law, using an international and European perspective, in order to apply these concepts in the following Chapters. Building this framework as an operational tool of analysis requires a high degree of simplification omitting many of the specificities which characterise the various national systems. As the first Chapter aimed at defining the empirical scope of our analysis, identifying the phenomenon of posting, this Chapter will trace the theoretical borders of my research. Thus its purpose is, first, to identify such a theoretical scope and, second, to break this scope down to categories which will then be used to study the posting phenomenon. Generally speaking, the definitions proposed through this Chapter are conceived for the limited scope of this research.

The aim here is to build tools to better understand the interactions between an empirical phenomenon (posting of workers) and the law, in the present case, collective labour law. Again, the role of this Chapter is to identify the boundaries of the present research and its main elements. As such, its rather abrupt closing should not come as a surprise, inasmuch as these pages are meant to provide the instruments through which the following analysis will be carried out. As a final note, since the posting phenomenon under Directive 96/71 deals exclusively with private sector workers, in developing my collective labour law framework I will not analyse those issues related to civil servants and public service in general.

The first task is once again to look for a definition. Meaning that the aim will be to define what collective labour law is. More precisely, I will try to look for a definition which can clarify the scope of this topic. Provided that the legal framework has to be used together with the industrial relations one, preference will be given to these definitions which entail a scope overlapping the one construed in the previous chapter when defining the industrial relations approach.

Evidently, a choice in terms of sources has to be made. Possibly every manual or syllabus of labour law is structured along the *summa divisio* between individual and collective labour law (sometimes including the third "branch" of the "labour market"), thus presenting a definition of both areas.[1] To operate this choice, I will prioritise those definitions formulated either in comparative cross-country analysis of labour law either in analysis of labour law in the context of transnational situations. Such a criterion derives from the struggle to avoid (as much as it is possible) a definition dictated by specific national experiences and path dependence.[2] Another reason for this choice lies in the very nature of our phenomenon. Posting of workers in the framework of directive 96/71, is necessarily a transnational phenomenon. Hence, its analysis should aim at maintaining its usefulness beyond the borders of a single national system.

I will now look to some of these definitions. We start with Kahn-Freund, who affirmed that "It [labour law] is however also concerned with collective relations between unions and other groups of workers and management, with the way the labour market is organised through understandings between them, the way rules are established through their agreements, and the way conflicts between them are fought and settled".[3] One can see that such a definition already sketches a categorisation of the "relations" introduced in its first passage. On the contrary the definition summarised by Rebhahn and also adopted by Dorssemont does not try to limit the scope to some pre-defined category: "Collective labour law is traditionally defined as all of the legal norms that govern the collective relationships between the organised employees' community and one or more employers,

1 *E.g.* S. Deakin and G.S. Morris, *Labour Law* (Oxford: Hart Publishing, 2009); Eklund, Sigeman, and Carlson, *Swedish Labour and Employment Law: Cases and Materials*; F. Carinci et al., *Diritto Del Lavoro Vol. 1. Il Diritto Sindacale* (Torino: UTET, 2006) and F. Carinci et al., *Diritto Del Lavoro Vol 2. Il Rapporto Di Lavoro Subordinato* (Torino: UTET, 2005); G. Auzero, E. Dockès and J. Pélissier, *Droit Du Travail* (Paris: Dalloz-Sirey, 2012); A.-V. Michaux, *Eléments de Droit Du Travail* (Bruxelles: Larcier, 2010).

2 The concept is used in its broader meaning; see S.J. Liebowitz and S.E. Margolis, "Path Dependence", in *Encyclopedia of Law and Economics, Volume I. the History and Methodology of Law and Economics*, ed. B. Bouckaert and G. De Geest (Cheltenham: Edward Elgar, 1999), 981–998 : "Most generally, path dependence means that where we go next depends not only on where we are now, but also upon where we have been. History matters." In this sense, our pre-existing experience of a specific legal system has an impact on our analysis of the law in general.

3 O. Kahn-Freund, "On Uses and Misuses of Comparative Law", *The Modern Law Review* 37, no. 1 (1974): 1–27, p. 21.

organised or not".[4] A third definition, by Servais, provides for an expansion in respect of the first two, including in the scope also the relations with public authorities: "Collective labour law concerns the relations between employers, organised or not, workers, whether organised in trade unions or in other forms, and eventually public authorities".[5] The fourth definition differentiates itself from the previous ones by focusing on the concept of "labour market organisation": "Labour law is in principle concerned with the legal rules which refers [(1) to employees in their relation to their employers, individual labour law, and] (2) to labour market organisations and their interrelations, collective labour law, which also includes the relations between trade unions and a single employer".[6] This necessity to include explicitly the relations between trade unions and the single employer also derives by the choice of the "labour market organisation" concept. Indeed, the individual employer could hardly be considered an organisation. In this sense the concept, though interesting, results somewhat difficult to handle in the context of the present research. One can easily see that all these definitions share a common "method", although to a different degree: their scope is mainly defined through the identification of the *actors* or collective labour law. This is most evident in the second definition, where every (collective) relationship is considered as included in the scope of collective labour law with the only condition of occurring between the actors of choice ("the organised employees' community and one or more employers, organised or not"). Thus *ex ante* these definitions seems to include every possible collective relation between these actors. However, if one looks at the *ex post* elaboration of the subject, the legal categories used to analyse the phenomenon provide for a higher degree of specification of this broad definition. I will soon present this second step.

For the purpose of this research, the simpler and broader definition which inspires the comparative work of Rebhahn is probably the most effective and easy to handle.

As said above, it is time now to break this broad scope of analysis into categories. Indeed the broad nature of the concept "relations" in my definition of choice requires some specification as our effort shift from the definition of the boundaries of our research to the analysis of the phenomenon. This exercise too requires choices. However once again one can see as this categorisation has

---

4 Dorssemont, "Collectief arbeidsrechtelijke aspecten van internationale detachering", pp. 525–526; R. Rebhahn, "Collective Labour Law in Europe in a Comparative Perspective (Part I)", *Journal of Comparative Labour Law and* 19, no. Part I (2004): 271–295, p. 271.

5 J.-M. Servais, *Droit Social de L'Union Européenne* (Brussels, Emile Bruylant, 2008), p. 224: "Collectives, ces relations, dites professionnelles, concernent les contacts qui se nouent entre les chefs d'entreprises, seuls ou groupés, les travailleurs organisés au sein de syndicats, ou représentés autrement, ainsi que, les cas échéant, les autorités publiques."

6 Adlercreutz and Nystrom, *Labour Law in Sweden*, p. 33. Though coming from a national perspective I consider this definition to be formulated in a context, the one of the International Encyclopaedia of Labour Law, mainly devoted at allowing the access to a given national system by people coming from a different one.

achieved a high degree of consensus. Thus I will follow this structure, organising the subject around four topics:

- Right or freedom of association;
- Right or freedom to take collective action;
- Right or freedom of collective bargaining;
- Right to information and consultation (including workers' representation).

I retain this structure from the comparative study of Rebhahn,[7] as well as from the analysis of Dorssemont dealing specifically with posted workers.[8] Every topic will be presented following the method presented above, hence through a high degree of simplification. Here I will try to make full use of internationally agreed instruments, as they already provide guidance in terms of shared conceptions of the rights at stake.

3.1 FREEDOM OF ASSOCIATION (AND THE ILO)

From a logical and chronological point of view freedom of association represents the first category of our analysis. The Declaration of Philadelphia itself explicitly recognises the pivotal nature of this right, identifying it both as an essential basis for sustained development[9] and as an instrument whose promotion is a fundamental task of the ILO.[10] In order to define the legal contents of this freedom (and right), I will focus on two main instruments developed at supranational level: ILO Convention No. 87 (and 98) and Article 11 of the European Convention on Human Rights. As it is evident, my interest here is limited to a specific aspect of this right: the freedom to form and join trade unions. As it has been summarised, this boils down to "a bundle of rights and freedoms relating to membership of association of employers and workers".[11]

---

7 Rebhahn, "Collective Labour Law in Europe in a Comparative Perspective (Part I)"; Rebhahn, "Collective Labour Law in Europe in a Comparative Perspective (Part II)", *Journal of Comparative Labour Law and* 19, no. Part II (2004): 107–132.

8 Dorssemont, "Collectief arbeidsrechtelijke aspecten van internationale detachering".

9 Declaration of Philadelphia, 1944, Article 1(b). The Declaration of Philadelphia was adopted by the International Labour Conference, in the context of the approaching end of World War II. The Declaration was then annexed to the Constitution of the ILO (contained in the Treaty of Versailles of 1919). See T. Novitz, *International and European Protection of the Right to Strike* (New York: Oxford University Press, 2003), pp. 99–102, and Supiot, *L'esprit de Philadelphie: La Justice Sociale Face Au Marché Total*, pp. 20–21.

10 Ibid., Article III.

11 B Creighton, "Freedom of Association", in *Comparative Labour Law and Industrial Relations in Industrialized Market Economies*, ed. Roger Blanpain (The Hague: Kluwer Law International, 2007), 275–322, p. 275. See also the comparative study F. Valdés Dal-Re (ed.), *Freedom of Association of Workers and Employers in the Countries of the European Union* (Madrid: Ministerio de Trabajo y Asuntos Sociales, 2006).

ILO Conventions No. 87 of 1948 on "Freedom of Association and Protection of the Right to Organise" (together with Convention No. 98 of 1949 on "Right to Organise and Collective Bargaining") were presented as the foundation of the right of association in a Report prepared by Brian Bercusson for the European Parliament in 1997,[12] dealing with trade union rights in the EU Member States (15 at that time). This was justified by the fact that all Member States had ratified this Convention. Today the situation is not different: all the 28 Member States have ratified this Convention. What is more, Convention 87 was included by the ILO Declaration on Fundamental Principles and Rights at Work[13] between those conventions (defined as "fundamental") whose respect and promotion is considered as inextricably connected with membership of the ILO itself, thus being applicable even as regards those members states which have not ratified such conventions.[14] Generally speaking, Conventions 87 and 98 represent the most important instruments for the international protection of freedom of association, due to their high degree of acceptance in the international community and to the role played in inspiring other instruments aimed at protecting the same right.[15]

Reading the text of Convention 87 one can see as it deals first and foremost with guarantees aimed at organisations (either of workers or employers) more than at individuals. The Convention guarantees:

- the right to establish and join organisations without prior authorisation (Article 2);
- right to draw up constitutions, elect representatives, organise activities and formulate programmes without interference by public authorities (Article 3);
- right of organisations not to be dissolved or suspended by administrative authority (Article 4);
- right to form and join federations and confederations, which may affiliate to international organisations (Article 5);
- right to acquire legal personality free of restrictive conditions (Article 7).

Article 9 provides for the only exception, *i.e.* the one granting the Members the possibility to exclude from the scope of these rights the members of the police

12 B. Bercusson, "Trade Union Rights in the EU Member States", Social Affairs Series (Brussels: European Parliament – Directorate General for Research, 1997).

13 ILO Declaration on Fundamental Principles and Rights at Work, adopted by the ILO Conference in June 1998.

14 In particular, these fundamental conventions include: Freedom of Association and Protection of the Right to Organise Convention, 1948 (No. 87), Right to Organise and Collective Bargaining Convention, 1949 (No. 98), Forced Labour Convention, 1930 (No. 29), Abolition of Forced Labour Convention, 1957 (No. 105), Minimum Age Convention, 1973 (No. 138), Worst Forms of Child Labour Convention, 1999 (No. 182), Equal Remuneration Convention, 1951 (No. 100), Discrimination (Employment and Occupation) Convention, 1958 (No. 111). See B. Langille, "The ILO and the New Economy: Recent Developments", *International Journal of Comparative Labour Law and Industrial Relations* 15 (1999): 229–257, pp. 229–232.

15 Creighton, "Freedom of Association", p. 276.

and/or of the armed forces. Together with the already recalled Article 2, Article 11 represents the most important individual aspect of the right of association. This Article obliges all Member States of the ILO "to take all necessary and appropriate measures to ensure that workers and employers may exercise freely the right to organise". This must be read in conjunction with Article 1 of Convention No. 98 which declares the right to protection against acts of anti-union discrimination and against interference with trade unions by other organisations and by employers.[16]

In my view, the posting phenomenon does not present particularly interesting interrelations with "trade union rights", defined as the rights aimed at guaranteeing the *foro interno*, the internal organisation and structure of a trade union (or an organisation of employers). To use the three-headed structure proposed by Bercusson in his report,[17] rights of *autonomy* thus present a lesser interest for the present research. On the contrary, rights of *action* (e.g. the ones regarding collective bargaining, collective action, representation) have shown a much higher degree of complexity in their encounter with the posting phenomenon. Finally, rights of *association* (as the right to join a union), in their individual declination, are also touched by the phenomenon, though more by its practical obstacles and hurdles than by the legal ones.

To this extent, since posted workers (in the context of a transnational provision of services) are bound to be working in a country different from their own, it is worth remembering that the ILO Committees have long held that Article 2 of Convention No. 87 implies that the freedom of association "should be guaranteed without discrimination of any kind based on occupation, sex, colour, race, beliefs, *nationality*, political opinion, etc."[18] (emphasis added). Even though in the context of the EU this may seem somewhat superfluous, one might wonder if guaranteeing the "freedom of association" of posted workers would also amount at guaranteeing the rights which the jurisprudence of the supervisory bodies of the ILO, or of other bodies supervising different instruments protecting this, has developed as "corollaries" of this freedom. The right to strike or to bargain collectively come to the mind.

To further explore the individual aspect of the freedom of association, I will now turn to Article 11 of the European Convention on Human Rights. Due to the

---

16 Bercusson, "Trade Union Rights in the EU Member States", pp. 8–9.

17 Ibid., p. 7.

18 ILO, *Freedom of Association: Digest of Decisions and Principles of the Freedom of Association Committee of the Governing Body of the ILO* (Geneva, 2006), para. 209.

nature of the rights protected under the Convention,[19] it is under this instrument that this individual dimension has been extensively developed.[20]

3.1.1 FREEDOM OF ASSOCIATION UNDER THE ECHR

Article 11 of the European Convention on Human Rights recognises the "freedom of assembly and association" through the following wording: "Everyone has the right to freedom of peaceful assembly and to freedom of association with others, including the right to form and to join trade unions for the protection of his interests." It is important to point out that, even though this Article has showed an high degree of expansive potential, being relied upon by the Court to protect other collective rights,[21] here we refer to it only in its stricter meaning.

In his analysis of the case law of the European Court on Human Rights (ECtHR) dealing with Article 11, Dorssemont[22] provides for a categorisation of this juridical production. Thus, under the label of the "individual dimension" of the freedom of association one finds the protection of the (so called) negative freedom of association, including the issue of closed shops, as well as the protection against acts of anti-union discrimination aimed at individual workers. On the other hand, the "collective side" includes the protection of the autonomy of trade unions *in foro interno* and of trade unions' action, *i.e.* of the right to be heard, the right to bargain collectively and the right to take collective action.[23]

Following the criteria described before, I will focus here only on those specific aspects which seem more likely to be relevant the posting phenomenon. Hence, I will leave aside the question related to closed shops and to the autonomy of trade unions. The right to collective bargaining and the right to take collective action will be analysed in their respective sections. This leaves on the table a limited number of issues.

First, looking at the "individual side" of Article 11, the question of the negative aspect of the freedom of association has to be analysed. The right not to join a trade union (or employers' organisation) has been developed both in relation with individual workers and employers. From the workers' point of view, the issue did arise in the context of closed shops. In present times, at least

19 See for example Novitz, *International and European Protection of the Right to Strike*, p. 262: "the institutional context [of the ECHR] created a judiciary which had imbibed a notion of human rights as the exercise of individual negative liberty, rather than collective positive freedom."

20 However, collective rights have in time found their way to the protection of art. 11, through the work of the court in Strasbourg. Those evolutions will be recalled in the next sections.

21 See European Court of Human Rights, 12 November 2008, *Demir and Baykara v. Turkey*; European Court of Human Rights, 21 April 2009, *Enerji Yapi-Yol Sen*, no. 68959/01, no. 34503/97.

22 F. Dorssemont, "The Right to Form and to Join Trade Unions for the Protection of his Interests under Article 11 ECHR", *European Labour Law Journal* 1, no. 2 (2010): 185–235.

23 Ibid., pp. 195, 198, 203, 206 and 210.

regarding the Member States of the EU, closed shops are no more of great practical interest. Also, for the scope of the present research, the employers' side of the question does represent a more interesting one.[24] The ECtHR had to deal with this issue in the cases of *Gustafsson*[25] and *Kellermann*.[26] Both cases dealt with a potential conflict between the negative freedom of association and the recourse to collective action (*in casu* a boycott) by trade unions aimed at forcing the employer to sign a collective agreement. This question is indeed interesting for the present research. Both *Laval* and *Rüffert* were concerned with the extension to posting employers of working conditions regulated by a collective agreement. Now, the Court in *Gustaffson* considered that Article 11 of the Convention "does not as such guarantee a right not to enter into a collective agreement".[27] A violation of Article 11 can only be entailed by a collective agreement directly affecting the freedom of association, whereas a compulsion simply causing economic damage "does not give rise to any positive obligation under Article 11". All in all, it seems that the concept of the negative freedom of association, as developed by the ECtHR, only encompasses disputes revolving around actual membership of trade unions or employers' associations.

Second, on the collective side, one has to consider the "right to be heard". Developed as the first inherent "corollary" to Article 11,[28] the right to be heard represents a *tertium genus*, to be distinguished from both information and collective bargaining. However, the actual content of such a right is elusive at best. On the one hand, it can be assimilated to the "trade union's version" of the right to freedom of speech, since it basically implies just the possibility for a trade union to make its position known to the employer. On the other hand, it has been argued that this right implies an added value in respect of the freedom of speech.[29] This added value is identified by the *Wilson* case as the "right to seek to persuade the employer to listen to what it has to say on behalf of its members".[30] Since, as we just said, this right is excluded from the scope of information, as well as from the one of collective bargaining, it is interesting to briefly analyse it here. This in order to "complete" the canvas of trade union rights. Thus, the scope of the right to be heard needs to be identified by differentiating it from its neighbours: freedom of speech, right to be consulted, right to collective bargaining. In respect of the first, the right to be heard implies an added value as it implies the obligation for the "receiver" of the "speech" to actually pay (some form of) attention. In this sense, it

---

24 As stressed in the conclusion of Chapter 1.

25 European Court of Human Rights, 2 July 2002, *Gustafsson v. Sweden*, 15573/89.

26 European Court of Human Rights, 1 July 2003, *A.B. Kurt Kellermann v. Sweden*, no. 41579/98.

27 European Court of Human Rights, 28 March 1996, *Gustafsson v Sweden*, no. 15573/89, para. 52.

28 European Court of Human Rights, 27 October 1975, *National Union of Belgian Police*, no. 4464/70; Dorssemont, "The Right to Form and to Join Trade Unions for the Protection of his Interests under Article 11 ECHR", p. 216.

29 Ibid., p. 217.

30 European Court of Human Rights, 2 July 2002, *Wilson, National Union of Journalists and Others v. United Kingdom*,15573/89, para. 44.

has been argued, the right to be heard protects not only the possibility to express the position of the trade union, but also the practical reception by the employer.[31] On the contrary, this right does not imply an obligation on the head of the receiver to provide an answer or to justify his reaction to the communication itself. This clearly differentiates the right to be heard from a process of consultation, as it was already evident in the *Belgian Police* case.[32] Finally, the ECtHR consistently held that the right to be heard was not to be confused with a right for the given trade union to be included in a process of collective bargaining. This clearly results from the *Wilson* case, where we were told that "The Court has not yet been prepared to hold that the freedom of a trade union to make its voice heard extends to imposing on an employer an obligation to recognise a trade union".[33] Also, in the *Demir and Baykara* judgement, the ECtHR, while recognising the right to collective bargaining as an essential element of the freedom of association,[34] listed the "the right for a trade union to seek to persuade the employer to hear what it has to say on behalf of its members"[35] as a different right. Thus, it seems safe to affirm that the right to be heard is conceived by the ECtHR as situated outside the process of collective bargaining.

3.2 COLLECTIVE ACTION

We turn now to "collective action"[36] (or "industrial action"). Trying again to follow a logical sequence, it is the quote by Kahn-Freund "there can be a strike without trade unions, but no trade union without strike"[37] which inspires this choice. Indeed, from an historical point of view, the struggle for recognition chronologically precedes the admission of trade unions representatives to the table of negotiations (or even the creation of such a table). Or, to quote another famous phrase: collective bargaining would be nothing but collective begging if trade unions did not have the right to strike.[38]

---

31 Ibid., p. 217.

32 *National Union of Belgian Police*, cit., para. 22: "If an organisation is not recognised as representative, it is barred from the consultation procedure but may nonetheless, *inter alia*, submit claims to the supervisory authority, *ask to be heard* by it, refer cases to it and make representations on behalf of its members" (emphasis added).

33 *Wilson, National Union of Journalists and Others v. United Kingdom*, cit., para. 44.

34 *Demir and Baykara v. Turkey*, cit., para. 154.

35 Ibid., para. 145, where the ECtHR refers to the right to be heard through the formula developed in *Wilson*, para. 44.

36 It is important to stress right from the start how the concept of "collective action" and that of "strike" are related to one another. In very brief, the strike, which will be defined *infra* in this section, can be considered as a *species* of the broader category of "collective action".

37 As cited by R. Ben-Israel, "Strikes, Lockouts and Other Kinds of Hostile Actions", in *International Encyclopaedia of Comparative Law. Volume XV*, ed. Bob Hepple (Tübingen: C.B. Mohr, 1997), 1–50, p. 14.

38 M. Weiss and M. Schmidt, "Germany – Collective Labour Law", in *International Encyclopaedia of Labour Law*, ed. R. Blanpain and M. Colucci, vol. 340, July 2008, 163–264, p. 211.

Once again I will focus on the international and supra-national dimension in order to draw the boundaries of the subject.[39] However, before starting, a first important distinction is needed. The concept of "collective action" includes many different forms of industrial struggle, since different systems of industrial relations know (or have known) different ways for the workers to exert pressure upon the employer. From the most "classical" strike, to boycotts, working to rule, and go-slows: the list could be long indeed. For quantitative reasons, the strike has had a larger role in the evolving jurisprudence (in a broader sense) regarding the right here at stake. Thus, I will focus on this kind of collective action, while leaving to a separate paragraph to deal with other kind of action. This also amount at leaving aside the employers' side of collective action (most commonly, the lockout), since the strike is necessarily carried out by workers.

In order to clarify the scope of the term "strike" itself, I refer to the definition emerging from the comparative work of the *International Encyclopaedia of Comparative Law*. There Ben-Israel distillates, from the analysis of a number of model countries, the definition of the strike as "a collective and concerted withholding of labour in pursuit of specific occupational demands exercised peacefully".[40] I will now analyse more deeply this definition through the contribution of the cited "jurisprudence". However, I will leave aside issues which, though relevant for the subject matter, lay outside of the scope of the present research. A good example is the debated issue of the right to strike of public servants, police and armed forces.

Notwithstanding what I just said about the logical primacy of the strike on other trade union practices (and, eventually, rights), it is interesting to note that no ILO Convention explicitly mention the right to strike. Still, one would be far from the truth in affirming that because of this the right here at stake is not protected by ILO standards. Building upon the Freedom of Association and Protection of the Right to Organise Convention (No. 87) of 1948,[41] the two supervisory bodies of the ILO, the Committee of freedom of Association (since 1952) and the Committee of Experts on the Application of Conventions and Recommendations (since 1959), have recognised the fundamental nature of this right.[42]

A similar process, though more slow and "impervious", characterises the European Convention on Human Rights. As for the ILO, this instrument does not

39 For a comprehensive analysis of the protection of the right to strike (and to take collective action) at European and international level, see the seminal work by Novitz, *International and European Protection of the Right to Strike*.

40 Ben-Israel, "Strikes, Lockouts and Other Kinds of Hostile Actions", p. 17. It is however important to note that in French the term *grève* (strike) is used also to define "working to rule" (*grève du zèle*) and other kind of collective actions.

41 Reference goes in particular to Article 3, which recognises the right of workers' and employers' organisations to freely organise their activities and programmes, and to Article 10, which defines the aims of such organisations as "furthering and defending the interests of workers and employers".

42 B. Gernigon, A. Odero and H. Guido, "ILO Principles Concerning the Right to Strike", *Int'l Lab. Rev.*, 1998, p. 8.

explicitly mention the right to strike, limiting itself to the protection of freedom of association (Article 11). Though the ECtHR has finally acknowledged the right to strike as a *corollaire indissociable* ("indissociable corollary"[43] of the right to form and join trade unions, this has happened only in 2009, with the *Enerji* case.[44] This stance has been confirmed in a later judgement.[45] However, the number of cases decided by the judges of Strasbourg dealing with collective actions remains limited,[46] thus reducing the contribution of the ECHR to our definitions.

In order to find an instrument *explicitly* mentioning the right to strike, one can turn to the European Social Charter[47] (ESC). In fact, the ESC, signed in Turin in 1961, is often referred to as the first binding international treaty to explicitly recognise the right to strike.[48] Article 6(4) of the Charter recognises the "the right of workers and employers to collective action in cases of conflicts of interest, including the right to strike, subject to obligations that might arise out of collective agreements previously entered into".[49] This provision was not changed on the occasion of the Revision of the Charter of 1996 (the Charter being afterwards referred to as Revised European Social Charter, RevESC). Two important observations stem from a superficial glance to the text. First, the protection offered by the Charter is not limited to the right to *strike*, encompassing the whole concept of "collective action". Second, whereas under the two instruments we saw before the right to strike/right to take collective action is developed as an "indissociable corollary" of the freedom of association, the (Rev)ESC stresses instead the link with collective bargaining: the rights protected under Article 6 are in fact recognised "with a view to ensuring the effective exercise of the right to bargain collectively [...]". However, as we will see below, the supervisory body of the (Rev)ESC, the European Committee of Social Rights (ECSR) has interpreted the concept of "collective bargaining" in a very broad way.

Before proceeding, it is necessary to point out that the question here is not to decide upon the fundamental nature of the right to strike in the international

---

43 K. Ewing and J. Hendy, "The Dramatic Implications of Demir and Baykara", *Industrial Law Journal* 39, no. 1 (2010): 2–51, p. 14.

44 European Court on Human Rights, 21 April 2009, Enerji Yapi-Yol Sen, no. 68959/01.

45 ECtHR, 8 April 2014, *National Union of Rail, Maritime and Transport Workers v. The United Kingdom*, no. 31045/10 (hereinafter *RMT*), para. 84: "what the above-mentioned cases illustrate is that strike action is clearly protected by Article 11".

46 See on the point F. Dorssemont, "The Right to Take Collective Action Under Article 11 ECHR", in *The European Convention on Human Rights and the Employment Relation*, ed. F. Dorssemont, K. Lörcher and I. Schömann (Oxford: Hart Publishing, 2013), 333–367.

47 About the ESC in general, see D.J. Harris and J. Darcy, *The European Social Charter (Procedural Aspects of International Law Series, V. 25)*, (Transnational Pub, 2001) and A.M. Świątkowski, *Charter of Social Rights of the Council of Europe* (The Hague: Kluwer Law International, 2007).

48 S. Evju, "The Right to Collective Action Under the European Social Charter", *European Labour Law Journal* 2, no. 3 (2011): 196–224, p. 197.

49 It is important to note that a country can be a party to the ESC without accepting Article 6(4). Austria, Greece, Luxembourg and Turkey, for example, did not accept Article 6(4), though they are parties to the ESC. See L. Samuel, *Fundamental Social Rights: Case Law of the European Social Charter* (Strasbourg: Council of Europe, 1997).

or European legal order. More modestly, my efforts in this passage are aimed at defining the legal boundaries of the previously mentioned definition of the strike.

3.2.1 CONCERTED AND COLLECTIVE

As far as the "concerted" part is concerned, the reference goes to the time preceding the actual strike. This brings us to the much debated issue of the holder of the right to *call* a strike. In particular, the question is whether the right to call a strike should be defined as a monopoly of trade unions or not. Here I will not even try to delve into the debate about the individual or collective nature of the right to strike. Given the aim of these paragraphs, I will go for a more "practical" approach, in particular by looking at the ECSR jurisprudence.

Evidently, reference to a "concerted" activity excludes that the calling of a strike can be conceived as an individual activity. So far so good. It is then the nature of the "organisation" involved in the calling which should be defined. All in all, dealing here with an attempt to define, it is impossible to leave outside from the scope of the right (or freedom) to strike the eventuality of a strike called by a group of workers not organised in a trade union.[50] The jurisprudence of the ECSR corroborates this choice. Since 1971, in the occasion of its conclusions about Germany, the ECSR held that "the Committee was of the opinion that a group of workers ought to be able to take strike action even outside the trade union framework".[51] To this one should add that on the afterwards the same Committee has considered as in conformity with Article 6(4) those systems characterised by a unions' monopoly on collective action. This as long as ("a small number of") employees may "easily form an organisation", "with very few formalities to be fulfilled".[52] In view of this, the definition of "strike" cannot leave aside the actions organised by group of workers not belonging to a trade union. Thus, the "withholding of labour" will be concerted either by a trade union or by an organised group of workers.[53]

As a side note, some European legal systems have set up procedures which can be seen as guaranteeing the "concerted" nature of the strike. In particular, I am referring to the obligation to take strike decisions by ballot.[54] Such an obligation has been considered in principle as compatible with the (Revised) European Social Charter as long as the balloting rules are not too complex or restrictive. For example, the requirement for a vote favourable to the action by the 50% + 1 of the

---

50 Novitz, *International and European Protection of the Right to Strike*, pp. 275–278.

51 Conclusions II (1971) 28 (Germany).

52 Conclusions XV-1 (2000) 566 (Sweden); see also ECSR, *Digest of the Case Law of the European Committee of Social Rights* (Strasbourg, 2008), p. 234.

53 Evju, "The Right to Collective Action Under the European Social Charter", pp 214–215, Świątkowski, *Charter of Social Rights of the Council of Europe*, p. 233.

54 Novitz, *International and European Protection of the Right to Strike*, pp. 283–284.

"workers concerned" has been repeatedly considered as infringing Article 6(4).[55] Also the ILO Freedom of Association Committee reached a similar conclusion, considering (in principle) acceptable "the obligation to observe a certain quorum and to take strike decisions by secret ballot".[56] The stance of the ILO Committee is similar to the ECSR (or vice versa) also inasmuch as it considers that the quorum and majority required in a ballot should not make it very difficult or impossible in practice to (lawfully) exercise the right to strike.[57] For example, a quorum of two-thirds of trade union members has been considered as too difficult to reach, especially for unions having a large number of member scattered over a large geographical area.[58] In view of the impact that factual element (such as the cited geographical structure of the workforce or the structure of collective bargaining) can have on the difficulty to reach quorums and majorities in balloting procedures, the issue have been generally examined on a case by case basis.[59] However, I am convinced that this issue should not have an impact on the definition I am trying to analyse here. This in view of a simple fact: balloting procedures, connected they may be to the "concerted" part of our definition, can only have an impact on the lawfulness (or lack thereof) of a strike. Whether a "a collective and concerted withholding of labour" is apprehended by the legal system as lawful or not, it will still be defined as a strike. Maybe, an unlawful or "wildcat" one, but a strike nonetheless.[60] Instead, it is at the elements which define such an action as a strike that I am looking in this paragraphs.

The "collective" aspect of the definition, seems to be far less problematic. While the "concerted" characteristic deals with the pre-strike phase, the "collective" one describes the way in which the strike is actually carried out. This simply boils down to the fact that the "withholding of labour", even though "physically" exercised by individuals, must be performed simultaneously by several employees in order to be perceived as a strike.[61]

Thus, at the end of this paragraph, the strike is now defined as a "a peaceful withholding of labour, organised by either a trade union or a group of workers and carried out simultaneously by a plurality of employees, in pursuit of specific occupational demands".

---

55 See ECSR Conclusions XVI-1 (2002) 140, and Conclusions XVII-1 (2004) 101 (Czech Republic); Conclusions 2004, 347 (Lithuania); Conclusions 2002, 134–136 (Romania).

56 *Freedom of association: Digest of decisions and principles of the Freedom of Association Committee of the Governing Body of the ILO*. Fourth (revised) edition, Geneva, para. 510.

57 See Gernigon, Odero, and Guido, "ILO Principles Concerning the Right to Strike", pp. 29–30.

58 *Freedom of association: Digest of decisions and principles of the Freedom of Association Committee of the Governing Body of the ILO*, 1996, cit., para. 511.

59 Ibid., p. 29.

60 L. François, *Théorie des Relations Collectives du Travail en Droit belge* (Bruxelles: Bruylant, 1980), pp. 41–42.

61 Ben-Israel, "Strikes, Lockouts and Other Kinds of Hostile Actions", p. 17.

3.2.2 WITHHOLDING OF LABOUR

This part of the definition represents the practical side of a strike. It is by the withholding of labour that pressure is exerted upon the employer in order to compel him to accept the strikers' demands.[62] In this sense, the economic cost of the action for both workers and their employer is implicit in the definition of strike. This may or may not be the actual means putting the recalled pressure upon the employer, since other means can be conceived in connection with the collective action (*e.g.* the effect on the public opinion).

Apart from this superficial glance, it is hard to be more specific in defining the nature of the "withholding". In this regard, the ILO Committee of Experts could only observe that "national law and practice vary widely in this respect", concluding that "Any work stoppage, however brief and limited, may generally be considered as a strike".[63] The only restriction provided is not much of a guidance, since it only reiterates the necessity for every collective action to be peaceful.[64] I will come back to this later, dealing with the "peaceful exercise" part of the definition. From a different angle, though still looking at the same Conclusions of the Committee of Experts, it is difficult to identify the "withholding" in the case of a work-to-rule or go-slow action.[65] Indeed, this topic is prone to trespassing, since this question essentially boils down to distinguishing the strike from other forms of collective action. No help comes from the ECSR either, where the issue has not been consistently analysed.[66]

As recalled, the issue of lawfulness is not at stake here. Looking from the point of view of a definition of the "strike", one might wonder if a stricter definition is a better tool to study the posting phenomenon. On the one hand, it seems safe to include, with the comfort of the ILO Committee jurisprudence, any work *stoppage*, even if brief or partial, in the concept of strike. Hence, for example, a collective and concerted refusal to work overtime could be included in the scope of such a definition. On the other hand, the answer is more difficult (again, as noted by the Committee of Experts) for those actions *not* involving an actual stoppage of work. However, from the point of view of a definition, to include these actions in the definition of "strike" would make it difficult to distinguish it from the broader category of "collective action".

---

62 Ibid., p. 17.

63 Freedom of association and collective bargaining. General Survey of the reports on the Freedom of Association and Protection of the Right to Organise Convention, 1948 (No. 87), and the Right to Organise and Collective Bargaining Convention, 1949 (No. 98), 1994, cit., para. 173–174.

64 Ibid.: "the Committee is of the opinion that restrictions as to the forms of strike action can only be justified if the action ceases to be peaceful".

65 Ibid.: "This is more difficult to determine when there is no work stoppage as such but a slowdown in work (go-slow strike) or when work rules are applied to the letter (work-to-rule)."

66 Evju, "The Right to Collective Action Under the European Social Charter", p. 203.

3.2.3 SPECIFIC OCCUPATIONAL DEMANDS

By defining the "demands" of the strike, this part of the definition deals with the objectives of the collective action. Keeping in mind that the various European legal systems present a wide range of differences on this topic, a categorisation has been proposed on the basis of the jurisprudence of the Supervisory Bodies of the ILO. It consists of three categories, on the basis of the demands pursued through the strike: occupational (including the protection or improvement of working and living conditions of the workers), trade union (aimed at protecting or improving trade unions rights) or political.[67] Since the first and second categories present less difficulties in being considered as protected under ILO Conventions, it is especially by distinguishing these from the third one that one can identify the stance of the ILO on the issue.

As a starting point, the Freedom of Association Committee holds that "strikes of a purely political nature [...] do not fall within the scope of the principles of freedom of association".[68] However, by looking at the subsequent Conclusions dealing with the "scope" of this "purely political nature", one can see that the tendency has been to narrow its extension. This because of the difficulty of drawing a clear demarcation line between political and occupational aims of a strike when, for example, political decisions adopted by a Government have (or can have) direct and over-reaching effects on working and living conditions of workers: "organisations responsible for defending workers' socio-economic and occupational interests should, in principle, be able to use strike action to support their position in the search for solutions posed by major social and economic policy trends which have a direct impact on their members and on workers in general, in particular as regards employment, social protection and the standard of living".[69]

Political strikes ("not a very clear concept in any way", in the words of a former member of the ECSR[70]) have been excluded from the scope of Article 6(4) by the ECSR since these strikes are considered to be "obviously quite outside the purview of collective bargaining"[71] This stems directly from the "functional

---

67 Gernigon, Odero, and Guido, "ILO Principles Concerning the Right to Strike", p. 13.

68 *Freedom of association: Digest of decisions and principles of the Freedom of Association Committee of the Governing Body of the ILO*, 1996, cit., para. 481. See Novitz, *International and European Protection of the Right to Strike*, pp. 294–297.

69 *Freedom of association and collective bargaining. General Survey of the reports on the Freedom of Association and Protection of the Right to Organise Convention, 1948 (No. 87), and the Right to Organise and Collective Bargaining Convention, 1949 (No. 98).* Report III (Part 4B), International Labour Conference, 81st Session, 1994, Geneva, para. 165.

70 Evju, "The Right to Collective Action Under the European Social Charter", p. 209.

71 ECSR Conclusions, C II (1971) 27. However, it must be noted that the Committee has not discussed the issue of strike aimed at criticising policy choices of a Government having an economic and social effect, see Novitz, *International and European Protection of the Right to Strike*, pp. 290–294; E. Kovács, "The Right to Strike in the European Social Charter", *Comparative Labor Law & Policy Journal* 26 (2006): 445–475, p. 451.

bond" between the right to strike and collective bargaining under Article 6 of the RevESC. However, a further look into the jurisprudence of the ECSR shows that the scope of "collective bargaining" (thus, of the "rightful" aims of a strike) is far from narrow. First, the Committee made it clear that the exercise of the right to strike cannot be limited *only* at situations involving the conclusion of a collective agreement.[72] Second, the very scope of the concept of "collective bargaining" has been broadened by the jurisprudence of the ECSR. In particular, virtually every negotiation between workers and their employer has been considered as "collective bargaining", following the statement present in the 1975 Conclusions: "any bargaining between one or more employers and a body of employees (whether *de jure* or *de facto*') aimed at solving a problem of common interest, whatever its nature may be, should be regarded as collective bargaining within the meaning of Article 6".[73] In this sense many different issues could be included in such a definition of collective bargaining, from conflicts about health and safety measures to collective dismissals. It must be noted that the ECSR held that Article 6(4) cannot be considered as covering a strike aimed at amending a collective agreement still in force. This can be found in the first Conclusions delivered by the Committee, stating that "This provision [Article 6(4)] recognises the right to collective action only in cases of conflicts of interest. It follows that it cannot be invoked in cases of conflicts of right, i.e., in particular, in cases of disputes concerning the existence, validity or interpretation of a collective agreement or its violation, e.g., through action taken during its currency with a view to the revision of its contents".[74] This vision is evidently inspired by those countries who see collective agreements as a social peace treaty.[75] The stance of the supervisory bodies of the ILO on this topic is different, though by no means conflicting. Indeed, the Committee on Freedom of Association having recognised that "the legislation in many countries does not establish any restrictions on the time when a strike may be initiated, stipulating only that the advance notice established by the law must be observed" whereas "other industrial relations systems are based on a radically different philosophy in which collective agreements are seen as a social peace treaty of fixed duration during which strikes and lockouts are prohibited under the law itself", explicitly stated that "both these options are compatible with the Convention and that the

---

72 ECSR Conclusions ii(1971) 28: "provisions are not consonant with the Charter when they are designed to restrict the right to strike solely to strikes to secure the conclusion of collective agreements [...]".

73 ECSR Conclusions IV (1975) 50.

74 ECSR Conclusions I (1969) 38.

75 See F. Schmidt and A.C. Neal, "Collective Agreements and Collective Bargaining", in *International Encyclopaedia of Comparative Law. Volume XV*, ed. Bob Hepple (Tübingen: C.B. Mohr, 1984), 1–127, p. 9: "The Collective Agreement as a Peace Instrument"; A. Jacobs, "The Law of Strikes and Lockouts", in *Comparative Labour Law and Industrial Relations in Industrialized Market Economies*, ed. Roger Blanpain (The Hague: Kluwer Law International, 2007), 633–687, p. 641.

choice should be left to the law and practice of each State".[76] Still, in the same Conclusion, the ILO Committee provided for a major deviation from the second model (the one based on the theory of collective agreement as peace treaties): "In both types of systems, however, workers' organisations should not be prevented from striking against the social and economic policy of the Government, in particular where the protest is not only against that policy but also against its effects on some provisions of collective agreements".[77] Under this light, a definition of the "specific occupational demands" pursued by a strike is bound to be broad, having to include, at least, collective actions in the occasion of a *sui generis* bargaining between workers and their employer, as well as a strike against the social and economic policy of a given Government.

The need for this broad definition is stressed also by the stance about "sympathy strikes", *i.e.* when workers come out in support of another strike. In such a situation, the "specific occupational demands" can sometimes only be traced back to solidarity (and in fact these actions are also called "solidarity strikes"). The ILO Committee of Expert, held that such actions should be permitted as long as the initial strike (the one which is being supported) is lawful.[78] What is more, both the ILO Committee of Experts and the ECSR consider a general prohibition on sympathy strikes as infringing their respective standards, since such a measure could "lead to abuses"[79] by preventing workers to take action "against their *de facto* employer".[80] Thus, since sympathy actions cannot be completely excluded by the definition of "strike", the scope of the "demands" should be interpreted in a sufficiently broad way in order to include this kind of action.

3.2.4 PEACEFUL EXERCISE

When it comes to the closing part of our definition the boundaries between the "lawfulness" aspect and the "definition" one became somewhat blurred. It is true that, generally speaking, every legal system recognising the right to strike submits

76 Freedom of association: Digest of decisions and principles of the Freedom of Association Committee of the Governing Body of the ILO, 1994, cit., para. 166–167.

77 Ibid.

78 Freedom of association and collective bargaining: General survey by the Committee of Experts on the application of the Conventions on freedom of association, the right to organise and collective bargaining and the Convention and Recommendation concerning rural workers' organisations. Report of the Committee of Experts on the Application of Conventions and Recommendations. Report III (Part 4B), International Labour Conference, 69th Session, 1983. Geneva, para. 217. See Gernigon, Odero, and Guido, "ILO Principles Concerning the Right to Strike", p. 16.

79 Freedom of association and collective bargaining. General Survey of the reports on the Freedom of Association and Protection of the Right to Organise Convention, 1948 (No. 87), and the Right to Organise and Collective Bargaining Convention, 1949 (No. 98), 1994, cit., para. 168. See also P. Germanotta, *Protecting Worker Solidarity Action: A Critique of International Labour Law* (London : The Institute of Employment Rights, 2002), pp. 10–11.

80 ECSR Conclusions XVI-1, vol. 2, para. 689.

such a right, at the very least, to the requirement of its peaceful exercise.[81] At the same time, from the point of view of the definition, recourse (for example) to physical violence or to destruction of property does fall outside of the concept of "strike".

Looking at the jurisprudence of the ILO Committee on Freedom of Association, the requirement here at stake plays the role of a first *filter*, in order to decide if a given action is protected by ILO Conventions. As it has already been recalled, the Committee accepted different form of collective action as long as they are conducted in a peaceful manner.[82]

In this sense, this part of the definition is less problematic. At least, it is not problematic as long as physical violence, destruction of property, assault or illegal confinement are involved. When it comes to other forms of violence which could be invoked, as for example, intimidation, the situation gets more obscure. This second issue has been analysed especially when dealing with the form of collective action (or, better, corollary to a collective action) known as "picketing". Thus, I will leave this discussion for the next paragraph.

3.2.5 OTHER FORMS OF COLLECTIVE ACTION

As recalled at the beginning of this Section, the different kinds of collective action are indeed many, so that it would be impossible to draw an exhaustive list of them. The creativity of the organisers is the only limit here. What is more, in view of the approach followed in these paragraphs, these "other forms" of collective action are far less widespread both geographically and quantitatively. Thus, there is no consistent body of international standards coming to our rescue. However, in a recent Decision the ECSR significantly stated that Article 6(4) "encompasses not only the right of withholding of work, but also other relevant means [...]. Both this components deserve a *comparable* degree of protection".[83] This shows the willingness of the ECSR to extend the protection elaborated for the right to strike to other forms of collective action, by means of analogy. Still, such a stance does not help in defining more precisely these "relevant means".

---

81 Ben-Israel, "Strikes, Lockouts and Other Kinds of Hostile Actions", p. 18.

82 Gernigon, Odero, and Guido, "ILO Principles Concerning the Right to Strike", p. 12. See *Freedom of association: Digest of decisions and principles of the Freedom of Association Committee of the Governing Body of the ILO*, 1996, cit., para. 496: "Noting that national law and practice vary widely in this respect, the Committee is of the opinion that restrictions as to the forms of strike action can only be justified if the action *ceases to be peaceful*" (emphasis added). See also Novitz, *International and European Protection of the Right to Strike*, p. 274.

83 European Committee of Social Rights, Complaint No 59/2009, European Trade Union Confederation (ETUC) / Centrale Générale des Syndicats Libéraux de Belgique (CGSLB)/ Confédération des Syndicats Chrétiens de Belgique (CSC)/ Fédération Générale du Travail de Belgique (FGTB) v. Belgium, para. 29 (emphasis added).

The most visible *fil rouge* between these "other forms", though hardly a surprising one, is the fundamental requirement of the peaceful exercise, which then marks the boundaries of the industrial dispute. In general, one should retain as many elements as possible from the definition of the strike, in order to define the scope of "collective action". In this sense, "collective and concerted" is almost a repetition (speaking of "collective action"), while the "specific occupational demands" are strictly intertwined with the "industrial" nature of the dispute, which would otherwise belong to the political arena more than to the employment/social one. Of the "peaceful exercise" we just said. Thus the only element which provides for the wide variety of possible actions is the "withholding of labour". As it is evident, go-slows or work-to-rules do not represent a withholding of labour; other actions may (and, historically, have been) in fact be founded on the very contrary principle. The reference goes to the "work-in",[84] which can be identified as an occupation of the premises of the enterprise where the employees try to continue the production by themselves. In order to catch all these various kinds of action one should have recourse to the broadest definition to substitute "withholding of labour". Instead, reference should be made to every "deviation from the standard pattern of production carried out without the management consent", keeping in mind that such a broad definition is bound to include actions that no legal system identifies as collective (or industrial) action.

That being said, there is at least one kind of collective action which has been the object of some attention both from the ILO and the RevESC supervisory bodies. Though in fact it must be conceived more as a corollary of a "principal" action, the picketing has made its way to the international bodies.[85] With picketing one generally means "the situation in which one or more employees, or union members, are present at or near a place connected with an industrial dispute", their objective being "either to persuade non-strikers and substitute workers not to work, or to persuade suppliers not to furnish goods or services to the employer in the dispute".[86] Such an action has been considered by the ILO Committee on Freedom of Association as being protected under ILO Conventions: "Taking part in picketing and firmly but peacefully inciting other workers to keep away from their workplace cannot be considered unlawful".[87] However, it is clear that the situation described in the definition has an high potential to degenerate into violence. Apart from this, it is worth mentioning another limit which is also mentioned by the ILO Committee in the same Conclusion cited above:

---

84 Ben-Israel, "Strikes, Lockouts and Other Kinds of Hostile Actions", p. 49.

85 European Committee of Social Rights, Complaint No. 59/2009, European Trade Union Confederation (ETUC)/ Centrale Générale des Syndicats Libéraux de Belgique (CGSLB) / Confédération des Syndicats Chrétiens de Belgique(CSC) / Fédération Générale du Travail de Belgique (FGTB) v. Belgium.

86 Ben-Israel, "Strikes, Lockouts and Other Kinds of Hostile Actions", p. 49.

87 *Freedom of association: Digest of decisions and principles of the Freedom of Association Committee of the Governing Body of the ILO*, 1996, cit., para. 587.

picketing workers should not attempt at interfering with the freedom to work of non-strikers.[88]

3.3 COLLECTIVE BARGAINING

The signing of collective agreements has represented and still represents the most important instrument in the hand of (generally speaking) trade unions to carry out the "de-commodification" of labour.[89] In very brief, a collective agreement tries to take working conditions out of competition, making it so that such conditions are not fixed following the interplay between supply and demand of labour. Instead, it is the power relationship between the "collectivity of workers" and the employer(s) that is taken into account when fixing the working conditions in a given collective agreement.

Collective bargaining does present itself, across the European countries, in many different ways.[90] Collective actions present many differences especially in terms of the regulations regarding their exercise, the practical nucleus being somewhat similar. Instead, collective bargaining in different countries does differ *also* in its practice: as for example, different countries witness processes of bargaining at different levels (industry or company, but also nationwide or at plant level).

Such a variety, has an impact both on the definition one may chose to embrace the phenomenon and on the jurisprudence of the different bodies we will look at to further specify the definition.

Looking in the *International Encyclopaedia of Comparative Law*, one finds that the definition revolves around the object (the collective agreement) more than the practice. Thus, a collective agreement is defined as: "an agreement between two parties (the employer side and the employee side) which they consider binding upon themselves".[91] Consequently, collective bargaining is defined as "negotiations which aim at the conclusion of a collective agreement".[92] Similarly,

---

88 Ibid.: "The case is different, however, when picketing is accompanied by violence or coercion of non-strikers in an attempt to interfere with their freedom to work". See also Jacobs, "The Law of Strikes and Lockouts", p. 657.

89 Esping-Andersen, *The Three Worlds of Welfare Capitalism*. See Rebhahn, "Collective Labour Law in Europe in a Comparative Perspective (Part I)", pp. 273–274.

90 For a comparative point view see Schmidt and Neal, "Collective Agreements and Collective Bargaining"; P.M. Sheldon, G. Bamber and E. Cordova, "Collective Bargaining", in *Comparative Labour Law and Industrial Relations in Industrialized Market Economies*, ed. Roger Blanpain and Chris Engles (The Hague: Kulwer, 1998), 405–436; Rebhahn, "Collective Labour Law in Europe in a Comparative Perspective (Part I)"; G. Bamber and P. Sheldon, "Collective Bagaining: an International Analysis", in *Comparative Labour Law and Industrial Relations in Industrialized Market Economies2*, ed. R. Blanpain (Den Haag: International, Kluwer Law, 2007), 585–632.

91 Schmidt and Neal, "Collective Agreements and Collective Bargaining", p. 3.

92 Ibid., p. 5.

Sheldon and Bamber define collective bargaining as "bipartite negotiations, where there is an intention to reach an agreement".[93] For a more extended definition, ILO Recommendation No. 91, in paragraph 2, defines collective agreements as "all agreements in writing regarding working conditions and terms of employment concluded between an employer, a group of employers or one or more employers organisations, on the one hand, and one or more representative workers' organisations, or, in the absence of such organisations, the representatives of the workers duly selected and authorised by them in accordance with national laws and regulations, on the other".[94] One can see that this definitions further specifies the parties of the agreement, while at the same time adding an element to the previous definition: the content of the agreement ("regarding working conditions and terms of employment"). On the other hand, Convention No. 154 defines collective bargaining as "all negotiations which take place between an employer, a group of employers or one or more employers organisations, on the one hand, and one or more workers' organisations, on the other, for: (a) determining working conditions and terms of employment; and/or (b) regulating relations between employers and workers; and/or (c) regulating relations between employers or their organisations and a workers' organisation or workers' organisations".[95] The two "couples of definitions" present different approaches. The first definition does not identify in any way the content of collective agreements, leaving the door open to any agreement between the two sides, with the sole requirement of both considering such an agreement as binding. Then, collective bargaining is restricted to the activity leading to a collective agreement. On the other hand, the second definition of collective agreement, considers the very content of these agreement as a requirement: collective agreement are only those agreement regulating working conditions and terms of employment. In the second couple the "opening" is provided by the definition of collective bargaining, which includes not only collective agreements (letter a) but also other kinds of agreements dealing with a different content (letters b and c). Both "couples" make use of the term "negotiations" in their definition of collective bargaining. In the context of the ILO this term was preferred upon "discussion", as it emphasised the objective of reaching an agreement,[96] with the intended meaning of "any form of discussion, formal or informal, that was designed to reach an agreement".[97] In the context of a comparative legal study, Bamber and Sheldon[98] accept a more specific definition of

---

93 Bamber and Sheldon, "Collective Bagaining: an International Analysis", p. 589.

94 ILO, *International Labour Conventions and Recommendations, 1919–1951. Vol. I* (Geneva, 1996), p. 656.

95 ILO, *International Labour Conventions and Recommendations, 1977–1995. Vol III* (Geneva, 1996), p. 93.

96 B. Gernigon, A. Odero and H. Guido, "ILO Principles Concerning Collective Bargaining", *International Labour Review*, 2000, p. 36.

97 ILO, *Record of Proceedings. International Labour Conference, 64th Session* (Geneva, 1978), para. 64–65, p. 25/9.

98 Bamber and Sheldon, "Collective Bagaining: an International Analysis", p. 586.

the term "bargaining": "a basic means of getting what you want from others. It is a back-and-forth communication designed to reach an agreement, when you and the other side have some interests that are shared and others that are opposed".[99]

Though the first couple of definitions does in fact *include* the second, the second presents a higher degree of clarity, and I will thus refer to it in the following paragraphs. Also, the definition of the process of "collective bargaining" as a process which is not bound to culminate in a "collective agreement" seems to be consistent with the broader interpretation given by the ECSR to the same concept.[100] Two main parts of both definitions require further clarification: the two "sides" of a collective agreement (or, of a process of collective bargaining, since we saw that the two scopes are only partially overlapping) and the possible contents of the agreement. However, I will start with a fundamental principle of collective bargaining, i.e. the principle of free and voluntary negotiations. This principle is laid down in Article 4 of Convention No. 98 and has been subsequently developed by the ILO Committees; the European Social Charter also mentions "voluntary negotiations" in its Article 6(2).

3.3.1 FREE AND VOLUNTARY NEGOTIATION

I start with this principle even though no mention of it is present in the couple of definitions presented before. This derives from the importance of the principle at stake, which, much through the work of the ILO, informs every element of collective bargaining.

As a starting point, one can point out that the Committee on Freedom of Association stated that such a principle is "a fundamental aspect of the principles of freedom of association".[101] In practice, this principle makes it so that any measure implying a compulsion to bargain would be considered as infringing the freedom to collective bargaining. Thus, the obligation to "encourage and promote" negotiations between employees' organisations and employers (or their organisation) should not be interpreted as to infringe the "voluntary" nature of these negotiations.[102]

---

99 R. Fisher, W.L. Ury and B. Patton, *Getting to Yes: Negotiating Agreement Without Giving In* (London: Penguin Books, 2011), p. xiii.

100 ECSR Conclusions IV (1975) 50: "any bargaining between one or more employers and a body of employees (whether *de jure* or *de facto*) aimed at solving a problem of common interest, whatever its nature may be, should be regarded as collective bargaining within the meaning of Article 6".

101 ILO, *Freedom of Association: Digest of Decisions and Principles of the Freedom of Association Committee of the Governing Body of the ILO*, 2006, para. 925.

102 Ibid., para. 927: "Nothing in Article 4 of Convention No. 98 places a duty on the government to enforce collective bargaining by compulsory means with a given organisation; such an intervention would clearly alter the nature of bargaining."

The ECSR, though it had less occasions to examine the matter, has held since its first Conclusions that "Whatever the procedures [to facilitate and encourage the conclusion of collective agreements] put in place are, collective bargaining should remain free and voluntary".[103]

A few exceptions to this principle have been accepted by the ILO Committees. For example, sanctioning unfair practices during negotiations or conducts against good faith have been accepted, insofar as they are proportionate.[104]

It is however important to keep in mind that the concept of "free and voluntary negotiation" makes reference to compulsion provided by the law, to be intended in the broader sense: legislation, intervention by public authorities, case law and so on. The voluntary character of negotiations is by no means harmed by the pressure eventually put on one of the "sides of the table" by means of collective action. The contrary would gave rise to the absurd situation where the right or freedom to take collective action is denied in the name of the very same collective bargaining which is one of the legitimate aims of the action itself. The European Court for the Human Rights had once to decide upon a much similar clash. This was in the *Gustaffson* case which has already been recalled *supra*. The ECtHR made it clear that compulsion through collective actions did not violate the negative freedom of association of the employer as long as this compulsion was aimed at the conclusion of a collective agreement and not to force the employer to associate himself to the employers' association.[105] Hence, one can draw the line between the protection of the freedom of association, which is protected against both legal and practical/economic compulsion, and voluntary negotiation, which is only protected against compulsion through legal obligations.

To exemplify the importance of this principle, one can look at the question of the different "levels" of collective bargaining. That is, the geographical scope of negotiations, which can take place at national level, regional level, branch level, company level, and so on to reach the level of a single establishment. On the topic the stance of the ILO Committees is clearly informed by the principle here at stake. Thus, the Committee on Freedom of Association stated that "According to the principle of free and voluntary collective bargaining embodied in Article 4 of Convention No. 98, the determination of the bargaining level is essentially a matter to be left to the discretion of the parties and, consequently, the level of negotiation should not be imposed by law, by decision of the administrative authority or by the case-law of the administrative labour authority".[106] Before, the Committee of Experts had concluded in a similar way by affirming that "the choice

---

103 ECSR, Conclusions I, Statement of Interpretation on Article 6(2), p. 35.

104 *318th Report of the Committee on Freedom of Association*. Document GB.276/1, Governing Body, 276th Session (November), Case No. 1931, para. 371. See Gernigon, Odero and Guido, "ILO Principles Concerning Collective Bargaining", p. 41.

105 *Gustafsson v. Sweden*, para. 52.

106 ILO, *Freedom of Association: Digest of Decisions and Principles of the Freedom of Association Committee of the Governing Body of the ILO*, para. 988.

[of the bargaining level] should normally be made by the partners themselves, since they are in the best position to decide the most appropriate bargaining level, including, if they so wish, by adopting a mixed system of framework agreements supplemented by local or enterprise-level agreements".[107]

3.3.2 PARTIES

Looking back to the definitions of collective bargaining provided before, one can see that the first definition contents itself of making reference to an "employer side" and an "employee side" to define the two parties of a collective agreement.[108] The definition provided by the ILO goes more into details. For the employer side, having accepted that this "side" can be represented by a single employer, it does not raise much of a problem to include a group of employers or an employers' organisation as possible parts of a collective agreement.[109] This is shown also by the (relative) lack of Conclusions of both the ILO and the ESC supervisory bodies on issues related to the employers' side of collective bargaining.

On the employees' side two main issues arise. The first is apparent from the definition provided by Recommendation 91: the question of a bargaining involving workers' representatives instead of representatives of workers' organisations (*i.e.* trade unions). The second issue is related to the eventual recognition of a most representative trade union.

I will analyse workers' representatives (thus to keep separated from trade unions' representatives, whether elected or not) more in detail in the next subsection. Here I will only deal with their possible role as actors in a process of collective bargaining. The definition provided by the ILO leaves it open for these representatives to conclude collective agreements, but *only* in a situation where no workers' organisation is present at the given level of collective bargaining. Furthermore, the Committee on Freedom of Association makes it clear that "direct negotiation between the undertaking and its employees, by-passing representative organisations where these exist, might in certain cases be detrimental to the principle that negotiation between employers and organisations of workers should be encouraged and promoted".[110] Indeed, the possible tension between

---

107 Freedom of association and collective bargaining. General Survey of the reports on the Freedom of Association and Protection of the Right to Organise Convention, 1948 (No. 87), and the Right to Organise and Collective Bargaining Convention, 1949 (No. 98), Report III (Part 4B), International Labour Conference, 81st Session, 1994. Geneva, para. 249.

108 Schmidt and Neal, "Collective Agreements and Collective Bargaining", p. 3.

109 This is also noted as relatively un-problematic by Rebhahn, "Collective Labour Law in Europe in a Comparative Perspective (Part I)", p. 274: "in all states [the USA and the EU-15 minus Luxembourg] apart from Austria, every employer can make a collective agreement for his enterprise on his own".

110 ILO, *Freedom of Association: Digest of Decisions and Principles of the Freedom of Association Committee of the Governing Body of the ILO*, para. 945.

workers' elected representatives and workers' organisations is apparent from the very wording of Convention No. 135 (Workers' Representatives Convention), which in Article 5 states that "Where there exist in the same undertaking both trade union representatives and elected representatives, appropriate measures shall be taken, wherever necessary, to ensure that the existence of elected representatives is not used to undermine the position of the trade unions concerned or their representatives". Under this light, it is clear that workers' organisation are considered, under ILO principles, as the "normal" actors in a process of collective bargaining. Workers' elected representatives may play a role "only when no organisation exists".[111] The preparatory works of the Collective Agreements Recommendation reveal (with no surprise) that the possibility for workers' representatives to conclude collective agreement should be considered as an option left open for "those countries in which trade union organisations have not yet reached a sufficient degree of development, and in order to enable the principles laid down in the Recommendation to be implemented in such countries".[112] However, dealing with a definition, such a stance does not amount at excluding agreements eventually reached between the employer and workers' representatives from the scope of "collective agreements".[113]

The second issue is related to the *composition* of the workers' side. Leaving aside the previous question, the workers' side of the negotiating table is occupied by bargaining agents representing trade unions. However, these agents may belong to a single trade union or to a plurality of organisations. Also, they may be deemed to represent only their members or all the workers covered by the eventual collective agreement. The ILO Committees have made it clear that both situations are compatible with ILO Conventions.[114] In this sense, the stance is neutral as regards our definition. Still, it is worth remembering here that several guarantees are to be put in place in case a system grants a special position to a "most representative union". In particular, the criteria to determine the representativeness should be objective and pre-established,[115] and the position should not be granted for an excessively long time period (implying the right for minority organisations to call for a new election or poll after a reasonable period of time).[116] Also, when

111 Ibid., para. 944.

112 ILO, *Record of Proceedings. International Labour Conference, 34th Session* (Geneva, 1951), p. 603; see Gernigon, Odero and Guido, "ILO Principles Concerning Collective Bargaining", p. 37.

113 See also Rebhahn, "Collective Labour Law in Europe in a Comparative Perspective (Part I)", p. 275: "only agreements with union are collective agreements *in the strict sense*" (emphasis added).

114 ILO, *Freedom of Association: Digest of Decisions and Principles of the Freedom of Association Committee of the Governing Body of the ILO*, para. 950: "Systems of collective bargaining with exclusive rights for the most representative trade union and those where it is possible for a number of collective agreements to be concluded by a number of trade unions within a company are both compatible with the principles of freedom of association."

115 Ibid., para. 926.

116 Ibid., para. 969.

criteria for picking an exclusive bargaining agent for a given unit are present, but no organisation does meet them, "collective bargaining rights should be granted to all the unions in the unit, at least on behalf of their own members".[117] Finally, requirements of representativeness (or other conditions) should not be set at a level which hinders the possibility for organisations to represent their members.[118] This view is maintained also by the ECSR.[119]

3.3.3 CONTENTS

The definition chosen before identifies the content of a collective agreement as related to working conditions and terms of employment. At the same time, the definition of collective bargaining presents a wider scope, including negotiations aimed at reaching a collective agreement (with the said content) or at regulating relations between employers and workers and/or at regulating relations between the employer (or the employers, or their organisations) and a workers' organisation (or workers' representatives).

That being said, the combination of the three categories makes it so that a definition of collective bargaining as potentially covering every aspect of the "labour sphere" must be accepted. A consistent stance of the ILO Committees confirm this view. Legislative intervention restricting the scope of negotiable issues have been repeatedly considered as non-conform to ILO Conventions.[120] The exclusion of working time, of clauses dealing with collective action, of job distribution, of leave or of job security fall in this category of non-conform interventions. Everything considered, one can see as Committee of Experts has warned that "measures taken unilaterally by the authorities to restrict the scope of negotiable issues are often incompatible with Convention No. 98".[121]

In the end, it is clear that the concept of "working conditions" is to be interpreted in a very broad way.[122] Thus, provided that to define in positive terms this wide scope amounts to an impossibly long listing, it is interesting to look at the negative side by turning the question: what is in principle excluded from

---

117 Ibid., para. 976.

118 Ibid., para. 978–980.

119 ECSR Conclusions 2006, Albania, p. 41–42: "It is open to States parties to require trade unions to meet an obligation of representativeness subject to certain general conditions. With respect to Article 6(2) such a requirement must not excessively limit the possibility of trade unions to participate effectively in collective bargaining."

120 Ibid., para. 912–923.

121 Ibid., para. 912.

122 As for example, it should include also matters which are normally considered "conditions of employment", such as promotions, transfers, dismissals and so on. See Gernigon, Odero and Guido, "ILO Principles Concerning Collective Bargaining", p. 39; P. Macklem, "The Right to Bargain Collectively in International Law: Workers' Right, Human Right, International Right?" in *Labour Rights as Human Rights*, ed. Ph. Alston (Oxford: Oxford University Press, 2005), 61–84, p. 67.

the scope of collective bargaining? Unfortunately the ILO *corpus* of decisions provides little guidance in this sense. Still, it seems that two limits can be safely identified: on the one hand, the subjects closely intertwined with the freedom of the employer to manage the enterprise[123] (*e.g.* the assignment of duties[124]), though this subject is obviously hard to define *per se*. On the other hand, mirroring the first exclusion in the public sphere, those issue which are related to the "management and operation of government business".[125] To this one should add, superfluous it may sound, that collective bargaining and/or collective agreement cannot provide for measures infringing the law (*e.g.* discriminatory clauses) or undercutting minimum standards set by the law itself.[126]

3.4 REPRESENTATION

The topic of (workers') representation is probably the most elusive of the bundle of rights I tried to define here. This is already apparent from ILO Convention No. 135 on "Workers' Representatives", which in Article 3 limits itself to define workers' representatives as "persons who are recognised as such under national law or practice". Though the Article continues, providing more guidance as to the scope of the concept at stake, this first approach reveals all the difficulty in finding a single definition of the concept of "workers' representatives". The European Social Charter is no different. In the Appendix[127] about Articles 21–22 (dealing with information and consultation), the definition provided for workers' representatives effectively mirrors the one provided by ILO Convention No. 135: "workers representatives means persons who are recognised as such under national legislation or practice".

However, the same Article 3 of Convention No. 135 provides with two possible categories which should then cover the whole topic of workers' representatives. The two categories[128] make reference to the distinction between the so called "single-channel" and "double channel" representation. In very brief (and thus rounding a

---

[123] ILO, *Report of the Committee of Experts on the Application of Conventions and Recommendations. General Report and Observations Concerning Particular Countries. Report III (Part 1A), International Labour Conference, 86th Session* (Geneva, 1998), p. 250.

[124] Gernigon, Odero and Guido, "ILO Principles Concerning Collective Bargaining", p. 40.

[125] ILO, *Freedom of Association: Digest of Decisions and Principles of the Freedom of Association Committee of the Governing Body of the ILO*, para. 920.

[126] Gernigon, Odero and Guido, "ILO Principles Concerning Collective Bargaining", p. 40.

[127] That forms integral part of the Charter, its provisions being equally obligatory: see Article N of the 1996 Revised Charter.

[128] "[...] (a) trade union representatives, namely, representatives designated or elected by trade unions or by members of such unions; or
(b) elected representatives, namely, representatives who are freely elected by the workers of the undertaking in accordance with provisions of national laws or regulations or of collective agreements and whose functions do not include activities which are recognised as the exclusive prerogative of trade unions in the country concerned".

good number of edges), the single-channel model entails in principle the absence of a distinction between the holders of the right to participate in the process of collective bargaining and the agents involved in the rights to information and consultation. Thus, the workers' representation is assured directly by trade unions' representatives. On the other hand, a double-channel model provides for distinct bodies and agents holding the two sets of rights, with information and consultation rights being exercised by elected workers' representatives while collective bargaining is generally left for trade unions representatives.[129] It is with this second situation in mind that Article 5 of Convention No. 135 has been drafted,[130] in order to guarantee trade unions' prerogatives from being by-passed through direct negotiations with workers' representatives.

Though this approach by the ILO has been criticised as being too abstract and oversimplified,[131] it still provides a welcome help in shedding some light upon the concept of "workers' representation". ILO Convention No. 135 features a clear-cut distinction between "representation" and "collective bargaining". True enough, as I just wrote, in a single-channel model both these prerogatives may be exercised by the same body, but this makes it not less evident that the two concepts must be kept separated. This view is confirmed by ILO Recommendation No. 94 (1952), which states that "Appropriate steps should be taken to promote consultation and co-operation between employers and workers at the level of the undertaking on matters of mutual concern *not within the scope of collective bargaining machinery*, or not normally dealt with by other machinery concerned with the determination of terms and conditions of employment" (emphasis added). Thus, sticking to our definition of "collective bargaining", we can say that workers' representatives are entrusted of negotiations aimed at "(a) determining working conditions and terms of employment; and/or (b) regulating relations between employers and workers; and/or (c) regulating relations between employers or their organisations and a workers' organisation or workers' organisations". It seems to me that this distinction can be generalised affirming that collective bargaining covers the "rule setting" aspect, while workers' representation refers primarily at the "day to day" life of the workplace, acting as a channel for workers' grievances as well as for information and consultation activities. It has also being proposed that the distinction could be found in the "cooperative" nature of the representative

129 G. Arrigo and G. Casale, "A Comparative Overview of Terms and Notions on Employee Participation", Labour Administration and Inspection Programme LAB/ADMIN, Working Document Number 8 (Geneva: International Labour Organization, 2010), pp. 22–23.

130 "Where there exist in the same undertaking both trade union representatives and elected representatives, appropriate measures shall be taken, wherever necessary, to ensure that the existence of elected representatives is not used to undermine the position of the trade unions concerned or their representatives and to encourage co-operation on all relevant matters between the elected representatives and the trade unions concerned and their representatives."

131 M. Tiraboschi and M. Biagi, "Forms of Employee Representational Participation", in *Comparative Labour Law and Industrial Relations in Industrialized Market Economies*, ed. R. Blanpain (The Hague: Kluwer Law International, 2007), 503–556, p. 504.

bodies, opposed to the "confrontation" of collective bargaining.[132] Even though this distinction may in some may describe some experiences, it falls short of adequately including the national systems characterised by a single-channel model.

In this sense, it is clear that "workers' representation" is a difficult concept to define *per se*. It can be defined through the method(s) for choosing the representatives, as in the cited Article 3 of ILO Convention No. 135. Otherwise, one can look at the activities actually carried out by the representatives, thus including under the label of "workers' representatives" the agents actually engaging in this activities, irrespective of the method through which they are chosen or elected. However, both methods can be used together. For the purpose of identifying a definition, Article 3 will provide the first filter, selecting only these bodies which fits with its second part. To further clarify the scope, I will then look at (some of) the functions which are included into this definition, characterising the representation of workers and distinguishing it from "collective bargaining".

In particular, I will focus on an area of collective labour rights which is intertwined with the topic of representation. Information and consultation do in fact represent a very coherent topic. For the first time in this overview of collective rights, a direct intervention by the European Union, in the form of Directive 2002/14,[133] makes it easier the identification of definitions to apply in the present work.

This choice leaves aside two areas. First, I will not deal a number of activities, related to the day-by-day life of the plant or company, carried out by workers' representatives. This in view of the difficulty of providing for a coherent analysis of such a broad (and varied) area. Second, I will not deal with the topic of co-determination or co-decision, though in some system of industrial relations this is the main aspect of workers' representatives activity. This choice is dictated by the very peculiar nature of this rights, as they can only be found in a limited number of systems while being completely absent from the others.[134]

---

132 R. Blanpain, "Representation of Employees at Plant and Eterprise Level", in *International Encyclopaedia of Comparative Law. Volume XV1*, ed. Bob Hepple (Tübingen: C.B. Mohr, 1994), 1–51, p. 12.

133 Directive 2002/14/EC of the European Parliament and of the Council of 11 March 2002 establishing a general framework for informing and consulting employees in the European Community - Joint declaration of the European Parliament, the Council and the Commission on employee representation Official Journal L 080 , 23/03/2002 P. 0029 - 0034. As a side note, Article 2 letter e of the Directive, defines "employees representatives" with the very same formula we saw before for ILO Convention No. 135 and the RevESC: "'employees' representatives' means the employees' representatives provided for by national laws and/or practices".

134 See Rebhahn, "Collective Labour Law in Europe in a Comparative Perspective (Part II)", pp. 124–131.

3.4.1 INFORMATION AND CONSULTATION

As regards the definition of the two terms composing the couple "information and consultation", EU Directive 2002/14 provides for the most straightforward formulation. Under Article 2 (Definitions) we find that "'information' means transmission by the employer to the employees' representatives of data in order to enable them to acquaint themselves with the subject matter and to examine it"[135] while 'consultation' means the exchange of views and establishment of dialogue between the employees' representatives and the employer". It seems to me that these two definitions can be safely accepted also when dealing with the approach to the subject matter followed by the ILO[136] and by the ESC.[137]

The ILO provides for less guidance in this field. Indeed, since information and consultation have not been developed as "corollaries" of the freedom of association, one cannot turn to the jurisprudence of the Supervisory bodies for clarification of the concept. Thus, it all boils down to some instruments, in particular a number of Recommendations,[138] which are connected to this topic. I have already recalled Recommendation No. 94, which prompts the members of the ILO to promote consultation between workers' and their employer at undertaking level, all the while making it clear that such consultation should deal with topic not covered by collective bargaining. Recommendation No. 129 provides for a number of guidelines about the subject matter. Here, the dissemination and exchange of information is linked with the creation of a climate of mutual understanding and confidence between workers' and their employer.[139] The measures for this dissemination are also left to the management to conceive, after consultation with

135 It is interesting to note that the means of communication, *i.e.* if the information must be in writing, is left undecided in the Directive. The same is true for the ESC. See F. Dorssemont, "Worker Involvement in Secondary EC Law Prior to the Recast Directive", in *The Recast of the European Works Council Directive*, ed. F. Dorssemont (Antwerp: Intersentia, 2010), 31–90, p. 39. On the other hand, C. Sachs-Durand, "Information and Consultation in the Recast Directive", in *The Recast of the European Works Council Directive*, ed. F. Dossemont (Antwerp: Intersentia, 2010), 313–326 considers that the information "should normally have a written character". This is inferred by the use of the word "transmission" in the text of the Directive.

136 See Arrigo and Casale, "A Comparative Overview of Terms and Notions on Employee Participation", pp. 17–18.

137 C. Kollonay-Lehoczky, "The Fundamental Right of Workers to Information and Consultation Under the European Social Charter", in *The Recast of the European Works Council Directive*, ed. F. Dorssemont and Th. Blanke (Antwerp: Intersentia, 2010), 3–30, p. 21.

138 Recommendation No. 94 (1952) on "Cooperation at the Level of the Undertaking"; Recommendation No. 113 (1960) on "Consultation (Industrial and National Levels)"; Recommendation No. 143 (1971) on the "Workers' Representatives"; Recommendation Number 129 (1967) on "Communications within the Undertaking"; Recommendation No. 166 (1982) on "Termination of Employment".

139 ILO Recommendation No. 129, para. 2(2): "This climate [of mutual understanding and confidence within undertakings] should be promoted by the rapid dissemination and exchange of information, as complete and objective as possible, relating to the various aspects of the life of the undertaking and to the social conditions of the workers."

workers' representatives.[140] More interestingly, the Recommendation stresses the importance of providing information and engaging in consultation *before* decisions on "matters of major interests" are *taken* by management.[141] This makes it clear that "information" cannot be conceived as an ex-post communication of decisions already taken. The same stance can be found in Recommendation No. 166: when dealing with "major changes in the undertaking" (involving terminations of employment) the employer should supply concerned workers' representatives "in good time" with "all relevant information on the major changes contemplated and the effects they are likely to have". Back to Recommendation No. 129, paragraph 15 provides for an extensive list of the topic which should be covered by the "information" rights.[142] These topics deal mainly with "working conditions" in the broader sense (including facilities, training, health and safety, "welfare"); however, information about the "general situation of the undertaking" (thus, the economic and financial situation) and the explanation of "decisions which are likely to affect directly or indirectly the situation of workers in the undertaking" are also included.

The European Social Charter presents an interesting evolution through the fifty years of its existence. In the first version of the ESC, consultation was only mentioned under Article 6.[143] Such a collocation however, implied a strong connection of this "consultation" procedure with collective bargaining. In fact, following the wording of Article 6(1), it is "with a view to ensuring the effective exercise of the right to bargain collectively" that "the Parties undertake to promote joint consultation between workers and employers". The recognition of an autonomous role for information and consultation came with the adoption of the Additional Protocol to the ESC, in 1988. Finally, with the adoption of the Revised European Social Charter, in 1996, the rights recognised under Articles 2

---

140 Ibid., para. 2(3): "With a view to the development of such a climate management should, after consultation with workers' representatives, adopt appropriate measures to apply an effective policy of communication with the workers and their representatives."

141 Ibid., para. 3.

142 "In particular, management should give information regarding: (a) general conditions of employment, including engagement, transfer and termination of employment; (b) job descriptions and the place of particular jobs within the structure of the undertaking; (c) possibilities of training and prospects of advancement within the undertaking; (d) general working conditions; (e) occupational safety and health regulations and instructions for the prevention of accidents and occupational diseases; (f) procedures for the examination of grievances as well as the rules and practices governing their operation and the conditions for having recourse to them; (g) personnel welfare services (medical care, health, canteens, housing, leisure, savings and banking facilities, etc.); (h) social security or social assistance schemes in the undertaking; (i) the regulations of national social security schemes to which the workers are subject by virtue of their employment in the undertaking; (j) the general situation of the undertaking and prospects or plans for its future development; (k) the explanation of decisions which are likely to affect directly or indirectly the situation of workers in the undertaking; (l) methods of consultation and discussion and of co-operation between management and its representatives on the one hand and the workers and their representatives on the other".

143 "All workers and employers have the right to bargain collectively."

and 3 of the said Protocol were included in the Charter itself, under Article 21 and 22. Also, workers' involvement in the specific matter of collective redundancies is guaranteed under Article 29. As regards the relationship of these "new" Articles with the (alleged[144]) precursor, it is important to note that the Committee (ECSR) supervising the application of the ESC stated that "for the States which have ratified both Article 6(1) and Article 22, consultation at enterprise level is examined under Article 22",[145] hence implying the character of a more specific provision for the latter.

Article 21 refers directly to both information and consultation in its wording.[146] The text of the Article expressly recognises the importance of the timing for both rights: information must be provided "at the appropriate time", while consultation must take place "in good time". However, no country has (so far) been found to be in violation of Article 21 for inappropriate timing of the information and consultation.[147] Both Article 21 and 22 refers to "workers' representatives" with the definition highlighted before. However, the rights provided are addressed to "workers or their representatives", even though the Explanatory Report[148] makes it clear that "the fact that they [the rights of information and consultation] are conferred upon one group does not mean that they cannot be conferred upon the other". As regards the distinction between trade unions' representatives and workers' representatives, the ECSR acknowledged the legitimacy of both these models for the purposes of information and consultation under the RevESC.[149] This, however, as long as all workers of the given undertaking see their rights guaranteed: models which are characterised by a trade unions' monopoly over representation are compatible with the RevESC as long as they also guarantee the rights of non-organised workers.[150] The material scope of the right to information seems rather different from ILO Recommendation No. 129, as Article 21(a) only makes reference to the "economic and financial situation of the undertaking". As for consultation, it should take place (Article 21(b) "on proposed decisions which could substantially affect the interests of workers, particularly on those decisions which could have an important impact on the employment situation in the undertaking". The two parts of Article 21 are in fact connected, so that the "information" is to be considered as the natural basis for an effective "consultation".[151] Looking at the material scope of the two rights, one can see that a distinction is traced in the RevESC: while information deals with economical an financial data, consultation is mainly connected with "occupational" aspects.

---

144 Ibid., pp. 6–8.
145 ECSR Conclusions 2004, Ireland, p. 264.
146 "Workers have the right to be informed and to be consulted within the undertaking."
147 Ibid., p. 22.
148 Explanatory Report, para. 29.
149 See for instance ECSR Conclusions XV-Add, Norway.
150 ECSR Conclusions XIII-3, Sweden.
151 Ibid., p. 21.

However, for our definition, it is not necessary to further specify the content of "information", or, better, the broad approach of ILO Recommendation No. 129 seems better suited to tackle a greater number of situations. On the other hand, "consultation" remains a more difficult concept to tackle. Its scope can be defined in a negative way, by placing it between the "right to be heard" (which, as we saw, does not imply a two-way exchange) and the "collective bargaining"[152] , which deals with the actual regulation of working conditions in the broader sense. The difference with the latter, apart from the eventual different actors involved in the process, can be traced to the (at least, potential) outcome of collective bargaining, *i.e.* a collective agreement.[153] The concept of "dialogue" found in the definition provided by EU Directive 2002/14 can be interpreted as an exchange between the employer and workers' representatives; in particular, as provided by Article 4(d), this implies the obligation for the employer to give a motivated answer to the opinions expressed by workers' representatives.

152 Dorssemont, "Worker Involvement in Secondary EC Law Prior to the Recast Directive", p. 39.

153 Although the English text of the Framework Directive does refer to the concept of agreement, stating, in Article 4, that the consultation must take place "with a view to reaching an *agreement*" (emphasis added). As stressed by ibid., in other language versions the terminology is clearer ("accord", "accordo", "acuerdo", "overeenstemming"), differentiating itself from the "traditional terminology used to indicate binding collective agreements".

CHAPTER 4
THE AGE OF INNOCENCE

The Drafting Process of the Posting of Workers Directive

As it was stressed in the introduction, the '90s represent the first "high tide" for the interest concerning posting of workers and the legal aspects of this phenomenon.[1] This period starts with the decision of the Court of Justice in the *Rush Portuguesa* case[2] and ends with the adoption of the Posting of Workers Directive (PWD).[3]

The Directive is completely silent about the relationship between posting of workers and industrial relations, as it contents itself of referring to the *outcomes* of industrial relations processes.[4] That being said, the PWD and its troubled drafting process (which spans, more or less, along the whole "high tide" period) do represent the first object of the analysis which will be carried out in the following pages.

This Chapter is focused on the drafting process as well as on the final text of the Directive. Hence, I will identify if and how the possible conflicts/interferences of the phenomenon with industrial relations (and with collective labour law norms) made their way to the table of negotiations. Furthermore, looking at the final text with the benefit of hindsight, those issues left unsolved by the Directive will also be stressed.

---

1 The title of this Chapter comes from K. Ahlberg, "The Age of Innocence – and Beyond", in *Cross-Border Services, Posting of Workers and Multilevel Governance*, ed. S. Evju (Oslo: Institutt for privaterett, 2013), 297–328.

2 Case C-113/89, *Rush Portuguesa v. Office National d'Immigration*, 27 march 1990.

3 Directive 96/71/EC of the European Parliament and of the Council of 16 December 1996 concerning the posting of workers in the framework of the provision of services.

4 See *supra*, p. 20.

4.1 A COMPLICATED BIRTH

The drafting of the Posting of Workers Directive has been thoroughly analysed by a number of Authors.[5] More modestly, the aim of this section is to summarise the process. Along this overview I will point out those elements of the PWD touching upon aspects of industrial relations and/or collective labour law. This will, more often than not, come down to pointing out the complete disregard for the potential interferences of the posting phenomenon with industrial relations and collective labour law. However, understanding the reasons behind this choice (or lack of attention) is important in order to fully assess the relationship here at stake.

4.1.1 IMPULSE(S)

The decision of the Court of Justice in *Rush Portuguesa*[6] has often been presented as the original impulse which set in motion the negotiations around the PWD.[7] The decision did play an important role in the drafting of the Directive. Still, the precise nature of the influence upon the process, is not straightforward. I will come back to this in the following paragraphs.

Eichhorst,[8] in his analysis of the drafting process, traces back the origin of the PWD to the activity of the European Federation of Building and Wood Workers (EFBWW) in the context of another Directive proposal, *i.e.* the directive on the liberalisation of public procurement.[9] Evju cites the same precedent,[10] while adding two more dimensions: the conflict of laws dimension and the 1989 Action Programme.

The first dimension, the one related to public procurement rules, refers to the debate around the inclusion of a *binding* social clause in the cited Directive on liberalisation of public procurement. This clause, requiring the application of terms and conditions of employment equal to those prevailing at the place of work,

---

5 W Eichhorst, "European Social Policy Between National and Supranational Regulation: Posted Workers in the Framework of Liberalized Services Provision", MPIfG Discussion Paper (Max-Planck-Institut für Gesellschaftsforschung, 1998); Kolehmainen, *The Posted Workers Directive: European Reinforcement of National Labour Protection*; Hellsten, "On the Social Dimension in Posting of Workers"; Evju and Novitz, "The Evolving Regulation: dynamics and Consequences".

6 The decision will be specifically analysed in the next Chapter, see p. 150. See also *supra*, p. 8, for a short summary which should hopefully be sufficient to understand the present Section.

7 Kolehmainen, *The Posted Workers Directive: European Reinforcement of National Labour Protection*, p. 112; Barnard, *The Substantive Law of the EU: The Four Freedoms*, p. 370; Evju and Novitz, "The Evolving Regulation: dynamics and Consequences", p. 14.

8 Eichhorst, "European Social Policy Between National and Supranational Regulation: Posted Workers in the Framework of Liberalized Services Provision", pp. 17–18.

9 Directive 89/440/EEC, OJ L 210/1 of 21 July 1989.

10 Evju, "Posting Past and Present. The Posting of Workers Directive – Genesis and Current Contrasts", pp. 9–10.

was shaped similarly to ILO Convention No. 94.[11] In the end the "social clause" was made optional, leaving it to contracting authorities to decide whether or not to include it in the tender.[12] The outcome falling short of the request put forward by the EFBWW, the same federation started lobbying for a different instrument, encompassing posting of workers in general (hence, not only in the context of public procurement). This new legislation was to be based on the application, from the very beginning of the posting, of the whole host state regulation (save for more favourable conditions provided in the home state) to posted workers.[13]

Conflict of laws

The second antecedent to the process which would led to the PWD is the conflict of laws dimension. Provided that the PWD can be described essentially as an instrument dealing with conflict of laws,[14] this dimension does represent an important piece of background for the drafting here at stake.[15] The first attempt at regulating the conflict of laws dimension in employment relationships dates back to 1972. At that time a proposal was drafted by the Commission,[16] though it took several years for the (amended) proposal to be actually put forward (1976). Due to divisions inside the Council[17] the proposal never made it into an actual piece

[11] Labour Clauses (Public Contracts) Convention, 1949 (No. 94), 29 June 1949. The "social clause" is enshrined in Article 2 of the Convention, which is worth quoting in full in view of its close connection with the PWD itself: "Contracts to which this Convention applies shall include clauses ensuring to the workers concerned wages (including allowances), hours of work and other conditions of labour which are not less favourable than those established for work of the same character in the trade or industry concerned in the district where the work is carried on: (a) by collective agreement or other recognised machinery of negotiation between organisations of employers and workers representative respectively of substantial proportions of the employers and workers in the trade or industry concerned; or (b) by arbitration award; or (c) by national laws or regulations". On the point see N. Bruun, A. Jacobs and M. Schmidt, "ILO Convention No. 94 in the Aftermath of the Rüffert Case", Transfer: European Review of Labour Law and Research 16, No. 4 (November 2010): 473-488.

[12] Directive 89/440/EEC, Article 18 inserting a new Article 22a into Directive 71/305/EC.

[13] See Evju, "Posting Past and Present. The Posting of Workers Directive – Genesis and Current Contrasts", p. 9; Eichhorst, "European Social Policy Between National and Supranational Regulation: Posted Workers in the Framework of Liberalized Services Provision", p. 19, stating more precisely that the proposal of the EFBWW was deemed to imply the application only of a "hard core of national standards".

[14] Dorssemont, "Collectief arbeidsrechtelijke aspecten van internationale detachering", pp. 531–532.

[15] Evju, "Posting Past and Present. The Posting of Workers Directive – Genesis and Current Contrasts", pp. 6–9. The conflict of laws dimension is also cursorily mentioned by Hellsten, "On the Social Dimension in Posting of Workers", p. 17.

[16] Proposition de règlement (CEE) du Conseil relatif aux dispositions concernant les conflits de lois en matière de relations de travail à l'intérieur de la Communauté, 23 mars 1972. The text of the proposal is only available in French.

[17] Hellsten, "On the Social Dimension in Posting of Workers", p. 17, refers especially to the British opposition to the proposal.

of legislation, and it was eventually withdrawn in 1981, after the adoption of the Rome Convention[18] in 1980.[19]

Notwithstanding its end, Evju and Novitz rightly point out how the proposal is interesting in a number of ways for the analysis of the PWD.[20] It thus important to notice that, while being based on Articles 48 and 49 EEC (now Articles 45 and 46 TFEU) and hence free movement of workers, the proposal would have also covered posted workers. Indeed, the first proposal (1972) did cover intra-company postings,[21] whereas the 1976 amended version presented an ever broader scope, covering "workers who are sent by their undertaking to other Member States to carry out temporary activities".[22] The 1972 version of the text left it to the parties to decide whether to apply the laws of the country of origin or of the host state.[23] The amended version on the contrary entailed the mandatory application of the "country of origin principle".[24] However, on both occasions, the "country of origin principle" (whether mandatory or optional) was "mitigated" by the mandatory application of a list of *lois de police* stemming from the host state regulations.[25] These lists are evidently predecessors of Article 3(1) of the PWD. In this sense it is interesting to compare the two texts, in order to examine the different formulations (see Table 4.1). Furthermore, and with more far reaching consequences for the possibility of the host state to apply its own regulations, the 1972 proposal left it to the host state to restrict the application of the country of origin principle, on the basis of public order, public security or public health.[26]

---

18 Rome Convention on the law applicable to contractual obligations, 1980.

19 Evju and Novitz stress the fact that the two instruments were not carried on in a co-coordinated way, ultimately proposing different rules. See Evju and Novitz, "The Evolving Regulation: dynamics and Consequences", p. 10.

20 Ibid., p. 13.

21 Article 4: "Lorsqu'une entreprise qui a son siège dans un état membre possède des établissements dans un autre état membre, il peut être convenu que les travailleurs transférés de l'état du siège de l'entreprise dans lesdits établissements [...]."

22 COM(75) 653 final, Amended proposal for a Regulation of the Council on the provisions of conflict of laws on employment relationships within the Community, 28 April 1976, Article 4.

23 Article 4 of the 1972 proposal: "il peut être convenu que les travailleurs transférés de l'état du siège de l'entreprise dans lesdits établissements ne relèveront pas du droit du travail applicable au lieu de l'établissement dans lequel ils sont occupés, mais du droit applicable au siège de l'entreprise".

24 Article 4 of the 1976 proposal: "Workers who are sent by their undertaking to other Member States to carry out temporary activities [...] shall continue to be governed by the labour laws in force at the place where the establishment sending workers is located."

25 The 1972 proposal explicitly lists the sources of such regulations, including "lois et règlements, les conventions collectives ou les usages en vigueur". This statement is not present in the 1976 version.

26 Article 4(2) of the 1972 proposal: "Tout État membre est habilité à prendre, dans le cadre de sa propre législation, des mesures justifiées par des raisons d'ordre public, de sécurité publique ou de santé publique en vue de restreindre l'application, sur son territoire, du droit en vigueur dans l'État où l'entreprise étrangère a son siège". This however without violating the free movement of workers: "Ces mesures ne peuvent toutefois pas être contraires aux dispositions relatives à la libre circulation des travailleurs arrêtées en vertu des articles 48 et 49 du traité instituant la Communauté économique européenne."

Table 4.1 Comparison between 1972 and 1976 proposals on conflict of laws in employment relationships – catalogues of lois de police

1972 Proposal, Article 4(2)	1976 Proposal, Article 8(1)
a) dispositions relatives aux interdictions de travailler les dimanches et jours fériés	a) provisions concerning time off per week and public holidays, provisions concerning work on Sundays and public holidays and night work
b) dispositions relatives à la durée maximale du travail journalier et hebdomadaire ainsi qu'à l'autorisation de dérogations dans ce domaine	b) provisions relating to the maximum daily and weekly working hours and permission to depart therefrom
c) dispositions relatives aux interdictions d'employer des enfants, des adolescents et des femmes	f) provisions concerning prohibitions and restrictions and other protective provisions with regard to the employment of children, adolescents, women and mothers and protective provisions for certain categories of workers, in particular severely handicapped people
d) dispositions relatives à la prévention des accidents du travail et à l'hygiène du travail	e) provisions on accident prevention at work and occupational medicine and hygiene
e) dispositions relatives à l'autorisation des pouvoirs publics à laquelle est subordonnée la fin de la relation de travail, dans la mesure où cette autorisation vise à prévenir le chômage	h) provisions concerning official approval of the termination of employment relationships
f) dispositions relatives au salaire minimum garanti par la loi ou par les conventions collectives et au paiement du salaire	d) provisions concerning minimum guaranteed wages and similar guaranteed payments by the employer, and payment of wages
g) dispositions relatives au congé minimum	c) provisions relating to minimum holidays
h) dispositions relatives à la nullité de certaines clauses des contrats de travail	j) provisions concerning the invalidity of restraints on competition, or similar clauses in contracts of employment which seek to restrain or prevent employment of the worker
i) dispositions relatives à l'organisation générale de l'entreprise, au service médical de l'entreprise, à l'exercice des droits syndicaux, à la représentation des travailleurs dans l'entreprise ainsi qu'à la protection particulière des représentants du personnel de l'entreprise	g) provisions concerning the protection of employees' representatives
	i) provisions concerning the business of hiring out workers

The most interesting finding of this comparison stems from the juxtaposition of letter *i* (1972) and letter *g* (1976). Whereas the former includes the exercise of collective labour rights as well as the norms regulating workers' representation (and the protection of representatives) into the *lois de police*, the latter only refers to the protection of workers' representatives. Casting an anticipated look to the final text of the PWD, also this last point is now absent from the list of Article 3(1). It is probably important not to over-stress the relevance of these proposals, since they were never approved by the Council. Still, the evident shift of conception between the two proposals is too tempting to be left aside. In sum, the 1972 proposal considered posted workers (though the denomination was not yet in use) as being, at least potentially, part of the host state system of industrial relations, and thus provided them with the very same guarantees enjoyed by their "stationary" colleagues. In the 1976 we are left with just the protection of "employees' representatives".[27]

Comparing the 1972 and 1976 proposals with the later development of the PWD reveals another difference worth stressing. Though, as it has been said, the scope and subject matter of the proposals does not overlap perfectly with the PWD, the points of convergence are still evident. In this sense, one can see as the proposals were in fact based on the *free movement* of workers.[28] The PWD on the contrary finds its basis in the freedom to provide services. The reason for this shift, which would have far reaching consequences in the case law following the adoption of the PWD, can (at least partially) be explained with the stance taken by the Court in *Rush Portuguesa* and in some preceding decisions.[29]

Speaking of the legal basis for the PWD, I will spend a few words to present the third "background" dimension highlighted by Evju,[30] *i.e.* the 1989 Action Programme.[31] The Programme was conceived as the instrument for the implementation of the Community Charter of the Fundamental Rights of Workers.[32] Here it is sufficient to point out that the Programme included, among the "New Initiatives" under the heading "Freedom of movement" a proposal for a "Community instrument on working conditions applicable to workers from another State performing work in the host country in the framework of the freedom

27 This is also quite puzzling, since provisions on "workers' representation" are not listed in the version of 1976.

28 Articles 48 and 49 EEC, now Articles 45 and 46 TFEU. In fact, the very drafting of the proposal started following the adoption of Regulation 1612/68, as the Council instructed the Commission "to examine thoroughly the problems raised by conflict of law rules with regard to labour law, in order to find the most suitable solutions as soon as possible", COM(76) 653 Final, Explanatory Memorandum, 3. See Ibid., pp. 9–10.

29 Case-279/80 *Criminal proceedings against Alfred John Webb*, 17 December 1981; Joined Cases C-62 and C-63/81 *Société anonyme de droit français Seco et Société anonyme de droit français Desquenne & Giral v. Etablissement d'assurance contre la vieillesse et l'invalidité*, 3 February 1982.

30 Evju, "Posting Past and Present. The Posting of Workers Directive – Genesis and Current Contrasts", pp. 10–11.

31 COM(89) 568 final. Communication from the Commission concerning its Action Programme relating to he Implementation of the Community Charter of Basic Social Rights for Workers, 29 November 1989.

32 Drafts tabled earlier in 1989, COM(89) 248 final and COM(89) 471 final.

to provide services, especially on behalf of a subcontracting undertaking".[33] There is however an important point to be highlighted in this context. As it has been stressed *supra*, one can perceive a "shift" in terms of legal basis for the regulation of the posting phenomenon, between the early developments and the actual PWD. The Action Programme does not escape from this dualism. In fact, the Programme itself did not provide for any guidance in terms of legal bases for the instruments proposed. Instead, this was left to the Preamble of the Community Charter to point out the Article of the Treaties which could be used as bases.[34] Looking at the Preamble one can clearly see that the freedom to provide services is not mentioned, whereas the freedom of movement of workers and the right of establishment are both listed.[35] This implies once again that the posting phenomenon was conceived, until the beginning of the '90s, as belonging to the free movement of workers, at least logically if not legally.

4.1.2 *RUSH* AND THE FIRST PHASE OF NEGOTIATIONS

A few months after the launching of the Action Programme, the Court of Justice delivered its decision in the *Rush Portuguesa* case. This decision has often been presented as a turning point in the history of the (still to be drafted) PWD.[36] Leaving the analysis of the decision for the next Chapter, there are two fundamental points that must be presented here, as they effectively shape (or catalyse) the following negotiations around the Directive.

The first point brings us back to the question of the legal basis. The Court, for the first time[37] explicitly places the phenomenon of posting of workers in the framework of the provision of services. As stressed by Novitz and Evju, "the Court effectively established a new legal basis for the movement of workers".[38] As it has been described in the Introduction, the Court considered that the Portuguese workers employed by Rush and posted to France would return to their home country after the completion of their work. Hence, not gaining at any time access to the labour market of the host state, they would not be covered by the dispositions on free movement of workers.[39]

33 COM(89) 568 final, pp. 21–22.
34 See Evju and Novitz, "The Evolving Regulation: dynamics and Consequences", p. 23.
35 Community Charter of Basic Social Rights for Workers, pp. 1–2.
36 Kolehmainen, *The Posted Workers Directive: European Reinforcement of National Labour Protection*, p. 112; Barnard, *The Substantive Law of the EU: The Four Freedoms*, p. 370; Evju and Novitz, "The Evolving Regulation: dynamics and Consequences", p. 14.
37 Though some precedent was already on this line of reasoning, see Joined Cases C-62 and C-63/81 *Société anonyme de droit français Seco et Société anonyme de droit français Desquenne & Giral v Etablissement d'assurance contre la vieillesse et l'invalidité*, 3 February 1982.
38 Ibid., p. 15.
39 *Rush Portuguesa*, para. 15.

This line of reasoning, effectively challenging the French regulation on work permits, was regarded as threatening national labour law regimes. However, the second point goes in the very opposite direction. As Gormley noted, the Court threw a "crumb of comfort", in answer to concerns about social dumping,[40] by stating that Member States were free to extend their legislation (or collective agreements) to all workers employed, even temporarily, on their territory.[41]

The decision in *Rush*, delivered on 27 March 1990, completes the background of the negotiations around the PWD. These would in fact start shortly afterwards, as the first draft of the Directive was presented by the Commission on 30 August 1991,[42] after a round of consultation with governments of the Member States and European social partners.[43]

The first round

The first draft was aimed at promoting the "transnational provision of services" through a "climate of fair competition [...] which cannot be attained without measures ensuring respect for the rights of workers". This balance between the promotion of the freedom to provide services (which provided the legal basis for the proposal) and the guarantee of workers' rights was to be achieved through the application to posted workers of a "hard core" of host country regulations. This was evidently in line with the proposals on conflict of laws in employment relations that have been presented *supra*. However it must be noted that the list of those "hard core" provisions was shorter than the 1976 proposal (which in its turn, was characterised by a shorter list than the 1972 one).[44] A further difference with the 1972 and 1976 proposals is that the 1991 draft did not include any reference to the notion of "public order" or "*lois de police*, though it followed the very same approach based on the "conflict of laws" dimension.[45]

---

40 L. Gormley, "Freedom of Establishment and Freedom to Provide Services. Workers and Services Distinguished", *European Law Review* 17 (1992): 63–67, p. 66.

41 *Rush Portuguesa*, para. 18.

42 OJ C 225/6 of 30 August 1991.

43 See Eichhorst, "European Social Policy Between National and Supranational Regulation: Posted Workers in the Framework of Liberalized Services Provision", p. 17.

44 Article 3(1)(b) of the 1991 draft included: "i) maximum daily and weekly hours of work, rest periods, work on Sundays and night work; (ii) minimum paid holidays; (iii) the minimum rates of pay, including overtime rates and allowances, but excluding benefits provided for by private occupational schemes; (iv) the conditions of hiring out of workers, in particular the supply of workers by temporary employment businesses; (v) health, safety and hygiene at work; (vi) protective measures with regard to the working conditions of pregnant women or women who have recently given birth, children, young people and other groups enjoying special protection; (vii) equality of treatment between men and women and prohibition of discrimination on the grounds of colour, race, religion, opinions, national origin or social background." It is interesting to note that already in this first draft it is impossible to find any reference to collective labour *rights*, though obviously the reference to "collective agreements" will remain in place. I have already stressed *supra*, p. 25, why this cannot be considered as a real "industrial relations" link.

45 Evju and Novitz, "The Evolving Regulation: dynamics and Consequences", p. 24.

Another important provision followed directly the list of "hard core provisions". Article 3(2) established a "grace period" of three months, meaning that for the first three months of posting the "country of origin" principle would apply to the employment relationship. This in order to avoid an excessively "rigid" instrument[46] which would impose financial costs on companies carrying out transnational works on a short-term basis.[47] The actual length of this "threshold" would soon become one of the most debated topic of the PWD.[48]

A third thorny issue was the identification of the sources of the "hard core" provisions. The draft only allowed for the extension to posted workers of conditions laid down either by law (regulation, administrative provisions) or by collective agreements "covering the whole of the occupation and industry concerned having an *erga omnes* effect and/or being made legally binding in the occupation and industry concerned".[49] Comparing this to the text of the 1972 proposal on conflict of laws in employment relations,[50] one can see that the further specification of collective agreements, would leave out those agreements not generally binding as well as the eventual *de facto* "generally applied" wages and working conditions.[51]

Finally, Article 2 identified the three categories of undertaking which would fall under the scope of the Directive.[52] This point was in fact less controversial. It can be safely said that this Article, apart of becoming Article 1 in the final version of the PWD, will not change much, nor attract much debate during the drafting process.

The draft was then sent to the Council, and referred to the Working Party for Social Affairs.[53] Evju and Novitz point out the important role that the Working Party has played in the drafting process,[54] while Eichhorst seems to consider this as secondary, focusing on the role of the European Parliament.[55] Also the Economic and Social Committee received the draft for consultation. In its opinion, delivered on December the 18th 1991,[56] the Committee commented on a number of points, generally fostering a strengthening of the Directive. In particular, the

46 Eichhorst, "European Social Policy Between National and Supranational Regulation: Posted Workers in the Framework of Liberalized Services Provision", p. 18.

47 European Industrial Relations Review, 213, p. 21.

48 If not the most debated. See Hellsten, "On the Social Dimension in Posting of Workers", p. 17.

49 Article 3(1)(a) of the 1991 draft.

50 Article 4(2): "[...] prévues par les lois et règlements, les conventions collectives ou les usages".

51 Eichhorst, "European Social Policy Between National and Supranational Regulation: Posted Workers in the Framework of Liberalized Services Provision", p. 18.

52 Article 2 of the 1991 draft.

53 The Working Party is comprised of specialised officials from the Member States, dealing with a number of issues connected to labour legislation and work environment issues, gender equality and social matters.

54 Evju and Novitz, "The Evolving Regulation: dynamics and Consequences", p. 25.

55 Eichhorst, "European Social Policy Between National and Supranational Regulation: Posted Workers in the Framework of Liberalized Services Provision", p. 18.

56 Opinion of the Economic and Social Committee on the proposal for a Council Directive concerning the posting of workers in the framework of the provision of services, 18 December 1991, OJ C 49/41, 24 February 1992.

Committee criticised the three months threshold, recommending a more clear commitment to prevent abuses. As for the Parliament, the Committee on Social Affairs, Employment and Work Environment delivered its final report in April 1992.[57] A final stance however was to be reached only at the beginning of 1993, after second report from the cited Committee,[58] due to contrasts between the Parliament itself and the Commission.[59] The compromise was included into the second draft put forward by the Commission.[60]

This new draft took into account a number of amendments proposed by the Parliament and had overall "a stronger social profile than its predecessor".[61] In particular, the new draft tried to tackle two issues that have been outlined *supra*. Following the critiques and comments coming both from the EP and the Economic and Social Committee, the threshold period was shortened to one month. Second, the Directive now allowed for "generally applicable" (in the area or in the profession or industry in question) collective agreements to be taken into account when applying the "hard core" provisions.[62] However, this rule was made subject to a *caveat*: the application of "generally applicable" collective agreements had to ensure the equality of treatment between the posting undertaking and national undertakings. With this, the Commission intended that only agreements applied by the great majority of national undertakings in the area, occupation or industry in question. This was to ensure that posting undertakings could compete with national undertakings on an equal footing.[63] Another novelty was the introduction of a "favourability clause",[64] implying the application of "terms and conditions of employment provided for by the law applicable which are more favourable to workers", the predecessor of Article 3(7) of the final text.[65]

---

57 EP Com 1 Report (I) from the Committee on Social Affairs, Employment and Work Environment of the European Parliament, A3-0161/92, 22 April 1992.

58 EP Com 2, and Doc. No. A3-0022/1993, OJ C 72/4, 15 March 1993.

59 Eichhorst points out two elements of contrast, the first being the threshold period, and the second the inclusion of "usually applied" wages and working conditions in the "hard core list"; see Eichhorst, "European Social Policy Between National and Supranational Regulation: Posted Workers in the Framework of Liberalized Services Provision", p. 18.

60 COM(93) 225 final, Brussels, 15 June 1993.

61 Evju and Novitz, "The Evolving Regulation: dynamics and Consequences", p. 26.

62 Article 3(4) of the 1993 draft: "For the purpose of paragraph 1 point (a), collective agreements or arbitration awards mean those which must be observed by all undertakings in the geographical area and in the profession or industry concerned. In the absence thereof, Member States may include those collective agreements or awards which are generally applicable in the area or in the profession or industry in question, provided that their application to the undertaking referred to in Article 2 ensures equality of treatment on matters itemised under paragraph 1 point (b) between that undertaking and national-level undertakings being in a similar position."

63 *European Industrial Relations Review*, 236, p. 23.

64 Article 3(3) of the 1993 draft.

65 It is on the basis of the 1993 formulation that Evju and Novitz argue that Article 3(7) was always conceived as referring to wages and working conditions stemming from the application of the home state's legislation and collective agreements. The expression "law applicable" seems indeed more clear in referring to the law applicable to the employment contract, hence the

4.1.3 DEADLOCKED

After the proposal of the second draft, however, the process witnessed a protracted slow-down, if not a complete stop. This was mainly due to the deep division inside the Council. This division revolved mainly around the threshold period. A number of countries, notably the ones characterised by higher labour costs (like France, the Netherlands, Belgium and Denmark) favoured a Directive without any "grace period".[66] This in view of the need to block (as much as possible) the possibilities for "social dumping" through the provision of services carried out by cheap labour. Indeed, the monitoring and enforcement of a grace period, notwithstanding its actual length, was considered as excessively difficult.[67] On the other side, net "exporters" of labour, Portugal and the United Kingdom in particular, did not want to lose their competitive advantage because of a far-reaching Directive covering the whole posting phenomenon from "day zero".[68] A third group (including Italy, Spain, Greece and Ireland) had a more nuanced (or shifting) stance.[69] Two other issues divided the Member States, though along different lines. First, the nature of the list presented under Article 3(1), *i.e.* whether the list should be considered as exhaustive or not. Second, the means which could be used to establish the minimum rights included in the "hard core". This second issue was particularly important for countries as Denmark or Italy, characterised by an industrial relations system relying on a high coverage of generally applicable (but not extended *erga omnes*) collective agreements.[70]

Obviously enough, these divisions hindered the progress of the second draft. Indeed, negotiations were "reactivated" only during the second half of 1994. The German presidency tried to propose a "diluted" draft.[71] Still, even the diluted

home state law. See Evju, and Novitz, "The Evolving Regulation: dynamics and Consequences", p. 35.

66 Eichhorst, "European Social Policy Between National and Supranational Regulation: Posted Workers in the Framework of Liberalized Services Provision", p. 18.

67 Hellsten, "On the Social Dimension in Posting of Workers", p. 17.

68 Eichhorst, "European Social Policy Between National and Supranational Regulation: Posted Workers in the Framework of Liberalized Services Provision", p. 19. However, Biagi points out that Portugal and the UK disagreed not just on the "grace period". In fact, we are told, they opposed the very idea of the directive, since it was not designed to promote freedom to provide services. See Biagi, "The 'Posted Workers' EU Directive: from Social Dumping to Social Protectionism", p. 175.

69 Eichhorst, "European Social Policy Between National and Supranational Regulation: Posted Workers in the Framework of Liberalized Services Provision", p. 19. Eichhorst however considers that this group was in general opposed to an excessively "strong" version of the Directive, as favoured by the first group.

70 Evju and Novitz, "The Evolving Regulation: dynamics and Consequences", p. 26.

71 In particular the proposal aimed at reducing the mandatory coverage to the construction sector. It also included a more flexible provision on the threshold period, leaving a larger margin to Member States to determine its actual length. See Eichhorst, "European Social Policy Between National and Supranational Regulation: Posted Workers in the Framework of Liberalized Services Provision", p. 19. The author stresses the fact that the limitation to the

version did not change the situation: no improvement was reached after two meetings of the Council on December 1994.

The French presidency, taking over for the first half of 1995, was also active, proposing a new text. Building upon the German proposal, the text tried to tackle the threshold issue by allowing the individual Member State to decide whether or not to apply national rules on minimum wages and holidays from "day one". From the German text the new proposal also retained the limitation of the mandatory application of rules laid down in collective agreements to the construction sector. Furthermore the "hard core" list was to be considered as "open". Once again, the proposal could not overcome the deadlock situation.[72] After an uneventful (for the PWD) Spanish presidency,[73] Italy took over for the first half of 1996. As Biagi puts it, after five years from the first draft, fortune would smile on the Italian presidency.[74]

Before proceeding with the Italian presidency however, it is necessary to look briefly at the national level. As pointed out by Eichhorst, the deadlocked situation at supranational level brought a number of Member States to regulate posting of workers through their own legislation.[75] Those Member States were, roughly speaking, the ones playing on the "no threshold side" (notably France, Belgium, The Netherlands, Luxembourg and, to some extent, Germany) together with some "new" Member States (Austria and Sweden). Here it would be impossible to give full account of the different regulations. Still it is important to note that this had an impact, at European level, on the drafting process described in these pages. This because, with the largest "importers" of labour (France and Germany) having passed a more or less restrictive regulation, the incentive for the "net exporters" to reach an agreement on the Directive would rapidly increase.[76] As an example, one can see that both the French[77] and the German[78] law decided in favour of the "zero day" option.

construction sector was due to the intense lobbying of German trade union and employers' association of this sector.

72 Evju and Novitz, "The Evolving Regulation: dynamics and Consequences", pp. 27–28.

73 *European Industrial Relations Review*, 264, p. 2.

74 Biagi, "Fortune Smiles on the Italian EU Presidency: talking Half-Seriously About the Posted Workers and Parental Leave Directives".

75 Eichhorst, "European Social Policy Between National and Supranational Regulation: Posted Workers in the Framework of Liberalized Services Provision", pp. 20 and ff.

76 W. Streeck, "The Internationalization of Industrial Relations in Europe: prospects and Problems", *Working Paper Series in European Studies* 1, no. 1 (1998): 1–40, pp. 28–29: "it appears that a main reason why the [Posting of Workers] Directive could at all be passed was the prior existence of various pieces of national and international law relevant to the subject, which made the actual 'value-added' of the Directive much smaller than may seem at first glance". Eichhorst, "European Social Policy Between National and Supranational Regulation: Posted Workers in the Framework of Liberalized Services Provision", p. 27.

77 Article 36 of the "Loi Quinquennale", creating a new Article L 341–5 in the Labour Code (Code du Travail).

78 Arbeitnehmer-Entsendegesetz, *German Bundesgesetzblatt*, I, 1996, pp. 227 and ff., 29 February 1996.

4.1.4 FORTUNE SMILING?

Italy's presidency did not start under the best auspices. In fact, Italy had only a "caretaker" government, following the resignation of Prime Minister Lamberto Dini.[79] Despite these worries, it was under the Italian presidency that the posted workers saga[80] ended (though in fact the Directive was finally approved under the Irish presidency). In this sense, the role of the Italian Minister of Labour, professor Tiziano Treu, and of his collaborator professor Marco Biagi, is often considered as pivotal in finally reaching an agreement over the text of the PWD.[81]

In February 1996 the Italian presidency tabled a new proposal containing the "Italian compromise",[82] whose main elements will soon be described. The Common Position was adopted in the Council on 3 June.[83] Several months afterwards, and already during the Irish presidency,[84] the Parliament, rejecting a number of amendments, approved the same Common Position.[85] The Directive was then adopted by the Council on 24 September,[86] with Portugal abstaining and the UK voting against. Finally, the PWD was duly signed on 16 December 1996, with a three years implementation deadline.

Several intermediate solutions characterised the "Italian compromise", thus allowing the saga to end, though its *happy* ending[87] may be questioned from the present point of observation.

The most visible issue to be tackled by the compromise was, not surprisingly, the question of the threshold. Biagi maintains that "to some extent", the Directive represented a victory for the "zero threshold" supporters.[88] Indeed, the final text provided for no grace period, as a point of departure. Together with this, it opened to some exception to this principle, either mandatory or optional. Article 3(2) provides that a grace period of eight days must be respected "in the case of initial assembly and/or first installation of goods where this is an integral part of a contract for the supply of goods and necessary for taking the goods supplied into use and carried out by the skilled and/or specialist workers of the supplying undertaking".[89] Three more optional exceptions are introduced in Articles 3(3),

---

79 *European Industrial Relations Review*, 265, p. 2.

80 Biagi, "The 'Posted Workers' EU Directive: from Social Dumping to Social Protectionism", p. 177.

81 Evju and Novitz, "The Evolving Regulation: dynamics and Consequences", p. 28; Hellsten, "On the Social Dimension in Posting of Workers", p. 18.

82 *European Industrial Relations* Review, 268, p. 2.

83 *European Industrial Relations Review*, 270, p. 2.

84 *European Industrial Relations Review* 271, p. 2.

85 *European Industrial Relations Review*, 274, p. 3.

86 Ibid., p. 14.

87 Biagi, "The 'Posted Workers' EU Directive: from Social Dumping to Social Protectionism", p. 177. It must be noted that the author did already cast some doubt: "All in all the posted workers saga ended happily. But at what price? The price paid for the enactment of the directive has been a watering down until the last minute."

88 Ibid., p. 176.

89 The exception to the exception being the construction sector, where no grace period applies.

3(4) and 3(5). First, Member States may, if they so decide and after *consulting* the social partners, introduce a one month threshold in relation to the application of minimum wages (and overtime rates). Second, Member States may *allow* collective agreements to establish a threshold up to one month and concerning one or more sectors of activity, as regards the application of minimum wages.[90] Third, Member States may exclude posting employers from the application of minimum annual holidays and minimum wage provisions, on the grounds that the amount of work to be performed is considered as "non-significant". Biagi stresses the fact that the complex structure of the threshold provisions is but a mirror of the complexity of the negotiations.[91] The same author gives credit to the Commission as regards the suggestion of this compromise to solve the issue of the threshold period.

A second point of debate, namely the "open" nature of the list of "hard core" provisions provided by Article 3(1) was finally closed by the compromise.[92] The list in itself was essentially unchanged from the previous drafts. However, two more paragraphs of Article 3, namely paragraph 7[93] and 10,[94] were considered as substantially "opening" the cited list. Still, as it was stressed Article 3(7), providing for a principle of "favourability" in the application of the "hard core" provisions, has been interpreted as referring to more favourable conditions applicable under the *home* state regulations.[95] On the other hand, Article 3(10) is clearly formulated as an opening clause, to permit the application of terms and conditions not included in the list of Article 3(1) provided that these are "public policy provision". Furthermore, the same paragraph allows the application of

---

90 These collective agreements, which are the same that can be taken into account to establish the hard core provisions, can also derogate from the choice of the Member State in the context of the *first* exception provided by paragraph Article 3(2).

91 Ibid., p. 179.

92 Though this "final" solution would prove itself "final" only as regards the actual *debate* on the issue, since from a legal point of view the following interventions of the Court of Justice would prove the weakness of this compromise. I will deal with the case law of the Court of Justice in the next Chapter.

93 "Paragraphs 1 to 6 shall not prevent application of terms and conditions of employment which are more favourable to workers."

94 "This Directive shall not preclude the application by Member States, in compliance with the Treaty, to national undertakings and to the undertakings of other States, on a basis of equality of treatment, of: – terms and conditions of employment on matters other than those referred to in the first subparagraph of paragraph 1 in the case of public policy provisions; – terms and conditions of employment laid down in the collective agreements or arbitration awards within the meaning of paragraph 8 and concerning activities other than those referred to in the Annex."

95 See Evju and Novitz, "The Evolving Regulation: dynamics and Consequences", p. 31, who point out how this nature was emphasised by the Member States along the negotiations. The Article was first introduced as Article 3(3) in the official draft of 1993; to this regard, see *European Industrial Relations Review*, 236, p. 23, where it is said (in the context of a summary of the 1993 draft) that "the intention is to ensure that any more favourable conditions provided for by the law which applies to the employment relationship – that is, *usually, the law of the worker's home country* – still apply" (emphasis added). *Contra* see the interpretations proposed in the Opinions of AG Mengozzi in Case C-341/05, *Laval*, para. 197–199, and of AG Bot in Case C-346/06, *Rüffert*, para. 81–83.

conditions laid down in collective agreements also to sectors other than the one of construction. In the words of Biagi, writing a few months before the final adoption of the Directive, this Article did characterise the list of "hard core" provisions as non-exhaustive: "Every Member State has the discretion to extend (unlimitedly?) the concept of 'public policy provisions'".[96] This Article was not included in any of the previous official drafts (1991 and 1993), neither can some "predecessor" be traced back in these texts. Evju and Novitz point out that the reference to "public policy provisions" was first discussed at the Labour and Social Affairs Council of 27 March 20 1995.[97]

The final relevant element of the compromise refers to the means by which the terms and provisions listed under Article 3(1) may be prescribed. Apart from "law, regulation or administrative provision", which were included from the very first draft of the Directive without raising any debate, the issue concerned which collective agreements could be relied upon to establish those conditions. The first draft, as it was highlighted *supra*, referred to collective agreements having an "erga omnes" effect.[98] The second official draft (1993) did not include any reference to the "erga omnes" requirement.[99] This change was made "in order to take into account the wishes overwhelmingly expressed by Parliament", as the very concept of "erga omnes" application was unknown in some Member States.[100] Furthermore, for those Member States who did not make use of universally binding agreements on

96 See Biagi, "Fortune Smiles on the Italian EU Presidency: talking Half-Seriously About the Posted Workers and Parental Leave Directives", p. 104. See also *European Industrial Relations Review*, 274, p. 15, where this point of the PWD is summarised as: "Member States are free, within limits, to add further elements to the list [of Article 3(1)]". *Contra*, see the Decision delivered by the Court of Justice in the Case C-319/06, *Commission of the European Communities v. Grand Duchy of Luxembourg*, 19 June 2008. This decision will be analysed in Chapter 5.

97 Evju and Novitz, "The Evolving Regulation: dynamics and Consequences", p. 36–37.

98 Articles 3(1)and 3(1)(a) of the 1991 draft: "Member States shall see to it that, whatever the law applicable to the employment relationship, the undertaking does not deprive the workers of the terms and conditions of employment which apply for work of the same character at the place where the work is temporarily carried out, provided that: (a) they are laid down by laws, regulations and administrative provisions, collective agreements or arbitration awards, covering the whole of the occupation and industry concerned having an *erga omnes* effect and/or being made legally binding in the occupation and industry concerned."

99 Articles 3(1) and 3(1)(a) of the 1993 draft: "Member States shall see to it that, whatever the law applicable to the employment relationship, the undertaking referred to in Article 2 does not deprive the workers of the terms and conditions of employment which apply for work of the same character at the place where the work is temporarily carried out, provided that: (a) they are laid down by laws, regulations and administrative provisions, collective agreements or arbitration awards within the meaning of paragraph 4". Paragraph 4 states that "For the purposes of paragraph 1 point (a), collective agreements or arbitration awards mean those which must be observed by all undertakings in the geographical area and in the profession or industry concerned. In the absence thereof, Member States may include those collective agreements or awards which are generally applicable in the area or in the profession or industry in question, provided that their application to the undertaking referred to in Article 2 ensures equality of treatment on matters itemised under paragraph 1 point (b) between that undertaking and national-level undertakings being in a similar position."

100 *European Industrial Relations Review*, 236, p. 23.

the local or sectoral level, the second draft allowed the application of "generally applicable" agreements (provided that their application respected the equality of treatment). Generally applicable collective agreements were intended by the Commission as covering the "great majority" of undertakings in the occupation or industry concerned, these being the real potential competitors of the posting undertaking.[101] Denmark was particularly concerned with this issue, since its system of industrial relations did not rely on any extension mechanism or "erga omnes" effect. The same was true for Sweden, after its joining the negotiations. Italy too was in a similar situation, though its position during the negotiations was less clear on the issue, finally managing to elaborate its preference only at the moment of the Italian presidency in 1996.[102]

The final compromise took into account these objections. Article 3(8) was intended to safeguard the Danish (and Swedish) and Italian systems of *de facto* generally applied collective agreements. The Article provides for two options in the case of absence, in a given Member State, of a "system for declaring collective agreements [...] to be of universal application". The first option covers those collective agreements "which are *generally* applicable to all similar undertakings in the geographical area and in the profession or industry concerned".[103] The second option, the so-called "Italian" clause, refers to those collective agreement "concluded by the most representative employers' and labour organisations at national level and which are applied throughout national territory". As for the 1993 draft, Member States who decided to base themselves on either of these options, must ensure that the application of these collective agreements respect

---

101 Ibid.

102 Ibid., p. 34.

103 This was the so-called Christophersen compromise. See Hellsten, "On the Social Dimension in Posting of Workers", p. 54: "[the compromise] was intended to safeguard the Danish (and later Danish-Swedish) system of a factual erga omnes effect of collective agreements". It is interesting to note that, answering the Danish concerns on a number of issues, going beyond the specific topic of the PWD, the Commissioner for social policy, Padraíg Flynn, wrote a letter to the Danish Trade Union Confederation. In this letter, among other topics, the Commissioner gave reassurance about the inclusion of what will become Article 3(8) of the PWD. What is more, the Commissioner assured that the Directive itself would have no impact on the legislation and practice of the Member States in the area of industrial actions. Letter of 11 May 1993 from Padraig Flynn to Bent Nielsen, President of the Danish LO (Trade Union Confederation). See Evju and Novitz, "The Evolving Regulation: dynamics and Consequences", pp. 39–40. Evidently, Recital 22 is a trace of this "reassurance", as it states that the "Directive is without prejudice to the law of the Member States concerning collective action to defend the interests of trades and professions". On the topic of Commissioner Flynn's reassurance to the Danish, and subsequently Swedish, social partners, see Ahlberg, "The Age of Innocence – and Beyond", p. 6.

the equality of treatment[104] between the posting undertakings and the national ones.[105]

4.2 NOT-SO-CLOSE ENCOUNTERS OF THE COLLECTIVE TYPE

Even this cursory look at the "adoption saga"[106] shows clearly enough how the *collective* dimension of the posting phenomenon played a minor role, often veering into complete forgetfulness.

As regards the drafting process itself, Biagi defines the enactment of the PWD as a "slap in the face of social dialogue at EU level".[107] With this caustic affirmation, Biagi stresses how the social partners at European level were very hesitant to actually take into their hands the negotiation of the PWD.[108] Eichhorst however points out that this solution was indeed hard to envisage. In particular, divisions inside UNICE made it difficult for the employers' association even to sit at the table of negotiations.[109]

On the other hand, reforms implemented at national level have been identified as the stepping stone for the achievement of the compromise on the Directive. On this basis, Streeck described the PWD as "the most telling illustration of the continuing primacy of national institutions in European industrial relations".[110] This was due also to the stance of the Court of Justice in *Rush Portuguesa*. The

104 Article 3(8): "Equality of treatment, within the meaning of this Article, shall be deemed to exist where national undertakings in a similar position: – are subject, in the place in question or in the sector concerned, to the same obligations as posting undertakings as regards the matters listed in the first subparagraph of paragraph 1, and – terms and conditions of employment laid down in the collective agreements or arbitration awards within the meaning of paragraph 8 and concerning activities other than those referred to in the Annex."

105 This in order to avoid what Biagi calls "social protectionism", meaning the situation where "industrialized nations erect trade barriers through the enforcement of domestic labour regulations". See Biagi, "The 'Posted Workers' EU Directive: from Social Dumping to Social Protectionism", p. 179. So defined, however, the concept of "social protectionism" is, at best, puzzling: it is hard to see how the non-discriminatory enforcement of domestic labour regulations could be interpreted as a protectionist measure. Also cf. *Rush Portuguesa*, para. 18. See also *infra*, in the next section.

106 To use the expression of Kolehmainen, *The Posted Workers Directive: European Reinforcement of National Labour Protection*.

107 Biagi, "The 'Posted Workers' EU Directive: from Social Dumping to Social Protectionism", pp. 176–177.

108 Ibid., p. 177. Biagi claims that it was originally the idea of the Italian presidency to encourage the European social partners to negotiate a solution for the posting phenomenon. This would have been carried out under the "shadow of the law", *i.e.* of a basic directive providing for a zero threshold to be enacted in the case the social partners could not reach an agreement.

109 Eichhorst, "European Social Policy Between National and Supranational Regulation: Posted Workers in the Framework of Liberalized Services Provision", p. 19.

110 Streeck, "The Internationalization of Industrial Relations in Europe: prospects and Problems", pp. 28–29.

"licence to regulate"[111] given to the Member States by the famous dictum of the Court[112] did throw the ball back into the national field, so that the findings of Streeck are not surprising.

4.2.1 THE FORGOTTEN "DROITS SYNDICAUX"

As it was mentioned above,[113] in order to find a direct reference to the collective side of labour law during the adoption saga one has to go back to 1972. The first proposal on conflict of laws in employment relations did include in the "hard core" list, the provisions concerning the exercise of "collective labour rights" or "trade unions rights"[114] as well as "workers representation".[115] However, this wording was to be reduced to "provisions concerning the protection of employees' representatives" in the 1976 draft of that instrument. Afterwards, the whole issue of collective labour rights will be removed from the drafting process of the PWD.

Dorssemont points out that this "disregard" follows in the steps of the Court of Justice.[116] Indeed the idea echoes the stance of the Court in *Rush Portuguesa*, where posted workers were defined as not gaining, at any time, access to the labour market of the host state.[117] The intrinsic temporary (and "alien") nature of their presence would then imply, following this line of reasoning, their complete indifference to the system of industrial relations in the host state, and, vice versa, the indifference of such a system to their presence.[118]

An important role in determining this outcome was (is) also played by the legal basis of the PWD. The first draft of the Directive did in fact refer to the right of *establishment*[119] as its legal basis. This was criticised by several Member

---

111 Evju, "Posting Past and Present. The Posting of Workers Directive – Genesis and Current Contrasts", p. 13.

112 *Rush Portuguesa*, para. 18: "Finally, it should be stated, in response to the concern expressed in this connection by the French Government, that Community law does not preclude Member States from extending their legislation, or collective labour agreements entered into by both sides of industry, to any person who is employed, even temporarily, within their territory, no matter in which country the employer is established; nor does Community law prohibit Member States from enforcing those rules by appropriate means."

113 See *supra*, p. 117.

114 Translating from the French "droits syndicaux".

115 Proposition de règlement (CEE) du Conseil relatif aux dispositions concernant les conflits de lois en matière de relations de travail à l'intérieur de la Communauté, 23 mars 1972, Article 4(2) letter (i): "dispositions relatives à l'organisation générale de l'entreprise, au service médical de l'entreprise, à l'exercice des droits syndicaux, à la représentation des travailleurs dans l'entreprise ainsi qu'à la protection particulière des représentants du personnel de l'entreprise".

116 Dorssemont, "Collectief arbeidsrechtelijke aspecten van internationale detachering", pp. 532–533.

117 *Rush Portuguesa*, para. 15.

118 This assumption seems very formalistic, I will come back to this critique while analysing the *Rush* decision in the next Chapter. See *infra*, p. 150.

119 Article 57(2) EEC, now Article 53(2) TFEU.

States.[120] In particular, a number of Member States, with France being the most ardent supporter, considered the free movement of *workers*[121] to be the right legal basis for the PWD. Instead, with the second draft (1993), the Commission included the freedom to *provide services* as a second legal basis for the Directive. This was maintained in the final version of the PWD. Apart from the stance of the Court of Justice, framing the posting phenomenon into the freedom of provide services, this choice has often been read in connection with the political necessity of enabling the qualified majority voting in the Council (thus circumventing the UK veto).[122] This decision evidently has far reaching legal consequences. Here it is interesting to stress just the fact that the (discarded) option of the free movement of workers would have implied a much clearer stance about the enjoyment of "collective" rights by posted workers. Indeed, Article 8 of Regulation 1612/68[123] guarantees the equal treatment of workers as regards joining professional associations and exercising collective labour rights (e.g., the right to vote for elected representatives). All in all, service *providers* and not their employees can rely on the freedom to provide services.[124] This implies that nor the Directive itself nor its legal basis can provide any guidance in the field of the possible relationship between posted *workers* and collective labour rights. As for the relationship between the service *provider* and collective labour rights of the host state, the choice for the freedom to provide services implies a preference for the identification of host state regulations with *obstacles* to this freedom.[125] This, obviously, trying to look at the still "virgin" Directive, ignoring the following case law delivered by the Court of Justice, which has, in a way, clarified some of these issues.

In the end, the Directive left open a number of questions. This is also due to the lack of definition of the "limited period" which should be a fundamental characteristic of a posting. As there is a thin line between the freedom to provide services and the freedom of establishment, notably in the case of a service provider which "spends a substantial period of time in the Member State where

---

120 Evju and Novitz, "The Evolving Regulation: dynamics and Consequences", p. 29.

121 Article 49 EEC, now Article 46 TFEU.

122 See for example Kolehmainen, *The Posted Workers Directive: European Reinforcement of National Labour Protection*, p. 150; Evju and Novitz, "The Evolving Regulation: dynamics and Consequences", p. 30.

123 Regulation (EEC) No. 1612/68 of the Council of 15 October 1968 on freedom of movement for workers within the Community, Article 8: "A worker who is a national of a Member State and who is employed in the territory of another Member State shall enjoy equality of treatment as regards membership of trade unions and the exercise of rights attaching thereto, including the right to vote [...]". See Article 8 of Regulation (EU) No 492/2011 of the European Parliament and of the Council, of 5 April 2011, on freedom of movement for workers within the Union.

124 See Barnard, *The Substantive Law of the EU: The Four Freedoms*, pp. 355–368.

125 Indeed, Biagi stresses how the Directive "prevents some Member Sates [...] from enacting domestic legislation without any limit", thus highlighting the role of the PWD in avoiding excessive "obstacles" to the provision of services. Biagi, "The 'Posted Workers' EU Directive: from Social Dumping to Social Protectionism", p. 179.

the service is provided"[126], the same can be said for the case of a posting lasting for several years.[127] In such a case the line between posting and free movement of workers becomes thin indeed.[128] Under this light the remarked silence of the Directive about collective labour law issues suddenly seems more problematic. In his contribution, Dorssemont has identified a number of potential tensions related to these issues.[129] The contribution, written at the peak of the second "high tide" of posting of workers (*i.e.*, in the post-*Laval* era), does point out a vast array of issues, arising both from the PWD and from its interpretation delivered by the Court of Justice. Here I will sketch the potential tensions between the posting phenomenon, as regulated by the PWD[130] and the articulations of collective labour law, following the structure presented in the previous Chapter.

Freedom of association

In the previous Chapter[131] it was anticipated that, among the bundle of rights[132] entailed by the freedom of association, the right of *association* is more prone to be "touched" by the posting phenomenon. Here it is interesting to focus on the right of posted workers to join a trade union (in the host state), as well as on the "negative" dimension of the same freedom, in respect of the posting employer.

As for the first topic, it seems unlikely that host state trade unions would refuse membership to a posted worker on the ground of its "mobile" situation.[133] As for an eventual legal limitation of the possibility for the posted worker to join a trade union in the host state, such an obstacle should be considered as infringing the freedom of association itself. Indeed, the body of decisions of the ILO supervisory bodies is clear in this regard. On the one hand, the Freedom of Association Committee considers the non discrimination as the very general principle, explicitly including the nationality in its listing of discriminatory

126 Barnard, *The Substantive Law of the EU: The Four Freedoms*, p. 355.

127 Speaking of the whole provision of services (evidently, including posted workers)the scenario is far from impossible especially in the construction sector, as it was pointed out *supra* (see p. 48). The story may be different for the single posted worker.

128 See for example Hellsten, "On the Social Dimension in Posting of Workers", p. 9: "the distinction made between posted workers who return back to their home (or living) state and those who do not return is artificial. In that thinking a worker moving on his own initiative for one day to the host state enters its labour market while a worker posted for a ten years project does not".

129 Dorssemont, "Collectief arbeidsrechtelijke aspecten van internationale detachering", with particular reference to the Belgian situation.

130 Thus trying to make abstraction from the case law, as I just said.

131 See *supra*, p. 84.

132 Creighton, "Freedom of Association", p. 276.

133 Though its not a legal argument, this eventuality would entail a risk of double membership fee for the posted worker -in case of a previous membership in the home state. Dorssemont argues that this potential situation could be solved through transnational agreements between trade unions. See Dorssemont, "Collectief arbeidsrechtelijke aspecten van internationale detachering", p. 536.

conditions.[134] On the other hand, the same Committee considers that the status of fixed term or contract employee should not deprive the worker of his right to form and join organisations of his own choosing.[135] It seems also reasonable to argue that such a restriction would also be sanctioned under Article 11 and 14 of the European Convention of Human Rights.

The second potential tension is related to the negative freedom of association of the posting employer. In fact, this brings us back to the case law of the European Court of Human Rights which was analysed in the previous Chapter.[136] The *Gustafsson*[137] and *Kellerman*[138] dealt with the question of the extension of standards set by collective agreement, whose content the employer had not the occasion to influence. One could argue that this is the case of the PWD, when the conditions of Article 3(1) are actually laid down in collective agreements.[139] The stance of the ECtHR on the issue is clear: the Court in *Gustafsson* considers that Article 11 of the Convention "does not as such guarantee a right not to enter into a collective agreement".[140]

Collective action

In analysing the relationship of the PWD with the right to take collective action, one has first to consider two elements stemming from the Directive itself. The first element is, not surprisingly, the 22th Recital of the Directive. The wording of the Recital could represent the final word on the issue, since it clearly states that the "Directive is without prejudice to the law of the Member States concerning collective action to defend the interests of trades and professions".[141] However, one cannot fail to notice that such a clause is inserted in a Recital, whose legal value is by no means evident. The second element is in a way the antecedent of

---

134 ILO, *Freedom of Association: Digest of Decisions and Principles of the Freedom of Association Committee of the Governing Body of the ILO*, 2006, para. 209.

135 Ibid., 2006, para. 255.

136 See *supra*, p. 86.

137 ECtHR, 2 July 2002, *Gustafsson v. Sweden*, 15573/89.

138 ECtHR, 1 July 2003, *A.B. Kurt Kellermann v. Sweden*, no. 41579/98.

139 However, one would probably be wrong by making this assumption. After all, the PWD does not entail an *extension* of collective agreements. Instead, it *refers* to the content of (certain typologies of) collective agreements in order to identify the applicable conditions under Article 3(1). This by no means implies that the posting employer becomes part of the collective agreement, nor of the employers' association who actually signed the agreement.

140 *Gustafsson v Sweden*, no. 15573/89, para. 52.

141 This clause would then became known as the "Monti clause", being inserted in the Council Regulation on the functioning of the internal market in relation to the free movement of goods among Member States, 7 December 1998, OJ L337/8, 12 December 1998, whose Article 2 states: "This Regulation shall not affect in any way the exercise of fundamental rights as recognised in the Member States, including the right or freedom to strike or to take other action covered by the specific industrial relations systems in Member States in accordance with national law and practices."

the first. Biagi[142] gives account of a statement of the Council and the Commission regarding Article 3.10. This Article, allowing the application to posted workers of terms and conditions stemming from public policy provisions, was thus presented as covering provisions dealing with "the legality of industrial action including strikes". This reference however, Biagi specifies, was dropped following a request of the Danish delegation.[143]

This implies, once again, that the Directive provides for no guidance about the relationship between the right at stake and posted workers. Two potential "tensions" can be singled out. The first is related to the possible use of posted workers as strike breakers. The second involves the participation of posted workers to a strike in the host state. A third issue, namely the case of a collective action called in order to obtain working conditions better than those "covered" by the PWD, will be analysed in the context of collective bargaining.

Dorssemont rules out the lawfulness of the first scenario (posted workers as strike breakers), on the basis of the analogy with the temporary agency regulations, both at European and national level.[144] Obviously, at least for the European level, this is true only after the adoption of the Temporary Agency Workers Directive.[145] Still, a look at the Digest of the ILO Freedom of Association Committee, suggest that such a possibility would also (at least) violate ILO standards regarding the protection of the right to strike. The Committee stated clearly that "the hiring of workers to break a strike in a sector which cannot be regarded as an essential sector in the strict sense of the term, and hence one in which strikes might be forbidden, constitutes a serious violation of freedom of association".[146] What is more, since the recourse to a service provider may avoid the label of "hiring out", the same Committee had the occasion to specify that also "the employment of the armed forces or of *another group of persons* to perform duties which have been suspended as a result of a labour dispute can, if the strike is lawful, be justified only by the need to ensure the operation of services or industries whose suspension would lead to an acute crisis".[147]

The second scenario involves the direct involvement of posted workers in a collective action. In a way, this necessarily implies a cross-border element, since the posted workers are still employed by their home state employer. This could

142 Biagi, "The 'Posted Workers' EU Directive: from Social Dumping to Social Protectionism", p. 177.

143 In a way the approach made its way to Recital 22 of the Directive. One can only wonder about the reason for the opposition from the Danish delegation, which was most probably due to the idea that the rights connected with industrial relations were best left outside of the legislative intervention of the European institutions.

144 See Dorssemont, "Collectief arbeidsrechtelijke aspecten van internationale detachering", p. 570.

145 Directive 2008/104/EC of the European Parliament and of the Council of 19 November 2008 on temporary agency work.

146 ILO, *Freedom of Association: Digest of Decisions and Principles of the Freedom of Association Committee of the Governing Body of the ILO*, 2006, para. 632.

147 Ibid., para. 636, emphasis added.

bring the legal issue under the umbrella of private international law, either in the form of contractual or non-contractual liability.[148] As regards the actual right to strike of posted workers, in principle it is hard to imagine a scenario where they would be denied this possibility. The main problem revolves around the identification of the law applicable to the (eventual) legal dispute stemming from the collective action. Apart from liability aspects, which law should be eventually relied upon in order to assess the legitimacy of the action? In this sense the PWD seems to complicate the picture. The Directive *restricts* the conditions applicable to posted workers to the list under Article 3(1), which does not include provisions related to collective labour law, including strikes and collective actions. At the same time, Article 3(10), covering "public policy provisions" (which could easily include the regulation of industrial conflicts) seems to require an *ex ante* choice of the host state. In the end, a collective action carried out by posted workers in the host state could be regulated by the law of the home state. Moreover, the specific situation of posted workers poses another problem. Since the very presence of the posted worker in the territory of the host state[149] is inextricably linked to the service provider, one might wonder whether the action of "sending back" in the home state the posted worker who took part in a collective action could be considered as a "penalisation". The ILO Committee used this broad concept (penalisation) when condemning acts of retaliation upon workers as a consequence of a legitimate collective action.[150] Still, it is unclear if the cited "sending back" could be defined as such.

Collective agreements and collective bargaining

It is important here to distinguish the process of collective bargaining from its outcome, *i.e.* collective agreements. The reason to stress this distinction in the context of the PWD, is that the Directive makes reference to collective agreements, whereas the process leading to their conclusion is ignored.

As it emerged from the analysis of the adoption saga, the role of collective agreements in setting the conditions to be applied to posted workers has been one of the most debated topics of the PWD. The first tension arises directly from this debate, being related to the different systems of extension (or lack thereof) of collective agreements. In fact, the second issue as well brings us back to a thorny issue of the Directive. In this case it is the "minimum" character of the PWD which comes to the mind. Thus, the second issue, possibly bridging the topic of

148 Dorssemont, "Collectief arbeidsrechtelijke aspecten van internationale detachering", pp. 565. See also F. Dorssemont and A. Van Hoek, "Collective Action in Labour Conflicts Under the Rome II Regulation (Part I)", *European Labour Law Journal* 2, no. 1 (2011): 48–75 and F. Dorssemont and A. Van Hoek, "Collective Action in Labour Conflicts Under the Rome II Regulation (Part II)", *European Labour Law Journal* 2, no. 2 (2011): 101–118.

149 Where, in the hypothesis, the collective action takes place.

150 ILO, *Freedom of Association: Digest of Decisions and Principles of the Freedom of Association Committee of the Governing Body of the ILO*, 2006, para. 660.

collective action with the one here at stake, is related to the possibility to try to obtain (through collective bargaining) conditions which are better than those covered by the PWD.

As it was just remarked, the issue of the collective agreements taken into account by the PWD has already been analysed in the context of the drafting process.[151] In that context, reassurance was given in particular to the Danish delegation, as regards the compatibility of their system of *de facto* generalised collective agreements with the PWD. This reassurance was then translated in Article 3(8). Still, the Directive seems much more tailored to fit those system characterised by some form of *centralised* setting of wages and working conditions.[152] On the contrary, those system characterised by an autonomous de-centralised system of collective bargaining and collective agreements, would find it hard (*rectius*, impossible) to impose their standards to foreign service providers posting their workers. This was a matter of concern for Sweden, which had joined the European Union in 1995. Indeed, in order to secure public support for the accession, the Swedish government sought reassurance from Commissioner Flynn[153] (who had already played a similar role in respect of Danish trade unions). For what it matters here, the Commissioner stated that the accession would not touch the Swedish system of industrial relations, simply because of Article 2.6 of the Social Protocol. This Article excluded the application of the Protocol itself (to became the social chapter of the Treaty) to "pay, the right of association, the right to strike or the right to impose lock out".[154] The Swedish government contented itself with this (rather vague) reassurance. The Directive was implemented without introducing a system of extension for collective agreements, thus relying on the "normal" means to get the service providers to sign a collective agreement in Sweden. The issue here at stake, *i.e.* the relationship of the PWD with a system of collective bargaining which did not feature an extension mechanism, was left unsolved. The highlighted reassurance clearly played a role in fostering the age of innocence.

The same "innocence" seems to underpin also the second issue. Biagi, commenting the Directive, considered Article 3(10) as basically allowing Member States to add items to the list of Article 3(1).[155] Still, the same Author, a few lines after this statement, affirms that the Directive will prevent Member States to "enact domestic legislation without any limit".[156] On the other hand,

---

151 See *supra*, p. 123.

152 See Dorssemont, "Collectief arbeidsrechtelijke aspecten van internationale detachering", pp. 554–555.

153 Ahlberg, "The Age of Innocence -and Beyond", pp. 301–302.

154 The Commissioner did in fact go further, affirming that non-compliance by firms or individuals (to European legislation and/or to its transposing norms) could be sanctioned "by recourse to the normal procedures in effect on the Swedish labour market". However, ibid., p. 303, points out that "he [Commissioner Flynn] is probably not even aware of the details of the law on industrial action in Sweden [...]".

155 Biagi, "The 'Posted Workers' EU Directive: from Social Dumping to Social Protectionism", p. 178.

156 Ibid., p. 179.

writing a few years after the adoption of the Directive,[157] Barnard states that the Directive will not deprive the service provider of its competitive advantage as it only imposes the respect of *minimum* wages and working conditions.[158] The issue of an actual process of collective bargaining covering posted workers or their working site and going beyond those minima was in general not dealt with. The fact that Article 3(10) requires a decision of the Member State in order to apply the public policy exception, would suggest that social actors are not, by themselves, entitled to bargain for wages and conditions beyond the minima covered by the Directive. This fits awkwardly with the principles of collective bargaining and of "free and voluntary negotiation". The body of decisions by the ILO Committee on Freedom of Association has not taken lightly restrictions to the practice of collective bargaining. This has often been analysed in cases where government policies aimed at containing inflation,[159] so that it would be too audacious to draw an analysis from this body of decisions. In the end, the diverging conceptions about the minimum or maximum character of the PWD, made it so that this potential tension was not addressed.

4.2.2 NOT A COMMODITY

It is very difficult to fit the scenario depicted by the PWD in the conceptual framework of industrial relations. All in all this seems to be coherent with the conceptual underpinning of the Directive. First, and foremost, with the idea of *Rush*, that posted workers are not part of the labour market of the host state. Accepting this assumption is indeed the twist in our tale. A number of consequences of this *choice* reverberate on the relationship between posting of workers and industrial relations.

Developed in the framework of the provision of services, the Directive itself imposes on the posting employer the respect of the social *policy* of the host state, instead of the collective autonomy of social actors.[160] The explanation given by the Commission in the context of the second draft of the PWD is in this sense revelatory.[161] The idea is that the service provider may (eventually) be subject to a number of *conditions*, as these can be measured in terms of equality of treatment

157 When the "clarifications" of the Court of Justice were yet to materialise.

158 Barnard, *EC Employment Law*, p. 179.

159 See for example, ILO, *Freedom of Association: Digest of Decisions and Principles of the Freedom of Association Committee of the Governing Body of the ILO*, 2006, para. 1024: "If, as part of its stabilization policy, a government considers that wage rates cannot be settled freely through collective bargaining, such a restriction should be imposed as an exceptional measure and only to the extent that is necessary, without exceeding a reasonable period, and it should be accompanied by adequate safeguards to protect workers' living standards."

160 Dorssemont, "Collectief arbeidsrechtelijke aspecten van internationale detachering", p. 542.

161 *European Industrial Relations Review*, 236, p. 23.

with potential national competitors. Industrial relations, on the contrary, never enter the picture their impact on competition being less measurable.

Notwithstanding this evident discrepancy, the PWD was saluted as being *neutral* towards different labour law systems.[162] This is true only inasmuch as one considers the neutrality as the absence of straight top-down harmonisation. The result however is quite different if one considers this from the point of view of industrial relations systems. Indeed, a given Member State, for example one lacking a system for extension of collective agreements, would not be forced by the PWD to change its system. This however only by accepting the creation of a "grey area" of employment relationship in its own territory. This Member State, in fact, would have to justify every legal burden coming from the "normal" functioning of its industrial relations system, under the narrow clause of Article 3(10) of the PWD.[163]

The same is true also for those system which, though fixing some minimum standard in a way "accepted" by the PWD, are characterised by a *practice* which sets higher standards at a different level of negotiations. As remarked by Barnard, in a situation where companies established in the host state pay their workers at rates above the mandatory minima, the service provider will retain (some of) its competitive advantage.[164] By creating those "islands" of (lower) working conditions, the legislator of the Directive does accept the implicit restriction of the scope of the system of industrial relations of the host country.[165] As it was highlighted in the first Chapter,[166] the recent *Study on the economic and social effects associated with the phenomenon of posting of workers in the EU* shows that lower labour costs are often one of the reasons underpinning the recourse to posted workers.[167] In this sense, the framework provided by the Directive makes it possible, by creating "islands" of wages and working conditions, to push back the de-commodification efforts of industrial relations.[168]

From a lawyer's perspective, it is more difficult to assess the impact on power relations and power resources[169] of the PWD itself. As a recent study has highlighted, "the problem is mainly due to other reasons than […] the PWD as

---

162 See for example Davies, "Posted Workers: Single Market or Protection of National Labour Law Systems?"; E. Kolehmainen, "The Directive Concerning the Posting of Workers: Synchronizations of the Functions of National Legal Systems", *Comparative Labor Law & Policy Journal* 20 (1998): 71–104, p. 97.

163 Also, the *Laval* case has shown that the Court of Justice does not allow trade unions to rely on this Article, in the name of their private nature. See *infra*, p. 189.

164 Barnard, *EC Employment Law*, p. 179.

165 Which is, in our definition, directly linked to the setting of wages and working conditions. See Dunlop, *Industrial Relations Systems*, p. 387, cited *supra*, p. 69.

166 See *supra*, p. 32.

167 IDEA Consult, and ECORYS Netherlands, *Study on the Economic and Social Effects Associated with the Phenomenon of Posting of Workers in the EU Final Report*, p. 135.

168 See *supra*, p. 63 ff.

169 See *supra*, p. 59.

such".[170] The very situation of posted workers, with all the social and economic hurdles which were summarised *supra*[171] has a deeper impact on these topics. On the other hand, looking from the perspective of the host state social actors and industrial relations system, the Directive could play a major role. This is largely due to what we just remarked, in terms of (legal) conception of posting of workers. The acceptance of the provision of service as general framework and the "lack of access" (to the labour market) idea are, in this sense, two sides of an heavy coin. However, the ripples caused by tossing this coin into the waters of industrial relations are much more visible through the case law developed by the Court of Justice. Hence, this issue will be analysed in the next Chapter.

4.2.3 INTERIM CONCLUSIONS

The silence of the PWD on collective labour law issues, though perfectly in line with the conception I just outlined, left on the table a number of unsolved questions. Some of these questions have been brought in front of the Court of Justice in the years following the adoption of the Directive. Other are still shrouded in darkness. From the present days' perspective, these problems are indeed evident.

The reasons underlying the silence also stand out quite clearly, when looking at the adoption saga. The whole debate was framed in terms of defence of labour standards more than of industrial relations systems ad practices. If the latter tension emerged, as for the Danish (and Italian) concerns, it was once again the issue of substantial standard setting[172] which dominated the requests. Paradoxically, even the outcome of the negotiations on the threshold period, the thorny issue *par excellence* during the adoption saga, could in a way have boosted the uncertainty. As the famous night, where all the cows are black, the "zero day" option puts in the same cauldron the briefest postings with service provisions lasting for years (as in certain construction contracts). From the point of view of industrial relations practices, the two situations are extremely different, with the latter implying the birth of a "industrial community"[173] which, at least potentially, could be integrated in the host state system of industrial relations. This was not foreseen during the negotiations. Taking into account the difficult struggle to conceive strategies aimed at posted workers,[174] the present days' perspective shows that the problem was at least underestimated: notwithstanding the stance

[170] Van Hoek and Houwerzijl, "Comparative Study on the Legal Aspects of the Posting of Workers in the Framework of the Provision of Services in the European Union", p. 35.

[171] See Chapter 1, p. 48.

[172] As opposed to the procedural aspect, *i.e.* to industrial relations practices.

[173] The "invisible villages" of Kontula, *Näkymätön Kylä*.

[174] See *supra*, p. 48.

of Court of Justice, posted workers do have an impact on the host state labour market.

The (relative) little quantitative significance of the phenomenon is one of the reasons for this lack of attention. Another reason was the idea that the European Union would, in time, reduce the disparities, in terms of wages and working conditions, between the Member States, thus eliminating the risk of social dumping.[175] The EU-28 perspective shows that the context has changed, or at least, how the reality stubbornly refused to conform itself to the prophecies of harmonisation. A different order of reasons (partially) explains the choice in favour of the freedom to provide services as legal basis, which, as we will see, would put pains thousandfold upon labour law. First, the Court played a major role in framing the debate,[176] with *Rush* being the clearest example of its understanding of the posting phenomenon as, essentially, a corollary of a provision of services. Second, the needs of the political debate, with the necessity to circumvent the UK veto on the Directive. It is almost striking to think that both these reasons were, in a way, completely contingent.[177] However, once framed in the provision of services, the simple institutional *inertia*[178] would have required a high degree of political willingness in order to steer back the posting of workers into the free movement dimension. As it should be clear by now, the political situation made it so that it was already difficult to reach the compromise here at stake.

Finally, a reason for the silence can be found in the old *innuendo*, which can be summarised as "industrial relations and collective labour law belong to the national level". True enough, the nature of the PWD, which has basically a conflict of laws dimension[179] did not suggest the inclusion of provisions aimed at the collective side of labour law. Still, the cited innuendo played a part. As it was recalled, Biagi gives account of the debate over Article 3(10). On the one hand, the Commission and the Council wanted to specify that "public policy provisions" included (among other topics) "the legality of industrial action, including strikes".[180] This reference was discarded, we are told, following a request

---

175 See for example, Barnard, *EC Employment Law*, p. 179: "the disparity between the rules of the different Member States in these core areas will be reduced as the Community passes further legislation in the social field".

176 In general on this role see S.K. Schmidt, "Law-Making in the Shadow of Judicial Politics", in *The 'Community Method'. Obstinate or Obsolete*, ed. R. Dehousse (Houndmills Basingstoke / Palgrave MacMillan, 2011), 43–59, p. 57.

177 On the one hand, a slightly different political stance of the UK could have permitted a completely different outcome. On the other, it has been remarked in the Introduction (page 9), and it will be further analysed in the next Chapter, as in *Rush* the Court simply could not rely on the free movement of workers, Portugal being still covered by the transitional measures after the accession.

178 See G. Falkner, "Introduction: The EU's Decision Traps and Their Exits", in *The EU's Decision Traps: Comparing Policies*, ed. G. Falkner (Oxford: Oxford University Press, 2011), 1–17, pp. 10–11.

179 Dorssemont, "Collectief arbeidsrechtelijke aspecten van internationale detachering", p. 531.

180 Biagi, "The 'Posted Workers' EU Directive: from Social Dumping to Social Protectionism", p. 177.

in this sense put forward by the Danish delegation.[181] On can only speculate at the reason for this request, but following the *innuendo*, it could be explained with the preference for the silence as a means to defend the national system of industrial relations, over the risk of mingling with the European level. As Ahlberg puts it, one might wonder if the Age of Innocence was founded on bluff, ignorance or naivety.[182]

Thus, it was left to the individual Member States (if they so decided) to modify their systems of collective labour law in order to make it easier/possible to integrate posted workers. This if one accepts the idea of *neutrality* of the PWD. Or, better, if one is convinced that this neutrality towards industrial relations system and collective labour regulations is still credible once the phenomenon is framed into the freedom to provide services. It will be then for the Court of Justice to end the Age of Innocence, as the analysis already fades into the next Chapter.

181 Ibid.
182 Ahlberg, "The Age of Innocence -and Beyond", p. 303.

CHAPTER 5

CHILDHOOD'S END

Thirty Years of Posting Case Law before the Court of Justice

In the previous Chapter a landmark case delivered by the Court of Justice, *Rush Portuguesa*,[1] marked the beginning of the Adoption Saga. The reference obviously goes beyond its chronological importance. Indeed, looking at the period preceding the drafting of the PWD, one can see how the Court of Justice played a major role in shaping the debate around the posting phenomenon. Some fundamental (legal) choices date back to that period, which would then have a major impact on the following debates. Just to cite the most important of these choices, one has to look at these "Prologues" of the PWD in order to find the roots of the integration of posted workers into the framework of the freedom to provide services.

Fast forwarding past the adoption of the Directive, the Court still played an important (if not the most important) role in shaping the legal framework of posting of workers. As it should be clear from the previous Chapter, the PWD itself left open a number of questions. Apart from the inevitable incomplete nature of the legal text, some of these questions stem directly from the need to reach a political compromise over the text of the Directive. In a way, from the day of its adoption, the PWD was being interpreted, by the very actors which took part in its drafting, in two opposing ways. On the one hand, the Directive could be interpreted as a *maximum*, as a ceiling for wages and working conditions applicable to posted workers by the host state. On the other hand, the Directive was interpreted as only providing for *minimum* conditions to be applied, leaving the host state substantially free to apply better conditions through the means provided by Articles 3(1) and 3(8).[2] It is in tackling (sometimes bluntly) these issues that the Court has played the role just mentioned. This especially during the "second high tide" period, starting on December 2007. It was at that time, in the halls of Luxembourg, that the Age of Innocence ended abruptly.

---

1 Case C-113/89 of 27 March 1990.

2 See *supra*, p. 125.

This Chapter will be devoted to the analysis of the contribution of the Court of Justice to the topic at stake.[3] This contribution has both a direct and an indirect impact on the relationship between posting of workers and industrial relations (and/or collective labour law). Not surprisingly, the first category (direct impact) encompasses those decisions where the Court had to examine a collective labour law issue, in connection with a posting situation.[4] The second category, i.e. the indirect impact, is less precise in its scope. Under this label I will include those decisions, concerning posting of workers, which do not touch upon collective labour law or industrial relations. However, these decisions *indirectly* influence this relationship, as they shape the broader legal framework of posting of workers. The aforementioned "attraction" of the posting phenomenon into the sphere of the provision of services comes to the mind.

The Chapter follows a chronological order, divided into three periods: decisions preceding the Adoption Saga, decisions delivered during the Adoption Saga and before the end of the implementation period,[5] and, finally, decisions concerning the Directive itself.

5.1 PROLOGUE(S)

As it was explained in the previous Chapter, the Posting of Workers Directive was not elaborated in a "legal void". If the decision in *Rush Portuguesa* has often been identified as the spark, igniting the legislative process,[6] one should not overlook the fact that other decisions delivered by the Court of Justice before the drafting of the PWD also played an important role in (pre)defining the boundaries of the discussion.[7]

The interest of these "prologues" is twofold. On the one hand, they do belong under the mentioned label of "indirect effect" on our subject matter. Indeed, by tackling the phenomenon for the first time in the European legal order, these judgements play a relevant role to this extent. On the other hand, to analyse these decisions allows for a complete understanding of the background of the negotiations about the PWD, which were discussed in the previous Chapter.

---

[3] In the next Chapter I will focus on the different, but strictly intertwined, topic of the relationship between fundamental freedoms and fundamental rights, which is also developed by the CJEU (partly) in the same decisions.

[4] Even less surprisingly, this category is somewhat limited from a quantitative point of view.

[5] 16 December 1999.

[6] See *supra*, p. 119.

[7] Schmidt, "Law-Making in the Shadow of Judicial Politics", p. 57.

None of the decisions which will be analysed in this section uses the wording "posted workers". In *Seco*[8] the expression "temporarily seconded workers" is used instead,[9] whereas *Webb*[10] and *Rush Portuguesa* do not provide a specific wording.[11]

5.2.1 THE STORY BEFORE THE STORY

The (legal) story of posting of workers is often presented as essentially beginning with the decision in *Rush Portuguesa*. Indeed, in the Introduction I defined this decision as the beginning of the first "high tide" for posting of workers. Keeping in mind the "resonance" of *Rush*, this can still be considered as essentially true. However, one should not overlook the story *before* the story, as it might hold a few surprises. In a way, it puts in a different light the "turning point" represented by *Rush*.

Indeed, as it has been said,[12] the decisions of the Court of Justice in *Webb* and *Seco*, represent the first step in the creation of a different framework for workers' mobility in the EU, separating posted workers from the broader context of free movement of workers. (now Article 45 TFEU). The cited "integration" of posted workers into the framework of the freedom to provide services thus started almost ten years before *Rush*, and fifteen before the adoption of the PWD.

Webb

The *Webb*[13] case concerns a temporary-work agency incorporated under English law posting workers (*i.e.* providing manpower) to the Netherlands.[14] Alfred John Webb, the manager of this agency, was accused of violating Article 1 of the Royal Decree of 10 September 1970, which prohibited the provision of manpower without previous authorisation (taking the form of a licence) by the Minister for Social Affairs. It is important to note that the Law on the provision of manpower of 31 July 1965 did provide that such an authorisation might be refused "only

---

8 Joined Cases 62 and 63/81, *Seco SA v. Établissement d'Assurance contre la Vieillesse et l'Invalidité*, 3 February 1982.

9 However, the French version refers to the fact that the employers "avaient à cette fin *détaché* temporarirement des travailleurs". Similarly, in the Italian version, the employers "*distaccavano* provvisoriamente lavoratori".

10 Case 279/80, *Criminal proceedings against Alfred John Webb*, 17 December 1980.

11 In *Webb* the Court does only look at the phenomenon as "provision of manpower" without any further specification deriving from the transnational context. The same is true for different language versions ("mise à disposition de main-d'œuvre", "fornitura di manodopera"). In *Rush Portuguesa*, the perspective of the employer prevails, so that the Court only refers to the possibility for the undertaking to "move with its own work-force" ("se déplacer avec son propre personnel", "trasferirsi col proprio personale").

12 S. Giubboni, "Libertà di circolazione dei lavoratori e libera prestazione dei servizi nell'ordinamento comunitario", *URGE Working Paper* 1 (2009), p. 5.

13 Case 279/80, *Criminal proceedings against Alfred John Webb*, 17 December 1980.

14 A scenario which, in the context of the PWD, would be covered by Article 1(3)(c).

when there is reasonable cause to fear that the provision of manpower by the applicant might harm good relations on the labour market or if the interests of the labour force in question are inadequately safeguarded".[15] The company held a licence for the provision of manpower under UK law.

In the context of the criminal proceeding against Mr. Webb, the Hoge Raad van de Nederlanden (Supreme Court of the Netherlands) refers three questions to the Court of Justice. First, the Hoge Raad asks if the provision of manpower should be considered as a "service" under Article 60 EEC Treaty (now Article 57 TFEU). Second, it asks if the Treaty prohibits a Member State from requiring a licence in order to provide manpower in its territory, and (third) if the fact that the service provider holds a licence in its home state should affect the answer to the second question.

The Court of Justice answers affirmatively to the first question, defining the provision of manpower as a service, covered by Article 60 EEC.[16] That being said, the Court also states that the employees of these agencies might (in some circumstances) still be covered by the provisions on free movement of *workers*.[17] This can be read as an answer to the concerns expressed, particularly by the French government, during the procedure, where it was pointed out that the provision of manpower was a "special kind of service" potentially interfering with the free movement of workers and with labour market regulations.

Passing to the second and third questions, the Court clarifies that Article 60 EEC, in stating that the service provider may pursue its activity "under the same conditions as are imposed by that State on its own nationals",[18] does not mean that "all national legislation applicable to nationals of that State and usually applied to the permanent activities of undertakings established therein may be similarly applied in its entirety to the temporary activities of undertakings which are established in other Member States".[19] Following this line of reasoning the Court had then to decide which measure could be applied to the service providers. In this sense, the Court uses an "embryonic" form of the test which would then characterise its jurisprudence in the field of fundamental freedoms.[20] In *Webb* this test has three steps: to be applicable, a measure has (first) to be justified by the "general good", insofar as (second) this interest is not already "safeguarded by the provisions to which the provider of service is subject in the Member State

15 *Webb*, para. 3.
16 Ibid., para. 11.
17 Ibid., para. 10.
18 The same wording is now present under Article 57 TFEU.
19 *Webb*, para. 16; here the Courts answers to the Danish and German governments, which had proposed an interpretation of Article 60 EEC as encompassing the full gamut of regulations applicable to national service providers. See Giubboni and Orlandini, *La Libera Circolazione Dei Lavoratori Nell'Unione Europea*, pp. 89–90.
20 See C. Barnard and S. Deakin, "Market Access and Regulatory Competition", in *The Law of the Single European Market: unpacking the Premises* (Oxford: Hart Publishing, 2002), 197–223, pp. 205 ff.

of his establishment"; third, it must be applied to "all persons or undertakings operating" in the State where the service is provided.[21]

In *Webb*, the Dutch regulation did pass the test. The Court considered that the license requirement was aimed at protecting "good relations on the labour market" and/or the "interests of the workforce affected",[22] which were considered as possible grounds justifying a restriction of the freedom to provide services. The Court also found that these interests were not sufficiently protected by the licensing system in the home state (UK);[23] finally, the Dutch regulation did not make any distinction based on the nationality of the provider.

The position of the actual posted workers was never in question in *Webb*. Two main points must be retained. On the one hand, though not particularly shocking, the "pure" provision of manpower is included under the freedom to provide services.[24] On the other hand, and more importantly, the Court clearly steers away from the "equal treatment" requirement, suggested by the wording of Article 60 EEC. The test applied however is still one aimed at tackling potential discriminations (direct or indirect).[25] This seems to be a more nuanced approach than the one proposed by AG Slynn in its opinion on the *Webb* case. The AG had in fact maintained that "the abolition of the restrictions on the freedom to supply services within the Community entails more than the abolition of discrimination on the grounds of nationality or place of establishment and extends to the *removal of all obstacles to the freedom to supply services*".[26]

Seco

As in *Webb*, the conflict between the freedom to provide services and a piece of social legislation is at stake in the *Seco*[27] case. In particular, the case concerns two French companies (Seco SA and Desquenne & Giral SA) posting their workers to Luxembourg in the context of railway construction and maintenance activities. These posted workers are not nationals of a Member State nor of a country

21 *Webb*, para. 17.

22 Ibid., para. 19. Barnard refers to these grounds for justification as "protection of workers", see C. Barnard, "Employment Rights, Free Movement Under the EC Treaty and the Services Directive", *Europa Institute Working Paper* 5 (2008): 1–30, p. 7.

23 See G. Druesne, "Liberté de prestation des services et travailleurs salariés", *Revue trimestrielle de droit européen*, 1982, p. 78.

24 As recalled, the Court pays tribute to the "special" nature of these service, leaving it open the possibility for the workers to be covered by the norms on free movement of workers.

25 Giubboni, "Libertà di circolazione dei lavoratori e libera prestazione dei servizi nell'ordinamento comunitario", p. 5.

26 Emphasis added. The formula resembles closely the so-called "market access" test, also because the AG referred to the mere risk that the procedure (of obtaining a licence) would make it *uneconomic* for a person or undertaking to supply services in another Member State. See Barnard, "Employment Rights, Free Movement Under the EC Treaty and the Services Directive", pp. 4–5.

27 Joined Cases 62 and 63/81, *Seco SA v. Établissement d'Assurance contre la Vieillesse et l'Invalidité*, 3 February 1982.

otherwise linked to the Grand Duchy. Following this posting and by virtue of the Social Insurance Code of Luxembourg the Établissement d'Assurance contre la Vieillesse et l'Invalidité (Old-age and Invalidity Insurance Institution, hereinafter EVI) required the French companies to pay some contribution under the old age and invalidity insurance scheme. The workers, being only temporarily employed in Luxembourg, are exempted from the contribution, while the employer was still liable for its part.[28]

During the procedure before the Luxembourgian judges, the companies claim that these rules are an obstacle to the freedom to provide services, as they require the posting employer to pay social contributions twice (once in the home state and once in Luxembourg), without providing any benefit for the workers being posted. The Cour de Cassation of the Grand Duchy of Luxembourg thus refers two questions to the Court of Justice. The first question is basically aimed at the cited conflict between the freedom to provide services and the regulation described above, whereas the second refers more specifically to a possible justification for the situation put forward by the EVI.[29] The Luxembourgian institution in fact maintained that the payment of the employer's share of social contributions was meant to offset its competitive advantage due to the possibility of *de facto* avoiding the regulation on minimum wages.[30]

In answering the first question, the Court of Justice refers to *Webb* in order to affirm that the freedom to provide services protected by Article 59 and 60 EEC (now Article 56 and 57 TFEU) prohibits "not only overt discrimination based on the nationality of the person providing a service but also all the form of *covert* discrimination which, although based on criteria which appear to be neutral, in practice lead to the same result".[31] This statement resembles closely the one formulated by the Court in the context of cases dealing with free movement of workers.[32] The Court thus identifies the regulation at stake as discriminatory. This is founded on two main arguments. First, the "double imposition", entailed by the fact that the employer is already liable to pay social security ("similar") contributions in the home country; second, the fact that the contribution to the EVI does not amount to a social security benefit for the workers posted in Luxembourg.[33] In doing so the Court discards the justification put forward by the EVI. The EVI maintained that the imposition of the contribution was justified

28 *Seco*, para. 3.

29 Ibid., para. 6.

30 This, maintains the EVI, because of the comparatively high wages of Luxembourg as well as the difficulty in practice to enforce the rules on minimum wages with regard to suppliers of services who temporarily introduce foreign labour into the Grand Duchy.

31 *Seco*, para. 8. With the wording "covert" discrimination the Court seems to refer to the same concept later identified with "indirect" discrimination; see Sjödin, "Labour Market Regulation as Restrictions. A Developmental Study of ECJ Case Law at the Interface Between Free Movement and Posting of Workers", p. 38.

32 Case 152–73, *Giovanni Maria Sotgiu v Deutsche Bundespost*, 12 February 1974. See Druesne, "Liberté de prestations de services et travailleurs salariés", p. 80.

33 *Seco*, para. 9–10.

a fortiori by the fact that, the posted workers being third-country nationals, the Grand Duchy could have simply denied their access to its territory (or to undertake paid employment there).[34] Furthermore, the same institution stated that these workers "who are not nationals of a Member State or persons treated as such, are outside the ambit of Community law. They cannot claim the benefit of the provisions on the free movement of persons and services". Both arguments were rejected by the Court, through the "incorporation" of the workers "into" the service provider.[35] In this sense, the reduction of workers to a mere "accessory" of the company, allows them to retain their right of access to the territory of the Grand Duchy.[36] Still, with this choice the Court of Justice widens the division between workers being "posted" abroad and workers covered by the provisions on free movement of workers. The second justification provided by the EVI represents the object of the second question raised by the Cour de Cassation. Basically this justification presented the double imposition as a counterbalance to the possibility (for posting employers) of eluding the regulations on minimum wages. The Luxembourgian institution thus proposed that the presence of a discrimination could only be ascertained by considering the final position of the service provider, all factors considered. The Court dismissed this argument on the basis that the double imposition was applied to all service providers, "irrespective of whether those persons have complied with the legislation on minimum wages".[37]

Though not fundamental in the decision, two more points must be stressed. In relation with the legal framework of posting of workers, it is important to notice that in *Seco* the Court for the first time affirmed the compatibility of the extension of "social regulations" to posted workers, with a statement worth quoting in full: "It is well-established that Community law does not preclude Member States from applying their legislation, or collective labour agreements entered into by both sides of industry relating to minimum wages, to any person who is employed, even temporarily within their territory, no matter in which country the employer is established, just as Community law does not prohibit Member States from enforcing those rules by appropriate means".[38] Such a statement represents an *obiter dictum* in the case at stake, which was only (very) loosely related to working conditions of posted workers.[39] However, coming to the second interesting point,

34 Ibid., para. 11.

35 Ibid., para. 12: "A Member State's power to control the employment of nationals from a non-member country may not be used in order to impose a discriminatory burden on an undertaking from another Member State enjoying the freedom under Articles 59 and 60 of the Treaty to provide services".

36 See L. Gormley, "Services and Double Social Security Contributions (Case Note on Seco)", *European Law Review*, 1982, 207–209, p. 208.

37 *Seco*, para. 14. The fact that the contribution would entail no benefit for the workers in question is also cited by the Court as an argument to dismiss the justification.

38 *Seco*, para. 14. This statement, as it was reminded in the Introduction (page 9), is very similar to the one in *Rush*, which will attract much more attention.

39 Hellsten, "On the Social Dimension in Posting of Workers", p. 10, explicitly defines this passage as an example of judicial activism. It is also interesting to note, as does Hellsten, that

this statement immediately makes much more sense if read alongside the opinion delivered in *Seco* by AG VerLoren van Themaat. In particular, the AG refers to the possibility to profit from "cost advantages [...] including lower labour costs" as "one of the fundamental features of the Common Market", which should then be protected in the field of the freedom to provide services.[40] In this sense, the *dictum* of the Court can be read as an answer to this conception, refusing the "cost advantage" argument put forward by the AG. This in the case where the service providers brings (or sends) their workforce in another Member State. As stressed by Hellsten,[41] the conception of the internal market which permeates the statement of the AG seems to be at odds with the whole idea of "upward harmonisation" embodied in Article 117 EEC[42] (now Article 151 TFEU).

5.2.2 *RUSH PORTUGUESA*

In a way, the facts as well the outcome of the *Rush* case are similar to *Webb* and *Seco*. The working conditions of posted workers were not discussed in the case here at stake; the question, all differences considered, was once again one of access. Still, *Rush Portuguesa* did draw much more attention than its predecessors. This can be partially explained by the fact that the dispute arose in the context of a posting phenomenon from a "new" to an "old" Member State. Indeed, the accession of Spain and (especially) Portugal in 1986 was surrounded by the (now well known) debate around the risk of "social dumping" and of potential disturbances to the labour market of the "old" Member States caused by the sudden influx of Portuguese workers. It is this kind of concerns which suggested the (transitional) limitation of the free movement of workers for the new Member States. These transitional measures, together with the freedom to provide services, come into question in *Rush*.

The facts were already summarised in the Introduction.[43] For a brief reminder, the dispute arose between Rush Portuguesa, an undertaking established in

---

the Court defines this principle as "well-established" in "Community law" without citing any specific provision of the Treaties nor pre-existing case law.

40 Opinion of AG VerLoren van Themaat in *Seco*: "It is *one of the fundamental features* of the Common Market, which is to be attained inter alia by the freedom to provide service, that when providing services in another Member State any employer may in principle make use of the cost advantages existing in his country, *including lower wage costs*, under the conditions of undistorted competition which constitute another objective of the Treaty" (emphasis added).

41 Ibid., p. 10.

42 "Member States agree upon the need to promote improved working conditions and an improved standard of living for workers, so as to make possible their *harmonisation while the improvement is being maintained.*
They believe that such a development will ensue *not only* from the functioning of the common market, which will favour the harmonisation of social systems, but also from the procedures provided for in this Treaty and from the approximation of provisions laid down by law, regulation or administrative action."

43 See *supra*, p. 8.

Portugal, and the French Office National d'Immigration (National Office of Immigration, hereinafter ONI). Rush Portuguesa was providing its services (posting its own Portuguese manpower) in France as subcontractor of a French undertaking, in the context of construction works. By virtue of the Act concerning the conditions of accession of the Kingdom of Spain and the Portuguese Republic and the adjustments to the Treaties[44] the freedom to provide services applied between Portugal and Spain and the "old" Member States, at the time of the facts (1986). On the contrary, Spanish and Portuguese workers were not covered yet by the provisions on free movement of workers, as the Act of Accession provided a transitional period until 1 January 1993.[45] The French labour inspectorate found that the workers employed by Rush were not in possession of the work permit required by the French labour code for third country nationals. Also, they had not been recruited by the ONI, which had an exclusive right to recruit third country nationals for work in France. A fine was thus issued by the ONI, to which Rush Portuguesa opposed in front of the Administrative Tribunal of Versailles.

Questions and observations

The French tribunal asks three questions. Two of these questions can be considered together, as does the Court of Justice. As it was identified by the AG in his opinion,[46] the French tribunal asks whether the limitation provided by the Act of Accession can be applied to undertakings based in Portugal wishing to move with their own workforce in order to provide a service in another Member State. In particular, the first question deals with the possibility to simply preclude this posting,[47] whereas the second envisages the possibility for the same Member State to subject service provider " to conditions, in particular relating to the engagement of labour in situ, the obtaining of work permits for its own Portuguese staff or the payment of fees to an official immigration body".[48] The third question relates to the qualification of the workers posted by Rush Portuguesa as "'specialized staff or employees occupying a post of a confidential nature' within the meaning of the provisions of the annex to Regulation No. 1612/68 of the Council of 15 October 1968". This question will ultimately prove irrelevant for the solution of the case and can be safely left aside.

In its observations, Rush Portuguesa concludes that the workers being posted to France should not be considered as "workers" within the meaning of Article 48 EEC (free movement of workers, now Article 45 TFEU) and of

---

44 O.J. 1987 L302/23.

45 Article 216 ff. of the Act of Accession.

46 Opinion of AG Van Gerven in *Rush Portuguesa*, para. 6.

47 It is however important to note that the question asked by the French tribunal specified that the presence of the Portuguese workers was characterised by the "understanding that the Portuguese workforce is to return, and does in fact return, immediately to Portugal once its task has been carried out and the provision of the services has been completed.

48 *Rush Portuguesa*, para. 5.

Regulation 1612/68.[49] This because the posted workers "did not look for work in France and have not entered the French labour market, seeing as they have a contract of employment in Portugal and, in the context of that employment, temporarily come to France in order to perform duties in the service of Rush, without however laying claim to the right to establish themselves for an indefinite period as workers in France". On the other side, France argues that only those workers in a "position of trust"[50] in the undertaking could be excluded from the application of the limitations provided by the Act of Accession. The Commission (followed, to a certain extent, by the AG) advocates an intermediate solution, basically broadening the definition of workers who could escape the limitation just recalled.[51]

The decision

The Court does not, in the end, follow any of the solution that I just outlined. Its decision however falls much closer to the position of the posting undertaking than to the ones put forward by the other parties.

The Court of Justice thus finds that the freedom to provide services (fully applicable to Portugal and Spain from the day of accession) also guarantees the right for the services provider to move freely with "all his staff", while at the same time precludes "from making the movement of staff in question subject to restrictions such as a condition as to engagement in situ or an obligation to obtain a work permit".[52] Those measures would discriminate against the service provider in relation to the undertakings established in the Member State of destination. Furthermore, they would affect the very possibility to provide the service. In this sense the Court refuses to "break down" the definition of "worker", as implicit in the solutions proposed by Rush Portuguesa, as well as by the French Government and the Commission. The "incorporation" of posted workers under the posting undertaking, and thus under the freedom to provide services, is consistent with the decisions delivered in *Webb* and *Seco* presented above.

---

49 Regulation (EEC) of the Council of 15 October 1968 on freedom of movement for workers within the Community.

50 "namely those who exercise management functions in the undertaking and are authorized to commit the undertaking as regards third parties", as reported by AG Van Gerven in his Opinion, para. 16.

51 This was based on the wording of the "General Programme for the elimination of restrictions on the freedom to provide services", established by the Council in 1962: "Before the end of the second year of the second stage of the transitional period provisions laid down by law, regulation or administrative action ...are to be amended ...where such provisions ...are liable to hinder the provision of services by such nationals, or by staff possessing special skills or holding positions of responsibility accompanying the person providing the services or carrying out the services on his behalf". See P. Rodière, "Note sur arrêt du 27 mars 1990 Société Rush Portuguesa Lda c. Office national de l'immigration", *Revue trimestrielle de droit européen* 26, no. 3 (1990): 635–640, particularly vocal in his critique of such a solution, which would greatly increase the uncertainty for service providers.

52 *Rush Portuguesa*, para. 12.

Though this reasoning is sufficient to reach a decision, the Court goes on to analyse the case from the point of view of the Act of Accession, and on the limitations imposed by the same Act on the free movement of workers.[53] The Court thus identifies the *purpose* of the limitations provided by the Act of Accession in preventing "disturbances on the employment [...] due to *large* and immediate movements of workers".[54] In order to deny the applicability of such a provision (in light of its purpose) to the case at stake, the Court makes a statement which will prove fundamental for the shaping of the posting phenomenon in the EEC/EU legal order. The posting of workers does not come under the scope of the cited provision, not just because the service provider is entitled to move with its staff, but also because "[...] such workers return to their country of origin after the completion of their work without at any time gaining access to the labour market of the host Member State".[55] This however, with the exception of those activities "which are specifically intended to enable workers to gain access to the labour market of the host Member State".[56]

Continuing in its *obiter dicta*, the Court also repeats (almost) verbatim a statement already present in *Seco*. Though working conditions were not at stake in the present decision, the Court states that "[...] Community law does not preclude Member States from extending their legislation, or collective labour agreements entered into by both sides of industry, to any person who is employed, even temporarily, within their territory, no matter in which country the employer is established; nor does Community law prohibit Member States from enforcing those rules by appropriate means".[57] Confronting this statement with the one in *Seco*, a single main differences strikes the eye. In *Seco* the Court referred to "legislation, or collective labour agreements entered into by both sides of industry relating to minimum wages" whereas in *Rush* the reference to "minimum wages" has been dropped, thus potentially offering a further-reaching "license to regulate" to Member States.[58]

---

53 Free movement of workers *not applicable* to the workers at stake, at least in the present dispute, as just summarised.

54 *Rush Portuguesa*, para. 13 (emphasis added).

55 *Rush Portuguesa*, para. 15. As noted by Rodière, "Note sur arrêt du 27 mars 1990 Société Rush Portuguesa Lda c. Office national de l'immigration", p. 638, the Court does nothing to justify this bold statement, contenting itself of a quite formalistic approach to the question. As Rodière puts it: "Supposons d'ailleurs que de nombreuses sociétés établies hors de France, y obitennent aisément des marchés de services temporaires et y détachent leur personnel, dira-t-on encore que cela n'intéresse pas le marché français de l'emploi? On peut le dire pour soixante personnes; et pour dix mille ou plus?".

56 *Rush Portuguesa*, para. 16–17. The reference here goes probably to the pure provision of manpower, which was already identified in *Webb* as a "special kind" of service.

57 Ibid., para. 18; cf. *Seco*, para. 14.

58 Gormley, "Freedom of Establishment and Freedom to Provide Services. Workers and Services Distinguished", pp. 66–67, refers to this statement (which "calmed French fears") when praising the balanced judgement delivered by the Court in the present case.

Background

The three decisions analysed above provide the scenario for the Adoption Saga. Though it is impossible to measure precisely their influence on the fundamental choices made during the negotiations of the PWD, several elements strike the eye after the tale told in the previous chapter.

First and foremost, the Court of Justice is adamant as to the inclusion of the posting phenomenon under the provision of services. This notwithstanding the statement in *Webb*, where the Court admitted that the employees posted through a transnational provision of manpower could be covered (in some circumstances, not better specified) by the provisions on free movement of workers.[59] *Rush* made it clear that an undertaking providing its services in another Member State could not be denied the right to do so by bringing its own manpower without being subject to any restriction (such as the obligation to obtain work permits).[60] The fact that the three cases were all developed from the "access to market" perspective of the service provider/posting undertaking clearly plays a role in this approach. Still, after the Prologues, the posting of workers as a legal phenomenon appears firmly entrenched in the provision of services. Obviously, this by no means amounts to denying the role played by the political advantage of basing the PWD on the provisions on the free movement of services.[61]

Not less important (though much more short-lived) is the second point. Through the *obiter dicta* in *Seco* and *Rush*, the Court creates a floodgate against the possible abuse of posting in terms of "social dumping". The reference goes to the possibility recognised to Member States to extend their regulations of (minimum[62]) wages and working conditions established either by legislation or by collective labour agreements (without further specification) to "any person who is employed, even temporarily, within their territory". This notwithstanding the country in which the employer is established.[63] Such a reasoning did conceive the posting of workers as *neutral* as regards working conditions, by preserving intact the territorial application of labour law. Put in this context, the list presented by Article 3(1) of the PWD seems to be a limitation of the "extension right" generously granted to host states by the Court of Justice in *Rush*.

The third point is somewhat more linked to the "conception" of the posting phenomenon than to actual (direct) legal effects. This point was only present in *Rush*, where the Court considered posted workers as not having access to the labour market of the host state.[64] With this statement the Court did even more

59 *Webb*, para. 10.

60 *Rush Portuguesa*, para. 12. See Barnard, *The Substantive Law of the EU: The Four Freedoms*, p. 367.

61 See *supra*, p. 131.

62 *Seco*, para. 14 only refers to minimum wages.

63 *Rush Portuguesa*, para. 18. Hellsten, "On the Social Dimension in Posting of Workers", p. 10, describes this as the "extension right".

64 *Rush Portuguesa*, para. 15.

strongly remove posted workers from the scope of free movement of workers. As it has been described, the phenomenon had so far been considered exclusively from the perspective of the posting undertaking wanting to accede the service market of the host state. By focusing on the intrinsically temporary presence of the posted worker, the Court introduces a differentiation with the mobility under the free movement of workers, characterised by a potential permanent staying. With this conception a brand-new ground for workers' mobility in the Community/EU is effectively created by the Court.[65]

The fourth point is more at odds with the final text of the PWD. Both in *Webb* and in *Rush* the Court had showed a certain amount of attention for the specific situation of temporary employment undertakings.[66] Both cases hinted at the possibility to include the workers being posted by these undertakings under the free movement of workers (implying the equal treatment). The PWD on the contrary explicitly covers these workers in its scope.[67] However, Article 3(9) of PWD acknowledges the "difference" of this category.[68]

5.2 DURING THE ADOPTION SAGA AND BEYOND

As it was described in the previous Chapter, after the *Rush* case we enter into the period characterised by negotiations around the PWD. However, before continuing with review of the case law related to posting of workers, it is necessary to give account to another legal evolution. Significantly the reference here is not to the Single European Act, nor to the Maastricht Treaty. Indeed, the attention remains into the field of the case law of the Court of Justice.

It is difficult to overstate the impact of the *Säger*[69] case for the evolution of the freedom to provide services in the EU.[70] Though giving full account of the

---

65 See Sjödin, "Labour Market Regulation as Restrictions. A Developmental Study of ECJ Case Law at the Interface Between Free Movement and Posting of Workers", pp. 27 ff.; Giubboni and Orlandini, *La Libera Circolazione Dei Lavoratori Nell'Unione Europea*, p. 6.

66 *Webb*, para. 10; *Rush Portuguesa*, para. 16–17.

67 Article 1(3)(c) of the PWD: "This Directive shall apply to the extent that the undertakings referred to in paragraph 1 take one of the following transnational measures: [...] (c) being a temporary employment undertaking or placement agency, hire out a worker to a user undertaking established or operating in the territory of a Member State, provided there is an employment relationship between the temporary employment undertaking or placement agency and the worker during the period of posting".

68 "Member States may provide that the undertakings referred to in Article 1(1) must guarantee workers referred to in Article 1(3)(c) the terms and conditions which apply to temporary workers in the Member State where the work is carried out".

69 Case C-76/90, *Criminal proceedings against Manfred Säger and Dennemeyer & Co. Ltd.*, 25 July 1991.

70 See for example C. Barnard and J. Scott, *The Law of the Single European Market: unpacking the Premises* (Oxford: Hart Publishing), 2002, pp. 370 ff.; Barnard, *The Substantive Law of the EU: The Four Freedoms*, pp. 273 ff.; Giubboni and Orlandini, *La Libera Circolazione Dei Lavoratori Nell'Unione Europea*, pp. 6 ff.; Sjödin, "Labour Market Regulation as Restrictions.

case goes beyond the scope of this Chapter, a brief reference to its main argument is necessary. The case has been presented as the turning point from a test of discrimination, to a test of "market access".[71] This has far-reaching consequences on the topic here at stake.

In *Säger* the Court held that the freedom to provide services entails: "not only the elimination of all discrimination against a person providing services on the ground of his nationality *but also* the abolition of any restriction, even if it applies without distinction to national providers of services and to those of other Member States, when it is *liable to prohibit or otherwise impede* the activities of a provider of services established in another Member State where he lawfully provides similar services".[72] These restrictions can then be justified only "by imperative reasons relating to the public interest" as long as their application is proportionate.[73] Finally, the Court identified the *effet utile* of the freedom to provide services in respect to the freedom of establishment, by stating that a "Member State may not make the provision of services in its territory subject to compliance with all the conditions required for establishment and thereby deprive of all practical effectiveness the provisions of the Treaty whose object is, precisely, to guarantee the freedom to provide services".[74]

Thus formulated, the "market access" test was able to tackle all the (even potential) obstacles to the freedom to provide services.[75] The threat posed to host state regulations in the social sphere extended to cover posted workers is apparent. Indeed, it did not take long for the Court to apply the "new" test to cases concerning posted workers.

5.2.1 *VANDER ELST*

The *Vander Elst* case[76] closely resembles *Rush Portuguesa*. As nobody remembers who comes in second place, *Vander Elst* is mostly analysed as a confirmation of the *Rush* case just presented. To a large extent the case is indeed a confirmation, the whole dispute resembling a *déjà-vu*. However, the decision delivered by the Court in front of comparable facts and legislation presents some deviation from *Rush*, which will be stressed in the following paragraphs.

A Developmental Study of ECJ Case Law at the Interface Between Free Movement and Posting of Workers", pp. 39 ff.

71 Barnard, "Employment Rights, Free Movement Under the EC Treaty and the Services Directive", pp. 4 ff.

72 *Säger*, para. 12, emphasis added.

73 Ibid., para. 15.

74 Ibid., para. 13.

75 Giubboni and Orlandini, *La Libera Circolazione Dei Lavoratori Nell'Unione Europea*, p. 7; Barnard, "Employment Rights, Free Movement Under the EC Treaty and the Services Directive", p. 5; S. Deakin, "Social Rights in a Globalized Economy", in *Labour Rights as Human Rights*, ed. Ph. Alston (Oxford: Oxford University Press, 2005), 25–60, p. 46.

76 Case C-43/93, *Raymond Vander Elst v. Office des Migrations Internationales*, 9 August 1994.

Facts

In 1989 the company directed by Mr. Vander Elst was carrying out demolition work involving the recovery of materials in Reims (France). This company was established in Belgium; in order to carry out the work it posted eight workers to France. Among them were four Moroccan workers, who had previously been employed continuously by the company of Mr. Vander Elst for several years. The company had obtained short-stay visas (valid for one month) for these workers.[77]

Following checks from the Labour Inspectorate, Mr. Vander Elst was fined by the Office des Migrations Internationales[78] (International Migration Office, hereinafter OMI). The French authorities considered that the short-stay visa did not enable the Moroccan workers to take up paid employment in France.

Mr. Vander Elst then brought action against this fine in front of the Tribunal Administratif Châlons-sur-Marne. Among other arguments, he claimed that the French provisions constituted a barrier to the freedom to provide services, incompatible with the Treaties.

Questions and observations

The two questions referred to the Court of Justice closely resemble the ones of *Rush*. Essentially the French tribunal asks whether the provisions on the freedom to provide services (Articles 59 and 60 EEC, now Articles 56 and 57 TFEU) allowed the application of the French regulation regarding third-country nationals to an undertaking, established in another Member State, posting its workers in the context of a provision of services.

Notwithstanding the similarity with *Rush*, a number of intervening governments (France, the Netherlands, Germany and the UK) argued that the two cases were different.[79] This in light of the fact that the Portuguese workers employed by Rush Portuguesa were nationals of a Member State, although covered by transitional period, thus justifying a broader protection of the freedom to provide services of their employer. AG Tesauro, having acknowledged the applicability of the *Rush* approach to the case at stake, rejected the arguments in favour of a distinguishing. As it was recalled *supra* for the Prologues, the AG states once again that the legal status of posted workers is "totally irrelevant", when assessing the freedom to provide services of the employer.

The intervening governments had proposed various grounds for refusing the extension of the *Rush* approach to third country nationals. Both the French and German governments maintained that allowing foreign service providers

77 *Vander Elst*, para. 3–4.

78 This institution was in fact the very same involved in the *Rush* case, having being renamed in 1988.

79 See S. Peers, "Indirect Rights for Third-Country Service Providers Confirmed", *European Law Review* 32 (1995): 303–309, p. 304.

to "post" third country nationals could "lead to disruption of the host country's labour market".[80] The AG, by referring to *Rush*, simply repeated that this objection had to be rejected, on the basis that posted workers do not "in any way gain access to the host country's labour market". Furthermore, the intervening governments argued that the regulations restricting the access of third country nationals being posted to a Member State were necessary to protect workers and prevent competition being distorted by a "race to the bottom" in working conditions. Again, *Rush* (in this occasion, together with *Seco*) provides the cornerstone for the answer of the AG. In very brief, AG Tesauro dismisses this objection because A) the "extension right" guarantees the possibility to apply "legislation or collective labour agreements [...] relating to minimum wages, to any person who is employed, even temporarily" in the territory of a Member State; and because B) since the Moroccan workers were employed in Belgium, the application of Belgian wages and working conditions would *already* "exclude any substantial risk of workers being exploited or of competition between undertakings being distorted".[81]

As regards the French provisions at stake, the AG insisted on the "double burden" which was imposed on the service provider, since the Moroccan workers were already employed in another Member State. The company had thus already "followed the legal procedures laid down in the State of establishment for engaging workers" and "born the attendant administrative and financial burdens".[82] The legislation at issue was considered by the AG as putting foreign service providers at disadvantage in competing with national providers and hence causing a (unjustified) restrictive effect on the freedom to provide services.

The decision

The Court largely follows the reasoning proposed by the AG, so that the outcome of *Vander Elst* (as more or less the whole case), does not differ from the one of *Rush Portuguesa*. Not surprisingly the Court finds that the freedom to provide services precludes a Member State to require a service provider established in another Member State to obtain work permits for its workers being posted, notwithstanding the fact that they are third-country nationals. The Court did not refer to the arguments put forward by the intervening government, nor to the reasoning of AG Tesauro in refusing them.

The short summary about *Säeger* presented *supra* comes in handy already in the present case. In *Vander Elst* the Court, for the first time in the context of posting of workers, applies the "market access" test,[83] leaving aside the test

80 Opinion of AG Tesauro in *Vander Elst*, para. 24.
81 Ibid., para. 30.
82 Ibid., para. 17.
83 *Vander Elst*, para. 14: "Article 59 of the Treaty therefore requires not only the elimination, against a person providing services who is established in another Member State, of all

of discrimination applied in the previous cases. Thus, the emphasis is placed on the "restrictive" nature of the French regulation, instead of its (indirectly) discriminatory impact, though the Court "hints" at the discriminatory effect of the *de facto* double imposition, citing *Seco*.[84]

However, the (potentially) far-reaching impact of the "market access" test appears somewhat reduced by the repetition of the "extension right" of *Seco/Rush Portuguesa*. Basically the Court repeats the formula used in *Seco*, to recognise the possibility for a Member State to extend its "legislation, or collective labour agreements entered into by both sides of industry relating to *minimum wages*, to any person who is employed, even temporarily, within their territory, no matter in which country the employer is established; nor does Community law prohibit Member States from enforcing those rules by appropriate means".[85] Indeed, the mention of *minimum* wages seems to imply a step back from the broader recognition of the "extension right" in *Rush Portuguesa*. Reading this passage side by side with the "market access" test just presented suggests that (at least) minimum wages should be *per se* excluded from the "restrictions" tackled by the cited test. In a way, this was consistent with the ongoing discussion around the PWD, which featured "minimum rates of pay" among the list of provisions to be extended to posted workers.[86] That being said, the picture gets more complicated when the Court states that the simple application of Belgian wages and working conditions would exclude the "risk of workers being exploited or of competition between undertakings being distorted".[87] Such a statement does not come from a comparison between wages and working conditions applicable in the two countries interested by the posting. Furthermore, in the same paragraph the Court refers to "the possibility of applying national rules of public policy governing the various aspects of the employment relationship to workers sent temporarily to France". This approach seems at odds with the "extension right" recognised just two paragraphs before, where the extension was by no means limited to "rules of public policy".

Finally, the Court repeats also the statement related to the lack of access of posted workers to the labour market of the host state.[88] The Court seems to focus

discrimination on the ground of his nationality but also the abolition of any restriction, even if it applies without distinction to national providers of services and to those of other Member States, when it is liable to prohibit or otherwise impede the activities of a provider of services established in another Member State where he lawfully provides similar services."

84 Ibid., para. 15. See Ibid., p. 306.

85 *Vander Elst*, para. 23, emphasis added.

86 Article 3(b)(iii) in the first and second draft, Article 3(c) in the final version.

87 *Vander Elst*, para. 25.

88 *Vander Elst*, para. 21: "Workers employed by an undertaking established in one Member State who are temporarily sent to another Member State to provide services do not in any way *seek* access to the labour market in that second State, *if* they return to their country of origin or residence after completion of their work." As a side note, one might stress the slight difference with the *Rush formula*. In *Vander Elst* the Court requires the return to the country of residence as a condition, whereas in *Rush* such a return was simply assumed as something inherent to the

on two conditions to justify this "lack of access", the temporary presence and the fact of being "habitually employed" by the posting undertaking in the state of residence. No further clarification is given on these conditions.[89]

5.2.2 *ARBLADE*

In the *Arblade*[90] case, arising out of another posting operation between France and Belgium, the Court of Justice had to analyse for the first time an actual question directly related to the application of minimum wages to posted workers. This minimum wage was established by an extended collective agreement, thus putting to test the extent of the "extension right" formulated in the *Seco*, *Rush Portuguesa* and *Vander Elst* decisions. Furthermore in this case the Court clarifies the test applied to restriction to provide services, shaping it as a four steps test.[91] Finally, it is important to keep in mind the fact that, even though the case was decided after the adoption of the PWD, the Directive itself was not applicable to the facts at stake, since its transposition period was not yet expired. However, the Directive was invoked in the case by the Belgian government, as a means to interpret "mandatory rules for the provision of minimum protection".[92]

Facts

Two French companies, Arblade & Fils SARL and Sofrage SARL, were carrying out construction works in Belgium. In order to do so, they posted their workers to the Belgian territory. In the context of checks carried out by the Belgian Labour Inspectorate the companies failed to produce a number of social documents requested by the said Inspectorate. The managers of these companies in fact considered that they were not obliged to produce those documents, having complied with the French legislation on the subject matter.

This gave rise to criminal proceedings against the managers of the two companies, M. Jean-Claude Arblade and M. Serge and M. Bernard Leloup. Civil liability was also involved for the two companies.

Following the questions referred by the Tribunal Correctionnel of Huy, the two cases were joined in front of the Court of Justice.

---

posting itself. The difference however does not seem to entail a different consideration of the phenomenon.

89 This lack of clarity was pointed out, by a commentator writing when the decision was delivered, as one of the main problems arising from the decision here at stake. See Peers, "Indirect rights for third-country service providers confirmed", p. 307.

90 Joined Cases C-369/96 and C-376/96, *Criminal proceedings against Jean-Claude Arblade, Arblade & Fils SARL and Bernard Leloup, Serge Leloup, Sofrage SARL*, 23 November 1999.

91 Hellsten refers to this as the "Arblade test"; see Hellsten, "On the Social Dimension in Posting of Workers", pp. 29 ff.

92 *Arblade*, para. 28.

Questions and observations

The questions raised by the Belgian tribunal in the two cases do overlap almost completely. The Court of Justice summarised these questions in three points. All these questions are related to the compatibility of obligations imposed on the service providers by Belgian regulations[93] with the freedom to provide services. The first point refers to the obligation to pay minimum wages fixed by collective agreement (having an *erga omnes* effect in the construction sector) as well as to pay "timbres-intempéries" and "timbres fidélité".[94] The second point analyses the obligation to keep a number of social documents, notably one recalling working regulation, a staff register and an individual account for each worker employed. The third point is a continuation of the second, considering the obligation to keep the cited documents at the residence in the Host State of a natural person acting as agent of the posting undertaking. This, however, in the circumstances provided by the questions, "where that undertaking is already subject, in the Member State in which it is established, to requirements which are comparable as regards their objective and which relate to the same workers and the same periods of activity".[95]

In their observations, the defendants held, among other arguments, that the obligation to pay minimum wages would *per se* deter "undertakings established in Member States which do not have a compulsory minimum wage or in which the amount of the minimum wage is lower than that applicable in Belgium from moving to Belgium since they will be subject to higher costs than they would if they did not move".[96] The Belgian government introduces the PWD into the dispute. By maintaining that the newborn Directive "crystallises the state of Community law in relation to the posting of workers in the framework of the provision of services",[97] the Belgian government suggests that the case at stake should be analysed in the light of the provisions of the Directive. The German, Finnish and Austrian governments, intervening in the procedure, consider that the application of minimum wages (fixed by collective agreements) should be considered as justified.

On the question regarding the application of minimum wages, AG Colomer recognises that *Arblade* is the first case dealing with the obligation for a service provider to pay the minimum wage in force in the host country. On the point the AG identifies two different kinds of minimum wages, industry-wide or nation-wide. However, in the end he considers that both these minimum wages

---

93 The Court, as well as the questions, further specify that these obligations are imposed, *inter alia*, by means of public-order legislation.

94 "Timbres intempéries" being a sum paid to the worker in case of bad weather conditions making the continuation of construction works impossible. "Timbres fidélité" are a sum paid to the worker at the end of the year. Both are indirectly paid by the employer, through a contribution to a specific fund.

95 *Arblade*, para. 27.

96 Reported by AG Colomer in his opinion, para. 30.

97 Ibid., para. 32.

can be applied to posted workers. This however, continues the AG, following a comparison between the wage applicable in the host country and the one applicable in the home country, in order to identify the most favourable disposition. This comparison should take into account the global situation of the worker under the two systems as regards his or her remuneration.[98]

The decision

With the "Arblade test" the Court delivers a coherent position regarding restrictions to the freedom to provide services. The test itself determines the answer to the question summarised before, so it should be presented first. The starting point for the test is the *Säger* formula. However, the formula is further broadened in this case, since the freedom to provide services now not only entails the abolition of any restriction which is liable to prohibit or impede the this freedom, but also of those restrictions liable to "render less advantageous the activities of a provider of services".[99] If the *Säger* formula seemed broad enough to threaten the application of every social regulation to posted workers, the new formulation makes this possibility even more likely. The existence of a restriction puts the test into motion.

The first step introduces the possible justifications for the restriction. The Court considers that "the freedom to provide services, as one of the fundamental principles of the Treaty, may be restricted only by rules justified by *overriding requirements relating to the public interest*".[100] This possibility is subject to three conditions, three more steps for the test. First, the restriction must be "applicable to all persons and undertakings operating in the territory of the State where the service is provided".[101] Second, the interest protected through the restriction must not be already "safeguarded by the rules to which the provider of such a service is subject in the Member State where he is established".[102] Finally, the rule entailing the restriction must be "appropriate for securing the attainment of the objective which they pursue and must not go beyond what is necessary in order to attain it",[103] *i.e.* its application must be *proportionate*.

The referring Tribunal had stressed, by formulating a specific question, that all the provisions at stake in the present case were considered by the Belgian legislator as "public order" legislation. The answer of the Court confirms the primacy of community law upon national legislation. Furthermore, the Court

98 Ibid., para. 77–81.

99 *Arblade*, para. 33.

100 Ibid., para. 34, emphasis added. In this sense the Court, at para. 36, reminds that the protection of workers is one of such overriding reasons.

101 Ibid.

102 Ibid.

103 Ibid., para. 35; in fact, in the wording of the Court, the proportionality test is not limited to restrictions, since it is directed to "the application of national rules to providers of services established in other Member States" in general.

essentially considers this norms of "public order" as whatever "simple" piece of national legislation causing a restriction to one of the fundamental freedoms.[104] In this sense, the concept of "public order legislation" or "*lois de police*" seems to be considered by the Court as a concept pertaining to community law, whose scope cannot thus be determined by the single Member State.[105]

On this background the Court answers the two sets of questions, on the one hand, those questions related to social documents; on the other the application of minimum wages (as well as of "timbres intempéries" and "timbres fidélité"). Dealing with the first set of question, the Court applied the test outlined before. First, the obligation to draw up social documents respecting Belgian regulations is struck down, failing the "equivalence test" (the second step of the test). The Court considers that the (justified) objective of social protection of workers could be safeguarded by "the production of social and labour documents kept by the undertaking in question in accordance with the rules applying in the Member State in which it is established".[106] Second, the Court upheld the obligation to keep social documents available throughout the period of activity, either on site or in an accessible and clearly identified place within the territory of the host state. This on the condition that the keeping of these documents is necessary "in order to enable it effectively to monitor compliance with legislation" of the host State, a test of necessity which is likely to be passed by similar measures. Third, the obligation to keep these documents available on the territory of the host state for a period of five years after the end of the provision of services is considered by the Court as failing the "proportionality test" (fourth step of the test), being possible to achieve the objective of social protection of workers with measures less restrictive of the freedom to provide services.[107]

The reasoning of the Court on the question dealing with the application of minimum wages to posted workers is much more truncated. Indeed, it seems clear that the Court does not apply the "Arblade test" reserved to the other requirements. This notwithstanding the fact that both service providers had observed that the obligation to pay minimum wages would (potentially) subject foreign undertakings to higher costs, thus restricting their freedom to provide services. A situation this which should have been caught in the net of the cited test. The Court refuses this argument, without however giving further clarification

---

104 Ibid., para 31. See M. Fallon, "Note sur CJCE 23 novembre 1999, Arblade", *Revue Critique de Droit International Privé* 89, no. 4 (2000): 728–737, p. 729; S. Francq, "Note sur CJCE 23 novembre 1999, Arblade", *Revue du Droit des Étrangers*, no. 106 (1999): 789–792, pp. 790–791.

105 Fallon, "Note sur CJCE 23 novembre 1999, Arblade", pp. 730–731.

106 *Arblade*, para 80. The Court also (somewhat superfluously) specifies that this is valid only inasmuch the obligations in the home state are comparable with the ones of the host state.

107 *Arblade*, para. 76–78.

as to whether the obligation could be considered as a restriction or not.[108] The reasoning on this point is in fact limited to the repetition of the formula used in *Seco* and *Vander Elst*, simply allowing Member States to extend "to any person who is employed, even temporarily, within their territory", minimum wages established by collective agreements or legislation.[109] The only requirement is that "those provisions must be sufficiently precise and accessible that they do not render it impossible or excessively difficult in practice for such an employer to determine the obligations with which he is required to comply".[110] Interestingly, a different fate awaited the provision on "timbres intempéries" and "timbres fidélité", which are considered in the light of the "Arblade test". This however after having decided that these entitlements were not part of the remuneration.[111] Thus, the Court finds that the payment of "timbres intempéries" and "timbres fidélité" cannot pass the "equivalence test", if the companies are already subject to " to obligations which are essentially comparable, as regards their objective of safeguarding the interests of workers, and which relate to the same workers and the same periods of activity".[112]

In a way, the different consideration of minimum wages can be read, as for the repetition of the *Seco* formula in *Vander Elst*, as consistent with the PWD. Though not applicable to the facts at stake, the Directive could have played a role in the decision,[113] a role which is made even more apparent by the fact that the "Arblade test" is not applied (without any explanation for this non-application) to the issue of minimum wages.

5.2.3 *MAZZOLENI*

"Once again unto the breach", the *Mazzoleni*[114] case brings us back to the border between France and Belgium, which has been incredibly productive in terms of legal disputes regarding posting of workers. The PWD is still not applicable to

108 See D. Martin, "Comments on Florus Ariël Wijsenbeek (Case C-378/97 of 21 September 1999) and Arblade (Joined Cases C-369/96 and C-376/96 of 23 November 1999", *European Journal of Migration and Law* 2, no. September 1999 (2000): 101–107, p. 106.

109 *Arblade*, para. 41.

110 *Arblade*, para. 43. Sjodin argues that this requirement was only dictated by the criminal nature of the proceedings against the managers of the companies. See Sjödin, "Labour Market Regulation as Restrictions. A Developmental Study of ECJ Case Law at the Interface Between Free Movement and Posting of Workers", p. 47.

111 A simple logical argument was applied here: since these entitlements were actually calculated as a percentage of the remuneration, they could not be considered as a part of the remuneration itself.

112 *Arblade*, para. 53–54. The equivalence test is left to the national court.

113 See on the role of legislation in this sense C. Kilpatrick, "Internal Market Architecture and the Accommodation of Labour Rights: As Good as It Gets?", *European Journal of Social Law* 1 (2012): 1–26, pp. 6 ff.

114 Case C-165/98, *Criminal proceedings against André Mazzoleni and Inter Surveillance Assistance SARL*, 15 March 2001.

the facts at stake, although the AG in his Opinion proposed to use the Directive as a tool to interpret the freedom to provide services. The peculiarity, at least at a superficial analysis, of *Mazzoleni* is that for the first time five employees among the actual posted workers were parties in the dispute. Moreover, if *Arblade* showed a high degree of compatibility between the solution delivered by the Court of Justice and the newly adopted Directive, the case here at stake seems to tell a somewhat different story.

Facts

The private security company Inter Surveillance Assistance SARL (hereinafter "ISA"), incorporated in France, employed 13 workers at a shopping mall located in Belgium. These workers were employed as security guards for the shopping mall, though some among them were not employed full-time in the Belgian territory.

A check carried out by the Belgian Social Law Inspectorate showed that the wage of ISA workers was lower than the minimum wage set by the Belgian collective agreement for the sector of private security services, extended by Royal Decree to all the undertakings operating in the sector.

The respect of these norms being covered by criminal sanctions, proceedings were brought against Mr. Mazzoleni (manager of ISA) and the company itself. Five workers also intervened in the proceeding to claim civil damages. ISA maintained that it was not required to comply with Belgian minimum wages, and that since its workers were employed in Belgium only for a fraction of their working-time they fell outside the scope of posting of workers. The Tribunal Correctionnel d'Arlon thus referred two questions to the Court of Justice.

Questions and observations

The first question raised by the Belgian Tribunal refers directly to the PWD. With this question, the Tribunal Correctionnel asks whether or not "part-time" posting is covered by the provisions of the PWD, particularly in connection with the situation of frontier workers. This question, as it will soon be clear, is the least important for the case.

The second question is directly related to minimum wages. Essentially this question seeks to "ascertain whether an undertaking established in a frontier region, some of whose employees may be required to perform, on a part-time basis and for *brief periods*, a part of their services in the adjacent territory of a Member State other than that in which the undertaking is established, is required to comply with the host Member State's national rules on minimum wages *where the workers enjoy comparable overall protection in the Member State of establishment although the minimum wage there is lower*".[115] The reference to the

[115] *Mazzoleni*, para. 19, emphasis added.

"overall protection" implies taking into account the global economical situation of the worker, thus including social and fiscal contributions and so on.

Intervening in the procedure, the governments of France, Germany and the Netherlands argue against the admissibility of the first question. They consider that the Directive could not provide individual rights, as the implementation period was not yet expired.[116] Furthermore, on the second question, all the intervening governments[117] as well as the Commission, maintain that the comparison between level of "protection" should only take into account the individual elements. Hence, the Belgian (gross) minimum wage could only be compared with the (gross) French one, refusing the concept of "overall protection" put forward by the posting undertaking.[118] AG Alber, in his opinion, concurs with this position. Finally, as the question of the duration of the posting was also introduced by the second question ("brief periods"), all the parties which had submitted observations[119] are adamant in defending the compromise just reached with the PWD. Thus they clearly argue in favour of the irrelevance of the short duration of the posting for the application of the Directive.[120]

Contrary to the position of France, Germany and the Netherlands, AG Alber suggests the Court to consider admissible the first question. This in light of the obligation to interpret national law "in such a way as to be compatible with the relevant directives".[121] As for the question of the application of minimum wages the AG goes on to apply the "Arblade test" to (the application of) minimum wages. Indeed, the AG considers that the extension of minimum wages to posted workers can by itself represent a restriction of the freedom to provide services.[122] The first and second step of the test are quickly considered as positively passed, as the application serves the interest of workers' protection (overriding requirement relating to public interest), and it's applied in a non-discriminatory way.[123] It is in analysing the proportionality of the Belgian measure that the AG had to evaluate the question of the "overall position" (as opposed to the comparison between individual elements) of the workers as well as the relevance of the length of posting. As it was stated before, the AG concurs with the intervening governments, as

116 Opinion of AG Alber in *Mazzoleni*, para. 10. The Belgian government, on the other hand, states that the freedom to provide services had to be examined "in the light of the directive"; Ibid., para. 11.

117 Austria, Belgium, France, Germany and The Netherlands.

118 Opinion of AG Alber in *Mazzoleni*, para. 7: "the employer also argues that the employees concerned would have enjoyed protection under the French system the same as or substantially comparable to that provided for under the Belgian system. French minimum wages might be lower, but the French taxation system was more favourable. The defendant argues that regard must be had to the *overall position*" (emphasis added).

119 Austria, Belgium, France, Germany, The Netherlands and the Commission.

120 Opinion of AG Alber in *Mazzoleni*, para. 56–62.

121 Ibid., para. 12.

122 Ibid., para. 18. The AG also stressed the fact that the previous case law, which allowed the application of minimum wages to posted workers (*Seco*, *Rush Portuguesa*, *Vander Elst*), had often analysed the question only in some *obiter dictum*; Ibid., para. 19.

123 Opinion of AG Alber in *Mazzoleni*, para. 31–32.

well as with the Commission, in opting for a comparison between individual elements, notably the gross minimum wage set by Belgian and French regulations. This under the point of view of the test of equivalence, in order to ensure that the interest at stake (protection of workers) was not already safeguarded by the rules of the home state. The question of the length of the posting comes into consideration in the fourth step.[124] In order to ascertain the relevance (or lack thereof) of the duration of the posting, the AG turns to the PWD. As it should be clear from the previous Chapter[125] the final compromise on the Directive had opted for the "zero day" option, meaning that no temporal threshold was in principle recognised for the application of the conditions included in the list of Article 3(1). Notwithstanding this clear choice, the AG considers that the presence of *exceptions* to this principle[126] clearly showed "the intention of the Community legislature that such an option be available". Thus, the duration of posting was to be taken into account in order to evaluate the proportionality of the measure here at stake.[127]

The decision

The Court does not follow the AG as regards the first question. It rapidly considers that since the implementation period was not yet expired at the time of the facts "it is not necessary to interpret its provisions for the purposes of the main proceedings".[128] The Court also discards the observation made by the Belgian government, arguing in favour of interpreting the treaty provisions on the freedom to provide services in the light of the PWD: in the whole case the Directive is mentioned only to deny the admissibility of the first question.

Answering to the second question, the Court refers to the *Säger* formula, expanding it to include measures liable to render "less attractive" the provision of services by an undertaking established in another Member State.[129] In this sense, a national measure is liable to "prohibit, impede or render less attractive the provision of services to the extent that it involves expenses and additional administrative and economic burdens". Having included "expenses" into the concept of restrictions, the Court prepares the stage to apply the "Arblade test", reminding that the protection of workers constitutes an overriding reason relating to the public interest.[130]

As in *Vander Elst* and *Arblade*, the *Säger* formula is followed by the "extension right". Once again the Court states that Community law does not preclude the

124 "Whether the measure goes beyond what is necessary in order to attain its objective", Opinion of AG Alber in *Mazzoleni*, para. 54.

125 See *supra*, p. 125.

126 See Articles 3(2), 3(3) and 3(4) of the PWD.

127 Opinion of AG Alber in *Mazzoleni*, para. 73.

128 *Mazzoleni*, para. 17.

129 Ibid., para. 22–24.

130 Ibid., para. 27.

extension of minimum wages to posted workers,[131] though the reference to *Rush Portuguesa* is finally left behind. The irony here is that it takes the Court no more than two paragraphs to deny this statement. By affirming that "there may be circumstances in which the application of such rules would be neither necessary nor proportionate to the objective pursued, namely the protection of the workers concerned"[132] the Court makes it clear that in some situation Community law may preclude the extension of minimum wages to posted workers.

For the rest, the Court applies the Arblade test as proposed by the AG. This, however, with an important deviation from the reasoning of the AG. In evaluating the *necessity* of the measure for the protection of workers, the Court, contrary to the position maintained by the AG, as well as by the intervening governments and by the Commission, decides in favour of the comparison between the "global" situation of posted workers under host state regulations. In particular, it states that "minimum wages" must be compared "in relation to remuneration, taxation and social security contributions".[133] The Court then adds further elements to be considered while evaluating the proportionality of the measure. First, the possibility that the application of the minimum wages of the host state may result in "an additional, disproportionate administrative burden". Second, the Court raises a warning which is important to keep in mind proceeding with the case law on posting of workers. The judges of Luxembourg refer to the risk that applying "different levels of wages to employees who are all attached to the same operational base and carry out identical work" could "result in tension between employees and even threaten the cohesion of the collective labour agreements that are applicable in the Member State of establishment".[134] Finally, the proportionality test[135] should also take into account the "duration of the provision of services".[136] Here the Court follows the reasoning of the AG. As recalled before, this seems to be at odds with the choice made in the PWD, with the "zero day option", which in fact was also brought to the attention of the Court by the intervening governments and by the Commission as well.

In the end, the Court sends the case back to the national judge, which will have to apply the test just outlined in order to ascertain which minimum wage should be applied to the workers of ISA. The choice in favour of the most favourable condition *in concreto*, meaning the comparison between the "global" position of workers under the two set of measures safeguards the protection of workers, comes at the expense of clarity. Indeed, the evaluation of the effects of taxation and social contributions would make it difficult for the employer to know in

131 Ibid., para. 28.
132 Ibid., para. 30.
133 Ibid., para. 35.
134 Ibid., para. 36.
135 It is worth remembering that the Court did not carry out the test, leaving it to the national Court to evaluate which minimum wage should be applied in the end.
136 *Mazzoleni*, para. 38.

advance which treatment must be applied to posted workers.[137] Once again, this is quite puzzling in the light of the choice made in the PWD; also, the Court itself reminded that the "additional, disproportionate administrative burden" which may be caused by the application of host state regulations dealing with minimum wages must be taken into account in order to evaluate the proportionality of this measures. By opting for the "global" comparison in the case at stake, the Court does not help in easing this burden.[138]

5.2.4 *FINALARTE*

The very broad formula inaugurated with *Säger*, when applied to posting of workers, had (has) the potential to put in question a large part of (if not every) host state regulation covering posted workers. To a certain extent, the questions originating the *Finalarte* case[139] show this potential in action. Provided that the PWD was not applicable to the facts at stake, the German Court, as it will be explained soon, questions the German law on posting of workers because of its aim of combating "unfair competitive conditions resulting from low pay competition in Europe" and "wage and social dumping".[140] Interestingly, the application of minimum wages is not among the subjects of *Finalarte*, making it clear that the referring court contested that a competition based on lower wages and working conditions could be considered as "unfair competition".[141]

Facts

Nine different actions were joined in the *Finalarte* case. All those actions regarded undertakings established in Member States other than the Federal Republic of Germany (Portugal and the United Kingdom) who posted workers to Germany during the year 1997, in the context of service provisions for construction works. These undertakings were thus subject to the scheme of paid

---

137 See P. Rodière, "Droit social. coordination des droits nationaux, loi applicable, compétence juridictionnelle", *Revue trimestrielle de droit europeen* 39, no. 3 (2003): 529–552, p. 544; E. Pataut, "Note Sur CJCE 15 Mars 2001, Mazzoleni", *Revue Critique de Droit International Privé*, 90, no. 3 (2001): 503–512, p. 506.

138 This position seems also to be at odds with the remark previously recalled about the "tension" between employees which could be caused by the application of different wages and working conditions in the same establishment. In itself, the "global comparison" seems to make this differences more likely to happen.

139 Joined Cases C-49/98, C-50/09, C-52/09 to C-54/98 and C-68/98 to C-71/98, *Finalarte Sociedade de Costrução Civil L.da and others v. Urlaubs und Lonhausgleichskasse der Bauwirtschaft*, 25 October 2001.

140 As reported by AG Mischo in his Opinion on *Finalarte*.

141 Opinion of AG Mischo in *Finalarte*, para. 33. On this point see also Hellsten, "On the Social Dimension in Posting of Workers", p. 12 and pp. 25 ff., where the argument put forward by the German court is labelled as "neo- or ultra liberal".

leave for the construction sector (hereinafter "the scheme"), governed by the Law on minimum holiday entitlement for workers (Mindesturlaubsgesetz für Arbeitnehmer – Bundesurlaubsgesetz) and by the collective agreement for the construction sector. In practice, the posting employers had to contribute to the Fund for paid leave for the construction sector (hereinafter, "the fund"), who in its turn would provide payment of holiday pay to the workers. Under this scheme, three main differences were identified between the treatment of national undertakings and service providers from a different Member State. First, national undertakings would pay themselves the holiday pay to their workers, being then entitled to claim reimbursement from the Fund. Second, the posting employers had to disclose more information to the Fund than national undertakings. Third, the definition of "business" applied to posting employers was different from the one applicable to national undertakings; for posting employers, it is the activity of their workers which defines their belonging to the scheme, whereas for national undertakings the criterion was the "prevalent activity" of the undertaking.

Some of the undertakings concerned by the case were acting in front of the Arbeitsgericht (Labour Court) Wiesbaden claiming the non-existence of their obligation towards the Fund, whereas others were acting as defendants, having received demands from the Fund to pay the contributions and to provide the information required for their workers being posted in the German territory.

Questions and observations

With its questions, the tribunal of Wiesbaden asks to the Court of Justice to state about the compatibility of the cited scheme with the freedom to provide services *and* the free movement of workers. In particular, the tribunal points out, first, the fact that the German provision grants an annual leave exceeding the minimum set by Council Directive 93/104/EC concerning certain aspects of the organisation of working time. Second, the German tribunal asks whether the differences of treatment between national undertakings and service providers established in another Member State, listed *supra*,[142] should be considered as incompatible with the freedom to provide services *and* the free movement of workers. Third, the national judge asks the Court to clarify the impact of the PWD on the previous questions.

In referring also to the free movement of workers, the tribunal of Wiesbaden anticipates the reasoning proposed by the posting undertakings beyond the Court of Justice. In brief, since the German regulations represent a cost for the service provider, the measure has the effect of rendering the provision of services less attractive, thus restricting the freedom to provide services. Hence, the employer

[142] 1) The fact that the Fund provides direct reimbursement to posted workers; 2) the broader obligation of information disclosure for the posting undertaking; 3) the different definition of "business" applied to service providers established in Member States other than the Federal Republic of Germany.

would be prevented from carrying out activities in Germany. This would cause a *loss of chances* for the workers, entailing a restriction of their freedom of movement.

The AG considers that the application of the law of the host state to the service provider is the "general principle", save for the exceptions laid down in the case law of the Court of Justice.[143] This on the basis of the recognition that, allowing service providers to "circumvent the level of social protection existing in the host Member State, that protection would, without doubt, ultimately being jeopardised because employers established in that Member State would seek a reduction of the level of protection in order to be able to compete on equal terms with undertakings providing services".[144] The AG points out that the Treaties do not place the principle of free competition on a higher footing than other objectives, notably the improvement of working conditions and of standard of living of workers, in a process of "harmonisation while the improvement is being maintained".[145] Under this light, the AG then considers the various questions referred. He applies the Arblade test to the German scheme, finding it compatible with the freedom to provide services, to the extent that an "identical or higher level of protection" is not afforded in the country of origin.[146] The same test is applied to the other differences of treatment between national undertakings and service providers established in another Member State. Thus, the direct reimbursement is considered as proportionate,[147] the obligation to provide additional information is sent back to the national court for the test of proportionality,[148] while the different definition of "business" is considered as discriminatory.[149] Finally, on the question relating to the Working Time Directive the AG refers to the minimum character of the Directive, suggesting to uphold the German regulation, providing a longer annual leave.[150] He also finds that the PWD to be irrelevant for the case at stake.[151]

The decision

Analysing the reference to the free movement of workers the Court quickly discards the argument put forward by the referring tribunal (as well as by the posting undertakings). This is done as quickly as a reference to the previous case law postulating the lack of access of the posted worker to the labour market of

---

143 Opinion of AG Mischo in *Finalarte*, para. 43.

144 Ibid., para. 42. The AG goes on to state that "the Treaty does not confer on undertakings the right when carrying out activities in another Member State to bring with them not only their staff and equipment but also the laws of their country of origin", para. 44.

145 Ibid., para. 50.

146 Ibid., para. 127.

147 Ibid., para. 171.

148 Ibid., para. 195.

149 Ibid., para. 214.

150 Ibid., para. 152.

151 Ibid., para. 226.

the host state.[152] The same sudden fate awaits the question related to the role of the PWD for the case at stake. The Court simply reminds that the Directive in question is not applicable, the time-limit for the implementation not having expired at the time of the facts.[153] Thus, the remaining questions are examined in the light of the provisions of the Treaty protecting the free movement of services.

The Court sets the stage for the analysis by summarising its case law on posting of workers.[154] It should be noted that the (usual) formula, stating that "a Member State may not make the provision of services in its territory subject to compliance with all the conditions required for establishment and thereby deprive the provisions of the Treaty",[155] seems at odds with the remarks of the AG concerning the risk of jeopardising the social protection of the host state, which would be entailed by the possibility for service providers to circumvent the social protection. While the AG argues in favour of the complete application (subject to the Arblade test) of social regulations, the Court seems to identify the added value of the provision of services precisely in the non-application of the full scale of these regulations to the service provider. Apart from the Opinion however, the case is nothing but a confirmation of the previous case law on the issue.[156]

The Court also ignores the reference of the German tribunal and of the posting undertakings to the "aims" of the German law on posting of workers,[157] stating that such "aims" are not conclusive. The actual content of the law has to be analysed objectively.[158]

In answering the first question, *i.e.* the one directly related to the applicability of the scheme for holiday pay, the Court upholds the German measure on a two-fold conditions, which will have to be verified by the national court. First, the national court will have to verify that the workers do not enjoy an *essentially similar* level of protection under the law of the Member State where their employer is established, so that the application of the national rules of the first Member State confers a genuine benefit on the workers concerned, which *significantly adds* to their social protection".[159] Second, the application of those rules must be proportionate to the interest pursued. In particular, the Court considers that "the national court should balance the administrative and economic burdens that the

152 *Finalarte*, para. 22. As noted by Martin, with this reply the Court avoids the problem of addressing the potential conflict between the rights granted by the Treaty to posted workers and to their employer. See D. Martin, "Comments on Gottardo (Case C-55/00 of 15 January 2002), Finalarte (Case C-49/98 of 25 October 2001) and Portugaia Costruções (Case C-164/99 of 24 January)", *Eur. J. Migration & L.* 4, no. 3 (August 2002): 369–375, p. 374.

153 Ibid., para. 25.

154 Ibid., para. 28–33.

155 Ibid., para. 29.

156 See Rodière, "Droit social. coordination des droits nationaux, loi applicable, compétence juridictionnelle", p. 546.

157 Cited *supra*, combating "unfair competitive conditions resulting from low pay competition in Europe" and "wage and social dumping".

158 *Finalarte*, para. 40–42.

159 Ibid., para. 53, emphasis added.

rules impose on providers of services against the increased social protection that they confer on workers compared with that guaranteed by the law of the Member State where their employer is established".[160] On the first condition one cannot fail to notice another discrepancy with the Opinion of the AG, as the cited Opinion refers to "an identical or higher level of protection".[161] The Court, requiring for the application of host state regulations that the workers do not enjoy an "essentially similar level of protection" and, furthermore, requiring that these regulations "significantly" add to the social protection of posted workers in respect of home state rules clearly opts for a stricter test. For the remaining questions the Court follows closely the solutions proposed by the AG summarised *supra*.[162]

5.2.5 *PORTUGAIA COSTRUÇÕES*

The case of *Portugaia Costruções*[163] is the last case presented here which was decided before the expiring of the transposition period. In itself this case has been analysed as a simple confirmation of the preceding case law.[164] This is certainly true for the first question (and for the answer given to that question). On the other hand, the answer given to the second question does introduce a new element for the evaluation of the "extension right", *i.e.* the application of minimum wages to posted workers. In fact, the question touches upon the very definition of minimum wage. What is more, in this case the Court of Justice for the first time is presented with the specificities of a system of collective bargaining. Much unfortunately, the analysis of this issue seems somewhat superficial, both in the Opinion of AG Mischo and in the decision delivered by the Court.

Facts

During the year 1997, Portugaia Costruções, an undertaking established in Portugal, carried out construction works in Germany. To do so, the undertaking posted several of its employees to Germany.

Following a check on the building site, the Employment Office of Tauberbischofsheim found that Portugaia was paying these posted workers a wage lower than the minimum wage. Under the German law on posting of workers (Arbeitnehmerentsendegesetz, or AEntG) these workers were covered by the collective agreement for the construction sector, declared universally binding.

---

160 Ibid., para. 50.

161 Opinion of AG Mischo in *Finalarte*, para. 227.

162 See p. 171.

163 Case C-164/99, *Portugaia Costruções L.da*, 24 January 2002.

164 *E.g.* Martin, "Comments on Gottardo (Case C-55/00 of 15 January 2002), Finalarte (Case C-49/98 of 25 October 2001) and Portugaia Costruções (Case C-164/99 of 24 January)", p. 374; Rodière, "Droit social. coordination des droits nationaux, loi applicable, compétence juridictionnelle", p. 547.

This collective agreement contained the minimum wage applicable to the sector and hence to the workers posted by Portugaia.[165]

The Employment Office thus ordered the payment of the difference between the hourly wage set by the collective agreement and the hourly wage actually paid by the posting undertaking. Portugaia appealed against this decision in front of the Amtsgericht (Local Court) of Tauberbischofsheim. In the context of this proceeding, the German judge referred two questions to the Court of Justice for a preliminary ruling.

Questions and observations

With the first question, the German court asks essentially if the German regulation is compatible with either the PWD or the provisions on the freedom to provide services. This in particular in light of the aims of the AEntG, already cited *supra*.[166]

The second question in its turn focuses on a specificity of the German "hierarchy" of collective agreements. Provided that a company agreement can derogate from a sectoral one,[167] the national judge asks the Court of Justice whether such a situation amounts to an unjustified restriction on the freedom to provide services. In the question referred it is highlighted that an employer established in a different Member State would *at least in fact* not be able to obtain such a derogation.[168] In sum, the German court asks the Court of Justice if the minimum wage established in the sectoral collective agreement can still be considered as a *minimum* in view of the possibility to derogate *in pejus* from it.

The government of The Netherlands, intervening in the procedure, submits that the PWD is not relevant for the case at stake, as made abundantly clear by the previous case law of the Court. The AG concurs with this analysis. In general, on the first question, the intervening governments (France, The Netherlands, Germany and Portugal) as well as the Commission consider that the aim put forward by the legislator should not be considered as conclusive to infer the existence of a restriction (or the lack of justification for a restriction); they also agree in suggesting the Court to upheld the German regulation. The posting undertaking argues that the minimum wage established for the construction sector is not justified by an overriding requirement of public interest. The reason for this is indeed interesting: Portugaia submits that the minimum wage is not justified because other sectors of industry (notably, steel industry and agriculture) are characterised by a lower level of minimum wages.[169] The AG however repeats his own Opinion formulated in the

165 *Portugaia Costruções*, para. 3–11.
166 *I.e.* the prevention of social dumping, the protection of the construction industry and the reduction of national unemployment.
167 For an overview see Weiss and Schmidt, "Germany – Collective Labour Law", pp. 180 ff.
168 *Portugaia Costruções*, para. 13, emphasis added.
169 Reported by AG Mischo in his Opinion, para. 29.

Finalarte case, stating that it is up to the Member State to determine the level of social protection to accord to their workers.[170]

Turning to the second question, the German government submits that such a question should be considered as inadmissible because of its purely hypothetical nature. Furthermore, it adds that the number of company-level agreements derogating *in pejus* from the sectoral one is very low, if it is even possible to identify any such agreement.[171] On the other hand, the French and Netherlands governments and the Commission consider such a situation as discriminatory and unjustified.[172] The AG agrees with this position.

The decision

The answer given by the Court to the first question is essentially a repetition of its previous case law, and in particular of *Finalarte*. The German regulation is analysed "objectively" and not from the angle of its explicit aims. Considered from the perspective of the case law analysed so far, it comes as no surprise that the Court ultimately upholds the German law on posting of workers.

The answer to the second question however undermines the usefulness of the first. Indeed, the Court considers that "the fact that, in concluding a collective agreement specific to one undertaking, a domestic employer can pay wages lower than the minimum wage laid down in a collective agreement declared to be generally applicable, whilst an employer established in another Member State cannot do so, constitutes an unjustified restriction on the freedom to provide services".[173]

The reasoning of the Court on the point is somewhat truncated, in comparison with the one proposed by the AG. Although the outcome is identical, it is worth focusing on an aspect which is ignored by the Court in the decision. Already in the question referred by the German court, it was stressed that it was impossible "*at least in fact*" for the posting employer to conclude a company agreement derogating from the sectoral one.[174] The AG recalls this in his Opinion, by pointing out that the posting undertaking "does not have any means *at least in practice* of avoiding the obligation to pay the minimum wage to its posted workers".[175] The same expression ("at least in fact") is present in the answer suggested to the Court. Looking at the decision on the second question from this perspective, it seems that the Court (and the AG) applied a slightly

170 Opinion of AG Mischo in *Portugaia Costruções*, para. 44.

171 Data from 2002 showed that only 2% of undertakings in the former West Germany and 4% in the former East Germany were covered by a company-wide agreement. See W. Ochel, "Decentralising Wage Bargaining in Germany – a Way to Increase Employment?", *CESifo Working Paper* 1069 (2003): 1–28, p. 7.

172 As reported by AG Mischo in his Opinion, para. 65.

173 *Portugaia Costruções*, para. 35.

174 Ibid., para. 13, emphasis added.

175 Opinion of AG Mischo in *Portugaia Costruções*, para. 76.

different standard in evaluating the restriction. On the one hand, the possibility for the German employer to conclude a company-wide agreement derogating from the sectoral minimum wage is considered strictly *de jure*, from the point of view of what is theoretically possible. This is made clear by the fact that the Court refuses the argument put forward by the German government that this possibility was *in practice* negligible, as a very low number of undertakings were in fact covered by a company agreement.[176] On the other hand, the impossibility for the posting undertaking to enjoy the same treatment is considered *de facto*, thus from the point of view of the objective difficulty for a foreign undertaking to conclude a company-wide collective agreement valid under the German system. Neither the Court nor the AG seems to consider if this possibility would have been theoretically open to the posting undertaking. This is the most important "impression" left by the first case dealing with an issue strictly connected with a system of industrial relations.

5.2.6 THE PRE-DIRECTIVE CASE LAW AND THE PWD

The case law analysed so far represents the framework for the interpretation of the posting phenomenon developed by the Court of Justice before the coming into force of the Posting of Workers Directive (16 December 1999). The Court repeatedly refused to take into account the PWD in the case law preceding the expiring of the transposition period.[177] Still, it is evident that this framework plays a role in the history "after the PWD". On the one hand, the Court had to decide upon issues which would then be regulated by the PWD. In this sense the corpus of precedents will influence the future decisions on similar issues, notwithstanding the novelty represented by the PWD. On the other hand, the compromise represented by the PWD was reached (as it was analysed in the previous Chapter) at the price of excluding some topics while formulating confusing provisions on others. The Court does play a major role in filling these gaps and/or "opening" these black-boxes.

The conceptual framework

Save for a brief afterthought in *Webb*,[178] the Court never really deviated from its "vision" of the posting phenomenon. In particular, posting of workers is consistently analysed under the freedom to provide services.

---

[176] *Portugaia Costruções*, para. 72. The data available, recalled *supra* (p. 175) also show that the argument of the German government was in fact well founded.

[177] 16 December 1999.

[178] *Webb*, para. 10: "[...] employees of agencies for the supply of manpower may in certain circumstances be covered by provisions of Articles 48 to 51 of the Treaty and the Community regulations adopted in implementation thereof [...]".

The fundamental concept here is first introduced with *Rush Portuguesa*, where the Court distinguishes posting from the free movement of workers in view of their lack of access to the labour market of the host state.[179] The Court did not find it necessary to further explain this distinction when asked, in *Finalarte*, to decide *also* on the basis of the free movement of workers, contenting itself of repeating the statement of *Rush*.[180]

In this sense, the final text of the PWD is coherent with the case law of the Court, being based exclusively on the provision on free movement of services. This however left undecided the issue about whether the posted workers themselves could claim the rights granted by the free movement of workers.

The scope

The Court never had the occasion to further explore the defining elements of posted workers. The formula just cited refers to the continuing employment relationship with the posting undertaking and the presence for a limited time ("temporarily") in the host state. As in the PWD, no "ceiling", *i.e.* maximum amount of time, was identified. At the same time, no threshold period was recognised for the workers to be considered as posted. Frontier workers, as in the *Mazzoleni* case, were hence potentially included in the scope of the posting phenomenon. This however not without a caveat, since the Court considers that the actual "duration of the provision of services" should be taken into account to examine the proportionality of the application of host state regulations to posted workers.[181] Though the PWD allows for some exceptions,[182] the (difficultly reached) general principle is the one of application of the whole Directive from "day one". No proportionality is mentioned for this application.

Another aspect was only analysed in *Webb*. There, temporary work agencies were identified as a special kind of service ("peculiar nature"), and hence potentially deserving a different treatment.[183] As recalled *supra*, the workers employed by these agencies could "in certain circumstances" be covered by the provisions on the free movement of workers.[184] Also in *Rush Portuguesa* the Court stated, in an obiter dictum, that "an undertaking engaged in the making available of labour, although a supplier of services within the meaning of the Treaty, carries on activities which are specifically intended to enable workers to gain access to

---

179 *Rush Portuguesa*, para. 15: "such workers return to their country of origin after the completion of their work without at any time gaining access to the labour market of the host Member State". The same statement was then repeated in *Vander Elst*, para. 21.

180 *Finalarte*, para. 22–23.

181 Ibid., para. 38.

182 Article 3(3) to 3(5).

183 *Webb*, para. 18.

184 Ibid., para. 10.

the labour market of the host Member State".[185] In a way this peculiar nature is acknowledged by the PWD. Indeed the final text of the Directive includes under its scope workers posted by a temporary work agency,[186] while Article 3(9) allows Member States to apply to posted workers covered by Article 1(3)(c) "the terms and conditions which apply to temporary workers in the Member State where the work is carried out".

Minimum wages

Article 3(1)(c) of the PWD includes "minimum rates of pay" in the hard nucleus of provisions which should be extended to posted workers. The only condition for the extension of minimum wages to posted workers is that these have to be established either by legislation or by collective agreements "declared universally applicable" or included within the meaning of Article 3(8).[187]

The Court in its turn has consistently upheld the "extension right" of minimum wages to posted workers. From *Seco*,[188] to (although with a broader formula) *Rush*,[189] to *Vander Elst*,[190] and so on for the following decisions,[191] minimum wages have escaped the fate reserved to other measures. Indeed, they were not analysed through the lenses of the restriction/justification test. The only exception is the *Mazzoleni* case,[192] which however was characterised by a rather specific situation of an undertaking established in a frontier region, posting its workers only for fractions of their working time. A condition to be respected by the minimum wage in order to be applicable to the posting employer was identified in *Arblade*.[193] However this condition, namely "be sufficiently precise and accessible" as to "not render it impossible or excessively difficult in practice for such an employer to determine the obligations with which he is required to

185 *Rush Portuguesa*, para. 16. In that occasion, the statement meant that those suppliers could be covered by the limitations provided by the Accession Treaty on the free movement of workers. This may be interpreted as a preference of the Court to consider employees sent in the context of a "pure provision of manpower" as covered by the provisions on the free movement of workers.

186 Article 1(3)(c): "This Directive shall apply to the extent that the undertakings referred to in paragraph 1 take one of the following transnational measures: [...] being a temporary employment undertaking or placement agency, hire out a worker to a user undertaking established or operating in the territory of a Member State, provided there is an employment relationship between the temporary employment undertaking or placement agency and the worker during the period of posting."

187 "Collective agreements or arbitration awards which are generally applicable to all similar undertakings in the geographical area and in the profession or industry concerned, and/or collective agreements which have been concluded by the most representative employers' and labour organizations at national level and which are applied throughout national territory."

188 Para. 14.

189 Para. 18.

190 Para. 23.

191 *Arblade*, para. 41; *Portugaia Costruções*, para. 21.

192 Where the Court left it to the national court to apply the proportionality test. See *Mazzoleni*, para. 28–31.

193 Para. 43.

comply", should probably be read in connection with the criminal prosecution at stake in *Arblade*.

In *Portugaia Costruções* the Court had to analyse a question relating to collective agreements setting the minimum wage. As it was recalled *supra*, the PWD only refers to the "universal" or "general" applicability of the collective agreement as a condition for the application of the minimum wage to posted workers. In *Portugaia* however, the Court does not analyse the issue from the angle of the applicability. On the contrary, the Court seems to offer a different *definition* of minimum wage. As it is evident from the decision, the Court defines the minimum wage as that wage from which it is *de jure* impossible to derogate.[194] Or, from a different perspective, if the possibility to derogate from a given minimum wage is available to national undertakings, posting employers should be able to access the same possibility, both *de jure* and *de facto*.[195] Such a definition seems to be able to "survive" the coming into force of the PWD, since the concept of "minimum wage" is not defined in the Directive.

Most favourable conditions

Article 3(7) of the PWD states that the Directive, in particular Article 3(1) to 3(6), "shall not prevent application of terms and conditions of employment which are more favourable to workers". At first blush, the Article seems to imply a simple comparison between the conditions applicable to the posted worker in the home state and the conditions (included in the list of "hard core provisions") applicable in the host state under the PWD.

However, in the two occasions where the Court was confronted with questions touching upon this "comparison" before the coming into force of the PWD, the picture got somewhat more complicated.

In *Finalarte* the Court seems to steer away from a simple comparison "if X > Y then X applies". First, looking to the conditions applicable to the posted workers in the home state, the Court states that these conditions should prevail inasmuch they provide a level of protection which is "essentially similar" to the one provided by the application of host state regulations.[196] This seems to imply that even if working conditions applicable in the home state provide a lesser protection to the worker, these conditions should be applied if the protection is not *significantly* lower. Second, to be applied the regulations of the host state must "significantly

194 *Portugaia Costruções*, para. 35: "[...] the fact that, in concluding a collective agreement specific to one undertaking, a domestic employer can pay wages lower than the minimum wage laid down in a collective agreement declared to be generally applicable, whilst an employer established in another Member State cannot do so, constitutes an unjustified restriction on the freedom to provide services."

195 Though it is quite hard to imagine how the latter element should be enforced.

196 *Finalarte*, para. 53.

add" to the social protection of posted workers.[197] As for the first condition, this implies a *quid pluris* from the simple "X > Y" comparison.

In another occasion, namely the *Mazzoleni* case, the Court specified the *components* of the comparison, at least in the context of minimum wages. Indeed, in the cited case, the Court proposed a much more complicated way to operate the comparison, though it should be kept in mind that the *Mazzoleni* case arose in a specific situation -frontier workers being posted for a limited amount of their working time. Still, the Court stated that the comparison should be carried out taking into account the "overall position" of posted workers "in relation to remuneration, taxation and social security contributions in the host Member State and in the Member State of establishment".[198] It is apparent that such a comparison would prove very difficult for the posting employer, making it harder to know in advance which wage and working conditions are applicable to its workers. True enough, the decision was delivered in a specific situation and before the coming into force of the PWD. However, it seems that the second element would not change much, as Article 3(7) does not specify further the kind of comparison which should be operated. As a final word on the topic, it is important to retain the fact that the Court always carried out the comparison in both ways, in order to apply "more favourable conditions", irrespective of their belonging to the state of establishment or to the one where the service is provided.

Public policy provisions and public order

Finally, in *Arblade* the Court had the occasion to consider the role of "public order" provisions, in particular when these provisions amount to a restriction to the freedom to provide services. This is interesting from the perspective of Article 3(10) of the Directive. The English version of this Article states that "This Directive shall not preclude the application by Member States [...] of: terms and conditions of employment on matters other than those referred to in the first subparagraph of paragraph 1 in the case of *public policy provisions* [...]". However, the French version makes it clear that the reference goes to provisions of public order, *i.e. lois de police*.[199]

It is evident from *Arblade* that these "public order" or "public policy" provisions were considered by the Court of Justice exactly as simple provisions of national law. No special consideration for their role can be found in the decision.[200]

197 Ibid.

198 *Mazzoleni*, para. 35.

199 "La présente directive ne fait pas obstacle à ce que les États membres, dans le respect du traité, imposent aux entreprises nationales et aux entreprises d'autres États, d'une façon égale: des conditions de travail et d'emploi concernant des matières autres que celles visées au paragraphe 1 premier alinéa, dans la mesure oú il s'agit de dispositions d'ordre public [...]".

200 As Fallon puts it: "ni plus ni moins que d'autres réglamentations nationales susceptibles d'entraver les échanges"; see Fallon, "Note sur CJCE 23 novembre 1999, Arblade", p. 729. See also Francq, "Note sur CJCE 23 novembre 1999, Arblade", p. 790.

In this sense, the Court considers that the concept of "public policy provisions" (or public order) has no autonomous existence and has to be interpreted in light of the Treaties.[201]

Once again, there is no reason to think that the coming into force of the PWD should change this position. On the contrary, the decision delivered in *Arblade* seems already to narrow the possibility provided by Article 3(10).[202]

5.3 POST-DIRECTIVE CASE LAW

The analysis of the case law directly involving the PWD brings us straight to the second high tide of the history of posting of workers. In this period, the Directive was propelled "from arcane legal obscurity to the front line of politics".[203] Because of this, to come back to these cases[204] is an exercise resembling the re-examination of a seven years old crime scene. What is more, the same scene has already been analysed by an host of forensic teams with the most various techniques.[205] Out of the metaphor, the following case law, notably the (in)famous *Laval* case[206] and its close successors (*Rüffert*[207] and *Commission v. Luxembourg*[208]) did spark an unprecedented attention, not only among legal scholars or practitioners. Indeed, the importance of these cases cannot be overestimated.

However, before proceeding with the analysis, I shall briefly turn to the Communication on "The implementation of Directive 96/71/EC in the Member States"[209] delivered by the Commission in 2003, which provides a temporal bridge between the pre- and post-directive case law. On the basis of Article 8 of the PWD[210] the Commission issued the Communication in order point out the (eventual) difficulties in its transposition. The resulting Communication

---

201 Fallon, "Note sur CJCE 23 novembre 1999, Arblade", p. 730.

202 Contrary to the interpretation of Biagi, who considered Article 3(10) as giving every Member State "the discretion to extend (unlimitedly?) the concept of 'public policy provisions'"; Biagi, "Fortune Smiles on the Italian EU Presidency: talking Half-Seriously About the Poste Workers and Parental Leave Directives", p. 104.

203 K. Ewing and C. Jones, "Introduction", in *The New Spectre Haunting Europe. the ECJ, Trade Union Rights and the British Government*, ed. K.D. Ewing and J. Hendy (London: Institute of Employment Rights, 2009), 1–5, p. 2.

204 I am speaking here of *Laval* and its fellowship.

205 The ETUI provides a comprehensive list of those commentaries at http://www.etui.org/Topics/Social-dialogue-collective-bargaining/Social-legislation/The-interpretation-by-the-European-Court-of-Justice/Reaction-to-the-judgements/Articles-in-academic-literature-on-the-judgements (last accessed 11 February 2014).

206 Case C-341/05, *Laval un Partneri Ltd v. Svenska Byggnadsarbetarefrbundet*, 18 December 2007.

207 Case C-346/06, *Dirk Rüffert v. Land Niedersachsen*, 3 April 2008.

208 Case C-319/06, *Commission of the European Communities v. Grand Duchy of Luxembourg*, 19 June 2008.

209 Brussels, 25.7.2003 COM(2003) 458 final.

210 "By 16 December 2001 at the latest, the Commission shall review the operation of this Directive with a view to proposing the necessary amendments to the Council where appropriate."

however, is largely focused on the case law delivered by the Court of Justice *before* the coming into force of the Directive.

From the start, the Commission identifies the aim of the PWD as "*abolish the obstacles* and uncertainties that impede implementation of the freedom to supply services, by improving legal certainty and facilitating identification of the employment conditions that apply to workers temporarily employed in a Member State other than the Member State whose legislation governs the employment relationship".[211] Looking side by side to the Communication and to the PWD itself, one may notice that the former never refers to Recital 5 of the Directive, where creating "a climate of fair competition" and "guaranteeing respect for the rights of workers" are included in the aims of the Directive. That being said, the Court refers to the case law of the Court of Justice to explain the distinction between posting of workers and free movement of workers. The reference, as it should be clear by now, goes to the "lack of access" to the labour market, first postulated in *Rush Portuguesa*.[212] Furthermore, the case law is referred to in order to introduce the "extension right". Interestingly, the Court refers to *Seco* and *Rush Portuguesa*, while implying the broader formula of the latter.[213]

In giving account of the Directive, the Commission seems to interpret it as a "minimum", in view of the use of the wording "minimum rules" or "minimum protective provisions" to identify the content of Article 3(1) of the PWD.[214] The Communication also makes it clear that the Directive entails an *obligation* for Member States to guarantee that these "minimum rules" are applied to workers being posted in their territory.[215]

The Communication focuses in particular on the applicable standards and on the question of collective agreements. With an eye to the post-Directive case law, it is important to stress the section dedicated to Article 3(8). The Commission makes it clear that a Member State who wishes to extend "generally applicable" collective agreements or collective agreements concluded by the most representative employers' and labour organisations, must *explicitly* mention this choice while implementing the PWD.[216] The Communication is clear in stating that without such explicit choice "those Member States which do not have collective agreements declared to be universally applicable within the meaning of

[211] Communication on the implementation of Directive 96/71/EC, p. 3, emphasis added.
[212] Ibid., p. 4; cf. *Rush Portuguesa*, para. 15.
[213] "Community law does not preclude Member States from extending their *legislation, or collective labour agreements* entered into by both sides of industry, to any person who is employed, even temporarily, within their territory, no matter in which country the employer is established, on condition that the rules of the EC Treaty, and in particular Article 49 are complied with", p. 4 and repeated at p. 7; cf. *Rush Portuguesa*, para. 18 and *Seco*, para. 14. The Commission refers to the first formula, whereas the second is limited to "minimum wages". The Court had always opted for the latter, from the *Vander Elst* case onwards.
[214] Ibid., pp. 5, 6, 13.
[215] Ibid., pp. 7, 11.
[216] Ibid., p. 12. The Commission also notes that *no* Member State, while transposing the Directive, made *any* reference to these options.

the first subparagraph of Article 3(8) of the Directive do not apply the terms and conditions of employment laid down in collective agreements to workers posted on their territory. In these countries, therefore, only the terms and conditions of employment laid down in legislative provisions apply to workers posted on their territory".

Turning to Article 3(10) the Commission recalls the case law of the Court on the clash between nationally defined "public policy" (or "public order") provisions and the freedom to provide services. On the one hand, the Commission recognises that the Treaty leaves an "area of discretion" to determine the scope of these "public policy" provisions. On the other hand, the very next sentence refers to the cited case law, stating that "the concept of public policy must be interpreted strictly and *should not be determined unilaterally* by each Member State".[217] Under this light the "area of discretion" seems somewhat narrow. The Commission also considers that the possibility offered by Article 3(10) must be interpreted "bearing in mind the objective of facilitating the free movement of services". Provided that the case law of the Court of Justice makes it easy for a social regulation to be considered as *restricting* such a free movement,[218] the interpretation put forward in the Communication seems to further reduce the margins for the recourse to Article 3(10). More precisely, the Communication clearly states that to apply the totality of the labour laws of the host country to posted workers exceeds the framework established by Community legislation.[219] To clarify what is actually *covered* by Article 3(10) the Commission refers to those provisions concerning "*fundamental rights and freedoms* as laid down by the law of the Member State concerned and/or by international law, such as *freedom of association* and *collective bargaining*, prohibition of forced labour, the principle of non-discrimination and elimination of exploitative forms of child labour, data protection and the right to privacy".[220] While taking note of the collective rights included in this list, it is important to stress the fact that this identification is justified by the Commission on the basis of ILO Conventions 87 and 98.[221]

Finally, the Communication deals with practical problems faced by Member States while applying the Directive. Here the main topic is the one related to monitoring problems and documents keeping.[222] The Commission accepts that the keeping of certain documents at the working site, for the construction sector, may be necessary in order to guarantee the effective protection of workers.

217 Ibid., p. 13, emphasis added. Cf. *Arblade*, para. 30–31.
218 As it will be recalled, the application of the host Member State's national rules to providers of services is liable to prohibit, impede or render less attractive the provision of services to the extent that it involves expense and additional administrative and economic burdens, *Finalarte*, para. 30; *Mazzoleni*, para. 24.
219 Communication on the implementation of Directive 96/71/EC, p. 14.
220 Ibid., emphasis added.
221 I extensively referred to these Conventions in Chapter 3.
222 See for example the issues raised by the *Arblade* and *Finalarte* cases, although the PWD was not yet applicable.

However, the Communication seems to imply that such a requirement will be made irrelevant by Article 4 of the PWD, entailing the cooperation between authorities in the host and home state in order to exchange information relating to posted workers.[223] Indeed, the Commission in its Communication places a good deal of faith in this system of cooperation, as in the conclusion it is stated that "Implementing the Directive may pose practical difficulties, but most of these should disappear in the course of time thanks to better information and better administrative cooperation between public authorities (Article 4 of the Directive)".

5.3.1 *LAVAL*

As it was pointed out, the first "high tide" of posting started with the *Rush Portuguesa* case. That case came after the 1986 enlargement of the European Community. Though the concept of "social dumping" was not yet omnipresent in the debate following the enlargement to Spain and Portugal, concerns related to the pressure upon social systems of the "old" Member States characterised the *Rush* case and its reception. The story almost repeated itself with *Laval*, though by no means as a farce.

The *Laval* case arose in a dispute involving an "old" (Sweden) and a "new" Member State (Latvia). The debate around "social dumping" was however much more widespread after the 2003 enlargement, epitomised by the figure of the "polish plumber". Such a debate was in fact (re)ignited by the infamous Bolkestein proposal, *i.e.* the first proposal of the Service Directive,[224] based on the "country of origin" principle.

However, for the present analysis, this is of *relative* importance. In fact, the decision delivered by the Court in *Laval* never considers the case from the point of view of the enlargement,[225] carefully avoiding even the mention of the word. The same is true for the opinion of AG Mengozzi. From a legal point of view, no transitional measure was to be considered in the dispute, since Sweden was among those Member States (together with Ireland and the UK) which opened their labour market to workers coming from the "new" Member States of EU-8.[226] In sum, this means that *Laval* was not decided on the basis of transitional measures.

---

223 "In any assessment of the justification of these measures, it must be expected that the Court will take fully into account the cooperation provided for in Article 4 of Directive 96/71, which should enable Member States to obtain all the information necessary in connection with transnational postings", p. 16.

224 Directive 2006/123/EC of the European Parliament and of the Council of 12 December 2006 on services in the internal market.

225 U. Belavusau, "The Case of Laval in the Context of the Post-Enlargement EC Law Development", *German Law Journal* 9, no. 12 (2008): 2279–2308, p. 2286.

226 Clearly enough, transitional measures only restricted free movement of workers, so that in the end they would not have been considered as applicable to the present case by the Court of

Provided that the case has been largely discussed, analysed and criticised, here I will stick to the descriptive structure employed for the previous cases, in order to keep the analysis into the boundaries of this Chapter.

Facts

Laval is a Latvian company working in the construction sector. In 2004 Laval posted around 35 workers to its (wholly owned) Swedish subsidiary, Baltic Bygg (hereinafter, Baltic). These workers were posted in order to carry out construction works for the municipality of Vaxholm. Following the posting, in June 2004, contacts were established between Bygettan, the Swedish trade union for the construction sector, and the management of Baltic and Laval.[227] Thus, negotiations started with the trade union asking Laval to sign a collective agreement covering the building site. The trade union required the signature of this collective agreement, essentially extending the collective agreement for the building sector (hence, a tie-in agreement) and also the guarantee that the employer would pay the posted workers a minimum salary equal to the average hourly wage for the Stockholm region. This request was backed by the threat of collective action. Following the refusal of Laval and Baltic to sign the agreement and to apply the required wage levels,[228] negotiations failed. The collective action eventually started in November 2004, in the form of a blockade of the building site. In the meantime Laval had signed two collective agreements with the Latvian building sector trade union. It must be noted that, though Swedish law considers unlawful to take industrial action in order to change an already existing collective agreement,[229] a specific law, known as *Lex Britannia*[230] allows such actions against an employer only covered by a collective agreement to which the MBL is not

Justice, following the precedent of *Rush Portuguesa*.

227 An outline of the Swedish industrial relations system was provided *supra* in Chapter 2, p. 75.

228 Laval refused to sign the collective agreement also on the basis that it would have been impossible to know in advance the wage level which should then be applied to the posted workers.

229 Section 42 of the Lag (1976:580) om medbestämmande i arbetslivet (Law on Workers Participation in Decisions, referred to as "MBL" in the English version of the Laval judgement); see Eklund, "A Swedish Perspective on Laval", pp. 553–554.

230 *Official Gazette* 1991:681, *Government Bill* 1990/91:162, om vissa fredspliktstegler (government bill). The law takes its nickname from a ship, the Britannia, which was the centre of a legal dispute ending with a judgement (AD 1989/20) of the Swedish Labour Court. This ship, owned by a German company and flying under Cypriot flag with a Philippine crew, was covered by a collective agreement signed by a Philippine trade union and a Philippine temporary agency. As the ship faced a boycott when calling at the port of Goteborg, which was aimed forcing the captain to sign a special collective agreement for the crew, the dispute ended up in front of the Labour Court. Here the collective action was declared unlawful as it was aimed at setting aside a collective agreement already in force. The Swedish trade union confederation then asked for a reform of the MBL in order to tackle such situations. This reform was hence named *Lex Britannia*. See Ahlberg, "The Age of Innocence – and Beyond", pp. 297–300.

applicable (hence, a "foreign" collective agreement). This was conceived explicitly as a tool to fight social dumping.[231]

Back to the facts, the Swedish construction trade union carrying out the collective action was then joined by the electricians' union intervening with a solidarity action in December 2004. The boycott of the latter union brought the work on the building site to a halt, so that the Vaxholm municipality ultimately cancelled the contract and Baltic became subject of liquidation proceedings.

The legal proceeding which would bring the dispute to the Court of Justice started in December 2004 in front of the Arbetsdomstolen (labour court). Laval asked the Swedish court to declare illegal both collective actions (the boycott and the blockade). Second, the Latvian employer asked to the labour court to order the immediate cessation of these actions. Third, it demanded compensation from the trade unions for the loss suffered. In order to answer to the claims raised by Laval, the Arbetsdomstolen referred two questions to the Court of Justice.

Questions and observations

Compared to the ten questions raised by its (heterozygote[232]) twin, *Viking*, the *Laval* case revolves around a mere two questions. The first one is probably the most relevant for its wide ranging effects. In this question the Court of Justice is asked to evaluate the compatibility of the collective action carried out by the Swedish trade unions with the freedom to provide services, inasmuch as this action is aimed at forcing the foreign service provider to sign a collective agreement which contains terms which go beyond what is permitted under the PWD. The second question deals with the *Lex Britannia*: the referring Court asks whether the Swedish legislation allowing collective action against an employer covered by "foreign" collective agreements is compatible with the freedom to provide services and the prohibition of discrimination on grounds of nationality.

The case at stake saw a great number of written observations submitted by parties other than the applicant and the defendant(s). In particular, 14 Member States[233] intervened in the procedure, as well as the EU Commission, the EFTA Surveillance Authority, the Republic of Iceland and the Kingdom of Norway. The intervening parties, and Member States in particular, were divided into two main groups (though one presented two sub-groups) much in line with the divide between "new Member States" (plus United Kingdom) and "old Member

---

231 Eklund, "A Swedish Perspective on Laval", p. 554.

232 It is worth stressing, since these cases are often presented as an inseparable couple, the *Viking* case does not refer to posting of workers (Case C-438/05), *Viking Line ABP v. The International Transport Workers' Federation and the Finnish Seaman's Union*).

233 The Kingdom of Belgium, the Czech Republic, the Kingdom of Denmark, the Federal Republic of Germany, the Republic of Estonia, the Kingdom of Spain, the French Republic, Ireland, the Republic of Latvia, the Republic of Lithuania, the Republic of Austria, the Republic of Poland, the Republic of Finland and the Kingdom of Sweden.

States" witnessed in the *Viking* case.[234] However, for the present case it seems more interesting to highlight the position taken by the different parties while presenting the final decision delivered by the Court. The same is (even more) true for the Opinion of AG Mengozzi, especially in light of the quite different solution that the same Opinion proposed for the dispute.

Decision 1: Revenge of the PWD

After having determined that the first question must be examined in the light of the PWD and of Article 49 EC (freedom to provide services, now Article 56 TFEU),[235] the Court goes on to analyse the actual transposition of the Directive by the Swedish state. As noted by Anne Davies,[236] this is already a puzzling beginning, provided that the PWD cannot be relied upon in a claim between private parties. In fact Laval did not base its claims on the Directive but exclusively on Article 49 EC. The *order* of arguments chosen by the Court can be interpreted as a sign of the willingness of the judges sitting in Luxembourg to address the (supposed) shortcomings of the Swedish transposition.[237] As AG Mengozzi puts it: "the national court raises, indirectly but necessarily, the question whether the Kingdom of Sweden did correctly transpose that measure".[238] On the point, a majority of the intervening parties was in favour of analysing the question from the angle of Article 49 EC and of the PWD.[239]

Keeping in mind the open questions highlighted at the end of Chapter 4,[240] in Laval the Court had the occasion to give an answer to many of those questions. Following the reasoning, the first issue to be addressed is the one related to the *means* to set the conditions listed under Article 3(1). This from the point of view of applicable collective agreements, thus (also) of Article 3(8). The Court here follows in the steps of the 2003 Commission's Communication summarised before. In this sense the Court states that the recourse to the possibilities provided by Article 3(8) must *explicitly* be decided by the Member State. Sweden had not

---

234 For an in-depth analysis of the submission in the *Viking* case, see Bercusson, "The Trade Union Movement and the European Union: Judgment Day", pp. 305–306: "new Member States making submissions were unanimous on one side of the arguments on issues of fundamental legal doctrine (horizontal direct effect, discrimination, proportionality) and the old Member States virtually unanimous on the other".

235 *Laval*, para. 61.

236 Davies, "One Step Forward, Two Steps Back? The Viking and Laval Cases in the ECJ", pp. 127–128.

237 A task which will in fact keep the Court of Justice busy along 24 paragraphs. *Laval*, para. 63–85. See further S Sciarra, "Viking E Laval: diritti Collettivi E Mercato Nel Recente Dibattito Europeo", *Lavoro E Diritto* XXII, no. 2 (2008): 245–269.

238 Opinion of AG Mengozzi in *Laval*, para. 139.

239 The German, Austrian, Belgium, Estonian, French, Icelandic, Latvian, Lithuanian and Polish Governments, and also the Spanish Government and Ireland (though intervening only on the first question).

240 See *supra*, pp. 125 ff.

made an explicit choice on this option while transposing the PWD.[241] Moreover, the Court affirms that wage levels included in the collective agreement, whose application was the aim of the collective action at stake, cannot be considered as *minima*, in the sense of Article 3(1) of the PWD. Hence, the Swedish transposition is essentially declared in breach of the PWD, which means, with the wording of the Communication, that "only the terms and conditions of employment laid down in legislative provisions apply to workers posted" on its territory.[242] In sum: since there is no "minimum wage" in the sense of Article 3(1) and 3(8), no wage can be considered as a minimum.[243] On its part Sweden submitted that its system of *de facto* generally applicable collective agreements, backed by the threat of collective action was able to ensure very high coverage and compliance with these agreements. The Austrian, Danish, Finnish, French, Icelandic and Norwegian Governments agreed with this approach.[244] The German, Irish and Spanish Governments and the EU Commission propose a "nuanced" approach to the Swedish position. They essentially maintain that the Swedish system can be considered as correctly transposing the PWD as long as the content of the collective agreements proposed/imposed to foreign service provides does not go beyond the list of matters of Article 3(1) or are covered by the "public policy option" of Article 3(10).[245] The Opinion of the AG seems closer to this second option. On the other side, Laval and the Estonian, Latvian, Lithuanian, Polish and Czech Governments took a position perfectly overlapping with the solution eventually affirmed by the Court.[246]

The Court then turns to the "opening clauses" of the PWD, namely Article 3.7 and 3.10. Here the aim of the PWD is identified in ensuring "a climate of fair competition between national undertakings and undertakings which provide services transnationally".[247] The Court also defines as unfair competition the situation in which "by applying to their workers the terms and conditions of employment in force in the Member State of origin as regards those matters [listed in Article 3(1)], undertakings established in other Member States would compete unfairly against undertakings of the host Member State in the framework of the transnational provision of services, if the level of social protection in the host Member State is higher".[248] The reference to the matters listed in Article 3(1) reveals a quite narrow understanding of unfair competition, which seems limited to the situation where the foreign service providers undercuts *minimum* level of protection, whereas other differences (which can be quite relevant) do not

---

241 In fact no Member State had done so, at least at the time of the 2003 Communication.
242 Communication on the implementation of Directive 96/71, p. 12.
243 Eklund, "A Swedish Perspective on Laval", pp. 558–559.
244 Opinion of AG Mengozzi in *Laval*, para. 166–167.
245 Ibid., para. 168.
246 Ibid., para. 169.
247 *Laval*, para. 74.
248 Ibid., para. 75.

come into consideration.[249] Coming to Article 3(7) the Court first notes that the collective agreement supported by the collective action contains "most favourable terms" in respect of the Swedish legislation. The text of Article 3(7), literally allowing the "application of terms and conditions of employment which are more favourable to workers", is then interpreted as only allowing the application of such more favourable conditions "pursuant to the law or collective agreements in the Member State of origin".[250] This in order to guarantee the *effet utile* of the PWD.[251] One is left to wonder how the *effet utile* of the Directive should be identified as limiting the regulatory powers of Member States and/or social actors to minimum conditions. Indeed, the AG had interpreted Article 3(7) in a way much closer to its literal meaning, by considering that the Article simply allowed the "application of terms and conditions of employment that are more favourable to workers"[252] covered by the PWD. On this basis, the AG went on to consider that a collective action aimed at concluding a collective agreement applying a wage rate "which applies in practice to domestic undertakings in the sector concerned" could not be considered as breaching the PWD, though the action should be assessed in light of Article 49 EC.[253] On the contrary, the Court only allows conditions which go beyond the minima of Article 3(1) if these are set in a collective agreement signed "of their own accord" by the posting undertaking.[254] The wording seems to imply that such agreement must be reached without the recourse to collective action, in a conception which artificially separates the result (collective agreement) from the means (collective action). I will come back to this in the conclusion of this Chapter.

That being said, the Court does also narrow the other "escape route", *i.e.* the possibility offered by Article 3(10) of the PWD to extend the list of Article 3(1) on matters covered by public policy. The reasoning seems in fact to have barred this route to social actors, as the Court simply and starkly affirms that social actors "not being bodies governed by public law, they cannot avail themselves of that provision by citing grounds of public policy".[255] In this sense, only national authorities can avail themselves of this option. From the wording of the Court it seems also that this choice, as for Article 3(8) must be made explicitly while

---

249 See Malmberg and Sigeman, "Industrial Action and EU Economic Freedoms: The Autonomous Collective Bargaining Model Curtailed by the European Court of Justice", p. 1136, who consider this definition of unfair competition as "the most important and controversial novelty in the judgement".

250 *Laval*, para. 81.

251 *Laval*, para. 80: "Nevertheless, Article 3(7) of Directive 96/71 cannot be interpreted as allowing the host Member State to make the provision of services in its territory conditional on the observance of terms and conditions of employment which go beyond the mandatory rules for minimum protection. [...] such an interpretation would amount to depriving the directive of its effectiveness."

252 Opinion of AG Mengozzi, para. 197.

253 Ibid., para. 198–199.

254 *Laval*, para. 81.

255 Ibid., para. 84.

transposing the Directive. In a way this also puts into question the role of social actors in transposing Directives, which was in fact reminded by the AG in his Opinion:[256] in light of *Laval*, such a transposition is relegated to a second-class instrument, as social actors cannot have recourse to public policy arguments. AG Mengozzi in his Opinion had suggested to leave it to the national court to examine whether the terms included in the collective agreement could be covered by Article 3(10). Hence, the fact that this agreement had been redacted by social actors is not considered as an obstacle in this sense.[257]

Decision 2: Collective action and the scope of EU Law

In the second step of its reasoning, the Court asserts its competence to decide upon a question related to the right to take collective action. Indeed, the Swedish and Danish Governments, as well as the trade unions involved in the dispute, had maintained that this right did fall outside the scope of Article 49 EC (freedom to provide services) in view of the explicit exclusion of competence of the EU to regulate the field.[258] The Court however quickly dismisses this argument, by stating that Member States must exercise their competence in a way which is consistent with Community law also in areas where the Union has no competence at all.[259] AG Mengozzi reaches a similar conclusion.[260]

Furthermore, the Danish and Swedish Government observe that the right to take collective action should be excluded from the scrutiny of the Court on the basis of both Article 49 EC and the PWD, in view of its status of fundamental right.[261] In answering this objection, the Court delivers a statement which *per se* makes *Laval* (similarly to *Viking*) a landmark judgement.[262] Citing a number of international and European texts,[263] the Court recognises the fundamental nature of the right to take collective action. Still, this recognition is used as an argument to include the right at stake under the scrutiny of the Court. This can be explained

256 Opinion of AG Mengozzi in *Laval*, para. 181.

257 Opinion of AG Mengozzi in *Laval*, para. 213–214.

258 Article 137(5) EC, now Article 153(5) TFEU.

259 *Laval*, para. 86–88.

260 Opinion of AG Mengozzi in *Laval*, para. 59.

261 *Laval*, para. 89.

262 Dorssemont, "The Right to Take Collective Action Versus Fundamental Economic Freedoms in the Aftermath of Laval and Viking. Foes Are Forever", p. 79.

263 "In that regard, it must be recalled that the right to take collective action is recognised both by various international instruments which the Member States have signed or cooperated in, such as the European Social Charter, signed at Turin on 18 October 1961 – to which, moreover, express reference is made in Article 136 EC – and Convention No 87 of the International Labour Organisation concerning Freedom of Association and Protection of the Right to Organise of 9 July 1948 – and by instruments developed by those Member States at Community level or in the context of the European Union, such as the Community Charter of the Fundamental Social Rights of Workers adopted at the meeting of the European Council held in Strasbourg on 9 December 1989, which is also referred to in Article 136 EC, and the Charter of Fundamental Rights of the European Union proclaimed in Nice on 7 December 2000."

on the basis of its previous case law on restrictions to fundamental freedoms caused by the exercise of fundamental rights,[264] where the Court had affirmed that such an exercise should be reconciled with "the requirements relating to rights protected under the Treaty".[265] What is more, the text of Article 28 of the Charter of Fundamental Rights of the European Union, recognising the right to take collective action, allows the Court to maintain that the exercise of this right must be "in accordance with Community law", hence allowing for restrictions stemming from it. Finally, the Court considers that also under Swedish law the right to take collective action can be restricted either by law or by collective agreement.[266] With a somewhat weak analogy, this situation is used by the Court as an argument in favour of the possibility to restrict the right to take collective action, without any attempt to evaluate the actual nature or extension of the restrictions allowed under Swedish law. AG Mengozzi similarly argues in his Opinion, both in terms of the recognition of the right to take collective action as a fundamental right (and general principle of Community law)[267] and of the competence of the Court of Justice to decide on the "clash" between this right and the freedom to provide services.[268] The AG however proposes a more specific analysis as to the nature of restrictions to this right. By referring to both Article 11(2) of the ECHR and to Article 52 of the Charter of Fundamental Rights, the AG considers that these restrictions "must be laid down in a legislative or regulatory measure, must be justified by the pursuit of an overriding general interest and must not affect the 'essence' of that right".[269]

Decision 3: Collective action v. freedom to provide services

having affirmed its competence to solve the conflict between the (fundamental) right to take collective action and the freedom to provide services, the Court concludes the analysis of the first question. By referring to the cited *Säger* formula[270] the Court identifies the collective action, "liable to make it less attractive, or more difficult" for posting service providers "to carry out construction work in Sweden", as a restriction to the freedom to provide services. Though the analogy seems somewhat flawed,[271] the Court corroborates this reasoning by referring

---

264 Case C-112/00 *Schmidberger* and Case C-36/02 *Omega*.
265 *Laval*, para. 94.
266 Ibid., para. 92.
267 Opinion of AG Mengozzi in *Laval*, para. 78,
268 Ibid., para. 85. The AG also highlights the fact that 15 states out of 17 intervening in the procedure had not raised doubts as to the applicability of Community law to the dispute at stake.
269 Ibid., para. 81.
270 *Laval*, para. 99.
271 F. Dorssemont and G. Orlandini, "Market Rules and the Right to Strike: a Different Approach", in *From Labour Law to Social Competition Law?*, ed. M. Rigaux, J. Buelens, and A. Latinne (Antwerp: Intersentia, 2014), 67–105, p. 74.

to its case law on professional associations:[272] trade unions are then considered as association exerting their "legal autonomy" in order to *regulate* collectively the *provision of services.*[273] Hence, their action must be analysed under the light of Article 49 EC. In this sense the Court does not apply here a genuine direct horizontal effect. The cited analogy makes it so that trade unions are not conceived as *private* parties, but as associations exerting regulatory powers, essentially on the basis of their "purely material" or "economic" power.[274] The Court does not follow the approach proposed by AG Mengozzi, which had argued in favour of a more explicit recognition of the direct horizontal application of the freedom to provide services.[275]

Having defined the recourse to collective action as a restriction, the Court undertakes a very similar path to the one seen in the *Arblade* test. Thus, in the wording of the Court, a restriction to the freedom to provide services "is warranted only if it pursues a legitimate objective compatible with the Treaty and is justified by overriding reasons of public interest; if that is the case, it must be suitable for securing the attainment of the objective which it pursues and not go beyond what is necessary in order to attain it".[276] One cannot fail to notice that the test applied is by no means influenced by the fact that the restriction comes from the exercise of a fundamental right.[277] As for the first step of the test, the Court recognises that the "protection of the workers of the host State against possible social dumping", falling into the broader objective of "protecting workers", constitutes a legitimate objective *in abstracto* compatible with the Treaty.[278] However, coming to the specific case, the Court considers that the collective action at stake "cannot be justified with regard to such an objective".[279] This conclusion is reached on the basis of two arguments. The first comes straight from the interpretation of the PWD provided in the first part of the decision: the collective action is aimed at applying to posted workers working conditions which go *beyond* and *above* the minima contained in "relevant legislative provisions" referred to in the PWD.[280] As it was highlighted before, the Court considers the application of the PWD as a necessary and sufficient protection against social dumping. Hence, the application

272 Cases C- 36/74 *Walrave and Koch*; C-415/93 *Bosman*; C-309/99, *Wouters and Others.*
273 *Laval*, para. 98; see L. Azoulai, "The Court of Justice and the Social Market Economy: the Emergence of an Ideal and the Conditions for Its Realization", *Common Market Law Review*, no. 2007 (2008): 1335–1356, p. 1346.
274 Dorssemont, "The Right to Take Collective Action Versus Fundamental Economic Freedoms in the Aftermath of Laval and Viking. Foes Are Forever", p. 74; Azoulai, "The Court of Justice and the Social Market Economy: the Emergence of an Ideal and the Conditions for Its Realization", pp. 1344–1346.
275 Opinion of AG Mengozzi in *Laval*, para. 222–229.
276 *Laval*, para. 101.
277 Dorssemont, "The Right to Take Collective Action Versus Fundamental Economic Freedoms in the Aftermath of Laval and Viking. Foes Are Forever", p. 81.
278 *Laval*, para. 103–107.
279 Ibid., para. 108.
280 Ibid., para. 111.

of higher standards than those referred to in Article 3(1) of the same Directive is unnecessary to attain the objective of "protection of the workers of the host State against possible social dumping". The second argument deals exclusively with the negotiations on pay. The Court, citing *Arblade*,[281] affirms that the Swedish system lacks of clarity as to the applicable wage, so that it makes "excessively difficult in practice" for the posting undertaking "to determine the obligations with which it is required to comply as regards minimum pay".[282] This second requirement seems to imply that the posting employer must be able to know in advance the conditions applicable to its posted workers. In this sense it seems correct to affirm that the Court has declared workplace-level bargaining as an unacceptable means of implementing the PWD,[283] and, more generally, of regulating working conditions of posted workers in the host state.

Decision 4: Lex Britannia

Turning to the second question the Court examines the *Lex Britannia* from the point of view of the freedom to provide services. The decision recognises that the law is aimed at combating social dumping.[284] However, the provision is considered as discriminatory as it fails to take into account foreign collective agreements "irrespective of their content".[285] The reference to the content seems to imply that the fault of the *Lex Britannia* is to allow collective action even in the case where the "foreign" collective agreement already applies conditions which are equal or better than those required by the PWD. The Court then looks for justifications for the discriminatory rule (grounds of public policy, public security or public health); in doing so, it once again examines the aims of the *Lex Britannia*, stating that the provision "is intended, first, to allow trade unions to take action to ensure that all employers active on the Swedish labour market pay wages and apply other terms and conditions of employment *in line with those usual in Sweden*, and secondly, to *create a climate of fair competition*, on an equal basis, between Swedish employers and entrepreneurs from other Member States".[286] Since these considerations do not fall into the grounds potentially justifying a discriminatory measure, the Court declares the *Lex Britannia* in breach of Articles 49 and 50 EC. Looking at the analysis it is interesting to stress the fact that the aims of the *Lex Britannia*, identified by the Court, fit perfectly into the framework of the

281 *Arblade*, para. 43. As a side note, it should be reminded that the *Arblade* case dealt with criminal proceeding, so that the "clarity requirement" seemed, at that time, dictated by the requirements of criminal law. Indeed, this condition for the application of host state measures was only mentioned in *Arblade*.

282 *Laval*, para. 110.

283 As noted by Davies, "One Step Forward, Two Steps Back? The Viking and Laval Cases in the ECJ", p. 144.

284 *Laval*, para. 113.

285 Ibid., para. 116.

286 Ibid., para. 118, emphasis added.

PWD as interpreted by the Court itself. Indeed, to guarantee a climate of fair competition is directly cited in Recital 5 of the PWD,[287] and the protection against social dumping had just been recognised by the Court as an overriding reason of public interest.[288]

The Opinion of AG Mengozzi on the point differs from the final decision reached by the Court. Indeed, the AG suggested to take into account the "foreign" collective agreement as a comparator, in order to ascertain whether the collective agreement supported by the collective action from the Swedish trade unions "involved a real advantage significantly contributing to the social protection of posted workers and did not duplicate any identical or essentially comparable protection available to those workers under the legislation and/or the collective agreement applicable to the service provider in the Member State in which it is established".[289] Seen in the light of the pre-Directive case law, the position of the AG follows the line of those cases, where the scrutiny of the Court was focused on the "real" advantage for posted workers entailed by the eventual application of host state wages and working conditions.[290] *Deviating* from this case law, the Court considers that the coming into force of the PWD leaves no space for such a comparison and for the application of more favourable conditions other than those stemming from home state legislation and collective agreements. With the PWD effectively limiting the application of host state wages and working conditions to the list of Article 3(1) the floor (of rights) became a ceiling.[291] Or, more precisely, floor and ceiling fused together.

5.3.2 *RÜFFERT*

Just a few months after *Laval*, the Court wrote another chapter in the evolving history of posting of workers. Though the lines of *Rüffert* are written in the same rhyme as *Laval*, the case here at stake does provide further insight on the Court vision of the PWD. In particular, the fact that no collective action was involved in *Rüffert* allows for a "cleaner"[292] analysis of the PWD itself, as well as of its relationship with the freedom to provide services (still embodied in Article 49 EC, now Article 56 TFEU).

---

287 "Whereas any such promotion of the transnational provision of services requires a climate of fair competition and measures guaranteeing respect for the rights of workers."

288 *Laval*, para. 103. It is important to stress the fact that an "overriding reason of public interest" cannot be relied upon in order to justify a discriminatory measure.

289 Opinion of AG Mengozzi in *Laval*, para. 307.

290 *E.g.*, *Mazzoleni*, para. 33–35; *Finalarte*, para. 50–53.

291 Eklund, "A Swedish Perspective on Laval", p. 566.

292 Davies, "Case C-346/06, Ruffert V Land Niedersachsen [2008] IRLR 467 (ECJ)", p. 293.

The *Rüffert* case hence has its rightful place in the so called *Laval quartet*, which from the point of view of posting becomes the *Laval trio*.[293] As in *Laval*, a number of parties submitted their observation in the *Rüffert* procedure. However, the divide witnessed in *Laval* and *Viking*, between new and old Member States is less apparent here. Also, the Opinion of AG Bot did propose a different solution for the case from the ones ultimately chosen by the Court, as Mengozzi did in *Laval*. It should be noted that AG Bot delivered his Opinion on the *Rüffert* case on 20 September 2007, hence *before* the actual decision in *Laval*.

Facts

In autumn 2003, following a public invitation to tender, the *Land* of Niedersachsen (Lower Saxony) awarded Objekt und Bauregie GmbH & Co. KG (hereinafter OuB), a German company, a contract for building works of the Göttingen-Rosdorf prison. In order to carry out the contract OuB had recourse to the Polish firm Pracownie Konserwacji Zabytków sp. zoo (PKZ) as subcontractor. PKZ posted around 53 Polish workers to the building site. During the execution of the contract, the German authorities investigated the situation of PKZ as it was suspected of paying its workers a wage well below (46,57%) the *applicable* collective agreement. Following the investigation, both parties terminated the contract, while the *Land* applied for application of a penalty against OuB for failure to comply with the obligations provided under the contract.

In fact, in this contract, between *Land* Niedersachsen and OuB, the latter undertook the obligation to pay its workers "at least the remuneration prescribed by the collective agreement at the place where these services are performed, as set out in the list of representative collective agreements referred to under No 01 'Construction industry' [...]".[294] The obligation extended also to the eventual subcontractors, holding the main contractor responsible. The identification of the applicable "collective agreement" is one of the most problematic point for the case at stake. Referring exclusively to the question of (minimum) wage, at the time of the facts the construction industry in Germany was covered by a collective agreement declared universally applicable, the *Tarifvertrag zur Regelung der Mindestlöhne im Baugewerbe im Gebiet der Bundesrepublik Deutschland* (TVM). However, the relevant collective agreement for the contract between the *Land* and OuB is a different one, namely the *Tarifvertrag zur Regelung der Löhne und Ausbildungsvergütungen* (TVLA), setting a higher wage level and a more detailed wage scale, which in its turn had *not* been declared universally applicable.[295] Finally, the law of Land Niedersachsen on the award of public

293 As the *Viking* case does not deal with posting of workers, involving a re-flagging phenomenon, hence raising question relating to the freedom of establishment.

294 Opinion of AG Bot in *Rüffert*, para. 35.

295 Indeed, the TVM allowed for higher wages to be set in collective agreement at a different level. See S. Francq et al., "Chronique de jurisprudence du Tribunal et de la Cour de Justice

contracts (*Niedersächsisches Landesvergabegesetz*) provides for a penalty in case of violation of the conditions for the awarding of the contract (including the respect of collective agreements cited before). These sanctions are represented by a contractual penalty up to the 10% of the contract itself. The law also specifies that the main contractor can be held responsible for violations on the part of a subcontractor "unless the contractor was not aware or could not have been aware of the non-fulfilment".[296] In the case at stake the penalty initially inflicted amounted to the 10% of the value of the contract (EUR 849343). M. Dirk Rüffert, acting as liquidator of OuB,[297] brought action in font of the Landgericht Hannover (Regional Court of Hanover) against the penalty, which was then confirmed for a reduced amount (1% of the value of the contract) by the Court. The case was then brought in front the Oberlandesgericht Celle for appeal, and in the context of this proceeding the German Court asked the Court of Justice for a preliminary reference.

Questions and observations

The formulation of the question referred by the national judge is already in itself quite striking. The German judge in its question qualifies the obligation to pay "the collectively agreed wage" as a restriction to the freedom to provide services *per se*, on the basis of the fact that such an obligation would deprive the foreign service provider of its competitive advantage, stemming from lower wage costs.[298] Moreover, the referring judge goes on to consider that the obligation only serves an economic (protectionist) objective, shielding the German building industry from competition.[299] Finally, the German court puts forward the "self exploitation right" argument, by stating that to respect the wage level fixed by the collective agreement in question would amount to depriving posted workers of employment possibilities.[300] Thus, the obligation, in the reasoning of the referring judge, cannot be justified in view of the protection of (posted) workers.

In fact, the whole line of reasoning is not new. There is a (surprising?) affinity between the present question and the one sent, by other German judges, in the cases forming the *Finalarte* decision.[301] In this sense, the formulation referred

des Communautés européennes. Concurrence", *Journal Du Droit International*, no. 1 (2009): 665–679, p. 668; C. Freitas da Costa, "Note sur C-346/06, Rüffert", *Revue du Droit de l'Union Européenne*, no. 3 (2008): 612–619, p. 613.

296 Opinion of AG Bot in *Rüffert*, para. 34.

297 OuB had in the meantime declared bankrupt.

298 Opinion of AG Bot in *Rüffert*, para. 41.

299 Hence "the obligation to pay the collectively agreed wage cannot be considered to meet overriding requirements relating to the public interest", ibid., para. 43.

300 Ibid., para. 44.

301 See *supra*, p. 171. On this reference see W. Däubler, "Posted Workers and Freedom to Supply Services. Directive 96/71/EC and German Courts", *Industrial Law Journal* 27 (1998): 264–268, p. 266: "a competition based on wages being 50% or 30% of those which are normally paid in the host country is just the contrary of 'maintaining the improvement'", referring

by the national judge has been criticised as already containing the answer, the German court not showing much doubts as to the answer which should be given to the question.[302] Provided that this use of the preliminary reference instrument is by no means rare, it is against this background that the Court develops its answer.

In the end, the referring judge asks the Court of Justice whether "Article 49 EC precludes an authority of a Member State from adopting a measure of a legislative nature requiring the contracting authority to designate as contractors for public works contracts only contractors which, when submitting their tenders, agree in writing to pay their employees, in return for performance of the services concerned, at least the wage provided for in the collective agreement in force at the place where those services are performed".[303]

As for *Laval*, I will refer to the Opinion of the AG while examining the decision ultimately delivered by the Court. Once again the Opinion proposed a very different solution for the case, from the one chosen by the Court. As it has been recalled before, the Opinion was delivered before the decision in *Laval*, and it is clear that the AG argues much in line with the case law preceding the coming into force of the PWD, which was analysed *supra*.

The decision

From the very beginning of the decision, the Court makes it clear that the question has to be assessed taking into consideration the PWD, though the referring judge had only mentioned Article 49 EC. This is in line with the Opinion of AG Bot as well as with the observations of the intervening Governments and of the Commission.[304] Indeed, the vast majority of the decision deals with the assessment of the *Land* regulation in light of the PWD,[305] while the analysis of its compatibility with the freedom to provide services is relegated to the closing paragraphs.[306]

The first step in the reasoning of the Court is devoted to the analysis of the wage level "fixed" by the law of *Land* Niedersachen, in the light of Articles 3(1) and 3(8) of the PWD. First of all, the Court considers that the mere reference to a collective agreement made in a legislative act is not sufficient to consider the wage

to Article 117 of the EEC Treaty of 1957 ("Member States agree upon the need to promote improved working conditions and an improved standard of living for workers, so as to make possible their harmonisation while the improvement is being maintained").

302 See S. Robin-Olivier, "Libre prestation de services, marchés publics et régulation sociale: le droit européen privilégie la concurrence fondée sur le coût du travail", *Revue trimestrielle de droit européen* 44 (2008), 485–495, pp. 486–487.

303 *Rüffert*, para. 17.

304 Ibid., para. 18; Opinion of AG Bot, para. 61–63.

305 *Rüffert*, para. 17–35.

306 Ibid., para. 35–42. See Davies, "Case C-346/06, Ruffert v. Land Niedersachsen [2008] IRLR 467 (ECJ)", p. 293.

level in itself as set by a law.[307] Hence, having ascertained that the wage level is ultimately set by a collective agreement, the Court turns to examine whether the collective agreement fulfils the criteria of Articles 3(1) and 3(8) of the PWD. By admission of *Land* Niedersachsen the TVLA had not been declared universally applicable.[308] At the same time, the fact that the German state has a system to declare a collective agreement as universally applicable (which had been used for the TVM) brings the Court to conclude that the other options provided by Article 3(8) could not be applied to the case at stake.[309] *Ad abundantiam*, the Court adds that the wage set (by reference) by the law of the *Land* cannot be considered as a minimum also because its coverage is limited to public contracts.[310] As side note, along the reasoning aimed at denying the "status" of "minimum wage" to the wage set under the TVLA and referred to by the law on public contracts, the Court refers exclusively to *Laval* as the relevant case law.[311]

The second step of the reasoning deals with Article 3(7) in order to ascertain if the rate of pay fixed by the TVLA can be considered as a "term and condition of employment which is more favourable to workers within the meaning of Article 3(7) of Directive 96/71".[312] Keeping in mind *Laval*, it comes as no surprise that the answer is negative. In fact the decision of the Court on the point is a direct quote from *Laval*.[313] The Court essentially repeats that Article 3(7) only applies to conditions stemming from the application of home state laws and collective agreements, the only exception being the possibility of agreement signed "of their own accord" by posting employers. The wording "the level of protection which must be guaranteed to workers posted to the territory of the host Member State is limited, in principle, to that provided for in Article 3(1), first subparagraph, (a) to (g), of Directive 96/71", is slightly misleading, the *must* having developed in a *can*. The solution resembles closely the one put forward by the Polish government in its observations.[314]

The interpretation of the PWD provided by the AG in his Conclusions differs greatly from the one ultimately reached by the Court in the Decision. Indeed, the AG considers the measure of the *Land* compatible with the PWD.[315] On the question of the "minimum" nature of the wage referred to by the law on public contracts, AG Bot highlights the fact that the TVM itself, in fixing the universally

---

307 *Rüffert*, para. 24.

308 In fact, following the structure of the German (federal) state and of its system of industrial relations, the *Land* is not competent for such an extension, as remarked by AG Bot in his Opinion, para. 129. See Francq, et al., "Chronique de jurisprudence du Tribunal et de la Cour de Justice des Communautés européennes. Concurrence", p. 670; Freitas da Costa, "Note sur C-346/06, Rüffert", p. 617.

309 *Rüffert*, para. 27.

310 Ibid., para. 29.

311 Ibid., para. 31.

312 Ibid., para. 32.

313 Cf. ibid., para. 33–34 and *Laval*, para. 80–81.

314 Opinion of AG Bot in *Rüffert*, para. 50.

315 Ibid., para. 97.

applicable minimum wages for the construction sector, refers explicitly to the possibility of *in melius* bargaining at decentralised level.[316] The AG refers to the text of the PWD affirming that "the concept of minimum rates of pay referred to in paragraph 1(c) is defined by the national law and/or practice of the Member State to whose territory the worker is posted",[317] evidently encouraging the Court to take into account the *practices* of the German system. The Opinion also reaffirms the minimum character of the PWD, something which would have been much more difficult after the decision in *Laval*. Essentially, the AG interprets Article 3(7) as authorising the enhanced protection of PWD in respect of the minima required by the PWD[318]; this with the only limitation of the compatibility with the freedom to provide services.[319] In proposing this interpretation of the PWD as a whole, AG Bot cites the 17th Recital of the PWD, which states that "[...] the mandatory rules for minimum protection in force in the host country must not prevent the application of terms and conditions of employment which are more favourable to workers".

Back to the Decision, the Court turns to the analysis under Article 49 EC. As it was stressed before, this part of the decision is less developed (and, ultimately, less relevant) than the one devoted to the PWD. In a way, this last step seems almost superfluous; as Paul Davies put it, "the Court virtually reaches the position that a protection which is not required by the Directive cannot be justified under Article 49 on the worker protection ground".[320] Having quickly assessed that the measure is a restriction of the freedom to provide services,[321] the Court considers if it can be justified. Three justifications were put forward by the *Land* and by the German Government: the protection of workers,[322] the protection of independence in the organisation of working life by trade unions and the necessity of ensuring the financial balance of the social security systems. The Polish government in its turn maintained that the only aim of the measure was to "shield German building undertakings from competition from other Member States", a "purely economic" aim which then could not justify the restriction to a fundamental freedom.[323] The first justification, the protection of workers, is dismissed by the Court on the grounds of lack of *necessity*. The Court considers that, the measure only being applicable to public contracts (hence, to a part of the construction sector) and exceeding the minimum wage set by the TVM, the wage fixed by the TVLA and referred to by the law on public contracts cannot be considered as *necessary* for

316 Ibid., para. 96.
317 Ibid., para. 78.
318 Ibid., para. 94.
319 Ibid., para. 99.
320 Davies, "Case C-346/06, Ruffert v. Land Niedersachsen [2008] IRLR 467 (ECJ)", p. 293.
321 *Rüffert*, para. 37.
322 Also supported by the German and Danish Governments, Ireland and the Cypriot, Austrian, Belgian, Finnish and Norwegian Governments.
323 Opinion of AG Bot in *Rüffert*, para. 51.

the protection of workers.[324] Indeed, the PWD thus becomes the only horizon for the protection of posted workers. The second argument, the protection of independence in the organisation of working life by trade unions, is dismissed by referring to the arguments used against the first justification.[325] The third justification is discarded not having been sufficiently proved.[326]

The AG in its turn also concurs with the existence of a restriction of the freedom to provide services.[327] However, the Opinion diverges from the Decision in that it considers the restriction justified on the basis of the overriding reasons of public interest of protection of workers and prevention of social dumping.[328] The AG then proposes the application of the test developed by the Court in its *previous* case law, in order to assess "whether those rules confer a genuine benefit on the workers concerned, which significantly augments their social protection".[329] AG Bot also discards the "self exploitation right" argument, as he considers that the guarantee of higher wages "is an appropriate means of protecting them", citing as a basis for this reasoning Article 136 EC (now Article 151 TFEU).[330] Finally, the AG considers the argument put forward by the Commission about the non-necessity of the wage level set by the TVLA, which is based on the assumption that, had the measure been *necessary*, it would have been applied to the whole sector and the whole state territory. The AG disagrees with the observation, citing the competence of the *Land*, which couldn't declare the collective agreement universally applicable. Also, the Opinion considers that

---

324 *Rüffert*, para. 39–40. The same conclusion on this point had been endorsed by the Commission and the French government; see the Opinion of AG Bot, para. 55–56. The same reasoning was repeated in a more recent case, which however did not involve a posting of workers; see Case C-549/13, *Bundesdruckerei GmbH v. Stadt Dortmund*: "the Court has already held that, in so far as it applies solely to public contracts, such a national measure is not appropriate for achieving that objective [the protection of workers] if there is no information to suggest that employees working in the private sector are not in need of the same wage protection as those working in the context of public contracts".

325 *Rüffert*, para. 41. The argument is in itself puzzling, provided that the protection of trade unions' independence do not overlap completely with the protection of workers.

326 *Rüffert*, para 42.

327 Opinion of AG Bot in *Rüffert*, para. 102.

328 Ibid., para. 106 and 109.

329 Ibid., para. 116–119. In fact the AG already answers the question by stating that "In this regard, it is evident from the order for reference that PKZ is accused of having paid the 53 employees engaged on the building site only 46.57% of the applicable minimum wage. In those circumstances, it appears to be established that compliance with the Landesvergabegesetz would have given these workers *genuine additional protection* by ensuring that they received a wage significantly higher than the wage they would normally be paid in the State in which their employer is established. This law therefore appears to me to ensure the protection of the posted workers", para. 118, emphasis added. See also Bruun, Jacobs and Schmidt, "ILO Convention No. 94 in the Aftermath of the Rüffert Case", pp. 477–478.

330 "[t]he Community and the Member States, having in mind fundamental social rights […], shall have as their objectives […] improved living and working conditions, so as to make possible their harmonisation while the improvement is being maintained, [and] dialogue between management and labour", Opinion of AG Bot in *Rüffert*, para. 121. The same Article had been cited to underpin a very similar reasoning by Däubler, "Posted Workers and Freedom to Supply Services. Directive 96/71/EC and German Courts", p. 266.

the supposed discrimination between workers employed in private contracts and their colleagues employed in public ones is not "relevant from the point of view of Community law".[331]

5.3.3 *COMMISSION V. LUXEMBOURG*

The decision delivered in the infringement procedure against the Grand Duchy of Luxembourg completes the "*Laval* trio". Though for the present research the case of *Commission v. Luxembourg*[332] is dwarfed by the importance of the two other members of the trio, the decision is interesting in its own right, especially as regards the interpretation of Article 3(10) of the PWD.[333]

Originating by an infringement procedure the case also clearly shows the position of the Commission on a number of issues stemming from the PWD. Also, the case, in condemning essentially the excessive broadness of the Luxembourgian regulation, was received as somewhat of a warning bell for those Member States who had transposed the PWD in a similar fashion.[334]

Here I will focus on the aspects which are relevant for their indirect impact, and in particular on the interpretation of Article 3(10).

The infringement procedure

The procedure started in April 2004, when the Commission raised, by formal letter of notice addressed to the Grand Duchy, a number of issues regarding the transposition of the PWD.[335] Notably, the Commission focused on four main topics. First, the Commission lamented the excessively broad interpretation of the possibility offered by Article 3(10) by the Luxembourgian legislator.[336] Second, the transposition of the PWD was deemed incomplete inasmuch as it restricted

---

331 Opinion of AG Bot in *Rüffert*, para. 129–130.

332 Case C-319/06 of 19 June 2008.

333 See Van Peijpe, "Collective Labour Law After Viking, Laval, Rüffert, and Commission v. Luxembourg", p. 93; Krebber, "Case C-319/06, Commission v. Luxembourg, Judgment of the Court (First Chamber) of 19 June 2008,[2008] ECR I-4323", p. 1728.

334 *E.g.*, the Kingdom of Belgium. See A. Defossez, "Détachement des travailleurs, ordre public et dumping social, suite et certainment pas fin", *Revue de la Faculté de Droit de l'Université de Liège* 4 (2008): 602–612, p. 605–607.

335 Transposed by Luxembourg with the Loi du 20 décembre 2002 portant 1: Transposition de la Directive 96/71/CE du Parlement européen et du Conseil du 16 décembre 1996 concernant le détachement de travailleurs effectué dans le cadre d'une prestation de services; 2. Réglementation du contrôle de l'application du droit du travail, Mémorial A, n° 154 du 21 décembre 2002, p. 3722.

336 In particular, the transposing law indicated as covered by public policy the following requirements: 1) Requirement of a written contract of employment or a corresponding document within the meaning of Directive 91/533; 2) Automatic adjustment of rates of pay to reflect changes in the cost of living; 3) Compliance with rules on part-time and fixed-term work; 4) Compliance with collective labour agreements.

the concept of "minimum rest periods" of Article 3(1) of the PWD to weekly rest periods. Third, the Commission criticised the obligation for posting undertakings to provide information to the Luxembourgian labour inspectorate (Inspection du travail et des mines) "prior to the commencement of work".[337] Finally, the requirement of designating an "ad hoc agent" residing in Luxembourg for the retention of relevant documents for monitoring purposes was considered as restricting the freedom to provide services. Not satisfied by the reasoned opinion receive in response to the formal letter of notice, the Commission commenced proceeding beyond the Court of Justice.

In the proceeding in front of the Court the Commission maintained the four topics of critique outlined above. On the interpretation of Article 3(10) the Commission relied on the Declaration No. 10 on the PWD.[338] In light of the Declaration, the Commission considered that Luxembourg had wrongly transposed the PWD by including provisions which could not be considered as covered by "public policy". The Government of Luxembourg contested the role of Declaration 10, on the basis that it had never been published on the *Official Journal*. However, the Government acknowledged the second complaint, limiting itself to point out that the incorrect transposition had been removed by an amendment dating May 2006.

The decision

The Court first analyses the question related to the scope of Article 3(10). The possibility offered by this Article is hence defined as a "double" derogation. First it is a derogation from the fundamental principle of the freedom to provide services.[339] Second, it is also a derogation from the *exhaustive* list of Article 3(1) of the PWD.[340] Thus, Article 3(10) must be interpreted (twice as) strictly. The Court considers, following in the steps of the 2003 Communication, that the scope of the "public policy" exception cannot be determined unilaterally by Member States.[341] AG Trstenjak states clearly that the narrow interpretation of "public

337 The Commission stressed the lack of clarity of the disposition, which also indicated that these information were to be provided "on demand" of the labour inspectorate.

338 Which was referred to also in the Communication of 2003 on "The implementation of Directive 96/71/EC in the Member States". The Declaration defined "public policy provisions" as "those mandatory rules from which there can be no derogation and which, by their nature and objective, meet the imperative requirements of the public interest. These may include, in particular, the prohibition of forced labour or the involvement of public authorities in monitoring compliance with legislation on working conditions".

339 *Commission v. Luxembourg*, para. 30.

340 Ibid., para. 31.

341 On the point see Francq et al., "Chronique de jurisprudence du Tribunal et de la Cour de Justice des Communautés européennes. Concurrence", pp. 674–675, who consider that two different concepts, namely "*lois de police*" and "public order" end up confused in the Decision.

policy provisions" is to be preferred "in the interests of the broadest possible implementation of the principle of the freedom to provide services".[342]

As the AG in her Opinion, the Court also considers that Declaration No 10 can be relied upon in order to support the interpretation of Article 3(10).[343] On this basis, the Court goes on to analyse the Luxembourgian legislation.

Unsurprisingly, all the topics included under first critique raised by the Commission were found to go beyond what is allowed under Article 3(10) in its narrowly interpreted scope. The requirement of a written contract, which was linked to Directive 91/533,[344] is considered essentially as a double burden.[345] The Court considers that posting undertakings are already subject to this obligation under the home state legislation, because of Directive 91/533. Thus, relying on its pre-PWD case law, the Court finds the requirement to be in breach of the Treaties and hence not covered by Article 3(10), the interest it is deemed to protect being already "safeguarded by the rules to which the provider [of services] is subject in the Member State where he is established".[346] As for the indexation of wages to the cost of living, the Court considers that the requirement outside the scope of Article 3(10) insofar as the indexation covers wages "other than minimum wages".[347] The public policy argument put forward by the Grand Duchy is discarded as not sufficiently proved. The Court adds that to rely on this option the Member State must show the existence of "a genuine and sufficiently serious threat to a fundamental interest of society" through "appropriate evidence or by an analysis of the expediency and proportionality of the restrictive measure adopted by that State, and precise evidence enabling its arguments to be substantiated".[348] Turning to the requirements related to the respect of rules on part-time and fixed term work, the Court refers to its reasoning as to the first topic (written contract). Thus, it points out that these areas being regulated by Directives,[349] the respect of these rules is already guaranteed by the monitoring in the home state.[350]

---

342 Opinion of AG Trstenjak in *Commission v. Luxembourg*, para. 46.

343 *Commission v. Luxembourg*, para. 32; Opinion of AG Trstenjak, para. 45: the AG points out that, the Government of Luxembourg being "the constitutional representative of a Member State represented in the Council", it cannot "deny having knowledge of the interpretative declarations which were recorded by that institution in the course of the legislative process".

344 Council Directive 91/533/EEC of 14 October 1991 on an employer's obligation to inform employees of the conditions applicable to the contract or employment relationship.

345 *Commission v. Luxembourg*, para. 41.

346 Ibid., para. 42–43.

347 *Commission v. Luxembourg*, para. 55. While generally the Decision do follow the Opinion delivered by AG Trstenjak, the same AG had suggested a different solution on this specific point, upholding the measure: "inasmuch as the Law of 20 December 2002 must be interpreted according to objective criteria, that is to say, as meaning that a general adjustment of pay is effected in line with developments in the cost of living which also operates to the benefit of the minimum wage, point (2) of Article 1(1) of the Law of 20 December 2002 fulfils the Community law requirements of Article 3(1)(c) of Directive 96/71".

348 *Commission v. Luxembourg*, para. 50–51.

349 Directives 97/81/EC and 1999/70/EC.

350 *Commission v. Luxembourg*, para. 60–61. In light of *Laval*, the measures could also be considered simply as falling outside the scope of the exhaustive list of Article 3(1). However,

The fourth topic included under the "public policy" argument is the requirement to respect all collective agreements. Here the Court contents itself of contesting the undefined and excessively broad nature of the reference, considering that a Member State cannot indicate a category of provisions as covered by "public policy" on the simple basis of their status.[351]

Skipping the second point of critique, the violation having being acknowledged by the Luxembourgian Government,[352] the third complaint deals with the lack of clarity of the prior notification requirement. The Court quickly finds the complaint well founded. The requirement of providing information "prior to the commencement of the work" "on *demand*" of the labour inspectorate and "within as short a period as possible"[353] is considered as confusing.[354] This is reinforced by the fact that failure to comply with the obligation may give rise to criminal proceedings.[355] The fourth complaint meets a similar fate. The obligation of designating an *ad hoc* agent residing in Luxembourg for the retention of documents necessary for monitoring is considered as a disproportionate restriction of the freedom to provide services. The Court refers to *Arblade* to point out that a less restrictive requirement could be put in place to guarantee the retention of necessary documents. In particular a worker could be designated for the role, whereas the requirement of residence in the territory of the host state cannot be justified.[356] On top of this, the Court adds that "the organised system for cooperation and exchanges of information between Member States provided for in Article 4 of Directive 96/71 *renders* superfluous the retention of the documents in the host Member State after the employer has ceased to employ workers there".[357]

---

it is interesting to note how the Court and the AG (para. 59 of her Opinion) consider that the existence of Directive regulating the topic excludes all possibility of application of the host state legislation. In this sense the Court and the AG seem oblivious of the nature itself of the instrument of Directives, provided that they do not entail, by definition, a total harmonisation of Member States legislations. Thus, it is theoretically possible (and common in practice) that different Member States transposed the same Directive ultimately granting different standards. The interpretation provided in the present case seems to imply that applying more favourable conditions than the ones provided by the transposition of a given directive in the home state of posted workers entails a violation of the Treaty and of the PWD. On the point see Ibid., p. 679.

351 *Commission v. Luxembourg*, para. 65.

352 Ibid., para. 71–74.

353 *Commission v. Luxembourg*, para. 75.

354 As pointed out by the AG in her Opinion, para. 76: "Difficulties in the practical implementation of Article 7(1) of the Law of 20 December 2002 may also result from the fact that the obligation to provide information and, thus, the administrative procedure itself ensues, in principle, only following the receipt of a 'demand' from the labour inspectorate, with it remaining unclear in that regard what role the undertaking is expected to play in anticipation of that procedure and whether possibly it must itself trigger that 'demand'."

355 *Commission v. Luxembourg*, para. 79.

356 Ibid., para. 89–90.

357 Ibid., para. 92, emphasis added. This is quite puzzling, as the lack of implementation of this system for administrative cooperation had been remarked by the same Commission in its 2003 Communication, p. 16. In fact, shortly before the Decision in the case here at stake the

5.3.4 *VICOPLUS*

After *Laval* and *Rüffert*, no "new" cases touching upon the relationship between posted workers and industrial relations (or collective labour law) were referred to the Court of Justice. However, the *Vicoplus* case,[358] decided in more recent times, does present some interesting aspects. In particular, this case provides some clarification as regards the scope of the PWD, notably in relation with temporary work agencies and the making available of labour, and of the concept of "impact on the labour market", which in itself was pivotal, as stressed before, in the shaping of the posting phenomenon by the Court of Justice.

True enough, the case arose in a contingent legal framework, namely during the application of transitional measures provided by the 2003 Act of Accession.[359] Still, the example of *Rush Portuguesa*, decided on the basis of a very similar situation, shows that the Court does not refrain from relying on its statements of principle, even if these are formulated in a specific legal context. From this perspective, I will focus on these points which (could) have an impact on the legal construction of the phenomenon in general. However, as it will be clear from the analysis of the decision, these questions are inextricable from the analysis of the transitional measures, as the Act of Accession is essentially the main legal basis, together with the PWD, relied upon by the Court to decide the case.

Facts

The three cases joined in *Vicoplus* arose in very similar situations. Essentially, three Polish companies[360] are fined by the State Secretary for Social Affairs and Employment (Staatssecretaris van Sociale Zaken en Werkgelegenheid) for employing Polish workers in the Netherlands without having obtained work permits for that purpose.[361] The requirement to obtain work permits, otherwise not applicable in the framework of a transnational provision of services, was

---

Commission had issued a Recommendation urging the Member State to implement such a system. See Commission Recommendation of 31 March 2008 on enhanced administrative cooperation in the context of the posting of workers in the framework of the provision of services, OJ C 85, 4.4.2008, p. 1–4. See also Defossez, "Détachement Des Travailleurs, Ordre Public Et Dumping Social, Suite Et Certainment Pas Fin", pp. 610–611.

358 Joined Cases C-307/09 to C-309/09, *Vicoplus and others v. Minister van Sociale Zaken en Werkgelegenheid*, 10 February 2011.

359 Act concerning the conditions of accession of the Czech Republic, the Republic of Estonia, the Republic of Cyprus, the Republic of Latvia, the Republic of Lithuania, the Republic of Hungary, the Republic of Malta, the Republic of Poland, the Republic of Slovenia and the Slovak Republic and the adjustments to the Treaties on which the European Union is founded, OJ 2003 L 236, p. 33.

360 Vicoplus SC PUH, BAM Vermeer Contracting sp.zoo, Olbek Industrial Services sp.zoo.

361 As required by the Dutch law on the employment of third country nationals (Wet arbeid vreemdelingen), Article 2(1).

specifically provided by the implementing decree[362] of the law on the employment of third country nationals (WAV), which extends the obligation to service providers whose service consists in the pure "making available of workers".

The Polish companies appealed against the decision of the State Secretary, first in front of the District Court (Rechtbank 's-Gravenhage) and then, the appeal having been dismissed, in front of the Raad van State (Council of State). The latter decided, in each of the three pending cases, to state proceedings and to refer two questions to the Court of Justice for a preliminary ruling.

Questions and observations

The first question raised by the Dutch judge refers to the compatibility of the requirement set out by the WAV and by its implementing decree with the freedom to provide services (Articles 56 and 57 TFEU). The second question asks for clarification over the meaning of "pure" making available of workers.[363]

Though the referring Court does not refer to it in its questions, AG Bot proposed to the Court to examine the questions first and foremost on the basis of the Act of Accession of 2003.[364] Indeed, the facts taking place between 2005 and 2006, the transitional measures provided in Annex XII of the Act were still in place. In particular, Chapter 2 of the Annex (paragraph 2) allowed the "old" Member States to restrict, in respect to the "new" Member States, the free movement of workers.[365] The AG identifies the aim of the provision, namely shielding the labour market of the "old" Member States from disturbances which could be caused by (potentially) large movement of workers from the "new" Member States gaining access to the said labour market.[366] On this basis AG Bot considers the provision as covering the situation at stake in the three cases forming *Vicoplus*, and hence suggests to the Court to uphold the Dutch legislation. The Court largely follows the Opinion of the AG on the point.

It is interesting to note that a different paragraph (No. 13) of Chapter 2 of the Annex, also gave the possibility, to Germany and Austria, to also restrict the freedom to *provide services* implying a "temporary movement of workers". On this basis the Danish and German governments did point out that, *a contrario*, the Kingdom of the Netherlands could not rely on paragraph 2 of the same Chapter to restrict the posting of workers in the context of a provision of services. The AG suggested the Court to discard this argument in light of the cited interpretation of the aim of the provision of paragraph 2.

---

362 Besluit uitvoering Wav (Decree on the implementation of the Wav) (Stb. 1995, No 406), as amended by the Decree of 10 November 2005 (Stb. 2005, No 577), Article 1e(1).

363 *Vicoplus*, para. 19.

364 Opinion of AG Bot in *Vicoplus*, para. 25.

365 *Vicoplus*, para. 38.

366 Opinion of AG Bot in *Vicoplus*, para. 51.

The decision

The Court analyses the questions raised by the Dutch judge in light of the Act of Accession. In the wording of the Decision, "if national legislation is justified pursuant to one of the transitional measures referred to in Article 24 of the 2003 Act of Accession, in this case the measure provided for in Chapter 2, paragraph 2, of Annex XII to that act, the question of the compatibility of that legislation with Articles 56 TFEU and 57 TFEU can no longer arise".[367] The Court provides for an interpretation of the hiring out of workers as essentially enabling "workers to gain access to the labour market of the host Member State".[368] Thus, as opposed to the posting of workers of Article 1(3)(a) of the PWD,[369] the hiring out of workers (or the "pure" making available of workers) "may have an impact on the labour market of the Member State of the party for whom the services are intended";[370] this notably because "a worker who has been hired out pursuant to Article 1(3)(c) of Directive 96/71 is typically assigned, during the period for which he is made available, to a post within the user undertaking which would otherwise have been occupied by a person employed by that undertaking".[371] Hence the Court considers that, in light of the aim of the restrictions provided by the Act of Accession,[372] the Dutch measure is an implementation of the said restriction, as it would be "artificial to draw a distinction with regard to the influx of workers on the labour market of a Member State according to whether they gain access to it by means of the making available of labour or directly and independently because in both cases that potentially large movement of workers is capable of disturbing that labour market".[373] Indeed, citing the *Webb* case, the Court affirms that these workers *may* be covered by the free movement of workers.[374]

Turning to the second question, the Court defines three criteria to identify a service as "hiring-out of workers". First, the continuing existence of an employment relationship between the temporary employment undertaking and the worker during the posting.[375] Second, the movement of workers must constitute "the very purpose" of the provision of services.[376] In this sense, the

367 *Vicoplus*, para. 24.
368 Ibid., para. 30.
369 The situation in which undertakings "post workers to the territory of a Member State on their account and under their direction, under a contract concluded between the undertaking making the posting and the party for whom the services are intended, operating in that Member State, provided there is an employment relationship between the undertaking making the posting and the worker during the period of posting".
370 *Vicoplus*, para. 28.
371 Ibid., para. 31.
372 Here the Court follows closely the interpretation of the AG. Ibid., para. 34.
373 Ibid., para. 35.
374 *Vicoplus*, para. 28. On the point, see A. Frankart, "Mesure de contrôle du détachement pendant la péeriode transitoire suivant l'adhésion à l'Union européenne", *Revue De Droit Social/Tijdschrift voor Sociaal Recht* 3 (2012), pp. 364–366.
375 *Vicoplus*, para. 44.
376 Ibid., para. 46; see also the Opinion of AG Bot, para. 65.

other scenarios of posting are on the contrary characterised by the fact that "the posting of workers by their employer to another Member State is *ancillary* to a provision of services undertaken by that employer in that State". Third, the worker being posted under Article 1(3)(c) of the PWD (hiring-out) does carry out his work "under the control and direction of the user undertaking".[377] On the other hand, the Court states that the fact that the worker returns to his home country after the conclusion of the provision of service does not amount at denying that the posting falls under Article 1(3)(c).[378] In a way, the Court seems to consider the latter as a *fil rouge* keeping together all the posting scenarios.

All in all, the Court seems to draw a line between the first scenario of posting, *i.e.* the posting of workers as a part of a provision of services by their employer, and the two remaining scenarios, the intra-group posting and the hiring-out of workers.[379] Article 1(3) letters (b) and (c) are thus included under the label of making available of transnational labour.[380] Following the reasoning of the Court, these two scenarios imply the *access* to the host state labour market, as workers made available through these channels are "typically assigned" to "a post within the user undertaking which would otherwise have been occupied by a person employed by that undertaking".[381] In the end, this is the criterion used by the Court to define the access to the labour market of the host state. On this basis, the two scenarios are considered as (partially?) overlapping with the free movement of workers.[382] The case at stake does not concern working conditions, so that it is still unclear whether this "partial" inclusion under the free movement of workers does entail the application of the right to equal treatment for the workers being posted, or if these workers will only be allowed the minima provided by the PWD.[383]

---

377 *Vicoplus*, para. 47. This is much in line with Article 1(1) of Directive 2008/104/EC of the European Parliament and of the Council of 19 November 2008 on temporary agency work, as remarked by the AG in his Opinion, para. 64. The Court however never refers to the cited Directive as a basis to interpret the definition of "hiring-out".

378 *Vicoplus*, para. 49.

379 Ibid., para. 39.

380 In a more recent case AG Bot proposed the Court to clarify this distinction, by distinguishing the approach of *Vicoplus*. See case C-91/13, *Essent Energie Productie BV v. Minister van Sociale Zaken en Werkgelegenheid*. Indeed following the Opinion of the AG, the Decision reached in *Vicoplus* would be confined to those situations covered by transitional measures (para. 113). However, the Court did not refer to this part of the Opinion in its decision, which moreover did not make reference to the PWD.

381 Ibid., para. 31.

382 Ibid., para. 28. As cited *supra*, the Court, para. 35, defines as "artificial" to distinguish between these posting scenarios and the influx of workers through their own independent movement.

383 Or, as a third option, if these workers will be covered by the principle of equal treatment, and possible exceptions thereof, provided by Article 5 of Directive 2008/104/EC on temporary agency work.

5.3.5 *PWD UNLEASHED*

Thirty years of case law on posting, and a decade of application of the PWD help shed some light upon the "black boxes" created by the Directive. From the point of view of 2014, the PWD looks very different from the instrument which saw the light in 1996, though its text has remained the same. From an instrument saluted as essentially protecting "national labour systems"[384] to a dangerous tool able to curtail one of these systems.[385] Indeed, the EU at 25 and then at 28 which witnessed the more recent case law on the topic is very different from the one which was negotiating the PWD in the middle of the nineties, though it is hard to measure the impact of the enlargement on the case law of the Court of Justice.

The case law preceding the coming into force of the PWD is in this sense useful to measure the different understanding of the phenomenon in the two periods. Notably, the comparison between the pre-PWD case law and the more recent one can be useful to actually assess the impact of the legislative intervention on the legal interpretation of the phenomenon by the Court of Justice.

All in all, the case law delivered by the Court, and especially the "Laval trio" touches upon many crucial issues that were left (to a greater or lesser extent) open by text of the PWD. Obviously, the *Laval* case itself represents the clearest expression of the encounter between posting of workers and industrial relations. However, the same decision has showed that the indirect effect of the interpretation of the PWD has also far reaching consequences on this relationship. In particular, the firm stance of the Court in the "Laval trio" in favour of the "maximum" character of the PWD seems able to interfere with all the issues connected with collective bargaining and collective action.

Scope

An underground river connects the early decision of *Webb* and the more recent *Vicoplus* case, its flow being partially noticeable also in *Rush Portuguesa*. The issue revolves around the concept of "making available of labour", including the (transnational) hiring-out of workers as its most evident form.

After *Rush Portuguesa* the flow was so difficult to notice that the Raad van State in *Vicoplus* asked the Court to confirm it, though it had never been explicitly denied. The Dutch court thus observed that "the Court did not, in the later judgments cited above, reproduce the view expressed in paragraph 16 of *Rush Portuguesa*".[386] In that paragraph, the Court of Justice acknowledged that "an undertaking engaged in the making available of labour, although a supplier

384 Davies, "Posted Workers: Single Market or Protection of National Labour Law Systems?", pp. 575–576.

385 Malmberg and Sigeman, "Industrial Action and EU Economic Freedoms: The Autonomous Collective Bargaining Model Curtailed by the European Court of Justice".

386 *Vicoplus*, para. 17.

of services within the meaning of the Treaty, carries on activities which are specifically intended to enable workers to gain access to the labour market of the host Member State".[387] With this statement, confirmed in *Vicoplus*, the Court introduced a distinction between different posting scenarios.

In fact, in the same *Rush* decision, the Court identified the criterion to exclude posted workers from the domain of the free movement of workers. This criterion, as it was remarked *supra*, revolves around the concept of "access to the labour market" of the host state.[388] Posted workers, we were told, *do not* gain access to the labour market of the host country, as (a) their presence is ancillary to the provision of services by their employer and (b) they return to their home country after the completion of their work. The exception to this assumption, already expressed in paragraph 16 of the *Rush* decision, is confirmed and developed further in *Vicoplus*. In particular, the criterion to draw the boundaries of this *exception* to the cited reasoning, is identified by the Court as follows: "a worker who has been hired out pursuant to Article 1(3)(c) of Directive 96/71 is typically assigned, during the period for which he is made available, to a post within the user undertaking which would otherwise have been occupied by a person employed by that undertaking".[389] In another paragraph of the same decision, the Court also includes under the umbrella of the "making available of transnational labour" the scenario of Article 1(3)(b) of the PWD, *i.e.* the intra-group posting.[390] Also, in identifying the hiring-out of workers, the Court considers that "the fact that the worker returns to his Member State of origin at the end of the posting cannot preclude that worker from having been made available in the host Member State".[391] On this basis, of the two assumptions affirming the lack of access of posted workers to the labour market of the host state, it seems that the second one[392] can be considered as superfluous. Following the reasoning of the Court, posted workers under Article 1(3)(c) *do* return to their home state after the provision of services but they nonetheless gain access to the labour market of the host state, because they are assigned "to a post within the user undertaking which would otherwise have been occupied by a person employed by that undertaking".

---

387 *Rush Portuguesa*, para. 16.

388 *Rush Portuguesa*, para. 15: "The situation is different, however, in a case such as that in the main proceedings where there is a temporary movement of workers who are sent to another Member State to carry out construction work or public works as part of a provision of services by their employer. In fact, such workers return to their country of origin after the completion of their work without at any time gaining access to the labour market of the host Member State."

389 *Vicoplus*, para. 31.

390 "This Directive shall apply to the extent that the undertakings referred to in paragraph 1 take one of the following transnational measures [...] (b) post workers to an establishment or to an undertaking owned by the group in the territory of a Member State, provided there is an employment relationship between the undertaking making the posting and the worker during the period of posting."

391 *Vicoplus*, para. 49.

392 Point (b) identified *supra*, *i.e.* the fact that posted workers return to the home state after the completion of their work.

Everything considered, the Court seems to carve a sub-category of posting for the scenarios of Article 1(3)(b) and 1(3)(c) of the PWD. At the very least, following *Vicoplus* this means that these scenarios are subject to the eventual limitations of the said free movement of workers. As for working conditions we are left with the non-decisive statement of *Webb*, repeated by the Court in *Vicoplus*: "*employees* of agencies for the supply of manpower *may* in certain circumstances be covered by the provisions of Articles 45 TFEU to 48 TFEU and the European Union regulations adopted in implementation thereof".[393] The reference to "employees" and not to their employers could be interpreted as a choice in favour of the application of the equal treatment provision stemming from the free movement of workers.[394] On the other hand, only workers can be covered by this fundamental freedom, so that the reference could not be formulated differently.

The Court evidently construes narrowly this exception to the theoretical framework of posting as not-accessing the host country's labour market. Indeed the reference to the possibility that the post occupied by the worker transnationally made available "would otherwise have been occupied by a person employed *by that undertaking*" seems artificial. The wording excludes the more general scenario in which the post would be occupied by another participant to the labour market of the host state, even if not already employed by the user undertaking. At the same time, the criterion is formulated and applied to the facts in *Vicoplus* without any enquiry by the Court about the actual situation in the user undertaking, so that "a person employed by that undertaking" could simply be interpreted as "a person hired by that undertaking to fill the specific post".

All in all, the *Vicoplus* case gives back the image of a two-headed legal interpretation of the posting phenomenon. On the one hand, the *pure* posting scenario, Article 1(3)(a) of the PWD,[395] where workers are *ancillary* to the provision of services by their employer. On the other, the scenarios overlapping, to a lesser or greater degree, with the free movement of workers, Articles 1(3)(b) and (c). This interpretation, though having an evident added value in respect of the pre-directive case law, is in line with the previous stance of the Court, as expressed in *Webb* and *Rush Portuguesa*.

---

393 *Vicoplus*, para. 28; *Webb*, para. 10, emphasis added.

394 See Frankart, "Mesure de contrôle du détachement pendant la péeriode transitoire suivant l'adhésion à l'Union européenne", pp. 364–366.

395 "This Directive shall apply to the extent that the undertakings referred to in paragraph 1 take one of the following transnational measures: (a) post workers to the territory of a Member State on their account and under their direction, under a contract concluded between the undertaking making the posting and the party for whom the services are intended, operating in that Member State, provided there is an employment relationship between the undertaking making the posting and the worker during the period of posting."

From floor to ceiling

The interpretation of the PWD as a "maximum" directive, (*i.e.* a ceiling) was without doubt the most staggering outcome of the *Laval* trio, at least regarding posting of workers *stricto sensu*. This development was particularly shocking from the point of view of those interpretations that welcomed the PWD as essentially protecting the ability of the host Member State to extend their level wages and working conditions to posted workers.[396]

As it was described before analysing *Laval*,[397] *Rüffert*,[398] and *Commission v. Luxembourg*,[399] the issue revolves around the interpretation of Articles 3(1), 3(7) and 3(10) of the PWD. The Court thus interpreted the items on the list of Article 3(1) as establishing the maximum protection which can be awarded to posted workers.[400] Also, the list is considered as exhaustive, with the only exception being Article 3(10) narrowly interpreted[401] and not covering trade union actions.[402]

Article 3(1) speaks of minima in relation to (a) rest periods, (b) paid annual holidays and (c) rates of pay (including overtime rates). The text of Article 3(7) is much more obscure in this regard, as it states that "Paragraphs 1 to 6 shall not prevent application of terms and conditions of employment which are more favourable to workers. [...]". Thus, the text in itself seemed open to the application by the host state of a higher degree of protection than the minimum provided by Article 3(1). Evju and Novitz maintain that such an interpretation would be "untenable", in light of the "intention of the legislator" highlighted by the previous drafts of the PWD and by working documents.[403] However, AG Mengozzi and Bot, in their Opinions respectively in *Laval* and *Rüffert*, both interpreted Article 3(7) as *allowing* the application of improved protection in the host state[404] with the only limit of the respect of freedom to provide services. AG Bot also referred to Recitals 13th and 17th to reinforce this interpretation. Recital 13th refers to the list of Article 3(1) "as a nucleus of mandatory rules for *minimum* protection", while Recital 17 essentially repeats the not-conclusive statement of Article 3(7) by

396 Davies, "Posted Workers: Single Market or Protection of National Labour Law Systems?", pp. 575–576; Biagi, "The 'Posted Workers' EU Directive: from Social Dumping to Social Protectionism"; *contra*, Barnard, *EC Employment Law*, p. 179, remarked that the PWD only allowed the extension of *minimum* conditions, thus safeguarding the (eventual) competitive advantage of posting undertakings.

397 See *supra*, p. 184.

398 See *supra*, p. 194.

399 See *supra*, p. 201.

400 *Laval*, para. 79–81; *Rüffert*, para. 32–34.

401 *Commission v. Luxembourg*, para. 28–31.

402 *Laval*, para. 84.

403 Evju and Novitz, "The Evolving Regulation: dynamics and Consequences", pp. 35 and 56. The second draft of the PWD (1993) in Article 3(3) states "Paragraph 1 shall not prevent application of the terms and conditions of employment *provided for by the law applicable* which are more favourable to workers."

404 Opinion of AG Mengozzi in *Laval*, para. 197–199; Opinion of AG Bot in *Rüffert*, paras. 81–84.

affirming that "the mandatory rules for minimum protection in force in the host country must not prevent the application of terms and conditions of employment which are more favourable to workers" without further specification.[405]

In fact, seen from the perspective of the previous analysis, both AGs seem to follow the pre-directive case law in interpreting the PWD. Thus the restrictions to the freedom to provide services at stake in both *Laval* and *Rüffert* were analysed through the "*Arblade* test",[406] as stated by AG Bot in his Opinion: "according to equally settled case law of the Court, such legislation, that is [a] applicable without distinction, may be justified under Article 49 EC where it meets [b] overriding requirements relating to the public interest in so far as [c] that interest is not safeguarded by the rules to which the provider of the service is subject in the Member State in which he is established and [d] in so far as it is appropriate for securing the attainment of the objective which it pursues and does not go beyond what is necessary in order to attain it".[407] This test was hence applied by the AGs in order to establish whether the application of better conditions could be justified under Article 3(8) while at the same time respecting the freedom to provide services. Looking briefly to the application of the test, the public interest was identified in the protection of workers and the fight against social dumping;[408] second, and limiting our overview to the issue of wages (which is shared by the two cases), both AG found that the application of higher wages than the ones applicable under the home state regulations provided a "genuine additional protection" for posted workers.[409] As regards point [d], hence the proportionality, AG Mengozzi considers the collective action at stake in *Laval* to be proportionate (as regards minimum wages) in so far as the wage level actually paid by Laval "was not the same as or essentially similar to that determined in accordance with the collective agreement".[410] Similarly, AG Bot concluded that the regulation of *Land* Niedersachsen was proportionate as "objectives of worker protection and the prevention of social dumping could not be achieved as effectively by means of less binding rules with a less restrictive effect on the freedom to provide services.".[411] Both AGs thus deliver a consistent interpretation of the PWD founded on the pre-directive case law involving posting of workers.

No trace of such a test can be found in both Decisions. Indeed, the Court makes it clear that host states are not allowed to impose a level of protection going beyond the ones pointed out in Article 3(1)[412] without any attempt to reconsider

---

405 On the point see also Van Peijpe, "Collective Labour Law After Viking, Laval, Rüffert, and Commission v. Luxembourg", pp. 99–100: "There is no ground for such interpretation [the one delivered by the Court on Article 3(7)] to be found in the text of the preamble."

406 *Arblade*, para. 33; see *supra*, p. 162.

407 Opinion of AG Bot in *Rüffert*, para. 105; similarly see AG Mengozzi in *Laval*, para. 263.

408 Opinion of AG Mengozzi in *Laval*, para. 249; Opinion of AG Bot in *Rüffert*, para. 115–116.

409 Opinion of AG Mengozzi in *Laval*, para. 264–265; Opinion of AG Bot in *Rüffert*, para. 118.

410 Opinion in *Laval*, para. 272–273.

411 Opinion in *Rüffert*, para. 124.

412 *Laval*, para. 81; *Rüffert*, para. 34.

its previous case law in light of the new Directive. *Rectius*, from the perspective of this case law the PWD seems to have had a *restrictive* effect on the possibilities left to Member States to extend their working conditions to posted workers.

This restrictive stance is also visible in the identification of what a minimum rate of pay *is*. On this point the text of the PWD shows once again its (intended?) minimalistic character, by stating, in Article 3(1) that "the concept of minimum rates of pay referred to in paragraph 1 (c) is defined by the national law and/ or practice of the Member State to whose territory the worker is posted".[413] The Court did not find it necessary to analyse the possible impact of this disposition. Instead, the boundaries of "minimum wage" are narrowly drawn.[414] This is however better analysed in the context of the issue related to the means which can be used to establish the conditions applicable to posted workers.

Collective agreements

Leaving aside the legislative instrument, the text of the PWD allows setting the standards applicable to post workers by three types of collective agreements. First, collective agreements which have been declared "universally applicable"[415]; second, "generally applicable" collective agreements;[416] third, collective agreements "concluded by the most representative employers' and labour organisations at national level and which are applied throughout national territory". The 2003 Communication of the Commission on the implementation of the PWD had specified that the choice among these methods must be made explicitly by the given Member State.[417] This stance was followed by the Court of Justice in *Laval*.[418] On the other hand, in *Rüffert*, the Court maintains that a Member State having system for declaring collective agreements "universally applicable" *cannot* (decide to) rely on the other options.[419] Thus, as Germany was considered to fall in the first scenario, the *Land* of Niedersachsen could not rely on the two other options provided by Article 3(8) in order to apply the higher regional minimum wage for

---

413 Referred to both by AG Mengozzi in his Opinion in *Laval*, para. 196, and by AG Bot in *Rüffert*, para. 78.

414 In fact, in the three cases composing the *Laval* trio, only in *Commission v. Luxembourg* a single measure was considered as effectively falling under the definition of "minimum wage", namely the automatic indexation of the minimum wage to the cost of living. See paras. 47 and 55.

415 "Collective agreements [...] which must be observed by all undertakings in the geographical area and in the profession or industry concerned."

416 "Collective agreements [...] which are generally applicable to all similar undertakings in the geographical area and in the profession or industry concerned."

417 Communication on "The implementation of Directive 96/71/EC in the Member States", p. 12; in absence of such a choice the Commission considered that those Member States "do not apply the terms and conditions of employment laid down in collective agreements to workers posted on their territory".

418 Para. 66.

419 *Rüffert*, para. 27.

the construction sector.[420] This is particularly puzzling from the point of view of the pre-directive case law. In particular, in the *Portugaia Costruções* case.[421] Back in 2002 the Court had found that "the fact that, in concluding a collective agreement specific to one undertaking, a domestic employer can pay wages lower than the minimum wage laid down in a collective agreement declared to be generally applicable, whilst an employer established in another Member State cannot do so, constitutes an unjustified restriction on the freedom to provide services".[422] Apart from the wording (*generally applicable*), it is clear from the decision of the Court that the minimum wage agreed at national level *can* be derogated at the enterprise level.[423] This means that these agreements do not meet the requirement of Article 3(8) to be considered "universally applicable": "collective agreements or arbitration awards which *must be observed* by *all undertakings* in the geographical area and in the profession or industry concerned". In *Rüffert* the Court never refers to *Portugaia Costruções*, which makes it impossible to clarify this apparent contradiction. In the meantime the German system of collective agreements seems to be caught in a *Catch-22*-like situation:[424] it has a system to declare a collective agreement as universally binding, thus it cannot rely on the other options; at the same time, the collective agreement declared "universally applicable" can be derogated at enterprise level and therefore is not universally applicable (in the meaning of the PWD).

In *Laval*, the Court repeatedly stated that Sweden, in the absence of a system to declare collective agreements universally binding, had not explicitly opted for one of the other possibilities offered by Article 3(8).[425] As a side note it is worth mentioning that, as noted by AG Mengozzi[426] in his Opinion, this

420 See Van Peijpe, "Collective Labour Law after Viking, Laval, Rüffert, and Commission v. Luxembourg", pp. 98–99; Francq et al., "Chronique de jurisprudence du Tribunal et de la Cour de Justice des Communautés européennes. Concurrence", pp. 676–677.

421 See *supra*, p. 173.

422 *Portugaia Costruções*, para. 35.

423 Following the principles of *Tarifautonomie* and *Tarifkonkurrenz*; on the point see Van Peijpe, "Collective Labour Law After Viking, Laval, Rüffert, and Commission v. Luxembourg", p. 99.

424 From the satirical novel by Joseph Heller, "There was only one catch and that was Catch-22, which specified that a concern for one's safety in the face of dangers that were real and immediate was the process of a rational mind. Orr was crazy and could be grounded. All he had to do was ask; and as soon as he did, he would no longer be crazy and would have to fly more missions".

425 *Laval*, paras. 66, 67 and 71.

426 Opinion in *Laval*, paras. 180–182. It is interesting to note that the possibility to implement EU directives through collective agreements was mentioned, back in the Age of Innocence, by Commissioner Flynn in his letter to the Swedish government. In the wake of the Swedish accession to the EU the government had asked for reassurance as to the implications of the Maastricht treaty for the Swedish system of industrial relations. The Commissioner answered, among other arguments, that "it goes without saying that, if directives [...] are adopted, then duly notified collective agreements at national level would be one way in which to implement them. And Sweden would most probably chose this way of implementation [...]. Non-compliance by firms or individuals could in this case be solved notably by recourse to the normal procedures in effect on the Swedish labour market". See Ahlberg, "The Age of Innocence – and Beyond", pp. 306–307.

greatly undermines the possibility of implementing the PWD through collective agreements, since social actors cannot themselves make the choice in favour of one of the three scenarios of Article 3(8).[427]

Though the Court states in *Laval* that Member States are in principle free to chose a "a system at the national level which is not expressly mentioned among those provided for in that directive, provided that it does not hinder the provision of services between the Member States",[428] it openly criticises the Swedish system. This especially on the basis of what the Court calls "case-by-case negotiations".[429] In this sense, the Court rules out all those systems which are based on negotiations at company level: making it impossible for the service provider to know *in advance* the working conditions applicable to posted workers, these systems are considered as restricting the freedom to provide services.[430] Also, such a system does not guarantee the equal treatment of national and foreign undertakings.[431]

However, whatever the procedural method chosen to apply working conditions to posted workers, these wages and working conditions *cannot* go beyond the list of Article 3(1). Thus, a collective agreement must set a *minimum* in order to be applied to posted workers, as highlighted in the previous paragraph. Still, *better* conditions *can* be applied to posted workers in a single specific situation:[432] a collective agreement signed in the host state by the posting undertaking "of its own accord".[433] The distinction drawn by the Court on the point thus implies a *summa divisio* between collective agreements which are *freely* signed by the posting employer and those which are forced upon him.[434] Thus, the issue moves to the territory of collective action.

Collective action

The clash between posting and collective action before the Court of Justice is at the heart of the *Laval* case. As it should be evident after the previous analysis of the decision, the issue must be analysed in the broader context of the relationship between fundamental social rights and fundamental freedoms. As it is even more evident, the importance of this topic requires an extensive analysis, that will thus

---

427 Evju and Novitz, "The Evolving Regulation: dynamics and Consequences", p. 57, consider this as "another illustration of *étatisme* having precedence over *collective autonomy*".

428 *Laval*, para. 68.

429 Ibid., paras. 69–70 and 100.

430 See Davies, "One Step Forward, Two Steps Back? The Viking and Laval Cases in the ECJ", p. 129.

431 *Laval*, para. 66. See Malmberg and Sigeman, "Industrial Action and EU Economic Freedoms: The Autonomous Collective Bargaining Model Curtailed by the European Court of Justice", p. 1141.

432 Apart from the more obvious situation where these workers enjoy better conditions under the home state regulations and collective agreements.

433 *Laval*, para. 81; *Rüffert*, para. 34.

434 On the point see Dorssemont, "The Right to Take Collective Action Versus Fundamental Economic Freedoms in the Aftermath of Laval and Viking. Foes Are Forever", p. 78.

be developed in the next Chapter. However, it is possible to anticipate here some considerations on the narrower topic of the relationship between collective action the PWD as construed by the Court of Justice.

The starting point is collective bargaining and collective agreements. The relationship between the latter and collective action, which is evident in the theoretical construction of the right to take collective action,[435] is both *denied* and re-affirmed in *Laval.* As it was examined in the above paragraph, the Court seems to consider that a collective agreement signed "of its own accord" by the employer would be perfectly acceptable. Thus, in a way it is the recourse to collective action which is ruled out, whereas a "peaceful" collective bargaining seems to be acceptable in the eye of the Court.[436] Hence, the link between collective action and the conclusion of collective agreements, which is otherwise inherent,[437] is broken.

On the other hand this link is re-affirmed when the Court examines the compatibility of the collective action put in place by the Swedish trade unions with the Treaties. Indeed, when the Court concludes that "Article 49 EC and Directive 96/71 are to be interpreted as precluding a trade union [...] from attempting, by means of collective action [...] to force a provider of services established in another Member State to enter into negotiations with it on the rates of pay for posted workers and to sign a collective agreement *the terms of which* lay down, as regards some of those matters, *more favourable conditions* than those resulting from the relevant legislative provisions, while other terms relate to matters not referred to in Article 3 of the directive",[438] it evidently uses the *content* of the collective agreement to assess the legitimacy of the collective action.[439] Thus, though the analysis of the collective action was conducted in light of the freedom to provide services (Article 49 EC, now Article 56 TFUE), the PWD still played a relevant role. Because of this, the (new?) *maximum* nature of this Directive has in itself far reaching consequences on the relationship of posting of workers with both collective action and collective agreements.

The functioning of the host system of industrial relations is thus put to the service of the PWD, as interpreted by the *Laval* trio. In the aftermath of these decisions, Malmberg and Sigeman considered that "the Laval judgement does not

---

435 See *supra*, p. 93.

436 *Laval*, para. 81.

437 Cf. the text of the RevESC which in the fourth paragraph of Article 6 (devoted to "the right to bargain collectively") guarantees the right "of workers and employers to collective action in cases of conflicts of interest".

438 *Laval*, para. 111.

439 Evju and Novitz, "The Evolving Regulation: dynamics and Consequences", p. 59, who remark that "given the way the Court framed its reasons, this 'excessiveness' of bargaining demands in itself was sufficient to render collective action disproportionate"; Dorssemont, "The Right to Take Collective Action Versus Fundamental Economic Freedoms in the Aftermath of Laval and Viking. Foes Are Forever", p. 84; Davies, "One Step Forward, Two Steps Back? The Viking and Laval Cases in the ECJ", p. 145: "the Court held that collective action could not be used to promote terms and conditions for posted workers which were more than the 'minimum core' of protection".

generally prohibit collective actions against foreign service providers, but rather restricts the demands that the host State trade union may put forward".[440] In this sense, these demands should be limited to the list of "minimum protection" of Article 3(1).[441] Still, this "minimum" seems difficult to meet if considered in light of the case law examined in this chapter. First, the "minimum" should be formulated so that the employer is able to know *ex ante* the conditions applicable to posted workers.[442] Second, the Court also hints that the *duration* of the eventual negotiations should be limited in time.[443] Third, the minimum must cover a whole sector of activity in its geographical area of application.[444] From this perspective, the scope for a system *not* falling into the three options provided by the PWD in Article 3(8) to validly apply (minimum) wages and/or working conditions to posted workers seems indeed narrow (to use an euphemism).[445] Consequently, all collective actions undertaken to support the signature of a collective agreement going beyond the minimum thus defined face a high risk to be considered as breaching the PWD (*hence* the Treaties). It is sadly ironic to compare this with the 22th Recital of the PWD, stating that the Directive is "without prejudice to the law of the Member States concerning collective action to defend the interests of trades and professions".

The freedom to provide services strikes back

The history told by the case law of the Court dealing with the PWD is an history of two revenges. First, the revenge of the legal basis, *i.e.* of the freedom to provide services, on the Directive itself and on all the black-boxes left by its adoption. It is

---

440 Malmberg and Sigeman, "Industrial Action and EU Economic Freedoms: The Autonomous Collective Bargaining Model Curtailed by the European Court of Justice", p. 2008.

441 Ibid.

442 *Laval*, para. 110.

443 Ibid., para. 100.

444 *Rüffert*, para. 29, where the Court rules out the application of collective agreements limited to public contracts. However, no further clarification is provided as to what would constitute a valid "sector".

445 Though, as recalled *supra*, the Court seems to leave the door open for these systems "not expressly mentioned among those provided for in that directive"; *Laval*, para. 68. What is more, the 2003 Declaration of the Commission on the Implementation of the PWD cast a shadow on this possibility. The Declaration, which was closely followed by the PWD on other matters such as the interpretation of Articles 3(7) and 3(8), states that "[Since no Member State's transposing legislation makes any mention of the options offered by the second sub paragraph of Article 3(8)], the Commission concludes that States which do not have collective agreements declared to be universally applicable within the meaning of the first subparagraph of Article 3(8) of the Directive *do not apply* the terms and conditions of employment laid down in collective agreements to workers posted on their territory. In these countries, therefore, *only* the terms and conditions of employment *laid down in legislative provisions* apply to workers posted on their territory". The wording of the Communication is pretty clear: in the eyes of the Commission (at least in 2003) in the absence of universally applicable collective agreements, Member States can explicitly opt for one of the possibilities offered by Article 3(8). In the absence of such a choice *no* collective agreement can be applied to posted workers.

a tale of lost innocence and shattered childhood's illusions. The second tale tells of a collision between two different worlds, where one side is armed with superior weaponry. It deals with the revenge of the black letter law on *practices* connected with industrial relations.[446]

The first tale emerges quite clearly if one compares the closing paragraphs of the previous Chapter[447] and the *Laval* trio examined here. Many of the questions left, more or less intentionally, open by the final text of the PWD found an answer in these cases, an answer that in general went in the direction of restricting the possibility for host states to extend their wages and working conditions to posted workers. As Davies puts it, the adoption of the PWD brought together three "largely inconsistent" rationales: the fight against social dumping (hence the protection of workers of the host state), the improvement of conditions of employment for posted workers and the promotion of the freedom to provide services.[448] The Court interprets the PWD "in the light of Article 49 EC"[449] (now Article 56 TFEU), hence as a tool to *abolish restrictions* to the fundamental freedom in question. The two other rationales (social dumping and protection of posted workers) are assimilated by this overarching "constitutional" reading of the Directive. Thus, the fight against social dumping is considered as satisfied by the application of the minimum conditions covered by the PWD as interpreted by the Court.[450] The second rationale (protection of posted workers) shares a similar fate, as the Court considers posted workers as sufficiently protected by the application of minimum wages and working conditions in force in the host state (*if* their application is compatible with the PWD itself).[451] Having "incorporated" the PWD under the long shadow of the freedom to provide services,[452] the Court applies its standard

446 In general on the complicated relation between flexible and informal practices with the internal market see R.D. Kelemen, *Eurolegalism: The Transformation of Law and Regulation in the European Union* (Harvard University Press, 2011), p. 23.

447 See *supra*, p. 125.

448 Davies, "Case C-346/06, Ruffert v. Land Niedersachsen [2008] IRLR 467 (ECJ)", pp. 294–295.

449 *Rüffert*, para. 43.

450 *Laval*, para. 75: "That provision thus prevents a situation arising in which, by applying to their workers the terms and conditions of employment in force in the Member State of origin as regards those matters [Article 3(1)], undertakings established in other Member States would compete unfairly against undertakings of the host Member State in the framework of the transnational provision of services, if the level of social protection in the host Member State is higher." On the point see Malmberg and Sigeman, "Industrial Action and EU Economic Freedoms: The Autonomous Collective Bargaining Model Curtailed by the European Court of Justice", p. 1136–1137.

451 *Laval*, para. 76–77: "the consequence of affording such minimum protection – if the level of protection resulting from the terms and conditions of employment granted to posted workers in the Member State of origin, as regards the matters referred to in Article 3(1), first subparagraph, (a) to (g) of Directive 96/71, is lower than the level of minimum protection afforded in the host Member State – is to enable those workers to enjoy better terms and conditions of employment in the host Member State".

452 The Opinion of AG Mengozzi in *Laval* is very clear on this point: "a measure that is incompatible with Directive 96/71 will, a fortiori, be contrary to Article 49 TEC, because that directive is intended, within its specific scope, to implement the terms of that article". See on this point

approach (breach, justification, proportionality).[453] However, in order to assess the breach, the Court conversely interprets the freedom to provide services "in light" of the PWD. The criterion to ascertain the existence of a breach is thus the "violation" of the PWD, *i.e.* the imposition (or the attempt to impose, as in *Laval*) of wages and working conditions going beyond what is permitted by Article 3(1) of the Directive, as interpreted by the Court. As it should be clear from the previous Chapter, the choice of the legal basis for the PWD responded largely to contingent political and legal constraints. The Directive was immediately perceived as fitting uncomfortably within the framework of the freedom to provide services,[454] as "the imposition of additional burdens on service providers hinders rather than facilitates the provision of services".[455] The decisions of the Court of Justice in the *Laval* trio now limit the (potential) diverging impact of the PWD in respect to the (unconstrained) freedom to provide services: the PWD is now domesticated.[456]

The second revenge is more subtle, at least in legal terms, not implying any deviation from legal texts or shift in interpretation. On the contrary, the stance of the Court is consistent if the pre-directive case law is taken into account. The question here is the marked preference of the Court of Justice for a formalistic interpretation of legal texts when it comes to consider the outcome of industrial relations *practices*. This was already made evident in the *Portugaia Costruções* decision. In that occasion, the Court considered the German system of collective agreements as violating the freedom to provide services inasmuch it allowed employers to derogate from "generally applicable" collective agreements (which had to be respected by posting undertakings). The German government had responded that the actual recourse to such a possibility was in fact *negligible*, being limited to around 2% of undertakings in West Germany (and 4% in East Germany), an argument well founded on available data. The Court did not even consider this submission, basing its decision on the formal legal regulation. The very same stance is visible in *Laval*. Once again, the AG brought to the attention of the Court the fact (submitted by the Government) that the overwhelming majority of undertakings in the Swedish construction sector were in fact covered

Dorssemont, "The Right to Take Collective Action Versus Fundamental Economic Freedoms in the Aftermath of Laval and Viking. Foes Are Forever", p. 76.

453 C. Barnard, "Social Dumping or Dumping Socialism?" *The Cambridge Law Journal* 67, no. 2 (June 2008), p. 264.

454 Biagi, "The 'Posted Workers' EU Directive: from Social Dumping to Social Protectionism", p. 175, points out that the UK and Portugal based their contrariety to the PWD (also) on the fact that it was not "a piece of legislation designed to promote freedom to provide services".

455 Barnard, *EC Employment Law*, p. 179. However, as the author notes, the Court never accepted the argument that whatever imposition of host state working standards would amount to a restriction of the freedom to provide services; nor the Court accepted the "self exploitation" argument, which implied that posted workers would be better protected by *lower* working conditions, since those would allow them to access more employment opportunities through the transnational competition. These arguments were put forward by the referring judges both in *Finalarte* and *Rüffert*, both analysed *supra*.

456 Krebber, "Case C-319/06, Commission v. Luxembourg, Judgment of the Court (First Chamber) of 19 June 2008,[2008] ECR I-4323", p. 1735.

by collective agreements, notwithstanding the lack of a formal system for the extension of these agreements.[457] On this basis the AG had maintained that the Swedish system of industrial relations ensured the equal treatment between foreign service providers and national undertakings through the functioning of its industrial relations system.[458] As for *Portugaia Costruções* the Court did not find it necessary to consider this observations, nor to spend time analysing the Swedish system of industrial relations and its practices. To a certain extent a similar stance pervades the *Rüffert* decision. The Court essentially considers the "social clause" designed by the German *Land* as going beyond what is allowed by the PWD and hence causing an excessive restriction to the freedom to provide services. Notwithstanding the fact that the practice of social clauses is in itself a widespread practice, a situation made evident by ILO Convention No. 94 devoted to this very topic,[459] the Court goes further in its critique of the German regulation. Among other arguments, the Court considers the regulation of the *Land* in breach of the Treaties as it applies "only to public contracts and not to private contracts".[460] However, the *Land*, which was the defendant in the case, could not have regulated wages and working conditions of workers employed under private contracts.[461] Thus, the *Land* had extended to the whole sector of its competence the application of the collective agreement. The Court did not consider the question of competences in its decision, nor the fact that the obligation would in fact cover every company wishing to "access" the market created by the tender. Finally, the disregard for the empirical reality permeates the stance of the Court about both the "lack of access to the labour market" approach to posting and its understanding of the nature of the PWD as not harmonising "the systems for establishing terms and conditions of employment in the Member States".[462] On the first issue, the Court has construed the "access to the labour market" as the situation in which a posted workers occupies "a post within the user undertaking which would otherwise have been occupied by a person employed by that undertaking".[463] Since they do not fall into this narrow category, workers posted under letter 1(3)(a) do not access the labour market. This is *artificial* in

---

457 Opinion of AG Mengozzi in *Laval*, para. 191: "there are around 9800 undertakings in Sweden with more than three employees, whereas around 11200 undertakings – and that figure thus includes undertakings employing fewer than three employees – are bound by collective agreements in the building sector".

458 See also *supra*, p. 75.

459 ILO Convention on labour clauses in public contracts (No. 94), 1949. On the point see extensively N. Bruun, A. Jacobs and M. Schmidt, "ILO Convention No. 94 in the Aftermath of the Ruffert Case", *Transfer: European Review of Labour and Research* 16, no. 4 (November 2010): 473–488.

460 *Rüffert*, para. 29; the same argument is repeated in Case C-549/13, Bundesdruckerei GmbH, para. 32.

461 See Francq et al., "Chronique de jurisprudence du Tribunal et de la Cour de Justice des Communautés européennes. Concurrence", pp. 676–677.

462 *Laval*, 68.

463 *Vicoplus*, para. 31.

two different ways. The first one is the line which it draws between such a worker and one moving under the free movement of workers, who could decide to come back to his home country after a short period of employment in another Member State.[464] Second, posting of workers *does* have an impact on the labour market of the host state, either in terms of "crowding out" of national workers either in terms of pressure on their wages and working conditions.[465]

At the end of this extensive examination, and in light of the "two revenges" just outlined, two main areas of impact of the legal framework of posting of workers on industrial relations can be identified. The first area is represented by the relationship between the freedom to provide services (and more generally, of "fundamental freedoms") and fundamental social rights. Though this issue is far broader than the simple posting phenomenon it does nonetheless influence the whole topic of collective labour law in its interaction with posted workers. The second area is the interpretation of the PWD as a maximum instrument delivered by the Court in the more recent case law. Both topics will be analysed in the following Chapters, starting (in a hierarchical order) from the complicated relationship between fundamental freedoms and fundamental (collective) social rights.

---

464 Hellsten, "On the Social Dimension in Posting of Workers", p. 9.

465 Cf. the German situation before the PWD highlighted by Eichhorst, "European Social Policy Between National and Supranational Regulation: Posted Workers in the Framework of Liberalized Services Provision", p. 22: "Germany was the host country of most of the posted workers from Western Europe after 1993, which led to high unemployment among nationals in the following years". More recently, see the study by IDEA Consult, and ECORYS Netherlands, *Study on the Economic and Social Effects Associated with the Phenomenon of Posting of Workers in the EU Final Report*, pp. 160 and 173.

CHAPTER 6
A CLASH OF KINGS

Fundamental Freedoms versus Fundamental Rights, again

The complicated relationship between fundamental freedoms and fundamental rights in the EU legal order is a much debated topic, especially in the aftermath of *Viking* and *Laval*.[1] The posting of workers phenomenon, when examined from the point of view of collective labour law, is completely immersed in this clash. On the one hand, posting of workers (in principle) takes place necessarily in the context of a transnational provision of services. This entails that a posting situation is always covered by the freedom to provide services, and more so taking into account the willingness of the Court to expand the reach of fundamental freedoms even in cases where the "cross-border element" is at best tenuous.[2] On the other hand, the rights at stake, which were identified in Chapter 3, can often be included in the catalogue of fundamental rights. The first section of this Chapter will further explore this inclusion.

Having ascertained the fundamental nature of the collective social rights at stake, it is clear that the legal framework stemming from the clash between

1 For a few examples see C. Barnard, "The Protection of Fundamental Social Rights in Europe After Lisbon: a Question of Conflicts of Interests", in *The Protection of Fundamental Rights in the EU After Lisbon*, ed. S. de Vries, U. Bernitz and S. Weatherill (Oxford: Hart Publishing, 2013), 37–57; Dorssemont, "The Right to Take Collective Action Versus Fundamental Economic Freedoms in the Aftermath of Laval and Viking. Foes Are Forever"; S. de Vries, "The Protection of Fundamental Rights Within Europe's Internal Market After Lisbon - An Endeavour for More Harmony", *Europa Institute Working Paper* 4 (2010): 1–46; J. Morijn, "Balancing Fundamental Rights and Common Market Freedoms in Union Law: Schmidberger and Omega in the Light of the European Constitution", *European Law Journal* 12, no. 1 (January 2006): 15–40; M. Avbelj, "European Court of Justice and the Question of Value Choices", *Jean Monnet Working Paper* 4 (2006): 1–84; A. Alemanno, "À la recherche d'un juste équilibre entre libertés fondamentales et droits fondamentaux dans le cadre du marché intérieur", *Revue du Droit de l'Union Européenne* 4 (2004): 709–751.

2 *E.g.* the oft cited *Carpenter* case: *Mary Carpenter v Secretary of State for the Home Department*, C-60/00. See N. Reich, "How Proportionate Is the Proportionality Principle? Some Critical Remarks on the Use and Methodology of the Proportionality Principle in the Internal Market Case Law of the ECJ", in *The European Court of Justice and the Autonomy of the Member States*, ed. H.-W. Micklitz and B. De Witte (Cambridge: Intersentia, 2012), 83–112, p. 87.

fundamental freedoms and fundamental rights is of paramount importance for legal appraisal of the relationship between posted workers and industrial relations. Provided that the topic of the clash is indeed huge, here I will only refer to the elements which are relevant for the instant research. Thus I will briefly present the stance delivered by the Court of Justice in relation to this topic through some well-known cases. Then I will proceed to analyse the different approach provided by other legal systems concerned with the protection of social rights, notably the ILO and the Council of Europe.

On this basis I will try to assess the role played by this ("constitutional") context in influencing the relationship between posting of workers and collective labour law, and hence industrial relations.

6.1 THE CLASH

The topic of the complicated relationship between fundamental (social) rights and fundamental freedoms of the internal market is at the same time unavoidable and impossible to deal extensively in the limited space of this Chapter. The limited objective here is to try to summarise the situation of this conflict as it stands, without delving -for the moment- into an assessment of its possible evolutions. In order to do so, I will first analyse the question related to the fundamental nature of collective social rights. This nature is evidently the gateway to introduce these rights into the overarching framework of the conflict here at stake. Then I will turn to the analysis of the case law of the CJEU. Finally I will introduce a few "legal events" which took place outside the forum of the CJEU and after *Viking* and *Laval* and which could (or should) have an impact on the approach developed by the CJEU in these cases.

6.1.1 COLLECTIVE *AND* FUNDAMENTAL SOCIAL RIGHTS

To identify the fundamental nature (or lack thereof) of the collective rights at stake I will follow a positivistic approach.[3] A positivistic approach means that fundamental rights are defined as such insofar as certain treaties (and eventually their monitoring bodies) at international or European level recognise them as such.[4] This is consistent with the approach followed by the Court of Justice in identifying those fundamental rights. Indeed, the Court "draws inspiration [from the constitutional traditions common to the Member States and] from the

3 V. Mantouvalou, "Are Labour Rights Human Rights?", *European Labour Law Journal* 3, no. 2 (2012): 151–172, pp. 152 ff.

4 Ibid., p. 151.

guidelines supplied by international treaties for the protection of human rights on which the Member States have collaborated or to which they are signatories".[5] Drawing directly from the topic at stake, in the renowned cases of *Viking*[6] and *Laval* the Court based its recognition of the right to strike as a fundamental right on the European Social Charter (ESC), ILO Convention 87 at the international level, and, at Community level, on the Community Charter of the Fundamental Social Rights of Workers (CCFSRW) and the Charter of Fundamental Rights of the European Union[7] (EUCFR).

Thus, this approach fits with the purpose of this analysis, *i.e.* to clarify that legal disputes arising from the encounter of posting of workers and industrial relations are most likely (if not bound) to be shaped as conflicts between fundamental rights and the (fundamental) freedom to provide services. It goes without saying that this is true in the context of EU law and under the current doctrine of the CJEU.

Freedom of association

The question is relatively simple for the freedom of association. Indeed, this freedom is protected by a number of instruments directed to the protection of fundamental rights.[8] The same holds substantially true for its declination in terms of trade union purposes, i.e. the freedom to form and join trade unions.

Here I will limit the analysis to the sources cited by the Court of Justice in *Viking* and *Laval*. A cursory glance to these sources reveals that the freedom of association for trade union purposes is protected under the European Social Charter,[9] under ILO Conventions,[10] as well as under the Community Charter of the Fundamental Social Rights of Workers[11] and the Charter of Fundamental

---

5 Case C-260/89 *ERT*, para. 41; Case C-274/99 *P. Connolly v Commission*, para. 37; Case C-94/00 *Roquette Frères*, para. 25; Case C-112/00 *Schmidberger*, para. 71; Case C-36/02, *Omega*, para. 33.

6 Case C-438/05, *Viking Line ABP v. The International Transport Workers' Federation and the Finnish Seaman's Union.*

7 Case C-438/05, *Viking*, para. 43; Case C-341/05, *Laval*, para. 90.

8 Creighton, "Freedom of Association", p. 275.

9 Article 5: "With a view to ensuring or promoting the freedom of workers and employers to form local, national or international organisations for the protection of their economic and social interests and to join those organisations, the Parties undertake that national law shall not be such as to impair, nor shall it be so applied as to impair, this freedom [...]".

10 Convention No. 87, Freedom of Association and Protection of the Right to Organise Convention, 1948 and Convention No. 98, Right to Organise and Collective Bargaining Convention, 1949.

11 Community Charter of the Fundamental Social Rights of Workers, adopted on 9 December 1989 by a declaration of all Member States, with the exception of the United Kingdom. Article 11: "Employers and workers of the European Community shall have the right of association in order to constitute professional organisations or trade unions of their choice for the defence of their economic and social interests. Every employer and every worker shall have the freedom to join or not to join such organisations without any personal or occupational damage being thereby suffered by him".

Rights of the EU.[12] Moreover, the freedom of association for trade union purposes is protected under the ECHR.[13] Hence, the positivistic approach followed by the Court in its case law suggests that the fundamental nature of the freedom of association cannot (realistically) be called into question.

This conclusion seems safe enough even though the Court of Justice itself never had the occasion to state over the nature of the (right to) freedom of association *for trade union purposes*, nor (*a fortiori*) over a conflict between this right and one of the fundamental freedoms protected by the Treaty. However, the fundamental nature of the right to freedom of association in its broader meaning has been recognised by the Court of Justice in the *Bosman* case.[14] In doing so the Court relied on Article 11 ECHR. It is well known that the same Article protects *specifically* the "right to form and to join trade unions for the protection of his interests".

In the event[15] of a conflict between this right and one of the so-called four freedoms, it is hence safe to affirm that the Court would scrutinise such a conflict as one between a fundamental right and a fundamental freedom.

---

12 Article 12 EUCFR: "Everyone has the right to freedom of peaceful assembly and to freedom of association at all levels, in particular in political, trade union and civic matters, which implies the right of everyone to form and to join trade unions for the protection of his or her interests [...]".

13 Article 11 ECHR: "1. Everyone has the right to freedom of peaceful assembly and to freedom of association with others, including the right to form and to join trade unions for the protection of his interests.
2. No restrictions shall be placed on the exercise of these rights other than such as are prescribed by law and are necessary in a democratic society in the interests of national security or public safety, for the prevention of disorder or crime, for the protection of health or morals or for the protection of the rights and freedoms of others. This Article shall not prevent the imposition of lawful restrictions on the exercise of these rights by members of the armed forces, of the police or of the administration of the State".

14 Case C-415/93, *Bosman*, para. 79: "As regards the arguments based on the principle of freedom of association, it must be recognized that this principle, enshrined in Article 11 of the European Convention for the Protection of Human Rights and Fundamental Freedoms and resulting from the constitutional traditions common to the Member States, is one of the fundamental rights". In the context of this case however, the Court considered that "the rules laid down by sporting associations to which the national court refers cannot be seen as necessary to ensure enjoyment of that freedom by those associations, by the clubs or by their players, nor can they be seen as an inevitable result thereof", so that a conflict between the newly found fundamental right and the fundamental freedom at stake (free movement of workers) was avoided. Also, Novitz stresses how the Court "did not elaborate on the scope of this freedom". See Novitz, *International and European Protection of the Right to Strike*, p. 252.

15 Though this event seems quite unlikely, provided that the exercise of the freedom of association for trade union purposes (or for other purposes, for what it matters) could hardly entail *per se* a restriction of one of the fundamental freedoms.

Collective action

As it should be evident, the approach here focuses on the recognition (or lack thereof) of a right as fundamental by the Court of Justice. Turning to the right to take collective action, this approach allows for a practical short-cut.

Indeed, one of the few positive elements (from the point of view of the labour lawyer) of *Viking* and *Laval* is that the fundamental nature of this right has now been recognised explicitly by the Court of Justice. The possibility envisaged by Antoine Jacobs in 1978[16] thus materialised at the end of 2007. At the same time the recognition of the right to take collective action by the Court of Justice confirmed all the dangers foreseen by Tonia Novitz in 2003.[17]

In both cases the Court affirmed that "the right to take collective action, including the right to strike, must therefore be recognised as a fundamental right which forms an integral part of the general principles of Community law the observance of which the Court ensures".[18] This on the basis of the international sources recalled *supra*.[19]

Looking at the sources cited by the Court one cannot fail to notice that, as it was already highlighted *supra*,[20] ILO Convention No. 87 does not *explicitly* protect the right to strike. However, the two bodies supervising the application of ILO standards have consistently stated that the right to strike is a necessary aspect of the freedom of association.[21] While referring to Convention No. 87 the Court of Justice did not acknowledge the (*sui generis*)"case law" of the ILO supervisory bodies, though it has evidently accepted their interpretation of the Convention. Without an explicit mention of such a choice however, the willingness of the Court to engage in a "dialogue" with the interpretation of international (and/or regional) treaties thus remains at best obscure.

---

16 A. Jacobs, "Towards Community Action on Strike Law", *Common Market Law Review* 15 (1978): 133–155.

17 Novitz, *International and European Protection of the Right to Strike*, pp. 258–260.

18 *Viking*, para. 44; *Laval*, para. 91.

19 Once again with the same wording between the two decisions: "In that regard, it must be recalled that the right to take collective action, including the right to strike, is recognised both by various international instruments which the Member States have signed or cooperated in, such as the European Social Charter, signed at Turin on 18 October 1961 – to which, moreover, express reference is made in Article 136 EC – and Convention No 87 concerning Freedom of Association and Protection of the Right to Organise, adopted on 9 July 1948 by the International Labour Organisation – and by instruments developed by those Member States at Community level or in the context of the European Union, such as the Community Charter of the Fundamental Social Rights of Workers adopted at the meeting of the European Council held in Strasbourg on 9 December 1989, which is also referred to in Article 136 EC, and the Charter of Fundamental Rights of the European Union proclaimed in Nice on 7 December 2000". See *Viking*, para. 43; *Laval*, para. 90.

20 See Chapter 3, p. 88.

21 Gernigon, Odero and Guido, "ILO Principles Concerning the Right to Strike", p. 8; Novitz, *International and European Protection of the Right to Strike*, pp. 123 and 192 ff.

Collective bargaining

A similar short-cut now characterises also the "right to bargain collectively".[22] Indeed, in the context of an infraction procedure initiated by the EU Commission against the Republic of Germany, the Court recognised the fundamental nature of this right.

The sources providing the basis for the recognition were only partially overlapping with the ones seen in *Viking* and *Laval*. The Court referred to the European Social Charter, the Community Charter of the Fundamental Social Rights of Workers and to the Charter of Fundamental Rights of the European Union.[23]

As it is evident, the reference to ILO sources was left out by the Court in the decision. This choice is in itself puzzling since, contrary to the right to strike, the right to bargain collectively is *directly* protected by ILO Convention 98.[24] Moreover, this Convention was included in the 1998 Declaration on Fundamental Principles and Rights at Work, committing all the Members of the ILO to respect, promote and realise in good faith the principles set out in the Convention. The second possible source visibly ignored by the Court was the ECHR, or, *rectius*, the case law of the European Court of Human Rights. In fact, just two years before *Commission v. Germany* was delivered, the ECtHR had stated that "the right to bargain collectively with the employer has, in principle, become one of the essential elements of the 'right to form and to join trade unions for the protection of [one's] interests' set forth in Article 11 of the Convention".[25]

Notwithstanding these *oversights*, and more generally the difficulty to identify the content of the fundamental right at stake, once again the explicit decision of the Court of Justice makes it possible to affirm without further analysis the fundamental nature of the right to bargain collectively.

---

22 See Case C-271/08, *Commission v. Federal Republic of Germany*, para. 37.

23 Ibid.: "the right to bargain collectively [...] is recognised both by the provisions of various international instruments which the Member States have cooperated in or signed, such as Article 6 of the European Social Charter, signed at Turin on 18 October 1961 and revised at Strasbourg on 3 May 1996, and by the provisions of instruments drawn up by the Member States at Community level or in the context of the European Union, such as Article 12 of the Community Charter of the Fundamental Social Rights of Workers adopted at the meeting of the European Council held in Strasbourg on 9 December 1989, and Article 28 of the Charter of Fundamental Rights of the European Union ('the Charter'), an instrument to which Article 6 TEU accords the same legal value as the Treaties".

24 Right to Organise and Collective Bargaining Convention, 1949 (No. 98). See Gernigon, Odero and Guido, "ILO Principles Concerning the Right to Strike.

25 *Demir and Baykara v. Turkey*, Application No. 34503/97, 12 November 2008, para. 154. On this point see M. Rocca, "Case C-271/08, Commission v. Germany [2010]", *European Labour Law Journal* 2 (2011): 76–79. More generally see A. Jacobs, "Article 11 ECHR: The Right to Bargain Collectively Under Article 11 ECHR", in *The European Convention on Human Rights and the Employment Relation*, ed. F. Dorssemont, K. Lörcher and I. Schömann (Oxford: Hart Publishing, 2013), 309–332; Ewing and Hendy, "The Dramatic Implications of Demir and Baykara".

Representation, workers involvement, information and consultation

The picture gets more complicated if one turns to those rights falling under the generic label of "representation" or "workers involvement". Indeed, the "short-cut" is only partially available for the right to information and consultation. Confronted, in the case of *Association de médiation sociale,*[26] with a question which defined such a right as "fundamental", the Court of Justice did not make an explicit statement[27] about the nature of the right to information and consultation. At the same time, this very silence may suggest that the CJEU implicitly agrees with the framing of the question proposed by the French Cour de Cassation, and hence with the fundamental nature of the right at stake.

Csilla Kollonay has defined the right "to be involved in matters of the workplace" as fundamental,[28] considering it as "akin to fundamental political rights". The author bases this claim on the recognition of the rights to information, consultation (and participation) in the CCFSRW,[29] in the EU Charter of Fundamental Rights,[30] and in the European Social Charter.[31] Looking at the

---

26 Case C-176/12m *Association de médiation sociale v Union locale des syndicats CGT, Hichem Laboubi, Union départementale CGT des Bouches-du-Rhône, Confédération générale du travail (CGT).*

27 Cf. with the statements about the nature of the right to take collective action or to bargain collectively quoted in the previous paragraphs.

28 Lehoczky, "The Fundamental Right of Workers to Information and Consultation Under the European Social Charter", p. 3.

29 Article 17: "Information, consultation and participation for workers must be developed along appropriate lines, taking account of the practices in force in the various Member States. This shall apply especially in companies or groups of companies having establishments or companies in several Member States of the European Community" and Article 18: "Such information, consultation and participation must be implemented in due time, particularly in the following cases: when technological changes which, from the point of view of working conditions and work organisation, have major implications for the work force are introduced into undertakings; in connection with restructuring operations in undertakings or in cases of mergers having an impact on the employment of workers; in cases of collective redundancy procedures; when trans-frontier workers in particular are affected by employment policies pursued by the undertaking where they are employed".

30 Article 27: "Workers or their representatives must, at the appropriate levels, be guaranteed information and consultation in good time in the cases and under the conditions provided for by Union law and national laws and practices."

31 Article 21: "With a view to ensuring the effective exercise of the right of workers to be informed and consulted within the undertaking, the Parties undertake to adopt or encourage measures enabling workers or their representatives, in accordance with national legislation and practice: a. to be informed regularly or at the appropriate time and in a comprehensible way about the economic and financial situation of the undertaking employing them, on the understanding that the disclosure of certain information which could be prejudicial to the undertaking may be refused or subject to confidentiality; and b. to be consulted in good time on proposed decisions which could substantially affect the interests of workers, particularly on those decisions which could have an important impact on the employment situation in the undertaking" and Article 22: "With a view to ensuring the effective exercise of the right of workers to take part in the determination and improvement of the working conditions and working environment in the undertaking, the Parties undertake to adopt or encourage measures enabling workers or their representatives, in accordance with national legislation and practice, to contribute: a. to the determination and the improvement of the working conditions, work organisation and

sources which were relied upon by the Court in recognising the fundamental nature of the right to bargain collectively, one could effectively draw a parallel.

However, the discrepancy between these three texts should not be overlooked. In this sense, it is evident that the right to be informed and consulted is indeed covered by the three sources. The same is not true when it comes to a more general right to be "involved" or to workers "participation" or even "representation": the EU Charter of Fundamental Rights is silent on these topics. Also, nor ILO sources[32] nor the ECHR could be resorted to in order to fill the place left empty by the EUCFR.[33]

Thus the positivistic approach shows here its limits.[34] One is left to wonder about the possible outcome of an eventual scrutiny by the Court of Justice aimed at ascertaining the fundamental nature (or lack thereof) of these rights. For the sake of speculation and on the basis of what I just summarised, one could lean towards a positive answer for the right to be informed and consulted. Indeed, the decision in *Association de médiation sociale* seems to go in this direction. On the other hand, one would only be taking wild guesses as regards rights to "workers involvement", "participation" and "representation".[35]

All in all, it is possible to affirm that a legal proceeding beyond the Court of Justice involving posting of workers *and* a collective labour right will *most probably* be analysed (exclusively or not) as a clash between a fundamental right and the freedom to provide services. Because of this conclusion, an analysis of the broader topic cannot be avoided.

6.1.2 *SCHMIDBERGER* AND *OMEGA*

This overview begins, however unsurprising it may be, with the earliest decisions delivered by the Court of Justice dealing with the clash between fundamental rights and fundamental freedoms. The issue first arose in the *Schmidberger*

working environment; b. to the protection of health and safety within the undertaking; c. to the organisation of social and socio-cultural services and facilities within the undertaking; d. to the supervision of the observance of regulations on these matters."

32 ILO Convention 135 (Workers' Representatives Convention) is not formulated in terms of rights of workers, being aimed instead at providing protection to the representatives.

33 For a practical overview see S. Clauwaert et al., "Fundamental Social Rights in the European Union: Comparative Tables and Documents" (Brussels: European Trade Union Institute, 2003).

34 Mantouvalou, "Are Labour Rights Human Rights?", pp. 155–156.

35 At the same time, these rights seem less likely to give rise to a clash with given fundamental freedom protected by the EU Treaty. More probably such a conflict would arise due to the *sanctions* surrounding rights and practises related to workers involvement, either in the form of secondary legal instruments protecting these rights or in the form of a collective action.

case,[36] soon to be followed by the *Omega* case.[37] In these decisions, fundamental rights, respectively the freedom of peaceful assembly and of expression, and the principle of human dignity, were invoked by a Member State[38] in order to justify a restriction to a fundamental freedom.[39]

In both cases the fundamental right ultimately prevailed over (or, *rectius*, did not succumb to) the fundamental freedom. This probably played a part in reassuring about the ability of the Court of Justice of actually shielding the exercise of fundamental rights stemming from the constitutional traditions of Member States and from international treaties from the effects of the freedoms related to the internal market. This reassurance notwithstanding, a number of critiques had already been moved at that time to the approach followed by the Court in solving the conflict here at stake.[40] Here I will only focus on those aspects which are directly related to this conflict.

Identifying the fundamental right

In the two cases the Court follows a different path in identifying the fundamental nature of the right at stake. In *Schmidberger*, the Court follows a fairly "standard" approach, referring to the ECHR which guarantees the rights of (peaceful) assembly and of expression.[41] In *Omega* this process is much more truncated. The Court refers the Opinion of AG Stix-Hackl without recalling the international sources cited by the said AG,[42] simply stating that "[...] the Community legal order undeniably strives to ensure respect for human dignity as a general principle of law. There can [...] be no doubt that the objective of protecting human dignity is compatible with Community law".[43] Thus it has been argued that in *Omega* the

---

36 C-112/00, *Eugen Schmidberger, Internationale Transporte und Planzüge v. Republik Österreich.* The well-known case deals with an action brought against the Austrian authorities for their failure to avoid traffic disruption on the Brenner motorway. This disruption was caused by a duly authorised demonstration of environmentalists groups, and lasted for 30 hours. The Court had thus to balance the restriction to the free movement of goods against the protection of the fundamental rights of peaceful assembly and of expression.

37 C-36/02, *Omega Spielhallen- und Automatenaufstellungs-GmbH v. Oberbürgermeisterin der Bundesstadt Bonn.* In the *Omega* case the Court had to assess a restriction to the freedom to provide services caused by the ban on a laser-dome activity (*i.e.* a simulated combat-like situation) ordered by the German police. The ban was justified by the German authorities the ground of protection of human dignity. Thus, it was this principle that had to be balanced against the freedom to provide services – which was at stake since the equipment was supplied by the British company Pulsar.

38 The Republic of Austria and the Federal Republic of Germany.

39 The free movement of goods and the freedom to provide services.

40 E.g. Alemanno, "À la recherche d'un juste équilibre entre libertés fondamentales et droits fondamentaux dans le cadre du marché intérieur", pp. 749–751; C. Brown, "Case C-112/00, Eugen Schmidberger, Internationale Transporte und Planzüge v. Austria", *Common Market Law Review* 40 (2003): 1499–1510, p. 1508.

41 ECHR, Article 10 and 11. See *Schmidberger*, para. 69, 71 and 77.

42 See Opinion of AG Stix-Hackl in *Omega*, para. 82–91.

43 *Omega*, para. 34.

Court relied much more on the (German) *national* constitutional protection of the principle of human dignity than on international sources.[44] Such a *self-restraint* in front of the national value choices surrounding the principle of human dignity will also be visible in the proportionality test applied by the Court in the case in question.[45]

The restriction

On the other hand, the Court follows a similar path in affirming the existence of a restriction to a fundamental freedom. Indeed, in both cases the Court simply *affirms* the existence of such a restriction[46] without further analysing *in concreto* whether the restrictive measure (either the ban or the demonstration) had affected the intra-community exchanges and to what extent. In *Omega* the restriction is identified in the ban on the laser-dome operations.[47] In *Schmidberger* the situation is reversed: the fact that the Austrian authorities did not ban the demonstration (*i.e.* did not themselves in first place restrict a fundamental right[48]) is considered by the Court "as constituting a measure of equivalent effect to a quantitative restriction which is, in principle, incompatible with the Community law obligations".[49]

There is no attempt by the Court to formulate a form of *threshold*, or *de minimis* rule,[50] let alone to develop a theory of "intrinsic" restrictive effect of the exercise of fundamental rights.[51] This is however perfectly in line with the *Säger* approach mentioned in Chapter 5.[52]

---

44 A. Bailleux, "Entrave Et Droits Fondamentaux", in *L'entrave et l'accès au Marché*, ed. D. Prieto (Brussels: Bruylant, 2011), 225–256, p. 251, speaks of "*exception d'ordre public constitutionnel*".

45 An approach highlighted by E. Spaventa, "Federalisation Versus Centralisation: tensions in Fundamental Rights Discourse in the EU", in *50 Years of the European Treaties: looking Back and Thinking Forward*, ed. M. Dougan and S. Currie, vol. 44, June (Oxford: Hart Publishing, 2009), 343–364, p. 25. The Author in fact urges the Court to show the same self-restraint in other cases dealing with the clash between fundamental rights and fundamental freedoms: "If the clash is between fundamental rights, regardless of the Community dimension, then the role of the European Court of Justice should be limited to a supervisory role, Omega-style, aimed at ensuring that claims containing a Community element are not treated in a different and more disadvantageous way than their purely domestic counterparts". Similarly, the "judicial deference" is noted by J. Fons and K. Lenaerts, "The Constitutional Allocation of Powers and General Principles of EU Law", *Common Market Law Review* 62, no. 47 (2010): 1629–1669, p. 1663.

46 Alemanno, "À la recherche d'un juste équilibre entre libertés fondamentales et droits fondamentaux dans le cadre du marché intérieur", p. 730.

47 *Omega*, para. 25.

48 Alemanno, "À la recherche d'un juste équilibre entre libertés fondamentales et droits fondamentaux dans le cadre du marché intérieur", pp. 731–732.

49 *Schmidberger*, para. 64.

50 Which could exclude those restrictions which stem only indirectly from the exercise of a fundamental right. See ibid., p. 717.

51 As in *Albany*.

52 See *supra*, p. 156.

Proportionality

Having ascertained a restriction of a fundamental freedom, the Court went on to apply a proportionality test[53] to the restricting measures. The application of the test does however differ between the two cases, reverberating the somewhat different consideration of the fundamental rights at stake highlighted *supra*.

In *Schmidberger* the Court states that "it is necessary to determine whether the restrictions placed upon intra-Community trade are proportionate in the light of the legitimate objective pursued, namely, in the present case, the protection of fundamental rights".[54] In this sense, the protection of fundamental rights is *in itself* a legitimate objective. This impression is reinforced by a previous statement of the Court, denying that the "specific aims *of the demonstration*" should be taken into account in the legal proceedings.[55] The Court then assesses the proportionality of the "measure", mainly by distinguishing the situation of *Schmidberger* from the one of the case known as *Spanish strawberries*.[56] The Court lists a number of factors upholding the Austrian decision. First, the authorisation for the demonstration was duly requested by the organisers, while the authorities decided not to ban it.[57] Second, the disruption of intra-community trade was limited in space and time ("a single route, on a single occasion and during a period of almost 30 hours").[58] Third, the *purpose of the demonstration*[59] was not to restrict intra-community trade, nor in general nor in connection to a specific product or source.[60] Fourth, supporting measures were taken by the authorities in order to minimise the inconveniences caused by the traffic disruption. In particular, *information* relating to the demonstration was provided in advance by the media.[61] Fifth, the Court affirms that "the isolated incident in question did not give rise to a general climate of insecurity such as to have a dissuasive effect on intra-Community trade flows as a whole".[62] Finally, the Court considers

---

53 *Schmidberger*, para. 79; *Omega*, para. 38.

54 *Schmidberger*, para. 82.

55 Ibid., para. 66. This has been criticised by Brown, "Case C-112/00, Eugen Schmidberger, Internationale Transporte und Planzüge v. Austria", pp. 1504–1505, reminding that the aims *of the demonstration* should indeed be relevant in assessing the breach of Community law. In the words of the Author: "Clearly, if demonstrators had decided to use the Brenner motorway as a space for performing drama or for promulgating neo-Nazi opinion, the authorities would [...] have been under an obligation, as a matter of both Community and Convention [the ECHR] law, to weigh that purpose in the balance".

56 Case C-265/95, *Commission of the European Communities v French Republic*. The case dealt with the lack of action from the French authorities in response to a widespread phenomenon of French citizens attacking Spanish imported agricultural goods.

57 *Schmidberger*, para. 84.

58 Ibid., para. 85.

59 This is quite in contrast with the previously affirmed disregard for the aims of the demonstration, as noted by Dorssemont, "The Right to Take Collective Action versus Fundamental Economic Freedoms in the Aftermath of Laval and Viking. Foes Are Forever", p. 17.

60 *Schmidberger*, para. 86.

61 Ibid., para. 87.

62 Ibid., para. 87.

the possible alternatives, coming to the conclusion that a) "an outright ban on the demonstration would have constituted unacceptable interference with the fundamental rights of the demonstrators to gather and express peacefully their opinion in public"[63] and b) even the impositions of limitations relating to the place or to the duration of the demonstration "could have been perceived as an excessive restriction, depriving the action of a substantial part of its scope".[64] Moreover the Court accepts the submission of the Republic of Austria, which basically insisted on the fact that "all the alternative solutions" would have risked "more serious disruption to intra-Community trade and public order", since the organisers could have turned to non-authorised demonstrations or outright acts of violence.[65] On the basis of these elements, the Court ultimately considered the authorisation by the Austrian authorities of the demonstration as a proportionate restriction to the free movement of goods.

As anticipated, the application of the proportionality test in *Omega* takes a different path, one that has been correctly defined as "state centric".[66] Indeed, having recognised a fundamental nature to the principle of (protection of) human dignity, the Court states that "the objective of protecting human dignity is compatible with Community law".[67] In introducing the proportionality test, the Court take a very "benevolent" approach towards the national measure (*in casu*, an outright ban of an economic activity), affirming that "it is not indispensable in that respect for the restrictive measure issued by the authorities of a Member State to correspond to a conception shared by all Member States as regards the precise way in which the fundamental right or legitimate interest in question is to be protected".[68] Instead, "the need for, and proportionality of, the provisions adopted are not excluded merely because one Member State has chosen a system of protection different from that adopted by another State".[69] That being said, the

63 Ibid., para. 89.

64 Ibid., para. 90.

65 Ibid., para. 92.

66 N. Shuibhne, "Margins of Appreciation: national Values, Fundamental Rights and EC Free Movement Law", *European Law Review* 34 (2009): 230–256, p. 254.

67 *Omega*, para. 34. Also, in the subsequent paragraph, the Court uses the same formula of *Schmidberger*, affirming that "the protection of fundamental rights" is *in itself* "a legitimate interest which, in principle, justifies a restriction of the obligations imposed by Community law".

68 *Omega*, para. 37.

69 Ibid., para. 38. As De Vries puts it "the Court first defines a typically German concept of human dignity as a general principle of EU law, and then, while applying the proportionality test, it shows a predominantly Member State-friendly approach". See De Vries, "The Protection of Fundamental Rights Within Europe's Internal Market After Lisbon – An Endeavour for More Harmony", p. 10. It is interesting to note that the measure was considered by the Court on grounds of "public policy". Thus, the State-friendly approach is particularly striking if compared to the stance of the Court in *Arblade*, para. 30–31, and even more in the later *Commission v Luxembourg*, para. 16 (both cases were analysed in the previous Chapter). There the Court embarked on a thorough scrutiny of the public policy exception put forward by the given Member State, affirming, in the latter case, that "the notion of public policy [...] cannot be unilaterally defined by each Member State".

proportionality test fits completely in the limited space of a single paragraph.[70] In the first part the Court simply accepts the definition provided by the Court of the appropriate level of protection of the fundamental right at stake.[71] In the second part the Court "completes" the test by stating that: "by prohibiting only the variant of the laser game the object of which is to fire on human targets and thus 'play at killing' people, the contested order did not go beyond what is necessary in order to attain the objective pursued by the competent national authorities". Thus, the test consists in assessing the national measure essentially on the basis on the level of protection of the fundamental right deemed as "correct" following the national conception of the said right. The Court seemingly does not even try to suggest that less restrictive measures could have guaranteed a sufficient level of protection without completely denying the freedom to provide services of Omega. Hence the difference with *Schmidberger*, where a number of elements were taken into account before upholding the Austrian (non)measure.

6.2 THE NEW WAVE

In 1977 MEP Goutmann addressed a written question to the EU Commission, essentially asking to clarify a potential conflict between the right to strike and the freedom of establishment.[72] The Commission laconically answered that "the principle of freedom of establishment neither affects nor is affected by the right to strike".[73] Thirty years later, the Court of Justice ruled that "Article 43 EC [freedom of establishment] is to be interpreted as meaning that, in principle, collective action initiated by a trade union or a group of trade unions against a private undertaking in order to induce that undertaking to enter into a collective agreement, the terms of which are liable to deter it from exercising freedom of establishment, *is not excluded from the scope of that article*".[74] The mere juxtaposition of the two texts shows the teeth marks of time over the relationship between fundamental freedoms of the internal market and collective social rights.

From the point of view of the relationship between fundamental freedoms and fundamental rights the *Viking* and *Laval* cases represent a new chapter of the history. The most evident difference between this new chapter and the one of *Omega* and *Schmidberger* lies in the subject relying on fundamental rights to

70 Ibid., para. 39.

71 "[...] according to the referring court, the prohibition on the commercial exploitation of games involving the simulation of acts of violence against persons, in particular the representation of acts of homicide, corresponds to the level of protection of human dignity which the national constitution seeks to guarantee in the territory of the Federal Republic of Germany".

72 The French Hersant press group had threatened to relocate the printing of several of its products to Belgium, close to the French border, in order to circumvent a collective action taking place in Paris.

73 See O.J. 1977, No. C 214/18 of 7 September 1977.

74 *Viking*, para. 55 (emphasis added).

justify a restriction of the fundamental freedoms. If in *Schmidberger* and *Omega* the action was brought against public authorities, in *Viking* and *Laval* trade unions were directly involved. This single difference however implies a sea change in the approach of the Court to the balancing at stake in both cases.[75] Hence, it is from the appraisal of trade union action by the Court of Justice that the analysis will start.

However, before passing on to the analysis, it is necessary to address the issue from a different point of view. Simply put, it has been suggested[76] that one should not "generalise" from *Viking* and *Laval*, since they both involve specific facts and peculiarities of national systems of industrial relations. On the one hand, these warnings rest on an evident truth: each decision is delivered on the basis of a specific set of facts and circumstances. On the other, one should not overlook the fact that the Court has been more than ready to "generalise" notwithstanding these necessary differences. Just to cite an example from the case law analysed in the previous Chapter, one can see as one of the conditions laid out in *Arblade* to apply working conditions to posted workers was that for those provisions to be "sufficiently precise and accessible that they do not render it impossible or excessively difficult in practice for such an employer to determine the obligations with which he is required to comply".[77] In the context of *Arblade* this requirement made perfectly sense, since the case dealt with a *criminal* proceeding, which in its turn was hence characterised by a higher necessity of legal certainty.[78] Still, the Court did not flinch when it extended the same requirement to the context of collective negotiations in *Laval*.[79] Another example comes from a case following the line of reasoning of *Viking* and *Laval*. In the *Commission v. Germany* case[80] the Court confirmed verbatim the approach of *Viking* and *Laval*, in the context of the right to bargain collectively, a choice which seems to go exactly in the direction of *generalising* the *Viking&Laval* reasoning to the balancing exercise of fundamental freedoms and fundamental (social) rights in general.[81]

---

75 As noted by L. Azoulai, "The Case of Fundamental Rights: a State of Ambivalence", in *The European Court of Justice and the Autonomy of the Member States*, ed. H.-W. Micklitz and B. De Witte (Cambridge: Intersentia, 2012), 207–217, p. 217.

76 Davies, "One Step Forward, Two Steps Back? The Viking and Laval Cases in the ECJ", p. 142; C. Barnard, "Viking and Laval: an Introduction", *Cambridge Yearbook of European Legal Studies* 10, no. 463–492 (2008), p. 491.

77 *Arblade*, para. 43.

78 T. Novitz, "A Human Rights Analysis of the Viking and Laval Judgments", *Cambridge Yearbook of European Legal Studies* 10 (2008): 541–561, p. 556.

79 *Laval*, para. 110.

80 Case C-271/08.

81 See P. Syrpis, "Reconciling Economic Freedoms and Social Rights – The Potential of Commission v. Germany (Case C-271/08, Judgment of 15 July 2010)", *Industrial Law Journal* 40, no. 2 (2011): 222–229, pp. 223–224; Rocca, "Case C-271/08, Commission V. Germany [2010]", p. 77.

6.2.1 TRADE UNIONS AND THE CJEU

The way in which the Court has apprehended trade unions in its reasoning plays a pivotal role in determining the rest of the decision. The Court of Justice, both in Viking and Laval held that Article 49 and Article 43 TEC (now Articles 56 and 49 TFEU), guaranteeing respectively the free provision of services and the freedom of establishment, can be invoked against trade unions.[82] In order for the Court to justify this argument, it stated that "the abolition, as between Member States, of obstacles to freedom to provide services would be compromised if the abolition of State barriers could be neutralised by obstacles resulting from the exercise of their legal autonomy by associations or organisations not governed by public law".[83] Hence, the Court extended the application of the free movement provisions of the Treaty to trade unions, on the basis of the (fragile) argument of their supposed regulatory power (or of their nature of quasi-public bodies).[84] In doing so however the Court explicitly rejected the claim that its interpretation applied only to quasi-public organisations or to associations exercising a regulatory task and having quasi-legislative powers.[85] Instead, it argued that it is sufficient for trade union to "*participate* in the drawing up of agreements *seeking* to regulate paid work collectively"[86] in order for them to be included under the scope of fundamental freedoms. Still, the Court itself refers to its previous case law dealing with sport associations,[87] in a way drawing a parallel between the task carried out by these "non-governmental regulatory bodies"[88] and the activity of trade unions. Such an assumption seems however a thin link over which to build the edifice of the Court's reasoning.

Indeed, it is apparent that there is a major difference between professional associations and trade unions: professional associations can impose rules on those who wish to participate in an economic activity, while trade unions do not have this power. Trade unions are far from being bodies able to regulate the access

---

82 Van Peijpe, "Collective Labour Law After Viking, Laval, Rüffert, and Commission v. Luxembourg", p. 97.

83 *Viking*, para. 57; *Laval*, para. 98.

84 Dorssemont and Orlandini, "Market Rules and the Right to Strike: a Different Approach", p. 70 ff.; Joerges and Rödl, "Informal Politics, Formalised Law and the Social Deficit of European Integration: Reflections After the Judgments of the ECJ in Viking and Laval", p. 14; Azoulai, "The Court of Justice and the Social Market Economy: the Emergence of an Ideal and the Conditions for Its Realization", p. 1344; Davies, "One Step Forward, Two Steps Back? The Viking and Laval Cases in the ECJ", pp. 136–137.

85 *Viking*, para. 64.

86 Ibid., para. 65 (emphasis added).

87 *Viking*, para. 34 and *Laval*, para. 98; Case C-36/74, *B.N.O. Walrave and L.J.N. Koch v. Association Union cycliste internationale, Koninklijke Nederlandsche Wielren Unie and Federación Española Ciclismo*; Case C-415/93, *Union Royale belge des sociétés de Football association ASBL v. Jean-Marc Bosman.*

88 A. Dashwood, "Viking and Laval: Issues of Horizontal Direct Effect", *Cambridge Yearbook of European Legal Studies* 10 (2008): 525–540, p. 527.

to labour market.[89] They can only negotiate with the employers' side (whether represented by a single employer or by an employers' association) on the terms of employment and even undertake collective action in order to put pressure towards the fulfilment of their demands, but they need the consent of the other party – namely the employer side – in order to reach a collective agreement.[90] True enough, also in the case of professional associations, the consent on the part of workers is needed in order to realise an economic activity. Still, the major difference lies at the relevant fact that professional associations have the power to set the rules, which employees are in principle free to accept, but in case they refuse to do so, it is them – namely the workers – who will not gain *access* to the market. In this regard, professional associations regulate access to the labour market.[91] On the contrary, trade unions enjoy only bargaining power which can be more or less effective depending on power relations in the specific dispute and in the society at large, but they *do not* have the power to legally impose terms, at least in western democracies.[92] As convincingly observed by Joerges and Rödl "the right to collective action does not imply the power to regulate market affairs unilaterally. Quite to the contrary, collective action is intended to compensate the absence of such a unilateral regulatory autonomy".[93]

The *vision* stemming from the decisions of the Court is thus puzzling. The Court of Justice concedes that trade unions are not "governed by public law"[94] but

89 A. Hinarejos, "Laval and Viking: The Right to Collective Action Versus EU Fundamental Freedoms", *Human Rights Law Review* 8, no. 4 (October 2008): 714–729, p. 722; Dorssemont, "The Right to Take Collective Action Versus Fundamental Economic Freedoms in the Aftermath of Laval and Viking. Foes Are Forever", p. 86.

90 Azoulai, "The Court of Justice and the Social Market Economy: the Emergence of an Ideal and the Conditions for Its Realization", p. 1346; Dorssemont, "The Right to Take Collective Action Versus Fundamental Economic Freedoms in the Aftermath of Laval and Viking. Foes Are Forever", p. 29. Also, AG Mengozzi in his Opinion is aware of this fundamental difference: "I willingly accept that the present case differs from the situations at issue in the judgments in which the Court has so far held that Article 49 EC was applicable to private persons. In those cases, it was the legality of the regulations and other rules drawn up by the entities in question that was examined", para. 158. However, the AG still considers that trade unions should be nonetheless "obliged to comply" with Article 49 TEC (now Article 56 TFEU) since "the Court considers that the principle of non-discrimination implemented by Article 49 EC applies to private persons as regards the drawing-up of (collective) agreements and the conclusion or the *adoption of other acts*", para 159 (emphasis added). Once again this seems to be a misunderstanding of the very nature of trade unions: it is impossible to conceive a collective *agreement* as an act *adopted* by a trade union, since it necessarily needs the consent of the employers' side.

91 Dashwood, "Viking and Laval: Issues of Horizontal Direct Effect", p. 529.

92 As noted by M. Schlachter, "National Reports: Germany", in *The Laval and Viking Cases: Freedom of Services and Establishment v. Industrial Conflict in the European Economic Area and Russia*, ed. R. Blanpain and A.M. Swiatkowski (Alphen aan den Rijn: Kluwer Law International, 2009), 63–72, p. 68. *Contra* see Dashwood, "Viking and Laval: Issues of Horizontal Direct Effect", p. 539, who considers that collective agreements backed by the threat of collective action can be considered as a form of regulation.

93 Joerges and Rödl, "Informal Politics, Formalised Law and the Social Deficit of European Integration: Reflections After the Judgments of the ECJ in Viking and Laval", p. 14.

94 *Viking*, para. 57; *Laval*, para. 98. Also this finding will prove double edged, as I describe *infra*.

it considers their legal autonomy to be "*conferred* [...] inter alia, *by national law*",[95] giving back the image of something similar to a delegation of power by the State.[96] Furthermore, trade unions are depicted as *regulating* collectively paid work and the provision of services[97] and hence included in the scope of fundamental freedoms.[98] Catherine Barnard has defined this approach as "extended vertical direct effect",[99] to distinguish it from a straight "horizontal effect". Trade unions are considered as covered by treaty provisions on fundamental freedoms *not* as simple private parties but as "non-governmental regulatory bodies", exercising an authority *functionally* equivalent to the public one.[100]

6.2.2 COLLECTIVE ACTION AND THE CJEU

From this point of view, the Court went on to assess the clash between the right to take collective action, considered as part of the regulatory action of trade unions, and fundamental freedoms.

Competence

The Court had to circumnavigate three orders of arguments denying its competence to judge over the said right. Indeed, the approach of the Court to this issue was contested for three reasons. First, because according to Article 137(5) TEC, now Article 153(5) TFEU, the Union has no competence to regulate the right to strike.[101] Not surprisingly, the Court firmly denied this exclusion.[102] However, a closer look at the argument leaves room for doubt. The Court affirms that "[...] even if, in the areas which fall outside the scope of the Community's competence, the *Member States* are still free, in principle, to lay down the conditions governing the existence and exercise of the rights in question, the fact remains that, when exercising that competence, the *Member States must nevertheless comply with*

95 *Viking*, para. 60.
96 As remarked by Dorssemont, "The Right to Take Collective Action Versus Fundamental Economic Freedoms in the Aftermath of Laval and Viking. Foes Are Forever", p. 84.
97 *Viking*, para. 65; *Laval*, para. 98.
98 Novitz, "A Human Rights Analysis of the Viking and Laval Judgments", p. 551.
99 Barnard, "Viking and Laval: an Introduction", p. 472.
100 H Schepel, "Constitutionalising the Market, Marketising the Constitution, and to Tell the Difference: On the Horizontal Application of the Free Movement Provisions in EU Law", *European Law Journal* 18, no. 2 (March 2012): 177–200, p. 186.
101 *Viking*, para. 39; *Laval*, para. 86. AG Mengozzi in his Opinion states explicitly that this lack of competence extends to the whole action of the EU: "If the effectiveness of Article 137(5) EC is to be upheld, the Community institutions could not of course resort to other legal bases in the Treaty in order to adopt measures designed to approximate the laws of the Member States in this field". See Malmberg and Sigeman, "Industrial Action and EU Economic Freedoms: The Autonomous Collective Bargaining Model Curtailed by the European Court of Justice", p. 1126.
102 *Viking*, para. 40; *Laval*, para. 87.

Community law". It is (also) in light of the failure of *Member States* to regulate the right to take collective action in compliance with Community law that the responsibility of *non-public* bodies as trade unions is affirmed. This leaves the impression that such a statement would have been more in line with a *Spanish Strawberries*-style approach (or *Schmidbergers*'s).

Second, the Court was confronted with the argument of the so-called "*Albany* immunity".[103] The argument was raised in *Viking*.[104] There the Court distinguished the case at stake from *Albany*, maintaining that the approach adopted in the latter applied only to competition law provisions and was not applicable to the free movement provisions of the Treaty. On the one hand the Court simply denies the possibility to extend *per analogiam* the *Albany* immunity beyond the limited scope of competition law. On the other hand, the Court takes the stance that "it cannot be considered that it is inherent in the very exercise of [...] the right to take collective action that those fundamental freedoms will be prejudiced to a certain degree".[105] This passage is particularly problematic. The Court here adopts a "unitarist" approach to fundamental social rights and fundamental freedoms of the internal market, meaning that the exercise of the former does not necessarily entail a restriction of the latter. On the one hand, this sits uncomfortably alongside the fact that the Court affirmed its competence to scrutinise the exercise of the right to take collective action *on the basis* of its restrictive nature as regards fundamental freedoms. However, now we are told that such a restriction is not *inherent* to the said exercise. Thus instead of first answering the question of whether the free movement provisions apply to trade unions' action, and then consider the possible limitations of both rights and freedoms at hand, the Court adopts the reverse logic.[106] On the other hand, to deny the inherent restriction to economic freedoms entailed by the exercise of the right to collective action seems to fall once again into the "disregard for the empirical reality" which was highlighted at the end of the previous Chapter. Indeed, this assumption has been criticised by a number of authors who consider

---

103 In the *Albany* case (C-67/96), the Court adopted the view that the social policy objectives pursued by collective agreements would be seriously undermined if management and labour were subject to *competition* law rules when seeking to improve jointly the terms and conditions of employment. Based on this argument, the Court ruled that such CAs by virtue of their nature and purpose should be considered to fall outside the scope of the competition law provisions. Therefore in *Albany* the Court chose to immunise *certain* collective agreements from the competition law provisions of the Treaty, namely those collective agreements whose purpose is to serve social policy objectives. See P. Syrpis and T. Novitz, "Economic and Social Rights in Conflict: Political and Judicial Approaches to Their Reconciliation", *European Law Review*, no. 3 (2008): 411–426, p. 419; B. Ryan, "The Charter and Collective Labour Law", in *Economic and Social Rights Under the EU Charter of Fundamental Rights – A Legal Perspective*, ed. T.K. Hervey and J. Kenner (Oxford: Hart Publishing, 2003), 67–90, pp. 82–84; B. Bercusson, "The Lisbon Treaty and Social Europe", *ERA Forum* 10, no. 1 (March 2009): 87–105, p. 293.

104 Para. 53.

105 Whereas in *Albany* the Court had recognised that collective agreements entailed an inherent restriction of competition.

106 Novitz, "A Human Rights Analysis of the Viking and Laval Judgments", p. 553.

that a restriction of the economic freedoms of the employer is indeed inherent in the exercise of the (fundamental) right to take collective action.[107] To deny this amounts to nothing less than construing the conflict between the exercise of the right to take collective action and the economic freedoms protected by the Treaties as *pathological*. Such an approach has more than an echo of a "unitarist" conception of capital-labour relationship, a vision which, as described in Chapter 2[108] has been consistently *denied* by industrial relations studies. If one considers industrial relations as "a field of tension between market pressures towards the commodification of labour (power) and social and institutional norms which ensure its (relative) 'decommodification'"[109] then the contrast with the wording of *Viking*[110] is staggering.

The third argument aimed at denying the competence of the Court of Justice to "balance" the right to take collective action and fundamental freedoms, is the one based on the fundamental nature of the former.

As it was explained *supra* it is in *Viking* and in *Laval* that the Court of Justice has recognised the right to take collective action as fundamental. Such a move did not however warrant any increased protection for the right at stake.[111] In fact the recognition was followed by a reference to *Schmidberger* and *Omega*, as the Court conceded that the protection of fundamental rights could in principle justify a restriction of one of the fundamental freedoms.[112] The Court however continues, in *Laval*: "As the Court held, in *Schmidberger* and *Omega*, the exercise of the fundamental rights at issue, that is, freedom of expression and freedom of assembly and respect for human dignity, respectively, does not fall outside the scope of the provisions of the Treaty. Such exercise must be reconciled with the requirements relating to rights protected under the Treaty and in accordance with the principle of proportionality".[113] The recognition of the right to take

107 C. Vigneau, "Le droit à l'action collective à l'épreuve des libertés économiques du Traité: la hiérarchisation des droits 'fondamentaux' dans l'ordre juridique communautaire", *La Semaine Juridique – Édition Générale*, no. 13 (2008): 33–36, p. 35; Dorssemont, "The Right to Take Collective Action Versus Fundamental Economic Freedoms in the Aftermath of Laval and Viking. Foes Are Forever", p. 71; Novitz, "A Human Rights Analysis of the Viking and Laval Judgments", pp. 550–551; Davies, "One Step Forward, Two Steps Back? The Viking and Laval Cases in the ECJ", p. 140; Bercusson, "The Trade Union Movement and the European Union: Judgment Day", p. 304.

108 See *supra*, p. 57 ff.

109 Hyman, "European Integration and Industrial Relations: a Case of Variable Geometry?", p. 10.

110 Para. 52: "[…] it cannot be considered that it is inherent in the very exercise of trade union rights and the right to take collective action that those fundamental freedoms will be prejudiced to a certain degree".

111 Novitz, "A Human Rights Analysis of the Viking and Laval Judgments", p. 542: "Indeed, it could be said that other aspects of the Viking and Laval judgments render judicial recognition of such a right negligible in terms of its practical effect".

112 *Viking*, para. 77; *Laval*, para. 93.

113 *Laval*, para. 94. In *Viking* the reasoning is similar though not as explicit: "Since the Community has thus not only an economic but also a social purpose, the rights under the provisions of the Treaty on the free movement of goods, persons, services and capital must be balanced against the objectives pursued by social policy, which include, as is clear from the first paragraph of

collective action as a fundamental right hence allows the Court to draw a parallel with its previous case law of *Schmidberger* and *Omega*. Also, Article 28 of the EU Charter of Fundamental Rights seems to play an important role in underpinning the reasoning of the Court. As suggested by Novitz, the very formulation of Article 28[114] implies "that entitlements under national law may be struck down by the European Court of Justice [...] to the extent that they are inconsistent with EC market freedoms". The Court extrapolates from this Article the generic possibility to subject the newly found fundamental right to "certain restrictions" not better specified, stemming either from Community law or from national law and practice.[115] Article 28 thus ends up transformed, by the hands of the Court, in something akin to a "Trojan horse", which "guarantees" the minimum possible protection for the right it is supposed to recognise.

The analogy with Omega and Schmidberger (and Spanish Strawberries)

The analogy with *Schmidberger* and *Omega* is one of the cornerstones of the Court's reasoning in both *Viking* and *Laval*. The reference to these previous cases both allows the Court to assert its competence to *balance* fundamental rights and freedoms and provides the Court with the tool to address the balancing, *i.e.* the proportionality test. Also, the Court relied again on *Schmidberger*, together with *Spanish Strawberries*, to base the argument that "restrictions may be the result of actions by individuals or groups of such individuals rather than caused by the State".[116]

Starting from the latter argument, one can see as this is not particularly convincing. Indeed, the two cases invoked as precedents by the Court both deal with *State* responsibility, being based, as Dashwood puts it, with "public inaction".[117] One might wonder about the outcome of an eventual action against the organisers of the demonstration at stake in *Schmidberger*, let alone against individual protesters.[118] Hence, either the Court is willing to push to the limit

Article 136 EC, inter alia, improved living and working conditions, so as to make possible their harmonisation while improvement is being maintained, proper social protection and dialogue between management and labour". It is known that the Court of Justice in *Viking* left the balancing exercise to the national court, though the former did in fact give a number of *hints* to the latter as to the outcome of the test (much in line with the approach of *Laval*).

114 "Workers and employers, or their respective organisations, have, in accordance with Union law and national laws and practices, the right to negotiate and conclude collective agreements at the appropriate levels and, in cases of conflicts of interest, to take collective action to defend their interests, including strike action".

115 D. Schiek, "Fundamental Rights Jurisprudence Between Member States' Prerogatives and Citizens' Autonomy", in *The European Court of Justice and the Autonomy of the Member States*, ed. H.-W. Micklitz and B. De Witte (Cambridge: Intersentia, 2012), 219–258, p. 240.

116 *Viking*, para. 62.

117 Dashwood, "Viking and Laval: Issues of Horizontal Direct Effect", p. 532.

118 As does M. Mörk, "An End to the Possibilities – on Horizontal Liability in Laval and the Limits of Judicial Rights Protection", in *The Protection of Fundamental Rights in the EU After Lisbon*, ed. S. de Vries, U. Bernitz and S. Weatherill (Oxford: Hart Publishing, 2013), 119–138, p. 130:

the identification of trade unions with the State, through their supposed role of "delegated regulatory bodies", or the answer to such hypothetical question is positive. Provided that the second option entails a complete and unrestrained horizontal effect of the fundamental freedoms (which has been avoided by the Court so far), the first case seems a more likely explanation. Thus, cases dealing with State responsibility are considered as relevant precedents inasmuch as trade unions do exert, in the reasoning of the Court, a regulatory task *equivalent* to that of the State, at least from the point of view of the restriction of fundamental freedoms.[119]

Leaving aside the nature of the defendant in these cases, both *Schmidberger* and *Omega* do reveal a number of notable differences when compared with *Viking* and *Laval*. The most evident of these differences is the margin of appreciation which was granted to the defendants in the earlier cases while being completely absent in the recent ones. This issue has been linked by a number of commentators to the different nature of the defendants.[120] In this sense trade unions are given the worst of both worlds. On the one hand they are considered regulatory bodies equivalent with states; on the other, not being states, they are not allowed a margin of appreciation when assessing restrictions to fundamental freedoms caused by the exercise of fundamental rights.[121] I will come back to this when analysing the proportionality test, in the next paragraph.

"if the strict standards laid down by the ECJ in *Laval* had been applied to the demonstrations, a national court could easily have established that the demonstrations were disproportionate infringements of Schmidberger's rights to the cross-border transport of goods on a highway (the demonstrators did not have to block the traffic, the demonstrations lasted too long, they should not have been planned in conjunction with a bank holiday etc.)". See also Dorssemont and Orlandini, "Market Rules and the Right to Strike: a Different Approach", pp. 80–81.

119 This point has already been analysed *supra*, when dealing with the Court's vision of trade unions.

120 Malmberg and Sigeman, "Industrial Action and EU Economic Freedoms: The Autonomous Collective Bargaining Model Curtailed by the European Court of Justice", p. 1130; Novitz, "A Human Rights Analysis of the Viking and Laval Judgments", p. 554; Barnard, "Viking and Laval: an Introduction", p. 486; Bercusson, "The Trade Union Movement and the European Union: Judgment Day", p. 304; S. Weatherill, "From Economic Rights to Fundamental Rights", in *The Protection of Fundamental Rights in the EU After Lisbon*, ed. S. de Vries, U. Bernitz and S. Weatherill (Oxford: Hart Publishing, 2013), 11–36, p. 28: "[...] disturbingly, the Court did not follow the model regularly preferred in the case law considered above: it left wholly out of account any margin of appreciation apt to permit recognition of local circumstances. This seems inconsistent with previous practice and constitutes the ruling's main weakness".

121 Barnard, "Viking and Laval: an Introduction", p. 475; Azoulai, "The Court of Justice and the Social Market Economy: the Emergence of an Ideal and the Conditions for Its Realization", p. 1350. As it was highlighted *supra*, while examining the decision in *Laval*, trade unions could not rely on Article 3(10) of the PWD, *i.e.* the "public policy exception", "not being bodies governed by public law". *Laval*, para. 84. See *supra*, p. 189. Cf. with *Bosman*, para. 86: "There is nothing to preclude individuals from relying on grounds of public policy, public security or public health. Neither the scope nor the content of those grounds is in any way affected by the public or private nature of the rules in question". Schepel reconciles the two statement by pointing out that Article 3(10) refers to the "application by Member States" of terms and conditions. See Schepel, "Constitutionalising the Market, Marketising the Constitution, and

Here it is worth noting two specific elements stemming from this different treatment. The first element is related to the *Omega* case. As it has been summarised *supra*, in this case the Court showed a lot of self-restraint in assessing the German ban. The German level of protection of human dignity was accepted as such.[122] This brought the Court to uphold a complete *ban* of an economic activity. It has been convincingly argued that such an approach derived from the relevance of the fundamental right at stake (respect for human dignity) in the context of the German legal system.[123] The fact that the protection of the right to take collective action is a key part of a national system of industrial relations did not move the Court to the slightest deference. This contrasting approach is made even more strident by the fact that a process of negotiations over working conditions (which, baked by collective action, was at stake in both cases) is logically *less* restrictive than the outright ban of an economic activity.[124]

The second element comes from *Schmidberger*. There a number of circumstances were considered favourably when assessing the (in)action of the Austrian authorities. In particular a) the demonstration was duly authorised[125]; b) the demonstration took place on a single occasion and for a limited duration[126]; c) the purpose of the demonstration "was not to restrict trade in goods of a particular type or from a particular source";[127] d) information was given in advance in order to limit inconveniences;[128] e) the event "did not give rise to a general climate of insecurity such as to have a dissuasive effect on intra-Community trade flows as a whole";[129] f) the imposition of limitations " would have been liable to cause much more serious disruption to intra-Community trade and public order, such as unauthorised demonstrations, confrontation between supporters and opponents

to Tell the Difference: On the Horizontal Application of the Free Movement Provisions in EU Law", pp. 197–198.

122 De Vries, "The Protection of Fundamental Rights Within Europe's Internal Market After Lisbon – An Endeavour for More Harmony", p. 40; Morijn, "Balancing Fundamental Rights and Common Market Freedoms in Union Law: Schmidberger and Omega in the Light of the European Constitution", p. 34.

123 Fons and Lenaerts, "The Constitutional Allocation of Powers and General Principles of EU Law", p. 1663.

124 This point was put forward by AG Mengozzi in his Opinion in the *Laval* case, para. 258: "[...] exercise of the right to take collective action in order to compel a service provider to subscribe to the rate of pay applied in the sector in question in the host Member State is, in principle, a less restrictive measure than automatic subjection to a similar rate of pay which, without being a minimum rate of pay, is set by national legislation, since it enables the service provider, within the framework of negotiation with the relevant trade unions, to arrive at a rate of pay that takes account of its own costs, without allowing it to apply, in any event, a rate of pay lower than that determined in accordance with the fall-back clause in the collective agreement". See also Schiek, "Fundamental Rights Jurisprudence Between Member States' Prerogatives and Citizens' Autonomy", p. 240.

125 *Schmidberger*, para. 84.

126 Ibid., para. 85.

127 Ibid., para. 86.

128 Ibid., para. 87.

129 Ibid., para. 87.

of the group organising the demonstration or acts of violence on the part of the demonstrators".[130] A good number of these "mitigating circumstances" can be found by looking at the facts of *Laval* and *Viking*. The actions were carried out in accordance with national regulations regarding the right to take collective action (a), and, when applicable, duly notified[131] (b). The employers thus knew in advance that they would be subject to a collective action (d). The actions were evidently not aimed against the foreign employer as such (c), nor the events could be seen as generating any widespread effect on intra-Community trade flows *as a whole* (e). Finally, very recent facts have shown that similar situations may easily give rise to unauthorised forms of protest[132] (e.g. wildcat strikes), so that also point (f) could have been considered. Indeed, the Court in *Laval* referred *a contrario* to point (b), when it found that the "unspecified duration" of negotiations about pay was an "aggravating condition" for the restriction. These points show as in *Schmidberger* the Court assessed the (in)action of the Austrian authorities using a *procedural* approach. In fact this is stated explicitly in the decision: "the specific aims of the demonstration are not in themselves material in legal proceedings such as those instituted by Schmidberger".[133] On the contrary, in both *Viking* and *Laval*, the test carried out by the Court is essentially *substantive*.

Restrictions, justifications... and cold water

Having affirmed its competence to a) scrutinise trade union action through the lenses of fundamental freedoms and b) strike the balance between fundamental freedoms and fundamental (social) rights in the process, the Court carried out its analysis. First it considered the collective action as entailing a *restriction* to fundamental freedoms and then applied the proportionality test.

As for the restriction, it is interesting to spend some time examining the *nature* of the restriction the Court identified in both cases. The point of departure is the *Säger* formula, following which the collective action is liable to make "less attractive" or "more difficult"[134] ("or even pointless".[135]) the exercise of the fundamental freedom at stake. It has already been stressed *supra* how such a formula has a extremely wide reach as regards the measures it "catches"

---

130 Ibid., para. 89–92.

131 *E.g.*, *Laval*, para. 33: "Since those negotiations were not successful, Byggettan requested Byggnads to take measures to initiate the collective action against Laval announced at the meeting of 15 September 2004. Notice was given in October 2004".

132 I am referring here to the East Lindsey Oil dispute which did take place in a situation similar to the one at stake in *Laval*. On the point see Barnard, "'British Jobs for British Workers': The Lindsey Oil Refinery Dispute and the Future of Local Labour Clauses in an Integrated EU Market".

133 *Schmidberger*, para. 66.

134 *Laval*, para. 99.

135 *Viking*, para. 72.

as restrictions.[136] This potential is evident in both cases, as the Court essentially *asserted* the existence of the restriction.[137]

Deakin has showed, analysing the *Laval* case, as this issue is "far from doubt-free".[138] The author summarises three scenarios which could justify the reasoning of the Court as regards the existence of a restriction, *i.e.* the fact that the collective action made "more difficult or less attractive" for Laval the exercise of the freedom to provide services. Under the first possibility, this exercise is more difficult or less attractive than "if the law allowing the industrial action had not existed"; second, "more difficult in relation to the situation faced by Swedish firms"; third, more difficult in relation to the situation which would have prevailed had Latvian law and/or Latvian collective agreements applied.[139] The reasoning of the Court falls in the third category, though the role of the PWD provides for a slightly different justification. The restriction, as it was described in the previous Chapter,[140] stems from the fact that the *demands* backed by the collective action go beyond the level of wages and working conditions *allowed* by the PWD (as interpreted by the Court). The problem here is that the PWD ends up playing multiple roles in the reasoning of the Court. At first it is used to assess the *existence* of a restriction; then (I will come to this in a moment) it is pivotal in the proportionality test applied to the collective action.

In *Viking* the Court found the Finnish collective action to be a restriction of the freedom of establishment "inasmuch as such action prevents both Viking and its subsidiary, Viking Eesti, from enjoying the same treatment in the host Member State as other economic operators established in that State",[141] while it was more obscure as to the transnational action of the ITF. Provided that this second action amounted at asking the affiliates (with the exclusion of the Finnish trade union) *not* to negotiate with Viking, the restriction seems to be construed as a violation of the "right" of Viking to negotiate with the Estonian trade unions.

However, since both actions were found in breach of the Treaty, the Court then passed to the next step: whether the collective action could be justified and its exercise was proportionate.

The approach to justifications shows another relevant divergence from the path traced in *Omega* and *Schmidberger*. In *Viking* the Court found that "the right to take collective action for the protection of workers is a legitimate interest which, in principle, justifies a restriction of one of the fundamental freedoms guaranteed by the Treaty" and that "the protection of workers is one of the

136 Reich, "How Proportionate Is the Proportionality Principle? Some Critical Remarks on the Use and Methodology of the Proportionality Principle in the Internal Market Case Law of the ECJ", p. 88. See p. 156.

137 Barnard, "Viking and Laval: an Introduction", p. 474; S. Deakin, "Regulatory Competition After Laval", *Cambridge Yearbook of European Legal Studies* 10 (2008): 581–610, p. 583.

138 Ibid., pp. 584 ff.

139 Ibid., p. 584.

140 See *supra*, p. 192.

141 *Viking*, para. 72.

overriding reasons of public interest recognised by the Court".[142] The right to take collective action is thus apprehended by the Court as strictly correlated with the "protection of workers".[143] However, the concept of "protection of workers" is interpreted by the Court in its narrowest meaning: the collective action can be considered as "aimed at protecting the jobs and conditions of employment" only if "jobs or conditions of employment" are "jeopardised or under serious threat".[144] Such a requirement implies that the right to take collective action can be justified only inasmuch it is aimed at protecting jobs and working conditions "as they stand".[145] Though the possibility may seem remote in times of austerity and internal devaluation, such a reasoning rules out the whole idea of *improving* working conditions through collective action. This fits uncomfortably with the "*promotion* of employment, *improved* living and working conditions, so as to make possible their harmonisation while the *improvement* is being maintained",[146] which should guide the action of the EU and of its Members in the social sphere. Turning to the transnational action of the ITF the Court rapidly found that "the restrictions on freedom of establishment resulting from such action cannot be objectively justified".[147] The reason for this adamant position is quite puzzling, so that it brings to the mind once again the "disregard for the empirical reality" already highlighted *supra*. The Court considered that the action could not be justified inasmuch it was "also applicable where the vessel is registered in a State which guarantees workers a higher level of social protection than they would enjoy in the first State".[148] The fact that *in practice* such a possibility is evidently only theoretical did not occur to the Court.[149] What is more, the Court here considers as restrictive the simple exercise (though concerted) of the freedom (not) to contract.[150] As noted by Dorssemont, an action which would have been perfectly legitimate if carried out by a single trade union (*i.e.* the refuse to engage in negotiations or to sign a collective agreement) becomes a restriction "once it is

142 *Viking*, para. 77.

143 Novitz, "A Human Rights Analysis of the Viking and Laval Judgments", p. 558 ff.

144 *Viking*, para. 81. See ibid., pp. 557–558; Barnard, "Social Dumping or Dumping Socialism?", pp. 482–483; G. Orlandini, "Trade Union Rights and Market Freedoms: the European Court of Justice Sets Out the Rules", *Labour Law & Policy Journal* 29 (2008): 573–604, p. 576.

145 Joerges and Rödl, "Informal Politics, Formalised Law and the Social Deficit of European Integration: Reflections After the Judgments of the ECJ in Viking and Laval", p. 15; N. Hős, "The Principle of Proportionality in Viking and Laval: an Appropriate Standard of Judicial Review?", *European Labour Law Journal* 1 (2010): 236–253, p. 246; Weatherill, "From Economic Rights to Fundamental Rights", p. 28.

146 Article 151 TFEU (Article 136 TEC at the time of the decision) (emphasis added). See Barnard, "The Protection of Fundamental Social Rights in Europe After Lisbon: a Question of Conflicts of Interests", pp. 40–41.

147 *Viking*, para. 88.

148 Ibid., para. 89.

149 Reich, "How Proportionate Is the Proportionality Principle? Some Critical Remarks on the Use and Methodology of the Proportionality Principle in the Internal Market Case Law of the ECJ", p. 104.

150 Dorssemont, "The Right to Take Collective Action Versus Fundamental Economic Freedoms in the Aftermath of Laval and Viking. Foes Are Forever", p. 93.

being undertaken in a coordinated way on a Community-Scale level".[151] So much for the development of a European system of industrial relations.[152]

In *Laval* the Court found that the "protection of the workers of the host State against possible *social dumping* may constitute an overriding reason of public interest".[153] Once again however the Court interprets the concept of "social dumping" in a restrictive way, so that the collective action undertaken by the Swedish trade unions does not ultimately fall into the scope of the justification. I already dealt with this interpretation while analysing the *Laval* decision in the previous Chapter.[154] As a reminder, the Court considers that the PWD is in itself a sufficient protection against social dumping. Hence, the PWD represents the yardstick to evaluate the collective action: going beyond what is permitted by the said Directive cannot be covered by the aim of protecting workers against social dumping.

Once again the distance of the *Viking&Laval* line of cases from the one set in *Omega* and *Schmidberger* is apparent by the analysis of the justifications. In the latter couple the Court considered the protection of a fundamental right as being a justification in *itself*. In *Schmidberger* this was apparently brought to its furthest consequence, as the Court stated that the aims of the demonstration (hence, of the exercise of the fundamental right) were not to be considered in assessing the proportionality of the restriction.[155] Both *Viking* and *Laval* showed a diametrically opposed approach. The exercise of a fundamental right did not warrant any specific consideration; instead it could only be justified on the basis of its aims.[156] Furthermore, the Court considered itself competent to assess these aims, and in particular to assess whether the collective action was

---

151 Ibid.

152 On the point it is interesting to note that Lenaerts (who was sitting as a judge in both *Viking* and *Laval)* has subsequently stated in a scientific Article that "had the Scandinavian trade unions in *Laval* and *Viking* reacted to cheaper labour coming from the Baltic States with a *transnational mindset*, perhaps *seeking to raise standards throughout the EU* rather than seeking to *exclude* workers from other Member States, the ECJ might have been more sympathetic to their claims". See Fons and Lenaerts, "The Constitutional Allocation of Powers and General Principles of EU Law", pp. 1666–1667 (emphasis added). Mörk has warned about the difficulty of assessing the "mindset" of a private (and collective) entity (see Mörk, "An End to the Possibilities – on Horizontal Liability in Laval and the Limits of Judicial Rights Protection", p. 136). Moreover, looking at *Viking*, one can easily see how the unions did in fact react with a "transnational mindset". How could an observer define differently the transnational solidarity organised under the umbrella of the ITF?

153 *Laval*, para. 103 (emphasis added). Later the Court adds that "In that regard, it must be observed that, in principle, blockading action by a trade union of the host Member State which is aimed at ensuring that workers posted in the framework of a transnational provision of services have their terms and conditions of employment fixed at a *certain level*, falls within the objective of protecting workers", para. 107 (emphasis added).

154 See *supra*, p. 192 ff.

155 *Schmidberger*, para. 66.

156 Novitz, "A Human Rights Analysis of the Viking and Laval Judgments", p. 554; Schiek, "Fundamental Rights Jurisprudence Between Member States' Prerogatives and Citizens' Autonomy", p. 240.

actually protecting workers. Considering the three steps of the proportionality test,[157] the Court found the collective action in *Laval* as lacking on the side of *suitability*. In *Viking* the situation is less clear. The Court seems to doubt as to the suitability of the action,[158] but it also sends back the case to the national court inviting to consider its *necessity*.[159] In this sense, the *purpose* of the collective action *stricto sensu*[160] becomes a fundamental element of its assessment by the Court of Justice. Before passing to analyse this role, it is useful to remind the warning of Bercusson, just before the dawn of the Judgment Day. The Author stressed the danger of applying a proportionality test on the basis of the demands backed by a given collective action: "It is difficult sensibly in practice to apply any test of proportionality to the demands made by the trade unions in that process. It is in the very nature of negotiations that both parties set demands at their highest and through negotiation over time seek a compromise, if necessary, with the assistance of mediation and conciliation. At what stage of this process and against what criteria is the test of proportionality to be applied?".[161] Another major issue with the approach restriction/justification/proportionality has been stressed by Anne Davies.[162] The Author notes that the *effectiveness* of a collective action can be measured in terms of its likelihood of persuading the employer to make concessions. This is to be achieved through the harm (or threat thereof) caused to the said employer by the collective action, so that engaging in collective bargaining becomes more efficient for the employer than facing a continued action. Hence the problem, and the reference to "cold water" at the beginning of this paragraph. To apply the proportionality test to such a situation amounts to a paradox akin to the ordeal of cold water:[163] either the accused sinks, then he

157 Suitability, necessity and proportionality *stricto sensu*. See for example Hös, "The Principle of Proportionality in Viking and Laval: an Appropriate Standard of Judicial Review?", pp. 241 and ff.; Reich, "How Proportionate Is the Proportionality Principle? Some Critical Remarks on the Use and Methodology of the Proportionality Principle in the Internal Market Case Law of the ECJ", pp. 96 ff.

158 *Viking*, para. 86.

159 Ibid., para. 87. Here the Court seems to introduce a requirement of *ultimum remedium*, *i.e.* that the collective action should represent the last resort of trade unions after having exhausted all the less restricting possibilities. See Barnard, "'British Jobs for British Workers': The Lindsey Oil Refinery Dispute and the Future of Local Labour Clauses in an Integrated EU Market", pp. 13–14; Davies, "One Step Forward, Two Steps Back? The Viking and Laval Cases in the ECJ", p. 143.

160 *I.e.*, not the generic "protection of workers" but the actual content of the collective agreement backed by the collective action.

161 Bercusson, "The Trade Union Movement and the European Union: Judgment Day", p. 304. Reich stresses how the proportionality test was "developed for state, not for private (even though collective) action. See Reich, "How Proportionate Is the Proportionality Principle? Some Critical Remarks on the Use and Methodology of the Proportionality Principle in the Internal Market Case Law of the ECJ", p. 109. See also Barnard, "The Protection of Fundamental Social Rights in Europe After Lisbon: a Question of Conflicts of Interests", pp. 47 ff., critical toward the application of the proportionality test in the field of industrial relations.

162 Davies, "One Step Forward, Two Steps Back? The Viking and Laval Cases in the ECJ", p. 143.

163 See for example R. Bartlett, *Trial by Fire and Water* (Oxford: Clarendon Press, 1986), pp. 22–23; J.H. Langbein, *Torture and the Law of Proof* (Chicago: University of Chicago Press, 1977),

or she was innocent, or he or she floats, then he or she is burned for witchcraft. Out of the metaphor: either the collective action is *not* effective, and thus it is less restrictive of the freedom of the employer, or it *is* effective, and is hence (more likely to get) caught in the test set up by the Court of Justice.

6.2.3 THE ROLE OF COLLECTIVE BARGAINING AND COLLECTIVE AGREEMENTS

It should be clear by now that the approach followed by the Court is largely (if not completely) focused on the actual *content* of the collective agreement backed by the collective action. At every step of the test, from the justification, through the suitability and ending with the necessity, the fundamental right to take collective action is never balanced *per se* against the fundamental freedom at stake. Instead, the specific aims of the action are scrutinised against the background of the Treaties[164] *and* of secondary legislation deemed to implement fundamental freedoms.[165] As it was explained *supra*, this constitutes a major deviation from the supposed "precedents" of *Schmidberger* and *Omega*.

In *Schmidberger* the Court employed a *procedural* approach, as it is made clear from the elements analysed in order to ascertain the responsibility (or, ultimately, lack thereof) of the Austrian government. The Court did not scrutinise the demonstration under its necessity and suitability in order to achieve a better protection of the environment. Nor did the Court engage in an interpretation of the concept of "protection of the environment". As I described *supra*, in both *Viking* and *Laval* the Court first re-defines the aims of the collective action, then scrutinise the *demands* backed by the action with a substantive test. On the one hand this brings us back to the problem highlighted above in relation with the risks of scrutinising the *demands* in a process of collective bargaining: a process of negotiation often (if not always) implies some changes to the initial positions of the parties.[166] To choose these initial demands as the tool to measure the proportionality of the collective action thus seems quite out of context. On the other hand, a substantive test is bound to intrude to a very high degree in the choices of social actors.[167] Hence the Court will essentially engage in a balancing of the (conflicting) interests of the parties, an exercise which is, ultimately, political.[168]

---

p. 210, n. 49 and literature cited.

164 Barnard, "Social Dumping or Dumping Socialism?", p. 482; Novitz, "A Human Rights Analysis of the Viking and Laval Judgments", p. 554.

165 *I.e.* the PWD in the *Laval* case.

166 Bamber and Sheldon, "Collective Bagaining: an International Analysis", pp. 586 ff.

167 Hős, "The Principle of Proportionality in Viking and Laval: an Appropriate Standard of Judicial Review?", p. 251.

168 See Davies, "One Step Forward, Two Steps Back? The Viking and Laval Cases in the ECJ", p. 146: "The rulings in *Viking* and *Laval* have the potential to involve the courts in a much more

Despite this relevant role of collective agreement (or, *rectius* of the demands) in assessing the proportionality of the collective action, the Court considers that the very same agreement would have been perfectly legitimate if it had been reached *without* the recourse to collective action.[169] Hence, it is the collective action which makes such contents dis-proportionate. As noted by Novitz, this is due to the understanding of trade union action by the Court of Justice.[170] Indeed, the Court seems to consider trade unions' action as "essentially coercive".[171] It is this view that catapults trade unions into the realm of regulatory bodies. The problem here, notwithstanding the constant interlinking of collective action and content of the collective agreement operated by the Court, is the divorce between the concept of collective action and of collective bargaining. In the understanding of the Court it is possible to identify a category of (in principle) "good" collective agreement (*i.e.* the ones reached without the recourse to collective action) opposed to a category of (in principle) "bad" ones, reached by "forcing" the employer through a collective action. This is, at best, puzzling, especially if one considers that the Court itself in *Viking* has acknowledged that the collective action "may be the trade unions' last resort to ensure the success of their claim to regulate the work of Viking's employees collectively" and should thus "be considered to be inextricably linked to the collective agreement the conclusion of which FSU is seeking".[172] Hence, collective action is inextricably linked with the conclusion of collective agreements, but the same collective action implies the metamorphosis of trade unions into regulatory bodies,[173] notwithstanding the fact that the exercise of the fundamental right to take collective action is not *inherently* restrictive of fundamental freedoms.[174]

The right to bargain collectively in the Laval & Viking era

Apart from its role in the assessment of the right to take collective action by the Court of Justice, (the right to) collective bargaining in itself came under the

politically sensitive set of questions as they seek to apply the proportionality test to unions' strike action".

169 *Laval*, para. 81: "[...]without prejudice to the right of undertakings established in other Member States to sign of *their own accord* a collective labour agreement in the host Member State, in particular in the context of a commitment made to their own posted staff, the terms of which might be more favourable [...]" (emphasis added). On the point see the vibrant critique of Dorssemont, "The Right to Take Collective Action Versus Fundamental Economic Freedoms in the Aftermath of Laval and Viking. Foes Are Forever", p. 33. See also Joerges, and Rödl, "Informal Politics, Formalised Law and the Social Deficit of European Integration: Reflections After the Judgments of the ECJ in Viking and Laval", p. 14.

170 Novitz, "A Human Rights Analysis of the Viking and Laval Judgments", pp. 552–553.

171 *Laval*, para. 99–100.

172 *Viking*, para. 36.

173 See Schepel, "Constitutionalising the Market, Marketising the Constitution, and to Tell the Difference: On the Horizontal Application of the Free Movement Provisions in EU Law", p. 187.

174 *Viking*, para. 52.

scrutiny of the Court in recent years. In fact, it took little less than two years to the CJEU to apply the doctrine developed in the two decisions to the right of collective bargaining. The occasion was provided by an infraction procedure brought against Germany.[175] The infraction procedure was directed against the direct awarding (by local authorities and local authority undertakings having more than 1218 employees[176]) of service contracts for the management of occupational old-age pensions, without call for tenders at European level. Those contracts were awarded to bodies which were directly identified by collective agreements. Such agreements were concluded between the Federation of Local Authority Employer Associations and ver.di (United Service Sector Union). This practice was considered by the Commission as being in breach of Council Directive 92/50/EEC relating to the coordination of procedures for the award of public service contracts,[177] in conjunction with Articles 23 to 55, of Directive 2004/18/EC of the European Parliament and of the Council on the coordination of procedures for the award of public works contracts, public supply contracts and public service contracts.[178] By explicitly referring to *Viking* and *Laval* the Court considered itself competent to solve the clash between economic freedoms and fundamental rights.[179] Apart from the reaffirmed loyalty to *Viking* and *Laval*, this decision is interesting for what it ignores. In the first place, still focusing on the question of balancing fundamental rights and fundamental freedoms, the court ignores the whole reasoning proposed on this point by the AG in her opinion. Indeed, AG Trstenjak proposed a rather different approach to the issue, an approach based on what could be defined as a "cross proportionality test". The AG, making reference to the solution delivered by the court in *Schmidberger*, argued in favour of a renewed centrality of the idea of equal ranking for conflicting fundamental freedoms and fundamental rights.[180] Following this reasoning, she proposes to the court to revise its approach (*i.e.* the one developed in *Viking* and *Laval*) to the balancing of fundamental rights and fundamental freedoms, by applying the proportionality test not only to the restriction to the latter arising from the exercise of the former, but also, the other way round, to the restriction of the

175 Case C-271/08, Commission v. Germany. See Syrpis, "Reconciling Economic Freedoms and Social Rights – The Potential of Commission V Germany (Case C-271/08, Judgment of 15 July 2010)"; Rocca, "Case C-271/08, Commission V. Germany [2010]".

176 It must be noted that the Commission in its reply redefined the subject-matter of its action "by requesting the Court to find a failure to fulfil those obligations because local authorities and local authority undertakings which had more than 2044 employees, in 2004 and 2005, more than 1827 employees, in 2006 and 2007, and more than 1783 employees, in the period from 2008, awarded such contracts directly, without a call for tenders at European Union level".

177 18 June 1992.

178 31 March 2004.

179 *In casu*, the freedom to provide services, since the two directives at stake are considered as an implementation of this freedom, and the right to collective bargaining, protected under Article 28 of the EU Charter of Fundamental Rights. *Commission v. Germany*, para 42–44.

180 See Opinion of AG Trstenjak in *Commission v Germany*, para. 195.

former caused by the eventual application of the latter.[181] It is worth noting that, in introducing this solution, the AG actually criticised the approach to the issue of *Viking* and *Laval*, on the ground that such an approach would sit "uncomfortably alongside the principle of equal ranking for fundamental rights and fundamental freedoms".[182] In doing so, she made vast reference to the widespread critique directed towards *Viking* and *Laval* by the European scholarship. That being said, the fact that the court completely ignored this part of the Opinion reinforces *a contrario* the loyalty to the solution delivered in *Viking* and *Laval*, provided that the application of the solution proposed by the AG could have brought to the very same outcome in the present case.[183]

Back to the case, Article 28 plays once again its "Trojan horse" role, since it provides the basis for the Court to affirm that also the constitutional protection enjoyed by the right to collective bargaining[184] has to bend the knee in front of EU law: "while it is true that the right to bargain collectively enjoys in Germany the constitutional protection conferred, generally, by Article 9(3) of the German Basic Law upon the right to form associations to safeguard and promote working and economic conditions, the fact remains that, as provided in Article 28 of the Charter, that right must be exercised in accordance with European Union law".[185] This comes as no particular surprise, as the pre-eminence of EU law has long been affirmed by the Court.[186] The actual application of this principle however is, in this case, more problematic. It was so that, after having confirmed its competence, the Court applied the proportionality test developed in *Viking* and *Laval*. Unsurprisingly the Republic of Germany was found in breach of the Directive (and hence of the freedom to provide services).

On its path to this solution, the Court had once again to circumvent the argument based on the "Albany immunity",[187] put forward by the Republic of Germany. The cornerstone of such a defence was the analogy between competition law (where the *Albany* doctrine was elaborated) and fundamental freedoms (at stake in the present case). The Court did not accept this reasoning, denying, plain and simply, the possibility of such an analogy, as it had already done in *Viking*.[188] Indeed the Court, in its distinguishing of the two sets of rules (competition and fundamental freedoms), carries the narrowing of the "Albany doctrine" to its

---

181 Ibid., para. 192 and 199.

182 Ibid., para. 183.

183 Syrpis, "Reconciling Economic Freedoms and Social Rights – The Potential of Commission V Germany (Case C-271/08, Judgment of 15 July 2010)", p. 228.

184 Article 9(3) of the German Basic Law.

185 *Commission v. Germany*, para 43.

186 Case C-26/62, *NV Algemene Transport- en Expeditie Onderneming van Gend & Loos v. Netherlands Inland Revenue Administration*; Case C-11/70, *Internationale Handelsgesellschaft mbH v. Einfuhrund Vorratsstelle für Getreide und Futtermittel.*

187 It is interesting to note that the facts in Albany were similar to the ones of the present decision, as the Court had to assess the compatibility of competition law with a collective agreement establishing a mandatory pension fund.

188 *Viking*, para 52.

furthest end. This is rather puzzling since in Albany the Court was already aware of the possible restriction of cross-frontier business and service,[189] while in the end it granted the immunity to (certain) collective agreements.

Paradoxically in a more recent judgement,[190] the Court had the occasion to confirm the Albany doctrine in its previous, "orthodox" version. In the *AG2R* case the Court of Justice had to decide upon the compatibility of a French sectoral agreement with the EU requirements in the field of anti-trust law. This sectoral agreement contained a provision for a mandatory health insurance, managed by AG2R Prévoyance. The dispute originates from the action brought by the insurer against an employer who refused to pay its contributions to the fund. Before the French tribunal the employer, among other arguments, claimed that the French legislation, allowing for an extension *erga omnes* of the cited agreement, was in breach of EU law. The Tribunal de Grande Instance of Perigueux then sent the case to the CJEU for a preliminary ruling on the issue. In very brief, the Court confirmed the compatibility of this scheme with competition law (Articles 101–106 TFEU). The decision is in fact a direct application of *Albany*, if not a repetition, even though the French legislation, not allowing for exemptions to the mandatory affiliation to the insurance, is even stricter than the Dutch one.[191] Hence, the paradox. Both the decision and the Opinion never make reference to *Commission v. Germany*. Visually, the gate preventing the intrusion of competition law in the field of collective bargaining stays (to a certain extent) high, strong and barred, while the surrounding walls are but a ruin, crumbled under the superior strength of economic freedoms. This amounts to a grotesque mimicry of the old idea that social policy was a matter for the individual Member States to handle. The combination of *Commission v. Germany* and *AG2R* makes it clear that a national employer cannot "escape" from (as in our cases) mandatory membership to an insurance/pension fund established in a CA applicable to its sector of activity. On the contrary, a foreign employer (or an eventual infringement procedure) could challenge the very same provision as restricting the freedom of establishment or the freedom to provide services with a much higher possibility of success.[192] Thus

189 See *Albany* para. 50: "Moreover, such an agreement affects trade between Member States in so far as it concerns undertakings which engage in cross-frontier business and deprives insurers established in other Member States of the opportunity to offer a full pension scheme in the Netherlands either by virtue of cross-frontier services or through branches or subsidiaries".

190 Case C-437/09, *AG2R Prévoyance v. Beaudout Père et Fils SARL*.

191 *AG2R*, para. 39: "Article 101 TFEU, read in conjunction with Article 4(3) EU, must be interpreted as not precluding the decision by the public authorities to make compulsory, at the request of the organizations representing employers and employees within a given occupational sector, an agreement which is the result of collective bargaining and which provides for compulsory affiliation to a scheme for supplementary reimbursement of healthcare costs for all undertakings within the sector concerned, without any possibility of exemption".

192 A situation which once again supports the risk of reverse discrimination towards national undertakings. See A. Lo Faro, "Toward a de-Fundamentalisation of Collective Labour Rights in European Social Law?" in *Before and After the Economic Crisis? What Implications for the 'European Social Model'?*, ed. M.-A. Moreau (Cheltenham: Edward Elgar, 2012), 203–216, p. 206.

the *Albany* doctrine is confined to competition law. On the one hand this approach seems formalistic: the restriction to competition and to economic freedoms derives from the very same exercise of the same right, namely the right to bargain collectively. It is difficult to conceive a collective agreement restricting competition while leaving untouched the (broader) economic freedoms. This brings back the paradox: those who can rely on fundamental freedoms to challenge collectively agreed standards may find themselves in a position of competitive advantage. On the other hand this situation shows once again the pre-eminence of economic freedoms, in their role of "constitutional" foundations of the EU.

6.3 THREE KINGS

I have highlighted before as the Court did refer to a number of international sources in order to recognise the fundamental nature of the rights to bargain collectively and to take collective action. At the same time and in both occasions, the Court decided not to engage in a true inter-textual interpretation, ignoring the body of (*sui generis*) "case law" developed by the supervisory bodies of the international instruments cited.[193]

Considering as acquired the stance[194] of the Court in respect to the case law *preceding* the decisions of both *Viking* and *Laval*[195] here I will focus on those evolutions which took place *after* the decisions at stake.

In particular, I will focus on the decisions delivered by the European Court of Human Rights, on the conclusions reached in two different occasions by the Committee for the Application of Conventions and Recommendations of the ILO and on a recent decision of the European Committee of Social Rights.

6.3.1 THE ILO

The CEACR conclusion which will retain my attention here are particularly interesting inasmuch as they do involve (as directly as possible) the decisions of the CJEU.

---

193 Novitz, "A Human Rights Analysis of the Viking and Laval Judgments", pp. 558–559. Though at the same time the CJEU cited ILO Convention 87, whose text does not recognise the right to take collective action. The right has instead been constantly recognised by ILO CFA and CEACR as protected by the same Convention. In a way, this is a confirmation of the role of those supervisory bodies, as stated by Dorssemont, "The Right to Take Collective Action Versus Fundamental Economic Freedoms in the Aftermath of Laval and Viking. Foes Are Forever", p. 90.

194 Though evidently not immune from critiques.

195 The situation for *Commission v. Germany* is, from a chronological point of view, only slightly different.

In both occasions it was a state member of the ILO (respectively the UK and Sweden) which was held accountable for the *effects* in its legal system of the decisions delivered by the CJEU.

BALPA

The dispute here at stake[196] (generally referred to as the "BALPA dispute") arose in the context of negotiations between British Airways and the British Air Line Pilots' Association. Following the Open Skies Treaty[197] (concluded in 2007 between the USA and the EU) British Airways was planning to launch a wholly owned subsidiary airline that would operate between Paris and (among others) the US. Along with this operation, the process of collective bargaining started: the thorny issue revolved around the working conditions to apply to the workers of the subsidiary. BALPA was ready to accept the principle by which the new subsidiary would need to operate with lower labour costs; still they were concerned by the possibility that this situation would provide a basis to subsequently undercut working conditions also within the "mother" company. Thus, collective bargaining started in the summer 2007. However, the negotiations failed and no agreement was reached. BALPA then called for strike action, holding a ballot which turned out clearly in favour of collective action. BA responded threatening to seek an injunction. It is at this point that the shadow of *Viking* and *Laval* appears on the scene. Indeed, the company alleged that any strike action would be unlawful because of the doctrine developed by the CJEU in the two decisions,[198] since such an action would be in violation of its freedom of establishment. Because of the complexity of the test involved in the *Viking&Laval* doctrine it was very likely that the injunction would have been granted.[199] What is more, when BALPA applied to the court in order to determine if BA claim was founded, the company counter-claimed, once again on the basis of the doctrine developed by the CJEU. The main threat behind this counter-claim revolved around a claim for unlimited damages, estimated by the company at £100 million *per day*. It was then clear for BALPA

---

196 For a more detailed account see K. Ewing and J. Hendy, "The ECJ Decisions and Trade Union Freedom: lessons from the United Kingdom", in *The New Spectre Haunting Europe. the ECJ, Trade Union Rights and the British Government*, ed. K.D. Ewing and J. Hendy (London: Institute of Employment Rights, 2009), 68–83.

197 This Treaty, for the part that is relevant for the dispute, allows an airline based in one EU Member State to operate flights to the USA from another EU State. Before the Treaty such a possibility faced significant obstacles.

198 Ewing and Hendy, "The Dramatic Implications of Demir and Baykara", p. 43. Writing in the aftermath of *Viking* and *Laval*, Barnard found that "the Court, the trade unions and even the employers have a lot to learn". Indeed, employers proved to be fast learners. Barnard, "Social Dumping or Dumping Socialism?", p. 492.

199 Ewing and Hendy, "The Dramatic Implications of Demir and Baykara", pp. 43–44: "Given that the test for the grant of an interim injunction is whether the claimant can demonstrate a serious issue to be tried and that the *status quo* should be maintained unless the balance of convenience disfavours it, it was plain that an interim injunction would be likely to be granted."

that even pursuing the action in court was futile: such an action would have likely required a long time to see its end, including a possible appeal and a reference to the CJEU. By that time the subsidiary would have been established. Also, the "life-threatening" amount of damages sought by the company meant that having recourse to industrial action before the end of the judicial procedure would have been far too dangerous for the union.[200] Because of this, BALPA discontinued its legal claim and the collective action was cancelled.

So far so good (more or less). However, this short chilling story is but the first half of the novel. There is indeed a second part, a twist in the plot. This second part is in fact directly connected with the chilling effect I referred to before.[201] At this point BALPA lodged a complaint before the ILO Committee of Experts on the Application of Conventions and Recommendations (CEACR). In this procedure the union was later joined by the International Transport Federation (ITF). The Committee delivered its conclusions in the occasion of the 2010 Report. These conclusions were defined by the ITF as ground-breaking.[202] In its conclusions, the Committee first discarded the objection raised by the UK Government, which had pointed out that the impact of *Viking&Laval* was a consequence of EU law.[203] Second, the Committee stressed the fact that it was not its task to "judge the correctness of the ECJ's holdings in Viking and Laval [...] but rather to examine whether the impact of these decisions at national level are such as to deny workers' freedom of association rights under Convention No 87".[204] However, after this careful disclaimer, the conclusions were a direct (as direct as it can be imagined in such a context) critique of the *Viking&Laval* doctrine. On a more "abstract" side, the Committee explicitly excluded the proportionality test from the catalogue of possible restrictions to the rights protected under Convention No. 87.[205] On the "practical" side, in the conclusions one finds a direct critique to the chilling effect entailed by the CJEU doctrine. In fact the Committee denounced that "the omnipresent threat of an action for damages that could bankrupt the union, possible now in the light of the Viking and Laval judgments, creates a

---

200 Though under British law (TULRCA 1992, s. 22) the amount of damages recoverable from a trade union in similar disputes is capped, the company argued that a claim based on EU law was incompatible with such a limitation, because of the principle which requires remedies for breach of EU law to be effective.

201 See *supra*, p. 73. Novitz, Hayes, and Reed, "Applying the Laval Quartet in a UK Context: chilling, Ripple and Distruptive Effects on Industrial Relations", pp. 227–230.

202 ITF, Right to strike over social dumping backed by key ILO body, 4 march 2010, http://www.itfseafarers.org/maritime_news.cfm/newsdetail/4256/region/1/section/0/order/1, (last accessed 30 April 2014).

203 International Labour Conference, 99th Session, 2010, Report of the Committee of Experts on the Application of Conventions and Recommendations, pp. 208–209.

204 Ibid., p. 209.

205 "The Committee observes that when elaborating its position in relation to the permissible restrictions that may be placed upon the right to strike, it has *never* included the need to assess the *proportionality* of interests bearing in mind a notion of freedom of establishment or freedom to provide services" (emphasis added), ibid.

situation where the rights under the Convention cannot be exercised".[206] Closing its conclusion the Committee stated that "the doctrine that is being articulated in these [*Viking* and *Laval*] ECJ judgments is likely to have a *significant restrictive effect* on the exercise of the right to strike in practice in a manner *contrary to the Convention*" (emphasis added).[207] It is clear that the recognition by the Committee of the chilling effect has played a pivotal role in reaching such a conclusion.

The "Lex Laval"

Trying to cope with the decision of the Court in *Laval*, Sweden in 2010 approved a number of amendments to its law regulating posting of workers, known as *Lex Laval*.[208]

These amendments were to provide an answer to the questions raised by the *Laval* decision. On the one hand, the objective was to preserve the Swedish system of industrial relations, so that a path-breaking intervention was out of question. On the other, the *Laval* decision represented a recent 'shock'. Hence, the objective of providing a CJEU-proof solution was also a relevant one. On top of this, as recalled by Malmberg,[209] the climate was made somewhat more tense by the fact that the Swedish private employers' organisation had partly financed the employer's side in the *Laval* case. The resulting amendments thus tried to "integrate" the points raised by the CJEU decision into the Swedish system, while leaving it as untouched as possible. As a result, posting undertakings are legally placed in a sort of "bubble", where the possibilities for collective action are subject to (more) stringent conditions. Those conditions are closely connected with the points highlighted in the analysis of the *Laval* decision.[210]

The first requirement to take (lawful) collective action against a posting undertaking with the aim of setting wages and working conditions of posted workers is linked with the issue of transparency/uncertainty. Thus, the demands backed by the collective action must correspond to wages and working conditions already provided by a "central branch agreement", *i.e.* a nationwide sector agreement.[211] The second condition deals with the minimum/maximum

---

206 Ibid.

207 On this point see also T. Novitz, "UK Implementation of the Posting of Workers Directive", in *Cross-Border Services, Posting of Workers and Multilevel Governance*, ed. S. Evju (Oslo: Institutt for privaterett, 2013), 329–358, pp. 347–348.

208 In fact, a series of amendments to the Swedish Posting of Workers Act (1999:678), amendments SFS 2012:857 and SFS 2013:351, as reported in Swedish Trade Union Confederation (LO) and Swedish Confederation of Professional Employees (TCO) v. Sweden Complaint No. 85/2012, para. 35.

209 J. Malmberg, "Posting Post-Laval: Nordic Responses", in *Before and After the Economic Crisis? What Implications for the 'European Social Model'?*, ed. M.-A. Moreau (Cheltenham: Edward Elgar, 2011), 25–39, p. 33.

210 See *supra*, p. 192.

211 Swedish Trade Union Confederation (LO) and Swedish Confederation of Professional Employees (TCO) v. Sweden Complaint No. 85/2012, para. 35.

character of the PWD, by limiting the said legitimate demands to minimum wages and other working conditions set by the central branch agreement. The third condition is aimed at taking into account foreign collective agreement, though it ultimately goes further than that. It forbids the collective action in the situation where the posting employer can 'show' that posted workers already enjoy wages and working conditions which are as good as the central branch agreement. Such an evidence hence bears no obligation for the posting employer to sign a collective agreement whatsoever, even in the home country.[212]

These amendments were scrutinised by the CEACR in the occasion of the 102nd Session of the International Labour Conference in 2013. In fact, the Committee also briefly analysed the outcome of the decision of the national judge in the *Laval* case. On this point the Committee urged the Government "to study possible solutions for compensation of the two unions" on the basis that those unions could not reasonably presume that the action would be found to be in violation of EU law.

The Conclusions analyse a number of questions strictly related to posting of workers. However these issues will be analysed in the next Chapter. Here I will focus on the more general topic of the relationship between fundamental (collective) social rights and fundamental freedoms. On this point the Committee essentially repeated its findings in *BALPA* as regards the proportionality principle.[213] Clearly enough the Committee considered (for the second time in a row) the proportionality test applied by the Court of Justice as falling outside the restrictions to the right to take collective action permitted under ILO conventions.

Furthermore, the Committee expressed its concern for the restriction of the permitted aims of collective actions to minimum conditions laid down in the PWD.[214] On the same point, the concern was extended to possibility for the employer to effectively stop the collective action just by showing that the employees' terms and conditions are as favourable as the minimum conditions of the PWD regardless the actual coverage by a collective agreement.[215]

---

212 K. Ahlberg, "Will Lex Laval Work?" *Nordic Labour Journal*, 2010, available at www.nordiclabourjournal.org/artikler/kommentar/comments-2010/article.2010-11-02.9464573364, last accessed on 12 February 2014.

213 International Labour Conference, 102nd Session, 2013 Report of the Committee of Experts on the Application of Conventions and Recommendations, p. 179: "As a general matter, the Committee recalls that when elaborating its position in relation to the permissible restrictions that may be placed upon the right to strike, it has never included the need to assess the proportionality of interests bearing in mind a notion of freedom of establishment or freedom to provide services".

214 Ibid., p. 180.

215 Making abstraction from the specificities of the case analysed, one might wonder how those concerns would apply in a *Viking*-like situation. In the end, the "legitimate" aims of the collective action were restricted to protecting the *existing* employment conditions, without any room left for eventual improvements, while an unilateral promise of the employer was considered as sufficient to cast some serious doubts as to the aim of protecting workers.

6.3.2 THE COUNCIL OF EUROPE

If the ILO system provided for some evolution *directly* linked to *Viking* and *Laval*, the situation under the system of the Council of Europe is at present slightly different. On the one hand, a *direct* connection can be found in the decision regarding the *Lex Laval* by the European Committee of Social Rights.

On the other hand no direct link can be found looking at the ECtHR. However, collective social rights were themselves interested by some very important decision from this Court in 2008 and 2009. Though the said direct link is missing, an indirect one has immediately been identified by many authors,[216] as the Strasbourg case law seemed to go in a very different direction than the one of the CJEU.

The European Court of Human Rights

The first, ground breaking, decision which has to be presented here is the *Demir and Baykara II* decision.[217] Provided that to give a full account of the case goes beyond the limited scope of this Chapter,[218] I will concentrate on two elements which are important for the analysis. The first point is methodological,[219] the second is substantial, and deals with the relationship of collective bargaining with the freedom of association protected by the ECHR.

As regards the methodology, with the "*Demir* approach" the ECtHR adopted an unprecedented[220] attitude toward the interpretation of the Convention. Indeed, the Grand Chamber, in its unanimous decision, made systematic reference to international labour standards[221] and to the case law of their supervisory

---

[216] *E.g.* Ewing and Hendy, "The Dramatic Implications of Demir and Baykara", p. 1: "the authors consider the apparent collision between the trade union rights established under the ECHR in *Demir and Baykara* and the trade union liabilities introduced under EU law by the *Viking* and *Laval* judgments of the European Court of Justice"; F. Dorssemont, "How the European Court of Human Rights Gave Us Enerji to Cope with Viking and Laval", in *Before and After the Economic Crisi? What Implications for the 'European Social Model'?*, ed. M.-A. Moreau (Cheltenham: Edward Elgar, 2011), 217–235.

[217] *Demir and Baykara v. Turkey*, Application No 34503/97, 12 November 2008.

[218] To summarise the facts very briefly, the *Demir* case concerned a collective agreement in the public sector which had been retroactively declared void, with the consequence (among others) that the workers had to repay the benefits obtained under the agreement. This was done because, though civil servants enjoyed the right to form and join trade unions, this did not include any right to engage in collective bargaining and to conclude valid collective agreements.

[219] See on this point K. Lörcher, "The New Social Dimension in the Jurisprudence of the European Court of Human Rights (ECtHR): The Demir and Baykara Judgment, Its Methodology and Follow-up", in *The European Convention on Human Rights and the Employment Relation*, ed. F. Dorssemont, I. Schömann and K. Lörcher (Oxford: Hart Publishing, 2013), 3–46.

[220] Ibid., pp. 9 ff., notes that this is both a "new" and a "consolidated" approach.

[221] The ILO in first place, with Conventions 98 and 151, then Article 6(2) of the ESC and Article 28 of the EUCFR.

bodies.[222] In the Conclusions of the *Demir* case, the ECtHR considers itself *bound* to such an interpretation, which should take into account a) elements of international law; b) the interpretation of these laws provided by the competent supervisory bodies; c) the practice of European states.[223] What is more, the Court stated that the fact that the respondent state had not ratified the instruments of letter a) and b) would not prevent the Court to make reference to these texts (and decisions) while interpreting the Convention.[224] The interlinking of Convention's right and international standards has been saluted as breathing new life into the international supervisory bodies of the ILO and the ESC.[225]

The importance of *Demir* however does not end with this methodological innovation. In fact, the decision also innovates in substantial terms. On the basis of the recalled international instruments the Court takes a step forward in respect to its previous case law,[226] by including the right to bargain collectively among the "essential elements" of the right to form and join trade unions.[227] Before *Demir*, the Court had often referred to the same right "just" as *one* of the means available to trade unions to protect the interests of their members.[228] Following

---

222 *E.g.*, para. 147: "[...] the ILO's Committee of Experts interpreted this provision as excluding only those officials whose activities were specific to the administration of the State. With that exception, all other persons employed by government, by public enterprises or by autonomous public institutions should benefit, according to the Committee, from the guarantees provided for in Convention No. 98 in the same manner as other employees, and consequently should be able to engage in collective bargaining in respect of their conditions of employment, including wages [...]"; para. 149: "According to the meaning attributed by the European Committee of Social Rights (ECSR) to Article 6(2) of the Charter, which in fact fully applies to public officials, States which impose restrictions on collective bargaining in the public sector have an obligation, in order to comply with this provision, to arrange for the involvement of staff representatives in the drafting of the applicable employment regulations".

223 *Demir and Baykara*, para. 85: "the Court, in defining the meaning of terms and notions in the text of the Convention, can and *must* take into account elements of *international law* other than the Convention, *the interpretation of such elements by competent organs*, and *the practice of European States* reflecting their common values. The consensus emerging from specialised international instruments and from the practice of Contracting States may constitute a relevant consideration for the Court when it interprets the provisions of the Convention in specific cases" (emphasis added).

224 Ibid., para. 86: " In this context, *it is not necessary for the respondent State to have ratified the entire collection of instruments that are applicable in respect of the precise subject matter of the case concerned.* It will be sufficient for the Court that the relevant international instruments denote a continuous evolution in the norms and principles applied in international law or in the domestic law of the majority of member States of the Council of Europe and show, in a precise area, that there is common ground in modern societies[...]" (emphasis added).

225 Ewing and Hendy, "The Dramatic Implications of Demir and Baykara", p. 7: "the ILO and ESC fora are thus now no longer processes for publicising grievances and causing some mild diplomatic embarrassment for national governments but important steps in building up the scope of ILO and ESC rights generally (as well as in particular cases), with a view to bringing proceedings in the ECtHR in Strasbourg under Article 11".

226 Ibid., p. 4; Dorssemont, "The Rght to Form and to Join Trade Unions for the Protection of His Interests Under Article 11 ECHR", pp. 218 ff.; Jacobs, "Article 11 ECHR: The Right to Bargain Collectively Under Article 11 ECHR", p. 311.

227 *Demir and Baykara*, para. 154.

228 See ECtHR, 6 February 1976, *Swedish Engine Drivers v. Sweden*, no. 5614/72, para. 40; ECtHR, 27 October 1975, *National Union of Belgian Police v. Belgium*, no. 4464/70, para. 38; ECtHR, 6

this recognition, the Court then assessed the restriction to this essential element under the strict conditions of Article 11(2) ECHR.[229] Once again the Court made reference to international standard to assess the proportionality of the Turkish measure,[230] ultimately finding it wanting on the "necessary in a democratic society" side.[231]

A few months after *Demir*, the said new methodological approach triggered another relevant evolution in the case law of the ECtHR regarding collective social rights. This time it was a simple Chamber that had to decide a case dealing with collective action.[232] The Court applied the *Demir* approach to the case at stake, by referring to ILO supervisory bodies' interpretation of ILO Convention No. 87, as well as to the ESC.[233] By doing so it recognised the link between collective bargaining and collective action. Since *Demir* had previously recognised the right to bargain collectively as an essential element of the right to form and join trade unions, this recognition seems to entail the inclusion (though somewhat tortuous) of the right to strike among the rights protected by Article 11 ECHR.[234] This is confirmed by the subsequent scrutiny of the Turkish ban carried out by the ECtHR. The ban itself is scrutinised as a *restriction* of Article 11. The Court recognised that the right to strike was not *absolute*, and could thus be subject to "certain restrictions".[235] As highlighted by Dorssemont,[236] the actual assessment of the legitimacy of the restrictions surpasses in importance the mere recognition of a right, as *Viking* and *Laval* have showed. As in *Demir*, the Court analysed the

February 1976, *Schmidt and Dahlström v. Sweden*, no. 5589/72, para. 36.

229 "No restrictions shall be placed on the exercise of these rights other than such as are prescribed by law and are necessary in a democratic society in the interests of national security or public safety, for the prevention of disorder or crime, for the protection of health or morals or for the protection of the rights and freedoms of others. This Article shall not prevent the imposition of lawful restrictions on the exercise of these rights by members of the armed forces, of the police or of the administration of the State."

230 *Demir and Baykara*, para. 165–168.

231 Ibid., para. 169. See Dorssemont, "The Right to Take Collective Action Under Article 11 ECHR", p. 336.

232 ECtHR, 21 April 2009, *Enerji Yapi-Yol Sen*, no. 68959/01. The *Enerji* originated from a circular emanating from the Turkish government which prohibited the participation of public sector employees to a national one day strike. Such a strike had been called by the Federation of Public Sector Trade Unions as a means to secure the right to collective bargaining for public sector employees.

233 *Enerji*, para. 24: "la Cour note également que le droit de grève est reconnu par les organes de contrôle de l'Organisation internationale du travail (OIT) comme le corollaire indissociable du droit d'association syndicale protégé par la Convention C87 de l'OIT sur la liberté syndicale et la protection du droit syndical (pour la prise en compte par la Cour des éléments de droit international autres que la Convention, voir *Demir et Baykara*, précité). Elle rappelle que la Charte sociale européenne reconnaît aussi le droit de grève comme un moyen d'assurer l'exercice effectif du droit de négociation collective".

234 Ewing and Hendy, "The Dramatic Implications of Demir and Baykara", p. 13; Dorssemont and Van Hoek, "Collective Action in Labour Conflicts Under the Rome II Regulation (Part I)", p. 230.

235 *Enerji*, para. 32.

236 Ibid., p. 231.

restriction under Article 11(2), a course which reinforces the understanding of the right to strike as something akin to an "essential element" of the freedom protected under Article 11 ECHR. Provided that the ban was prescribed by law, the Court found that the Turkish government had not demonstrated how such a broad restriction was necessary in a democratic society.[237]

The fact that the right to strike is protected under Article 11 ECHR has been confirmed in a more recent decision.[238] Indeed, by referring to its previous case law[239] the ECtHR affirmed that "what the above-mentioned cases illustrate is that *strike action is clearly protected by Article 11*".[240] Interestingly, such a confirmation was delivered in the context of a decision which ultimately did not accept the claims of the trade unions' side. The *RMT* decision did also confirm the *Demir* approach, that is the fundamental role of the *sui generis* case law of the ECSR and of the CEACR for the interpretation of the rights and freedoms protected by the ECHR.[241] Indeed, the role of the CEACR was the object of a specific critique raised by the UK government.[242] The ECtHR appears to be of a different opinion on the point.[243] Finally, the ECtHR again examined the restrictions to the right to strike under the light of Article 11(2).[244]

The European Social Charter

Turning to the ESC the link with the CJEU case law is once again more direct. Indeed the reclamation presented by Swedish Trade Union Confederation (LO) and Swedish Confederation of Professional Employees (TCO) to the European Committee of Social Rights[245] involved precisely the effects (the "transposition")

---

237 *Enerji*, para. 32: "La Cour relève que le Gouvernement n'a pas démontré la nécessité dans une société démocratique de la restriction incriminée".

238 ECtHR, 8 April 2014, *National Union of Rail Maritime and Transport Workers v. The United Kingdom*, no. 31045/10; hereinafter *RMT*. In fact, also the UK government explicitly conceded that "in light of the recent case-law of this Court, the right under Article 11 to join a trade union normally implied the ability to strike", para. 62.

239 In particular: *Karaçay v. Turkey*, no. 6615/03, 27 March 2007; *Dilek and Others v. Turkey*, nos. 74611/01, 26876/02 and 27628/02, 17 July 2007; *Urcan and Others v. Turkey*, nos. 23018/04, 23034/04, 23042/04, 23071/04, 23073/04, 23081/04, 23086/04, 23091/04, 23094/04, 23444/04 and 23676/04, 17 July 2008; *Enerji Yapı-Yol Sen v. Turkey*, no. 68959/01, 21 April 2009. This was also confirmed in a more recent decision. See *Veniamin Tymoshenko and others v. Ukraine*, no. 48408/12, 2 October 2014, para 77–78: "The Court considers, and this was the common ground between the parties, that the ban on the proposed strike action constituted an interference with the applicants' right to freedom of association under Article 11 of the Convention. Having regard to its case-law illustrating that strike action is clearly protected by Article 11 [...], the Court sees no reasons for holding otherwise".

240 *RMT*, para. 84, emphasis added.

241 Ibid., para. 76.

242 Ibid., para. 70.

243 Ibid., para. 97.

244 Ibid., para. 78.

245 *Swedish Trade Union Confederation (LO) and Swedish Confederation of Professional Employees (TCO) v. Sweden*, Complaint No. 85/2012, 12 July 2012. I analysed this decision in M. Rocca,

of *Laval* in the Swedish legal system. The intervention of European and international workers' and employers' associations[246] revealed the importance of this complaint. In particular, the complaint was initiated on a parallel path in respect of the aforementioned procedure beyond the CEACR. In a way, the fact that the former procedure was concluded before the verdict of the ECSR had an impact on the latter.[247]

The risk of chilling effect was put forward by the Swedish trade unions, providing the background for different arguments. In particular, it was submitted that the test articulated in *Laval* made it impossible for trade unions to know in advance whether the collective action will be considered as lawful or not, and hence to escape the risk of potentially very high damages.[248] Moreover, in the *Laval* dispute, neither the CJEU nor the Swedish Labour Court took into account that the collective action had been considered as lawful by a Swedish court in 2004. The LO and TCO submit that the decline in the number of collective agreement reached with posting employers after 2007 is a direct consequence of this situation.[249]

A second argument is particularly interesting when compared with the outcome of the procedure beyond the CEACR. The Swedish trade unions submitted that, by placing restriction on the recourse to collective action and on the legitimate content of collective agreements backed by those actions, the *Lex Laval* hampered the ability of trade unions to act on behalf of its members, in the situation where a posted worker is effectively organised by the given trade union. Notwithstanding the remoteness of this eventuality, the complaint argued that the Swedish legislator, when drafting the *Lex Laval*, considered that the test applied by the CJEU was independent of "whether the [posted] workers are organised by the trade union or not".[250]

"A Clash of Kings The European Committee of Social Rights on the 'Lex Laval'... and on the EU Framework for the Posting of Workers", *European Journal of Social Law* 3 (2013): 217–232.

246 The ETUC, Businesseurope and the International Organisation of Employers (IOE).

247 In fact, the ETUC made a number of references to the CEACR conclusions in its Observations, pp. 5 ff. On the contrary, the only reference to the CEACR made in the Observations submitted by IOE and BUSINESSEUROPE is meant to deny its role in providing an authoritative interpretation (p. 35).

248 Complaint No. 85/2012, para. 81.

249 Ibid., para. 82.

250 Ibid., para. 77. Cf. with the Conclusions of the CEACR on the *Lex Laval*: "The Committee therefore requests the Government to review with the social partners the 2010 amendments made to the Foreign Posting of Employees Act so as to ensure that workers' organizations *representing foreign posted workers* are not restricted in their rights simply because of the nationality of the enterprise" (emphasis added).

The third and fourth argument focused respectively on the violation of the duty to *promote* collective bargaining[251] and on the overstepping of the allowed restrictions to the right to take collective action.[252]

It is interesting to note that in its submission the Government tried to "hide behind the EU".[253] As highlighted before, the UK Government put forward the same objection in the BALPA case.[254] The argument however was dismissed by the CEACR,[255] and it met the very same fate in the subsequent Conclusions about the *Lex Laval.* A second point worth stressing is that both the Swedish Government and IOE-BUSINESSEUROPE in their submission argued in favour of the compatibility of the *Lex Laval* (and more broadly of the *Laval* doctrine) with the ESC (also) on the basis of a decoupling of collective bargaining and collective action. Indeed, both parties remarked that posting employers remain free to conclude collective agreement on a *voluntary* basis, with voluntary clearly indicating without being "forced" by a collective action (or a threat thereof).

Coming to the actual decision delivered by the ECSR I will present the arguments following the order in which they are examined in the decision. Hence I will first analyse the question of collective social rights (right to take collective action, right to bargain collectively).[256] Then I will turn to the question of the protection of posted workers as migrant workers.[257] Having reasserted the importance of the collective rights at stake not just as ends in themselves, but also in their role of stepping stones for the enjoyment of other fundamental

---

251 Article 6: "With a view to ensuring the effective exercise of the right to bargain collectively, the Parties undertake: [...] 2. to *promote*, where necessary and appropriate, machinery for voluntary negotiations between employers or employers' organisations and workers' organisations, with a view to the regulation of terms and conditions of employment *by means of collective agreements* [...]" (emphasis added).

252 Article G: "1. The rights and principles set forth in Part I when effectively realised, and their effective exercise as provided for in Part II, shall not be subject to any restrictions or limitations not specified in those parts, except such as are prescribed by law and are necessary in a democratic society for the protection of the rights and freedoms of others or for the protection of public interest, national security, public health, or morals.
2. The restrictions permitted under this Charter to the rights and obligations set forth herein shall not be applied for any purpose other than that for which they have been prescribed."

253 "Further, the Swedish Government would like to stress that the legislative changes were considered necessary in order for the Swedish legislation to comply with EU law on freedom to provide services and non-discrimination, as interpreted by the ECJ in the Laval case".

254 "The Committee notes the Government's indication in its reply that BALPA's application is misdirected and misconceived because any adverse impact of Viking and Laval would be a consequence of the European Union law, to which the United Kingdom is obliged to give effect, rather than of any unilateral action by the United Kingdom itself". See *supra*, p. 257.

255 "The Committee wishes to make clear that its task is not to judge the correctness of the ECJ's holdings in Viking and Laval as they set out an interpretation of the European Union law, based on varying and distinct rights in the Treaty of the European Community, but rather to examine whether the impact of these decisions at national level are such as to deny workers' freedom of association rights under Convention No. 87".

256 *Swedish Trade Union Confederation (LO) and Swedish Confederation of Professional Employees (TCO) v. Sweden*, Complaint No. 85/2012, para. 107–125.

257 Ibid., para. 132–142.

rights protected by the Charter,[258] the Committee stresses the fact that the contracting parties cannot satisfy themselves of recognising those rights. The concept of promoting collective bargaining is thus highlighted by the ECSR.[259] At the same time the Committee remarks the importance of preserving the *autonomy* of social actors, in particular as regards the legitimate methods used to defend the interest of workers. On this background, the ECSR goes on to analyse the limitations provided by the *Lex Laval*. It then notes that the limitation to minimum working condition as regards the legitimate demands of a collective action (and the legitimate contents of an eventual collective agreement backed by such an action) do impose a "substantial limitation" to the rights at stake.[260] This, coupled with the practical difficulty to bargain with an employer established abroad, bring the Committee to the conclusion that the amendments constituting the *Lex Laval* are not in conformity with the obligation to promote collective bargaining between social actors.[261] The reasoning, as well as the conclusion, is similar for the right to take collective action[262] protected by Article 6(4) ESC. The ESCR places the emphasis on the possibility for trade unions to "strive for the *improvement* of existing living and working conditions of workers".[263] The restriction of legitimate demands to minimum wages and working conditions is thus defined as a violation of the very *substance* of the right protected by the ESC. The same reasoning is extended to the restrictive effect of the eventual "evidence" showed by the employer of the application of wages and working conditions at least as good as the minimum ones.[264] By referring to Article G[265] the Committee considers that restrictions to the right to take collective action in the name of the exercise of economic freedoms should be *proportionate,*[266] provided that those freedoms "cannot be treated, from the point of view of the system of values, principles and fundamental rights embodied in the Charter, as having a greater *a priori* value than core labour rights".[267]

---

258 Ibid., para. 109.
259 Ibid., para. 111.
260 Ibid., para. 112.
261 Article 6(2) ESC.
262 *Swedish Trade Union Confederation (LO) and Swedish Confederation of Professional Employees (TCO) v. Sweden,* Complaint No. 85/2012, para. 116.
263 Ibid., para. 120 (emphasis added).
264 Ibid., para. 123.
265 Which deals with restrictions to the rights protected by the Charter: "[t]he rights and principles set forth in Part I when effectively realised, and their effective exercise as provided for in Part II, shall not be subject to any restrictions or limitations not specified in those parts, except such as are prescribed by law and are necessary in a democratic society for the protection of the rights and freedoms of others or for the protection of public interest, national security, public health, or morals".
266 *Swedish Trade Union Confederation (LO) and Swedish Confederation of Professional Employees (TCO) v. Sweden,* Complaint No. 85/2012, para. 121. Here the Committee highlights once again the importance of the possibility to strive for the improvement of living and working conditions, including "*equal treatment* of workers regardless of nationality or any other ground" (emphasis added).
267 Ibid., para. 122.

The Committee then turns to analyse the issue under the point of view of the protection of *migrant* workers. The Committee was asked to consider the question under Article 19(4) by the Swedish trade unions in their submission. This Article requires the signatory parties to assure *equal treatment* in a number of fields to "workers lawfully within their territories". The matters covered by this obligation include "remuneration and other employment and working conditions" as well as "membership of trade unions and enjoyment of the benefits of collective bargaining". As recalled by Świątkowski,[268] the provision is inspired by Article 6(1) of ILO Convention No. 97 (Migration for Employment Convention) of 1949. Similarly to Article 19(4) of the ESC, this provision makes reference to immigrants "lawfully within" the territory of the signatory party. It is interesting to note that BUSINESSEUROPE and the IOE affirmed the non-applicability of Article 19(4) to posted workers on the basis of another ILO Convention (No. 143),[269] which is supplementing the aforementioned Convention No. 97. Convention No. 143 in fact *excludes* "employees of organisations or undertakings operating within the territory of a country who have been admitted temporarily to that country at the request of their employer to undertake specific duties or assignments, for a limited and defined period of time, and who are required to leave that country on the completion of their duties or assignments" from the definition of 'migrant workers'. However, the ECSR in its reasoning emphasises the literal version included in the ESC. Thus, on the basis of the understanding of "migrant worker" as a worker "coming from another State and lawfully within the territory of the host State", the Committee goes on to analyse the situation of posted workers. On this background, the inevitable conclusion is that, notwithstanding the differences between posted workers and other migrant workers, posted workers are indeed migrant workers, falling in the scope of application of Article 19(4).[270] Having thus included posted workers in the category of "migrant workers" the Committee presents the logical conclusion of such a finding. Posted workers have the *right* "to receive treatment not less favourable than that of the national workers of the host State in respect of remuneration, other employment and working conditions, and enjoyment of the benefits of collective bargaining".[271] Furthermore, the limitations to the right to take collective action introduced by the *Lex Laval* are bound to hinder the reaching of equal treatment.[272] Also, the *comparator* for the equal treatment should be the actual Swedish worker with "comparable occupational experience and skills",[273] while minimum wages and

268 Światkowski, *Charter of Social Rights of the Council of Europe*, p. 348.

269 *Swedish Trade Union Confederation (LO) and Swedish Confederation of Professional Employees (TCO) v. Sweden*, Complaint No. 85/2012, Case document No. 5, Observations by the International Organisation of Employers (IOE) and BUSINESSEUROPE, para. 44.

270 *Swedish Trade Union Confederation (LO) and Swedish Confederation of Professional Employees (TCO) v. Sweden*, Complaint No. 85/2012, para. 134.

271 Ibid..

272 Ibid., para. 135.

273 Ibid., para. 136.

working conditions as those identified by the *Lex Laval* normally do not take into account those characteristics. Hence, according only minimum protection to posted workers, as well as economic and social rights which are more limited than the ones guaranteed to national workers, constitutes a discriminatory treatment.[274] Concluding the decision, the ECSR shows its perfect awareness about the legal context in which the posting phenomenon takes place. In this sense, the *Lex Laval* is framed in the context of the internal market, as the aims of the less favourable treatment of posted workers are correctly identified with the facilitation of cross border movement of services and the guarantee of the freedom to provide services abroad.[275] Those objectives however "cannot be treated as having a greater a priori value than labour rights",[276] meaning that they cannot justify, under the ESC, the discriminatory treatment of (migrant) posted workers.

6.4 YOU ARE HERE

The complicated relationship between fundamental social rights and fundamental freedoms of the internal market is hence the stage for a conflict (or, at least, a divergence) of standards of protection of the said social rights[277] between the EU legal order and other European and international orders. As it is evident, the issue raises a huge number of legal questions as to the relationship between these legal orders[278] which is impossible to analyse here. I will however come back to this intricate situation while turning to the possible evolutions in the concluding Chapters.

Here I will just add two more remarks about the situation as it stands. The first, which starkly emerges from the analysed disputes beyond the ECSR and the CEACR, is the unpleasant situation of Member States. Indeed, in these *fora*, both the United Kingdom and Sweden tried to use what I called the "hiding behind the EU" argument. That is to say that both Member States justified their (potential) violation of ESC or ILO standards (also) in the name of their obligation to apply EU law, as interpreted by the CJEU. As it was described *supra*, these argument was dismissed by both the CEACR and the ECSR. Member States thus find themselves, as the dilemma goes, between a rock and a hard place.[279] Though one

274 Ibid., para. 141.

275 Ibid., para. 140.

276 Ibid.

277 F. Fabbrini, "Europe in Need of a New Deal: On Federalism, Free Market and the Right to Strike", *Georgetown Journal of International Law* 43 (2012): 1–73, p. 70.

278 See A. Bücker, W. Warneck and F. Dorssemont, "The Search for a Balance: analysis and Perspectives", in *Reconciling Fundamental Social Rights and Economic Freedoms After Viking, Laval and Rüffert*, ed. Andreas Bücker and Wiebke Warneck (Baden-Baden: Nomos Publishers, 2011), 315–360, pp. 331 ff.

279 In fact, the EU Treaties did envisage the possibility of a conflict between EU law and obligation stemming from international treaties signed by Member States *before* the accession to the Community. Article 351 TFEU thus states: "The rights and obligations arising from agreements

could argue about the "hardness" of the ILO/ESC systems of sanctioning, the metaphor surely holds for a possible conflict between EU and ECHR standards.[280] In the light of the *Demir* approach, a conflict with ILO/ESC standards could in fact become a conflict with the ECHR.

The second remark shows how the stance of the CJEU *to this day* seems to increase the likelihood of such a conflict. As it was already pointed out, the Court proved rather reluctant at referring to the body of decisions of the supervisory bodies of both the ESC and of ILO Conventions, while referring to those instruments in *Viking* and *Laval*. For example, at the time of the decisions, the ECSR had already ruled out the "proportionality test" from the restrictions allowed under the ESC.[281] More recently, such a choice became even more evident in *Commission v. Germany* (2010). In acknowledging the fundamental nature of the right to bargain collectively neither the Court nor the AG did mention the *Demir* judgement,[282] which had been delivered two years before. In this sense the *Commission v. Germany* (2010) decision represents a missed occasion for the CJEU to engage in (some form of) "dialogue" with the ECtHR.

In the light of this reluctance, one cannot ignore the legislative attempt at tackling the issue at EU level. This attempt came chronologically in the middle of the divergence. The (first and only) draft of the so-called "Monti II" proposal was in fact presented in the early 2012, thus after the ECtHR decisions in *Demir* and *Enerji* and after the CEACR Conclusions in the *BALPA* dispute, but before the disputes involving the *Lex Laval*.

6.4.1 THE "MONTI II" PROPOSAL

On the 21st of March 2012, the EU Commission put forward a proposal for a Council Regulation on the exercise of the right to take collective action within the context of the freedom of establishment and the freedom to provide services.[283]

concluded before 1 January 1958 or, for acceding States, before the date of their accession, between one or more Member States on the one hand, and one or more third countries on the other, shall not be affected by the provisions of the Treaties. To the extent that such agreements are not compatible with the Treaties, the Member State or States concerned shall take all appropriate steps to eliminate the incompatibilities established. Member States shall, where necessary, assist each other to this end and shall, where appropriate, adopt a common attitude [...]". ILO Convention No. 87 (1948) as well as the ECHR (1950) were concluded (and signed by a majority of Member States) before the accession to the Community. See ibid., p. 338. However, the possibility offered by Article 351 TFEU remains at best obscure and largely unexplored.

280 Or, as Ewing and Hendy put it: "the mouth-watering possibility of a high noon conflict between the two [the CJEU and the ECtHR]". See Ewing and Hendy, "The Dramatic Implications of Demir and Baykara", p. 3.

281 See ECSR, XVI-1, Conclusion with regard to Belgium.

282 The Court relied instead on the EUCFR, the ESC and the Community Charter of Fundamental Social Rights of Workers.

283 COM(2012) 130, 21 March 2012. See N. Bruun, A. Bücker and F. Dorssemont, "Balancing Fundamental Social Rights and Economic Freedoms: Can the Monti II Initiative Solve the

The process of drafting this proposal had been a long one. Indeed, it saw the light more than four years after the "Judgment Day" of *Viking* and *Laval*. This long period had been punctuated by negotiations, reports and documents.[284] The intention of addressing the situation created by *Viking* and *Laval* was also mentioned by President Barroso in its speech (in the quality of candidate for re-election) beyond the European Parliament.[285]

The proposal however never came into force. In fact it proved quite short-lived, since it was ultimately withdrawn by the Commission on 12 September 2012, following the difficulties in finding the necessary political support.[286] Still, the "Monti II" proposal remains an unavoidable object of analysis since it clearly depicts (or depicted) the possible point of compromise at the European level on a legislative answer to *Viking* and *Laval*.[287]

Multiple Montis

Starting from its "nickname" it is worth remembering that the "Monti II" proposal took such a denomination from Mario Monti, former Commissioner for the Internal Market, former Commissioner for Competition (now) former Prime Minister of Italy and "only" President of the Bocconi University at the time of the "Monti Report". This is due to two different reasons. First, as it was stated before, Mr. Monti was the author of one of the preparatory documents, the Report *A New Strategy for the Single Market at the Service of Europe's Economy and Society* of May 2010, where he addressed the issue of *Viking* and *Laval* in a specific section. Second, and more importantly, logic has it that to have a "Monti II" one usually needs a "Monti I". This first episode was the Regulation on the functioning of the internal market in relation to the free movement of goods among Member States.[288] More specifically, the reference goes to Article 2 of this Regulation. Since

EU Dilemma?", *International Journal of Comparative Labour Law and Industrial Relations* 28, no. 3 (2012): 279–306; J. Malmberg and C. Johansson, "The Commission's Posting Package", *SIEPS – European Policy Analysis*, no. 8 (2012): 1–16; M. Rocca, "The Proposal for a (so-Called) 'Monti II' Regulation on the Exercise of the Right to Take Collective Action Within the Context of the Freedom of Establishment and the Freedom to Provide Services", *European Labour Law Journal* 1 (2012): 19–34.

284 See for example *A New Strategy for the Single Market At the Service of Europe's Economy and Society*, Report to the European Commission by Mario Monti, 9 May 2010, hereinafter, "Monti Report"; Communication by the Commission, *A Single Market Act – Twelve levers to boost growth and strengthen confidence*, COM (2011) 206, 13 April 2011; EP resolution of 22 October 2008 on challenges to collective agreements in the EU, 2008/2085(INI); EESC Opinion, SOC/360 – EESC 970/2010.

285 José Manuel Durão Barroso, Speech/09/391, http://europa.eu/rapid/pressReleasesAction.do?reference=SPEECH/09/391 (last accessed 30 July 2013).

286 The reasons surrounding the choice of the Commission are in fact interesting in their own right. They will be presented in the next paragraphs, after the analysis devoted to the text of the proposal.

287 The proposal is also historical in its own right, since it was the first attempt of the EU legislator to *directly* intervene in the field of the right to take collective action.

288 Regulation of 7 December 1998, OJ L337/8, 12 December 1998.

"Monti I" obliged Member States to take all necessary and appropriate actions in order to avoid interruptions to the functioning of the internal market caused by private individuals, Article 2 was included in the legal instrument to exclude the right (or freedom) to strike from its scope. It states: "This Regulation may not be interpreted as affecting in any way the exercise of fundamental rights as recognised in Member States, including the right or freedom to strike. These rights may also include the right or freedom to take other actions covered by the specific industrial relations systems in Member States". This solution (known, uncreative it may be, as "Monti clause") was proposed in the… Monti Report as a possible answer to the questions raised by *Viking* and *Laval*.[289]

The proposal itself consisted of just four articles. Article 1 on the scope and the subject matter of the Regulation; Article 2, laying down the general principles applicable to the relationship between fundamental rights and economic freedoms; Article 3 dealing with dispute resolution mechanism (either already present at State level or elaborated by the European social actors) and Article 4 establishing an alert mechanism. In view of the limited scope of this Chapter I will focus on the first two Article of the short-lived proposal.

Thus, Article 1 presented the subject matter of the Regulation which then "lays down the general principles and rules applicable at Union level with respect to the exercise of the fundamental right to take collective action within the context of the freedom of establishment and the freedom to provide services". So far so good. The picture already gets complicated with the second part of Article 1. Here the "Monti clause" found its place: "This Regulation shall not affect in any way the exercise of fundamental rights as recognised in the Member States, including the right or freedom to strike or to take other action covered by the specific industrial relations systems in Member States in accordance with national law and practices […]". It is clear that such a clause was directly inspired by the one (recalled before) included in the "Monti I" Regulation.[290] However, the different context made the "transplant" more impervious than anticipated. While the Regulation on the free movement of goods (*i.e.* "Monti I") was aimed at regulating *other* areas of EU law and *could* be used in order to impose limitations on the right to strike (hence the clause was included to avoid this possibility), the purpose of the present proposal, from its very *title*, was to regulate precisely *the exercise of the right to take collective action* (within the context of the freedom of establishment and the freedom to provide services). This resulted in, at least, a puzzling outcome. Indeed it is difficult to see how regulating the exercise of the right to take collective action

289 Monti Report, p. 72: "[…] introduce a provision to guarantee the right to strike *modelled on Art. 2 of Council Regulation(EC) No 2679/98* and a mechanism for the informal solutions of labour disputes concerning the application of the Directive" (emphasis added).

290 On the point see in general G. Orlandini, "The Free Movement of Goods as a Possible 'Community' Limitation on Industrial Conflict", *European Law Journal* 6, no. 4 (2000): 341–362; G. Orlandini, *Sciopero E Servizi Pubblici Essenziali Nel Processo d'integrazione Europea. Uno Studio Di Diritto Comparato E Comunitario* (Torino: Giappichelli, 2003), pp. 245–302.

without *affecting*, in any way, such an exercise would even be possible. A second possible critique to this Article regards once again the wording of the (displaced) "Monti clause". By "immunising" the exercise of the right (or freedom) to take collective action from "this Regulation" the clause seemed to quite miss the objective. The restrictions to this right came before this Regulation, and came directly from the interpretations given by the CJEU to Articles present in the Treaty itself. *In sum*, it is difficult to find an *effet utile* for this new (but already defunct) "Monti clause".[291]

Article 2 laid down the general principle which should govern the relationship between fundamental rights and economic freedoms, hence striking at the very heart of the matter at stake in this Chapter. It is hence worth quoting its text in full: "The exercise of the freedom of establishment and the freedom to provide services enshrined in the Treaty shall respect the fundamental right to take collective action, including the right or freedom to strike, and conversely, the exercise of the fundamental right to take collective action, including the right or freedom to strike, shall respect these economic freedoms". This Article was conceived as a tool to restate the equal footing of fundamental rights and economic freedoms. However, since conflicts between the two may arise, Recitals 11–13 bring back the instrument to solve these conflicts, the principle of proportionality.[292] Thus, Article 2 can be understood as an attempt at "completing" the proportionality test applied by the CJEU in *Viking* and *Laval* with a "third limb",[293] where the proportionality of the restrictions imposed on fundamental rights should also be assessed. From a theoretical point of view, this is evidently a step forward towards a more balanced approach. However, it is difficult to see how this could work in practice. The problem is that the "recourse" to economic freedoms never needs to be justified in itself: *e.g.*, in *Viking*, the shipping company did not need to justify its decision to re-flag the Rossella, nor it would need to justify it under the new Regulation (had it come into force). On the contrary, it is the very *recourse* to the

291 Fabbrini has proposed to interpret the clause as referring to "intra-State labour-management disputes in which the EU freedom of establishment and freedom to provide services are not at play", *i.e.*, in the wording of the Author, purely internal situations. See F. Fabbrini and K. Granat, "Yellow Card but No Foul: The Role of the National Parliaments Under the Subsidiarity Protocol and the Commission Proposal for an EU Regulation on the Right to Strike", *Common Market Law Review* 50, no. 2 (2013): 115–144, p. 133. However, this interpretation just makes the clause (in principle) completely superfluous, as purely internal situations are by definition outside the scope of fundamental freedoms of the internal market.

292 Recital 13: "A fair balance between fundamental rights and fundamental freedoms will in the case of conflict only be ensured when a restriction imposed by a fundamental right on a fundamental freedom is not permitted to go beyond what is appropriate, necessary and reasonable to realise that fundamental right. Conversely, a restriction imposed on a fundamental right by a fundamental freedom cannot go beyond what is appropriate, necessary and reasonable to realise the fundamental freedom". As a side note, it is interesting to stress the fact that the principle of proportionality, which is evidently one of the most important point of the whole problem, is absent from the legal text of the Proposal.

293 See Barnard, "The Protection of Fundamental Social Rights in Europe After Lisbon: a Question of Conflicts of Interests", pp. 50–51.

right to take collective action (in the context of the freedom of establishment or the freedom to provide services) that will require justification.[294] On the point it has been suggested by Catherine Barnard that this "cross-proportionality test" should be completed by yet another limb, considering whether the application of proportionality could result in undermining the essence of the right being protected.[295] This suggestion echoes Article 52(1) of the EU Charter of Fundamental Rights,[296] which, dealing with the permissible limitations to the rights recognised by the Charter, states that the limitations must respect the *essence* of these rights. In light of this, one should also notice that the content of this Article is repeated almost verbatim in Recital 12 of the proposal. Keeping in mind that the legal value of Recitals is by no means clear, the inclusion of this "test" in the approach of the Court would have provided for a more solid foundation for a balancing of fundamental rights and economic freedoms. A word of warning is however appropriate: in the end going down this road could amount at protecting *only* the essence, a minimal hard nucleus, of those fundamental rights facing economic freedoms.

Competence, yellow cards and fundamental rights

The "Monti II" proposal not only represented the first attempt at regulating the right to take collective action at EU level. It was also the first time that the specific procedure introduced by the Lisbon Treaty with Protocol No. 2[297] (Subsidiarity Protocol) was activated. In the context of this procedure twelve national parliaments[298] decided to produce a "reasoned opinion" (so-called "yellow card") regarding the respect (*rectius*, the lack thereof) of the principle of subsidiarity by the proposal put forward by the Commission.

Provided that the number of "yellow cards" reached the threshold established by Protocol No. 2[299] the Commission had to "review" the proposal in order to

294 Bruun, Bücker, and Dorssemont, "Balancing Fundamental Social Rights and Economic Freedoms: Can the Monti II Initiative Solve the EU Dilemma?, pp. 289–290.

295 C. Barnard, "A Proportionate Response to Proportionality in the Field of Collective Action", *European Law Review* 2, no. 37 (2012): 117–135.

296 "Any limitation on the exercise of the rights and freedoms recognised by this Charter must be provided for by law and respect the essence of those rights and freedoms. Subject to the principle of proportionality, limitations may be made only if they are necessary and genuinely meet objectives of general interest recognised by the Union or the need to protect the rights and freedoms of others".

297 Protocol No. 2 on the application of the principles of subsidiarity and proportionality. For a more detailed analysis of the topic see Fabbrini, "Europe in Need of a New Deal: On Federalism, Free Market and the Right to Strike".

298 Seven unicameral and five chambers. The Member States whose parliament (or chamber) produced a reasoned opinion were Belgium, Denmark, Finland, France, Latvia, Luxembourg, Malta, the Netherlands, Poland, Portugal, Sweden and the United Kingdom.

299 A third of the total votes available, as stated by Article 7(2) of Protocol No.2: "where reasoned opinions on a draft legislative act's non-compliance with the principle of subsidiarity represent at least one third of all the votes allocated to the national Parliaments in accordance with the

decide whether to "maintain, amend or withdraw the draft".[300] As it was already mentioned before, the Commission ultimately decided to withdraw the proposal.

However, the contents of the reasoned opinion, as well as the letter of withdrawal by the Commission are interesting in completing the picture of the "Monti II" proposal, especially as regards the question of the competence of the EU to regulate the area of collective action. Also, with a direct connection with the topic of the Chapter, a number of the "yellow cards" do contain reference to "fundamental rights" arguments. This makes immediately apparent an issue which was highlighted by Fabbrini and Granat.[301] Indeed, the boundaries of the procedure, in principle limited to control the respect of the principle of subsidiarity, were forced by the vast majority of reasoned opinion issued by national parliaments (or chamber). In order to summarise the situation I have organised the arguments backing the yellow cards in three categories: arguments based on the non-respect of the subsidiarity principle; arguments based on the (lack of) competence of the EU to regulate the field; arguments based on the substantial contents of the proposal (often connected with fundamental rights). Table 6.1 gives account of these categories. For every one of these categories, an "x" indicates that the argument is only cursory mentioned in the reasoned opinion, while an "**X**" is used to point out those arguments which are pivotal in the issuing of the "yellow card".

The Table shows clearly that critiques about the non-respect of the principle of subsidiarity are mentioned in the vast majority of the reasoned opinions. Still, a good number of these yellow cards contents itself of mentioning the question of subsidiarity[302] while focusing the analysis on other issues. The most striking example is the reasoned opinion of the *Asembleia da República* of Portugal, which considers the violation of the subsidiarity principle demonstrated by the fact that "in its present format, this Proposal for a Regulation restricts the right to exercise collective action [...]".

second subparagraph of paragraph 1, the draft must be reviewed". The total votes being 54 (2 for each unicameral parliament or 1 for each chamber of bi-cameral parliament), the proposal was met with a total of 19 negative reasoned opinions.

300 Article 7(2) of Protocol No. 2.

301 Fabbrini, and Granat, "Yellow Card but No Foul: The Role of the National Parliaments Under the Subsidiarity Protocol and the Commission Proposal for an EU Regulation on the Right to Strike", pp. 135–139.

302 Belgium, Finland, France, Luxembourg, Latvia, Malta, Sweden.

Table 6.1 Yellow Cards concerning the so-called "Monti II" proposal

Country	Subsidiarity	Competence	Content
Belgium	x	X	X
Denmark	X	X	
Finland	x	x	X
France	x	X	
Latvia	x	X	x
Luxembourg	x	x	X
Malta	x		X
The Netherlands	x	X	X
Poland	X		X
Portugal		X	X
Sweden	x	X	X
United Kingdom	X		

The question of the competence of the EU in the field of collective action did attract much stronger critiques. The best example here is the reasoned opinion delivered by the Belgian *Chambre des Représentants*, which affirmed (somewhat overextending) that the whole "*droit du travail*" is "*une question nationale par excellence*". Playing on a similar tune, the French *Senat* directly referred to the explicit exclusion of Article 153(5) TFUE, to suggest that the only acceptable intervention in the field would be one "immunising" the right to take collective action from the direct and indirect effects of EU law. If one looks to the explanatory memorandum accompanying the proposal, it is clear that the thorny issue of competence was known to the drafters. However, they ultimately decided that it could be circumvented by basing the proposal on a different legal basis (*in casu* Article 352 TFEU[303]). The explanatory memorandum states that the very

[303] "If action by the Union should prove necessary, within the framework of the policies defined in the Treaties, to attain one of the objectives set out in the Treaties, and the Treaties have not provided the necessary powers, the Council, acting unanimously on a proposal from the Commission and after obtaining the consent of the European Parliament, shall adopt the appropriate measures. Where the measures in question are adopted by the Council in accordance with a special legislative procedure, it shall also act unanimously on a proposal from the Commission and after obtaining the consent of the European Parliament". On the point, it is worth recalling that AG Mengozzi in his Opinion in the *Laval* case (para. 57) had warned against such a course of action, stating that "If the effectiveness of Article 137(5) EC [now 153(5) TFEU] is to be upheld, the Community institutions *could not of course resort to other legal bases in the Treaty in order to adopt measures designed*" (emphasis added).

existence of the CJEU rulings of *Viking* and *Laval* is a sufficient basis to consider the EU competent to regulate the right to take collective action.[304] The number of critiques directed at the non-respect of EU competences by the reasoned opinion show at least a divergent interpretation between the Commission and national parliaments.[305]

Finally, to the furthest end of the spectrum in respect of the supposed function of the procedure established by Protocol No. 2, one can find the question of content. Two groups of critiques can be identified. The first one focused on the disruptive effects that the proposal could have had on *existent* systems of dispute resolution at national level (DK, FI, LU, MT, NL, SE[306]). The second group of critiques focuses on the non-compliance of the restrictions to the right to take collective action established by the proposal with the respect of international standards from the ILO or the ESC[307] (BE, FI, LV, LU). Both groups of critiques are sometimes reinforced by the remark that the proposal represents a simple *repetition* of the decisions of the Court in *Viking* and *Laval* (FI, LU, MT, PL).

From this short overview of the arguments put forward by the yellow cards, it seems safe to affirm that those often went beyond the limits of a control of subsidiarity.[308] The political relevance of the proposal at stake can in fact explain this "misuse" by national parliaments. The letter of the Commission announcing the withdrawal of the proposal does in fact acknowledge this situation. Indeed, the letter states that "the Commission has not found based on this assessment that the principle of proportionality has been breached".[309] Instead, the withdrawal is motivated by the fact that the proposal "is unlikely to gather the necessary political support within the European Parliament and Council to enable its adoption".[310] In this sense the yellow cards seem to have played a different role than the one initially conceived by Protocol No. 2, signalling a political disagreement with the proposal.

---

304 "Article 153(5) TFEU excludes the right to strike from the range of matters that can be regulated across the EU by way of minimum standards through Directives. However, the Court rulings have clearly shown that the fact that Article 153 does not apply to the right to strike does not as such exclude collective action from the scope of EU law".

305 Moreover, the same CJEU in the *Tobacco Advertising* case stated that "Other articles of the Treaty may not, however, be used as a legal basis in order to circumvent the express exclusion of harmonisation laid down in Article 129(4) of the Treaty"; Case C-376/98, *Germany v. Parliament and Council*, para. 79. On the point see G. Conway, "Articles Conflicts of Competence Norms in EU Law and the Legal Reasoning of the ECJ", *German Law Journal* 11, no. 2 (2010): 966–1005, pp. 970–971.

306 It is interesting to find here re-united all the "Scandinavian" Member States.

307 *E.g.* the *Chambre des Représentants* of Belgium states that those restrictions go "au-delà de ce qui est autorisé par la Charte Sociale Européenne avec entre autres un test de proportionnalité entre action collective (grève) et liberté d'établissement et libres prestations de services, qui ne semble pas opportun de maintenir".

308 Fabbrini, "Europe in Need of a New Deal: On Federalism, Free Market and the Right to Strike", pp. 139 ff.

309 Brussels, 12 September 2012, Ares(2012)1058907.

310 Ibid.

Fundamental rights from the ivory tower

The reference to international standards made by some of the yellow cards brings to the fore the question of the relationship of the proposal with the legal events highlighted before. A simple look to the calendar reveals that the proposal saw the light *after* the ECtHR decisions of *Demir* and (more pertinently) *Enerji*, as well as after the conclusions of the CEACR regarding the *BALPA* dispute.

In fact, the explanatory memorandum attached to the proposal in a way acknowledges the novelty represented by the said case law of the ECtHR. The memorandum refers to this case law in order to justify the acquired fundamental nature of the right to take collective action.[311] At the same time the Explanatory Memorandum proposes an interpretation of the said case law which strikes as rather superficial. In a way, the whole issue comes down to the expression 'certain restrictions'. On this term, the Explanatory Memorandum seems to suggest a perfect parallel between the case law of the two Courts (the CJEU and the ECtHR). In the wording of the Memorandum: "[...] as recognised by the Court of Justice and the European Court of Human Rights, the right to strike is not absolute and its exercise may nonetheless be subject to *certain restrictions*[...]" (emphasis added). Now, as it was summarised before, the two approaches do not lend themselves to such a light-hearted equivalence.[312] On the one hand, the court of Strasbourg considers the right to take collective action as the starting point, assessing the limitation to this right on the basis of Article 11(2) ECHR. On the other, the judges of Luxembourg interpret the (fundamental) right to strike as a limitation of the fundamental freedoms, so that the exercise of this right should be considered as legitimate, only inasmuch as it is carried out in a proportionate way.[313] Though one *could* pick-and-choose some signs of an effective convergence between the two approaches,[314] more evident signs of *divergence* should not be overlooked. In particular, the *Demir* approach, coupled with the possible unanimous rejection of the *Viking&Laval* doctrine by both the CEACR and the

---

311 Explanatory memorandum, p. 4. Interestingly, such a reference is not present among the Recitals; the case law of the ECtHR is cited there only as regards the right to collective bargaining (hence, *Demir*), in Recital No. 2.

312 Dorssemont, "How the European Court of Human Rights Gave Us Enerji to Cope with Viking and Laval", pp. 225–226.

313 *Viking*, para. 74; *Laval*, para. 96.

314 This (unlikely?) process of convergence could be envisaged as the result of a one-way influence. In particular, the firm position of the CJEU in *Viking* and *Laval* could exert an influence upon Strasbourg, paving the way for an interpretation of the "protection of [...] rights and freedoms of others" to include the fundamental freedoms of the EU legal order. Even though the decision in *Enerji* seems to go into another direction, one should not overlook the different stance of the Court in *UNISON* (Application No. 53574/99) and in *Federation of Offshore Workers' Trade Unions and Others v. Norway* (Application No. 38190/97) where an economic interest was at least taken into account while assessing the proportionality of the restriction of the right to take collective action. On the point see Dorssemont, "The Right to Take Collective Action Under Article 11 ECHR", p. 360.

ECSR, suggests a certain scepticism about the possibility for a progressive shift of Strasbourg towards a *Viking&Laval*-like approach.

Speaking of the CEACR and of the ECSR, it is impossible not to notice that the Explanatory Memorandum also made explicit reference to ILO Convention No. 87 and to the ESC. If for the second the Memorandum makes no attempt whatsoever to take into account the interpretation provided by the ECSR, it is perhaps much more surprising (in light of the actual proposal) to find the *BALPA* dispute mentioned in the same Memorandum.[315] The Conclusions of the CEACR are recalled in order to highlight the problem caused by the CJEU rulings. Since this mention clearly rules out the possibility of the drafters overlooking the Conclusions on the *BALPA* dispute, the question arises almost spontaneously: how can the reaffirmed loyalty to the proportionality test contained in Recitals 12 and 13 of the proposal be reconciled with the direct critique of this same test by the CEACR? In the absence of divinatory powers one can only guess. It is even more interesting to observe that the ultimate abortion of the proposal avoided the situation in which the application of a EU Regulation by a Member State could amount to a violation of ILO standards. At the same time, the failure to provide a legislative answer allowed the *Viking* and *Laval* era to continue.

6.4.2 THE ICE AGE

Answering the question of a Finnish MP, Commissioner Andor explained that the Commission would not try again its luck on the subject of the Monti II proposal.[316] Indeed, the Commissioner affirmed that workers' rights already enjoy a sufficient protection on the basis of the objectives of EU social policy[317] and of the EU Charter of Fundamental Rights.[318] Hence, the Commission appears to be satisfied with leaving the situation unchanged, though (as it should be remembered) President Barroso actually promised an intervention in the form of a Regulation while speaking in front of the European Parliament.[319] The saga of the Monti II proposal sadly confirms once more the fundamental asymmetry between the judicially-driven de-regulation and the legislative attempts to re-regulate.[320]

315 Explanatory Memorandum, p. 9.

316 Answer given by Mr. Andor on behalf of the Commission, 19 November 2012, E-008617/2012.

317 Article 151 TFEU: "[...] promotion of employment, improved living and working conditions, so as to make possible their harmonisation while the improvement is being maintained, proper social protection, dialogue between management and labour, the development of human resources with a view to lasting high employment and the combating of exclusion [...]".

318 Which, as it is clear from the decisions of the Court, was already taken into account in *Viking*, *Laval* and *Commission v Germany*. In every occasion the role of the Charter has been to *justify* the restriction to the fundamental right at stake.

319 Strasbourg, 15 September 2009.

320 F.W. Scharpf, "The Asymmetry of European Integration, or Why the EU Cannot Be a 'Social Market Economy'", *Socio-Economic Review* 8 (2010): 211–250, p. 210. This point will be developed further in Chapter 7. See *infra*, p. 282.

The decisions of the Court played a relevant role in framing the debate around the Monti II proposal. Indeed, those actors which were in favour of restricting fundamental (collective) social rights[321] could easily activate "veto-points", since in the absence of a legislative intervention the matter would remain "regulated" by the case law of the CJEU. On the other side, those in favour of a higher protection of social rights (*i.e.* of a real equal footing with economic freedoms of the internal market) could only block a deeply unsatisfactory proposal. Also, the rejection of the proposal allows the Commission to "wash its hands", having proved its goodwill in trying to solve the situation.

The Monti Report showed some hope about the coming into force of the Lisbon Treaty.[322] This was based on two elements: the new objective of the "social market economy" and the now binding nature of the EU Charter of Fundamental Rights. The first element seems way to broad and fuzzy to have an actual impact on the case law of the Court. As for the second, it is impossible not to notice that the Charter was mentioned and taken into account in the case law at stake (*Viking*, *Laval*, *Commission v. Germany*). In fact, the Charter provided a *justification* for the restriction of fundamental rights ("in accordance with Community law"). Moreover, in a recent decision[323] the Court relied on Article 16 of the Charter,[324] protecting the freedom to conduct a business, to interpret restrictively the protection offered by Directive 2001/23.[325] Hence, as noted by Barnard, the Lisbon Treaty "has not fundamentally changed the position as set out in *Viking* and *Laval*".[326] Provided that the situation has not changed, one should keep in mind previous analyses which considered the approach of the Court to the issue at stake as ultimately *inevitable*.[327]

---

321 See for example the submission of BUSINESSEUROPE (together with the IOE) in the procedure concerning the *Lex Laval* (ECSR): "In line with the ECJ's interpretation in the Viking and Laval rulings, BUSINESSEUROPE and the IOE believe that it is logical that trade unions' industrial action be submitted to an objective test. Collective action should have a *legitimate objective* and be *necessary* for *'overriding reasons of public interest'*. Its use should also be *proportionate*, considering its interaction with *interests*/rights/freedoms of other parties" (emphasis added).

322 "The ECJ rulings pre-date the entry into force of the Lisbon Treaty, which explicitly sets out the social market economy as an objective for the Union and makes the European Charter of Fundamental Rights legally binding at Treaty level. These elements should shape a new legal context, in which the issues and the concerns raised by the trade unions should hopefully find an adequate response".

323 Case C-421/11, *Mark Alemo Herron and Others v Parkwood Leisure Ltd.*

324 "The freedom to conduct a business in accordance with Community law and national laws and practices is recognised". It is impossible not to remark the risk of using such a disposition as an interpretative tool for Directive conceived to *protect* workers rights.

325 Council Directive 2001/23/EC of 12 March 2001 on the approximation of the laws of the Member States relating to the safeguarding of employees' rights in the event of transfers of undertakings, businesses or parts of undertakings or businesses.

326 Barnard, "The Protection of Fundamental Social Rights in Europe After Lisbon: a Question of Conflicts of Interests", p. 46.

327 V. Skouris, "Fundamental Rights and Fundamental Freedoms: The Challenge of Striking a Delicate Balance", *European Business Law Review*, 2006, 225–240, pp. 237 ff.; Barnard, "Viking and Laval: an Introduction", p. 486. *Contra*, see Dorssemont and Orlandini, "Market Rules and the Right to Strike: a Different Approach", p. 84: "[...]*Viking* and *Laval* do not represent the

Hence, we still live in the *Viking&Laval* era, where the approach shaped by the CJEU in these decisions (and confirmed in *Commission v. Germany*) to the relationship between fundamental freedoms and fundamental (collective) social rights is *inevitable*. The meaning of this can be quickly summarised through two references. The first one is to the Explanatory Memorandum of the Monti II proposal. Dealing with the possible *abuse* of the approach developed in *Viking* and *Laval*, the Memorandum states that "such a broad risk of liability to damages on the basis of a rather hypothetical situation or one where there are no cross-border elements would render the use by trade unions of their right to strike rather difficult, if not impossible, in situations where the freedom of establishment or the freedom to provide services *does not even apply*".[328] Now, going beyond the situation in which fundamental freedoms do not even apply, one should consider the other side of the coin. That is to say, consider the meaning of the statement for situations where fundamental freedoms *do* apply, as it is the case for situations involving posted workers. The formulation could then sound more or less like this: such a broad risk of liability to damages in a situation where *there are* cross-border elements, would render the use by trade unions of their right to strike rather difficult, if not impossible, in situations where the freedom of establishment or the freedom to provide services *do apply*. This second formulation, which is *implicit* in the one put forward by the drafters of the Monti II regulation has more than a resemblance to the critiques formulated by the CEACR in both the *BALPA* and the *Lex Laval* disputes.[329] Indeed, the chilling effect seems to be the *leitmotif* of the *Viking&Laval* era.

Along this Chapter the specific issue of posted workers has been left somewhat in the background, in order to analyse the broader legal context. However, as I explained in the beginning, it seems likely that any encounter between posted workers and industrial relations can (given the willingness of at least one the parties concerned) turn into a conflict between fundamental (social) rights and fundamental freedoms of the internal market. Hence, the situation would be heavily influenced by the framework analysed here. What is more, it would be influenced by such a situation even *before* the conflict actually takes place, as per the characteristic impact of the chilling effect. This is however only a half of the problem. The other part is the actual interpretation of the PWD provided by the Court in the case law analysed in the previous chapter. As it is evident from *Laval*, the Directive itself plays a relevant role in interpreting (and being interpreted through) the freedom to provide services. The next Chapter is hence devoted to the impact of the (interpretation of) the PWD.

---

logic of the previous ECJ case law and are not the inevitable application of the principles on internal market".

328 Explanatory Memorandum, p. 12 (emphasis added).

329 "The Committee takes the view that the omnipresent threat of an action for damages that could bankrupt the union, possible now in the light of the Viking and Laval judgements, creates a situation where the rights under the Convention cannot be exercised".

CHAPTER 7

"REAL PWD" AND NATIONAL INDUSTRIAL RELATIONS

Stuck with Negative Integration

Writing in 1997 Fritz Scharpf referred to the Posting of Workers Directive as an example of the possibility to "limit the impact of negative integration".[1] In the same year a very similar view was expressed by Paul Davies, who considered the PWD as an instrument to protect the systems of labour regulation of the host states.[2] In 2007, just a few months before the *Laval* case, Phil Syrpis similarly presented the directive, highlighting in particular its implicit political message (addressed to the Court), *i.e.* "the importance which the political institutions attach to the integrity of national labour law systems".[3] Then the triad of decisions of 2007–2008 occurred. In 2010 Scharpf thus wrote that those decisions showed the limits of the PWD, which could not "prevent the Court from invoking the Treaty-based freedom of services provision to strike down wage regulations that had been considered allowable under the directive".[4] After *Laval*, *Rüffert* and *Commission v. Luxembourg* he considered that the use of (secondary) legislation could not stop the judicial-driven negative integration, those attempts being bound "to be frustrated by the subsequent evolution of the case law".[5] Similarly Paul Davies, commenting the *Rüffert* decision, had the occasion to revisit the rationale(s) of the PWD.[6] He concluded that of the possible rationales of the PWD (anti-dumping and/or protection of posted workers) the Court had relied on a different one: the promotion of the freedom to provide services.[7] From floodgate

---

1 F.W. Scharpf, "Balancing Positive and Negative Integration: The Regulatory Options for Europe", *MPIfG Working Paper* 97/8, no. November (1998): 1–26, p. 8.

2 Davies, "Posted Workers: Single Market or Protection of National Labour Law Systems?, pp. 591 ff.

3 P. Syrpis, *EU Intervention in Domestic Labour Law* (Oxford: Oxford University Press, 2007), p. 124.

4 Scharpf, "The Asymmetry of European Integration, or Why the EU Cannot Be a 'Social Market Economy'", p. 227.

5 Ibid.

6 Davies, "Case C-346/06, Ruffert v. Land Niedersachsen [2008] IRLR 467 (ECJ)".

7 Ibid., p. 294.

against negative integration, the PWD came to be understood as a tool to foster such an outcome, and this in particular because of the ambiguities surrounding its legal basis.[8]

After the decisions of 2007–2008 the concept of negative integration has often correlated with the PWD, as interpreted by the CJEU.[9] On the one hand, this is strictly connected with the broader issue analysed in the previous Chapter. On the other, the PWD itself and its interpretation are particularly relevant for the specific question. Before moving to this second topic however, I will briefly outline the concept of negative integration, with a particular attention to its meaning for the field of industrial relations.

7.1 NEGATIVE INTEGRATION

From a conceptual point of view, negative integration can be easily defined. Indeed, most authors refer to it as the process of elimination of national barriers to intra-community trade, as well as of distortions of competition created by national regulations.[10] Majone suggests to take into account also other more "positive" aspects of negative integration, such as the limitation of monopolies, the protection of consumers' interests and the fight against discrimination.[11] Here however I will stick with the first more limited but widespread definition. Opposed to "negative integration" one finds the concept of "positive integration". Such concept encompasses the processes aimed at market regulation at the EU level, hence entailing the elimination of trade barriers through the setting up of common standards.[12] Negative integration characterises judicial intervention, whereas positive integration can generally be carried out only by political institutions.

As with many dichotomies, the distinction is not clear-cut. In particular, it has been stressed that every judicial intervention does (at least, theoretically) provide

---

8 Malmberg, "Posting Post Laval International and National Responses", p. 20–21.

9 Joerges and Rödl, "Informal Politics, Formalised Law and the Social Deficit of European Integration: Reflections After the Judgments of the ECJ in Viking and Laval", p. 19; Malmberg and Sigeman, "Industrial Action and EU Economic Freedoms: The Autonomous Collective Bargaining Model Curtailed by the European Court of Justice", p. 1145; Bücker, Warneck and Dorssemont, "The Search for a Balance: analysis and Perspectives", p. 124; S. Evju, "The FORMULA Project: Introduction and Backdrop", in *Cross-Border Services, Posting of Workers and Multilevel Governance*, ed. S. Evju (Oslo: Institutt for privaterett, 2013), 9–18, p. 14.

10 Scharpf, "Balancing Positive and Negative Integration: The Regulatory Options for Europe", p. 15; T. Perisin, *Free Movement of Goods and Limits of Regulatory Autonomy in the EU and WTO* (The Hague: T.M.C. Asser Press, 2009), p. 8; Syrpis, *EU Intervention in Domestic Labour Law*, p. 17 only refers to "barriers to trade".

11 G. Majone, *Dilemmas of European Integration* (Oxford: Oxford University Press, 2005), p. 155.

12 Scharpf, "Balancing Positive and Negative Integration: The Regulatory Options for Europe", p. 15; Perisin, *Free Movement of Goods and Limits of Regulatory Autonomy in the EU and WTO*, p. 8.

a window of opportunity for re-regulation at EU level.[13] A striking example of this possible "pendulum" between negative and positive integration, comes straight from the tale of the short-lived Monti II proposal. Indeed, the Explanatory Memorandum explicitly states that "Article 153(5) TFEU excludes the right to strike from the range of matters that can be regulated across the EU by way of minimum standards through Directives. However, the Court rulings have clearly shown that the fact that Article 153 does not apply to the right to strike does not as such exclude collective action from the scope of EU law".[14] Though I described in the previous Chapter how this argument was in the end rejected by a number of national parliaments,[15] one could hardly find a better exemplification of the interrelations between the two means of furthering market integration in the EU.

7.1.1 A DESERT CALLED INTEGRATION?

The most visible instrument of negative integration, and also the more directly connected with the issue at stake here, is (are) the test(s) developed by the Court of Justice to tackle national measures infringing the fundamental freedoms of the internal market. In this sense, the relationship between different tests and different models of integration has been convincingly described.[16] In very brief, the taxonomy envisages two possible approaches to the said test, as well as two approaches to the re-regulation by at European level through positive integration. The two different tests, are represented, on the one hand, by a "narrow" anti-discriminatory test, aimed at tackling exclusively protectionist measures, and on the other by a "broad" restriction-based test, which catches as many national measures as possible.[17] In their interplay with different approaches at re-regulation[18] the two tests give rise to the three models of integration described by Maduro[19] summarised in Table 7.1.

---

13 Majone, *Dilemmas of European Integration*, pp. 155–156; P.C. de Sousa, "Negative and Positive Integration in EU Economic Between Strategic Denial and Cognitive Dissonance?", *German Law Journal* 13, no. 8 (2012): 979–1012, p. 989.

14 Proposal for a Council Regulation on the exercise of the right to take collective action within the context of the freedom of establishment and the freedom to provide services, COM(2012) 130 final, Explanatory Memorandum, p. 11.

15 See *supra*, p. 273.

16 Ibid., pp. 987 ff.

17 Ibid., p. 1001.

18 Either favourable at the re-regulation through European-wide standards or hostile to such an intervention. This second position can be based in its turn either on the objective of protecting national pluralism or on the preference of an lightly regulated market.

19 M. Maduro, *We the Court: The European Court of Justice and the European Economic Constitution* (Oxford: Hart Publishing, 1998), pp. 109 ff. Here I do not present the further distinction as regards the decentralised constitutional model proposed by de Sousa. See de Sousa, "Negative and Positive Integration in EU Economic Between Strategic Denial and Cognitive Dissonance?", pp. 987 ff.

Table 7.1 Models of Integration

Model	Test	Positive Integration
Centralised Constitutional	Broad	Strong
Competitive Constitutional	Broad	Limited
Decentralised Constitutional	Narrow	Limited

Hence, the first model calls for broadly construed judicial tests as tools to pave the way to a re-regulation at European level.[20] The second model instead denies the desirability of such a de-regulation, "constitutionalising", as Maduro puts it[21] negative integration. By impeding re-regulation at higher level, while enforcing at the same level the integration of markets, this model closely resembles the theorisations of "market preserving federalism" put forward by neoliberal thinkers.[22] Finally, the third model argues in favour of limited competencies for re-regulation at European level. This would also be coupled with a narrower judicial tests, essentially aimed at avoiding protectionists measures.[23]

Now, the origin of the posted powers saga does not fit squarely into the taxonomy. Indeed, the first judicial intervention was all but inspired at negative integration. The *obiter dictum* of *Rush Portuguesa*[24] did in fact allow the continued existence of national regulation concerning working conditions of posted workers. As it was described *supra*, the PWD was similarly welcomed at the time of its adoption.[25] However, starting with the second "high tide", the story seems easier to accommodate in the categories presented before. As I pointed out in the beginning of this Chapter, it was in the aftermath of the *Laval* case with its contemporaries *Rüffert* and *Commission v. Luxembourg*, that the whole issue was transferred to the field of negative integration. After the difficulties of the

20 Maduro, *We the Court: The European Court of Justice and the European Economic Constitution*, pp. 110–113.

21 Ibid., p. 109.

22 See A. Harmes, "Neoliberalism and Multilevel Governance", *Review of International Political Economy* 13, no. 5 (December 2006): 725–749, p. 727: "This [market preserving federalism] is achieved either by 'bringing the economy up' through greater capital mobility and the centralization of 'market enabling' policy competencies or by 'pushing the polity down' through decentralization of 'market-inhibiting' policy competencies".

23 Maduro, *We the Court: The European Court of Justice and the European Economic Constitution*, pp. 126–129.

24 *Rush Portuguesa*, para. 18: "[...] Community law does not preclude Member States from extending their legislation, or collective labour agreements entered into by both sides of industry, to any person who is employed, even temporarily, within their territory, no matter in which country the employer is established; nor does Community law prohibit Member States from enforcing those rules by appropriate means".

25 See *supra*, p. 4.

posting package[26] we witness a situation which closely reminds the second model of integration.

Origin of asymmetry

The outlined outcome is not particularly surprising if one follows the analysis developed by Scharpf, and in particular his reference to the asymmetry of EU action.[27] The concept of "asymmetry" refers here to the institutional configuration favouring negative over positive integration.[28] The case law of the Court of Justice is identified as the main vector of negative integration. First, because the four freedoms, the "constitutional" drive of much of the case law,[29] entail an approach aimed at market-making. In the hand of the Court, the only possible form of this intervention is thus the lifting of restrictions to the said freedoms,[30] and *in casu* to the freedom to provide services. Second, Scharpf noted how the Court is necessarily invested by cases focusing on the interests of more mobile players, its legal reasoning hence showing a bias in favour of the interests of such parties, as opposed to diffused interests of parties benefiting from national laws and regulations.[31]

This however can only explain a half of the asymmetry. As noted *supra*, de-regulation enforced by the Court of Justice may well be followed by re-regulation at EU level.[32] Hence, to complete the asymmetry one has to look at the obstacles and hurdles of the process of re-regulation, for the moment making abstraction

26 On the one hand, the Monti II Regulation, which was analysed in the previous Chapter, and on the other the Enforcement Directive (Proposal for Directive concerning the enforcement of the provision applicable to the posting of workers in the framework of the provision of services), COM(2012) 131, which is still being discussed. I will come back to this second part of the "package" in the next Chapter.

27 F.W. Scharpf, "Negative and Positive Integration in the Political Economy of European Welfare States", in *Governance in the European Union*, ed. Gary Marks et al. (London: SAGE Publications, 1996), 15–39, p. 33; Scharpf, "The Asymmetry of European Integration, or Why the EU Cannot Be a 'Social Market Economy'".

28 Ibid., p. 214. In this work Scharpf splits the concept into two parts, the first highlighting the asymmetry between legislative and judicial lawmaking, while the second refers to the relationship negative/positive integration. However, if one accepts that the Court of Justice cannot (generally) bring about positive integration, and that, hence, judicial lawmaking is bound to foster negative integration, the distinction seems somewhat superfluous.

29 Scharpf, "Negative and Positive Integration in the Political Economy of European Welfare States", p. 18; de Sousa, "Negative and Positive Integration in EU Economic Between Strategic Denial and Cognitive Dissonance?", p. 979.

30 F.W. Scharpf, "The Joint-Decision Trap Revisited", *JCMS: Journal of Common Market Studies* 44, no. 4 (November 2006): 845–864, p. 854.

31 Scharpf, "The Asymmetry of European Integration, or Why the EU Cannot Be a 'Social Market Economy'", p. 221.

32 Even though the new regulation may differ greatly from the previously existent national ones, provided the very different constellation of players at the different levels. See de Sousa, "Negative and Positive Integration in EU Economic Between Strategic Denial and Cognitive Dissonance?", p. 984; Scharpf, "The Asymmetry of European Integration, or Why the EU Cannot Be a 'Social Market Economy'", p. 103.

from the specific situation of industrial relations. Once again, the argument rests on two main pillars. The first is the one known as the joint-decision trap.[33] Such a trap springs when two conditions are met: a) "central government decisions are directly dependent upon the agreement of constituent governments" and b)"the agreement of constituent governments must be unanimous or nearly unanimous".[34] For what it matters here, a situation characterised by the joint-decision trap is vulnerable to non-agreement, with the individual governments loosing their independent capabilities for action in such a case.[35] The second pillar (which is, in fact, strictly intertwined with the first) is represented by the increased heterogeneity of the EU. To put it simply, the successive enlargements of the EU makes it more and more difficult to find agreement and hence to re-create at supranational level what the Court has struck down at the national one.[36] This is particularly true in the context of posting of workers as framed by the case law of the Court. Indeed, as it was analysed *supra*[37] Member State interventions in the most relevant cases showed a clear divide between "new" Member States (joined by the UK) and "old" ones.

On this background, the Court emerges as moving into a vast "zone of discretion".[38] Though, as Alter puts it, "legal rulings gain in influence via [...] 'political follow-through',[39] such a follow-through may well be represented by a legislative blockage.[40] What is more, intervention at the level of secondary legislation may not even be enough to change the judicial regulation of a given topic.[41] Such a situation follows those cases where the CJEU interprets the Treaties, and it is defined by Falkner as "court-decision trap".[42] Indeed, the court-

---

33 The concept was famously formulated by Scharpf, drawing from the analysis of the German federal experience. See F.W. Scharpf, "The Joint-Decision Trap: Lessons from German Federalism and European Integration", *Public Administration* 66, no. 3 (September 1988): 239–278, then revised (and confirmed) in Scharpf, "The Joint-Decision Trap Revisited".

34 Scharpf, "The Joint-Decision Trap: Lessons from German Federalism and European Integration", p. 254.

35 Ibid., p. 258.

36 M. Höpner and A. Schäfer, "Embeddedness and Regional Integration: Waiting for Polanyi in a Hayekian Setting", *International Organization* 66, no. 3 (July 2012): 429–455, p. 432; Kelemen, *Eurolegalism: The Transformation of Law and Regulation in the European Union*, p. 24.

37 See *supra*, Chapter 5, especially the *Laval* and *Rüffert* cases.

38 A. Stone Sweet, *The Judicial Construction of Europe* (Oxford: Oxford University Press, 2004), p. 26; M. Höpner, "Political Answers to Judicial Problems? Europe After Viking, Laval and Rüffert", in *Viking-Laval-Rüffert: Economic Freedoms Versus Fundamental Social Rights – Where Does the Balance Lie?* (Notre Europe, 2008), p. 445.

39 K. Alter, *The European Court's Political Power: Selected Essays* (Oxford: Oxford University Press, 2009), p. 17.

40 Kelemen, *Eurolegalism: The Transformation of Law and Regulation in the European Union*, p. 27.

41 Bruun, Bücker and Dorssemont, "Balancing Fundamental Social Rights and Economic Freedoms: Can the Monti II Initiative Solve the EU Dilemma?", p. 284.

42 Falkner, "Introduction: The EU's Decision Traps and Their Exits", p. 11. In this case only a change in the Treaties could effectively influence the interpretation provided by the Court. See also Scharpf, "The Asymmetry of European Integration, or Why the EU Cannot Be a 'Social Market Economy'", p. 217.

decision trap seems to characterise several aspects of the topic of posted workers, in particular those analysed in the previous Chapter.[43] All in all, provided that the possibilities for re-regulation are blocked, the intervention of the Court has essentially de-regulatory effects.[44]

Negative integration and industrial relations

Looking specifically at the legal aspects connected with industrial relations, the outcome just outlined appears even more as an inevitable destiny. As it is well known, in a number of these areas the EU has no competence at all. Indeed, its competence is been explicitly denied by the Treaties. The reference here goes to Article 153(5) TFEU, which excludes "pay, the right of association, the right to strike or the right to impose lock-outs" from the competences of the EU under the chapter of "Social Policy".

True enough, one could try to argue that the wording seems to exclude those areas from EU competences exclusively when regulating matters of Social Policy. Hence, the EU could legitimately regulate the same areas with measures based on different competences, and in particular on the ones stemming from the completion of the internal market. As it was explained before,[45] this was the strategy of the Commission with the "Monti II" proposal. Such a choice was particularly daring, inasmuch as the proposal was not even based on an "internal market" competence,[46] but instead on Article 352 TFEU, in the wording of the Explanatory Memorandum: "reserved for cases where the Treaties do not provide the necessary powers to implement actions necessary, under the policies defined in the Treaties, to attain one of the objectives of the Treaties".[47] The point is, the "policy" whose implementation would have required powers not provided for by the Treaties was *not* specified in the Explanatory Memorandum. However, it is

---

43 Though the Commission resorted to the Monti II proposal (a Regulation) as a possible solution to the issue of the relationship between fundamental social rights and fundamental freedoms. See Rocca, "The Proposal for a (so-Called) 'Monti II' Regulation on the Exercise of the Right to Take Collective Action Within the Context of the Freedom of Establishment and the Freedom to Provide Services", p. 29.

44 De Sousa, "Negative and Positive Integration in EU Economic Between Strategic Denial and Cognitive Dissonance?", p. 989.

45 See *supra*, p. 275 ff.

46 And here the saga of the posting of workers Directive has probably (at least) taught an important lesson: a (more or less) protective instrument approved on an "internal market" legal basis will be interpreted as an...internal market instrument.

47 Article 352 TFEU stating that: "If action by the Union should prove necessary, within the framework of the policies defined in the Treaties, to attain one of the objectives set out in the Treaties, and the Treaties have not provided the necessary powers, the Council, acting unanimously on a proposal from the Commission and after obtaining the consent of the European Parliament, shall adopt the appropriate measures. Where the measures in question are adopted by the Council in accordance with a special legislative procedure, it shall also act unanimously on a proposal from the Commission and after obtaining the consent of the European Parliament".

difficult to see how a policy different from the social one could have provided for a basis for an intervention on the right to take collective action.[48] Thus here lies the problem with such an approach: it is daring indeed to argue that the Treaty has not provided the necessary powers to attain one of the objectives of a policy, when the same Treaty explicitly excludes the area envisaged by the intervention from that specific policy.

What is more, this has been if anything reinforced by the reaction of the national parliaments, intervening under the procedure set up by the Protocol on subsidiarity (while evidently distorting the same procedure). As I showed in the previous Chapter, no less than 9 national parliaments (or single chambers of bicameral national parliaments) have criticised the "Monti II" proposal from the point of view of EU competence (*i.e.* of lack thereof). In a way this has vindicated the warning of AG Mengozzi in *Laval*, where he considered that the exclusion of Article 153(5) TFEU (back then, Article 137(5) TEC) could not simply be circumvented by legislating on a different legal basis.[49] All in all the possibility of re-regulation seems essentially blocked, even from a legal point of view, in a good number of topics covered by industrial relations: completely, for the right to take collective action and the freedom of association, and partially for collective bargaining.[50]

On the other hand, the political choice in favour of economic liberalisation did found its perfect instrument in the case law of the Court of Justice. As highlighted by Kelemen,[51] the creation of the single market under the flag of liberalisation was bound to clash with "informal, flexible regulatory practices at national level *for their lack of transparency and legal certainty*".[52] Industrial relations practices and outcomes do belong among those informal and flexible regulatory practices, though it took a relatively long amount of time for them to encounter the hard law of negative integration.[53] With re-regulation blocked by the said asymmetry both in legal and political terms, it simply takes a broad judicial test to drive the issue towards the competitive constitutional model of "market preserving federalism".

48 Bruun, Bücker and Dorssemont, "Balancing Fundamental Social Rights and Economic Freedoms: Can the Monti II Initiative Solve the EU Dilemma?", pp. 301–302.

49 Opinion of AG Mengozzi in *Laval*, para. 57: "if the effectiveness of Article 137(5) EC is to be upheld, the Community institutions could not of course resort to other legal bases in the Treaty in order to adopt measures designed to approximate the laws of the Member States in this field".

50 Since the topic of wages is excluded from re-regulation. Indeed, this topic is crucial for industrial relations and collective bargaining, as argued by P. Marginson and K. Sisson, *European Integration and Industrial Relations: Multi-Level Governance in the Making* (London: Palgrave Macmillan, 2004), p. 246.

51 Kelemen, *Eurolegalism: The Transformation of Law and Regulation in the European Union*, pp. 22–23.

52 The statement has more than an echo of the *Laval* decision, where the Court condemns the unspecified duration of negotiations surrounding the conclusion of a collective agreement. See *Laval*, para. 100.

53 Joerges and Rödl, "Informal Politics, Formalised Law and the Social Deficit of European Integration: Reflections After the Judgments of the ECJ in Viking and Laval", p. 2.

As I discussed in Chapter 5 while analysing the evolution of the case law on posting of workers, the broad test embodied by the *Säger* formula[54] can definitely be described as a broad test, and its potential in terms of negative integration and de-regulation has been perfectly highlighted in the *Laval* and *Rüffert* cases.[55]

Keeping in mind the interpretation of trade union action provided by the Court,[56] the *Säger* formula is bound to catch in its net a large range of activities connected with industrial relations practices, inasmuch as those as considered as liable to "make it less attractive, or more difficult" the transnational provision of services.[57] The concepts of "*less* attractive" and "*more* difficult" do raise the obvious question of the comparator. Indeed, as Deakin puts it, "more difficult or less attractive than what?".[58] I have already presented the possible answers to such a question in the previous Chapter.[59] Bringing back the question in the field of posting of workers, the PWD represents the yardstick by which the *impact* of industrial relations has to be measured. Hence, before proceeding with the analysis one has to look once again at the PWD as used and interpreted by the Court of Justice, in order to assess the potential impact of negative integration on a system of industrial relations.

7.2 THE ROLE OF THE PWD

The Directive plays at least two different roles in the case law of the Court of Justice which shaped the legal framework of posting of workers in the almost-twenty years since its adoption. This is especially visible in the more recent case law, extensively presented in Chapter 5. First, the Directive is used to determine the existence of a restriction to the freedom to provide services. In both *Laval*[60] and *Rüffert*,[61] the

---

54 See *supra*, pp. 155 ff.

55 All analysed in Chapter 5. Also, the *Viking* case legitimately belongs to this group.

56 Which considers trade unions as carrying out a regulatory task. See *supra*, Chapter 6, p. 240.

57 *Laval*, para. 99.

58 Deakin, "Regulatory Competition After Laval", p. 584.

59 See *supra*, p. 246.

60 *Laval*, para. 99: "In the case in the main proceedings, it must be pointed out that the right of trade unions of a Member State to take collective action by which undertakings established in other Member States may be forced to sign the collective agreement for the building sector – *certain terms of which depart from the legislative provisions and establish more favourable terms and conditions of employment as regards the matters referred to in Article 3(1), first subparagraph, (a) to (g) of Directive 96/71 and others relate to matters not referred to in that provision* – is liable to make it less attractive, or more difficult, for such undertakings to carry out construction work in Sweden, and therefore constitutes a restriction on the freedom to provide services within the meaning of Article 49 EC" (emphasis added).

61 *Rüffert*, para. 37: "[...] by requiring undertakings performing public works contracts and, indirectly, their subcontractors to apply the minimum wage laid down by the 'Buildings and public works' collective agreement, a law such as the Landesvergabegesetz may impose on service providers established in another Member State where minimum rates of pay are lower an additional economic burden that may prohibit, impede or render less attractive the provision of their services in the host Member State. Therefore, a measure such as that at

Court states that the measure at stake does represent a restriction inasmuch as it applies to the service provider working conditions which go beyond the *minima* established by the Directive (either by providing more favourable conditions or regulating matters not included in the Directive).

Second, the Directive strikes back when the Court considers the possible *justifications* for the restriction to the freedom to provide services. In *Laval*, the Court states that the protection of workers against *social dumping* is in principle an overriding reason of public interest, thus able to justify a restriction of the freedom to provide services.[62] However, the concept of "social dumping" is defined by the Court, through the PWD, in a rather narrow way. Simply put, the Court considers that the respect of minimum conditions listed by the PWD is in itself sufficient in order to avoid social dumping and unfair competition.[63] The *Rüffert* case follows a similar pattern. In this case the Court considers the "protection of workers" as a possible justification for the restriction.[64] Once again the justification is denied, though the PWD does not play a direct role in the reasoning. The Court states that the measure at stake cannot be considered as covered by the objective of "protecting workers" because it only covers public contracts, whereas, had it been *necessary* for such a protection, it would have covered the entire construction sector.[65] The Court also mentions the fact that the rate of pay established exceeds the *minimum* one set at national level.

As it is apparent, if the PWD provides the yardstick, it is the *aim* of the intervention which is to be measured against it. Whether this intervention takes the form of a collective action (a boycott) or an extension of collective agreement through the means of public procurement clauses, it is the actual content of the collective agreement which is scrutinised by the Court. As opposed to the

---

issue in the main proceedings is capable of constituting a restriction within the meaning of Article 49 EC".

62 *Laval*, para. 103.

63 Cf. *Laval*, para. 75 "That provision [Article 3(1)] thus prevents a situation arising in which, by applying to their workers the terms and conditions of employment in force in the Member State of origin as regards those matters, undertakings established in other Member States would compete unfairly against undertakings of the host Member State in the framework of the transnational provision of services, if the level of social protection in the host Member State is higher" and 108 "however, as regards the specific obligations, linked to signature of the collective agreement for the building sector, which the trade unions seek to impose on undertakings established in other Member States by way of collective action such as that at issue in the case in the main proceedings, the obstacle which that collective action forms cannot be justified with regard to such an objective [the protection of workers against social dumping]. [...] [T]heir employer is required, as a result of the coordination achieved by Directive 96/71, to observe a nucleus of mandatory rules for minimum protection in the host Member State". See on the point Malmberg, and Sigeman, "Industrial Action and EU Economic Freedoms: The Autonomous Collective Bargaining Model Curtailed by the European Court of Justice", pp. 1136–1137 and 1144.

64 *Rüffert*, para. 38.

65 *Rüffert*, para. 40. In a way this can be considered as a reference to the system set up by the PWD at Article 3(8), when referring to collective agreements which cover "similar undertakings in the geographical area and in the profession or industry concerned".

Schmidberger case, where only *procedural* aspects[66] were taken into account by the Court, here one witnesses a substantive evaluation. The PWD hence has become the needle's eye through which the *aims* of industrial relations practices have to pass in order to be considered compatible with the freedom to provide services. *Or*, in order to be considered as justified once their restrictive nature has been assessed. That is why I will now re-read the PWD in the light of the case law and of the other legal events I described in the preceding Chapters. The objective is to try to assess how the PWD actually looks in the present days, though here and there the assessment can only be based on a prospective interpretation on the basis of a very limited case law.

7.2.1 LIVING UNDER THE "REAL PWD"

The focus for this reconstruction is thus almost exclusively the case law of the Court of Justice. Indeed, the so-called Posting Package did not, and does not, touch upon the parts of the PWD which I will present here. I already examined in detail the tale of the Monti II Regulation, while the Enforcement Directive[67] has yet to see the light. This second legislative intervention however, is essentially aimed at regulating the areas of monitoring, administrative cooperation, exchange of information and judicial handling of complaints, thus leaving untouched the substantive "core" of the PWD.

As per the disclaimer I just put forward, the Directive will be re-assessed in light of a number of cases which in itself remains pretty limited. However, for the vast majority of the topics I will present here, the interpretation has at least been confirmed in more than a single case, and often adamantly so.

The scope

Two points are worth mentioning as regards the first Article of the Directive. In first place, it amounts at making explicit a contradiction with the original text. Article 1(1) states that the Directive applies to posting of workers "in the framework of the transnational provision of services". However, Article 1(3)(b)[68]

---

[66] *E.g.*, the fact that the demonstration had been authorised ad that information had been given in advance. In general the Court considered that "the specific aims of the demonstration are not in themselves material in legal proceedings", *Schmidberger*, para. 66. See *supra*, p. 246.

[67] Directive 2014/67/EU of the European Parliament and of the Council on the enforcement of Directive 96/71/EC concerning the posting of workers in the framework of the provision of services and amending Regulation (EU) No 1024/2012 on administrative cooperation through the Internal Market Information System ("the IMI Regulation"), 15 May 2014.

[68] "This Directive shall apply to the extent that the undertakings referred to in paragraph 1 take one of the following transnational measures: [...] (b) post workers to an establishment or to an undertaking owned by the group in the territory of a Member State, provided there is an employment relationship between the undertaking making the posting and the worker during the period of posting".

covers situation which may fit difficultly under the provision of services. This was made apparent by the *Laval* case. As remarked by Deakin, in the *Laval* case, the contractual relationship for the renovations ran between the municipality of Vaxholm and Baltic, a Laval subsidiary *established in Sweden*.[69] Hence, this relationship was not characterised by a "transnational provision of services". Indeed, the posting happened between Laval and its subsidiary, coherently with the scenario of Article 1(3)(b). However, the Court did not examine this relationship. Hence, we do not know whether this posting did in fact take place in the framework of a transnational provision of services or not. In particular, whether the posting was provided for *remuneration*.[70] Looking at the issue from downstream, one has just to take note of the fact that the scope of the PWD may result as somewhat broader than the strict definition of "transnational provision of services", especially in those cases characterised by an Article 1(3)(b) scenario of posting. The question gets more complicated upstream, where the scope of the freedom to provide services ends up broader, carried on the shoulders of the PWD. This however falls outside the boundaries of the present analysis.

The second point also deals partly with Article 1(3)(b) together with Article 1(3)(c).[71] Following the *Vicoplus* decision, those two situations have been considered as potentially falling in the category, carved in the *Rush Portuguesa* decision,[72] of "activities which are specifically intended to enable workers to gain access to the labour market of the host Member State".[73] In *Vicoplus* this was considered as a sufficient condition to extend the limitation on free *movement of workers* provided by transitional measures to workers being posted by a temporary employment agency. The *caveat* here is that extrapolating from *Vicoplus* may indeed amount at building on quicksand. First the case was decided by a single Chamber of the CJEU. Second, it dealt with the specific (and temporary) situation of transitional measures following the accession of Poland to the European Union.[74] That being said, the identification of those activities "intended to enable workers to gain

69 *Laval*, para. 27. See Deakin, "Regulatory Competition After Laval", pp. 587–588. Similarly, in *Rüffert*, the dispute arose between the German liquidator of a German company and a German *Land*. The said German company had indeed made use of a Polish subcontractor, but this relationship is never analysed in the case.

70 As stated in the definition of Article 57 TFEU. See ibid., p. 599.

71 "This Directive shall apply to the extent that the undertakings referred to in paragraph 1 take one of the following transnational measures: (c) being a temporary employment undertaking or placement agency, hire out a worker to a user undertaking established or operating in the territory of a Member State, provided there is an employment relationship between the temporary employment undertaking or placement agency and the worker during the period of posting".

72 *Rush Portuguesa*, para. 16.

73 *Vicoplus*, para.

74 In a more recent case dealing with third country nationals the AG urged the CJEU to clarify exactly this point. See Opinion of AG Bot in Case C-91/13, *Essent Energie Productie BV v. Minister van Sociale Zaken en Werkgelegenheid*, para 97–99. The Court however did not analyse this point in its decision.

access to the labour market of the host state",[75] may provide for a higher leeway for the inclusion of those workers in the industrial relations practices of the host country. It is worth noting that the interplay between the PWD and the Temporary Agency Work Directive[76] seems to depict workers posted by a temporary-work agency as a *tertium genus* between posted workers and workers covered by the free movement. Following the wording of Article 5, those workers are entitled (save exception[77]) to (basic) working conditions that are "at least those that would apply if they had been recruited directly by that undertaking to occupy the same job". The application of (national dispositions transposing) Article 5 should then court-circuit Article 3 of the PWD as regards applicable working conditions.[78]

The list of Article 3(1)

Much attention has been devoted to the fact that the Court interpreted the list contained in Article 3(1) as an *exhaustive* one.[79] However, this was achieved more through the narrowing of the possibility of extension offered by Article 3(10), than through the interpretation of the Actual text of the Article in question. Hence, I will present the state of the case law on the point when dealing with the "opening clause" of Article 3(10).

Evidently, not much is left of Article 3(1) once one leaves aside the list of conditions of employment that have to be applied to posted workers. Still, it is interesting to spend a few words on the last passage of the said Article. This passage defines "minimum rates of pay" (one of the items of the list) by referring to "national law and/or practice of the Member State to whose territory the worker is posted". Once again, a clear marker of the (initial) deference of the Directive towards national arrangements in terms of employment conditions. Taking into account the case law of the Court however, this passage has to be reconsidered, as the effective space left to national law and *practice* to determine what is the minimum wage for an occupation has been exceptionally narrowed. That is, "national law and/or practice" can only identify "minimum rates of pay" which

---

75 Which in the reasoning of the Court is marked by the fact that "a worker who has been hired out pursuant to Article 1(3)(c) of Directive 96/71 is typically assigned, during the period for which he is made available, to a post within the user undertaking which would otherwise have been occupied by a person employed by that undertaking"; see *Vicoplus*, para. 31. Because of this, and going as back as the *Webb* decision (para. 10), "such activities may *have an impact on the labour market* of the Member State of the party for whom the services are intended" (emphasis added).

76 Directive 2008/104/EC of the European Parliament and of the Council of 19 November 2008.

77 As allowed by Articles 5(3) and 5(4).

78 See M. Schlachter, "Transnational Temporary Agency Work: How Much Equality Does the Equal Treatment Principle Provide?", *The International Journal of Comparative Labour Law and Industrial Relations* 28, no. 2 (2012): 177–197, pp. 188 and 197.

79 C. Kilpatrick, "The ECJ and Labour Law: A 2008 Retrospective", *Industrial Law Journal* 38, no. 2 (June 2009): 180–208, p. 196; Sjödin, "Labour Market Regulation as Restrictions. A Developmental Study of ECJ Case Law at the Interface Between Free Movement and Posting of Workers", p. 49.

are covered by the means provided by Articles 3(1) and 3(8). In this sense, the Directive has been interpreted as to completely pre-empt the concept of minimum rates of pay. Only minimum rates of pay can be applied to posted workers, and only rates of pay which are established by the means identified by the Directive can be considered as a minimum.

On the same topic, in *Commission v. Luxembourg* the Court accepted without much discussion that the automatic indexation of minimum wages would fall into the definition of "minimum rates of pay". The same indexation applied to wages different from *the* minimum one, however, was considered as falling outside what it is *prima facie*[80] allowed by the PWD.[81]

What once was opened now it is closed: more favourable conditions and public policy

The interpretation of Article 3(7)[82] and 3(10)[83] provided by the CJEU prompted much of the comments about the turning of the PWD from a "floor" to a ceiling".[84] That is changing an instrument of minimal protection to a restriction of state prerogatives in terms of extending labour regulations to posted workers.

Not much should be said about Article 3(7). Apart from future legislative interventions or judicial corrections the "new" form of this Article is pretty straightforward. Since the former seems well outside the foreseeable future and the latter appear unlikely in the same time span, in view of a crystal clear stance

80 The Court then went on to scrutinise the justification put forward by the Grand Duchy. However, it found that the provision could not be considered as covered by "public policy" on the basis of the generic reasons of "protecting the purchasing power of workers and good labour relations". *Commission v. Luxembourg*, para. 53–55.

81 *Commission v. Luxembourg*, para. 47: "the requirement […] concerning the automatic adjustment of rates of pay *other than the minimum wage* to the cost of living does not fall within the matters referred to in the first subparagraph of Article 3(1) of Directive 96/71" (emphasis added).

82 "Paragraphs 1 to 6 shall not prevent application of terms and conditions of employment which are more favourable to workers".

83 This Directive shall not preclude the application by Member States, in compliance with the Treaty, to national undertakings and to the undertakings of other States, on a basis of equality of treatment, of: – terms and conditions of employment on matters other than those referred to in the first subparagraph of paragraph 1 in the case of public policy provisions".

84 Eklund, "A Swedish Perspective on Laval", p. 566; Malmberg and Sigeman, "Industrial Action and EU Economic Freedoms: The Autonomous Collective Bargaining Model Curtailed by the European Court of Justice", pp. 1140–1141; A. Asteriti, "Social Dialogue, Laval-Style", *European Journal of Legal Studies* 5, no. 2 (2012): 57–79, p. 71.

in both *Laval*[85] and *Rüffert*,[86] I will just provide what can be defined as the new text of the Article at stake:

> Paragraphs 1 to 6 shall not prevent application of terms and conditions of employment laid down by law or collective agreements in the Member State of origin which are more favourable to workers

As for the possibility offered by Article 3(10), it has also been restricted in several ways. First, only "bodies governed by public law"[87] can invoke this Article in order to justify the application of terms and conditions which go above or beyond the list of Article 3(1). This should be read as excluding in particular trade unions[88] from availing themselves of Article 3(10). Second, those bodies who can actually have recourse to the possibility offered by this Article (basically, legislators and administrative bodies), must provide "appropriate evidence" as to the "expediency and proportionality" of the measure,[89] and proof that "there is a genuine and sufficiently serious threat to a fundamental interest of society".[90] Third, the scope of the very concept of public policy "cannot be determined unilaterally by each Member State",[91] and it is subject to scrutiny from the Court of Justice. In this sense, the scrutiny does not seem to differentiate itself from the classical restriction/justification test deployed by the Court to evaluate national restrictions to fundamental freedoms.[92] Indeed, the possibility of justification for

---

85 *Laval*, para. 81 "nevertheless, Article 3(7) of Directive 96/71 cannot be interpreted as allowing the host Member State to make the provision of services in its territory conditional on the observance of terms and conditions of employment which go beyond the mandatory rules for minimum protection. As regards the matters referred to in Article 3(1), first subparagraph, (a) to (g), Directive 96/71 expressly lays down the degree of protection for workers of undertakings established in other Member States who are posted to the territory of the host Member State which the latter State is entitled to require those undertakings to observe" and 82 "[...] the level of protection which must be guaranteed to workers posted to the territory of the host Member State is limited, in principle, to that provided for in Article 3(1), first subparagraph, (a) to (g) of Directive 96/71, *unless, pursuant to the law or collective agreements in the Member State of origin, those workers already enjoy more favourable terms and conditions of employment as regards the matters referred to in that provision*" (emphasis added).

86 *Rüffert*, para. 33–34.

87 *Laval*, para. 82–84.

88 *Laval*, para. 84: "the terms of the collective agreement for the building sector in question were in fact established through negotiation between management and labour; *not being bodies governed by public law*, they cannot avail themselves of that provision by citing grounds of public policy in order to maintain that collective action such as that at issue in the main proceedings complies with Community law" (emphasis added). See Azoulai, "The Court of Justice and the Social Market Economy: the Emergence of an Ideal and the Conditions for Its Realization", p. 1351; Davies, "One Step Forward, Two Steps Back? The Viking and Laval Cases in the ECJ", p. 130; Dorssemont, "The Right to Take Collective Action Versus Fundamental Economic Freedoms in the Aftermath of Laval and Viking. Foes Are Forever", p. 74.

89 *Commission v. Luxembourg*, para. 51.

90 Ibid., para. 50.

91 Ibid. See also, in relation to *Arblade* but perfectly mirroring the reasoning in *Commission v. Luxembourg*, Fallon, "Note sur CJCE 23 novembre 1999, Arblade", pp. 730–731.

92 See Ibid., p. 729; Francq, "Note sur CJCE 23 novembre 1999, Arblade", p. 790.

"public policy" provisions seems, if anything, narrower than *simple* restrictions, as "fundamental interest of society" appears as a higher standard than a mere "legitimate objective".

Applicable collective agreements

Last but by no means least, one has to turn to the question of applicable collective agreements. Indeed, it is difficult to overstate the importance of Article 3(8) in the "Real PWD". To put it shortly, the content of collective agreements is the measure of all things, as regards the relationship of industrial relations practices with posting of workers. *Laval* is the most coherent and spectacular example of this statement. Along the decision, the collective action of the Swedish trade unions is examined through the lenses of its objectives. That is, through the content of the collective agreement(s) whose conclusion represented the aim of the action. The compatibility of these contents with the PWD is, as it was explained *supra*, the yardstick by which to measure both the restrictive nature of the collective action[93] and its possible justification in terms of EU law.[94] More marginally, in *Rüffert* the CJEU considered that the *Landesvergabegesetz* adopted by Land Niedersachsen could not be considered as a law fixing (minimum) rates of pay.[95] This because the law in question merely provided for a reference to a collective agreement. Hence, the Court considered that the legislative veil had to be pierced, and went on to examine the compatibility of the collective agreement with the PWD.

The determination of which collective agreement *can* actually be applied to posted workers is thus a fundamental issue. I will now turn once again to the PWD, trying to assess the present state of the "options" for applying collective agreements to posted workers.[96] A good number of conditions for this extension can be identified in the case law.

First, as it was stated in the 2003 Communication,[97] the Court considers that a Member State must *explicitly* opt for one of the extension mechanisms.[98] Lacking

93 If the content of collective agreement goes above or beyond what is admissible under the PWD, then the action entails a restriction to the freedom to provide services.

94 The protection of workers against social dumping is ensured by the respect of the PWD. Setting wages or working conditions above the levels of the said Directive cannot be justified in light of such an objective.

95 *Rüffert*, para. 24.

96 Article 3(8): a) "collective agreements or arbitration awards which must be observed by all undertakings in the geographical area and in the profession or industry concerned"; b) "collective agreements or arbitration awards which are generally applicable to all similar undertakings in the geographical area and in the profession or industry concerned"; c) "collective agreements which have been concluded by the most representative employers' and labour organizations at national level and which are applied throughout national territory".

97 The implementation of Directive 96/71/EC in the Member States, Brussels, 25 July 2003 COM(2003) 458 final, p. 12. See *supra*, p. 181.

98 *Laval*, para. 66–67.

such an explicit mention, the Member State simply waivers the possibility to apply collective agreements to posted workers.[99]

Second, if a given Member State is equipped with a legal instrument to declare collective agreements to be of "universal application",[100] the same country cannot avail itself of one of the other options provided by Article 3(8).[101] It must be highlighted that the Court appears particularly formalistic in this requirement. If such a system of extension does exist, so to say, in the black letter law, the other options are closed. This regardless the effective use the national system in question actually does of such an instrument. This may be of particular interest for those Member States characterised by a "deviation" of industrial relations practices from formal legal instruments. I will come back to this in the next Section.

Third, social clauses in public procurement contracts can only impose the application of collective agreements which also cover the private sector[102] pursuing one of the available options under Article 3(8). It is important to remind that this applies regardless of the fact that national undertakings wanting to respond to the public offer would have to respect the collective agreement imposed by such a social clause.[103] On the other hand, a collective agreement generally applicable at regional level should be able to pass this test, as long as the other conditions are met.

The fourth and last point is the more difficult to assess, stemming also from a case preceding the coming into force of the PWD. At the same time it potentially has far reaching consequences. Hence, one should proceed with caution. As it was described in Chapter 5[104] in the *Portugaia Costruções* case the Court had to deal with a question concerning the possibility to derogate *in pejus* from generally applicable collective agreements. The Court concluded that the possibility for domestic employers to derogate from the generally applicable minimum wage "constitutes an unjustified restriction on the freedom to provide services",[105] if the same possibility is not open to posting employers. With all due caution, this

99 From the 2003 Communication, p. 12: "since no Member State's transposing legislation makes any mention of the options offered by the second subparagraph of Article 3(8), the Commission concludes that those Member States which do not have collective agreements declared to be universally applicable within the meaning of the first subparagraph of Article 3(8) of the Directive do not apply the terms and conditions of employment laid down in collective agreements to workers posted on their territory. In these countries, therefore, only the terms and conditions of employment laid down in legislative provisions apply to workers posted on their territory".

100 *I.e.*, falling in the baseline scenario of Article 3(8).

101 *Rüffert*, para. 27: "[...] regarding the second subparagraph of Article 3(8) of Directive 96/71, it is clear from the actual wording of that provision that it is applicable *only* where there is no system for declaring collective agreements to be of universal application [...]" (emphasis added).

102 *Rüffert*, para. 28–29.

103 As rightly pointed out by Bruun, Jacobs and Schmidt, "ILO Convention No. 94 in the Aftermath of the Ruffert Case", p. 478.

104 See *supra*, p. 175.

105 *Portugaia Costruções*, para. 35.

stance seems likely, also in light of the more recent case law, to have an impact on PWD-related cases. At the same time, when facing a similar question the Court is likely to stick to its formalistic approach, so as to examine the *legal* possibility of *in pejus* bargaining without paying attention at the actual relevance of these derogations in statistical terms.[106]

Thus, if such an approach has an impact, this can be envisaged in three different, and potentially concurring, ways. First, the Court could simply consider that a national or sectoral collective agreement allowing for derogations at lower level cannot be extended to posted workers, not meeting the conditions of the three categories provided by the Directive. That is to say, those agreement would not be considered as universally/generally applicable. Second, the possibility of derogation, in particular in the field of minimum wages, could have an impact on the "minimum" character of the wages and working conditions set by the agreement. Following the reasoning of *Rüffert*, had it *really* been a minimum, it would not have allowed for derogations.[107] Both the first and this second possible impact obviously would reverberate on accepted justifications of restrictions to the freedom to provide services, following the multifaceted role of the PWD in this regard. The third possibility is admittedly the less likely to materialise. The formulation of the decision in *Portugaia* provides scope for another possibility. That is, the obligation for Member States allowing for the derogations here at stake to allow the service provider to negotiate and possibly conclude a collective agreement derogating from superior agreements. There is an obvious (further) bifurcation in this line of reasoning, and a relevant one at that. Would this lower level collective agreement have to be negotiated in the host country or would a home country agreement be considered as sufficient? The answer provided by the Court in relation to the *Lex Britannia* in the *Laval* case seems to suggest the second possibility. As it is well known, the Court considered the *Lex Britannia* as discriminatory, inasmuch as it failed "to take into account [...] collective agreements to which undertakings that post workers to Sweden are already bound in the Member State in which they are established".[108] However, the same *Laval* case also suggests that the third scenario of potential impact of the *Portugaia* line of reasoning is quite unlikely to materialise. What ultimately stems from *Laval* is the preference for a formal scrutiny of the content of collective agreements which has to be extended to posting undertaking, as opposed to an involvement of these undertakings into the national system of industrial relations of the host state on

[106] This was already the approach in *Portugaia*, where the Court ignored the argument put forward by the German government, submitting that the incidence of undertaking-specific agreement was negligible. See Opinion of AG Mischo, para. 72–73.

[107] Cf. *Rüffert*, para. 40. On the point, it is interesting to refer to the comment of Sophie Robin-Olivier, criticising the Court for not distinguishing between "minimum wage" (*salaire minimum*) and "basic income" or "social minimum" (*minimum d'existence*). See Robin-Olivier, "Libre prestation de services, marchés publics et régulation sociale: le droit européen privilégie la concurrence fondée sur le coût du travail", p. 489.

[108] *Laval*, para. 116.

a non-discriminatory basis.[109] In this sense the first and second possibility seem more in line with the recent case law on posting: either a collective agreement allowing *in pejus* derogations would be considered as not universally/generally applicable, or as not setting a "real" minimum floor for wages and working conditions.

7.3 CHANGE OR DESIST?

Delivering his Opinion in the Laval case, AG Mengozzi suggested caution to the CJEU when dealing with the industrial relations system of a Member State. Indeed, he considered that Community law, *in casu* embodied by its sharpest edge, the fundamental freedoms, should refrain from encroaching upon a specific national approach at regulating industrial relations.[110] As it should be abundantly clear by now, the Court of Justice did not heed the call.

The PWD is theoretically neutral as to the material content of rules for minimum protection.[111] Ironically, this is repeatedly acknowledged by the Court of Justice along the case law analysed here.[112] The problem, taking into account the "real" Directive just summarised, is what this *neutrality* actually means after the interpretation of the CJEU. Hence, the Directive remains neutral if with this one defines the absence of legal harmonisation, whether of industrial relations or of their outcomes. However, the situation appears quite different if from the formal plan one turns to look at the actual likelihood of the different industrial relations systems to "fit" into the conditions set up by the Court. From this second point of view, the Directive appears far from neutral, presenting a clear bias in favour of centralised systems of collective bargaining featuring quasi-legislative extended collective agreements.[113] On the other hand de-centralised and/or autonomous systems are untouched by the Directive itself. That is, *as long as* they refrain in their turn from "touching" posted workers.

In the second context the PWD thus comes to serve exclusively its "internal market" rationale, at the expense of the protection of posted workers.[114] In the

109 Incidentally, such was the solution proposed in *Laval* by AG Mengozzi, who argued in favour of the substantial equivalence of the Swedish system in terms of application of the PWD, since the industrial relations practices faced by Laval and Baltic where essentially the same that a Swedish undertaking would face in a similar situation. See Opinion of AG Mengozzi in *Laval*, para. 201–202.

110 Opinion of AG Mengozzi in *Laval*, para. 260: "I do not think that, at its present stage of development, Community law can encroach upon [the Swedish] approach to employment relationships through the application of one of the fundamental freedoms of movement provided for in the Treaty".

111 Van Hoek and Houwerzijl, "Comparative Study on the Legal Aspects of the Posting of Workers in the Framework of the Provision of Services in the European Union", p. 13.

112 E.g. *Laval*, para. 60.

113 Ibid., p. 24.

114 Davies, "Case C-346/06, Ruffert v. Land Niedersachsen [2008] IRLR 467 (ECJ)", p. 294.

Rüffert case posted workers were being paid some 46%[115] of the wage which would have been applied to a non-posted worker performing the same job in the same geographical area. In fact, this percentage could have been lower,[116] since the Court never considered the case from this perspective. Or, more precisely, when it did consider the legitimate interest of "protecting workers",[117] it did so to *deny* the extension of the wage at stake, thus effectively depriving posted workers of minimum protection.

Living in the "real PWD" world, it is almost ironic to look back to a pair of recitals accompanying the Directive itself. First and foremost, Recital 12,[118] quoting verbatim the well known *obiter dictum* of the *Rush* case. Indeed, the reports on the possibility for Member States of extending "legislation or collective agreements [...] to any person who is employed even temporarily on their territory" appear now to have been...greatly exaggerated. The perfect partner to compose a couple which has not aged well is Recital 22.[119] Evidently, the duel against this fruit of the Age of Innocence has been decided by first blood in the *Laval* case. Under the rule of the "real PWD" it is hard to deny that the same Directive (teamed with Treaty provision on the freedom to provide services) can indeed cause prejudice to the law concerning collective action. The follow-up of the *Laval* decision in the Swedish context provides the perfect example as to the obsolescence of these Recitals. It also shows what is left of the supposed *neutrality* of the PWD with respect of national systems.

7.3.1 POSTED WORKERS IN THE BUBBLE?

As it was highlighted before,[120] the amendments constituting the so-called *Lex Laval* were to provide an answer to the questions raised by the Laval decision.

Leaving aside for a moment the intricate situation created by the concentric clash of legal order regarding the issue here at stake[121] the example of the *Lex Laval* needs to be briefly analysed in the perspective of the "real PWD" highlighted before. As I just stressed, with these amendments the Swedish government decided to "internalise" the restrictions created by the *Laval* decision. Hence,

115 *Rüffert*, para. 11.

116 For example, had the posting undertaking been established in a different Member State, as Romania or Bulgaria, the wage differential would have been greater.

117 *Rüffert*, para. 38.

118 "Whereas Community law does not preclude Member States from applying their legislation, or collective agreements entered into by employers and labour, to any person who is employed, even temporarily, within their territory, although his employer is established in another Member State; whereas Community law does not forbid Member States to guarantee the observance of those rules by the appropriate means".

119 "Whereas this Directive is without prejudice to the law of the Member States concerning collective action to defend the interests of trades and professions".

120 See in Chapter 6, *supra*, p. 258.

121 See *supra*, pp. 255 ff.

the law regarding collective action applied to posting undertakings becomes plain and simply *different* than the one applied through the rest of the Swedish territory. So much for the absence of prejudice of Recital 22. Also, the possibility to apply "collective agreements" (in Recital 12 without further specification) to posted workers is severely hampered. The reference to "minimum rate of pay or other minimum conditions" shows the non-neutral aspect of the application of the PWD. Indeed, the very wage structure of Swedish agreements makes it so that a reference to minimum wages implicitly entails a lower treatment for posted workers in respect of workers performing the same job and having similar work experience and/or qualifications.[122] The recent study on the legal aspects of posting of workers affirmed that limiting the applicable minimum wage to the "lowest level of pay in every national labour law system [...] would surely go too far since it would rob the Directive of much of its effectiveness with regard to offering adequate protection to workers as well as creating a level playing field for competition".[123] Indeed, such a situation resembles closely (though not perfectly) the one put in place in order to adapt the Swedish system to the *Laval* decision.

7.3.2 IMPACTS

The Swedish example shows the distance with the call of Scharpf to refuse to comply with the rulings of the CJEU in *Viking* and *Laval* in order to "force" a political solution to the un-balance created by those decisions.[124] With the right setting in terms of actors' preferences, the way opened by the honed blade of negative integration may be used by national actors to tilt the balance of power to their advantage. The approach of the Court of Justice, favouring *state* intervention over the practices of industrial relations makes this even more true. The perfect example comes from the interpretation of Article 3(8) of the PWD. Following the reasoning of the CJEU, in order to make use of one of the "alternative" options for extending collective agreements a Member State is required to *explicitly* opt for one of the alternative methods.[125] This seems to presuppose a legislative intervention.[126] Indeed, the Commission had already clarified this approach in its 2003 Communication on the implementation of the PWD.[127] Hence, the simple

[122] See further ECSR, Decision on Admissibility and the Merits, 3 July 2013, *Swedish Trade Union Confederation (LO) and Swedish Confederation of Professional Employees (TCO) v. Sweden*, Complaint No. 85/2012 para. 82.

[123] Van Hoek and Houwerzijl, "Comparative Study on the Legal Aspects of the Posting of Workers in the Framework of the Provision of Services in the European Union", p. 63.

[124] F.W. Scharpf, "The Only Solution Is to Refuse to Comply with ECJ Rulings", *Social Europe Journal* 4, no. 1 (2008): 16–21.

[125] *Laval*, para. 66.

[126] Van Hoek and Houwerzijl, "Comparative Study on the Legal Aspects of the Posting of Workers in the Framework of the Provision of Services in the European Union", p. 25.

[127] COM(2003) 458 final, "Since no Member State's transposing legislation makes any mention of the options offered by the second subparagraph of Article 3(8), the Commission concludes

inaction of a government pursuing a self-conscious agenda of undermining trade unions' role in regulating the labour market would effectively provide an insurmountable obstacle for the exercise of collective social rights.

All in all, the negative integration potential of the posting phenomenon remains dependant from the system of industrial relations of the receiving country. Evidently, such a potential does unfold to the greater extent in respect of those system characterised by an autonomous de-centralised system of collective bargaining. As for the title of the present Section, these systems must either change or desist. This means either changing the way in which (minimum) wages and working conditions are set, or refrain from extending a part of these conditions to posted workers. As explained before, the *Lex Laval* perfectly represents this second possibility. Such a choice, as well as inaction, however entails a different kind of pressure for the industrial relations system. Once it is accepted that undertakings employing posted workers enjoy a competitive advantage with respect to their less mobile colleagues,[128] in the form of lower wages and/or worse working conditions, undertakings employing the latter group of workers face a "reverse discrimination".[129] This situation may remain negligible in quantitative terms. On the other hand it *could* entail (particularly in certain sectors) a pressure for lower national standards and/or for escaping the national system of industrial relations and collective bargaining. In this sense the legal framework shaped by the CJEU for posting of workers may prove itself as a tool to foster changes in industrial relations systems. After "change or desist", the alternative would sound like "centralise or disintegrate". It should also be noted that a similar, though less apparent, pressure might extend to Member States characterised by a more "centralised" system of industrial relations. This second possibility is related to the "structure" of minimum wages in the various national systems. The tension has been highlighted in the study on the legal framework for posting of workers.[130] In very brief, different systems provide for different "levels" of minimum wages,

that those Member States which do not have collective agreements declared to be universally applicable within the meaning of the first subparagraph of Article 3(8) of the Directive do not apply the terms and conditions of employment laid down in collective agreements to workers posted on their territory. In these countries, therefore, only the terms and conditions of employment laid down in legislative provisions apply to workers posted on their territory". However, the Commission did never initiate an infringement procedure for the failure of a Member State to provide adequate protection to posted workers, though the wording of the PWD *requires* Member States to guarantee (for example) the application of minimum wages ("Member States shall ensure").

128 See IDEA Consult, and ECORYS Netherlands, *Study on the Economic and Social Effects Associated with the Phenomenon of Posting of Workers in the EU Final Report*, pp. 8, 135, 160. Though the study is not conclusive, it clearly states, at page 135, that "companies in receiving countries are mainly driven by the lower costs of using foreign-service providers and the subsequent effect this has on their competitiveness [...]".

129 Lo Faro, "Toward a de-Fundamentalisation of Collective Labour Rights in European Social Law?", p. 206.

130 Van Hoek and Houwerzijl, "Comparative Study on the Legal Aspects of the Posting of Workers in the Framework of the Provision of Services in the European Union", pp. 62–63.

depending on seniority and qualifications. It remains to be seen whether the Court of Justice would accept the extension of the entire "pyramid" to posted workers, or if it would condemn the extension of whatever wage surpassing the lowest level set by the applicable law or collective agreement. The said study appears sceptic as to this possibility, though a more pessimistic attitude appears fuelled by the *Laval* judgement.[131] One might add even more fuel to pessimism by looking to the decision in the *Rüffert* and *Commission v Luxembourg* cases. In the former, the Court considered the wage imposed by the *Land* for public contracts as falling outside the legitimate interest of "protection of workers" since it went beyond the national minimum wage and its applications was *mandatory* only for public works.[132] Such a stance may suggest a preference of the CJEU for the lowest minimum wage as the only *necessary* measure for ensuring the protection of (posted) workers. Second, in the case against Luxembourg, the Court of Justice found the automatic adjustment to the cost of living of wages "other than the minimum wage" as breaching the PWD.[133] Evidently, both decisions are not conclusive, as an analogy on this basis would amount at stretching too much the CJEU wording. Still, the possibility for a decision finding the application of a multi-layered wage structure to a posting undertaking as going beyond the application of "minimum wages" cannot be ruled out. In the end, also the last paragraph of Article 3(1),[134] leaving the definition of the concept of "minimum rates of pay" to national law and practice, may be destined to obsolescence.

Law in the Books v. Law in Action

Another tension highlighted by the case law of the Court of Justice has to be mentioned here. This tension could in fact provide another possibility for negative integration to travel on the wings of posting of workers. The tension I am referring to comes down to the distance between the so-called "law in the books" and the "law in action". This situation is highlighted more clearly by the *Rüffert* case. In that occasion the Court considered that a Member State can make use of the possibility offered by Article 3(8) PWD, third and fourth subparagraphs,[135] "*only* where there is *no* system for declaring collective agreements to be of universal

131 Ibid., p. 63.

132 *Rüffert*, para. 40: "The case file submitted to the Court contains no evidence to support the conclusion that the protection resulting from such a rate of pay – which, moreover, as the national court also notes, exceeds the minimum rate of pay applicable pursuant to the AEntG – is necessary for a construction sector worker *only when he is employed in the context of a public works contract but not when he is employed in the context of a private contract*" (emphasis added).

133 *Commission v Luxembourg*, para. 47.

134 "For the purposes of this Directive, the concept of minimum rates of pay referred to in paragraph 1 (c) is defined by the national law and/or practice of the Member State to whose territory the worker is posted".

135 *I.e.*, the possibility to rely on generally applicable collective agreements or on agreements concluded by the most representative trade unions and employers' organisations.

application".[136] The Court decided not to explore the practical situation, relying of a formalistic assessment of the legislation. I already pointed out[137] how this emerges as a coherent approach by the Court of Justice in dealing with question relating to industrial relations. The best examples are those offered by the *Portugaia Costruções* case, where the negligible impact of *in pejus* bargaining was ignored, and by the *Laval* case, where the Court disregarded the widespread application of collective agreements in the Swedish system.[138]

This approach may be problematic for those Member States characterised by a *de facto* situation deviating from established legal instruments, in particular as regards the extension of collective agreement. The Italian situation is probably the most spectacular example of this possibility. The Italian Constitution indicates a method to extend collective agreements as to make them "universally applicable" (*erga omnes*).[139] However, due to a number of factors which go beyond the scope of this work,[140] this method was *never* implemented in the Italian legal order. Still, to a formalistic analysis, the legal possibility for universal application of collective agreements does indeed exist. It should be noted that Italy extends to posted workers sectoral collective agreements signed by most representative trade unions and employers' organisations, thus making use of the possibility offered by the fourth subparagraph of Article 3(8) PWD.[141] As noted by Orlandini,[142] the Italian government in the past gave the impression to interpret the extension of collective agreements to posted workers as limited to those matters covered by Article 3(1). Still, on the basis of *Rüffert* it remains unclear whether reference to minimum conditions established by collective agreements covered by the fourth subparagraph of Article 3(8) would at all be considered as acceptable when an instrument to extend collective agreements "universally" is present in the legal system. Thus, this "discrepancy" between law in the books and law in action is

---

136 *Rüffert*, para. 27, emphasis added. Van Peijpe criticises the interpretation of the German situation delivered by the Court, since "universally applicable" agreements under German law could still be derogated by agreements at lower level. See Van Peijpe, "Collective Labour Law After Viking, Laval, Rüffert, and Commission v. Luxembourg", pp. 98–99.

137 See *supra*, p. 220.

138 Though it was urged to do the contrary by the Opinion of AG Mengozzi.

139 Article 39 of the Italian Constitution, fourth paragraph: "I sindacati registrati hanno personalità giuridica. Possono, rappresentati unitariamente in proporzione dei loro iscritti, stipulare contratti collettivi di lavoro con efficacia obbligatoria per tutti gli appartenenti alle categorie alle quali il contratto si riferisce".

140 See G. Pera, *Problemi Costituzionali del Diritto Sindacale Italiano* (Milano: Feltrinelli, 1960), pp. 19–141; U. Romagnoli and T. Treu, *I Sindacati in Italia dal '45 a Oggi: Storia di una Strategia* (Bologna: Il Mulino, 1977), pp. 18–43.

141 Article 3 of d.lgs 72/2000, transposing the PWD in the Italian system. See further G. Orlandini, "Il rapporto di lavoro con elementi di internazionalità", *WP C.S.D.L.E. Massimo D'Antona.IT*, no. 137 (2012): 1–72, pp. 51 and ff.

142 G. Orlandini, "Main Features Relating with Posted Workers in Italy", in *Evaluating Application of the Directive on the Posting of Workers Within the Framework of the Provision of Services*, vol. 3, March, 2010, 1–13, available at www.dialogue-social.fr/files_upload/documentation/201101141445190.1_orlandini-en.pdf, last accessed 30 December 2013.

another possibility for a system to be exposed to the negative integration potential of posting of workers.

Escape trajectory?

Along this Chapter, multiple possibilities for the posting phenomenon to deliver negative integration upon a national system of industrial relations have been highlighted. These scenarios give back the picture of a preference of the Court of Justice for centralised systems characterised by institutionalised methods for extending collective agreements through public intervention, either at nationwide or sectoral level. Moreover, these systems should also make possible for the posting undertaking to know in advance which (minimum) wages and working conditions it will have to apply to its posted workers (transparency). Third, the possibility to derogate from minimum standards extended to posted workers through collective agreements at company level entails the risk of seeing the "minimum" nature of those standards denied, or their application considered as discriminatory. Limiting the focus to minimum wages, it appears that the greater the degree of de-centralisation of a system of industrial relations the harder it will be to extend *whatever* minimum wage to posting employers.

In the previous Chapter I have showed how the approach of the CJEU to the conflict between fundamental social rights and fundamental freedoms is increasingly out of touch with the evolution of regional and international protection of the former. It appears now that the interpretation of the PWD is in its turn out of touch with the evolutionary trends of industrial relations in Europe. This is increasingly true in the present context. I will come back to this in the next Chapter, when the interpretation of the CJEU will be analysed on the background of these future perspectives, and of the self-conscious role that EU institutions are playing in this field.

Still, without the need to look at the future, such a trend was identified well before the end of the Age of Innocence and the renewed interest for the posting phenomenon. It has been highlighted, as back as 1998, that the creation of the European Monetary Union (which has recently welcomed its 18th member), entails a pressure towards so-called Americanisation of the labour market of Member States.[143] In particular an "Americanised" labour market is defined as one where "collective bargaining would have a diminished role in wage setting", bringing about a highly decentralised wage setting.[144] Writing in 2004 Sisson and Marginsson also refer to this tendency towards decentralisation through EU

143 A. Martin, "EMU and Wage Bargaining: the Americanization of the European Labour Market?", *European Trade Union Institute Discussion and Working Papers DWP* 1, no. 3 (1998): 1–41.

144 Ibid., p. 1.

Member States.[145] They concluded that sectoral (multi-employer) bargaining was not going to disappear completely, mutating instead in a "framework" allowing for deviations at company level,[146] following what Traxler defined as organised decentralisation.[147] However, in light of the analysis carried out so far, it seems clear that the "organised" or "dis-organised" nature of decentralisation is largely irrelevant as to the scrutiny of the CJEU of a national system of industrial relations.

Hence, more and more national systems are bound to (at least potentially) feel the bite of negative integration on the living flesh of their systems of industrial relations. What it is troubling is that, taking into account the said evolution of collective bargaining, as time goes by the objective of protecting posted workers will be largely (or completely) sacrificed to the promotion of the internal market of services. Moreover, as collective bargaining[148] is the "measure of all things"[149] in the reasoning of the Court of Justice, every increase in decentralisation will further restrict the legitimate recourse to collective action in the field of posting of workers. Now, one could be tempted to ignore the "trend" toward decentralisation, since it simply emerges from the economic reality.[150] However, this approach is becoming less and less tenable, if it ever was, as EU institutions are increasingly and self-consciously promoting (or imposing) decentralisation of collective bargaining systems in the EU Member States. The next Chapter, turning to the present and future context of the posting phenomenon, will analyse this *schizophrenic* situation.

---

145 Marginson and Sisson, *European Integration and Industrial Relations: Multi-Level Governance in the Making*, pp. 143 ff.

146 Ibid., pp. 170.174.

147 F. Traxler, "Farewell to Labour Market Associations? Organised Versus Disorganised Decentralization as a Map for Industrial Relations", in *Organised Industrial Relations in Europe: What Future?*, ed. F. Traxler and C. Crouch (Avebury: Aldershot, 1995).

148 More precisely, as the demands put forward in the form of (proposed) collective agreements.

149 See *supra*, p. 296.

150 Marginson, and Sisson, *European Integration and Industrial Relations: Multi-Level Governance in the Making*, pp. 149 ff.

CHAPTER 8

THE FUTURE IN CONTEXT

De-centralisation during the Great Recession and Three Future Scenarios

In the previous Chapters I have highlighted the obstacles to the exercise of collective social rights which have been created by the EU legal framework for posting of workers. Sparing a moment for a quick glance backwards, the story thus far reads as follows. The PWD saw the light after a protracted negotiation, which culminated in a compromise featuring a number of "black boxes".[1] The Court of Justice consistently analysed the posting phenomenon as an *accessorium* of the freedom to provide services continued with the same approach, confirmed by the choice of legal basis for the PWD, when confronted with the new Directive.[2] In the rapidly changing context following the 2004 enlargement,[3] the Court put into motion the second "high tide"[4] with the decisions delivered in 2007–2008. These decisions tackled the said "black boxes" and, in light of the legal basis, proceeded to interpret the PWD as an instrument to foster the free provision of services across the EU. The exercise of (fundamental) collective social rights, in the context of posting, was analysed as a simple restriction to the freedom to provide services.[5] The Court considered the PWD as the yardstick by which the exercise of those rights had to be measured,[6] so that every practice of industrial relations aimed at extending to posted workers whatever wage or working conditions going beyond or above the ones exhaustively identified by the Directive would be deemed unlawful. As it was highlighted in the previous Chapter, this is particularly problematic for those countries not fitting into the model(s) shaped

1 Chapter 4.

2 Chapter 5.

3 And also, in the changing composition of the CJEU itself. See Kilpatrick, "The ECJ and Labour Law: A 2008 Retrospective", p. 185; R. Hyman, "Trade Unions, Lisbon and Europe 2020: from Dream to Nightmare", *LEQS Paper*, no. 45 (2011), p. 18; A. Dufresne and J.-M. Pernot, "Les syndicats européens à l'épreuve de la nouvelle gouvernance économique", *Chronique Internationale de L'IRES* 143–144 (2013): 3–29, p. 6.

4 The first being the one which brought to the adoption of the PWD.

5 Chapter 6.

6 Chapter 7.

by the text of the PWD and in the interpretation provided by the CJEU. That is to say, countries characterised by de-centralised systems of collective bargaining and by multi-layered structures of minimum wages. These countries would then face a difficult choice: either re-structure their system of industrial relations, towards a more centralised one featuring a higher degree of public intervention, or accept the existence of pockets of economic activity excluded *de jure* from the exercise of collective social rights of national actors.

The purpose of this Chapter is twofold. The first objective is to put this situation in context. On the one hand, to better understand the increasing scope of negative integration in connection with the posting phenomenon. On the other hand, to consider the true extent of the said alternative "change or desist". The second objective is an attempt to look to the future evolution of the issue at stake. This will be done by identifying three possible scenarios: a) a baseline scenario, which considers the *legal* framework (both legislative and judge-made) as static; b) an (admittedly unlikely) scenario of legislative intervention; c) a judge-centred scenario which explores the possibilities for a *revirement* of the case law analysed thus far.

Evidently, the concept of "context" must be delimited to be of any use in our analysis. The most obvious reference would be to the dire economic situation of the EU. However, this will only briefly be considered in its broader implications. Instead, it is to a by-product of the Great Recession that the attention will be devoted. Hence, I will focus on the impact on systems of collective bargaining of two intertwined instruments, both involving (completely or prevalently) an important role for EU institutions. First, the reforms imposed to countries which had recourse to international helping packages.[7] Second, the reforms fostered by Country Specific Recommendations formulated by the Commission, and adopted by the Council in the framework of the European Semester.[8] Finally, while analysing the context I will also turn briefly to the proposed Enforcement Directive. However, this proposal will be taken into account more as a reflection of the previous analysis, than as an element effectively shaping the context.

8.1 THE CONTEXT, SELECTED CHAPTERS

Giving a full account of the impact of the Great Recession upon industrial relations in the EU would go "above and beyond" the scope of the present research.

---

7 Greece, Ireland, Portugal, but also Romania, Latvia and Hungary. See ibid., pp. 9–10.

8 A. Jolivet, F. Lerais and C. Sauviat, "La dimension sociale aux prises avec la nouvelle gouvernance économique européenne", *Chronique Internationale de L'IRES* 143–144 (2013): 30–52; T. Schulten and T. Müller, "A New European Interventionism? The Impact of the New European Economic Governance on Wages and Collective Bargaining", in *Social Developments in the EU 2012*, ed. D. Natali and B. Vanhercke (Brussels: ETUI; OSE Publications, 2013), pp. 181–214.

However, one cannot ignore how the crisis shaped the whole European political debate. Though the second "high tide" of posting of workers arose between the end of 2007 and spring 2008, it should be evident that the subsequent discussions and negotiations were heavily influenced by the long shadow of the crisis, which finds it conventional start with the sudden collapse of Lehman Brothers.[9] Hence, the EU institutions' *understanding* of the crisis had a major impact on the attempts to provide an answer to the decisions delivered by the CJEU. What is more, the analysis of such an understanding shows a great deal of coherence between the solutions proposed to overcome the Great Recession and the (non) handling of the posting of workers issue. On the other hand, one cannot deny the fact that the much more devastating effects of the crisis, and of the supposed solutions[10] soon wiped the comparatively minor issue of posting of workers out of the political table. Still, the topic managed to make a comeback with the recent debate around the Enforcement Directive, though this too can be linked with the effects of the *political* crisis of the EU, as I will argue in the Section devoted to this proposal.

As I just stressed, a crisis which for Europe is worse than the one of 1929,[11] clearly permeates whatever discourse about labour regulations and/or industrial relations. Hence, a brief analysis is in order. The Great Recession started, both in the reality and in the public discourse, as a financial crisis.[12] This understanding did not last for long. Landing on the European side of the Atlantic, the crisis was quickly hijacked. The financial flows, going from EU so-called "core" countries towards the "periphery",[13] had in the meantime experienced a sudden stop, so that there were growing concerns as to the ability of the "periphery" to refinance its public debts. The confidence inspired by the adoption of the Euro, together with the rigidities entailed by a currency union, thus showed their double-edged nature.[14] No matter that much of the public debt was in fact the result of bank bailouts (especially in Spain and Ireland[15]), that those growing private financial inflows in

---

9 The financial services firm filed for bankruptcy on 15 September 2008.

10 *I.e.* the approach which goes under the name of "austerity".

11 P. Krugman, "Europe's Second Depression", The Coscience of a Liberal (Blog), 29 March 2013, http://krugman.blogs.nytimes.com/2013/03/29/europes-second-depression/, last accessed 10 January 2014.

12 C. Degryse, "The New European Economic Governance", *ETUI Working Paper* 14 (2012): 1–86, p. 79.

13 One of the many expressions indicating the group of countries composed by Greece, Ireland, Portugal, Spain and Italy (as the order suggest, GIPSI being another possibility).

14 P. Krugman, *End This Depression Now!* (New York: W.W. Norton & Company, 2013), p. 160: "What actually happened, however, was the mother of all asymmetric shocks. And it was the creation of the euro itself that caused it".

15 See for example Y. Varoufakis, *The Global Minotaur: America, Europe and the Future of the Global Economy (Economic Controversies)* (London: Zed Books, 2013), p. 154; C. Degryse and P. Pochet, "Worrying Trends in the New European Governance", in *Social Developments in the European Union 2011*, ed. D. Natali and B. Vanhercke (Brussels: ETUI; OSE Publications, 2011), 81–108, pp. 81 and 89; Degryse, "The New European Economic Governance", p. 70: "before the crisis Ireland had had a budget surplus since 1997. The only Irish deficit year during this period was 2002, with a very modest -0.4 per cent of GDP. But in 2010 it reached -32.4 per cent of GDP because of the bailout of the financial sector".

the periphery had provided the needed demand to absorb the external surpluses of the so-called "core" countries,[16] and that many of the GIPSI countries had in fact entered the Great Recession with low deficits and comparatively low level of public debts.[17] What is more, ECB Vice-president Vitor Constancio affirmed clearly that the European crisis had *not* originated from public debts or fiscal profligacy in the GIPSI countries.[18] Instead, he pointed out that the true cause should be found in *private* debt and bank behaviour, with huge flows of credits going from the "core" to the "periphery" during the first Euro decade, coupled with the sudden stop of those flows caused by the international financial crisis originated in the

---

16 Varoufakis, *The Global Minotaur: America, Europe and the Future of the Global Economy (Economic Controversies)*, pp. 202–206; P. de Grauwe, "Design Failure in the Eurozone – Can They Be Fixed?", *European Economy. Economic Papers* 491 (2013), p. 7: "It is important to stress here that the booms in the South allowed the Northern European countries to accumulate large current account surpluses. These were financed by credit that the Northern European countries granted to the South. Thus in a way it can be said that Northern Europe behaved like the automobile salesman who sells cars to his customers by providing them with cheap credit. It is important to recognize this because in the North of Europe the irresponsibility of Southern countries to take on too much debt is often stressed. The truth is that for every foolish debtor there must be a foolish creditor".

17 See Krugman, *End This Depression Now*, pp. 165–166; Varoufakis, *The Global Minotaur: America, Europe and the Future of the Global Economy (Economic Controversies)*, p. 167: "While Greece was, indeed, running a large deficit, Ireland was a paragon of fiscal virtue. Spain was even running a surplus when the Crash of 2008 hit, and Portugal was no worse than Germany in its deficit and debt performance", but, continues Varoufakis, " who cares about the truth when lies are so much more fun, not to mention useful to those who are desperate to shift the spotlight from the real locus of the Crisis – the banking sector?".

18 Speech by Vítor Constâncio, Vice-President of the ECB, at the Bank of Greece conference on "The crisis in the euro area", Athens, 23 May 2013, text available at www.ecb.europa.eu/press/key/date/2013/html/sp130523_1.en.html, last accessed 12 January 2014: "Beginning with the first perspective on the causes, the oldest narrative of the crisis, progressively corrected by academics but still popular with some segments of public opinion, goes more or less like this: There was essentially nothing wrong with the initial design of EMU, and the crisis resulted mostly from the fact that several peripheral countries did not respect that design – in particular the fiscal rules of the Stability and Growth Pact – which generated the sovereign debt crisis. This is the 'it was mostly fiscal' narrative, which can be easily connected to two of the others: fiscal indiscipline led to economic overheating, wage and price increases implied loss of competitiveness, and this then led to the balance of payment crises. Although this is an internally coherent narrative, it is not correct, especially as a main driver of the crisis. First, there is no strong correlation between whether a Member State respected or not the Stability and Growth Pact before the crisis, and the yields being demanded by financial markets today. For instance, Germany and France did not respect the Pact in 2003–4; Spain and Ireland respected it more or less fully until 2007. Second, there was no uniform increase in overall government debt during the first years of the common currency in the countries that are now under sovereign stress. In fact, in a number of those it declined, and in some of them it declined substantially. For instance, from 1999–2007, public debt in Spain declined from 62.4% of GDP to 36.3% of GDP. In Ireland, over the same period, public debt fell from 47.0% of GDP to 25.0% of GDP. While at relatively high levels, public debt also went down in Italy (from 113.0% of GDP to 103.3% of GDP) and increased only slightly in Greece".

US.[19] Still, the EU having identified the illness in public expenditure[20] and in the southern laziness,[21] the prescription was internal devaluation[22] under the label of "austerity" policies. Nobel laureate Paul Krugman described these policies as the bleeding inflicted by middle-age "doctors" to their patients, with the implication that, improvements failing to materialise, the patient would have to undergo… more bleeding.[23] However, it is not the aim of this extremely succinct account to provide an evaluation of these policies. At the risk of oversimplifying, austerity generally entailed (and entails) spending cuts and more or less direct interventions on wage-setting mechanism in order to promote/enforce wage moderation (or outright reduction[24]) and competitiveness.[25] For the topic here at stake, it meant an unprecedented role for EU institutions in influencing the legal framework of industrial relations in several Member States,[26] as far reaching reforms of collective bargaining were imposed by Memoranda or suggested by Country Specific Recommendations.

---

19 Ibid.: "[…]I hope I have been clear about what I consider the prime drivers of the European crisis, namely the role of the financial sector and of the international financial crisis. Without the strain on public finances generated by the recession that ensued and by balance sheet losses of European banks, Euro area governments would not have been so vulnerable to stress in sovereign bond markets. In other words, without the banks' behaviour and the financial crisis, the sovereign debt crisis at least would not have been so severe".

20 C. Degryse, M. Jepsen and P. Pochet, "The Euro Crisis and Its Impact on National and European Social Policies", *ETUI Working Paper* 05 (2013), p. 14.

21 Ireland moving somewhat to the south for the occasion.

22 That is, lowering wages and labour costs in order for the "periphery" countries to restore their competitiveness and heal their economic woes by moving into surplus (*i.e.* becoming net exporters of goods and services). On the point see P. Pochet and C. Degryse, "The Programmed Dismantling of the 'European Social Model'", *Intereconomics* 47, no. 4 (2012): 200–217, p. 216; N. Roubini, "Eurozone Crisis: Here Are the Options, Now Choose", EconoMonitor (Blog), 9 November 2011, available at www.economonitor.com/nouriel/2011/11/09/eurozone-crisis-well-at-least-we-have-options/; R. Janssen, "Internal Wage Devaluation – The IMF Admits It Does Not Work", Social Europe (Blog), 16 December 2013, available at www.social-europe.eu/2013/12/internal-wage-devaluation/.

23 P. Krugman, "Revenge of the Optimum Currency Area", *NBER Macroeconomics Annual* 27 (2012): 1–14, available at http://krugman.blogs.nytimes.com/2012/12/11/bleeding-europe: "it really is like medieval medicine, where you bled patients to treat their ailments, and when the bleeding made them sicker, you bled them even more".

24 As for the public sector and general minimum wage in Greece. See C. Karakioulafis, "Grèce: les syndicats dans la ligne de mire de La Troïka", *Chronique Internationale de L'IRES* 143–144 (2013): 121–132.

25 The underlying idea being that GIPSI countries *and Europe as a whole* should move to external surpluses. See for example F. Saraceno, "Incomprenhensible? Really?", Sparse Thoughts of a Gloomy European Economist (Blog), 5 November 2013 available at http://fsaraceno.wordpress.com/2013/11/05/incomprehensible-really/, and F. Saraceno, "Free Riders in Frankfurt", Sparse Thoughts of a Gloomy European Economist (Blog), 28 November 2013, available at http://fsaraceno.wordpress.com/2013/11/28/free-riders-in-frankfurt/.

26 Dufresne and Pernot, "Les syndicats européens à l'épreuve de la nouvelle gouvernance économique", p. 3.

8.1.1 DECENTRALISATION FOR EVERYONE

Along the years of the Great Recession, the EU underwent a number of fundamental changes, trying to cope with the worsening economic conditions of its members. Some of those changes took the form of legislative interventions, Directives, Regulations, changes in the Treaties and a brand new intergovernmental treaty. They became known as the New Economic Governance. Other changes are related to the direct participation of the EU Commission and of the ECB, together with the International Monetary Fund, to the so-called Troika, managing the relationship with those countries which needed to call for financial rescue plans.

After the wake-up call of the first international loan provided to Greece in order to avoid (postpone) the perspective of an outright default (May 2010), EU Member States and institutions sought to improve economic coordination and governance. In September 2010 the Commission proposed five Regulations and a Directive (the so-called "Six Pack"[27]), focused on fiscal and budgetary question,[28] as well as on macroeconomic imbalances.[29] In March 2011 another piece is added to the puzzle, with the adoption of the so-called Euro Plus Pact,[30] signed by 23 Member States,[31] calling in particular for closer monitoring of wage dynamics in order to restore competitiveness[32] and "soft" coordination of tax policies.[33]

---

[27] See Degryse, "The New European Economic Governance", pp. 29–30; A. Verdun, "The Building of Economic Governance in the European Union", *Transfer: European Review of Labour and Research* 19, no. 1 (January 2013): 23–35, p. 31; E. Mazuyer, "Les questions de l'emploi et du travail dans une Union Européenne en crise", in *Quel Droit Social Dans Une Europe En Crise?*, ed. M.-C. Escande Varniol et al. (Brussels: Larcier, 2012), 31–60, pp. 56–58.

[28] Regulation of the European Parliament and the Council amending Regulation (EC) No. 1466/97 on the strengthening of budgetary surveillance and coordination of economic policies; Council Regulation amending Regulation (EC) No. 1467/97 regarding speeding up and clarifying the implementation of the excessive deficit; Regulation of the European Parliament and Council Directive on the effective enforcement of budgetary surveillance in the euro area; Directive of the Council on the requirements for the fiscal framework of the Member States Council Directive 2011/85/EU.

[29] Regulation (EU) No 1176/2011 of the European Parliament and of the Council on the prevention and correction of macroeconomic imbalances; Regulation (EU) No 1174/2011 of the European Parliament and of the Council on enforcement measures to correct excessive macroeconomic imbalances in the euro area. In a way this approach validates the finding that the crisis was also caused by imbalances in trade and credit flows between the "core" and the "periphery".

[30] European Council, Conclusion 24–25 March 2011, EUCO 10/1/11 REV 1, Brussels, 20 April 2011. See further ibid., pp. 55–56.

[31] Hence, all Member States at that time excluding Czech Republic, Hungary, Sweden and the United Kingdom.

[32] Euro Plus Pact, p. 16. See Schulten and Müller, "A New European Interventionism? The Impact of the New European Economic Governance on Wages and Collective Bargaining", p. 184; S. Deakin, "The Lisbon Treaty, the Viking and Laval Judgments and the Financial Crisis: In Search of New Foundations for Europe's 'Social Market Economy'", in *The Lisbon Treaty and Social Europe*, ed. N. Bruun, K. Lörcher, and I. Schömann (Oxford: Hart Publishing, 2012), 19–44, p. 34.

[33] Degryse, "The New European Economic Governance", p. 47.

Furthermore, in December 2011 25 Member States[34] agreed on the Treaty on Stability, Coordination and Governance in the Economic and Monetary Union (TSCG), best known as "Fiscal Compact".[35] Finally, the "Two Pack"[36] was adopted in March 2012. These two Regulations only concern Eurozone Members. They complement the "Six Pack", and implement a closer surveillance on budgetary policies.

Following this panoply of new instruments, the economic governance of the EU looks very different from the one which witnessed the unravelling of the Great Recession. The mere enumeration of the instruments adopted in the period 2010–2013 makes it impossible to give full account of the measures introduced.[37] Table 8.1, quoting (and translating) Jolivet and Sauviat,[38] provides a summary of these measures.

Table 8.1 Economic governance in the crisis (Jolivet and Sauviat, 2013)

Year	Instrument	Countries	Criteria and sanctions
2011	"Six Pack"	EU (27)	- If public debt > 60% of GDP must be reduced by at least 0.5% each year. Otherwise excessive deficit/ imbalances procedure; - Reinforced sanctions in case of excessive deficit; - European semester, early warning mechanism based on macroeconomic scoreboard.
2012	"Fiscal Compact"	EU (25)	- Maximum deficit allowed limited to 0.5%; - "Golden rule" (i.e. balanced budget) must be introduced at constitutional level or equivalent; - Public debt beyond 60% of GDP must be reduced by 1/20th of the outstanding part per year; - In case of violation, quasi-automatic sanctions (unless reversed by qualified majority in the Council).
2013	"Two Pack"	Eurozone	- Strengthened surveillance on public budgets and macroeconomic indicators for countries facing an excessive deficit procedure or under financial help programme.

34 Representing, at the time, all the Member States minus the UK and the Czech Republic.

35 See ibid., pp. 57–59.

36 Regulation (EU) No. 473/2013 of the European Parliament and of the Council of 21 May 2013 on common provisions for monitoring and assessing draft budgetary plans and ensuring the correction of excessive deficit of the Member States in the euro area; Regulation (EU) No. 472/2013 of the European Parliament and of the Council of 21 May 2013 on the strengthening of economic and budgetary surveillance of Member States in the euro area experiencing or threatened with serious difficulties with respect to their financial stability.

37 For a more detailed account, see Degryse, "The New European Economic Governance"; Verdun, "The Building of Economic Governance in the European Union"; Jolivet, Lerais, and Sauviat, "La dimension sociale aux prises avec la nouvelle gouvernance économique européenne".

38 Ibid., p. 33.

Among all these measures, I will focus on a specific instrument, the Country Specific Recommendations (CSRs). These Recommendations are formulated by the Commission and then adopted by the Council in the context of the new European Semester introduced by the Six Pack.[39] CSRs are thus formulated following the submission (in April each year) to the Commission by Member States of budgetary plans and economic reforms.[40] These recommendations may however be backed by the full force of the New Economic Governance in the case of Member States undergoing a procedure for excessive deficit. In such a scenario, the failure to implement the measures "suggested" by the Commission may open the way to sanctions, which can only be *reversed* by a qualified majority vote in the Council.[41] Leaving aside the question of their binding force, those Recommendations will be analysed in their relationship with collective bargaining systems. The objective is to better understand the "vision" of the Commission when it comes to the direction of collective bargaining reforms.

However, CSRs will be postponed to make place to another set of instruments, namely the reforms (related to collective bargaining) imposed by the different Memoranda of Understanding (MoU) signed between the Troika and Member States in need of financial help. These countries are Greece, Ireland, Romania, Portugal, Hungary and Latvia.[42] Indeed, these instruments are, as of today, the *most binding* of all, provided that the difficult situation of these countries makes Memoranda the kind of offer you can't refuse.[43] As two thirds of the Troika are actually EU institutions, the aim of this analysis is similar and concurrent with that highlighted before in respect to CSRs.

Alas, one has to immediately spoil the suspense surrounding to the "vision" of collective bargaining which is made clear by those instruments. The perfect "spoiler" is in fact represented by an analytical[44] document produced by DG ECFIN, the report on "Labour Market Developments in Europe 2012".[45] In listing reforms considered as "employment-friendly", the report devotes a section to collective bargaining.[46] The passage is worth quoting in full:[47]

---

39 See further Mazuyer, "Les questions de l'emploi et du travail dans une Union Européenne en crise", pp. 53–54.

40 S. Clauwaert, "The Country-Specific Recommendations (CSRs) in the Social Field – An Overview and Initial Comparison", *ETUI Background Analysis* 2 (2013), pp. 5–6.

41 Degryse, "The New European Economic Governance", p. 58; Schulten and Müller, "A New European Interventionism? The Impact of the New European Economic Governance on Wages and Collective Bargaining", p. 184.

42 See Dufresne and Pernot, "Les syndicats européens à l'épreuve de la nouvelle gouvernance économique", p. 9.

43 In particular in the situation shaped by the "*nein*-cubed": no bail-out, no interest rate relief, no default. See Varoufakis, *The Global Minotaur: America, Europe and the Future of the Global Economy (Economic Controversies)*, p. 206.

44 As opposed to "policy" related documents, as the CSRs.

45 European Commission, Labour Market Developments in Europe 2012, European Economy, No. 5, pp. 103–104.

46 In the report "wage bargaining framework".

47 The emphasis is added.

> Reforms potentially leading to better employment outcomes (henceforth employment-friendly reforms) [...] are distinguished as follows:
> - "decrease statutory and contractual minimum wages",
> - "*decrease the bargaining coverage*",
> - "decrease (automatic) extension of collective agreements",
> - "reform the bargaining system *in a less centralized way*, for instance by removing or limiting the favourability principle",
> - introduce/extend "the *possibility to derogate from higher level agreements* or to negotiate *firm-level agreements*",
> - promote measures which "result in an overall reduction in the wage setting power of trade unions".

Though data regarding economic and occupational performance of different systems of collective bargaining is far from conclusive,[48] a situation apparently known also to DG ECFIN,[49] the choice seems clear. The Commission, at least in this document, marks a strong preference for de-centralisation, to be achieved with all the means at the disposal of the legislator. Hence, making it more difficult to extend collective agreements, reversing the hierarchy between the levels of collective bargaining (*i.e.* giving precedence to the application of lower level collective agreements), introducing opening clauses in higher level collective agreements and/or the possibility to derogate from those agreements through lower level ones and, finally, achieving a generalised reduction of wage setting power of trade unions. After the previous Chapters, and in particular after the identification of those systems of collective bargaining which appear more prone to experience negative integration in the field of posting of workers, this should ring a bell. However, now that the desired (as it seems, at least by the Commission) destination has been revealed, one has to analyse the steps of the journey.

With a little help from my..."friends"

On May 2010 the Eurozone, the IMF and the ECB agreed on a 110€ billion loan to Greece, which, following the crisis dynamic sketched before, was tethering on the brink of default. During the preceding months Greece had to borrow at increasingly unsustainable levels, after the announcement of the newly elected prime minister that the country's deficit was about the double of what had been declared by the previous government.[50] The loan was accompanied by a number of

48 See for example the account provided by Marginson and Sisson, *European Integration and Industrial Relations: Multi-Level Governance in the Making*, pp. 12–14.

49 See Schulten and Müller, "A New European Interventionism? The Impact of the New European Economic Governance on Wages and Collective Bargaining", pp. 185, referring to European Commission (2011), Assessing the links between wage setting, competitiveness and imbalances, Note for the Economic Policy Committee, Brussels, Document No. Ares (2011)666366, p. 17.

50 12% of GDP instead of 6.5%. See Varoufakis, *The Global Minotaur: America, Europe and the Future of the Global Economy (Economic Controversies)*, pp. 206–207.

measures which the Greek government would have to implement.[51] Thus the new vocabulary of austerity and Memorandum of Understanding entered the public discourse, to be used with a certain frequency in the years of the Great Recession. Indeed, after May 2010, a vast number of EU Member States announced austerity measures and austerity budgets, along the lines of cutting public expenditure, freezing wages in the public sectors, freezing or cutting pensions, increasing taxes and privatisations.[52] In July 2010 Romania received aid from the IMF and hence had to implement a similar policy. A few months later (November 2010), Ireland officially requested financial aid from the EU and the IMF. Once again, the aid, in the form of a 85 billion EUR loan was granted. Needless to say, the measures requested in exchange continued on the same tune. After Ireland, Portugal found itself on the front line of the financial collapse. Though its prime minister had declared in March 2011 that the country would not need financial aid, a rescue plan was eventually requested the following month. The ensuing austerity plan saw the light in May 2011; in the meantime, the situation in Greece had further deteriorated so that a second rescue plan was needed. Also, though Italy and Spain were not interested by a full-scale rescue plan, and by the inseparable MoU, during summer 2011 they had to face increasingly unsustainable interest rates to refinance their public debt. To avoid the collapse of two of the most important economies of the Eurozone, the ECB started buying state bonds on the secondary market. At the same time (August 2011), a "secret" letter was sent to the Italian and Spanish governments, unsurprisingly asking for the implementation of a number of austerity measures. The letter was so secret that one of the most renown of Italian newspapers, *Il Corriere della Sera*, would publish it in September.[53] In November 2011 also Hungary was forced to ask for financial aid from the EU and the IMF, followed, in June 2012, by Cyprus. This ends the count of countries interested by financial aid from the IMF and/or the EU, and thus forced to adopt austerity policies. To these countries, one can add Italy and Spain in relation to the "secret" letter of summer 2011, though the situation is very different from a strictly legal point of view.

As said before, under the label of "austerity measures" one can find a vast array of instruments, supposedly aimed at improving the budgetary situation of a country (by reducing public debt and deficit in relation to GDP) and its competitive position (by lowering labour costs). To assess their effectiveness in

---

51 See Degryse, "The New European Economic Governance", p. 25: "The Commission, the ECB and the IMF demanded that the Greek government impose an unprecedented austerity plan, raise VAT from 21 to 23 per cent, raise taxes on fuel, alcohol and tobacco by 10 per cent, freeze wages and pensions in the public sector and raise the minimum retirement age".

52 Krugman, *End This Depression Now*, Chapter Eleven "Austerians", pp. 174 ff.; Degryse, "The New European Economic Governance", p. 27.

53 *Corriere della Sera*, 29 September 2011, Letter of Mario Draghi and Jean-Claude Trichet to the Italian Government. As Professor Albus Percival Wulfric Brian Dumbledore would put it: the letter is a complete secret, so, naturally the whole country knows.

relation to these objectives is not the aim of the present analysis.[54] Instead it is interesting to analyse those austerity packages in order to identify those measures having an impact on collective bargaining structures.

Now, the point of departure does matter when assessing a *shift* in existing structures. In this sense, Central-Eastern EU countries were already characterised by a more de-centralised system of collective bargaining, which also presented lower level of coverage.[55] Thus, the space for implementing those "employment friendly" policies was more limited. Nevertheless, Romania had been characterised by a more continental model, with mechanism to extend national and sectoral collective agreement, resulting in a high coverage.[56] The Memorandum of Understanding[57] for Romania demanded reform of the "wage setting systems" in order to "better reflect productivity developments in the medium term". This was implemented by dismantling nationwide agreements and by reducing the coverage of sectoral agreements through the introduction of conditions for the extension *erga omnes*.[58] More specifically, a sectoral agreement would now be valid only in respect of employers which are members of a signatory organisation, while the applicability to non-associated employers requires the said agreement to be already applicable to at least the 50% of the workforce in the sector.[59]

Collective bargaining in Greece was directly affected by austerity measures from the very first MoU.[60] In October 2010 a presidential decree introduced a "special company-related agreement", which is in fact a company level agreement. The novelty lies in the fact that those agreements can derogate *in pejus* from

54 However, from the point of observation of spring 2014, those policies appear to have utterly failed. I will leave aside, and that is already revelatory, the historically high unemployment levels in the EU (10.7%), the Eurozone (12%) and in the "rescued" countries in particular (27.8% in Greece; 25.8% in Spain; 18.6% in Hungary; 17.5% in Cyprus; 15.4% in Portugal. Eurostat data, January 2014), and the almost non-existent growth of GDP of the EU, also in comparison with the US (for 2013 respectively 0.1% and 1.6%. Eurostat data, November 2013)). Looking at debt to GDP ratios one can see the counter-productive nature of these policies. Indeed *all* the countries interested by austerity measures have seen their position worsen to this extent. See Grauwe, "Design Failure in the Eurozone – Can They Be Fixed?", p. 2.

55 G. Meardi, "Peripheral Convergence in the Crisis? Southern and Eastern European Labour Markets and Industrial Relations", *Paper for the SASE Annual Meeting*, no. June (2012): 1–13, p. 2.

56 Around 90%. See V. Delteil and M. Bănărescu, "Roumanie – Le modèle social sous la pression des bailleurs de fonds: les syndicats à la recherche de nouvelles 'tutelles'", *Chronique Internationale de L'IRES* 143–144 (2013): 133–151, p. 142.

57 Memorandum of Understanding Between the European Union and Romania, Brussels/Bucharest, 28/29 June 2011, p. 13.

58 Clauwaert and Schomann, "The Crisis and National Labour Law Reforms – a Mapping Exercise", Country Report: Romania (January 2013).

59 *I.e.* that employers members of a signatory organisation employs at least 50% of the workforce in the sector.

60 See S. Deakin and A. Koukiadaki, "The Sovereign Debt Crisis and the Evolution of Labour Law in Europe", in *Resocialising Europe in a Time of Crisis*, ed. Nicola Countouris and Mark Freedland (Cambridge: Cambridge University Press, 2013), 163–188, pp. 180–181.

sectoral ones.[61] However, with another round of austerity measures, the company-related agreement was ditched in favour of a more comprehensive approach. Act No. 4024/2011, adopted in October 2011, established a generalised priority for company level agreements, which would then prevail over a conflicting sectoral agreement, even if the latter is more favourable to the worker. The same Act also suspended the possibility of extending *erga omnes* sectoral agreements, while also introducing the possibility to conclude company agreements with "association of workers" representing at least 3/5 of the workforce.[62] Furthermore, on February 2012 a new austerity budget limited the ultra-activity of expired sectoral agreements to three months. Thus, if a new agreement is not reached before this deadline, wages and working conditions will be no more regulated by the sectoral agreement, falling back to minima established by legislation.[63] After three rounds of Troika-driven austerity and six years of Great Recession, Greece now looks as a completely de-centralised system,[64] with an increasingly evident drop in collective agreements both at sectoral and company level (as shown in Figure 8.1[65]).

61 Clauwaert and Schomann, "The Crisis and National Labour Law Reforms – a Mapping Exercise", Country Report: Greece (January 2013); Karakioulafis, "Grèce: les syndicats dans la ligne de mire de la Troïka", pp. 124–125; A. Koukiadaki and L. Kretsos, "Grèce/Greece", in *Quel Droit Social Dans Une Europe En Crise?*, ed. M.-C. Escande Varniol et al. (Brussels: Larcier, 2012), 189–231, pp. 213–214.

62 Report on the High Level Mission to Greece (Athens, 19–23 September 2011) by the ILO, p. 18. See also Achtsioglou, "Greece 2010–2012: labour in the Maelstrom of Deregulation", p. 126.

63 Clauwaert and Schomann, "The Crisis and National Labour Law Reforms – a Mapping Exercise", p. 4.

64 Though they decreased the bargaining coverage, decreased the extension of collective agreements, reformed the bargaining system in a less centralised way, introduce the possibility to derogate from higher level agreements and to negotiate firm-level agreements, and, most surely, resulted in an overall reduction in the wage setting power of trade unions, the "employment friendly" side of those measures somewhat failed to materialise, unemployment in Greece currently being at 27.4% (Eurostat, September 2013 data).

65 From T. Schulten, "The Impact of the Troika Policy on Wages and Collective Bargaining", *Public Hearing on "Employment and Social Aspects of the Operations and Role of the Troika in Euro Area Programme Countries"*, European Parliament (9 January 2014).

Figure 8.1 Number of collective agreements in Greece during the Great Recession

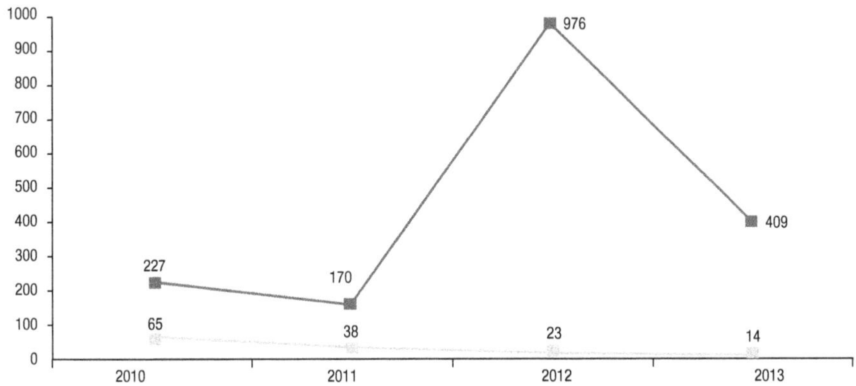

Collective bargaining was also among the topics touched by the MoU between Portugal and the Troika. Democratic Portugal had been characterised by a high level of coverage, in spite to relatively low level of representativeness of workers' and employers' associations, achieved through administrative extension of sectoral agreement.[66] It was by intervening on this very tension that the MoU had it deepest impact. True enough, the Memorandum also asked (and obtained[67]) a reform in the sense of decentralisation of collective bargaining,[68] by allowing workers' councils to negotiate company level agreements. However this was implemented in Portugal by maintaining a trade union monopoly over such a possibility.[69] The intervention regarding the extension mechanism[70] had more far-reaching consequences. Implemented by the Portuguese government by Regulation No. 90/2012, this reform required a coverage of at least 50% of the employees in a specific sector in order for a sectoral agreement to be extended *erga omnes*.[71] In the Portuguese context this made the extension of collective agreements more difficult, thus reducing the incentives to reach an agreement whatsoever.[72] Hence, more than a decentralisation, Portugal is currently

---

66 M. do R. Palma Ramalho, "Portuguese Labour Law and Industrial Relations During the Crisis November 2013 Project", *ILO Working Paper*, no. 54 (2013), p. 3.

67 The changes were introduced by Law No. 23/2012.

68 Memorandum of Understanding Between the European Union and Portugal, Brussels/Lisbon, 17 May 2011, p. 24.

69 *I.e.* workers' councils had to obtain the acquiescence of trade unions in order to negotiate a company level agreement.

70 Ibid.

71 Eurofund, Dramatic decline in collective agreements and worker coverage, available at http://www.eurofound.europa.eu/eiro/2013/02/articles/pt1302029i.htm (last accessed 17 January 2014).

72 A situation only made worse by the dire economic context.

witnessing a disintegration of collective bargaining, with the number of workers covered shrinking dramatically, as shown by Figure 8.2.[73]

Figure 8.2 Number of workers covered by collective agreements in the private sector

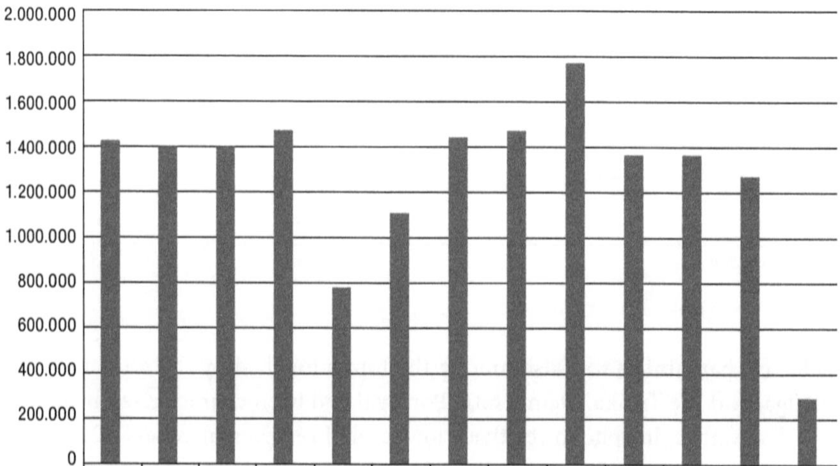

	2000	2001	2002	2003	2004	2005	2006	2007	2008	2009	2010	2011	2012
Serie 1	1.462	1.396	1.385	1.512	758,9	1.125	1.454	1.521	1.894	1.397	1.407	1.236	327,6

Italy and Spain are somewhat mixed cases. They did not sign a MoU, so they do belong to the second group of countries, *i.e.* those affected by Country Specific Recommendations. However, limited to the event of the "secret" letters sent by the ECB during the fiery summer 2011, they have also received their own "Memorandum", in the form of the desiderata of the ECB. The content of the Spanish letter has not been revealed, but it is considered as resembling the Italian one, at least for the part dealing with collective bargaining.[74] The letter addressed to the Italian government requested a reform of the collective bargaining system, "allowing firm-level agreements to tailor wages and working conditions to firms' specific need and increasing their relevance with respect to other layers of negotiations".[75] Thus, both countries will be analysed in both groups. In the next one I will focus on CSRs they respectively received, while here I will present those reform which appears as direct consequences of the ECB intervention.

---

73 From Palma Ramalho, "Portuguese labour law and industrial relations during the crisis November 2013 Project".

74 Meardi, "Peripheral Convergence in the Crisis? Southern and Eastern European Labour Markets and Industrial Relations", p. 3.

75 See P. Loi, "Italie/Italy", in *Quel Droit Social Dans Une Europe En Crise?*, ed. Marie-Cécile Escande Varniol et al. (Brussels: Larcier, 2012), 261–282, p. 267.

In June 2011 the Spanish government approved Royal Decree 7/2011, which gave precedence to company agreement over higher level agreements. This however was limited by the fact that those higher level agreements could pre-empt such a possibility, explicitly excluding areas from *in pejus* derogation from company agreements.[76] However, this was not the end of the story. In February 2012 the new Government of the conservative *Partido Popular* passed a new reform (among many other topics) of collective bargaining.[77] This time, company level agreements were simply to be given precedence over higher level ones.[78] Moreover, the ultra-activity of collective agreements was brought down from being unlimited to only last for two years. After the expiration of such a period, and without a new agreement, the rights established by a collective agreement would lose their binding force. As it should be apparent, once again a system of collective bargaining was being turned upside down, and once again, as shown in Figure 8.3,[79] this entailed a spectacular decrease of the number of workers covered by a collective agreement whatsoever.

Figure 8.3 Workers covered by collective agreements in Spain

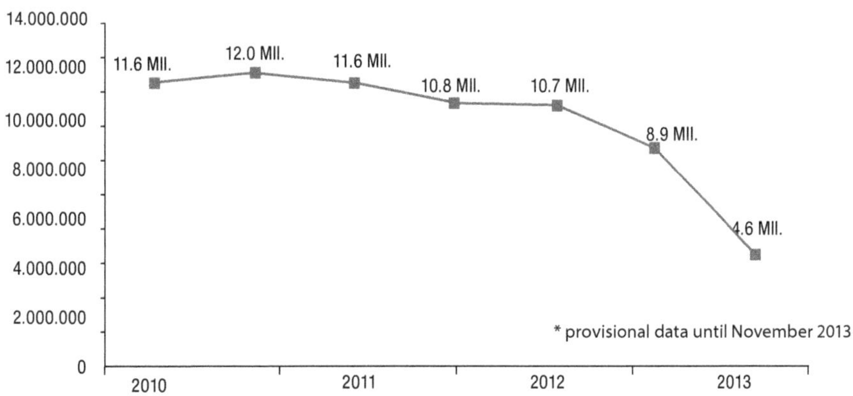

The Italian situation is more confused. That is due to the intertwining of multiple crises: the Great Recession, with the intervention of the ECB, the final months of

76 Clauwaert and Schomann, "The Crisis and National Labour Law Reforms – a Mapping Exercise", Country Report: Spain, p. 4; J.M. Miranda Boto and R. Rodrìguez Contreras, "Espagne/Spain", in *Quel Droit Social Dans Une Europe En Crise?*, ed. Marie-Cécile Escande Varniol et al. (Brussels: Larcier, 2012), 131–155, p. 151.

77 Law 3/2012.

78 Meardi, "Peripheral Convergence in the Crisis? Southern and Eastern European Labour Markets and Industrial Relations", p. 5; Clauwaert and Schömann, "The Crisis and National Labour Law Reforms – a Mapping Exercise", Country Report: Spain, p. 7; Deakin and Koukiadaki, "The Sovereign Debt Crisis and the Evolution of Labour Law in Europe", pp. 182–183.

79 From Schulten, "The Impact of the Troika Policy on Wages and Collective Bargaining".

the Berlusconi IV government, the recent FIAT case which was shaking the very foundations of the Italian system of industrial relations.[80] Thus, in strict correlation with the last of these crises, Italian trade unions and employers' associations had, a few months before the "secret" letter, reached an agreement which went in the direction of organised decentralisation of collective bargaining.[81] However, after the "secret" letter,[82] the Government approved a decree[83] going in the direction of a dis-organised decentralisation. The decree[84] in fact allowed company level agreements to derogate, on a number of important matters,[85] not only from national agreements but also from legislative dispositions. The social actors reacted with a new agreement, on 21 September, re-affirming their intention of allowing derogations only on the basis of the previous agreement.[86] More recently the same workers' and employers' organisations agreed upon a text which consolidate the previous agreements in order to establish the rules for their application.[87] However, the interplay between this text and the law gives rise to some question. In particular, the more recent inter-professional agreement, in regulating company level agreements, allows negotiations on the subjects and with the procedures established by sectoral agreements *or* by the law.[88] For the moment it is particularly difficult to assess the nature of the system of collective bargaining emerging from this concentric clash between legal dis-organised decentralisation and collectively agreed organised decentralisation. On the other hand, a *formalistic* approach would find in the law sufficient arguments to decide that in Italy sectoral agreements *and* statutory minima *can* be derogated at company level. Such a situation, read in the light of the previous analysis of the CJEU case law on posting, could be sufficient to deny the extension of minimum wages and working conditions to posted workers.

---

80 That is to say, the *de facto erga omnes* effect of Italian collective agreements. See Loi, "Italie/Italy", pp. 275–277. See further, E. Ales, "Dal 'caso FIAT' al 'caso Italia'. Il diritto del lavoro 'di prossimità', le sue scaturigini e i suoi limiti", *WP C.S.D.L.E. Massimo D'Antona.IT*, no. 134 (2011): 1–30.

81 Accordo interconfederale fra CONFINDUSTRIA e CGIL, CISL e UIL del 28 giugno 2011, point 7: "company level agreements can derogate […] from regulations established by national agreements, respecting the limits and procedures established by the same national agreements" (my translation).

82 See also U Rehfeldt, "Italie – des recommandations européennes à la résistance syndicale", *Chronique Internationale de L'IRES* 143–144 (2013): 93–132, p. 95.

83 Decreto Legge 13 agosto 2011 n. 138.

84 Article 8.

85 In particular, on the use of a-typical contract, working time and dismissals (with the exclusion of pregnant workers, discriminatory dismissals and dismissal in the occasion of marriage).

86 See Meardi, "Peripheral Convergence in the Crisis? Southern and Eastern European Labour Markets and Industrial Relations", p. 4.

87 *Testo Unico sulla Rappresentanza*, signed by CONFINDUSTRIA, CGIL, CISL, UIL, 10 January 2014.

88 Ibid., p. 21, my translation: "la contrattazione collettiva aziendale si esercita per le materie delegate e con le modalità previste dal contratto collettivo nazionale di lavoro di categoria o dalla legge".

Country-specific recommendations

The first round of CSRs was delivered in the context of the European Semester 2011. Looking at the numbers,[89] 117 recommendations were adopted in 2011, 137 in 2012 and 142 in 2013. Of these Recommendations, a large share deals with the "social field", (respectively, 54, 61 and 57). It is important to note that countries covered by a MoU were not included in CSRs. Wage policies play a fundamental role in the prescriptions delivered by EU institutions which should (supposedly) help Member States to overcome the Great Recession. Indeed, in the context of the EMU, so-called "internal devaluation" has been presented as the one of the main drivers to improve the competitive position of "deficit" countries *vis-à-vis* their European competitors.[90] More specifically, in relation to the scope of the present analysis, collective bargaining structures were often targeted by EU interventions (as we just saw) or by its Recommendations.[91] Thus, the Euro Plus Pact explicitly suggests to "review the wage setting arrangements, and, where necessary, *the degree of centralisation in the bargaining process*, and the indexation mechanisms".[92] A number of CSRs issued by the Commission and approved by the Council make this approach more apparent. It should also be noted that several countries did not receive Recommendations dealing with wage policy at all. In particular, a large part of countries outside the Eurozone avoided this kind of Recommendations,[93] together with the "core" countries of Austria and The Netherlands.

If one keeps in mind what was stated in opening this paragraph, that "Memorandum" countries were not interested by Country Specific Recommendations, this leaves an indeed short list of countries. Hence, the attention will be focused on three countries which, in the wake of the Great Recession, were characterised by a more centralised system of collective bargaining, namely Spain, Italy and Belgium. The Spanish and Italian cases have already been presented before; however, the analysis of the CSRs addressed to these countries remains interesting. Indeed, the point of the whole exercise is not just to assess the actual *impact* of EU intervention in national collective bargaining systems. Instead, the point is to identify the vision of the said systems fostered by EU institutions (and in particular by the Commission).

---

89 From the research carried out by the ETUI. See Clauwaert, "The Country-Specific Recommendations (CSRs) in the Social Field – An Overview and Initial Comparison", p. 8.

90 K. Armingeon and L. Baccaro, "Political Economy of the Sovereign Debt Crisis: The Limits of Internal Devaluation", *Industrial Law Journal* 41, no. 3 (2012): 254–272, p. 256.

91 Schulten and Müller, "A New European Interventionism? The Impact of the New European Economic Governance on Wages and Collective Bargaining", p. 186.

92 European Council, "The Euro Plus Pact: stronger economic policy coordination for competitiveness and convergence, Conclusions", 20 April 2011, EUCO 10/1/11, p. 16, emphasis added. See further C. Barnard, "The Financial Crisis and the Euro Plus Pact: A Labour Lawyer's Perspective", *Industrial Law Journal* 41, no. 1 (2012): 98–114.

93 Czech Republic, Denmark, Estonia, Lithuania, Poland, Slovakia, United Kingdom.

In the case of Belgium CSRs were particularly precise and direct in 2012 as to the need to de-centralise the system of collective bargaining, whereas both in 2011 and 2013 the wording was more nuanced.[94] In fact, in these two years the focus was on the necessity for wages to follow the dynamic of productivity.[95] Thus, in 2012 the Recommendation was clear in requesting to "take steps to reform […] the system of wage bargaining and wage indexation", in order to ensure "the implementation of ex post correction mechanisms foreseen in the 'wage norm'" and to facilitate "the use of opt-out clauses from sectoral collective agreements to better align wage growth and labour productivity developments at local level". As said before, 2013 Recommendations uses a less direct wording. However, the reference to the necessity "to ensure that wage setting is responsive to productivity developments, reflects *local* differences in productivity and labour market conditions" still implies a de-centralisation of collective bargaining. A similar conclusion can be found in the outcome of the macroeconomic imbalances procedure for 2014.[96]

The effects (both immediate and repeated) of the ECB letter on the Spanish system make it so that CSRs aimed at this country only mention collective bargaining in 2011. Hence, before the double reform (described *supra*) satiated the hunger for de-centralisation, the 2011 Recommendations suggested (emphasis added) to "proceed with the implementation of a comprehensive reform of the collective bargaining process and the wage indexation system to ensure that wage growth better *reflects productivity* developments as well as *local- and firm-level* conditions and to *grant firms enough flexibility to internally adapt working conditions* to changes in the economic environment". A similar pathway was followed by the Recommendations addressed to Italy. As it seems, the mix of the reform passed in the summer 2011 and the agreements between social actors, placated the Commission. Thus, only in 2011 a Recommendation in this sense

---

94 This notwithstanding the fact that wage development in Belgium were not showing a problematic trajectory. See Degryse, Jepsen and Pochet, "The Euro Crisis and Its Impact on National and European Social Policies", p. 33. Nor, it was performing badly during the crisis, as highlighted by Degryse, and Pochet, "Worrying Trends in the New European Governance", p. 96.

95 CSR of 2011: "Take steps to reform, in consultation with the social partners and in accordance with national practice, the system of wage bargaining and wage indexation, to ensure that wage growth better reflects developments in labour productivity and competitiveness."; CSR of 2013: "To restore competitiveness, pursue the on-going efforts to reform the wage setting system, including wage indexation; in particular, by taking structural measures, in consultation with the social partners and in accordance with national practice, to ensure that wage setting is responsive to productivity developments, reflects local differences in productivity and labour market conditions, and provides automatic corrections when wage evolution undermines cost-competitiveness."

96 European Commission, Occasional Papers 172, March 2014, Macroeconomic Imbalances (Belgium): "Yet, the existence of sizeable sectoral differences with regard to productivity means that introducing productivity in the wage setting at the inter-professional, national level would seriously distort figures. Incorporating it at lower levels would therefore be more appropriate. This would require a more decentralized procedure than currently applied with the determination of a national wage norm".

was adopted, going in the very same direction as the one addressed to Spain which was just quoted.[97]

These three examples stand out, since Italy and Spain effectively implemented far reaching reforms in the direction of de-centralisation, while Belgium decided differently and was rewarded with the repetition of the Recommendations in this sense. However, in particular in the 2011 round, other countries were interested by Recommendation to reform their wage setting systems. In those cases the de-centralisation direction is less evident. Hence, 2011 CSR for Cyprus recommended to reform collective bargaining so that wage growth could better reflect "developments in labour productivity and competitiveness". The Recommendations was dropped in 2012 (in favour of a more specific intervention on wage indexation). The next round of CSRs saw Cyprus in the group of MoU countries. Luxembourg received a very similar recommendation in 2011, 2012 and 2013, as well as Malta (in 2011 and 2012). However, in these cases the Recommendations make no reference to the necessity to de-centralise the system, or to take into account "local" or "firm level" specificities.

Method in madness?

The idea emerging from the intervention described above is a coherent and self-conscious policy choice of several EU institutions[98] in favour of a strongly de-centralised system of collective bargaining.[99] In the first place, one might wonder at the coherence of such a choice. Indeed, if wages are seen as a macroeconomic lever, an increased *centralisation* would make it easier to actually control their tendencies. Unless, as it seems to be the case, the idea is that in the present conditions, de-centralised bargaining will in fact be very efficient in simply driving down wages. However, it is not on *this* lack of coherence that the present work will have to focus.

---

97 CSR to Italy, 2011: "Take further steps, based on the 2009 agreement reforming the collective bargaining framework and in consultation with the social partners in accordance with national practices, to ensure that wage growth better reflects productivity developments as well as *local and firm conditions*, including *clauses that could allow firm level bargaining to proceed in this direction*" (emphasis added).

98 The ECB, the Commission and the Council, whether acting directly, through CSRs or as members of the Troika.

99 See Deakin and Koukiadaki, "The Sovereign Debt Crisis and the Evolution of Labour Law in Europe", pp. 184–185; Schulten and Müller, "A New European Interventionism? The Impact of the New European Economic Governance on Wages and Collective Bargaining", p. 200; Jolivet, Lerais and Sauviat, "La dimension sociale aux prises avec la nouvelle gouvernance économique européenne", p. 43; Clauwaert and Schömann, "The Crisis and National Labour Law Reforms – a Mapping Exercise", pp. 13–14.

Figure 8.4 Centralisation and decentralisation trends in industrial relations during the Great Recession

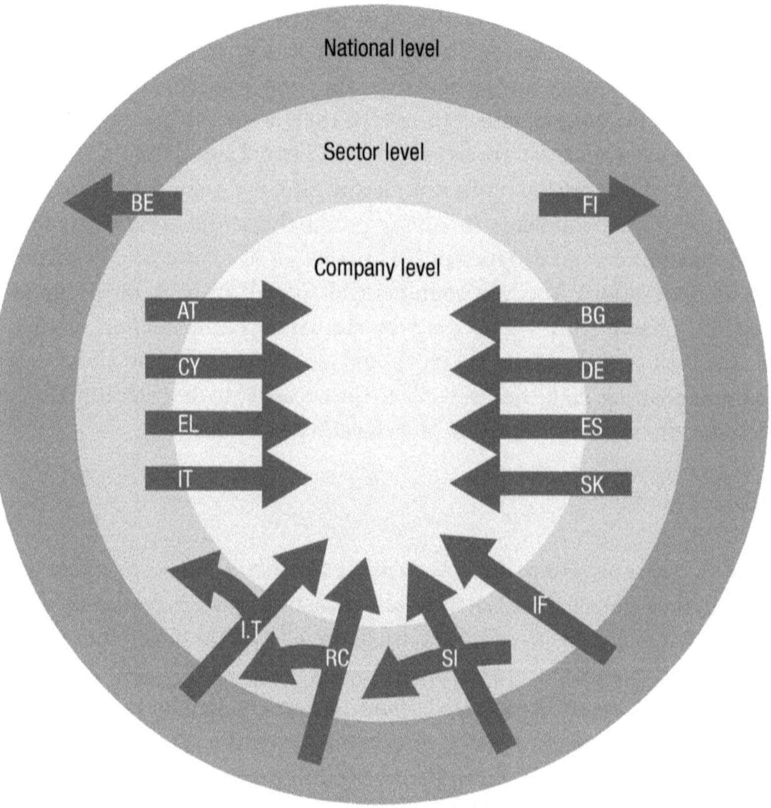

Instead, though it should be clear by now, the incoherence that I want to stress here is the one between the CJEU approach in the field of posting and the said self-conscious choice in favour of decentralisation of collective bargaining. After years of Great Recession we do live increasingly in a decentralised world, in terms of collective bargaining. The shift is nicely summarised by the graph prepared by the Eurofund[100] shown in Figure 8.4.

However, it is not the simple, though widespread, tendency towards decentralisation that gives rise to the lack of coherence. The tendency in itself "simply" shows that the PWD, with the limited options of Article 3(8) and their formalistic interpretation provided by the CJEU, is bound to increasingly leave posted workers without an effective protection, all the while exposing the host country national undertaking to an increased competition based on lower labour costs and worse working conditions. Still, it is far more striking to verify that the

[100] Eurofound, "Impact of the Crisis on Industrial Relations" (Dublin, 2013), p. 24.

Commission, the Council and the ECB, in their respective role, and the CJEU seem to be pulling in diametrically opposed direction. It is evident that posting of workers is a minor issue when compared to the economical onslaught of the Great Recession, so that the impact of the political choice in favour of de-centralisation upon the topic at stake in the present work is easily left aside. Nonetheless, such an impact is real and potentially far reaching, and it comes straight from political choices from EU institutions which have been consistently confirmed during the last four years. What is more, all along the years of the Great Recession, the discussion upon the posting package went on, so that the "building site" of a reform of the framework for posting of workers was in fact open. Still, while the Commission was delivering one Country Specific Recommendation after the other urging to de-centralise collective bargaining systems, or while it was concocting Memoranda which would impose the same effect, it did not find it appropriate to take such a move into account when dealing with posting of workers.

Without resorting to conspiracy theories, it is quite clear that there *is* a lot of method in this … incoherence. In a policy (that of EU institutions in the face of the crisis) dominated by the need to drive down labour costs in order to regain competitiveness, an increased pressure on the host country wages and working conditions brought about by the means of posting is perfectly at home. Indeed, once the basic policy is "workers of Europe, compete!",[101] all the lack of coherence suddenly disappears. As decentralisation is in fact a means to an end, namely the possibility to reduce wages and worsen working conditions during an economic crisis in order to regain competitiveness *vis-à-vis* other Eurozone countries, an increasingly ineffective PWD is another tool to foster competition between workers and thus put pressure on the same wages and working conditions.

8.1.2 THE ENFORCEMENT DIRECTIVE

While looking forward at the possible scenarios for the future of posting, the so-called Enforcement Directive[102] needs to be mentioned. With raising fears about the probable advance of nationalist, anti-EU parties in a number of Member States, the adoption of the Directive was seen as a tool to show proof of the ability of the EU to tackle actual problems. What is more, for the parties situated to the

---

101 R. Janssen, "Workers Of Europe, Compete!", Social Europe (Blog), 22 August 2013, available at www.social-europe.eu/2013/08/workers-of-europe-compete/.

102 Directive 2014/67/EU of the European Parliament and of the Council on the enforcement of Directive 96/71/EC concerning the posting of workers in the framework of the provision of services and amending Regulation (EU) No 1024/2012 on administrative cooperation through the Internal Market Information System ("the IMI Regulation"), 15 May 2014.

left of the centre, the said adoption could be pointed out as the sign that Social Europe is alive and kicking.[103]

In its declaration on 15 September 2009, EC President Barroso (speaking in the occasion of his re-election to the post) devoted a passage of his speech to posting of workers.[104] However, in that occasion he announced a Regulation to solve the issues related to fundamental rights, whereas a revision of the Directive itself was to be considered only as an *extrema ratio*. However, the Monti Report, commissioned by M. Barroso, suggested a two headed solution to tackle the posting problem. The first[105] then found its realisation (and demise) in the Monti II proposal, which was analysed before.[106] The second part of the solution proposed instead to clarify the *implementation* of the PWD, with a view to strengthening "dissemination of information on the rights and obligations of workers and companies, administrative cooperation and sanctions". This second part was to be embodied by the Enforcement Directive.

Proposed simultaneously with the Monti II Regulation, the debate on the Enforcement Directive somewhat lagged behind the one about the first instrument. However, after the shipwreck of the Monti II proposal, the attention went back to the Enforcement Directive, partly for the reasons I stated above, *i.e.* for the necessity to show that *something* was being done on the issue. The proposal tabled by the Commission was discussed and amended by the EP, where a compromise was found on the 20 of July 2013. The Lithuanian Presidency (second half of 2013) included the Enforcement Directive among its priorities.[107] The EPSCO (Employment, Social Policy, Health and Consumer Affairs) Council was not able

103 This was also stated by Commissioner Andor, in his keynote speech delivered on the 7 February 2014 at the Macroeconomic Institute of the Hans Boeckler Foundation (IMK), available at www.social-europe.eu/2014/02/address-social-imbalances-europe/, last accessed 19 February 2014: "it's adoption before the European elections would indeed send a very strong signal of the EU's capacity to address social questions".

104 "I have clearly stated my attachment to the respect of fundamental social rights and to the principle of free movement of workers. The interpretation and the implementation of the posted workers Directive falls short in both respects. That is why I commit to propose as soon as possible a Regulation to resolve the problems that have arisen. This Regulation will be co-decided by the EP and the Council. A Regulation has the advantage of giving much more legal certainty than the revision of the Directive itself, which would still leave too much room for diverging transposition, and take longer to produce real effects on the ground. If we discover during the preparation of the Regulation that there are areas where we need to revisit the Directive itself: I will not hesitate to do so. And let me be clear: I am committed to fighting social dumping in Europe, whatever form it takes".

105 "Introduce a provision to guarantee the right to strike modelled on Art. 2 of Council Regulation(EC) No 2679/98 and a mechanism for the informal solutions of labour disputes concerning the application of the directive".

106 See *supra*, Chapter 6, p. 269.

107 Press Release: Lithuanian Presidency priorities as presented in EP committees, 8–12 July 2013, p. 3: "Employment, especially youth employment, creating a European platform to combat undeclared work, protection of workers, particularly posted workers, and pensions portability were among the priorities of the Lithuanian Presidency".

to find a common position on the text resulting from the EP amendments,[108] divergences resulting in particular from national control measures applicable to posted workers and from the proposed joint and several liability for subcontractors. Interestingly, in the same occasion, the EPSCO Council acknowledged that the lack of integration "into the industrial relations of the host member state" was a matter of concern also for supervision and control of their working conditions. In fact, a few days before the EPSCO meeting, several European trade unions federations[109] had addressed a letter to the competent Ministers. In very brief, the letter asked for a number of improvements in relation to the text resulting from the EP amendments. In the absence of those improvements, the federations expressed their preference for an outright rejection of the proposal, in order to "guarantee that the proposed Enforcement Directive is not worsening the current situation". EPSCO council reached an agreement on a common position on the 9 of December 2013, so that negotiations could start with the European Parliament over the text. It is interesting to highlight that this agreement was saluted, particularly in some "old" Member States, as a victory for Social Europe, to the point that *Libération* wrote that *"c'est donc une victoire du camp des 'régulateurs' face au camp des libéraux"*.[110] Michel Sapin, French Minister of Labour declared *"cette journée marque un progrès pour la défense de notre modèle social, pour la défense des travailleurs et pour le refus du dumping social"*.[111] A similar situation can be identified in Italy[112] and in Belgium,[113] just to cite a few examples. The Directive was finally adopted on 15 May 2014. I will soon come to the actual content of the Directive. The instrument however can safely be described as focusing mainly on procedural elements and on monitoring and control. It leaves untouched the PWD itself, and, for the most part[114] every *substantive* issue dealing with wages and working conditions applicable to posted workers. Thus, even taking at face value the improvement of sanctions and control, the possibility of social dumping is only barely touched by the proposed Directive. It is worth noting that European trade union federations[115] as well as the ETUC[116] did not share the enthusiasm

---

108 Council meeting, Employment, Social Policy, Health and Consumer Affairs, Luxembourg, 15 October 2013.

109 EFBWW, EFFAT, ETF, IndustriALL, Uni Europa, EPSU.

110 Roughly, "that's a victory for the regulator against the liberals", *Libération*, 9 December 2013.

111 This day marks a progress for the defence of our social model, for the defence of workers and for the refusal of social dumping.

112 *Internazionale*, 10 December 2013, "Una sconfitta per gli ultra-liberali" (A defeat for ultra-liberals).

113 *La Libre Belgique*, 9 December 2013, "Dumping social : Monica De Coninck très satisfaite".

114 And the almost entirety for what has been analysed in this work.

115 *E.g.*, EFBWW, EPSCO agreement on the Enforcement Directive – A disappointing agreement with low ambitions, available at www.efbww.org/default.asp?Index=899&Language=EN; EFFAT, European labour ministers' agreement privileges internal market over rights of posted workers, 11 December 2013, available at www.effat.org/en/node/10758, last accessed 20 January 2014.

116 ETUC, Statement by the ETUC on the EPSCO Council compromise on the enforcement of the posting of workers directive, 10 December 2013, available at www.etuc.org/a/11821, last

about the common position reached by the EPSCO. This reinforces the impression I expressed before, that the need to approve a Directive is more pressing than the actual interest for the *content* of the same instrument. Another reason for the over-dramatisation of the debate over the Enforcement Directive can be found in the political decision not to emend the PWD itself. This choice made it so that under the label of procedural requirements, control measures and sanctions, and more in general of fighting *abuses*, a rearguard battle for re-balancing the legal framework for posting was being fought.

A quick look at the content

The analysis of the actual text of the (proposed) Enforcement Directive will necessarily be brief. Indeed, as it was stressed before, only few passages of the proposal refer to either collective aspects or substantive ones. The largest part of the Directive, unsurprisingly, deals with administrative cooperation, monitoring and sanctions.

In the Recitals[117] the *minimum* character of the protection offered by the PWD is suggested, somewhat confirming the attempt to "influence" the interpretation of the PWD through the Enforcement Directive. On the collective side, a "Monti clause" apparently found its way into the text of the proposal.[118] As it should be clear, the inclusion of such a clause in the Enforcement Directive does not appear as particularly useful. True enough, this is in line with the said attempt at "influencing without amending". Nevertheless, fundamental rights, as the right to take collective action and the right to bargain collectively, are in fact affected by the interpretation of the fundamental freedoms, as it was highlighted while analysing the "Monti II" proposal.

The text of the proposal, in defining "competent authority" for the purposes of the Directive[119] only refers to "any authority or *body*", which should cover those systems where labour inspections are carried out by trade unions. Strictly related to the issue of the applicability of "structured" minimum wage,[120] the proposal

accessed 20 January 2014: "unfortunately the agreement reached in the council does not set this key principle with the necessary legal clarity".

117 Recital 3, "[the PWD] establishes a core set of clearly defined terms and conditions of work and employment which must be complied with by the service provider in the Member State to which the posting takes place to ensure the minimum protection of the posted workers concerned".

118 Article 1(2): "This Directive shall not affect in any way the exercise of fundamental rights as recognised in Member States and at Union level, including the right or freedom to strike or to take other action covered by the specific industrial relations systems in Member States, in accordance with national law and/or practice. Nor does it affect the right to negotiate, conclude and enforce collective agreements and to take collective action in accordance with national law and/or practice".

119 In particular, for inspections.

120 That is to say, a situation in which several levels of minimum wages are provided by law or collective agreements for different categories based on age or skills.

implicitly takes position in favour of the full applicability of different (minimum) wage categories to posting undertaking.[121] The bottom line is that the proposal does not bring much to the table for the topic here at stake. This is coherent with the fact that issues related to "collective" labour law, *rectius* to the right to take collective action, were to be covered by the "Monti II" Regulation.

8.2 SCENARIOS

On the basis of the analysis carried out so far I will now try to sketch some possible scenarios for the evolution of the topic. Evidently, reality has the habit of defying predictions. This is particularly true for the present context, still characterised by economic and social tensions as well as by ongoing discussion dealing with the very foundations and future direction of the EU. Thus, I will put forward the four points characterising the context of the scenarios.

- the legislative framework for posting of workers, in particular the PWD;
- the CJEU approach to posting;
- the decentralisation direction, backed by the EU Commission and the Troika (or by its future mutations);
- a political equilibrium in the new European Parliament which is essentially similar to the past one, save for an increased presence of so-called anti-EU and/or nationalist MEPs.

The first scenario considers all these points as fixed. The second analyses the situation following a change in legislative framework. The third one looks instead at the possibility of a *revirement* of the CJEU in its approach to posting of workers.

In drawing the three scenarios I will devote limited attention to the likelihood of their actual materialisation. In fact, such an exercise would require taking into account a number of elements which go beyond the limited scope of the present work. However, on the basis of the analysis carried out so far, the "baseline" scenario (Scenario 1) comes out as the more likely, while the second (legislative changes) stands on the opposite end of the scale of probabilities. The third scenario represents the "wild card", as a change of direction in the CJEU

---

121 Article 5(4): "Where, in accordance with national law, traditions and practices, the terms and conditions of employment referred to in Article 3 of Directive 96/71/EC are laid down in collective agreements in accordance with Article 3 paragraphs 1 and 8 of that Directive, Member States shall ensure that these terms and conditions are made available in an accessible and transparent way to service providers from other Member States and to posted workers, and may involve the social partners in this respect. The relevant information should, in particular, cover the *different minimum rates of pay* and their constituent elements, the method used to calculate the remuneration due and, where relevant, the *qualifying criteria for classification in the different wage categories*" (emphasis added).

case law remains harder to guess. Hence, the analysis will focus on those legal elements which (should) suggest such a change.

8.2.1 SCENARIO 1: MUDDLING THROUGH

The first scenario does not bring much to the table. It is in fact a simple recollection of the analysis carried out so far, coupled with the inertia of both legal and political situation. Thus, as it was highlighted before,[122] the ideological push towards more decentralisation on the part of EU institutions will also continue. In the context of an economic recession (or depression), the eventual Recommendations will continue to bear a lot of weight, hence ensuring an impact on national systems of industrial relations.

The preference for centralised systems was already present in the original text of the PWD. However, the "black boxes" contained in the same text made it possible for the Age of Innocence to last for a good decade. After the round of cases of 2007–2008[123] this preference is even more clear. With Article 3(7) extremely narrowed down and Article 3(10) tamed, the PWD effectively pre-empts the full range of wages and working conditions which can be extended to posted workers.

As it was said before,[124] this context makes the whole edifice of industrial relations practices dependant upon the evaluation of the *demands* fostered by those practices. Those demands become the "measure of all things", meaning that if they go beyond or above what is allowed by the PWD, the whole practice risks to be considered as violating the Treaty provisions on freedom to provide services. Here one should focus on Article 3(8). The intervention of the Troika, as well as the Recommendations prepared by the Commission and adopted by the Council have sought to reduce the scope for both generally applicable sectoral collective agreements and for agreements reached by most representative social actors, and in this they have been successful.

The reduced coverage of sectoral agreements will probably trigger a more stringent analysis of what is "generally" applicable. At the moment of the drafting of the PWD, the Commission gave the impression of referring to agreements complied with by the *majority* of undertakings in the industry or occupation concerned.[125] It is unclear how the CJEU would scrutinise such a situation. From the analysis of the case law, the Court seems to favour a formalistic approach, engaging with the legal construction of the system and not with its actual empirical characteristics. Thus, one is left to wonder about the fate of a system still characterised by generally (in theory) applicable collective agreements, which are however not respected by the majority of undertakings. Provided

122 See *supra* in this Chapter.
123 See Chapter 5, p. 181 ff.
124 See *supra*, Chapter 7, p. 296.
125 *European Industrial Relations Review*, 236, p. 23.

that "employment friendly" policies should be aimed at *reducing* the scope of collective bargaining, it is probably safe to assume that more systems will not fit in the categories of Article 3(8). One should also keep in mind that company level bargaining has been ruled out in *Laval,*[126] at least as long as the demands do not mirror perfectly otherwise applicable standards set by legislation or collective agreements falling in one of the categories set by Article 3(8).

Sooner or later, also opening clauses will come under scrutiny. These clauses, which are included in the instruments for the said "employment friendly policies",[127] allow for derogations from higher level agreements. The issue brings us back to the discussion related the *Portugaia Costruções* case.[128] It seems that opening clauses will not be sufficient to change the nature of a collective agreement;[129] instead, the fact that an undertaking is allowed to derogate from a minimum wage or another condition set by an agreement (at sectoral or intersectoral level) may call into question its "minimal" nature. On the other hand we have the generalised legal possibility for company level agreements to derogate from sectoral ones. Whether such a possibility is used in practice or not, the said formalistic approach would probably conclude that these sectoral agreements are not generally applicable.[130] Needless to say, such a situation would entail that a collective action aimed at applying the sectoral standard would be considered as an excessive restriction to the freedom to provide services.

Thus, in this scenario, posting undertakings will be progressively construed as legally excluded from national industrial relations. The Swedish "solution" of the *Lex Laval* provides a good example of this outcome. One might argue that this would sacrifice the objective of protecting posted workers. However, this potential rationale for the Directive has been already somewhat neglected in the 2007–2008 case law.[131]

In this scenario, one can also imagine a dynamic similar to the one witnessed in the negotiations of the Enforcement Directive. That is to say, the attempt of "correcting" the PWD and the case law of the Court through other secondary instruments. Moreover, the more the "physiology" of posting escapes national systems for setting wages and working conditions, the more one can expect an increased (over)attention for pathological situation, this lack of trust leading to over-regulation[132] in the attempt to tackle frauds and bogus posting.

---

126 Davies, "One Step Forward, Two Steps Back? The Viking and Laval Cases in the ECJ", p. 129.

127 See *supra*, p. 315.

128 See Chapter 5, p. 175.

129 Meaning that a generally applicable agreement will still be considered as a ... generally applicable agreement, even though it includes opening clauses.

130 This was the situation of *Portugaia Costruções*.

131 As pointed out by Davies, "Case C-346/06, Ruffert v. Land Niedersachsen [2008] IRLR 467 (ECJ)", p. 294.

132 See Kelemen, *Eurolegalism: The Transformation of Law and Regulation in the European Union*, p. 23.

Finally, one should never forget of the evocative power which the "polish plumber" already showed in the occasion of the European Constitution referenda. The ever increasing ability of posting undertakings to legally employ workers with remunerations below the average pay and/or with worse working conditions may turn out as a political disaster for the EU. One should keep in mind that the workers in the *Rüffert* case were being paid 46% of the regional minimum wage.[133] I will come back to this in the concluding comments in the next Chapter.

8.2.2 SCENARIO 2: LEGISLATIVE CORRECTIONS AT PRIMARY AND SECONDARY LEVEL

Coming to the second Scenario, one could easily chose to give creativity free rein. Indeed, in imagining potential legislative solution for the tensions stressed along the previous Chapters, as the saying goes "the sky's the limit". However, a pure exercise of creativity, no matter how perfect the solutions found in the process, would ultimately be pointless. Indeed, the second Scenario is included mainly to show that an effective legislative correction is particularly unlikely.

Without repeating the analysis carried out before,[134] this is due to the asymmetry between negative and positive regulation, and between "rights of the market" and right of the social sphere.[135] Moreover, peculiar to the posting phenomenon, the constellation of interests at stake makes it so that the dividing lines do not run simply along different political sides. The most obvious tension is the one between "importers" and "exporters" of posted workers. Another, more obvious, clash is the one between the social actors at EU level, in particular between BUSINESSEUROPE and the ETUC. To have a look at the depth of this divide one can examine the observations submitted by both organisations to the European Committee of Social Rights, in the occasion of the procedure related to the *Lex Laval*.[136] Simply put, BUSINESSEUROPE defended the approach developed by the CJEU, both in relation to posting and to the relationship between fundamental freedoms and fundamental social rights.[137] The ETUC stood on the opposite side, urging the ESC to condemn these approaches.[138]

---

133 *Rüffert*, para. 11.

134 See *supra*, Chapter 7, p. 283.

135 See Scharpf, "The Asymmetry of European Integration, or Why the EU Cannot Be a 'Social Market Economy'".

136 See *supra*, p. 265.

137 *Swedish Trade Union Confederation (LO) and Swedish Confederation of Professional Employees (TCO) v. Sweden*, Complaint No. 85/2012, Case document No. 5, Observations by the International Organisation of Employers (IOE) and BUSINESSEUROPE.

138 *Swedish Trade Union Confederation (LO) and Swedish Confederation of Professional Employees (TCO) v. Sweden*, Complaint No. 85/2012, Case document No. 4, Observations by the European Trade Union Confederation (ETUC).

This constellation of interests makes it difficult to find a compromise which is capable to withstand the scrutiny of the vast array of veto players, and will most probably continue to do so in the foreseeable future. Furthermore, the short-cut of adopting a "social" instrument with an "internal market" legal basis has already proved extremely dangerous. Hence, the bottom line is that in re-regulating the posting phenomenon, the asymmetry is able to unfold its full potential.

All in all, the second Scenario shows a strong tendency to collapse on the first one. Thus, here I will just present two proposals for legislative intervention, both at secondary and primary level. Those were put forward by the ETUC, the choice being somewhat forced by the simple fact that, as stated before, the employers' side seemed more than content to simply defend the line traced by the CJEU.[139]

Amending the PWD

The Eight Proposals[140] drafted by the ETUC Expert Group on Posting go in the general direction of allowing Member States to apply the principle of equal treatment to posted workers.

Thus, the first proposal aimed at clarifying the objectives of the PWD[141] as well as to include social policy as a further legal basis for the Directive.[142] The second proposal essentially identified a "Monti clause"[143] to be included in the PWD. The objective of the third proposal is to restrict the scope of posting of workers, in particular by excluding intra-group posting[144] and by better defining

139 BUSINESSEUROPE, Policy Briefing 3 April 2012, available at www.businesseurope.eu/content/default.asp?PageID=568&DocID=30086 (last accessed 2 February 2014). "BUSINESSEUROPE strongly supports proper enforcement of the Posting of Workers Directive. But measures to improve enforcement should not impose disproportionate burdens on companies, and should not create additional barriers in the single market. […] There is no need for an EU Regulation on the exercise of the right to take collective action, because *ECJ rulings have provided legal clarity*" (emphasis added).

140 A Revision of the Posting of Workers Directive: Eight proposals for improvement, Brussels, 31 May 2010, available at www.etuc.org/IMG/pdf/final_report_ETUC_expert_group_posting_310510_EN.pdf (last accessed 2 February 2014).

141 Ibid., p. 20, new Article 1: "The purpose of this Directive is to guarantee the protection of workers, as well as to ensure a climate of fair competition in the internal market".

142 Ibid., in the Preamble: "Having regard to the Treaty on the Functioning of the European Union establishing the European Community, and in particular Articles 53(2), 62, 151 and 153 thereof".

143 Ibid., p. 22, new Article 1: "This Directive may not be interpreted as affecting in any way the exercise of fundamental rights as recognised in Member States and in international treaties, including the right or freedom to strike and the right to collective bargaining These rights may also include the right or freedom to take other actions covered by the specific industrial relations systems in Member States".

144 Ibid., p. 24.

the concept of both posting[145] and of provision of services.[146] The fourth proposal aims at (re)affirming the *minimum* character of the PWD,[147] also by re-opening the possibility of Article 3(7) to apply more favourable wages and working conditions applicable in the *host* country to posted workers.[148] Proposal number five deals with Article 3(8) by expanding the instruments available for setting wages and working conditions to be extended to posted workers.[149] Proposal number six deals with public procurement,[150] while the seventh proposal aims at

145 Ibid., p. 26, new Article 2: "The undertaking posting a worker within the meaning of Art.1.3 shall in particular demonstrate
– that the worker is habitually employed in another Member State than the Member State of posting and will return there after the period of posting;
– that the worker is not sent to replace a posted worker performing the same or similar task in order to circumvent rules regarding the temporary nature of the posting".

146 Ibid., p. 25, new Article 2: "'transnational provisions of services' means the cross border provision of a service, within the meaning of Articles 49 and 50 EC, and involving real economic activity in the Member State of establishment of the service provider.
This Directive does not cover situations where most or all of the services of an undertaking are directed at the territory of a particular Member State but the place of establishment is maintained outside that Member State".

147 Ibid., p. 29, in the new Article 3 all references to "minimum" conditions are deleted.

148 Ibid., p. 30, new Article 3(7): "Paragraphs 1 to 6 shall not prevent application of terms and conditions of employment of the host country or of the country of origin of the posted worker which are more favourable to workers, in particular through the exercise of the fundamental right of workers and employers, or their respective organisations, to negotiate and conclude collective agreements at the appropriate levels and to take collective action to defend their interests, including strike action, to protect and improve the living and working conditions of workers including the right to equal treatment" and "This Directive is without prejudice to the Member States' right to apply or introduce legislative, regulatory or administrative provisions, in areas harmonised by minimum provisions in EC law, which are more favourable to workers or to promote or permit collective agreements concluded between the social partners which are more favourable to workers".

149 Ibid., p. 35, new Article 3(8): "Member States may also, if they so decide, in accordance with their national law and practice, base themselves on:
– collective agreements or arbitration awards which are generally applicable, including on the basis of public procurement law, to a majority of similar undertakings and/or similar workers in the geographical area and in the profession or (part of the) industry concerned, and/or
– collective agreements or arbitration awards which are generally applied to a majority of similar undertakings and/or similar workers in the geographical area and in the profession or industry concerned or a part thereof, and/or
– collective agreements which have been concluded by the most representative employers' and labour organisations at national and other relevant levels and which are applied in the geographical area and in the profession or (part of the) industry concerned".

150 Ibid., p. 39, new Article 3(10): "This Directive shall not preclude the application by Member States, in compliance with the Treaty, to national undertakings and to the undertakings of other States, on a basis of equality of treatment, of:
[...]
– terms and conditions of employment regarding the matters referred to in Article 3.1. as well as regarding other matters in the case of public contracts, as defined in Article 1.2 (a) of Directive 2004/17/EC and Article 1.2 (a) of Directive 2004/18/EC".

re-expanding the notion of public interest in Article 3(10).[151] Finally, the eighth and last proposal deals with enforcement.[152]

I will not enter into much detail as to the proposed modifications of the PWD. It is however apparent that, as it was stated before, the direction of those amendments is to clarify the minimum character of the PWD, hence allowing collective action and collective bargaining to go beyond minimum wages and working conditions. Furthermore, the list of collective agreements which can be *prima facie* applied to posted workers is also extended. These modifications would essentially take away the yardstick from the test employed by the CJEU. Keeping in mind what it was stated before as to the role of the PWD in the reasoning of the Court,[153] (minimum) wages and working conditions applicable under the PWD were in fact needle's eye through which the demands put forward by collective bargaining and action had to "pass". However, once one takes out the PWD from the table, we go back to the balancing process between fundamental freedoms and fundamental (social) rights. Hence, to *Schmidberger* and *Omega*, but also, more relevant inasmuch as it deals with trade unions and not with public action, to *Viking*. Still, if one looks at the test deployed in *Viking*, the amended PWD would provide a solid coverage as to the justification of an eventual collective action. In particular, the new PWD would surely help in justifying the restriction on the basis of an overriding reason of public interest (*i.e.*, the protection of workers). At the same time the CJEU could still consider the restriction as going beyond what is necessary to achieve the objective of protecting workers. It is probably for this very reason that the ETUC paired the proposal for a revision of the PWD with the so-called "Social Progress Protocol", which entails an intervention at the level of the Treaties.

The Social Progress Protocol

For what it matters here, the Social Progress Protocol proposed by the ETUC[154] can be described as an "*über*-Monti clause". Indeed, Article 3(1) of the proposal[155]

---

151 Ibid., pp. 41–42, new Article 3(10): "This Directive shall not preclude the application by Member States, or, in accordance with the practice in the Member State, by management and labour, to national undertakings and to the undertakings of other States, of
– terms and conditions of employment on matters other than those referred to in the first subparagraph of paragraph 1 in the case of social and public policy provisions, including provisions which are appropriate to the attainment of the protection of workers, equal treatment, the prevention of social dumping, or fair competition".

152 Ibid., pp. 44–49.

153 See *supra*, p. 289.

154 ETUC, Proposal for a Social Progress Protocol, 18 March 2009, available at www.etuc.org/a/5175 (last accessed, 2 February 2014); see also A. Bücker, "A Comprehensive Social Progress Protocol Is Needed More Than Ever", *European Labour Law Journal* 4, no. 1 (2013): 4–23.

155 Bücker rightly warns against focusing exclusively on Article 3 when assessing the Protocol. Though I completely agree with the advice, Article 3 remains the most relevant part for the topic here at stake. See Ibid., p. 19.

is in fact a "Monti clause", covering both fundamental freedoms and competition rules.[156] From the point of view of our topic, it is evident that such a clause would guarantee the exercise of collective social rights in the field of posting of workers. It would also represent a complete U-turn of the legal construction of the relationship between fundamental freedoms and fundamental rights.

As to the political feasibility of the Protocol, the years of the Great Recession has not provided the most favourable environment to envisage such a change in the Treaties. The Monti Report defined the idea of seeking Treaty changes as unrealistic "in the short term".[157] However, the story shows that some Treaty changes are more realistic than others, since the Treaties were in fact amended in the process of creating the New Economic Governance.[158] Instead, together with the asymmetry recalled before, it was the "hijacking" of the crisis which made it extremely unlikely for the Social Protocol to be discussed, let alone approved and implemented. Indeed, the whole concept of the Union improving "living and working conditions of its population as well as any other social condition" and ensuring "that improvements are being maintained"[159] was definitely out of place at a time when the reduction of labour costs, coverage of collective agreements and social rights were being presented as the EU-strategy for crisis stricken countries.

In opening this section I put forward the four points which form the context for those scenarios. Hence, looking to the new composition of the European Parliament, I assumed (much for simplicity's sake) that the political equilibrium of the EP has not been radically changed by those elections. To this one has to add the increased presence of anti-EU/nationalist MEPs. In this light it is interesting to consider that the protection of collective social rights from the effects of fundamental freedoms may easily be presented as the defence of *national* prerogatives from the "invasion" of EU law. Since industrial relations *are* deeply rooted into national economic, social and political history, their shielding via the Social Progress Protocol could, in a way, appeal to nationalist/euro-sceptic parties and groups.

8.2.3 SCENARIO 3: A GAME OF COURTS

The third Scenario deals with the judicial pathway.[160] The elements on which it is based were largely dealt with in Chapter 6. In particular, I will focus on those legal

---

156 "Nothing in the Treaties, and in particular neither economic freedoms nor competition rules shall have priority over fundamental social rights and social progress as defined in Article 2. In case of conflict fundamental social rights shall take precedence".

157 Monti Report, p. 70.

158 In particular to authorise the establishment of the European Stability Mechanism under EU law. See Degryse, "The New European Economic Governance", pp. 35–36.

159 ETUC, Proposal for a Social Progress Protocol, Article 2(1)(a) and 2(1)(d).

160 Bücker, Warneck and Dorssemont, "The Search for a Balance: analysis and Perspectives", pp. 331 ff.

evolutions which may be relied upon by the CJEU itself in order to re-assess both the question of posted workers and the broader topic of the relationship between fundamental rights and fundamental freedoms. Those new elements come from different legal orders than the EU, namely the Council of Europe and the ILO.

The legal relationship of those systems with the EU is not easily assessed. For the European Convention of Human Rights a more clear-cut answer could have been provided by the accession of the EU to the Convention, which was in fact envisaged[161] by the Lisbon Treaty. Indeed, four years have passed since the commitment to such accession was included in the Treaties. A draft of the accession protocol was published,[162] but then the negotiations faced a sudden stop, due to the afterthoughts of some Member States. Two years after, an agreement was reached over the draft accession agreement,[163] which is now awaiting the opinion of the Court of Justice.

However, I will focus directly on the "inputs" coming from the European Court of Human Rights, from the European Committee of Social Rights and from the ILO Committee for the Application of Conventions and Recommendations. Leaving aside the question of the legal relationship between those institutions and the CJEU, it should be clear that an open clash with these legal systems should not be taken lightly by the Court of Justice. And what we are witnessing closely resembles an open clash.

Emerging consensus on collective social rights

In the years after the *Laval* quartet, the right to take collective action was repeatedly object of remarkable decisions delivered by several international bodies. First the Court of Human Rights, then the ILO Committee of Experts on the Application of Conventions and Recommendations and finally the European Committee for Social Rights. Both the CEACR and the ECSR had to deal with a direct clash between the *effects* of the quartet and the rights protected by the respective documents. These decisions have been presented in Chapter 6.[164] Hence I will simply mention these important evolutions. The order is circular: first the ECtHR with the *Enerji* case, then the CEACR and afterwards the ECSR. The circle will be closed by the reference to *Demir*, which has the potential of opening the case law of the ECtHR to the evolutions of the other bodies I just mentioned.

161 Or imposed, if one looks at the text of Article 6(2) TEU: "The Union shall accede to the European Convention for the Protection of Human Rights and Fundamental Freedoms. Such accession shall not affect the Union's competences as defined in the Treaties".

162 Draft legal instruments on the accession of the European Union to the European Convention on Human Rights, 19 July 2011, www.coe.int/t/dghl/standardsetting/hrpolicy/Accession/Working_documents/CDDH-UE_2011_16_final_en.pdf (last accessed 8 February 2014).

163 Council of Europe, press release, "Milestone reached in negotiations on accession of EU to the European Convention on Human Rights", 5 April 2013, wcd.coe.int/ViewDoc.jsp?Ref=DC-PR041(2013) (last accessed 8 February 2014).

164 See *supra*, p. 256 (for the CEACR); p. 260 (for the ECtHR); p. 263 (for the ECSR).

Thus, in *Enerji*[165] the ECtHR followed the doctrine developed by ILO supervisory bodies and considered the right to strike as a "*corollaire indissociable*"[166] of the right to form and join trade unions (protected under Article 11 ECHR). On this basis, the ECtHR went on to analyse the restriction to the right to strike imposed by the Turkish government[167] under Article 11(2).[168] The same approach was followed by the ECtHR in the *RMT* case. Though the outcome was not favourable to trade unions, the Court confirmed that the right to strike is protected under Article 11 and that the restrictions to its exercise must comply with Article 11(2). In *Enerji* the ECtHR found that the restriction was not *necessary* in a democratic society. Apart from the (ground-breaking) recognition of the right to strike, it is apparent that a scrutiny which involves the restriction *of* this right[169] goes into a completely different direction than the one of the CJEU, where (the exercise of the) right to strike *is* the restriction. The limited possibility for considering the approach of the Court of Justice as compatible with the limits imposed by Article 11(2) would be to consider the "protection of [...] rights and freedoms of others" as including the fundamental freedoms of the EU legal order.[170] Even though the decision in *Enerji* seems to go into another direction, one should not overlook the different stance of the ECtHR in *UNISON*,[171] where an economic interest was at least taken into account while assessing the proportionality of the restriction of the right to take collective action.[172] However, the reference to both ILO Convention 87 and the European Social Charter in *Enerji*[173] suggests that this eventuality is quite remote. Even more so if one takes into account the recent decisions of the ECSR and the CEACR.

The position of the ILO Committee of Experts can be rapidly presented, since it has already been described in Chapter 6. In both the *BALPA* and the *Lex Laval* decisions, the CEACR openly condemned the proportionality test as a means to

---

165 ECtHR, 21 April 2009, *Enerji Yapi-Yol Sen*, no. 68959/01. See Dorssemont, "How the European Court of Human Rights Gave Us Enerji to Cope with Viking and Laval".

166 Ibid., para. 24.

167 Ibid., para. 32.

168 "No restrictions shall be placed on the exercise of these rights other than such as are prescribed by law and are necessary in a democratic society in the interests of national security or public safety, for the prevention of disorder or crime, for the protection of health or morals or for the protection of the rights and freedoms of others. This Article shall not prevent the imposition of lawful restrictions on the exercise of these rights by members of the armed forces, of the police or of the administration of the State."

169 See further Ewing and Hendy, "The Dramatic Implications of Demir and Baykara", p. 14; Dorssemont, "The Right to Take Collective Action Under Article 11 ECHR", p. 352 ff.

170 See Rocca, "The Proposal for a (so-Called) 'Monti II' Regulation on the Exercise of the Right to Take Collective Action Within the Context of the Freedom of Establishment and the Freedom to Provide Services", p. 24.

171 ECtHR, 10 January 2002, *UNISON v. UK*, no. 53574/99. See also ECtHR, 27 June 2002, *Federation of Offshore Workers' Trade Unions and Others v. Norway*, no. 38190/97; ECtHR, 28 October 2011, Trofimchuk v. Ukraine, no. 4241/03. See Dorssemont, "The Right to Take Collective Action Under Article 11 ECHR", pp. 357–360.

172 *UNISON*, p. 11.

173 *Enerji*, para. 24.

restrict the right to take collective action in light of economic freedoms,[174] though it always referred to the *effects* of EU law on national situations, since the EU is not member of the ILO.

The ECSR similarly decided when assessing the compatibility of the *Lex Laval* with the European Social Charter. The Committee found the restrictions to the right to take collective action imposed by the Swedish "transposition" of *Laval* as disproportionate. In affirming this, it remarked that EU fundamental freedoms, notwithstanding their importance in the EU legal order, could not be considered as having a greater value than fundamental social rights.[175] Somewhat translating in the EU context the stance of the ECtHR in *Enerji*, the Committee stated that eventual restrictions to fundamental social rights should undergo a proportionality test, as required by Article G of the ESC.[176]

As I said before, the circle ends where it began, with the European Court of Human Rights. In *Demir and Baykara*,[177] the ECtHR opened an important channel to the *corpus* of decisions of the ECSR[178] and of other supervisory bodies, as the CEACR.[179] The ECtHR referred to the interpretation provided by those bodies of their respective international agreements (ILO Conventions and the European Social Charter), in order to assess the emerging consensus (and the

---

174 International Labour Conference, 99th Session, 2010, Report of the Committee of Experts on the Application of Conventions and Recommendations (The United Kingdom), pp. 208–209 and International Labour Conference, 102nd Session, 2013 Report of the Committee of Experts on the Application of Conventions and Recommendations (Sweden), p. 178: "the Committee recalls that when elaborating its position in relation to the permissible restrictions that may be placed upon the right to strike, it has never included the need to assess the proportionality of interests bearing in mind a notion of freedom of establishment or freedom to provide services".

175 *Swedish Trade Union Confederation (LO) and Swedish Confederation of Professional Employees (TCO) v. Sweden*, Complaint No. 85/2012 para. 122: "[...] the facilitation of free cross-border movement of services and the promotion of the freedom of an employer or undertaking to provide services in the territory of other States – which constitute important and valuable economic freedoms within the framework of EU law – cannot be treated, from the point of view of the system of values, principles and fundamental rights embodied in the Charter, as having a greater a priori value than core labour rights, including the right to make use of collective action to demand further and better protection of the economic and social rights and interests of workers. In addition, any restrictions that are imposed on the enjoyment of this right should not prevent trade unions from engaging in collective action to improve the employment conditions, including wage levels, of workers irrespective of their nationality".

176 Ibid., para. 121: "[t]he Committee further considers that legal rules relating to the exercise of economic freedoms established by State Parties either directly through national law or indirectly through EU law should be interpreted in such a way as to not impose *disproportionate restrictions* upon the exercise of labour rights as set forth by, further to the Charter, national laws, EU law, and other international binding standards. In particular, national and EU rules regulating the enjoyment of such freedoms should be interpreted and applied in a manner that recognises the fundamental importance of the right of trade unions and their members to strive both for the protection and the improvement of the living and working conditions of workers, and also to seek equal treatment of workers regardless of nationality or any other ground" (emphasis added).

177 ECtHR, 12 November 2008, *Demir and Baykara v. Turkey*, no. 34503/97.

178 *Demir and Baykara v. Turkey*, para. 50 and 149.

179 Ibid., para. 38, 43, 101, 122, 147 and 166.

"continuous evolution") regarding the rights protected by the ECHR.[180] *In casu* such emerging consensus brought the ECtHR to consider the right to bargain collectively as an "essential element" of the right to form and join trade unions,[181] protected by Article 11 ECHR.

From the decisions just outlined, it appears that there is an emerging consensus, going in the very opposite direction of the limitations to the right to take collective action imposed by the Court of Justice through the means of the proportionality test.[182] It is also worth mentioning that in *Demir* the European Court of Human Rights, deciding a case against Turkey, took into account Articles 5 and 6 ESC though Turkey had not ratified those Articles. In the (hopefully, unlikely) event of a given Member State unilaterally denouncing ILO Conventions or (relevant Articles of) the ESC to solve a contrast with EU Treaties (under the procedure of Article 351 TFEU[183]), this choice would not *per se* impede the ECtHR to take into account those Articles when assessing the restrictions imposed on collective social rights. Hence, such a choice would not constitute the emergency exit from the clash.

Posted workers, different takes

The specific issue of posted workers is evidently more limited than the epic clash between fundamental rights and fundamental freedoms. As such, the ECtHR provides no guidance on this topic. On the other hand, both the CEACR and the ECSR, as recalled before, had to decide on the *Lex Laval*, which directly regulates the posting phenomenon. Hence, a number of useful elements can be identified in those decisions to assess the compatibility of the EU legal framework for posting with international labour standards.

The CEACR analysed the question on the basis of its mandate, hence exclusively from the collective side. From this perspective, the ILO Committee focused on three problems of the new Swedish legislation dealing with posted workers. First, the limitation to minimum conditions as regards the demands

180 Ibid., para. 85–86. On the point see Lörcher, "The New Social Dimension in the Jurisprudence of the European Court of Human Rights (ECtHR): The Demir and Baykara Judgment, Its Methodology and Follow-up"; M. Schlachter, "The European Social Charter: could It Contribute to a More Social Europe?" in *Resocialising Europe in a Time of Crisis*, ed. N. Contouris and M. Freedland (Cambridge: Cambridge University Press, 2013), 105–117, p. 115.

181 *Demir and Baykara*, para. 154.

182 See further *supra*, Chapter 6, p. 245 ff.

183 "The rights and obligations arising from agreements concluded before 1 January 1958 or, for acceding States, before the date of their accession, between one or more Member States on the one hand, and one or more third countries on the other, shall not be affected by the provisions of the Treaties.
To the extent that such agreements are not compatible with the Treaties, the Member State or States concerned shall take all appropriate steps to eliminate the incompatibilities established. Member States shall, where necessary, assist each other to this end and shall, where appropriate, adopt a common attitude".

backed by a collective action.[184] Second, the Committee pointed out that the *Lex Laval* did not take into account the situation in which Swedish trade unions effectively have members among posted workers.[185] In such a situation the trade union would be prohibited to its rights to represent its member(s). Finally, the CEACR criticised the possibility offered by the Swedish legislation to a posting employer to impede the collective action by merely "showing" that wages and working conditions applied to posted workers are essentially similar to the minima allowed by the PWD. In such a situation the said posting employer could completely avoid signing a collective agreement whatsoever, whether in the home or in the host country.

As described in Chapter 6, the ECSR criticised the *Lex Laval* and, indirectly, the EU legal framework for posting, from two different angles. On the one hand, from the side of collective rights of trade unions in the host state. In this sense, as it was partly anticipated in the previous paragraph, the ECSR considered the restriction to (the demands of) collective action to *minimum* conditions as disproportionate.[186] In particular the European Committee of Social Rights stressed the importance of allowing trade unions to take collective action in order to seek *equal treatment*[187] and the *improvement* of existing working conditions.[188] On the other hand, the second line of critique deals with the individual rights of posted workers. Indeed, by defining posted workers as migrant workers,[189] the ECSR decided clearly in favour of their right to *equal treatment vis-à-vis* the comparable worker of the host state.[190] To limit the conditions applicable to posted workers to minimum ones, "for the sake of enhancing free cross border movement of services and advantages in terms of competition within a common market zone",[191] would amount to a discriminatory treatment.[192] Moreover, to be *equal*, the treatment of posted workers should be measured upon "that of Swedish workers with comparable occupational experience and skills".[193]

---

184 International Labour Conference, 102nd Session, 2013 Report of the Committee of Experts on the Application of Conventions and Recommendations (Sweden), 178: 179: "The Committee does observe with concern, however, that the amendments to the Foreign Posting of Employees Act restrict recourse to industrial action to conditions corresponding to the PWD minimum conditions".

185 Ibid.

186 *Swedish Trade Union Confederation (LO) and Swedish Confederation of Professional Employees (TCO) v. Sweden*, Complaint No. 85/2012 para. 121–123.

187 Ibid., para. 121.

188 Ibid., para. 122–123.

189 Ibid., para. 134.

190 Ibid., para. 134–136.

191 Ibid., para. 141.

192 Ibid., para. 140–141.

193 Ibid., para. 136.

Reconciliation

Article 3(7) of the Posting of Workers Directive, as it should be well known by now, literally allows the application of "terms and conditions of employment which are more favourable to workers". In *Laval* and *Rüffert* the CJEU decided that, contrary to the Opinion of the AG in both cases,[194] Article 3(7) only covered more favourable conditions set by laws or collective agreement of the *home state* of the posting undertaking. In particular, in both cases the Court stated that "Article 3(7) of Directive 96/71 cannot be interpreted as allowing the host Member State to make the provision of services in its territory conditional on the observance of terms and conditions of employment which go *beyond* the mandatory rules for *minimum* protection" because "such an interpretation would amount to *depriving the directive of its effectiveness*".[195]

Dealing with the *Lex Laval*, which essentially limits wages and working conditions applicable to posted workers to "rules for minimum protection", the ECSR found that "the Swedish legislation, in respect of remuneration and other working conditions, does not secure for posted workers the *same treatment* guaranteed to other workers with permanent employment contracts; and for this reason it is not in conformity with the Charter".[196] Or, if one prefers to look at the question from the point of view of collective social rights: "the Committee considers that national legislation which prevents a priori the exercise of the right to collective action, or permits the exercise of this right only in so far as it is necessary to obtain given minimum working standards would not be in conformity with Article 6(4) of the Charter [...] if the substance of this right is to be respected, trade unions must be allowed to strive for the improvement of existing living and working conditions of workers, and its scope should not be limited by legislation to the attainment of minimum conditions".[197] As we saw, the CEACR expressed a similar critique.

The mere juxtaposition of these statements brings the observer to a pressing, though somewhat rhetorical, question:[198] is the entire PWD-system, shaped by the case law of the CJEU, in violation of the obligations stemming from the European Social Charter[199] and from ILO Conventions? Or, more specifically, is

---

194 AG Mengozzi in *Laval*, para. 197–198; AG Bot in *Rüffert*, para. 79–81, as Claire Kilpatrick puts it "a textbook illustration of the pre-*Laval* approach to posting of workers". See Kilpatrick, "Internal Market Architecture and the Accommodation of Labour Rights: As Good as It Gets?", p. 19.

195 *Laval*, para. 80; *Rüffert*, para. 33 (emphasis added).

196 *Swedish Trade Union Confederation (LO) and Swedish Confederation of Professional Employees (TCO) v. Sweden*, Complaint No. 85/2012 para. 136.

197 Ibid., para. 121.

198 I analysed this issue in Rocca, "A Clash of Kings The European Committee of Social Rights on the 'Lex Laval'...and on the EU Framework for the Posting of Workers".

199 On this point see the statement included in the Report "State of Democracy, Human Rights and the Rule of Law in Europe", SG(2014)1 – FINAL, by the Secretary General of the Council of Europe: "In 2013 the European Committee of Social Rights found a breach, inter alia, of

the *quantum* of competitive advantage awarded to posted workers by EU law[200] in contrast with the obligation of protecting and promoting the rights to collective bargain and action and the equal treatment for migrant workers? In light of the decisions presented in the previous paragraphs one can hardly avoid answering for the affirmative. Having being delivered in direct connection with the effects of EU law, the decisions of the ECSR and of the CEACR open the door to a conflict of unprecedented latitude.

As regards the rights to collective bargaining and action, in light of the growing consensus described above, the Court of Justice (and hence the EU) appears to be falling behind more specialised bodies in protecting fundamental social rights (in the clash with economic freedoms). Even the moderate correction proposed by AG Trstenjak in her Opinion[201] on the *Commission v Germany*[202] case was completely disregarded by the CJEU. No assessment of the restrictions imposed to fundamental social rights was carried out by the Court of Justice. Such a stance went in the opposite direction of the approach of the ECtHR in *Enerji* and *Demir*, which were both delivered *before* the *Commission v Germany* decision.

As highlighted in the previous paragraphs, such a situation does not lend itself to a simple legal solution, for the *network*[203] of legal orders connecting the EU, the Council of Europe and the ILO cannot be apprehended by a straight hierarchical approach. Hence, to mend the wounds left behind by the *Laval* quartet and pave the way for a reconciliation, the Court of Justice should go beyond the simple superficial reference to international texts. In order to avoid conflicts,[204] it would have to engage in a true analysis of the interpretation of those texts provided by their supervisory bodies.[205] It goes without saying that such a change of attitude

---

the right to bargain collectively and the right to strike important corollaries of the right to organise. The measures in question had been adopted as a result of a judgment of the Court of Justice of the European Union. The decisions of the States Parties (resulting directly or indirectly from EU law) must conform to the rights enshrined in the Charter. Therefore we see an urgent need to find pragmatic solutions to settle conflicts between the two sets of standards".

200 Barnard, *EC Employment Law*, p. 179.

201 Opinion of AG Trstenjak in *Commission v. Germany*, para. 192 and 198.

202 C-271/08. See further Syrpis, "Reconciling Economic Freedoms and Social Rights – The Potential of Commission v. Germany (Case C-271/08, Judgment of 15 July 2010)"; Rocca, "Case C-271/08, Commission v. Germany [2010]".

203 Bücker, Warneck and Dorssemont, "The Search for a Balance: analysis and Perspectives", p. 332.

204 Barnard, "The Protection of Fundamental Social Rights in Europe After Lisbon: a Question of Conflicts of Interests", p. 43.

205 Though, as stated by de Búrca, so far "there has been a remarkable lack of reference on the part of the Court of Justice to other relevant sources of human rights law and jurisprudence". G. de Búrca, "After the EU Charter of Fundamental Rights: The Court of Justice as a Human Rights Adjudicator?", *Maastricht Journal of European and Comparative Law* 20 (2013): 168–184, p. 173. Specifically about the (lack of) reference to the ESC see J.-F. Flauss, "'Les Interactions Normatives Entre Les Instruments Européens Relatifs À La Protection Des Droits Sociaux'",

would have far reaching implications which would go far beyond the scope of the present research.

In this perspective, it is interesting to look at the possibilities offered by the EU Charter of Fundamental Rights. The recourse to this instrument would allow the CJEU to integrate the "emerging consensus" without leaving the boundaries of EU law. Here I will just look into the interplay of Article 28 and Article 52(1) EUCFR. As it is well known, the former recognises the rights to collective bargaining and action, while the latter regulates the possibility to restrict the exercise of the rights recognised in the Charter. In doing so Article 52(1) recalls the necessity for those restrictions to a) respect the "essence" of the right, b) undergo a proportionality test. Now, keeping in mind the newly found legal value of the EUCFR, one could draw inspiration from the "emerging consensus" to interpret the "essence" of the rights to collective bargaining and action. The ECSR made it easy to find this inspiration. In its decision about the *Lex Laval*, the Committee stated that "if the *substance* of this right is to be respected, trade unions must be allowed to strive for the improvement of existing living and working conditions of workers, and its scope should not be limited by legislation to the attainment of minimum conditions".[206] As for the proportionality test, the limits shaped by the *Enerji* case, *i.e.* those of Article 11(2) ECHR, are the most obvious reference. Also, allowing collective action to strive for conditions going above the minimum ones could also represent an answer to the violation of the principle of equal treatment for migrant workers.

Furthermore, the ECSR found the limitation to minimum conditions to be a disproportionate restrictions to the rights protected, among others, by Article 28 EUCFR. The same limitations were noted with concern by the CEACR. Thus, once that striving for equal treatment is included in the essence/substance of the rights to collective bargaining and action, it remains to be seen what lies outside this scope. Also in this sense the decision of the ECSR could provide an interesting inspiration for the CJEU. In particular, the Committee found that the prohibition of collective actions backing *discriminatory objectives* would be *prima facie* legitimate under the system of values established by the ESC.[207] The Court of Justice would thus be perfectly equipped to tackle those actions backing discriminatory or outright xenophobic demands.[208]

---

in *Droits Sociaux et Droit Européen. Bilan et Prospective de la Protection Normative*, ed. J.-F. Flauss (Brussels: Nemesis, 2002), 89–114, p. 109.

206 *Swedish Trade Union Confederation (LO) and Swedish Confederation of Professional Employees (TCO) v. Sweden*, Complaint No. 85/2012 para. 120.

207 *Swedish Trade Union Confederation (LO) and Swedish Confederation of Professional Employees (TCO) v. Sweden*, Complaint No. 85/2012 para. 119.

208 See also Dorssemont and Orlandini, "Market Rules and the Right to Strike: a Different Approach", p. 83. However, to allow this, a *limited* review of the demands, though always risky for the autonomy of social actors, will have to be accepted. Lacking this, it would be possible to hide a xenophobic purpose behind artificially high demands. To this extent, statistical data about (in particular) wages and working conditions, which have proved useful in identifying discriminations, could provide an instrument to sanction eventual protectionist behaviours.

CHAPTER 9
THE LEGACY

'Alas! there are some wounds that cannot be wholly cured' said Gandalf.
'I fear it may be so with mine' said Frodo.
'There is no real going back. Though I may come to the Shire, it will not seem the same; for I shall not be the same. I am wounded with knife, sting, and tooth, and a long burden. Where shall I find rest?'

— J.R.R. Tolkien, *The Return of the King*

In 2011 a book was published, honouring the memory of Brian Bercusson and Yota Kravaritou. The title of this book reads *Before and After the Economic Crisis - What Implications for the 'European Social Model'?*. For the second part of the title, a rather *final* "implication" was suggested by ECB President Mario Draghi. Speaking to *The Wall Street Journal* in the beginning of 2012 he declared the European Social Model "already gone".[1] As for the first part, writing in 2014, one cannot but appreciate the "optimism of the will" of the title. Indeed, the aftermath of the Great Recession is still failing to materialise for a majority of EU countries.

The legacy of tensions[2] bequeathed by the *Laval* quartet has if anything worsened during the years of the crisis. The fact that the impact of the Great Recession essentially (and rightly) monopolised the attention should not deceive. The questions raised by the legal framework for posting of workers did not receive an answer during the years which separates the present times from the Judgement Day.[3] In the meantime, the tension between fundamental economic freedoms and fundamental social rose to an unprecedented level. Similarly, the tension between the *reality* of collective bargaining systems, and the EU expectations regarding their evolution, became apparent. Finally, the crisis *narrative* shaped by EU institutions has fuelled a wave of sympathy for nationalist and anti-EU parties

1 *The Wall Street Journal*, Q&A: ECB President Mario Draghi, 23 February 2012, available at http://blogs.wsj.com/eurocrisis/2012/02/23/qa-ecb-president-mario-draghi/. On the point see P. Pochet and C. Degryse, "Monetary Union and the Stakes for Democracy and Social Policy", *Transfer: European Review of Labour and Research* 19, no. 1 (January 2013): 103–116, pp. 113–114.

2 C. Joerges, "Democracy and European Integration: A Legacy of Tensions, a Re-Conceptualisation and Recent True Conflicts", *EUI Working Paper*, no. 25 (2007).

3 Bercusson, "The Trade Union Movement and the European Union: Judgment Day".

across the Member States. This overarching issue is also worth mentioning, as it may profit from the unsolved questions in the field of posted workers. The reference obviously goes to the role played by the "polish plumber" figure in the debate about the Treaty establishing a Constitution for Europe. These concluding pages will be devoted to these tensions.

9.1 THE EU AND THE INTERNATIONAL PROTECTION OF SOCIAL RIGHTS: FAIR-WEATHER COMMITMENT?

As the mere number of pages devoted to the "Game of Courts" in the previous Chapter may have suggested, I consider such a scenario as the more likely among the ones implying a legal change. That is, more likely than a legislative intervention tackling the issues identified in Chapters 6 and 7. Backing this impression is the *embarrassing* situation in which EU law finds itself at present in relation with international standards of protection for fundamental social rights and human rights.

Indeed, the commitment to "the strict observance and the development of international law" is embedded in the Treaty on European Union.[4] Just to mention a more recent example, the Commission recently stated that "the EU promotes, in *all its policies*, the ratification and *effective implementation* of ILO Conventions on core labour standards".[5] The idea is that, much beyond the actual *legal* impact, ILO Conventions bear a high degree of legitimacy and hence political weight. Even more so considering that the conflict involves Convention 87 which is included among the Fundamental Principles and Rights at Work.[6] The same is true in particular for the European Convention of Human Rights, and by extension for the European Court of Human Rights. This role is confirmed by the direct

---

4 Article 3(5): "In its relations with the wider world, the Union shall uphold and promote its values and interests and contribute to the protection of its citizens. It shall contribute to peace, security, the sustainable development of the Earth, solidarity and mutual respect among peoples, free and fair trade, eradication of poverty and the *protection of human rights*, in particular the rights of the child, as well as to the *strict observance and the development of international law*, including respect for the principles of the United Nations Charter" (emphasis added). A similar commitment is repeated in Article 21(1) TEU.

5 European Commission, press release, Working conditions: time for Member States to implement the ILO domestic workers convention, 28 January 2014, emphasis added. See on the point G. Casale, "International Labour Standards and EU Labour Law", in *Resocialising Europe in a Time of Crisis*, ed. N. Countouris and M. Freedland (Cambridge: Cambridge University Press, 2013), 81–104, pp. 86 ff.

6 Adopted in 1998, the ILO Declaration on Fundamental Principles and Rights at Work the Declaration commits Member States (of the ILO) to respect and promote principles and rights related to the freedom of association and the effective recognition of the right to collective bargaining, the elimination of forced or compulsory labour, the abolition of child labour and the elimination of discrimination in respect of employment and occupation, whether or not they have ratified the relevant Conventions.

reference to the Convention included in the EU Charter of Fundamental Rights.[7] Though the case law of the ECtHR is not mentioned explicitly by the EUCFR, the interpretation provided by the Presidium is clear in this regard.[8] The recognition of the European Social Charter is less striking but still recognisable in its own right. Both the TFEU[9] and the Community Charter of Fundamental Social Rights of Workers[10] refer to this instrument. Also, the ESC somewhat completes the circle, meaning that it would have been difficult to violate *other* instruments through action in the topic at stake. The tension is as evident as it can be as regards the ILO and the ESC legal systems, considering the conclusions analysed *supra*.[11] As for the European Court of Human Rights, to the very least one can affirm that the ECtHR in *Enerji* accepted to review restrictions *to* the right to take collective action, while the CJEU in *Laval* and *Viking* (and in general, in its "fundamental rights" case law) analyses the very exercise *of* the fundamental/human right as a restriction to fundamental freedoms. It should be evident that the very credibility of the CJEU as a "human rights adjudicator"[12] is at stake in such a conflict.

The movement resembles the "pendulum" between market and society described by Polanyi.[13] Obviously, this reference is limited to the "dynamic" aspect, without any pretence to draw a real analogy. Thus, as the reasons of the (internal) market prevailed in the decisions of the CJEU, it was their very triumph to put into motion the counter-move, *i.e.* the reaction of the guardians of fundamental social rights.

Indeed, the present topic is not alone in showing this dynamic. The action of EU institutions[14] is repeatedly clashing with the protection of fundamental social

---

7 Articles 52(3) and 53.

8 Explanations relating to the Charter of Fundamental Rights, *Official Journal of the European Union* (OJEU), 14 December 2007, No. C 303, pp. 17–35, available at http://eurlex.europa.eu/LexUriServ/LexUriServ.do?uri=OJ:C:2007:303:0017:0035:EN:PDF (last accessed 15 February 2014), p. 18: "the reference to the ECHR covers both the Convention and the Protocols to it. The meaning and the scope of the guaranteed rights are determined not only by the text of those instruments, *but also by the case-law of the European Court of Human Rights* and by the Court of Justice of the European Union. The last sentence of the paragraph is designed to allow the Union to guarantee more extensive protection. In any event, the level of protection afforded by the Charter may never be lower than that guaranteed by the ECHR" (emphasis added).

9 Article 151: "The Union and the Member States, having in mind fundamental social rights such as those set out in the European Social Charter signed at Turin on 18 October 1961 and in the 1989 Community Charter of the Fundamental Social Rights of Workers, shall have as their objectives the promotion of employment, improved living and working conditions, so as to make possible their harmonisation while the improvement is being maintained, proper social protection, dialogue between management and labour, the development of human resources with a view to lasting high employment and the combating of exclusion".

10 "Whereas inspiration should be drawn from the Conventions of the International Labour Organization and from the European Social Charter of the Council of Europe".

11 See Chapter 6, pp. 255 ff.; and Chapter 8, pp. 338 ff.

12 De Búrca, "After the EU Charter of Fundamental Rights: The Court of Justice as a Human Rights Adjudicator?".

13 Polanyi, *The Great Transformation: The Political and Economic Origins of Our Time*, pp. 150–151.

14 In particular, the EU Commission and the ECB.

rights in another relevant context. This brief excursion hence brings us to Greece. Here I will not give an account of the measures demanded by the so-called Troika in the context of the financial help provided to Greece.[15] What is interesting is that those measures started another swing of the pendulum. Following the complaints of Greek trade unions, the impact of the multiple Memoranda upon social rights has been scrutinised both in light of ILO Conventions and of the ESC. A High Level Mission of the ILO examined the Greek situation in September 2011, while the Committee on Freedom of Association (CFA) decided upon the complaint raised by the Greek trade unions in November 2012. In both occasions the results of the Memoranda were openly criticised. Referring just to a few relevant passages, the High Level Mission was particularly concerned by the changes imposed to industrial relations[16] and by the general lack of attention towards employment itself as an objective for economic measures.[17] The CFA in its turn condemned the Government intervention on collective bargaining, and in particular on the *results* of bargaining processes.[18] Turning to the ESC,[19] the European Committee for Social Rights decided upon several complaints from the Greek trade unions in 2012. Five complaints were raised by pensioners' unions,[20] following legislative interventions essentially aimed at cutting pensions and other bonuses for retired persons. In each case, the ECSR unanimously concluded that the measures violated Article 12(3) of the Charter.[21] Another complaint addressed the introduction of "special apprenticeship contracts" for young boys and girls,[22]

15 Some of those measures, as well as a sketched account of the context, were described in the previous Chapter. See *supra*, p. 308.

16 Report on the High Level Mission to Greece (Athens, 19–23 September 2011), para. 304–307.

17 Ibid., para. 330–332: "the mission has been struck by the reports that in discussions with the Troika employment objectives rarely figure".

18 International Labour Office, 316th Session, Geneva, 1–16 November 2012, 365th Report of the Committee on Freedom of Association, Complaints against the Government of Greece presented by the Greek General Confederation of Labour (GSEE), the Civil Servants' Confederation (ADEDY), the General Federation of Employees of the National Electric Power Corporation (GENOP-DEI-KIE) and the Greek Federation of Private Employees (OIYE), supported by the International Confederation of Trade Unions (ITUC), in particular para. 990–995: "The suspension or derogation by decree -without the agreement of the parties- of collective agreements freely entered into by the parties violates the principle of free and voluntary collective bargaining established in Article 4 of Convention No 98."

19 See O. De Schutter, "L'adhésion de l'Union Européenne à la Charte sociale européenne", Report, 8 July 2014, pp. 14–17.

20 *Pensioners' Union of the Agricultural Bank of Greece (ATE)*, Complaint No. 80/2012; *Panhellenic Federation of pensioners of the Public Electricity Corporation (POS-DEI)*, Complaint No. 79/2012; *Pensioners' Union of the Athens-Piraeus Electric Railways (I.S.A.P.)*, Complaint No. 78/2012; *Panhellenic Federation of Public Service Pensioners (POPS)*, Complaint No. 77/2012; *Federation of employed pensioners of Greece (IKA-ETAM)*, Complaint No. 76/2012. All were decided on the 7 December 2012.

21 "With a view to ensuring the effective exercise of the right to social security, the Contracting Parties undertake: […] to endeavour to raise progressively the system of social security to a higher level".

22 Decision on the Merits, *General Federation of employees of the national electric power corporation (GENOP-DEI) and Confederation of Greek Civil Servants' Trade Unions (ADEDY) v. Greece*, Complaint No. 66/2011, 23 May 2011.

characterised by (heavily) reduced safeguards in terms of labour law and social security. Once again unanimously, the Committee concluded that there had been violation of Articles 7(7),[23] 10(2),[24] 4(1)[25] and 12(3) ESC.

Falling outside the scope of the present research, the aim of this short digression is to show the full extent of the tension between the EU and fundamental social rights in the era of the Great Recession. As far as austerity measures and Memoranda are concerned, the "legal" solution for those tensions is not straightforward. Instead, coming back to the topic at stake in this work, the conflict *generated* by the CJEU decision could, at least in principle, be solved by the very same Court. That would at least restore some of the supposed commitment of the EU to the respect of international law (or to the "effective implementation of ILO Conventions on core labour standards"), and also have an impact on the legitimacy of its action. I will come back to this last point in a few paragraphs.

9.1.1 GOOD TIME FOR A CHANGE (OF APPROACH)

Writing about the *Laval* quartet, the Monti Report expressed some hope as to the ability of the (coming into force of the) Lisbon Treaty to shape a new legal context, in which the issues and the concerns raised by the trade unions should hopefully find an adequate response".[26] The *Commission v Germany* case[27] delivered a few months after the Report showed that this hope was somewhat misplaced. True enough, the new Treaty was not applicable *ratione temporis* to the infringement procedure. However, the CJEU did acknowledge the new status of the EUCFR, by stating that Article 6 TEU accorded to this instrument the same legal value as the Treaties.[28] As it is known, the Court then applied the very same *Viking&Laval* approach to solve the clash between the right to bargain collectively and the freedom to provide services, notwithstanding the Opinion

---

23 "With a view to ensuring the effective exercise of the right of children and young persons to protection, the Contracting Parties undertake: [...] to provide that employed persons of under 18 years of age shall be entitled to not less than three weeks' annual holiday with pay".

24 "With a view to ensuring the effective exercise of the right to vocational training, the Contracting Parties undertake: [...] to provide or promote a system of apprenticeship and other systematic arrangements for training young boys and girls in their various employments".

25 "With a view to ensuring the effective exercise of the right to a fair remuneration, the Contracting Parties undertake: to recognise the right of workers to a remuneration such as will give them and their families a decent standard of living". In particular, the Committee found (para. 57–65) that the "special apprenticeship contract" allowed the payment of a minimum wage below the poverty level.

26 Monti Report, p. 70. This hope was based on the fact that "The ECJ rulings pre-date the entry into force of the Lisbon Treaty, which explicitly sets out the social market economy as an objective for the Union and makes the European Charter of Fundamental Rights legally binding at Treaty level".

27 Case C-271/08.

28 *Commission v. Germany*, para. 37.

of the AG which proposed a "correction" of this approach.[29] It is worth noting that, as for *Viking&Laval*, the *Commission v Germany* case was decided by the Grand Chamber. This is to stress that the coming into force of the Lisbon Treaty probably is *not* the legal novelty which will suggest a *revirement* to the CJEU. One could also notice that this case was delivered some two years after *Demir.* Still, the fact that the European Court of Human Rights had just recognised the right to bargain collectively, *i.e.* the (fundamental) right at stake in *Commission v Germany*, was completely absent from the Court's reasoning as well as from the Opinion.

In order to recognise the fundamental nature of the rights to take collective action (*Viking&Laval* and to bargain collectively (*Commission v. Germany*), the Court referred to international instruments.[30] Among those were the European Social Charter and ILO Convention No. 87. The inclusion of ILO Convention No. 87 to justify the fundamental nature of the right to take collective action suggests that the CJEU is aware of the role of the *sui generis* case law developed by the supervisory bodies of those international instruments. Indeed, as it is well known, the *text* of Convention No. 87 does *not* mention the right to strike.[31] However, this reference remains completely and utterly implicit. Never along those cases the position expressed by the supervisory bodies either of the ILO Convention or of the ESC is mentioned. What is more, also the mere textual reference to those international instruments appears inspired by a *pick and choose* attitude. Thus, though the CJEU referred to Article 6 of the ESC (both for the right to take collective action and for the right to bargain collectively), the Court did not go as far as to mention Article G of the same instrument, which regulates the restrictions to the rights recognised by the Charter.[32] This is true even for the EUCFR. As for Article 6 ESC, Article 28 EUCFR played a role in all the cases mentioned before, providing yet another basis for the recognition of the fundamental nature of the rights at stake. Once again the CJEU did not acknowledge the existence of an Article regulating the limitations to the right protected by the EUCFR. Indeed, Article 52(1)[33] stipulates that these limitations must undergo a proportionality test. No sign of such a test can be found in the

---

29 See Opinion of AG Trstenjak in *Commission v. Germany*, para. 183 ff.

30 *Viking*, para. 43; *Laval*, para. 90; *Commission v. Germany*, para. 37.

31 Dorssemont, "The Right to Take Collective Action Versus Fundamental Economic Freedoms in the Aftermath of Laval and Viking. Foes Are Forever", p. 44.

32 "The rights and principles set forth in Part I when effectively realised, and their effective exercise as provided for in Part II, shall not be subject to any restrictions or limitations not specified in those parts, except such as are prescribed by law and are necessary in a democratic society for the protection of the rights and freedoms of others or for the protection of public interest, national security, public health, or morals".

33 "Any limitation on the exercise of the rights and freedoms recognised by this Charter must be provided for by law and respect the essence of those rights and freedoms. Subject to the principle of proportionality, limitations may be made only if they are necessary and genuinely meet objectives of general interest recognised by the Union or the need to protect the rights and freedoms of others."

decisions. This is particularly striking for *Commission v Germany*, since to apply the proportionality test *also* to the restrictions imposed on the fundamental right at stake was the solution suggested by the AG in her Opinion.[34] The only basis to justify the restrictions is found by the CJEU on the same Article 28, which states that the rights to take collective action and to collective bargaining must be exercised "in accordance with Union law and national laws and practices".[35]

On this background, it takes a particularly optimistic clairvoyant to foresee a change of approach by the CJEU as a consequence of the unprecedented tension identified before. The first pre-requisite would be for the CJEU to engage in a true analysis of the *dynamic* nature of the international instruments to which it has so far superficially referred. This could be achieved *implicitly*, if an open commitment to a *Demir*-like methodology[36] seems too far-reaching.[37] As highlighted before, the CJEU has already, although to a very limited extent, done so, in order to consider the right to strike as protected by ILO Convention No. 87.

In the meantime Member States find themselves in a particularly uncomfortable position. Both the CEACR and the ECSR did not allow them to "hide behind the EU". The CEACR, in both BALPA[38] and *Lex Laval*[39] conclusions, made it clear that its task was limited to examining the *impact* of EU law on the rights protected by ILO Convention No. 87. Similarly, the ECSR placed itself "downstream" in respect of EU law, assessing the "compliance of a national situation with the Charter, including when the transposition of a European Union directive into domestic law may affect the proper implementation of the Charter".[40] This reasoning was extended by analogy "to national provisions based on preliminary rulings given by the CJEU".[41] Interestingly, the ECSR also denied

---

34 Opinion of AG Trstenjak in *Commission v. Germany*, para. 190: "A fair balance between fundamental rights and fundamental freedoms is ensured in the case of a conflict only when the restriction by a fundamental right on a fundamental freedom is not permitted to go beyond what is appropriate, necessary and reasonable to realise that fundamental right. Conversely, however, nor may the restriction on a fundamental right by a fundamental freedom go beyond what is appropriate, necessary and reasonable to realise the fundamental freedom". See further Syrpis, "Reconciling Economic Freedoms and Social Rights – The Potential of Commission v. Germany (Case C-271/08, Judgment of 15 July 2010); Rocca, "Case C-271/08, Commission v. Germany [2010]".

35 *Viking*, para. 44; *Laval*, para. 91; *Commission v. Germany*, para. 43.

36 See Lörcher, "The New Social Dimension in the Jurisprudence of the European Court of Human Rights (ECtHR): The Demir and Baykara Judgment, Its Methodology and Follow-up".

37 Though Schlachter argues that the Court should be bound by such a methodology under Article 52(3) EUCFR. See Schlachter, "The European Social Charter: could It Contribute to a More Social Europe?", p. 116.

38 International Labour Conference, 99th Session, 2010, Report of the Committee of Experts on the Application of Conventions and Recommendations (The United Kingdom), p. 209.

39 International Labour Conference, 102nd Session, 2013 Report of the Committee of Experts on the Application of Conventions and Recommendations (Sweden), p. 178.

40 *Swedish Trade Union Confederation (LO) and Swedish Confederation of Professional Employees (TCO) v. Sweden*, Complaint No. 85/2012 para. 72.

41 Ibid., para. 73.

the existence of a "presumption of conformity" of EU law with the ESC.[42] Among other arguments, the Committee stressed the different situation as regards the European Convention on Human Rights, since the EU "has not taken steps to accede to the European Social Charter".[43] Hence, Member States cannot free themselves from the obligations stemming from those international instruments by referring to their duty to implement EU law and to apply the decisions of the CJEU. As it is evident, the issue could be looked at from the opposite angle. That is, by analysing the possibility for a Member State to oppose to the EU their obligation to respect ILO Conventions and the ESC. As it was mentioned in the previous Chapter, this situation is regulated by Article 351 TFEU. The Article refers to "rights and obligations arising from agreements concluded before 1 January 1958 or, for acceding States, before the date of their accession". ILO Convention No 87 falls in this category for all Member States but Italy and Luxembourg.[44] For the European Social Charter the picture gets much more complicated, due to the "dual" nature of the instrument, with the Revised ESC being ratified at a much later date. De Schutter argued that, in the case of a Member State having ratified both instruments, the ratification date of the Revised ESC would be the one to take into account, hence "resetting" the clock in respect of Article 351.[45] The ETUC supported a different approach in its submission to the *Lex Laval* case,[46] arguing in favour of a "continuity" of the two instruments (the "no-reset" option in Table 9.1). The situation stemming from these different approaches is summarised in Table 9.1.

---

42 Cf. the stance of the European Court of Human Rights, in the case of *Bosphorus Hava Yollari Turizm ve Ticaret Anonim Şirketi v. Ireland*, 30 June 2005, no. 45036/98.

43 Ibid., para. 74.

44 Which have ratified it respectively on 13 March 1958 and 3 March 1958.

45 O. De Schutter, "L'adhésion de l'Union Européenne à la Charte sociale européenne révisée", *EUI Working Paper*, no. 11 (2004): 1–44, pp. 8–9; an updated version of this paper is now available. See De Schutter, "L'adhésion de l'Union Européenne à la Charte sociale européenne" (2014), www.coe.int/t/dghl/monitoring/socialcharter/Presentation/PublicationCSEUEODeSchutterJuly2014_en.pdf.

46 *Swedish Trade Union Confederation (LO) and Swedish Confederation of Professional Employees (TCO) v. Sweden*, Complaint No. 85/2012, Case document No. 4, Observations by the European Trade Union Confederation (ETUC), para. 52: "The ratification of the RESC (1998) took place after Sweden's entry into the EU (1995). One might therefore think that EU law overrides the Charter's provisions. However, this would not be correct taking into account Article B of the RESC which stipulates that any given provision of the 1961 ESC remains the same after ratification of the RESC [...] Since Sweden had already accepted Article 6 and 19(4) ESC when ratifying the ESC (1962) it remains bound to these provision irrespective of the later RESC's ratification. Therefore Article 351(1) TFEU applies and these obligations have remained valid ever since".

Table 9.1 ESC/(Rev)ESC and Article 351 TFEU

	Before EU Accession	After EU Accession
Only ESC	Austria, Croatia, Czech Republic, Denmark, Greece, Hungary, Latvia, Poland, Slovakia, Spain, United Kingdom	Germany, Luxembourg
Only (Rev)ESC	Bulgaria, Estonia, Lithuania, Romania, Slovenia	
Both (reset)	Cyprus	Belgium, Finland, France, Ireland, Italy, Malta, Netherlands, Portugal, Sweden
Both (no-reset)	Cyprus, Finland, Ireland, Malta, Sweden	Belgium, France, Italy, Netherlands, Portugal

Thus, first of all, the possibility offered by Article 351 TFEU[47] would only be available to some Member State. It would not help to clarify the relationship between fundamental rights and fundamental freedoms for the whole EU legal order. Second, in the event of a Member State effectively invoking Article 351 TFEU, the outcome of such a situation would be far from clear. De Schutter notes that it could potentially lead to the obligation for the Member State to unilaterally denounce the conflicting international agreement.[48] For the ESC this could be achieved more easily, since the Charter allows for the "selective" ratification of its articles.[49] ILO Convention No. 87 would put up a fiercer fight in this regard. Indeed, in light of its inclusion in the 1998 Declaration on Fundamental Principles and Rights at Work makes its respect an obligation directly stemming from the membership of the ILO itself. It seems safe to affirm that the eventuality of EU Member States being forced to leave *en masse* the ILO is almost unthinkable, though the years of the Great Recession somewhat changed our perception of what is "unthinkable" in Europe.[50]

47 This possibility was also explored in relation to the contrast between the *Rüffert* decision and ILO Convention No. 94. See Bruun, Jacobs and Schmidt, "ILO Convention No. 94 in the Aftermath of the Ruffert Case", p. 480.

48 De Schutter, "L'adhésion de l'Union Européenne à la Charte sociale européenne" (2014), p. 19–20.

49 See further, O. De Schutter, "The Two Lives of the European Social Charter", in *The European Social Charter: a Social Constitution for Europe*, ed. O. De Schutter (Brussels: Bruylant, 2010), 11–37.

50 *E.g.*, "drastic reductions to municipality budgets have led to a scaling back of several activities (e.g., mosquito spraying programmes), which, in combination with other factors, has allowed the re-emergence of locally transmitted malaria for the first time in 40 years" or "a 21% rise in stillbirths between 2008 and 2011 [...] attributed to reduced access to prenatal health services for pregnant women". The quotes come from a recent Article about on the effect of austerity on healthcare in Greece, published on The Lancet. See further A. Kentikelenis et al., "Greece's Health Crisis: from Austerity to Denialism", *The Lancet* 383, no. 9918 (February 2014): 748–753.

The role of the European Court of Human Rights in this game is partly dependent upon the fulfilment by the EU of its obligation to accede to the ECHR. The accession will in fact shape the relationship between the two apical European Courts. Before that, it remains to both Courts to define their respective relationship.[51] The CJEU has not the best of records when it comes to referring to the case law of Strasbourg.[52] Furthermore, a "precedent" in the field of collective social rights is quite alarming in this respect. In the *Werhof* case[53], the CJEU referred to the ECtHR decision in *Gustafsson,*[54] in order to support its conclusion that the "negative" freedom of association would be violated by the application of a collective agreement.[55] Since the collective agreement at stake did *not* deal with membership of an organisation whatsoever, it can be safely said that the interpretation given to *Gustafsson* by the CJEU is in direct contrast with the actual content of the ECtHR decision. Indeed, in *Gustafsson* the ECtHR stated that "Article 11 of the Convention does not as such guarantee a right not to enter into a collective agreement".[56] As for the ECtHR, it has showed particular restraint when assessing a (supposed) violation of the Convention caused by an act stemming from EU law.[57] Hence, while we await for the accession of the EU to the ECHR to materialise, a direct clarification appears rather difficult. Leaving aside the actual *outcomes*, what strikes the eye is the sheer distance between the approaches of the two Courts. At the apex of the European legal systems we thus have, on the one hand, a Court, the ECtHR, who has adopted a methodology which is open to the contribution of other supervisory bodies of international instruments. This Court analyses the restrictions *to* the right to take collective action and to bargain collectively through Article 11(2) ECHR. On the other hand, the CJEU in its decisions on the same rights included only cursory references to the *text* of international agreements. Moreover, its lip service to (supposedly) fundamental rights has only gone as far as to allow the exercise of these rights to potentially justify a restriction to the fundamental freedoms of the internal market.

---

51 See further, F. Dorssemont, "A Judicial Pathway to Overcome Laval and Viking", *OSE Research Paper*, no. September (2011).

52 De Búrca, "After the EU Charter of Fundamental Rights: The Court of Justice as a Human Rights Adjudicator?", pp. 173–174: "there has been a remarkable lack of reference on the part of the Court of Justice to other relevant sources of human rights law and jurisprudence. Apart from a very occasional and increasingly selective use of the case law of the European Court of Human Rights, there have been virtually no references to other human rights jurisprudence or rulings".

53 Case C-499/04, *Hans Werhof v. Freeway Traffic Systems GmbH & Co. KG.*

54 ECtHR, *Gustaffson v Sweden*, Application no. 15573/89.

55 *Werhof*, para. 34.

56 *Gustafsson*, para. 52. See on this point Dorssemont, "The Right to Form and to Join Trade Unions for the Protection of His Interests Under Article 11 ECHR", pp. 203–204.

57 See on this point S. Douglas-Scott, "A Tale of Two Courts: Luxembourg, Strasbourg and the Growing European Human Rights Acquis", *Common Market Law Review* 43, no. 3 (2006): 629–665.

Article 52(3) of the EUCFR is intended, in the words of the Explanations provided by the Praesidium,[58] "to ensure the necessary consistency between the Charter and the ECHR by establishing the rule that, in so far as the rights in the present Charter also correspond to rights guaranteed by the ECHR, the meaning and scope of those rights, including authorised limitations, are the same as those laid down by the ECHR". The Explanations however make it clear that this reference *includes* the case-law of the European Court of Human Rights.[59] Furthermore, the Explanations refer to the case law of the ECtHR in correlation with Article 28 EUCFR[60] (collective bargaining), meaning that the "correspondence" between the EUCFR and the ECHR should not be considered from a merely textual point of view. The Explanations have no binding legal value, though they are "a valuable tool of interpretation intended to clarify the provisions of the Charter". Following this "valuable tool" it would seem that the CJEU is under the obligation of interpreting "authorised limitations" to the rights protected by Article 28 EUCFR in accordance with the case law of the ECtHR. Article 53 EUCFR seems also relevant for the topic here at stake. This Article should ensure that the Charter is not interpreted as to restrict human rights and fundamental freedoms as recognised by (among others) "international agreements to which the Union or all the Member States are party, including the European Convention for the Protection of Human Rights and Fundamental Freedoms". Apart from the ECHR, whose role is already recognised by Article 52(3), it is worth considering in this light the ESC and ILO Convention No. 87. As it was highlighted before, all Member States are parties to the latter instrument. Provided that the CEACR has made abundantly clear that Article 28 (among other sources) has been interpreted by the CJEU as "restricting or adversely affecting" the rights protected by the said Convention, the next step would be to ask oneself whether the interpretation provided by the Committee is included in the "level of protection" of Article 53. The Explanations are less clear on this Article, so that they do not provide an answer to this question. Turning to the ESC, it is unclear if it would be considered as an international agreement to which *all* Member States are party.[61] The question, as was discussed before, revolves around the "reset" or "no-reset" options presented in Table 9.1. In the end, the analysis of De Schutter would suggest to answer for

58 Explanations relating to the Charter of Fundamental Rights, Official Journal of the European Union (OJEU), 14 December 2007, No C 303, pp. 17–35, available at http://eurlex.europa.eu/LexUriServ/LexUriServ.do?uri=OJ:C:2007:303:0017:0035:EN:PDF (last accessed 15 February 2014).

59 Ibid., p. 18.

60 Ibid., p. 11.

61 Schlachter argues in favour of such an interpretation: "Article 53 of the EU Charter of Fundamental Rights refers the Court to instruments relevant for the interpretation of fundamental rights, including the ESC, as an international treaty signed by all EU Member States". See Schlachter, "The European Social Charter: could It Contribute to a More Social Europe?", p. 116.

the negative.[62] All in all, the potential of Article 53 remains thus more obscure than the one of Article 52(3). This once again confirms the more important role recognised to the European Court of Human Rights by the EU legal order. In light of this, of the eventual accession of the EU to the ECHR, and of the ability to take into account the position of both the CEACR and the ECSR (courtesy of the *Demir* approach), the ECtHR could find itself in the position to be the ultimate adjudicator in the tension here at stake.

9.2 A ROOM THAT HAS NO FLOOR: THE PWD AND THE DE-CENTRALISATION OF COLLECTIVE BARGAINING

The second tension, namely the one between the trend towards de-centralisation of collective bargaining and the EU framework for posting of workers, lends itself more difficultly to an exclusively legal analysis. The explicit choice in favour of de-centralisation of collective bargaining operated by EU institutions during the years of the Great Recession poses mainly a political problem when assessed on the background of posting. As it was analysed in the previous Chapter, the problem comes down to a question of contrasting messages. On the one hand, the PWD, and much more strongly its interpretation provided by the CJEU, favours a centralised approach when it comes to extending the content of collective agreements to posted workers. On the other, Memoranda and Country Specific Recommendations pushed in the very opposite directions during the last three years. Indeed, also the recent reviews under the procedure for macroeconomic imbalances provided yet another occasion to reinforce the message for some Member State. Belgium is the best example in this sense.[63] In the review of the Spanish imbalances, it was stated that "Before the 2012 labour reform, Spain's collective bargaining system featured an intermediate degree of centralisation (at the sectoral and regional level), which did not allow for a sufficient adaptation to the macroeconomic conditions, nor to the microeconomic conditions of the company", hence suggesting that even an "intermediate degree of centralisation" would not satisfy the Commission.[64] Indeed, the political direction seems rather clear. Whether or not in connection with this choice on the part of EU institutions, recent reforms of collective bargaining, especially among the GIPSI countries, have moved in this direction.

---

62 De Schutter, "L'adhésion de l'Union Européenne à la Charte sociale européenne" (2014), p. 19–20.

63 European Commission, Occasional Papers 172, Macroeconomic Imbalances: Belgium (2014), p. 26.

64 European Commission, Occasional Papers 176, Macroeconomic Imbalances: Spain (2014), p. 51.

This creates two sets of problems in connection with the legal framework for posting shaped by the PWD and by the CJEU. The first one deals with the role of collective agreements in the reasoning of the CJEU when assessing the exercise of collective rights in the field of posted workers. The second set of problems is related to the objective of protecting posted workers.

As to the first set, the role of collective agreements in the reasoning of the CJEU was described in Chapter 7.[65] Without repeating what was already analysed before, the fact that the *demands* of the collective action did fall outside the scope of the PWD was particularly relevant in the reasoning of the Court in *Laval*.[66] The reference goes to the concept of collective agreements as the "measure of all things". The interplay of this stance with the de-centralisation is definitely dangerous for the application of the rights to take collective action and of collective bargaining. Following the reasoning of the Court, in the absence of PWD-applicable collective agreements, *no* collective action can be undertaken against the posting employer.[67] This because such an action will prove impossible to justify either for the objective of protecting posted workers[68] or of fighting social dumping.[69] Both objectives are considered by the CJEU as sufficiently protected by the formal application of the PWD.

For countries characterised by an "employment friendly" de-centralised system of collective bargaining, along the lines suggested by the DG ECFIN,[70] the situation would get quite difficult. Once the bargain coverage is reduced beyond a certain threshold, it would be difficult to consider sectoral or nationwide agreements as generally applicable, let alone universally. This is the situation which characterises the countries which recently implemented reforms of collective bargaining, described in the previous Chapter,[71] such as Romania, Portugal, Spain and Greece. The only option left open by such a situation would be the one of extending collective agreements "concluded by the most representative employers' and labour organisations at national level and which are applied throughout national territory", if these agreements are effectively available. Indeed, the absence of reference to "general applicability" would seem to suggest a different requirement in terms of coverage. However, a different problem arises in this respect. Provided that many of the reforms either required

65 See *supra*, p. 296.
66 *Laval*, para. 110–111.
67 Or, for what it matters, no restriction to the freedom to provide services could be justified on this basis.
68 Ibid., para. 107–110.
69 Ibid., para. 113–118.
70 European Commission, Labour Market Developments in Europe 2012, European Economy, No. 5, pp. 103–104: a) decrease the bargaining coverage or (automatic) extension of collective agreements; b) reform the bargaining system in a less centralised way, for instance by removing or limiting the "favourability principle", or introducing/extending the possibility to derogate from higher level agreements or to negotiate firm-level agreements; c) reduced wage setting power of trade unions.
71 See *supra*, p. 312 ff.

by Memoranda or suggested by "secret" letters and CSR implied a reversal of the hierarchy of collective agreements, it is worth considering such a situation. Now, in *Laval* the CJEU condemned the *Lex Britannia* as discriminatory on the ground that it ignored collective agreements concluded in the home state to which the posting undertaking was already bound.[72] The problem here is the impact of such a reasoning on a Member State wishing to extend to posted workers collective agreement concluded at national level by most representative employers, if these agreements can be derogated by company/plant agreements. Following *Laval*, in such a situation posting undertakings should be allowed to derogate to these agreements at national level through the plant/company agreements concluded in the home state. This impression is nothing but reinforced by the similar approach in the pre-Directive decision of *Portugaia Costruções*.[73] In fact, the same finding seems to apply also for the other options of Article 3(8), *i.e.* for systems relying on generally or universally applicable collective agreements. In the case of a possibility to derogate to those agreements by plant/company agreement, such an option, following the *Laval/Portugaia* reasoning, should also be open to collective agreements concluded in the home state. This means that, following the approach proposed by DG ECFIN and by Memoranda/CSR, (minimum) wages and working conditions applicable to posting undertaking would rapidly come down to those which allow for no derogation. In our hypothesis this would only cover legislative provisions. On this point it is important to consider the example of the Italian system. This system offers today, at least formally,[74] the possibility for company agreements to derogate also from *legislative* dispositions in a number of subjects.[75]

Hence, for this first issue, a de-centralised system like the one supported by the Commission and the Troika would essentially revive, in those areas not covered by legislative disposition allowing for no derogation, a sort of "country of origin principle" for wages and working conditions. That is, a country of origin principle backed by the application of country of origin collective agreements at plant/company level. Some authors referred to this outcome of the *Laval*, *Rüffert* and *Commission v. Luxembourg* decisions, by highlighting the contrast with the

[72] *Laval*, para. 116–120.

[73] In particular, para. 77: "The fact that, in concluding a collective agreement specific to one undertaking, a domestic employer can pay wages lower than the minimum wage laid down in a collective agreement declared to be generally applicable, whilst an employer established in another Member State cannot do so, constitutes an unjustified restriction on the freedom to provide services".

[74] Most representative social actors have agreed not to make use of this disposition.

[75] Decreto-legge 13 agosto 2011, n. 138, coordinato con la legge di conversione 14 settembre 2011, n. 148, recante: "Ulteriori misure urgenti per la stabilizzazione finanziaria e per lo sviluppo", Article 8(2) and 8(2-*bis*). Those subjects are: the use of a-typical contract, working time and dismissals (with the exclusion of pregnant workers, discriminatory dismissals and dismissal in the occasion of marriage).

expulsion of the country of origin principle from the Service Directive.[76] The disregard for this political choice, which followed one of the very few moment of a European public opinion mobilisation,[77] is obviously not a legal argument. Instead, it is a clear reminder of how the attempts to "influence" the approach of the CJEU to the PWD by intervening on *other* instruments and relying on the power of the "democratic imprimatur"[78] are probably doomed. The more recent example of this attempt is the inclusion of a "Monti clause" in the Enforcement Directive.[79] Another important outcome of this "diagonal"[80] possibility of derogation is the creation of a direct competition between industrial relations system. Such a situation, which already characterises the EU construction,[81] is exacerbated by the interplay between de-centralisation and the case law of the CJEU on posting. From the point of view of posted workers, this same interplay might prove toxic to their protection. Indeed, in the absence of a minimum wage which can be validly extended to posted workers and which allows no derogation, their wages could be lawfully fixed at a level which is below the poverty line[82] for the given country.

The second issue also stems from the question of applicable collective agreements. The Court of Justice has construed the test applied to collective action as to make the action legitimate only if the demands it puts forward respect the PWD. Building on the scenario I just outlined, one can easily see that the restriction of the applicable agreements, through de-centralisation and possibilities for derogation, thus restricts also the possibility to have recourse to (legitimate) collective action, or, for what it matters, to other collective rights which could cause a restriction to the freedom to provide services. This reasoning can be extended

---

76 See for example, Barnard, "Employment Rights, Free Movement Under the EC Treaty and the Services Directive", p. 168; Malmberg, "Posting Post Laval International and National Responses", p. 7.

77 See A. Crespy, "Legitimizing Resistance to EU Integration: Social Europe as a Europeanized Normative Frame in the Conflict over the Bolkestein Directive", *Les Cahiers Européens de Sciences Po.* 3 (2010): 1–24, p. 4.

78 C. Kilpatrick, "Internal Market Architecture and the Accommodation of Labour Rights: As Good as It Gets?" *European Journal of Social Law*, no. 1 (2012): 1–26, pp. 7.

79 Directive 2014/67/EU of the European Parliament and of the Council on the enforcement of Directive 96/71/EC concerning the posting of workers in the framework of the provision of services and amending Regulation (EU) No 1024/2012 on administrative cooperation through the Internal Market Information System ("the IMI Regulation"), 15 May 2014, Article 1(2): "This Directive shall not affect in any way the exercise of fundamental rights as recognised in Member States and by Union law, including the right or freedom to strike or to take other action covered by the specific industrial relations systems in Member States, in accordance with national law and practices. Nor does it affect the right to negotiate, conclude and enforce collective agreements and to take collective action in accordance with national law and practices".

80 *I.e.*, the possibility to use a plant/company agreement negotiated in the context of a different industrial relations system to derogate a nationwide/sectoral agreement of the host state.

81 See Marginson and Sisson, *European Integration and Industrial Relations: Multi-Level Governance in the Making*, pp. 9–10.

82 Defined as the 50% of median adjusted household disposable income.

to the right to bargain collectively, when it is backed by the threat of collective action.[83] In our scenario this would effectively make posting undertaking as "dead zones" for collective labour rights and for the host state industrial relations. In fact, this situation was the one openly criticised by the European Committee on Social Rights when dealing with the *Lex Laval.* Indeed, the Committee stated that " from the point of view of the system of values, principles and rights embodied in the Charter, the facilitation of free cross-border movement of services and the promotion of the freedom of an employer or undertaking to provide services in the territory of other States – which constitute important and valuable economic freedoms within the framework of EU law – cannot be treated as having a greater a priori value than labour rights [...], including the right for posted workers to receive from the host State treatment not less favourable than that of other workers, in respect of the enjoyment of the benefits of collective bargaining".[84] On the same line the Committee added that "excluding or limiting the right to collective bargaining or action with respect to foreign undertakings, for the sake of enhancing free cross border movement of services and advantages in terms of competition within a common market zone, constitutes, according to the Charter, discriminatory treatment on the ground of nationality of the workers".[85] Indeed, the creation of these "dead zones" where workers and (posting) employers are *de jure* excluded from the scope of fundamental rights, such as the right to take collective action and to bargain collectively, is a by-product of the said interplay. That is, the result of the combination of a political choice from EU institutions[86] in favour of complete de-centralisation of collective bargaining and of a legal construction of the posting phenomenon delivered by the Court of Justice.

The question is thus how to reconcile the reality of increasingly de-centralised systems of collective bargaining with the approach of the Court of Justice in order to avoid the complete obliteration of collective social rights. In this perspective it would fall upon the Court of Justice to adapt its reasoning to the ever changing reality, even more so when this change is in fact supported by other EU institutions. Obviously, this is intertwined with the first tension. Indeed, bringing its case law in line with the interpretation of ILO Convention No. 87 and of the ESC provided by the respective supervisory bodies would probably solve also the second tension. However, a more specific and less far-reaching solution could also be envisaged. In fact, it *has* been envisaged, with two slightly different formulations by Syrpis

83 The only "safe" negotiation being the one in which the posting employer signs a collective agreement on its own accord. See *Laval*, para. 81.

84 *Swedish Trade Union Confederation (LO) and Swedish Confederation of Professional Employees (TCO) v. Sweden*, Complaint No. 85/2012 para. 140.

85 Ibid., para. 141.

86 Either acting in the context of the Troika or drawing CSR or analysing macroeconomic imbalances of Member States.

and Novitz[87] and Dorssemont and Orlandini.[88] Syrpis and Novitz propose "to hold that private parties, including trade unions, are bound by free movement provisions when they are exercising regulatory tasks which would otherwise be exercised by public authorities in the state in question".[89] In the Authors' example, the "setting of a minimum wage on a national or sectoral basis" would fall into this category, while "collective bargaining in respect of particular establishments" would not. Similarly, Orlandini and Dorssemont propose a distinction between the *extension* of collective agreements and the exercise of collective bargaining.[90] Hence, only collective agreements whose application is "mandatory by law" should be considered as possible obstacles to fundamental freedoms. Instead those agreements which are applicable to the (posting) employer only following a process of negotiations in which he or she is involved cold not be considered as such, since any restriction would be stemming from the exercise of the employer's freedom of contract.[91] By excluding that this kind of agreements can represent a restriction, both approaches would exclude the collective action eventually aimed at their conclusion from the scrutiny of the CJEU. Dorssemont and Orlandini also stress the fact that collective actions would still have to respect the principle of non-discrimination, so that "any industrial action aiming to create obstacles to the execution of a contract of service by a company based abroad for the sole purpose of defending national companies (and employees) should be considered discriminatory, irrespective of the working conditions applied to foreign workers or the ones that could be applied if the employer accepted to take part in collective bargaining".[92] This is in line with the approach of the European Committee of Social Rights, considered that a general ban on collective actions having discriminatory objectives would not be *prima facie* contrary to the ESC.[93]

These solutions have the merit of demanding from the CJEU only a limited deviation from its own case law, whereas solving the first tension would require a re-thinking of the whole approach to the balancing exercise. The basic idea would be to separate the destinies of public action from the activity of trade unions. Only the former should hence be assessed through the lenses of the PWD-as-a-ceiling.

87 Syrpis and Novitz, "Economic and Social Rights in Conflict: Political and Judicial Approaches to Their Reconciliation".

88 Dorssemont and Orlandini, "Market Rules and the Right to Strike: a Different Approach".

89 Syrpis and Novitz, "Economic and Social Rights in Conflict: Political and Judicial Approaches to Their Reconciliation", p. 421.

90 Dorssemont and Orlandini, "Market Rules and the Right to Strike: a Different Approach", p. 78.

91 Ibid., pp. 73–74.

92 Ibid., p. 83.

93 *Swedish Trade Union Confederation (LO) and Swedish Confederation of Professional Employees (TCO) v. Sweden*, Complaint No. 85/2012 para. 119: "the prohibition of certain types of collective action, or even the introduction of a general legislative limitation of the right to collective action in order to prevent initiatives aimed at achieving illegitimate or abusive goals (e.g. goals which do not relate to the enjoyment of labour rights, or relate to discriminatory objectives) would not be necessarily contrary to Article 6(4) of the Charter".

Such a conclusion seems also logic in view of the tension here at stake. The EU as a whole cannot preach the employment-friendly virtues of de-centralisation and then witness its Court of Justice condemn the fact that an undertaking "may be forced, by way of collective action, into negotiations with the trade unions of unspecified duration at the place at which the services in question are to be provided".[94] What is more, to free the right to take collective action and to bargain collectively in respect of posting undertakings from the scrutiny of the Court shaped in *Laval* may not have too much of an impact on a majority of posting situations. Indeed looking at this issue in more empirical terms, as it was showed in Chapter 1,[95] posting employers have a definitely upper hand when it comes to bargaining power in respect of trade unions in the host country. A shift in attitude in this regard could thus have a relevant symbolic importance while its impact on the economic reality of posting would remain relatively moderate.

9.3 FINALE

At the end of this journey, it is apparent that posting of workers represented the battleground for a clash of a much broader scope. A phenomenon of relatively small proportions[96] brought to the fore, in the words of the Monti Report, "an old split that had never been healed: the divide between advocates of greater market integration and those who feel that the call for economic freedoms and for breaking up regulatory barriers is code for dismantling social rights protected at national level".[97] This split has not healed in the field of posting. In the meantime it has widened to an unprecedented extent, following the decisions of EU institutions in dealing with the Great Recession.

The relatively small dimension of the posting phenomenon, coupled with the fundamental nature of the clash taking place in its context, makes it a perfect candidate for some form of symbolic message. A better equilibrium between fundamental social rights and fundamental freedoms of the internal market in this area could provide a sign of life for "Social Europe", whatever the actual meaning of such a label may be. The economic impact would be limited, a dwarf if compared to the choice in favour of austerity, but it would nonetheless intervene on a very visible topic. True enough, the issue of social dumping, the "dead zones" created by the EU legal framework for posting, are arguments with a much greater impact on the so-called "core" EU countries. Still, if one looks at the results of the last elections for the European Parliament, it is in those countries,

94 *Laval*, para. 100.
95 See *supra*, p. 48.
96 See *supra*, pp. 32 ff.
97 Monti Report, p. 68.

not in the devastated GIPSI periphery, that anti-EU parties are gaining ground.[98] In this context, the *de jure* exclusion of equal treatment for posted workers may represent a time-bomb. It just takes some particularly outrageous case to make it to the media; even less than that, as the "polish plumber" scarecrow has showed. Thus, if a U-turn, *i.e.* equal treatment for posted workers, is at present difficult to conceive, to reinstate equal treatment at least as a legitimate *aim* of collective action could do much to mend the wounds left by the *Laval* quartet. This could be achieved by different approaches, as I have showed in this final Chapter.

Moreover, the first tension highlighted in this Chapter poses serious question in terms of "output legitimacy"[99] of the EU itself. Unfortunately, the steps to take to bring in line the EU legal order with the systems of values and rights embodied by the ESC and by ILO Convention No 87 appear at present somewhat out of reach. The likelihood of legislative intervention has showed all its limits in this regard with the failure of the "Monti II" proposal. Once again it would fall to an independent institution, *in casu* the CJEU, to do "whatever it takes" to save the situation. However, the willingness of the EU judges to do so can be questioned. The most recent precedent remains *Commission v. Germany*, which reads as a loyalty oath to *Viking&Laval*. This could theoretically damage also the legitimacy of the CJEU itself, as regards it ability to protect fundamental and human rights, suggesting a less deferential attitude to the constitutional courts of Member States. This possibility has been envisaged by Dorssemont,[100] and it has become somewhat less abstract at a time when the German Constitutional Court openly questions the Outright Monetary Transactions (OMT) operation of the ECB.[101] Also, the Portuguese Constitutional Court has played an important role in striking down several austerity measures imposed by the Memorandum. In this sense it is interesting to look at the reasoned opinion of the Portuguese *Assembleia da República* on the "Monti II" proposal. The opinion states that "placing social rights and economic rights on an equal footing in the field of fundamental rights, which this initiative upholds, is contrary to constitutional tradition in Portugal and to the interpretation followed in decisions in Portugal's Constitutional Court, as well as in general principles of doctrine". The simple possibility of an open conflict with a national constitutional court should suggest

---

98 *E.g.* France (FN), The Netherlands (PVV), Finland (Finns Party), Austria (FPOE), Sweden (SD) and Denmark (DPP) (together, less surprisingly, with the UK). One might be tempted to conclude that the EU-narrative for the crisis, based on the distinction between the profligate periphery and the productive core was quite effective in convincing the voters ... in the core.

99 See further F.W. Scharpf, "Legitimacy in the Multilevel European Polity", *MPIfG Working Paper* 1 (2009): 1–40; F.W. Scharpf, "Political Legitimacy in a Non-Optimal Currency Area", *MPIfG Discussion Paper* 15 (2013): 1–39.

100 Dorssemont, "A Judicial Pathway to Overcome Laval and Viking", pp. 16 ff.

101 Which has often been pointed out as the move which effectively saved the Euro. See P. De Grauwe, "Why The ECJ Should Reject The German Constitutional Court's Ruling", *Social Europe (Blog)*, 11 March 2014; W. Münchau, "Germany's Constitutional Court Has Strengthened the Eurosceptics", *Financial Times*, 9 February 2014.

a more balanced approach to the CJEU. Unfortunately such a change of mind has not happened so far, for lack of "good cases" to do so, the optimist would say.

Still, the lack of optimism in this regard does not come from lack of legal arguments to underpin this change, as these would readily be available to the CJEU. Instead, it is the coherence of the present configuration of posting of workers (in its relationship with fundamental social rights) with the present policy direction of the EU that makes a change of mind less likely. In an environment focused on competitiveness based on wage moderation,[102] posted workers provide a useful pressure on (some economic sectors[103] of) core countries, while the same moderation in the periphery is ensured by high levels of unemployment. Furthermore, the "market access test"[104] applied to the exercise of collective social rights is yet another brick in the wall of a construction resembling more and more a "market preserving federalism"[105] with the introduction of the reforms going under the label of "New Economic Governance". In 2013 a Report by J.P. Morgan pointed out that "constitutions and political settlements in the southern periphery, put in place in the aftermath of the fall of fascism, have a number of features which appear to be unsuited to further integration in the region",[106] including "constitutional protection of labour rights". In this sense the *Viking&Laval* doctrine would surely prove useful to overcome those "constitutional problems". Hopefully this pessimistic vision will prove the wrong one.

To conclude, the relatively small phenomenon of posting of workers indeed represents the unlikely battleground for a conflict about the very nature of the EU construction. As such, it remains tangled in a web of issues, both legal and socio-economic. It would be virtually impossible to provide an exhaustive

---

102 Janssen, "Workers Of Europe, Compete!".

103 The best example being the construction sector, where the large presence of posted workers greatly enhances competition between workers, in a sector otherwise quite shielded from international competition.

104 J. Snell, "The Notion of Market Access: a Concept or a Slogan?", *Common Market Law Review* 47 (2010): 437–472, pp. 467 ff.

105 Höpner and Schäfer, "Embeddedness and Regional Integration: Waiting for Polanyi in a Hayekian Setting", p. 435; Harmes, "Neoliberalism and Multilevel Governance", p. 737. A market-preserving federalism should be characterised by "(F1) a hierarchy of governments, that is, at least "two levels of government rule the same land and people", each with a delineated scope of authority so that each level of government is autonomous in its own, well-defined sphere of political authority; (F2) the autonomy of each government is institutionalized in a manner that makes federalism's restrictions self-enforcing; [...] (F3) subnational governments have primary regulatory responsibility over the economy; (F4) common market is ensured, preventing the lower governments from using their regulatory authority to erect trade barriers against the goods and services from other political units; (F5) the lower governments face a hard budget constraint, that is, they have neither the ability to print money nor access to unlimited credit. This condition is not met if the central government bails out the lower one whenever the latter faces fiscal problems".

106 J.P. Morgan, "The Euro Area Adjustment: about Halfway There", *Europe Economic Research*, 28 May 2013, 1–16, p. 2. The Report further defines the problem: "the political systems in the periphery were established in the aftermath of dictatorship, and were defined by that experience. Constitutions tend to show a strong socialist influence, reflecting the political strength that left wing parties gained after the defeat of fascism".

analysis of every strand of this web. In fact, some of these issues remain at present undecided. In particular, it remains to be seen if and how the new EU Commission and the new European Parliament will try to intervene (again) on the posting phenomenon. From another angle, the eventual accession of the EU to the ECtHR will (would) surely provide an occasion to re-examine the overarching question of the relationship between the fundamental freedoms of the EU internal market and the protection of fundamental (social) rights. Finally, it is in the context of the posting phenomenon that the conflict between EU law and the rights and values protected by ILO Conventions and by the ESC became evident.[107] Time will tell if the Court of Justice will be willing to do "whatever it takes" to ensure that the interpretation of EU law respects international standards of protection for social and labour rights.

But that is another story and shall be told another time.

the triangle tingles and the trumpet plays slow...

---

107 Report "State of Democracy, Human Rights and the Rule of Law in Europe", SG(2014)1 – FINAL, by the Secretary General of the Council of Europe: "In 2013 the European Committee of Social Rights found a breach, inter alia, of the right to bargain collectively and the right to strike important corollaries of the right to organise. The measures in question had been adopted as a result of a judgment of the Court of Justice of the European Union. The decisions of the States Parties (resulting directly or indirectly from EU law) must conform to the rights enshrined in the Charter. Therefore we see an urgent need to find pragmatic solutions to settle conflicts between the two sets of standards".

BIBLIOGRAPHY

Achtsioglou, E. "Greece 2010–2012: labour in the Maelstrom of Deregulation." *Transfer: European Review of Labour and Research* 19, no. 1 (January 2013): 125–127.

Adlercreutz, A and B Nystrom. *Labour Law in Sweden*. Alphen aan den Rijn: Kluwer Law International, 2010.

Ahlberg, K. "The Age of Innocence – and Beyond." In *Cross-Border Services, Posting of Workers and Multilevel Governance*, edited by Stein Evju, 297–328. Oslo: Institutt for privaterett, 2013.

—. "Will Lex Laval Work?" *Nordic Labour Journal*, 2010.

Alemanno, A. "À la recherche d'un juste équilibre entre libertés fondamentales et droits fondamentaux dans le cadre du marché intérieur" *Revue du Droit de l'Union Européenne* 4 (2004): 709–751.

Ales, E. "Dal 'caso FIAT' al 'caso Italia'. Il diritto del Lavoro 'di prossimità', le sue scaturigini e i suoi limiti" *WP C.S.D.L.E. Massimo D'Antona.IT*, no. 134 (2011): 1–30.

Alter, K. *The European Court's Political Power: Selected Essays*. Oxford: Oxford University Press, 2009.

Anderson, B.N. Clark and V. Parutis, "New EU Members?: Migrant Workers' Challenges and Opportunities to UK Trades Unions: a Polish and Lithuanian Case Study." London: TUC, 2007.

Anderson, B., M. Ruhs, B. Rogaly and S. Spencer. "Central and East European Migrants in Low-Wage Employment in the UK." *Joseph Rowntree Foundation*. London: Joseph Rowntree Foundation, 2006.

Armingeon, K. and L. Baccaro. "Political Economy of the Sovereign Debt Crisis: The Limits of Internal Devaluation." *Industrial Law Journal* 41, no. 3 (2012): 254–272.

Arrigo, G. and G. Casale. "A Comparative Overview of Terms and Notions on Employee Participation." Labour Administration and Inspection Programme LAB/ADMIN, Working Document Number 8, Geneva: International Labour Organization, 2010.

Asteriti, A. "Social Dialogue, Laval-Style." *European Journal of Legal Studies* 5, no. 2 (2012): 57–79.

Auzero, G.E. Dockès and J. Pélissier. *Droit Du Travail*. Paris: Dalloz-Sirey, 2012.

Avbelj, M. "European Court of Justice and the Question of Value Choices." *Jean Monnet Working Paper* 4 (2006): 1–84.

Avci, G. and C. McDonald. "Chipping Away at the Fortress: Unions, Immigration and the Transnational Labour Market." *International Migration* 38, no. 2 (June 2000): 191–213.

Azoulai, L. "The Case of Fundamental Rights: a State of Ambivalence." In *The European Court of Justice and the Autonomy of the Member States*, edited by Hans-W. Micklitz and Bruno De Witte, 207–217. Cambridge: Intersentia, 2012.

—. "The Court of Justice and the Social Market Economy: the Emergence of an Ideal and the Conditions for Its Realization." *Common Market Law Review*, no. 2007 (2008): 1335–1356.

Bailleux, A. "Entrave Et Droits Fondamentaux." In *L'entrave Et L'accès Au Marché*, edited by D. Prieto, 225–256. Brussels: Bruylant, 2011.

Bain, G. and H. Clegg. "A Strategy for Industrial Relations Research in Great Britain." *British Journal of Industrial Relations* 12, no. 1 (1974): 91–113.

Bamber, G. and P. Sheldon. "Collective Bagaining: an International Analysis." In *Comparative Labour Law and Industrial Relations in Industrialized Market Economies*, edited by Roger Blanpain, 585–632. Den Haag: International, Kluwer Law, 2007.

Barnard, C. "A Proportionate Response to Proportionality in the Field of Collective Action." *European Law Review* 2, no. 37 (2012): 117–135.

—. "'British Jobs for British Workers': The Lindsey Oil Refinery Dispute and the Future of Local Labour Clauses in an Integrated EU Market." *Industrial Law Journal* 38, no. 3 (August 2009): 245–277.

—. *EC Employment Law*. Oxford: Oxford University Press, 2000.

—. "Employment Rights, Free Movement Under the EC Treaty and the Services Directive." *Europa Institute Working Paper* 5 (2008): 1–30.

—. "Social Dumping or Dumping Socialism?" *The Cambridge Law Journal* 67, no. 02 (June 2008).

—. "The Financial Crisis and the Euro Plus Pact: A Labour Lawyer's Perspective." *Industrial Law Journal* 41, no. 1 (2012): 98–114.

—. "The Protection of Fundamental Social Rights in Europe After Lisbon: a Question of Conflicts of Interests." In *The Protection of Fundamental Rights in the EU After Lisbon*, edited by Sybe de Vries, Ulf Bernitz, and Stephen Weatherill, 37–57. Oxford: Hart Publishing, 2013.

—. *The Substantive Law of the EU: The Four Freedoms*. Oxford: Oxford University Press, 2007.

—. "Viking and Laval: an Introduction." *Cambridge Yearbook of European Legal Studies* 10, no. 463–492 (2008).

Barnard, C. and S. Deakin. "Market Access and Regulatory Competition." In *The Law of the Single European Market: unpacking the Premises*, 197–223. Oxford: Hart Publishing, 2002.

Barnard, C. and J. Scott. *The Law of the Single European Market: unpacking the Premises*, Oxford: Hart Publishing, 2002.

Bartlett, R. *Trial by Fire and Water*. Oxford: Clarendon Press, 1986.

Belavusau, U. "The Case of Laval in the Context of the Post-Enlargement EC Law Development." *German Law Journal* 9, no. 12 (2008): 2279–2308.

Ben-Israel, R. "Strikes, Lockouts and Other Kinds of Hostile Actions." In *International Encyclopaedia of Comparative Law. Volume XV*, edited by Bob Hepple, 1–50. Tübingen: C.B. Mohr, 1997.

Bercusson, B. "The Lisbon Treaty and Social Europe." *ERA Forum* 10, no. 1 (March 2009): 87–105.

—. "The Trade Union Movement and the European Union: Judgment Day." *European Law Journal* 13, no. 3 (May 2007): 279–308.

—. "Trade Union Rights in the EU Member States." Social Affairs Series. Brussels: European Parliament – Directorate General for Research, 1997.

Bernaciak, M. "Social Dumping: political Catchphrase or Threat to Labour Standards?" *ETUI Working Paper* 6 (2012): 1–40.

Bevort, A. and A. Jobert. *Sociologie Du Travail: les Relations Professionelles*. Paris: Armand Colin, 2008.

Biagi, M. "Fortune Smiles on the Italian EU Presidency: talking Half-Seriously About the Poste Workers and Parental Leave Directives." *The International Journal of Comparative Labour Law and Industrial Relations* 12, no. 2 (1996): 97–109.

—. "The 'Posted Workers' EU Directive: from Social Dumping to Social Protectionism." In *Labour Law and Industrial Relations in the European Union*, edited by Roger Blanpain, 173–180. The Hague: Kluwer Law International, 1998.

Blanpain, R. *European Labour Law*. The Hague: Kluwer Law International, 2010.

—. *Freedom of Services in the European Union: Labour and Social Security Law: the Bolkestein Initiative*. The Hague: Kluwer Law International, 2006.

—. "Representation of Employees at Plant and Eterprise Level." In *International Encyclopaedia of Comparative Law. Volume XV1*, edited by Bob Hepple, 1–51. Tübingen: C.B. Mohr, 1994.

Brown, C. "Case C-112/00, Eugen Schmidberger, Internationale Transporte Und Planzüge v. Austria." *Common Market Law Review* 40 (2003): 1499–1510.

Bruun, N., A. Bücker and F. Dorssemont. "Balancing Fundamental Social Rights and Economic Freedoms: Can the Monti II Initiative Solve the EU Dilemma?" *International Journal of Comparative Labour Law and Industrial Relations* 28, no. 3 (2012): 279–306.

Bruun, N., A. Jacobs and M. Schmidt. "ILO Convention No. 94 in the Aftermath of the Ruffert Case." *Transfer: European Review of Labour and Research* 16, no. 4 (November 2010): 473–488.

Bruun, N., C.-M. Jonsson and E. Olauson. "Consequences and Policy Perspectives in the Nordic Countries as a Result of Certain Important Decisions of the Court of Justice of the EU." In *Reconciling Fundamental Social Rights and Economic Freedoms After Viking, Laval and Rüffert*, edited by Andreas Bücker and Wiebke Warneck, 385. Baden-Baden: Nomos Publishers, 2011.

de Búrca, G. "After the EU Charter of Fundamental Rights: The Court of Justice as a Human Rights Adjudicator?" *Maastricht Journal of European and Comparative Law* 20 (2013): 168–184.

Bücker, A. "A Comprehensive Social Progress Protocol Is Needed More Than Ever." *European Labour Law Journal* 4, no. 1 (2013): 4–23.

Bücker, A., W. Warneck and F. Dorssemont. "The Search for a Balance: analysis and Perspectives." In *Reconciling Fundamental Social Rights and Economic Freedoms After Viking, Laval and Rüffert*, edited by Andreas Bücker and Wiebke Warneck, 315–360. Baden-Baden: Nomos Publishers, 2011.

Carinci, F., R. De Luca Tamajo, P. Tosi and T. Treu. *Diritto Del Lavoro Vol 2. Il Rapporto Di Lavoro Subordinato*. Torino: UTET, 2005.

—. *Diritto Del Lavoro Vol. 1. Il Diritto Sindacale*. Torino: UTET, 2006.

Çaro, E., L. Bernsten, N. Lillie, I. Wagner, "Work/Life Experience of Posted Migrant Construction Workers in a Pan-European Labour Market," no. August (2013): 1–17.

Casale, G. "International Labour Standards and EU Labour Law." In *Resocialising Europe in a Time of Crisis*, edited by Nicola Countouris and Mark Freedland, 81–104. Cambridge: Cambridge University Press, 2013.

Castles, S. and G. Kosack. *Immigrant Workers and Class Structures in Western Europe*. Oxford: Oxford University Press, 1985.

Clauwaert, S. and I. Schomann. "The Crisis and National Labour Law Reforms – a Mapping Exercise." *Transfer: European Review of Labour and Research* 19, no. 1 (January 2013): 121–124.

Clauwaert, S., I. Schömann, W. Düvel and C. Wörgotter. "Fundamental Social Rights in the European Union: Comparative Tables and Documents." Brussels: European Trade Union Institute, 2003.

Clauwaert, S. "The Country-Specific Recommendations (CSRs) in the Social Field – An Overview and Initial Comparison." *ETUI Background Analysis* 2 (2013).

Clegg, H. *The Changing System of Industrial Relations in Great Britain*. Oxford: Blackwell, 1979.

—. *Trade Unionism Under Collective Bargaining: A Theory Based on Comparisons of Six Countries*. Oxford: Blackwell Publishers, 1976.

Colling, T. and M. Terry. "Work, the Employment Relationship and the Field of Industrial Relations." In *Industrial Relations. Theory and Practice*, edited by Trevor Colling and Michael Terry, 1–24. New York: John Wiley & Sons, 2010.

Commons, J.R. *Legal Foundations of Capitalism*. New York: McMillan, 1924.

Conway, G. "Articles Conflicts of Competence Norms in EU Law and the Legal Reasoning of the ECJ." *German Law Journal* 11, no. 2 (2010): 966–1005.

Da Costa, I. "La théorie des relations industrielles aux Etats-Unis. De Dunlop au débat actuel." In *Les Systèmes de Relations Professionnelles*, edited by Jean-Daniel Reynaud, François Eyraud, Catherine Paradeise, and Jean Saglio, 25–42. Paris: Editions du Centre National de la Recherche Scientifique, 1990.

Creighton, B. "Freedom of Association." In *Comparative Labour Law and Industrial Relations in Industrialized Market Economies*, edited by Roger Blanpain, 275–322. The Hague: Kluwer Law International, 2007.

Cremers, J. *In Search of Cheap Labour in Europe. Working and Living Conditions of Posted Workers*. CLR Studies. Bruxelles: European Institute for Construction Labour Research, 2011.

Crespy, A. "Legitimizing Resistance to EU Integration: Social Europe as a Europeanized Normative Frame in the Conflict over the Bolkestein Directive." *Les Cahiers Européens de Sciences Po*. 3 (2010): 1–24.

Crouch, C. *Industrial Relations and European State Traditions*. Oxford: Oxford University Press, 1993.

—. *Trade Unions: The Logic of Collective Action*. Waukegan: Fontana Press, 1982.

Dashwood, A. "Viking and Laval: Issues of Horizontal Direct Effect." *Cambridge Yearbook of European Legal Studies* 10 (2008): 525–540.

Davies, A. "One Step Forward, Two Steps Back? The Viking and Laval Cases in the ECJ." *Industrial Law Journal* 37, no. 2 (June 2008): 126–148.

Davies, P. "Case C-346/06, Ruffert V Land Niedersachsen [2008] IRLR 467 (ECJ)." *Industrial Law Journal* 37, no. 3 (September 2008): 293–295.

—. "Posted Workers: Single Market or Protection of National Labour Law Systems?" *Common Market Law Review* 34 (1997): 571–602.

Däubler, W. "Posted Workers and Freedom to Supply Services. Directive 96/71/EC and German Courts." *Industrial Law Journal* 27 (1998): 264–268.

De Grauwe, P. "Why The ECJ Should Reject The German Constitutional Court's Ruling." *Social Europe (Blog)*, 11 March 2014.

De Schutter, O. "L'adhésion de L'Union Européenne à la Charte sociale européenne." Report, 8 July 2014.

De Schutter, O. "L'adhésion de l'Union Européenne à la Charte sociale européenne révisée." *EUI Working Paper*, no. 11 (2004): 1–44.

—. "The Two Lives of the European Social Charter." In *The European Social Charter: a Social Constitution for Europe*, edited by Olivier De Schutter, 11–37. Brussels: Bruylant, 2010.

Deakin, S. "Regulatory Competition After Laval." *Cambridge Yearbook of European Legal Studies* 10 (2008): 581–610.

—. "Social Rights in a Globalized Economy." In *Labour Rights as Human Rights*, edited by Philip Alston, 25–60. Oxford: Oxford University Press, 2005.

—. "The Lisbon Treaty, the Viking and Laval Judgments and the Financial Crisis: In Search of New Foundations for Europe's 'Social Market Economy'." In *The Lisbon Treaty and Social Europe*, edited by Niklas Bruun, Klaus Lörcher and Isabelle Schömann, 19–44. Oxford: Hart Publishing, 2012.

Deakin, S. and A. Koukiadaki. "The Sovereign Debt Crisis and the Evolution of Labour Law in Europe." In *Resocialising Europe in a Time of Crisis*, edited by Nicola Countouris and Mark Freedland, 163–188. Cambridge: Cambridge University Press, 2013.

Deakin, S. and G.S. Morris. *Labour Law*. Oxford: Hart Publishing, 2009.

Defossez, A. "Détachement des travailleurs, ordre public et dumping social, suite et certainment pas fin." *Revue de La Faculté de Droit de L'Université de Liège* 4 (2008): 602–612.

Degryse, C. and P. Pochet. "Worrying Trends in the New European Governance." In *Social Developments in the European Union 2011*, edited by David Natali and Bart Vanhercke, 81–108. Brussels: ETUI-OSE Publications, 2011.

Degryse, C. "The New European Economic Governance." *ETUI Working Paper* 14 (2012): 1–86.

Degryse, C.M. Jepsen and P. Pochet. "The Euro Crisis and Its Impact on National and European Social Policies." *ETUI Working Paper* 05 (2013).

Delteil, V. and M. Bănărescu. "Roumanie – Le modèle social sous la pression des bailleurs de fonds: les syndicats à la recherche de nouvelles 'tutelles'." *Chronique Internationale de L'IRES* 143–144 (2013): 133–151.

Dolvik, J.E. and J. Waddington. "Organizing Marketized Services: Are Trade Unions Up to the Job?", *Economic and Industrial Democracy* 25, no. 1 (February 2004): 9–40.

Dorssemont, F. and A. Van Hoek. "Collective Action in Labour Conflicts Under the Rome II Regulation (Part I)." *European Labour Law Journal* 2, no. 1 (2011): 48–75.

—. "Collective Action in Labour Conflicts Under the Rome II Regulation (Part II)." *European Labour Law Journal* 2, no. 2 (2011): 101–118.

Dorssemont, F. "A Judicial Pathway to Overcome Laval and Viking." *OSE Reasearch Paper*, no. September (2011).

—. "Collectief Arbeidsrechtelijke Aspecten van Internationale Detachering." In *Handboek Europese Detachering En Vrij Verkeer van Diensten*, edited by Yves Jorens, 525–576. Brugge: Die Keure, 2009.

—. "How the European Court of Human Rights Gave Us Energy to Cope with Viking and Laval." In *Before and After the Economic Crisi? What Implications for the 'European Social Model'?*, edited by Marie-Ange Moreau, 217–235. Cheltenham: Edward Elgar, 2011.

—. "The Right to Form and to Join Trade Unions for the Protection of His Interests Under Article 11 ECHR." *European Labour Law Journal* 1, no. 2 (2010): 185–235.

—. "The Right to Take Collective Action Under Article 11 ECHR." In *The European Convention on Human Rights and the Employment Relation*, edited by Filip Dorssemont, Klaus Lörcher and Isabelle Schömann, 333–367. Oxford: Hart Publishing, 2013.

—. "The Right to Take Collective Action Versus Fundamental Economic Freedoms in the Aftermath of Laval and Viking. Foes Are Forever." In *European Union Internal Market and Labour Law: Friends or Foes?*, edited by Marc De Vos, 88:45–104. Antwerp: Intersentia, 2009.

—. "Worker Involvement in Secondary EC Law Prior to the Recast Directive." In *The Recast of the European Works Council Directive*, edited by Filip Dorssemont, 31–90. Antwerp: Intersentia, 2010.

Dorssemont, F. and G. Orlandini. "Market Rules and the Right to Strike: a Different Approach." In *From Labour Law to Social Competition Law?*, edited by Marc Rigaux, Jan Buelens and Amanda Latinne, 67–105. Antwerp: Intersentia, 2014.

Douglas-Scott, S. "A Tale of Two Courts: Luxemgourg, Strasbourg and the Growing European Human Rights Acquis." *Common Market Law Review* 43, no. 3 (2006): 629–665.

Dribbusch, H. "European Migrant Workers Union Founded." Dublin: European Foundation, 2004.

Druesne, G. "Liberté de prestation des services et travailleurs salariés." *Revue Trimestrielle de Droit Européen*, 1982, 75-81.

Dufresne, A. and J.-M. Pernot. "Les syndicats européens à l'épreuve de la nouvelle gouvernance économique." *Chronique Internationale de L'IRES* 143–144 (2013): 3–29.

Dunlop, J.T. *Industrial Relations Systems*. New York: Henry Holt; Company, 1958.

—. "The Task of Contemporary Wage Theory." In *New Concepts in Wage Determination*, edited by W. Taylor and Frank C. Pierson, 131–134. New York: McGraw Hill, 1957.

—. *Wage Determination Under Trade Unions*. London: Macmillan Co, 1944.

ECSR. *Digest of the Case Law of the European Committee of Social Rights*. Strasbourg, 2008.

Edwards, P. *Conflict at Work: A Materialist Analysis of Workplace Relations*. Oxford: Blackwell Pub, 1986.

—. "The Employment Relationship and the Field of Industrial Relations." In *Industrial Relations: theory and Practice*, edited by Paul Edwards, 1–36. New York: John Wiley & Sons, 2003.

Eichhorst, W. "European Social Policy Between National and Supranational Regulation: Posted Workers in the Framework of Liberalized Services Provision." MPIfG Discussion Paper. Max-Planck-Institut für Gesellschaftsforschung, 1998.

Eklund, R. "A Swedish Perspective on Laval." *Comparative Labor Law & Policy Journal* 29, no. 4 (2008): 551–572.

Eklund, R., T. Sigeman and L. Carlson. *Swedish Labour and Employment Law: Cases and Materials*. Uppsala: Lustu Forlag, 2008.

Esping-Andersen, G. *The Three Worlds of Welfare Capitalism*. Princeton: Princeton University Press, 1990.

Eurofound. "Impact of the Crisis on Industrial Relations." Dublin, 2013.

Evju, S. "Posting Past and Present. The Posting of Workers Directive - Genesis and Current Contrasts." *FORMULA Working Paper* 8, no. 8 (2009): 1–65.

—. "The FORMULA Project: Introduction and Backdrop." In *Cross-Border Services, Posting of Workers and Multilevel Governance*, edited by Stein Evju, 9–18. Oslo: Institutt for privaterett, 2013.

—. "The Right to Collective Action Under the European Social Charter." *European Labour Law Journal* 2, no. 3 (2011): 196–224.

Evju, S. and T. Novitz. "The Evolving Regulation : dynamics and Consequences." *FORMULA Working Paper* 33, no. 33 (2012): 1–89.

Ewing, K. and J. Hendy. "The Dramatic Implications of Demir and Baykara." *Industrial Law Journal* 39, no. 1 (2010): 2–51.

—. "The ECJ Decisions and Trade Union Freedom: lessons from the United Kingdom." In *The New Spectre Haunting Europe. the ECJ, Trade Union Rights and the British*

Government, edited by K.D. Ewing and J. Hendy, 68–83. London: Institute of Employment Rights, 2009.

Ewing, K. and C. Jones. "Introduction." In *The New Spectre Haunting Europe. the ECJ, Trade Union Rights and the British Government*, edited by K.D. Ewing and J. Hendy, 1–5. London: Institute of Employment Rights, 2009.

Fabbrini, F. and K. Granat. "Yellow Card but No Foul: The Role of the National Parliaments Under the Subsidiarity Protocol and the Commission Proposal for an EU Regulation on the Right to Strike." *Common Market Law Review* 50, no. 2 (2013): 115–144.

Fabbrini, F. "Europe in Need of a New Deal: On Federalism, Free Market and the Right to Strike." *Georgetown Journal of International Law* 43 (2012): 1–73.

Falkner, G. "Introduction: The EU's Decision Traps and Their Exits." In *The EU's Decision Traps: Comparing Policies*, edited by Gerda Falkner, 1–17. Oxford: Oxford University Press, 2011.

Fallon, M. "Note Sur CJCE 23 Novembre 1999, Arblade." *Revue Critique de Droit International Privé* 89, no. 4 (2000): 728–737.

Fisher, R., W.L. Ury and B. Patton. *Getting to Yes: Negotiating Agreement Without Giving In*. London: Penguin Books, 2011.

Flanders, A. *Industrial Relations: What Is Wrong with the System? An Essay on Its Theory and Future*. London: Faber; Faber, 1965.

—. *Management and Unions*. London: Faber; Faber, 1970.

Flauss, J-F. "'Les Interactions Normatives Entre Les Instruments Européens Relatifs À La Protection Des Droits Sociaux'." In *Droits Sociaux Et Droit Européen. Bilan Et Prospective de La Protection Normative*, edited by J-F Flauss, 89–114. Bruxelles: Nemesis, 2002.

Fons, J. and K. Lenaerts. "The Constitutional Allocation of Powers and General Principles of EU Law." *Common Market Law Review* 62, no. 47 (2010): 1629–1669.

Fox, A. *Beyond Contract: Work, Power and Trust Relations*. London: Faber; Faber, 1974.

—. "Industrial Relations: a Social Critique of Pluralist Ideology." In *Man and Organization: The Search for Explanation and Social Relevance*, edited by John Child, 264. Crows Nest: Allen & Unwin, 1973.

—. *Industrial Sociology and Industrial Relations*. London: H.M.S.O., 1966.

Francq, S. "Note sur CJCE 23 novembre 1999, Arblade." *Revue Du Droit Des Étrangers*, no. 106 (1999): 789–792.

Francq, S., C. Florence, C.J. Berr and C. Prieto. "Chronique de jurisprudence du Tribunal et de la Cour de justice des Communautés européennes. Concurrence." *Journal Du Droit International*, no. 1 (2009): 665–679.

François, L. *Théorie Des Relations Collectives Du Travail En Droit Belge*. Bruxelles: Bruylant, 1980.

Frankart, A. "Mesure de contrôle du détachement pendant la péeriode transitoire suivant l'adhésion à l'Union Européenne." *Revue De Droit Social/Tijdschrift Voor Sociaal Recht* 3 (2012).

Freitas da Costa, C. "Note sur C-346/06, Rüffert." *Revue Du Droit de L'Union Européenne*, no. 3 (2008): 612–619.

Ganesh, A.R. "Appointing Foxes to Guard Henhouses: the European Posted Workers' Directive." *Columbia Journal of European Law*, 2008, 123–142.

Germanotta, P. *Protecting Worker Solidarity Action : A Critique of International Labour Law*. London : The Institute of Employment Rights, 2002.

Gernigon, B., A. Odero and H. Guido. "ILO Principles Concerning Collective Bargaining." *International Labour Review*, 2000.

—. "ILO Principles Concerning the Right to Strike." *Int'l Lab. Rev.*, 1998.

Giubboni, S. "Libertà di circolazione dei lavoratori e libera prestazione dei servizi nell'ordinamento comunitario." *URGE Working Paper* 1 (2009).

Giubboni, S. and G. Orlandini. *La Libera Circolazione Dei Lavoratori Nell'Unione Europea*. Bologna: Il Mulino, 2007.

Giugni, G. *Introduzione Allo Studio Dell'autonomia Collettiva*. Milano: Giuffré, 1960.

Gormley, L. "Freedom of Establishment and Freedom to Provide Services. Workers and Services Distinguished." *European Law Review* 17 (1992): 63–67.

—. "Services and Double Social Security Contributions (Case Note on Seco)." *European Law Review*, 1982, 207–209.

Grainger, H. "Trade Union Membership 2005." *DTI Publications*, 2005.

Grauwe, P de. "Design Failure in the Eurozone – Can They Be Fixed?" *European Economy. Economic Papers* 491 (2013).

Greer, I., Z. Ciupijus and N. Lillie. "The European Migrant Workers Union and the Barriers to Transnational Industrial Citizenship." *European Journal of Industrial Relations* 19, no. 1 (February 2013): 5–20.

Hansen, J. and S. Andersen. "East European Workers in the Building and Construction Industry. Recruitment Strategies and Effects on Wages, Employment Terms and Agreements." Employment Relations Research Centre (FAOS), 2008.

Harmes, A. "Neoliberalism and Multilevel Governance." *Review of International Political Economy* 13, no. 5 (December 2006): 725–749.

Harris, D.J. and J. Darcy. *The European Social Charter (Procedural Aspects of International Law Series, V. 25,)*. Transnational Pub, 2001.

Hellsten, J. "On the Social Dimension in Posting of Workers." *Publication of Labour Administration*, no. 301 (2006): 1–134.

Hinarejos, A. "Laval and Viking: The Right to Collective Action Versus EU Fundamental Freedoms." *Human Rights Law Review* 8, no. 4 (October 2008): 714–729.

Höpner, M. "Political Answers to Judicial Problems? Europe After Viking, Laval and Rüffert." In *Viking-Laval-Rüffert: Economic Freedoms Versus Fundamental Social Rights – Where Does the Balance Lie?* Notre Europe, 2008.

Höpner, M. and A. Schäfer. "Embeddedness and Regional Integration: Waiting for Polanyi in a Hayekian Setting." *International Organization* 66, no. 03 (July 2012): 429–455.

Hös, N. "The Principle of Proportionality in Viking and Laval: an Appropriate Standard of Judicial Review?" *European Labour Law Journal* 1 (2010): 236–253.

Hyman, R. "European Integration and Industrial Relations: a Case of Variable Geometry?" *Antipode*, 2001.

—. *Industrial Relations: a Marxist Introduction*. London: Macmillan, 1975.

—. "The Europeanisation – or the Erosion – of Industrial Relations." *Industrial Relations Journal*, 2001.

—. *The Political Economy of Industrial Relations: Theory and Practice in a Cold Climate.* London: Macmillan, 1989.

—. "Theory and Industrial Relations." *British Journal of Industrial Relations* 32, no. 2 (June 1994): 165–180.

—. "Trade Unions, Lisbon and Europe 2020: from Dream to Nightmare." *LEQS Paper*, no. 45 (2011).

IDEA Consult and ECORYS Netherlands. *Study on the Economic and Social Effects Associated with the Phenomenon of Posting of Workers in the EU Final Report. Labour.* European Commission, 2011.

ILO. *Freedom of Association: Digest of Decisions and Principles of the Freedom of Association Committee of the Governing Body of the ILO.* Geneva, 2006.

—. *International Labour Conventions and Recommendations, 1977–1995. Vol III.* Geneva, 1996.

—. *International Labour Conventions and Recommendations, 1919–1951. Vol. I.* Geneva, 1996.

—. *Record of Proceedings. International Labour Conference, 34th Session.* Geneva, 1951.

—. *Record of Proceedings. International Labour Conference, 64th Session.* Geneva, 1978.

—. *Report of the Committee of Experts on the Application of Conventions and Recommendations. General Report and Observations Concerning Particular Countries. Report III (Part 1A), International Labour Conference, 86th Session.* Geneva, 1998.

J.P. Morgan. "The Euro Area Adjustment: about Halfway There." *Europe Economic Research*, 28 May 2013, 1–16.

Jacobs, A. "Article 11 ECHR: The Right to Bargain Collectively Under Article 11 ECHR." In *The European Convention on Human Rights and the Employment Relation*, edited by Filip Dorssemont, Klaus Lörcher, and Isabelle Schömann, 309–332. Oxford: Hart Publishing, 2013.

—. "The Law of Strikes and Lockouts." In *Comparative Labour Law and Industrial Relations in Industrialized Market Economies*, edited by Roger Blanpain, 633–687. The Hague: Kluwer Law International, 2007.

—. "Towards Community Action on Strike Law." *Common Market Law Review* 15 (1978): 133–155.

Janssen, R. "Internal Wage Devaluation – The IMF Admits It Does Not Work." Social Europe (Blog), 16 December 2013.

—. "Workers Of Europe, Compete!" Social Europe (Blog), 22 August 2013.

Joerges, C. "Rethinking European Law's Supremacy." *EUI Working Paper* 12 (2005).

Joerges, C. "Democracy and European Integration: A Legacy of Tensions, a Re-Conceptualisation and Recent True Conflicts." *EUI Working Paper*, no. 25 (2007).

Joerges, C. and F. Rödl. "Informal Politics, Formalised Law and the Social Deficit of European Integration: Reflections After the Judgments of the ECJ in Viking and Laval." *European Law Journal* 15, no. 1 (January 2009): 1–19.

Jolivet, A., F. Lerais and C. Sauviat. "La dimension sociale aux prises avec la nouvelle gouvernance économique européenne." *Chronique Internationale de L'IRES* 143–144 (2013): 30–52.

Kahn-Freund, O. *Labour and the Law.* 2nd Revise. London: Stevens & Sons Ltd, 1977.

—. "On Uses and Misuses of Comparative Law." *The Modern Law Review* 37, no. 1 (1974): 1–27.

Karakioulafis, C. "Grèce: les syndicats dans la ligne de mire de la Troïka." *Chronique Internationale de L'IRES* 143–144 (2013): 121–132.

Kaufman, B. "Paradigms in Industrial Relations: Original, Modern and Versions In-Between." *British Journal of Industrial Relations* 46, no. 2 (June 2008): 314–339.

—. "The Core Principle and Fundamental Theorem of Industrial Relations." *The International Journal of Comparative Labour Law and Industrial Relations* 23, no. 1 (2007): 5–33.

—. "The Social Welfare Objectives and Ethical Principles of Industrial Relations." In *The Ethics of Human Resources and Industrial Relations*, edited by J. Budd and J. Scoville, 23–59. Champaign: Labour; Employment Relations Association, 2005.

—. "The Theoretical Foundation of Industrial Relations and Its Implications for Labor Economics and Human Resource Management." *Industrial and Labor Relations Review* 64, no. 1 (2010).

Kelemen, R.D. *Eurolegalism: The Transformation of Law and Regulation in the European Union.* Harvard University Press, 2011.

Keller, B. "The German Approach to Industrial Relations: A Literature Review." *European Journal of Industrial Relations* 2, no. 2 (July 1996): 199–210.

Kentikelenis, A., M. Karanikolos, A. Reeves, M. McKee and D. Stuckler. "Greece's Health Crisis: from Austerity to Denialism." *The Lancet* 383, no. 9918 (February 2014): 748–753.

Kilpatrick, C. "Internal Market Architecture and the Accommodation of Labour Rights: As Good as It Gets?" *European Journal of Social Law* 1 (2012): 1–26.

—. "Internal Market Architecture and the Accommodation of Labour Rights: As Good as It Gets?" *European Journal of Social Law*, no. 1 (2012): 1–26.

—. "The ECJ and Labour Law: A 2008 Retrospective." *Industrial Law Journal* 38, no. 2 (June 2009): 180–208.

Kolehmainen, E. "The Directive Concerning the Posting of Workers: Synchronizations of the Functions of National Legal Systems." *Comparative Labor Law & Policy Journal* 20 (1998): 71–104.

—. *The Posted Workers Directive : European Reinforcement of National Labour Protection.* Florence: European University Institute, 2002.

Kontula, A. *Näkymätön Kylä.* Helsinki: Into, 2010.

Koukiadaki, A. and L. Kretsos. "Grèce/Greece." In *Quel Droit Social Dans Une Europe En Crise?*, edited by Marie-Cécile Escande Varniol, Sylvaine Laulom, Emmanuelle Mazuyer, and Pascale Vielle, 189–231. Brussels: Larcier, 2012.

Kovács, E. "The Right to Strike in the European Social Charter." *Comparative Labor Law & Policy Journal* 26 (2006): 445–475.

Krebber, S. "Case C-319/06, Commission V. Luxembourg, Judgment of the Court (First Chamber) of 19 June 2008,[2008] ECR I-4323." *Common Market Law Review* 46, no. 5 (2009): 1725.

Krugman, P. *End This Depression Now!* New York: W. W. Norton & Company, 2013.

—. "Europe's Second Depression:" The Coscience of a Liberal (Blog), 29 March 2013.

—. "Europe's Second Depression: a Correction." The Coscience of a Liberal (Blog), 29 March 2013.

—. "Revenge of the Optimum Currency Area." *NBER Macroeconomics Annual* 27 (2012): 1–14.

Lallement, M. *Sociologie Des Relations Professionnelles.* Paris: La Découverte, 1996.

Langbein, J.H. *Torture and the Law of Proof.* Chicago: University of Chicago Press, 1977.

Langille, B. "The ILO and the New Economy: Recent Developments." *International Journal of Comparative Labour Law and Industrial Relations* 15 (1999): 229–257.

Lehoczky, C.K. "The Fundamental Right of Workers to Information and Consultation Under the European Social Charter." In *The Recast of the European Works Council Directive*, edited by Filip Dorssemont and Thomas Blanke, 3–30. Antwerp: Intersentia, 2010.

Léonard, É. "Le modèle belge et l'Union européenne." In *Dynamiques de La Concertation Sociale*, edited by Étienne Arcq, Michel Capron, Évelyne Léonard, and Pierre Reman, 389–404. CRISP, 2010.

Liebowitz, S.J. and S.E. Margolis. "Path Dependence." In *Encyclopedia of Law and Economics, Volume I. the History and Methodology of Law and Economics*, edited by Boudewijn Bouckaert and Gerrit De Geest, 981–998. Cheltenham: Edward Elgar, 1999.

Lillie, N. and I. Greer. "Industrial Relations, Migration, and Neoliberal Politics: The Case of the European Construction Sector." *Policy & Society* 35 (2007): 551–581.

Lillie, N. and M. Sippola. "National Unions and Transnational Workers: the Case of Olkiluoto 3, Finland." *Work, Employment & Society* 25, no. 2 (June 2011): 292–308.

Lo Faro, A. "Toward a de-Fundamentalisation of Collective Labour Rights in European Social Law?" In *Before and After the Economic Crisis? What Implications for the 'European Social Model'?*, edited by Marie-Ange Moreau, 203–216. Cheltenham: Edward Elgar, 2012.

Loi, P. "Italie/Italy." In *Quel Droit Social Dans Une Europe En Crise?*, edited by Marie-Cécile Escande Varniol, Sylvaine Laulom, Emmanuelle Mazuyer, and Pascale Vielle, 261–282. Brussels: Larcier, 2012.

Lörcher, K. "The New Social Dimension in the Jurisprudence of the European Court of Human Rights (ECtHR): The Demir and Baykara Judgment, Its Methodology and Follow-up." In *The European Convention on Human Rights and the Employment Relation*, edited by Filip Dorssemont, Isabelle Schömann, and Klaus Lörcher, 3–46. Oxford: Hart Publishing, 2013.

Lucio, M.M. and R. Perrett. "The Diversity and Politics of Trade Unions' Responses to Minority Ethnic and Migrant Workers: The Context of the UK." *Economic and Industrial Democracy* 30, no. 3 (July 2009): 324–347.

Macklem, P. "The Right to Bargain Collectively in International Law: Workers' Right, Human Right, International Right?" In *Labour Rights as Human Rights*, edited by Philip Alston, 61–84. Oxford: Oxford University Press, 2005.

Maduro, M. *We the Court: The European Court of Justice and the European Economic Constitution*. Oxford: Hart Publishing, 1998.

Majone, G. *Dilemmas of European Integration*. Oxford: Oxford University Press, 2005.

Malmberg, J. "Posting Post Laval International and National Responses." Centre for Labor Studies. Uppsala, 2010.

—. "Posting Post-Laval: Nordic Responses." In *Before and After the Economic Crisis? What Implications for the 'European Social Model'?*, edited by Marie-Ange Moreau, 25–39. Cheltenham: Edward Elgar, 2011.

—. "The Collective Agreement as an Instrument for Regulation of Wages and Employment Conditions." *Stability and Change in Nordic Labour Law* 43 (2002): 189–213.

Malmberg, J. and C. Johansson. "The Commission's Posting Package." *SIEPS - European Policy Analysis*, no. 8 (2012): 1–16.

Malmberg, J. and T. Sigeman. "Industrial Action and EU Economic Freedoms: The Autonomous Collective Bargaining Model Curtailed by the European Court of Justice." *Common Market Law Review* 45 (2008): 1115.

Mantouvalou, V. "Are Labour Rights Human Rights?" *European Labour Law Journal* 3, no. 2 (2012): 151–172.

Marginson, P. and K. Sisson. *European Integration and Industrial Relations: Multi-Level Governance in the Making*. London: Palgrave Macmillan, 2004.

Marsden, D. *A Theory of Employment Systems: Micro-Foundations of Societal Diversity*. Oxford: Oxford University Press, 1999.

Martin, A. "EMU and Wage Bargaining: the Americanization of the European Labour Market?" *European Trade Union Institute Discussion and Working Papers DWP* 1, no. 3 (1998): 1–41.

Martin, D. "Comments on Florus Ariël Wijsenbeek (Case C-378/97 of 21 September 1999) and Arblade (Joined Cases C-369/96 and C-376/96 of 23 November 1999." *European Journal of Migration and Law* 2, no. September 1999 (2000): 101–107.

—. "Comments on Gottardo (Case C-55/00 of 15 January 2002), Finalarte (Case C-49/98 of 25 October 2001) and Portugaia Costruções (Case C-164/99 of 24 January." *Eur. J. Migration & L.* 4, no. 3 (August 2002): 369–375.

Marx, K. and F. Engels. *Marx and Engels Collected Works - Volume 20*. New York: International Publishers, 1986.

Massey, D., J. Arango, G. Hugo, A. Kouaouci, A. Pellegrino and E. Taylor. "Theories of International Migration: A Review and Appraisal." *Population and Development Review* 19, no. 3 (1993): 431–466.

Mazuyer, E. "Les questions de l'emploi et du travail dans une Union européenne en crise." In *Quel Droit Social Dans Une Europe En Crise?*, edited by Marie-Cécile Escande Varniol, Sylvaine Laulom, Emmanuelle Mazuyer, and Pascale Vielle, 31–60. Brussels: Larcier, 2012.

Meardi, G. "Peripheral Convergence in the Crisis? Southern and Eastern European Labour Markets and Industrial Relations." *Paper for the SASE Annual Meeting*, no. June (2012): 1–13.

Michaux, A.-V. *Eléments de Droit Du Travail*. Bruxelles: Larcier, 2010.

Miranda Boto, J.M. and R. Rodrìguez Contreras. "Espagne/Spain." In *Quel Droit Social Dans Une Europe En Crise?*, edited by Marie-Cécile Escande Varniol, Sylvaine Laulom, Emmanuelle Mazuyer, and Pascale Vielle, 131–155. Brussels: Larcier, 2012.

Morijn, J. "Balancing Fundamental Rights and Common Market Freedoms in Union Law: Schmidberger and Omega in the Light of the European Constitution." *European Law Journal* 12, no. 1 (January 2006): 15–40.

Mörk, M. "An End to the Possibilities – on Horizontal Liability in Laval and the Limits of Judicial Rights Protection." In *The Protection of Fundamental Rights in the EU After Lisbon*, edited by Sybe de Vries, Ulf Bernitz and Stephen Weatherill, 119–138. Oxford: Hart Publishing, 2013.

Münchau, W. "Germany's Constitutional Court Has Strengthened the Eurosceptics." *Financial Times*, 9 February 2014.

Novitz, T. "A Human Rights Analysis of the Viking and Laval Judgments." *Cambridge Yearbook of European Legal Studies* 10 (2008): 541–561.

—. *International and European Protection of the Right to Strike*. New York: Oxford University Press, 2003.

—. "UK Implementation of the Posting of Workers Directive." In *Cross-Border Services, Posting of Workers and Multilevel Governance*, edited by Stein Evju, 329–358. Oslo: Institutt for privaterett, 2013.

Novitz, T., L. Hayes and H. Reed. "Applying the Laval Quartet in a UK Context: chilling, Ripple and Distruptive Effects on Industrial Relations." In *Reconciling Fundamental Social Rights and Economic Freedoms After Viking, Laval and Rüffert*, edited by Andreas Bücker and Wiebke Warneck, 195–244. Baden-Baden: Nomos Publishers, 2011.

Ochel, W. "Decentralising Wage Bargaining in Germany – a Way to Increase Employment?" *CESifo Working Paper* 1069 (2003): 1–28.

Orlandini, G. "Il rapporto di lavoro con elementi di internazionalità." *WP C.S.D.L.E. Massimo D'Antona.IT*, no. 137 (2012): 1–72.

—. "Main Features Relating with Posted Workers in Italy." In *Evaluating Application of the Directive on the Posting of Workers Within the Framework of the Provision of Services*, 3:1–13. March, 2010.

—. *Sciopero E Servizi Pubblici Essenziali Nel Processo d'integrazione Europea. Uno Studio Di Diritto Comparato E Comunitario*. Torino: Giappichelli, 2003.

—. "The Free Movement of Goods as a Possible 'Community' Limitation on Industrial Conflict." *European Law Journal* 6, no. 4 (2000): 341–362.

—. "Trade Union Rights and Market Freedoms: the European Court of Justice Sets Out the Rules." *Labour Law & Policy Journal* 29 (2008): 573–604.

Palma Ramalho, M. do R. "Portuguese Labour Law and Industrial Relations During the Crisis November 2013 Project." *ILO Working Paper*, no. 54 (2013).

Pataut, E. "Note sur CJCE 15 mars 2001, Mazzoleni." *Revue Critique de Droit International Privé2* 90, no. 3 (2001): 503–512.

Pedersini, R. *Trade Union Strategies to Recruit New Groups of Workers*. Dublin: European Foundation for the Improvement of Living; Working Conditions, 2010.

Pedersini, R. and M. Pallini. *Posted Workers in the European Union*. Dublin: European Fondation for Improvement of Living and Working Conditions, 2010.

Peers, S. "Indirect Rights for Third-Country Service Providers Confirmed." *European Law Review* 32 (1995): 303–309.

Pera, G. *Problemi Costituzionali Del Diritto Sindacale Italiano*. Milano: Feltrinelli, 1960.

Perisin, T. *Free Movement of Goods and Limits of Regulatory Autonomy in the EU and WTO*. The Hague: T.M.C. Asser Press, 2009.

Piore, M.J. *Birds of Passage: Migrant Labor and Industrial Societies*. Cambridge: Cambridge University Press, 1980.

Pochet, P. and C. Degryse. "Monetary Union and the Stakes for Democracy and Social Policy." *Transfer: European Review of Labour and Research* 19, no. 1 (January 2013): 103–116.

Pochet, P. and C. Degryse. "The Programmed Dismantling of the 'European Social Model'." *Intereconomics* 47, no. 4 (2012): 200–217.

Polanyi, K. *The Great Transformation: The Political and Economic Origins of Our Time*. Boston: Beacon Press, 1957.

Portes, A. and J. Walton. *Labor, Class, and the International System*. New York: Academic Press, 1981.

Rebhahn, R. "Collective Labour Law in Europe in a Comparative Perspective (Part I)." *Journal of Comparative Labour Law and* 19, no. Part I (2004): 271–295.

—. "Collective Labour Law in Europe in a Comparative Perspective (Part II)." *Journal of Comparative Labour Law and* 19, no. Part II (2004): 107–132.

Rehfeldt, U. "Italie - Des recommandations européennes à la résistance syndicale." *Chronique Internationale de L'IRES* 143–144 (2013): 93–132.

Reich, N. "How Proportionate Is the Proportionality Principle? Some Critical Remarks on the Use and Methodology of the Proportionality Principle in the Internal Market Case Law of the ECJ." In *The European Court of Justice and the Autonomy of the Member States*, edited by Hans-W. Micklitz and Bruno De Witte, 83–112. Cambridge: Intersentia, 2012.

Rocca, M. "A Clash of Kings The European Committee of Social Rights on the 'Lex Laval'... and on the EU Framework for the Posting of Workers." *European Journal of Social Law* 3 (2013): 217–232.

—. "Case C-271/08, Commission V. Germany [2010]." *European Labour Law Journal* 2 (2011): 76–79.

—. "The Proposal for a (so-Called) 'Monti II' Regulation on the Exercise of the Right to Take Collective Action Within the Context of the Freedom of Establishment and the Freedom to Provide Services." *European Labour Law Journal* 1 (2012): 19–34.

Rodière, P. *Droit Social de L'Union Européenne*. Paris: L.G.D.J., 1998.

—. "Droit social. Coordination des droits nationaux, loi applicable, compétence juridictionnelle." *Revue Trimestrielle de Droit Europeen* 39, no. 3 (2003): 529–552.

—. "Note sur arrêt du 27 mars 1990 Société Rush Portuguesa Lda C. Office national de l'immigration." *Revue Trimestrielle de Droit Européen1* 26, no. 3 (1990): 635–640.

Romagnoli, U and T Treu. *I Sindacati in Italia Dal '45 a Oggi: storia Di Una Strategia.* Bologna: Il Mulino, 1977.

Roubini, N. "Eurozone Crisis: Here Are the Options, Now Choose." EconoMonitor (Blog), 9 November 2011.

Ruiter, D.W.P. "A Basic Classification of Legal Institutions." *Ratio Juris* 10, no. 4 (December 1997): 357–371.

Ryan, B. "The Charter and Collective Labour Law." In *Economic and Social Rights Under the EU Charter of Fundamental Rights - a Legal Perspective*, edited by Tamara K. Hervey and Jeff Kenner, 67–90. Oxford: Hart Publishing, 2003.

Sachs-Durand, C. "Information and Consultation in the Recast Directive." In *The Recast of the European Works Council Directive*, edited by Filip Dossemont, 313–326. Antwerp: Intersentia, 2010.

Samuel, L. *Fundamental Social Rights: Case Law of the European Social Charter.* Strasbourg: Council of Europe, 1997.

Saraceno, F. "Free Riders in Frankfurt." Sparse Thoughts of a Gloomy European Economist (Blog), 28 November 2013.

—. "Incomprenhensible? Really?" Sparse Thoughts of a Gloomy European Economist (Blog), 5 November 2013.

Scharpf, F.W. "Balancing Positive and Negative Integration: The Regulatory Options for Europe." *MPIfG Working Paper* 97/8, no. November (1998): 1–26.

—. "Legitimacy in the Multilevel European Polity." *MPIfG Working Paper* 1 (2009): 1–40.

—. "Negative and Positive Integration in the Political Economy of European Welfare States." In *Governance in the European Union*, edited by Gary Marks, FW Scharpf, Philippe G. Schmitter, and Wolfgang Streeck, 15–39. London: SAGE Publications, 1996.

—. "Political Legitimacy in a Non-Optimal Currency Area." *MPIfG Discussion Paper* 15 (2013): 1–39.

—. "The Asymmetry of European Integration, or Why the EU Cannot Be a 'Social Market Economy'." *Socio-Economic Review* 8 (2010): 211–250.

—. "The Joint-Decision Trap Revisited." *JCMS: Journal of Common Market Studies* 44, no. 4 (November 2006): 845–864.

—. "The Joint-Decision Trap: Lessons from German Federalism and European Integration." *Public Administration* 66, no. 3 (September 1988): 239–278.

—. "The Only Solution Is to Refuse to Comply with ECJ Rulings." *Social Europe Journal* 4, no. 1 (2008): 16–21.

Scheele, A. *Non-Permanent Employment, Quality of Work and Industrial Relations.* Dublin: European Foundation for the Improvement of Living and Working Conditions, 2002.

Schepel, H. "Constitutionalising the Market, Marketising the Constitution, and to Tell the Difference: On the Horizontal Application of the Free Movement Provisions in EU Law." *European Law Journal* 18, no. 2 (March 2012): 177–200.

Schiek, D. "Fundamental Rights Jurisprudence Between Member States' Prerogatives and Citizens' Autonomy." In *The European Court of Justice and the Autonomy of the Member States*, edited by Hans-W. Micklitz and Bruno De Witte, 219–258. Cambridge: Intersentia, 2012.

Schlachter, M. "National Reports: Germany." In *The Laval and Viking Cases: Freedom of Services and Establishment V. Industrial Conflict in the European Economic Area and Russia*, edited by Roger Blanpain and Andrzej Marian Świątkowski, 63–72. Alphen aan den Rijn: Kluwer Law International, 2009.

—. "The European Social Charter: could It Contribute to a More Social Europe?" In *Resocialising Europe in a Time of Crisis*, edited by Nicola Contouris and Mark Freedland, 105–117. Cambridge: Cambridge University Press, 2013.

—. "Transnational Temporary Agency Work: How Much Equality Does the Equal Treatment Principle Provide?" *The International Journal of Comparative Labour Law and Industrial Relations* 28, no. 2 (2012): 177–197.

Schmidt, F. and A.C. Neal. "Collective Agreements and Collective Bargaining." In *International Encyclopaedia of Comparative Law. Volume XV*, edited by Bob Hepple, 1–127. Tübingen: C.B. Mohr, 1984.

Schmidt, S.K. "Law-Making in the Shadow of Judicial Politics." In *The 'Community Method'. Obstinate or Obsolete*, edited by Renaud Dehousse, 43–59. Houndmills (Basingstoke): Palgrave Macmillan, 2011.

Schulten, T. "The Impact of the Troika Policy on Wages and Collective Bargaining." *Public Hearing on "Employment and Social Aspects of the Operations and Role of the Troika in Euro Area Programme Countries"* European Parliament (9 January 2014).

Schulten, T. and T. Müller. "A New European Interventionism? The Impact of the New European Economic Governance on Wages and Collective Bargaining." In *Social Developments in the EU 2012*, edited by David Natali and Bart Vanhercke, 181–214. Brussels: ETUI; OSE Publications, 2013.

Sciarra, S. "Viking e Laval: diritti collettivi e mercato nel recente dibattito europeo." *Lavoro E Diritto* XXII, no. 2 (2008): 245–269.

Servais, J.-M. *Droit Social de L'Union Européenne*. Emile Bruylant, 2008.

Sheldon, P.M., G. Bamber and E. Cordova. "Collective Bargaining." In *Comparative Labour Law and Industrial Relations in Industrialized Market Economies*, edited by Roger Blanpain and Chris Engles, 405–436. The Hague: Kulwer, 1998.

Shuibhne, N. "Margins of Appreciation: national Values, Fundamental Rights and EC Free Movement Law." *European Law Review* 34 (2009): 230–256.

Sjödin, E. "Labour Market Regulation as Restrictions. A Developmental Study of ECJ Case Law at the Interface Between Free Movement and Posting of Workers." In *Cross-Border Services, Posting of Workers and Multilevel Governance*, edited by Stein Evju, 19–84. Oslo: Institutt for privaterett, 2013.

Skouris, V. "Fundamental Rights and Fundamental Freedoms: The Challenge of Striking a Delicate Balance." *European Business Law Review*, 2006, 225–240.

Snell, J. "The Notion of Market Access: a Concept or a Slogan?" *Common Market Law Review* 47 (2010): 437–472.

Sorge, A. "The Evolution of Industrial Democracy in the Countries of the European Community." *British Journal of Industrial Relations* 14, no. 3 (1976): 274–294.

de Sousa, P.C. "Negative and Positive Integration in EU Economic Between Strategic Denial and Cognitive Dissonance?" *German Law Journal* 13, no. 8 (2012): 979–1012.

Spaventa, E. "Federalisation Versus Centralisation: tensions in Fundamental Rights Discourse in the EU." In *50 Years of the European Treaties: looking Back and Thinking Forward*, edited by M. Dougan and S. Currie, 44:343–364. June. Oxford: Hart Publishing, 2009.

Stone Sweet, A. *The Judicial Construction of Europe*. Oxford: Oxford University Press, 2004.

Streeck, W. "The Internationalization of Industrial Relations in Europe: prospects and Problems." *Working Paper Series in European Studies* 1, no. 1 (1998): 1–40.

Supiot, A. *L'esprit de Philadelphie : La Justice Sociale Face Au Marché Total*. Paris: Seuil, 2010.

Syrpis, P. *EU Intervention in Domestic Labour Law*. Oxford: Oxford University Press, 2007.

—. "Reconciling Economic Freedoms and Social Rights –The Potential of Commission v. Germany (Case C-271/08, Judgment of 15 July 2010)." *Industrial Law Journal* 40, no. 2 (2011): 222–229.

Syrpis, P. and T. Novitz. "Economic and Social Rights in Conflict: Political and Judicial Approaches to Their Reconciliation." *European Law Review*, no. 3 (2008): 411–426.

Świątkowski, A.M. *Charter of Social Rights of the Council of Europe*. The Hague: Kluwer Law International, 2007.

Tiraboschi, M. and M. Biagi. "Forms of Employee Representational Participation." In *Comparative Labour Law and Industrial Relations in Industrialized Market Economies*, edited by Roger Blanpain, 503–556. The Hague: Kluwer Law International, 2007.

Torreblanca, J.I. and M. Leonard. "The Continent-Wide Rise of Euroscepticism." *European Council of Foreign Relations Policy Memo*, 2013, 1–10.

Traxler, F. "Farewell to Labour Market Associations? Organised Versus Disorganised Decentralization as a Map for Industrial Relations." In *Organised Industrial Relations in Europe: What Future?*, edited by F. Traxler and Colin Crouch. Avebury: Aldershot, 1995.

Valdés Dal-Re, Fernando, ed. *Freedom of Association of Workers and Employers in the Countries of the European Union*. Madrid: Ministerio de Trabajo y Asuntos Sociales, 2006.

Van Hoek, A. and M. Houwerzijl. "Comparative Study on the Legal Aspects of the Posting of Workers in the Framework of the Provision of Services in the European Union." Brussels, 2011.

Van Peijpe, T. "Collective Labour Law After Viking, Laval, Rüffert, and Commission v. Luxembourg." *International Journal of Comparative Labour Law and Industrial Relations* 25, no. 2 (2009): 81–107.

Vandaele, K. and J. Leschke. *Following the 'Organising Model' of British Unions? Organising Non-Standard Workers in Germany and the Netherlands.* European Trade Union Institute, 2010.

Varoufakis, Y. *The Global Minotaur: America, Europe and the Future of the Global Economy (Economic Controversies).* London: Zed Books, 2013.

Verdun, A. "The Building of Economic Governance in the European Union." *Transfer: European Review of Labour and Research* 19, no. 1 (January 2013): 23–35.

Vigneau, C. "Le Droit à l'action collective à l'épreuve des libertés économiques du Traité: la hiérarchisation des droits 'fondamentaux' dans l'ordre juridique communautaire." *La Semaine Juridique – Édition Générale*, no. 13 (2008): 33–36.

Visser, J. "Union Membership Statistics in 24 Countries." *Monthly Labor Review* 129, no. 1 (2006): 38–49.

Vries, S de. "The Protection of Fundamental Rights Within Europe's Internal Market After Lisbon – An Endeavour for More Harmony." *Europa Institute Working Paper* 4 (2010): 1–46.

Weatherill, S. "From Economic Rights to Fundamental Rights." In *The Protection of Fundamental Rights in the EU After Lisbon*, edited by Sybe de Vries, Ulf Bernitz, and Stephen Weatherill, 11–36. Oxford: Hart Publishing, 2013.

Weiss, M. and M. Schmidt. "Germany – Collective Labour Law." In *International Encyclopaedia of Labour Law*, edited by Roger Blanpain and Michele Colucci, 340:163–264. July, 2008.

Wood, S.J., A. Wagner, E.G.A. Armstrong, J.F.B. Goodman and J.E. Davis. "The 'Industrial Relations System' Concept As a Basis for Theory in Industrial Relations." *British Journal of Industrial Relations* 13, no. 3 (November 1975): 291–308.

Wrench, J. "Trade Union Responses to Immigrants and Ethnic Inequality in Denmark and the UK: the Context of Consensus and Conflict." *European Journal of Industrial Relations* 10, no. 1 (March 2004): 7–30.

www.ingramcontent.com/pod-product-compliance
Ingram Content Group UK Ltd.
Pitfield, Milton Keynes, MK11 3LW, UK
UKHW051925100926
8556IPUK00022B/1381

9 781780 683072